W9-CCB-877

# NOVA SCOTIA AND ATLANTIC CANADA

12th Edition

Where to Stay and Eat
for All Budgets

Must-See Sights
and Local Secrets

Ratings You Can Trust

Fodor's Travel Publications    New York, Toronto, London, Sydney, Auckland
www.fodors.com

## FODOR'S NOVA SCOTIA AND ATLANTIC CANADA

**Editors:** Caroline Trefler (Lead Editor), Denise Leto

**Editorial Contributors:** Susan MacCallum-Whitcomb, Keith Nicol, Penny Phenix

**Production Editor:** Emily Cogburn

**Maps & Illustrations:** David Lindroth, Mark Stroud, *cartographers;* Bob Blake, Rebecca Baer, *map editors;* William Wu, *information graphics*

**Design:** Fabrizio La Rocca, *creative director;* Guido Caroti, *art director;* Tina Malaney, Chie Ushio, Nora Rosansky, Jessica Walsh, *designers;* Melanie Marin, *associate director of photography*

**Cover Photo:** Peggy's Cove: Garry Black/Masterfile

**Production Manager:** Angela L. McLean

### COPYRIGHT

Copyright © 2012 by Fodor's Travel, a division of Random House, Inc.

Fodor's is a registered trademark of Random House, Inc.

All rights reserved. Published in the United States by Fodor's Travel, a division of Random House, Inc., and in Canada by Random House of Canada, Limited, Toronto. Distributed by Random House, Inc., New York.

No maps, illustrations, or other portions of this book may be reproduced in any form without written permission from the publisher.

12th Edition

ISBN 978-0-307-92835-1

ISSN 1558–8173

### SPECIAL SALES

This book is available at special discounts for bulk purchases for sales promotions or premiums. Special editions, including personalized covers, excerpts of existing books, and corporate imprints, can be created in large quantities for special needs. For more information, write to Special Markets/Premium Sales, 1745 Broadway, MD 3-2, New York, NY 10019, or e-mail specialmarkets@randomhouse.com.

### AN IMPORTANT TIP & AN INVITATION

Although all prices, opening times, and other details in this book are based on information supplied to us at press time, changes occur all the time in the travel world, and Fodor's cannot accept responsibility for facts that become outdated or for inadvertent errors or omissions. So **always confirm information when it matters**, especially if you're making a detour to visit a specific place. Your experiences—positive and negative—matter to us. If we have missed or misstated something, **please write to us.** Share your opinion instantly through our online feedback center at fodors.com/contact-us.

PRINTED IN UNITED STATES

10 9 8 7 6 5 4 3 2 1

# CONTENTS

About This Book. . . . . . . . . . . . . . 5

What's Where. . . . . . . . . . . . . . . . 6

When to Go . . . . . . . . . . . . . . . . 8

Province Picker. . . . . . . . . . . . . . 9

Top Attractions . . . . . . . . . . . . . 10

Top Experiences . . . . . . . . . . . . 11

If You Like. . . . . . . . . . . . . . . . . 12

Quintessential Nova Scotia &
Atlantic Canada . . . . . . . . . . . . . 14

Quintessential Canada. . . . . . . . . 16

1 NOVA SCOTIA . . . . . . . . . . . . . . 17

Welcome to Nova Scotia . . . . . . . 18

Halifax. . . . . . . . . . . . . . . . . . . . 25

South Shore and
Annapolis Valley. . . . . . . . . . . . . 43

The Eastern Shore and
Northern Nova Scotia. . . . . . . . . 73

Cape Breton Island. . . . . . . . . . . 88

2 NEW BRUNSWICK. . . . . . . . . . . 109

Welcome to New Brunswick . . . 110

Saint John. . . . . . . . . . . . . . . . 116

The Fundy Coast. . . . . . . . . . . . 127

The Acadian Coast and
St. John River Valley. . . . . . . . . 150

St. John River Valley. . . . . . . . . 162

Fredericton . . . . . . . . . . . . . . . 168

3 PRINCE EDWARD ISLAND. . . . 179

Welcome to
Prince Edward Island . . . . . . . . 180

Charlottetown. . . . . . . . . . . . . . 186

Central Coastal Drive. . . . . . . . . 200

Points East Coastal Drive. . . . . . 211

North Cape Coastal Drive . . . . . 218

4 NEWFOUNDLAND
AND LABRADOR. . . . . . . . . . . 227

Welcome to
Newfoundland and Labrador. . . 228

St. John's, Newfoundland. . . . . . 234

Avalon Peninsula . . . . . . . . . . . 251

Eastern Newfoundland. . . . . . . . 258

Gander and Around . . . . . . . . . 267

Western Newfoundland . . . . . . . 272

UNDERSTANDING NOVA SCOTIA
AND ATLANTIC CANADA. . . . 285

Books and Movies . . . . . . . . . . 286

French Vocabulary . . . . . . . . . . 287

Menu Guide . . . . . . . . . . . . . . . 291

TRAVEL SMART NOVA SCOTIA
AND ATLANTIC CANADA . . . . 295

INDEX. . . . . . . . . . . . . . . . . . . . 309

ABOUT OUR WRITERS . . . . . . . 320

## MAPS

Halifax..................... 29

South Shore and
Annapolis Valley............. 44

Eastern Shore and
Northern Nova Scotia......... 72

Cape Breton Island........... 88

Downtown Saint John ........ 120

The Fundy Coast............ 129

Fundy National Park......... 140

Acadian Coast and
St. John River Valley......... 151

Fredericton ................ 169

Charlottetown.............. 190

Central Coastal Drive......... 201

Points East Coastal Drive...... 213

North Cape Coastal Drive ..... 220

St. John's.................. 237

Avalon Peninsula ........... 252

Eastern Newfoundland
and Gander................ 259

Western Newfoundland....... 273

# ABOUT
# THIS BOOK

## Our Ratings

At Fodor's, we spend considerable time choosing the best places in a destination so you don't have to. By default, anything we recommend in this book is worth visiting. But some sights, properties, and experiences are so great that we've recognized them with additional accolades. Orange **Fodor's Choice** stars indicate our top recommendations; black stars highlight places we deem **Highly Recommended;** and **Best Bets** call attention to top properties in various categories. Disagree with any of our choices? Care to nominate a new place? Visit our feedback center at www.fodors.com/feedback.

## Hotels

Hotels have private bath, phone, and TV, and do not offer meals unless we specify that in the review. We always list facilities but not whether you'll be charged an extra fee to use them.

> For expanded hotel reviews,
> visit **Fodors.com**

## Restaurants

Unless we state otherwise, restaurants are open for lunch and dinner daily. We mention dress only when there's a specific requirement and reservations only when they're essential or not accepted—it's always best to book ahead.

## Credit Cards

We assume that restaurants and hotels accept credit cards. If not, we'll note it in the review.

## Budget Well

Hotel and restaurant price categories from ¢ to $$$$ are defined in the opening pages of the respective chapters. For attractions, we always give standard adult admission fees; reductions are usually available for children, students, and senior citizens.

---

| Listings | | Hotels & Restaurants | Outdoors |
|---|---|---|---|
| ★ Fodor's Choice | ✉ E-mail | **Hotels** | ✗ Golf |
| ★ Highly recommended | 🖾 Admission fee | **& Restaurants** | ⛺ Camping |
| | ⏱ Open/closed times | ⊡ Hotel | |
| ⊠ Physical address | | ↵ Number of rooms | **Other** |
| ✛ Directions or Map coordinates | Ⓜ Metro stations | ⌂ Facilities | 🅒 Family-friendly |
| ⊡ Mailing address | ▭ No credit cards | ⭐ Meal plans | ⇨ See also |
| ☎ Telephone | | ✗ Restaurant | ⊠ Branch address |
| 🖶 Fax | | ⚑ Reservations | ☞ Take note |
| ⊕ On the Web | | 🏛 Dress code | |
| | | ⚞ Smoking | |

# WHAT'S WHERE

**1 Nova Scotia.** Nova Scotia is the land of lighthouses and lobster traps: throw a dart at the map and you'll likely hit one or the other. But there are inland highlights, too, like sylvan orchards and dramatic highlands. If you're looking for urban amenities, the capital—hip, historic Halifax—is the largest city in Atlantic Canada and has the region's broadest range of dining and nightlife options.

**2 New Brunswick.** Fronted by the Bay of Fundy, New Brunswick is a fine place to witness the action of the world's highest tides as they rise and fall a phenomenal 14.5 meters (48 feet) twice daily. Beyond the bay, the province boasts rivers, mountains, and dense forests—all of which offer abundant adventure opportunities—plus two rich cultures (English and French) and more than four centuries of history.

**3 Prince Edward Island.** PEI is rightly nicknamed "The Gentle Island" because it's generally prettier and more pastoral than its neighbors. PEI's rich red soil supports thriving farms, while its sandy warm-water beaches and nostalgia-inducing towns are a magnet for vacationers. Being largely flat, Canada's smallest province is also hugely popular with cyclists and golfers.

**4 Newfoundland and Labrador.** This province is rugged and remote (Newfoundland sits alone in the North Atlantic; Labrador is tucked into northern Québec). It's also relatively cold, which allows for iceberg watching in summer, great snow sports in winter, and wildlife viewing year-round. Nevertheless, a warm welcome is assured: people here have been greeting visitors since the Vikings arrived 1,000 years ago.

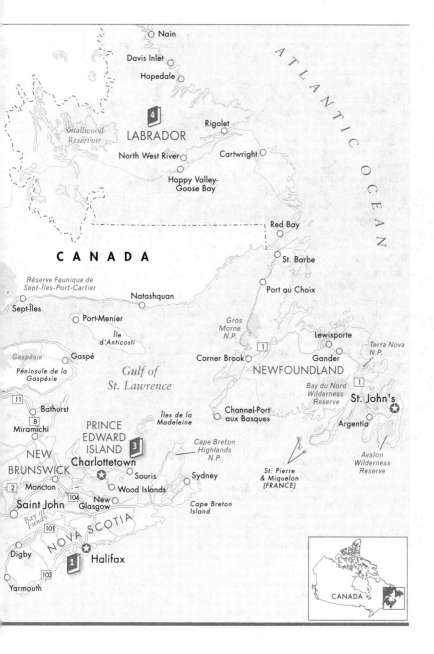

Nain

Davis Inlet

Hopedale

4

Rigolet

*Smallwood Reservoir*

LABRADOR

North West River          Cartwright

Happy Valley-
Goose Bay

Red Bay

C A N A D A

St. Barbe

*Réserve Faunique de
Sept-Îles-Port-Cartier*

Natashquan

Port au Choix

Sept-Îles

Port-Menier

*Gros
Morne
N.P.*

Lewisporte

*Terra Nova
N.P.*

*Île
d'Anticosti*

*Gaspésie*        Gaspé

Corner Brook          Gander

*Péninsule de la
Gaspésie*

*Gulf of
St. Lawrence*

NEWFOUNDLAND

*Bay du Nord
Wilderness
Reserve*

St. John's

11

Bathurst

*Îles de la
Madeleine*

Channel-Port
aux Basques

1

8

Miramichi

PRINCE
EDWARD
ISLAND

3

*Cape Breton
Highlands
N.P.*

Argentia

NEW
BRUNSWICK

Charlottetown

*Avalon
Wilderness
Reserve*

2        Moncton

Souris

Sydney

St. Pierre
& Miquelon
(FRANCE)

104

Wood Islands

Saint John      New
Glasgow

*Cape Breton
Island*

*Bay of
Fundy*

101

N O V A   S C O T I A

Digby

1        Halifax

103

Yarmouth

CANADA

# WHEN TO GO

July and August, when long, warm days let you fully enjoy attractions and activities, are the most popular months to visit Atlantic Canada. Beaches beckon in summer, sites open their doors for extended hours, and outfitters go full tilt, offering both soft and extreme outdoor adventures. As an added bonus, the seafood is freshest during those sunny days (or at least it seems so when you're eating at a waterside café) and the calendar is packed with festivals. Fall brings bountiful harvests, excellent whale-watching, and, of course, brilliant foliage. The trees, which start turning in late September, are at their most dazzling in October, and events like Cape Breton's Celtic Colours International Festival are scheduled to coincide with the vivid display.

Although many outlying inns and eateries close for the coldest months, there is a lot to do in Atlantic Canada during the winter. Snowmobilers and skiers, for example, can chill in northern New Brunswick, which gets as much as 400 centimeters (157 inches) of snow annually, and wildlife lovers can take dogsled rides in Labrador to view the world's largest caribou herd. March and April are the months for maple syrup and north-bound migratory birds, but travelers typically avoid this time as the weather is often frosty and wet. Late spring, though, is lovely. Apple trees bloom, wildflowers reappear, and seasonal tourism operations reopen, while the visitor-to-local ratio remains low.

## Climate

As a general rule, spring arrives later in coastal regions than inland, and nights are cool by the water even in summer. The balmiest land temperatures are recorded in July and August, while the ocean is at its warmest in August and early September.

Autumn can last well into November, with warm, clear days and crisp nights. Most of Atlantic Canada is blanketed by snow in winter.

As far as main cities go, it may be handy to note that St. John's is uncommonly cold and Halifax, due to the Gulf Stream, is relatively moderate in winter.

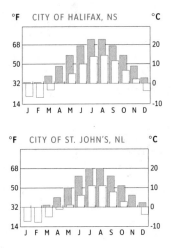

# PROVINCE PICKER

Not sure which of the four Atlantic provinces is right for you? All have hospitable people and stunning scenery, but not every one might offer that unique mix of attributes that makes it ideal for your trip. Use this chart to compare how each province will measure up to your idea of the perfect vacation. Remember, if you're looking for big cosmopolitan cities and TMZ-worthy nightlife, you'd be better off in a different part of the world.

| | Nova Scotia | New Brunswick | Prince Edward Island | Newfoundland and Labrador |
|---|:---:|:---:|:---:|:---:|
| Cold-water beaches | ◑ | ◑ | ○ | ● |
| Warm-water beaches | ◑ | ● | ● | ○ |
| Water sports | ● | ● | ● | ● |
| Snow sports | ◑ | ● | ○ | ● |
| Golfing | ● | ◑ | ● | ◑ |
| National parks | ● | ● | ◑ | ● |
| Rugged coastline | ● | ● | ◑ | ● |
| Scenic drives | ● | ● | ● | ● |
| Lighthouses | ● | ● | ● | ● |
| Lobster | ● | ● | ● | ● |
| Iceberg-watching | ○ | ○ | ○ | ● |
| Whale-watching | ● | ● | ○ | ● |
| Bird-watching | ● | ● | ● | ● |
| Historic sites | ● | ● | ◑ | ◑ |
| Museums | ● | ● | ◑ | ◑ |
| Arts and crafts | ● | ● | ● | ● |
| Wineries and distilleries | ● | ○ | ○ | ○ |
| Spas | ◑ | ◑ | ◑ | ◑ |
| Cool capitals | ● | ◑ | ◑ | ◑ |

● = Noteworthy, ◑ = Some, ○ = Little or none

# TOP ATTRACTIONS

### Halifax Waterfront Boardwalk, Nova Scotia

Halifax is the heart of Atlantic Canada and the **Halifax Waterfront Boardwalk** constitutes that city's soul, so it's only logical to take a good, long look. Shops, restaurants, and must-see attractions (including the Maritime Museum of the Atlantic and the Historic Properties) line its length while boats of every description ply the busy harbor behind it.

### Lunenburg, Nova Scotia

Timeless is a word that's often used to describe **Lunenburg**, on Nova Scotia's South Shore. Little wonder: the colorful Old Town retains a "long ago" vibe courtesy of the UNESCO World Heritage designation that has protected hundreds of 18th- and 19th-century buildings in Lunenburg's downtown core. Wandering its steep streets can feel like the next best thing to time travel.

### Hopewell Rocks, New Brunswick

To understand why the Bay of Fundy was named Canada's official entry in the "New Seven Wonders of Nature" contest, check out New Brunswick's **Hopewell Rocks**. At high tide, they appear to be nothing more than a cluster of islands. Six hours later, when the tallest tides on the planet pull back, the rocks are funky-looking megaliths that tower above the bare ocean floor.

### Beaverbrook Art Gallery, New Brunswick

The world-class collection in Fredericton's **Beaverbrook Art Gallery** rivals that of some Europe galleries. Works by painters such as Thomas Gainsborough, Salvador Dalí, Eugéne Delacroix, Sir Joshua Reynolds, and Canada's own Group of Seven, as well as Emily Carr, grace the walls of this riverfront museum, which was bequeathed by Lord Beaverbrook (aka Max Aitken)—a New Brunswick man who rose to prominence as a British press baron in the first half of the twentieth century.

### Anne's Land, Prince Edward Island

On PEI it's virtually impossible to avoid a certain redheaded orphan. If you weren't weaned on "Anne with an E," brush up on her backstory by taking in **Anne of Green Gables—The Musical** at Charlottetown's Confederation Centre. The tuneful tearjerker, based on L.M. Montgomery's classic book, has played to packed houses every summer since 1965 and shows no sign of waning in popularity, especially since the new Duchess of Windsor, née Kate Middleton, professed her love of the character.

### Cape Spear, Newfoundland

Late-night revelers love to throw back beers and bellow sea songs on pub-packed George Street in St. John's. Early risers, conversely, flock to **Cape Spear**: a National Historic Site 11 km (7 mi) away, where a lighthouse marks the easternmost point of this eastern province. Arrive at dawn and you'll be the first person in North America to see the new day break.

### Gros Morne National Park, Newfoundland

Newfoundland's seafaring history goes back to Viking days, but the Rock's natural history extends further. At **Gros Morne National Park** you can see evidence at the Tablelands, a formation created millions of years ago when the North American and North African continental plates collided, and at Western Brook Pond, a fjord carved by the last ice age.

# TOP EXPERIENCES

### Drive the Cabot Trail
The **Cabot Trail** on Nova Scotia's Cape Breton Island qualifies as one of the most dramatic drives in the world. Timid motorists should note that tackling its vertiginous, ocean-hugging turns—and the potential need to dodge a stray moose—is no easy task. Sound brakes and steady nerves are required. Yet the sheer beauty of this 298-km (185-mi) stretch amply rewards the effort.

### Sample Nova Scotia's Divine Wines
Samuel de Champlain and his thirsty crew planted Nova Scotia's first grapevines in 1611. Today the province boasts a burgeoning number of grape growers and boutique winemakers, the bulk of them concentrated in the Annapolis Valley. Learn more about the award-winning fruits of their labors by heading to an area winery. Several of them, including **Domaine de Grand Pré** in Wolfville, **Sainte Famille Winery** in Falmouth, and **Jöst Vineyards** in Malagash, offer tours and tastings.

### Ride New Brunswick Rapids . . . Rapidly
When incoming tides from the Bay of Fundy meet an outflowing river in Saint John, New Brunswick, the former pushes the latter backward, creating a phenomenon known as the **Reversing Rapids**. Thrill seekers can suit up in a slicker and brave the resulting whitewater on a wet-and-wild jet boat ride. A new zip line course that runs beside the rapids offers a breathtaking aerial alternative.

### Go Biking on PEI
Is pedal power your thing? Prince Edward Island's **Confederation Trail**, a gently graded recreational path that follows an abandoned railroad bed, positively begs to be biked. The route covers the island from tip to tip, in the process winding past vivid green fields, stands of yellow birch, red clay cliffs, white sand beaches, and the shimmering blue sea.

### Get the Inside Scoop on PEI
I scream. You scream. Everyone screams for PEI-based **Cows Ice Cream**. Polish off a double-decker cone (made from a family recipe, the ice cream incorporates premium ingredients and comes in more than 32 flavors); then pick out a cute Cows T-shirt to take home as a souvenir. Choices include one honoring the 2011 "Royal Honey*moo*n" and another featuring Atlantic Canadian hockey icon "Sidney *Cows*by."

### Chase Bergs in Newfoundland
Board a tour boat for a quick cruise around Newfoundland's **Notre Dame Bay**: it's billed as "The Iceberg Capital of the World." The optimal time to see one of these 100- to 200-thousand-ton mountains of ice float serenely by is June and early July. Latecomers, however, will be pleased to hear that the welcome mat for humpback whales stays out here through September.

### Work Up an Appetite, Region-Wide
Somehow a meal tastes so much better when you've had a hand in making it. When simply eating fresh seafood won't suffice, you can always trap, hook, harvest, or (in the case of clams) dig for your dinner, thanks to innovative hands-on programs like those offered by **Fundy Adventures** in Nova Scotia, **Shediac Bay Cruises** in New Brunswick, or **Tranquility Cove Adventures** on PEI (*see Chapters 1-3 for more information*).

# IF YOU LIKE

## Blissful Beaches

It's good news for beach lovers that Canada's easternmost provinces are shaped by the sea. Along the shoreline you'll encounter everything from pebbly coves to classic crescent beaches and several variations on the theme, including shores backed by rare parabolic dunes and ones composed of "singing sand" that squeaks when you walk on it (check out Basin Head, PEI, for that).

Top PEI picks—like touristy **Cavendish** and pristine **Prince Edward Island National Park**—are justifiably famous. Lapped by the warmest waters north of the Carolinas, they draw swimmers, sun worshipers, sand-castle builders, and bird-watchers.

On the opposite side of Northumberland Strait, eastern New Brunswick has a fine selection, too, the best of the bunch being **Parlee Beach** in Shediac, a 3-km (2-mi) expanse of sand that inevitably pulls in crowds. **New River Beach**, on the province's Bay of Fundy side, is another good bet, provided you don't mind chilly water: you'd better beware the tides, too, otherwise that grand strand might disappear, leaving you, um, stranded.

Nova Scotia has a little bit of everything. Big waves entice surfers to the **Eastern Shore**, just above Halifax, whereas the **South Shore** has lovely protected inlets and long stretches of powdery white sand. **Cape Breton's western shore** has its own little-known gems, many of them framed by mountain vistas.

Given **Newfoundland and Labrador's rugged coast** and cool temperatures, you'll probably spend more time *on* the water there than *in* it. Kayaking, sailing, and canoeing are popular activities—and watching the marine life isn't a bad way to spend the day, either.

## Scenic Drives

It's no surprise that Atlantic Canada earns an A+ for scenery. Crashing surf, forest-clad mountains, rolling farmland, meandering rivers: it's all here. Sublime vistas are so numerous that you don't even have to get out of your car to appreciate them. Designated scenic routes that highlight the best of the best make auto touring easy.

Nova Scotia alone has 11 "Scenic Travelways," including the self-explanatory **Lighthouse Route** and **Marine Drive.** If you only have time for one, make it the **Cabot Trail.** Although it may sound cliché, Cape Breton's rollercoaster-ish coastal highway proves the journey really is more important than the destination: it's widely regarded as one of the most beautiful roads on earth.

Prince Edward Island counters with three scenic drives of its own, the most popular being the **Central Coastal Drive,** which loops through top sites like Cavendish, Prince Edward Island National Park, and Charlottetown, taking in vintage Victoria and other less traveled villages along the way.

Among New Brunswick's five routes are ones that showcase the world's highest tides (the **Fundy Coastal Drive**) and oldest mountains (the **Appalachian Range Route**). Other options, such as the River Valley Scenic Drive with its covered bridges and open-deck cable ferries, are equally remarkable.

Similarly, Newfoundland and Labrador's celebrated scenery can be seen all through the province. In particular, the **Discovery Trail,** near Clarenville, passes some of Newfoundland's most historic communities, while the long **Labrador Frontier Circuit** reveals how great the great outdoors actually is.

## Novel Excursions

When Prince William and his bride made their first official trip abroad, Kate reportedly asked that PEI be put on their itinerary, specifically so that she could see locales from a favorite childhood book—**Anne of Green Gables.** In doing so, the Duchess of Cambridge reinforced that Green Gables *is* the place to be. She also reminded the world about this region's strong literary connections.

L.M. Montgomery, who was born and buried on Prince Edward Island, introduced her irrepressible title character in 1908. Today, fans flock to associated sites such as Silver Bush, Avonlea, and, of course, the Cavendish farm that gave the series its name: a bucolic spot that is as fertile as Anne's imagination.

Over in Nova Scotia, Cape Breton has provided a backdrop for Alistair MacLeod, Lynn Coady, and *Oprah Book Club* alum Anne-Marie MacDonald. The latest literary pilgrimage site, however, is the Shelburne/Birchtown area on the South Shore. It featured prominently in a novel that's been described as Canada's answer to *Roots*—Lawrence Hill's **The Book of Negroes** (published in the U.S. as *Someone Knows My Name*).

In New Brunswick, Acadian writer Antonine Maillet's witty charwomen, **La Sangouine**, is popular enough to inspire a cultural park near Bouctouche. As for Newfoundland and Labrador, the spirit of that place was, ironically, best captured by an American. Annie Proulx's **The Shipping News** conjures up evocative images of foggy vistas and flipper pie, both of which are plentiful in Trinity Bay where the movie adaptation was filmed.

## Living History

With all due respect to Columbus, it was Viking explorer Leif Eriksson who "discovered" North America when he landed in Newfoundland in 1000 AD. By the 1600s, the French and English were duking it out in the remaining three provinces. Hence this region is rife with history, and there are many spots where you can step back in time.

The Viking settlement at **L'Anse aux Meadows,** in Newfoundland, is now a UNESCO World Heritage Site featuring excavated sod huts, interpretive programs, and a visitor center filled with artifacts. At nearby **Norstead** you can enter Norse-style buildings, board a full-scale Viking boat, and perhaps throw an ax with the aid of a costumed staffer.

In Nova Scotia's Annapolis Valley, history buffs can hit the pause button at **Port Royal,** a reconstruction of the fur-trading post built by the French in 1605, before proceeding to Cape Breton to ogle the mighty fortress they erected at **Louisburg** more than a century later. Elsewhere on that island you can learn about the Scottish connection (remember, Nova Scotia is Latin for "New Scotland") at the open-air **Highland Village Museum.**

New Brunswick, meanwhile, has sprawling living-history museums devoted to both French- and English-speaking colonials—**Acadian Historical Village** and **Kings Landing Historical Settlement,** respectively. **Metepenagiag Heritage Park** tells another part of the story by focusing on the Miramichi River's traditional Mi'kmaq culture. In PEI's **Confederation Hall** state-of-the-art technology explains how the country of Canada was created during the Charlottetown Conference of 1864.

# QUINTESSENTIAL
# NOVA SCOTIA & ATLANTIC CANADA

## Eat Succulent Seafood

Atlantic salmon, Digby scallops, Malpeque Bay oysters—this part of Canada is nirvana for seafood fans. Nothing, however, makes true aficionados swoon like fresh local lobster. Fast-food junkies can try a McLobster while Food Channel aficionados can buy lobster right off the wharf and boil it themselves. In some places, visitors curious about crustaceans can learn how to haul in traps before devouring the catch. Want to get right down to business? You'll find lobster ready to eat in simple dockside eateries and haute-cuisine restaurants almost everywhere. Perhaps the most satisfying feasts are the communal lobster suppers hosted each summer by rural churches and community centers: look for signs posted in coastal areas. At these unpretentious gatherings tables are long, prices are low, and the ambience is unforgettable.

## See Illuminating Lighthouses

Nowhere is the marine heritage of Atlantic Canada more evident than in the 400-plus lighthouses that stand sentry on the coast. Each has its own claim to fame. Newfoundland's Cape Spear Light, for example, marks the continent's most easterly point; the one at Peggy's Cove, near Halifax, is one of the continent's most photographed. Amazing views of ferries, fishing boats, and, occasionally, spouting whales set New Brunswick's Swallowtail Light apart. But PEI's Cape Bear lighthouse has a sadder distinction: it received the first SOS from the *Titanic* as she sank in 1912. Though designed to be seen from afar, many of these structures now offer visitors up-close experiences. Some house museums, crafts shops, or restaurants. A few—like Newfoundland's Quirpon, Nova Scotia's Cape d'Or, and PEI's West Point—even offer accommodations.

If you want to genuinely *experience* Atlantic Canada, as opposed to merely seeing it, you must first learn what makes Atlantic Canadians tick. Sampling these tried-and-true activities will give you the inside track.

## Learn the Lingo

Canada's multicultural model isn't a melting pot so much as a simmering stew that enables each group to maintain its distinctive character. In this region one result is a unique linguistic mélange. For most folks English is the mother tongue, yet in northern New Brunswick (Canada's only officially bilingual province), French predominates. Ditto for Nova Scotia's Acadian Coast and parts of PEI, so you may want to practice your *bonjour* and *merci* before arriving. Gaelic is added to the mix in Cape Breton, which is home to North America's only Gaelic college: you won't be on the island long before someone wishes you *ciad mille failte* (a hundred thousand welcomes). Newfoundland famously has a lingo all its own. You best twig to it, too, or you might be a chucklehead and decline if invited out for a scoff and a scuff (dinner and a dance).

## Slow Down

You might as well ease your foot off that gas pedal: in Atlantic Canada, no one's in a hurry to get anywhere. Despite their quick wits, people here choose to move at a slower pace and will happily interrupt almost any activity to chat with a friend, a neighbor—or you, if given a chance. Such behavior can frustrate travelers intent on sticking to a strict itinerary. If you're open to opportunities, though, you'll not only see firsthand how friendly Atlantic Canadians are, you'll likely also come away with in-the-know info on hidden back roads, undiscovered eateries, and one-of-a-kind events. Taking time out may mean you have to pare back the destinations you cover or drop some attractions from your sightseeing checklist. Well, so be it. After all, this is a vacation, not The Amazing Race. Slow down and savor the experience.

# QUINTESSENTIAL CANADA

## Learn to Say "Eh"

Canada's "Eh" is as emblematic as France's "zut, alors," except in Canada, people actually say "eh," and say it all the time. Master this verbal tic and you'll fit in anywhere. The wonderful thing about "eh" is its versatility. There's the interrogatory "eh" ("You want to go to a movie, eh?"), the consensus-seeking "eh" ("This is good pie, eh?"), the inquisitive "eh" ("She's got a new boyfriend, eh?"), the solo "eh," which translates as "Repeat, please," and the simple punctuation "eh" that can be dropped randomly into long narratives to reassure the listener that it's a dialogue, not a soliloquy. Then there's the conciliatory "eh"—perhaps the oddest one of all. Canadians drop it in at the end of insults to change an imperative like "Take off" (or worse) into more of a suggestion than a command. And really, it does take the edge off, eh?

## A "Large Double-Double"

Forget that fancy mocha-choca latte, nothing says Canada more clearly than a "large double-double" (shorthand for a big cup of joe with two creams and two sugars) at Tim Hortons with a maple-glazed donut on the side. Despite the fact that the chain is now owned by an American conglomerate and that most people under 40 have forgotten that its founder was hockey great Tim Horton of the Toronto Maple Leafs, Timmy's is still a national institution. You'll see its trademark logo splashed on signs everywhere from Vancouver, BC, to Happy Valley, Newfoundland. Indeed the only thing in Canada more prevalent than Timmy's is taxes, and you can learn something curious about the latter by visiting the former. Buy one doughnut as a treat and you'll be taxed. Buy six and you won't because they count as groceries.

# Nova Scotia

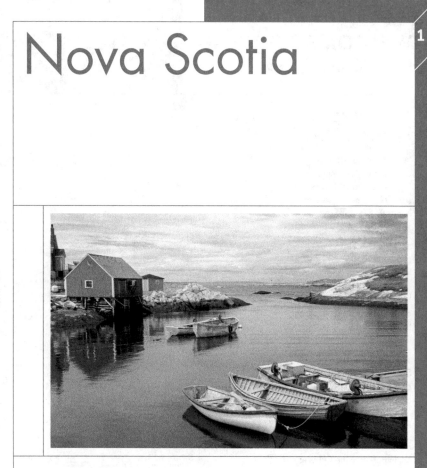

## WORD OF MOUTH

"IMO, Cape Breton Island is the most scenic part of Nova Scotia. If I were you, I would definitely spend some time there . . . We stayed in Baddeck. We spent all day driving around the Cabot Trail and hiked along the Skyline Trail. . . . You could spend a night or two in Halifax . . . the waterfront is nice. . . . We also visited Annapolis Royal while staying in Wolfville, and toured Grand Pre National Park."

—Kwoo

# WELCOME TO NOVA SCOTIA

Dock street, Shelburne

## TOP REASONS TO GO

★ **See the Coast:** There are postcard-perfect fishing villages and sprawling sandy beaches. The water is inviting, too, for kayaking, sailing, or whale-watching.

★ **Dine on Crustaceans:** This province is shaped liked a lobster claw, a happy coincidence since the lobster here is so delicious. Mussels and oysters are also plentiful, and Digby lays claim to the world's finest scallops.

★ **Shop for Crafts:** Nova Scotians—from the quilters at Suttles and Seawinds in Mahone Bay to the students of Halifax's Centre for Craft & Design—create high-quality products.

★ **Experience the Culture:** Cape Breton "kitchen parties" combine music and dancing, allowing you to sample the region's rich Celtic culture. For a French-tinged alternative, substitute a rollicking Acadian *soiree*.

★ **Enjoy the Camaraderie:** Bluenosers (the long-standing nickname for Nova Scotians) are famously friendly and very social. So be responsive—with a little encouragement you'll likely be embraced like long lost kin.

**1 Halifax.** The Halifax Regional Municipality is Atlantic Canada's biggest city and—as Nova Scotia's capital—has been a military, commercial, political, and cultural powerhouse for over 250 years. Its downtown showcases the best of old and new through waterfront restaurants, pubs, galleries, heritage properties, and modern office towers.

**2 South Shore and Annapolis Valley.** The South Shore, on the Atlantic coast, is "classic" Nova Scotia, complete with weathered fishing villages, craggy coves, and white-sand beaches. The Annapolis Valley, on the Bay of Fundy side, is more pastoral and better known for orchards, vineyards, and picturesque farming villages.

1

Sheep, Fortress of Louisbourg, Cape Breton

Clam digging on the Bay of Fundy

QUEBEC

## GETTING ORIENTED

Nova Scotia is all but surrounded by water, save for the narrow stretch of land that links it to the rest of Canada. Secondary highways hug the coastline and meander through historic, small towns, while "100-series" arterial highways offer the fastest travel routes. Halifax, the capital, sits on the eastern coast, roughly in the middle of the province's mainland. Southwest of the city, the South Shore runs all the way to Yarmouth. The Annapolis Valley, beside the Bay of Fundy, is the eastern spine of Nova Scotia. The central and northern areas lie beside Northumberland Strait (on a fine day you can see across to PEI); while the northernmost region, Cape Breton Island, is connected to the remainder of the province by a 1.6-km (1-mi) causeway.

**3 Eastern Shore and Northern Nova Scotia.** The area east and north of Halifax reveals remarkable variety within a relatively short distance. The sparsely populated Eastern Shore has pounding surf, thick forests, and remote cranberry barrens, while Northumberland Strait boasts hiking trails, and sandy warm-water beaches.

**4 Cape Breton.** The Island of Cape Breton is the Celtic heart of Nova Scotia, where music and dancing are a part of daily life. The gritty, industrial past of its towns and cities is a sharp contrast to the unspoiled natural beauty that defines the rural areas. The island is home to the Cabot Trail, a spectacular drive through the Cape Breton Highlands.

By Susan
MacCallum-
Whitcomb

It was Thomas Chandler Haliburton who first said "seeing is believing," and the observation applies to his home province because it's hard to fathom such a variety of cultures and landscapes packed into an area smaller than West Virginia without witnessing it firsthand. For many, Nova Scotia evokes images of seascapes. To the south and east, the Atlantic crashes against rocky outcrops or washes placidly over white sand. To the west, Fundy tides recede to reveal mud flats, then rush back in a ferocious wall of water. To the north, warm, relatively shallow Northumberland Strait flows between Nova Scotia and PEI providing a livelihood for fishermen on both sides.

Within the perimeter drawn by that convoluted coastline, however, lie the rolling farmlands of the Annapolis Valley, which yields vintner's grapes, apples, corn, peaches, and plums. In the middle of the province, dense forests are interspersed with blueberry patches, cranberry bogs, and, in spring and summer, open fields of wildflowers—purple and blue lupines, yellow coltsfoot, pink fireweed—that blanket the ground with color. In Cape Breton are highlands that rival Scotland's rugged rock-rimmed inlets, and mountains that plunge dramatically down to meet the waves.

The people of Nova Scotia are equally diverse. The original inhabitants, the Mi'Kmaqs, have been here for 10,000 years and remain a major cultural presence. In the early days of European exploration, they were joined by the French and English who settled on the shores and harvested the sea. Later, waves of immigrants came: Germans in Lunenburg County; Highland Scots displaced by their landlords' preference for sheep; New England Loyalists fleeing the American Revolution; blacks arriving as freemen or escaped slaves; then Ukranians, Poles, West Indians, Italians, and Lebanese drawn to the industrial centers of Halifax and Sydney.

That multicultural mélange accounts for the fact that you'll see Gaelic signs in Mabou and Iona, German sausage and sauerkraut prominently featured on menus in Lunenburg, and Francophones proudly flying their own tricolor flag in Acadian communities. It also helps explain why Nova Scotians, who originally hailed from so many different places themselves, are so famously hospitable to "people from away."

# PLANNING

**1**

## DISCOUNTS AND DEALS

The Nova Scotia Museum Pass lets you visit 27 provincially-run sites (including popular picks like Halifax's Maritime Museum, Lunenburg's Fisheries Museum, and Cape Breton's Highland Village) as many times as you want for a full year. Priced at C$43 for adults and C$85 for a family of four, the passes are an excellent value. Call ☎ *800/632–1114* or go to ⊕ *www.museum.gov.ns.ca* for details.

## DRIVING ROUTES AND HIKING TRAILS

Hiking, biking, and horseback riding routes make inland exploring a breeze; kayak and canoe routes let you splash out with ease; and there are snowmobile and cross-country skiing options, too. The province's trail site (⊕ *www.trails.gov.ns.ca*) will put you on the right path.

Motorists can sample Nova Scotia's sensational scenery by following any of the province's 11 Scenic Travelways. There are five in Cape Breton and six on the mainland, all clearly identified by roadside signs with icons that correspond to route names. Nova Scotia Tourism's encyclopedic *Doers and Dreamers Guide* has the lowdown (☎ *902/425–5781 or 800/565–0000* ⊕ *www.novascotia.com*).

## FESTIVALS

Nova Scotia annually hosts some 600 festivals and, at first glance, you'd think 599 were devoted to food. June's **Shelburne County Lobster Festival** and July's **Lobster Carnival** in Pictou are followed by a **Seafest** in Yarmouth that celebrates all things fishy. Not to be outdone, Digby turns the spotlight on **scallops** in August. The farm-filled Annapolis Valley brackets the fishing season by offering an **Apple Blossom Festival** in May and **Pumpkin Fest** in October. Many other events, however, highlight the diversity of the Nova Scotian people. In June, a **multicultural festival** on the Halifax waterfront showcases more than two dozen ethno-cultural groups. Antigonish honors its Scottish heritage with the **Highland Games** in July, and there is a rollicking **Acadian fête in Clare** each August. Halifax focuses on a different type of diversity during its mid-summer LGBT **Pride Week**.

Music lovers have several festivals to choose from.

The nine-day **Celtic Colours International Festival** (☎ *902/562–6700 or 877/285–2321* ⊕ *www.celtic-colours.com*), in Cape Breton, spans the first and second weekends in October, and showcases the very best Celtic musicians and dancers, while fall colors are at their peak. International artists and homegrown talent shine in performances staged in more than three dozen island communities. Ticket prices range from C$20 to C$90. Workshops and seminars covering all aspects of Gaelic language, lore, history, crafts, and culture complement the joyful noise.

**The Royal Nova Scotia International Tattoo** (✉ *Metro Centre, 1800 Argyle St.* ☎ *902/420–1114 or 800/563–1114* ⊕ *www.nstattoo.ca* ✆ *C$34–$70*), generally considered the city's signature event, is a celebration of military instruments (brass and drums) and military-inspired music that runs the first week of July. The extravaganza features 1,700-plus performers from around the globe.

The internationally acclaimed **Scotia Festival of Music** (☎ 902/429–9467 ⊕ *www.scotiafestival.ns.ca*) presents classical musicians via concert and master classes each June. The **TD Halifax Jazz Festival** (☎ *902/492–2225* ⊕ *www.jazzeast.com*), with an eclectic selection of jazz styles, takes place in mid-July. Some concerts are free.

Prefer more traditional tunes? Lunenburg and Wolfville stage **folksy festivals** in August and September, respectively. In October, Cape Breton pulls out the fiddles and pipes during the **Celtic Colors International Festival**, and the capital counters with the **Halifax Pop Explosion**.

Shoppers will enjoy the Lunenburg **Folk Art Festival** (⊕ *www.nsfolkart-festival.com*), in late July or early August.

**The Halifax International Busker Festival** (☎ 902/422–9262 ⊕ *www.buskers. ca*) has been bringing street performers to the waterfront area for more than two decades. It's an 11-day event that takes place every August and includes more than 50 acts and events for all ages. The first week of September, the **Atlantic Fringe Festival** (☎ *902/435–4837* ⊕ *www. atlanticfringe.ca*) presents numerous theatrical shows in a variety of venues downtown. Eastern Canada also has a burgeoning film industry, the product of which is presented at the **Atlantic Film Festival** (☎ 902/422–3456 ⊕ *www.atlanticfilm.com*) during the third week in September. Admission to films often includes entry to a party or gala event following the screening.

Knowing a good thing when they see it, townspeople honor the magnificent mollusk during **Digby Scallop Days** (⊕ *www.digbyscallopdays. com*), a five-day festival in early August replete with parades, fireworks, and food.

## GETTING HERE AND AROUND
### BY AIR
Halifax's Stanfield International Airport is Atlantic Canada's largest airport. Ground transport into Halifax takes 30 to 40 minutes. Limousine and taxi services, as well as car rentals, are available on-site. Airporter Inc., which has regular bus service to most major city hotels, charges C$19.50 one-way. Regular taxi fares into Halifax are C$53 each way. If you book ahead with Share-A-Cab, the fare is around C$30, depending on your time of arrival, but you must share your car with another passenger.

Visitors proceeding on to other Nova Scotian destinations can take shuttles to the South Shore, Annapolis Valley, and Cape Breton. Cape Breton–bound travelers short on time can also fly into Sydney's own airport.

**Contacts Airporter Inc.** (☎ *902/873-2091* ⊕ www.airporter.biz). **Halifax Stanfield International Airport** (☎ *902/873-4422* ⊕ www.hiaa.ca). **J.A. Douglas McCurdy Sydney Airport** (☎ *902/564-7720* ⊕ www.sydneyairport.ca). **Share-A-Cab** (☎ *902/429-5555 or 800/565-8669* ⊕ www.atyp.com/ashareacab).

### BY BUS
Because of conflicting schedules, getting to Nova Scotia by bus can be problematic, but Greyhound, entering through New Brunswick, does connect with Acadian—which, in turn, provides service between Nova

Scotian communities. Shuttle buses offering transport between Halifax and Sydney include Cape Shuttle and Scotia Shuttle.

**Contacts Acadian** (☎ 800/567–5151 ⊕ *www.acadianbus.com*). **Greyhound Canada** (☎ 800/661–8747 ⊕ *www.greyhound.ca*). **Cape Shuttle** (☎ 902/539–8585 *or* 800/349–1698 ⊕ *www.capeshuttleservice.com*). **Scotia Shuttle** (☎ 902/435–9686 *or* 800/898–5883 ⊕ *www.atyp.com*).

### BY CAR

The only overland route to Nova Scotia crosses the Isthmus of Chignecto: a narrow neck of land that joins the province to New Brunswick. The TransCanada Highway (Highway 2 in New Brunswick) becomes Highway 104 in Amherst, the first town after the border. From there you can make it to Halifax (connecting to Hwy. 102 at Truro) in two hours. Alternately, you can opt for a scenic drive up Route 6 (which runs along the coast of Northumberland Strait) or down Route 2 (which hugs the Fundy Shore).

### BY SEA

Car ferries connect Nova Scotia with New Brunswick, PEI, and Newfoundland *(see the Travel Smart chapter for specifics and timing)*. Cruise ships often dock in Halifax and Sydney as well.

**Contacts Bay Ferries Ltd.** (☎ 877/359-3760 *or* 888/249-7245 ⊕ *www.nfl-bay. com*). **Cruise Halifax** (☎ 902/426-8222 ⊕ *www.cruisehalifax.ca*). **Marine Atlantic** (☎ 800/341-7981 ⊕ *www.marine-atlantic.ca*). **Port of Sydney** (☎ 902/564-0800 ⊕ *www.portofsydney.ca*).

### BY TRAIN

Via Rail offers overnight service from Montréal to Halifax six times a week.

**Contacts Via Rail** (☎ 888/842-7245 ⊕ *www.viarail.ca*).

## LOCAL FLAVORS: NOVA SCOTIA

This province's verdant landscapes and churning seas are a feast for the eyes and also provide a feast for the table. Nova Scotians contend that the best meals are made using local ingredients (Lunenburg lobster, Digby scallops, Atlantic salmon, Annapolis Valley apples . . .) and recipes handed down through generations. If you're serious about discovering down-home favorites, seek out dishes with curious names like Hodge Podge (a summer staple of beans, peas, carrots, and baby potatoes, cooked in cream), Solomon Gundy (a pickled-herring pâté), *rappie* pie (a hearty chicken stew with dried, shredded potatoes), and blueberry grunt (a steamed pudding featuring Nova Scotia's finest berries). Looking for something a bit more sophisticated? A growing number of dining establishments, especially in Halifax and the southern part of the province, are putting their own spin on Nova Scotia classics, fusing time-honored ingredients with contemporary flair. The province's *Taste of Nova Scotia: Culinary Adventure Guide* (⊕ *www.tasteofnovascotia. com*) will help you find them. A companion Adventures in Taste app is also available, free, at ⊕ *www.adventuresintaste.ca*.

For local libations, try a beer (or two) from the growing number of microbreweries. Propeller, Garrison, Keltic, and Rudder's all draw on the history of the region and produce distinctive, tasty ale, lager, stout, and more. Local wines are growing in popularity and reputation as well. Try Jost from Malagash, Sainte Famille Winery from Falmouth, and Domaine de Grand Pré near Wolfville. And what better way to cap a Nova Scotian dinner than with a dram of the acclaimed Glen Breton, North America's original single-malt whiskey. (Nova Scotia may mean "New Scotland," but you still can't call it "Scotch" unless it's actually produced in Scotland.) In Gaelic, they call single-malt *Uisge beatha* ("the water of life"): one sip of Glen Breton and you'll know why.

### THE SPORTS ENTHUSIAST'S ADDRESS BOOK

Nova Scotian sporting associations can be an invaluable resource for active travelers province-wide. In addition to the individual commercial outfitters we list throughout the chapter, these are some good provincial resources.

**Canoeing and Kayaking** (☎ 902/425–5454 Ext. 316 ⊕ www.ckns.ca).

**Cycling** (☎ 902/425–5450 Ext. 316 ⊕ www.bicycle.ns.ca).

**Golfing** (☎ 902/468–8844 ⊕ www.nsga.ns.ca or ☎ 866/404–3224 ⊕ www.golfnovascotia.com).

**Hiking** (☎ 902/425–5450 Ext. 325 ⊕ www.novascotiatrails.com).

**Sailing** (☎ 902/425–5450 Ext. 312 ⊕ www.nsya.ns.ca).

**Surfing** (☎ No phone ⊕ www.surfns.com).

### TOURS

Multiday packaged bus tours to and within Nova Scotia are available through Ambassatours Gray Line. **Ambassatours Gray Line** (☎ 902/423–6242 or 800-565-7173 ⊕ www.ambassatours.com).

### VISITOR INFORMATION

**Halifax Tourism** (⊕ www.halifaxinfo.com).

**Nova Scotia Tourism** (⊕ www.novascotia.com).

**Tourism Cape Breton** (⊕ www.cbisland.com).

| WHAT IT COSTS IN CANADIAN DOLLARS | | | | |
|---|---|---|---|---|
| | ¢ | $ | $$ | $$$ | $$$$ |
| Restaurants | under C$8 | C$8–C$12 | C$13–C$20 | C$21–C$30 | over C$30 |
| Hotels | under C$75 | C$75–C$125 | C$126–C$175 | C$176–C$250 | over C$250 |

Restaurant prices are per person for a main course at dinner. Hotel prices are for two people in a standard double room in high season.

### WHEN TO GO

Spring comes late in Nova Scotia: trees don't get leafy until mid-May, and it takes until mid-June for temperatures to heat up. As a result, many find July and August to be the ideal months here, but even then, come prepared: you'll soon understand why Bluenosers say, "If you don't like the weather, wait a minute." Bring a raincoat for morning fog and showers, a sweater to keep the ocean breezes at bay at night, and your bathing suit for the blazing sun in between. Autumn has its own charm: September has warm days, refreshingly cool nights, and hot events like Halifax's Atlantic Film and Atlantic Fringe festivals. Late September through October is peak time for foliage fans. The downside is that wildlife cruises, cycling tours, and kayaking outfitters generally only operate from mid-June through September. Keep in mind, too, that outside major tourist centers, many resorts, inns, and B&Bs close after Canadian Thanksgiving (Columbus Day in the United States) and don't reopen until Victoria Day in late May. Some shops, restaurants, and sites are also seasonal.

### WHERE TO SEE WHALES

The two best places for whale watching are on the Bay of Fundy, from Digby down to Digby Neck, or in Cape Breton, on Pleasant Bay. There are other spots to go whale-watching (Halifax, for instance) but the chances of sightseeing are not as great.

# HALIFAX

*1,137 km (705 mi) northeast of Boston; 275 km (171 mi) southeast of Moncton, New Brunswick.*

It was Halifax's natural harbor—the second largest in the world after Sydney, Australia's—that first drew the British here in 1749, and today most major sites are conveniently located either along it or on the Citadel-crowned hill overlooking it. That's good news for visitors because this city actually covers quite a bit of ground.

Since amalgamating with Dartmouth (directly across the harbor) and several suburbs in 1996, Halifax has been absorbed into the Halifax Regional Municipality, and the HRM, as it is known, has 400,000 residents. That may not sound like a lot by U.S. standards, but it makes Nova Scotia's capital the most significant Canadian urban center east of Montréal. Haligonians will tell you that it's also the most interesting—and they have a point, at least as far as Halifax proper is concerned.

The old city manages to feel both hip and historic. Previous generations had the foresight to preserve much of it, culturally as well as architecturally, yet students from five local universities keep it from being stuffy. In addition to the energetic arts-and-entertainment scene the students help create, visitors also benefit from enviable dining, shopping, and museum-hopping options.

There's easy access to the water, too, and despite being the focal point of a busy commercial port, Halifax Harbour doubles as a playground. It's a place where container ships, commuter ferries, cruise ships, and tour boats compete for space, and where workaday tugs and fishing vessels tie up beside glitzy yachts. Like Halifax as a whole, the harbor represents a blend of the traditional and the contemporary.

### GETTING HERE AND AROUND

Halifax is an intimate city that's large enough to have the trappings of a capital, yet compact enough to be explored with ease. Because most sites are comparatively close, walking is a good way to get around. The caveat is that streets connecting the waterfront to Citadel Hill are steep. If you're not prepared for a nine-block uphill hike, grab a cab. Rates begin at C$3 and increase based on mileage and time. (A crosstown

# NOVA SCOTIA GREAT ITINERARIES

Don't let the fact that Nova Scotia is Canada's second-smallest province fool you. Driving (the only feasible way to go if you venture beyond pedestrian-friendly Halifax) will likely take longer than you expect. Aside from being so irregularly shaped, Nova Scotia is riddled with harbors and inlets that complicate the highway system. These recommended routes—all starting and ending in Halifax—hit the highlights.

### IF YOU HAVE 3 DAYS

Spend your first full day in **Halifax**. Explore downtown, leaving time to linger on the harborfront boardwalk, and have a fun evening out in one of the many pubs and clubs. Don't stay out too late, though—you'll need to be up early to beat the crowds to **Peggy's Cove**. From there, head down to the "Holy Trinity" of South Shore towns: Chester, Mahone Bay, and Lunenburg. Have a coffee break in **Chester** before proceeding to lovely **Mahone Bay** for lunch and boutique browsing. In **Lunenburg** visit the Fisheries Museum and sign on for one of the boat tours departing from its dock. Next, drive on to the Liverpool area (an hour away) where you'll stop for the night. Depending on your preferences, you can dedicate the morning of Day 3 to blissful beaches or immediately veer northwest on Highway 8, which connects Liverpool to Annapolis Royal. Hikers can dally en route at **Kejimkujik National Park and Historic Site**. History buffs can drive 90 minutes straight through, thereby allowing more time to visit the heritage sites in and around **Annapolis Royal** and **Wolfville**. Given that Halifax is about 200 km (124 mi) from the former and 90 km (56 mi) from the latter, completing the loop and returning to the capital for your final night is easy.

### IF YOU HAVE 5 DAYS

Stick to the above itinerary but, rather than continuing on to Halifax at the end of Day 3, bed down at a **Wolfville** inn. As you've already seen the Atlantic and Bay of Fundy, it seems unsporting not to add Northumberland Strait to your itinerary. So, on the morning of Day 4, take the pretty three-hour drive cross-country to **Pictou**. There you can visit Hector Heritage Quay, where the Scots landed in 1773, and take a dip in the strait's warm salty water. On the morning of Day 5, explore a bit more of the **Sunrise Trail** by car or kayak, then make the two-hour trek back to **Halifax**.

### IF YOU HAVE 7 DAYS

Cape Breton Island is a nice place to spend a week, or a lifetime, but you *can* cover the basics in two days. Follow the route above, perhaps overnighting in **Pictou** (FYI: As the Caribou ferry terminal is minutes away, Pictou is a good launch pad for PEI-bound tourists, too) before backtracking to Halifax. A 235 km (146 mi) journey west and north—stopping on the way in music-loving **Mabou**—puts you in **Margaree Harbour**. Then, take the **Cabot Trail** to **Ingonish** (the cliff-hugging trail rates as one of the world's most dramatic drives). On Day 6, be in **Louisbourg** by lunch and devote the afternoon to this reconstructed 18th-century French fortress. An easier alternative is to stay on the Cabot Trail to **Baddeck**, allowing time to visit Alexander Graham Bell's former home before making the 2½-hour return trip to Pictou.

trip should cost C$7 to $8, depending on traffic.) You can usually hail one downtown or pick one up at a hotel stand. Otherwise, call **Casino Taxi** or **Yellow Cab.**

July through mid-October, you can save your energy—and money— by hopping **FRED**, a complimentary shuttle (it stands for "Free Rides Everywhere Downtown") provided by the Downtown Halifax Business Commission. From 10:30 am to 5 pm daily, the bright green bus makes a 40-minute loop traversing the waterfront from Pier 21 to Casino Nova Scotia, and going uphill as far as the Spring Garden Road shopping district.

If you want to combine transportation with narration, **Ambassatours Gray Line** runs a series of coach tours throughout Halifax (including ones aboard double-decker buses) as well as to outlying communities like Peggy's Cove and Lunenburg. Virtually every local cab company also gives customized driving tours.

Boat tours are popular as well, with the broadest selection being offered from the boardwalk by **Murphy's Cable Wharf**. It sails various vessels mid-May to late October, among them a 23-meter (75-foot) ketch and a Mississippi-style sternwheeler. Murphy's even has an amphibious Harbour Hopper for those who want to see by land *and* water. If you're traveling with kids, try a Big Harbour tour aboard Theodore Tugboat. Theodore is a seafaring version of Thomas the Tank Engine, and even children unfamiliar with the Canadian character will get a kick out of the tugboat's broad grin and bright red cap. Costs and durations of these trips vary, but a basic tour of Halifax Harbour ranges from C$15 to $25. An affordable alternative to a Murphy's tour is to take the **Metro Transit Commuter Ferry** from the boardwalk terminal at Lower Water Street across the harbor to downtown Dartmouth. Inaugurated in 1752, it's North America's oldest saltwater ferry service and, at C$2.25 for a 20-minute ride, a real deal. Dartmouth—once Halifax's "Twin City" and now part of the HRM—is straight across the harbor and accessible from Halifax proper by passenger ferry or by car via the Angus L. Macdonald and A. Murray MacKay Bridges. Motorists can avoid bridge traffic by taking a land route that loops around the Bedford Basin.

### ESSENTIALS

**Boat Tours Metro Transit Commuter Ferry** (☎ 902/490–4000 ⊕ www. halifax.ca/metrotransit). **Murphy's Cable Wharf** (☎ 902/420–1015 ⊕ www. murphysonthewater.com).

**Bus Tours Ambassatours Gray Line** (☎ 902/423–6242 or 800/565–7173 ⊕ www.ambassatours.com).

**Taxi and Bus Contacts Casino Taxi** (☎ 902/429–6666 or 902/425–6666 ⊕ www.casinotaxi.ns.ca). **FRED** (☎ 902/423–6658 ⊕ www.downtownhalifax. ns.ca). **Yellow Cab** (☎ 902/420–0000 or 902/422–1551).

## TOP ATTRACTIONS

**Art Gallery of Nova Scotia.** In an 1867 Italianate-style building that saw service as a post office, bank, and headquarters for the Royal Canadian Mounted Police, the provincial art gallery has an extensive permanent collection of more than 14,000 works. Some are primarily of historical

## A GOOD WALK

Starting your walk at the **Halifax Citadel National Historic Site** is practical because, as the city's highest point, it puts you on a downhill course. More importantly, visiting the star-shaped fortress—built in the 1800s as an outpost for the then-expanding British Empire—is like taking a crash course in civic history. After exploring the site, descend the stairs (a more direct route for pedestrians than the road) to the **Town Clock**, which has been keeping time for more than two centuries.

From here, cross Brunswick Street and head down Carmichael, passing the Metro Centre (Halifax's main sporting venue) and the World Trade and Convention Centre en route to the Grand Parade. Once used for military drills, the leafy rectangle is now the setting for summertime picnics and free concerts. Anchoring its right end is **St. Paul's Church** (dating from 1750, it's the country's oldest Protestant church); the Second Empire–style stone building on the left end is City Hall. As you exit the park, Carmichael Street becomes St. George. Follow it two blocks down to Hollis, then make a short detour to see the impressive collection of folk art in the **Art Gallery of Nova Scotia. Province House**, Canada's oldest legislative building, is just across the street and is also open for tours. Walking another two

blocks down lands you on Water Street, where you'll find the **Historic Properties**, a cluster of restored warehouses linked by cobblestone lanes, containing shops and eateries.

If you go straight through, you will reach the **Halifax Waterfront Boardwalk**, which runs all the way over to Marginal Road. This is where decision-making gets difficult. Depending on your tastes (and budget) you might board a sightseeing boat at Cable Wharf, hop the **Metro Transit Commuter Ferry** to the Dartmouth side of the harbor, take in the action from a waterfront restaurant, or simply ogle the tugboats and transatlantic yachts that often tie up here. Whatever you choose, be sure to leave time for the **Maritime Museum of the Atlantic**, where you can learn about Nova Scotia's seafaring past. A final stop lies to the south, just off the boardwalk: the Port of Halifax seawall development, which includes the cruise ship terminal, the new **Seaport Farmers' Market**, and **Pier 21**, a former immigration depot that now houses **Canadian Museum of Immigration**. You could spend several hours in Pier 21 alone, so if you're staying in the city longer, save this for another day. Instead, cap your walking tour with a libation in a local pub. Halifax is said to have more pubs per capita than anywhere else in Canada.

interest; others are major works by contemporary Canadian painters like Christopher Pratt, Alex Colville, and Tom Forrestall. The gallery's heart, however, is an internationally recognized collection of maritime folk art by artists such as woodcarver Sydney Howard and painter Joe Norris. This is also the actual home of the late painter Maude Lewis (Canada's answer to Grandma Moses), whose bright, cheery paintings cover the tiny structure inside and out. A guided tour of the collection is given daily at 2:30, with an extra one added Thursdays at 7. The gallery's gift shop carries an excellent selection of arts and crafts. ⊠ *1723 Hollis St.*

Alexander Keith's
Nova Scotia
Brewery . . . . . . . **11**

Anna Leonowens
Gallery . . . . . . . . . . **9**

Art Gallery of
Nova Scotia . . . . . **5**

Canadian Museum
of Immigration
at Pier 21 . . . . . **13**

Government
House . . . . . . . . . **12**

Halifax Citadel
National
Historic Site . . . . **3**

Halifax Public
Gardens . . . . . . . . . **1**

Halifax
Waterfront
Broadwalk . . . . . **8**

Historic
Properties . . . . . . **7**

Maritime
Museum of
the Atlantic . . . **10**

Mary E. Black
Gallery . . . . . . . . **14**

Nova Scotia
Museum of Natural
History . . . . . . . . . . **2**

Point Pleasant
Park . . . . . . . . . . . **15**

Province
House . . . . . . . . . . . **6**

St. Paul's
Church . . . . . . . . . . **4**

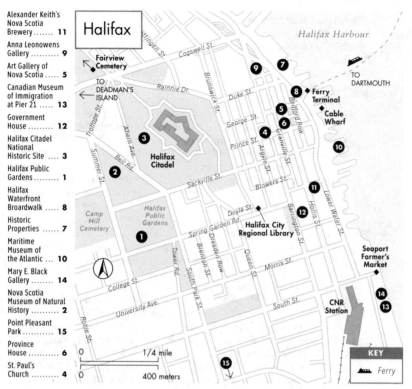

☎ 902/424–5280 or 902/424–7542 ⊕ www.artgalleryofnovascotia.ca
C$12; Thurs. evening by donation ⊙ Mon.–Wed. and Fri.–Sun.
10–5, Thurs. 10–9; Nov.–Apr., closed Mon.

Ⓒ **Canadian Museum of Immigration at Pier 21.** Affectionately dubbed
★ "Canada's Front Door," nearly a million immigrants entered Canada
through Pier 21 between 1928 and 1971. The pier is now a national
museum where the immigrants' experience is recreated. In addition to
the expected photos and artifacts, there are several innovative exhibits:
for instance, the holographic multimedia presentation detailing immigrants' arrival is shown inside a *faux* ship. Beside it sits a Canadian
National train car, and in each of its compartments you can hear different first-person accounts from immigrants who continued westward
from Halifax. (The train itself is stationary, but these oral histories are
definitely moving.) The museum's many hands-on displays have built-
in kid appeal, and special activities, like having "passports" stamped
at various stations, are designed to engage young visitors. A research
center, gallery, café, and gift shop are on-site as well. ⊠ *1055 Marginal
Rd.* ☎ *902/425–7770 or 855/526–4721* ⊕ *www.pier21.ca* C$8.60
⊙ *May–Oct., daily 9:30–5:30; Nov., daily 9:30–5; Dec.–Mar., Tues.–
Sat. 10–5; Apr., Mon.–Sat. 10–5.*

○ **Halifax Citadel National Historic Site.** You can't miss the Citadel, literally or
Fodor'sChoice figuratively. Erected between 1826 and 1856 on Halifax's highest hill, it
★ still dominates the skyline and, as Canada's most-visited National Historic Site, is a magnet for tourists. The present citadel with its dry moat
and stone ramparts was the fourth defensive structure to be built on the
site, and was once linked to smaller forts and gun emplacements on the
harbor islands and the bluffs above the harbor entrance. (A multimedia
presentation that runs every 15 minutes recounts that story.) Today you
can visit its barracks, guard room, and powder magazine before heading
for the parade ground to watch reenactors, sporting kilts and tall feather
"bonnets," practice their drills. Tours that help bring the history of both
the fort and the city to life go on throughout the day in high season, but
the best time to visit is just before noon when the Noon Gun is fired—
a tradition since 1857. Before leaving the Citadel, pause to enjoy the
view. In front of you are the spiky downtown, crowded between the
hilltop and the harbor; the wooded islands at the harbor's mouth; and
the naval dockyard under the Angus L. Macdonald Bridge, the nearer
of the two bridges connecting Halifax proper with Dartmouth. Behind
you is the 235-acre Halifax Common with its ball fields, tennis courts,
playground, skateboard park, and open green. The last of these has
served as a summertime venue for performers like the Rolling Stones,
Keith Urban, and the Black Eyed Peas. Worried about losing track
of time? Don't be. Simply keep an eye on Citadel Hill's **Town Clock.**
Given to Halifax by Prince Edward, Duke of Kent (the military com-
mander here from 1794 to 1800), it has ticked in its octagonal tower
for more than 200 years. ⊠ *Citadel Hill* ☎ *902/426–5080* ⊕ *www.pc.gc.
ca* ⚑ *June–mid-Sept. C$11.70; May and mid-Sept.–Oct. C$7.80; rest
of year grounds only, free* ⊙ *May, June, Sept., and Oct., daily 9–5; July
and Aug., daily 9–6.*

○ **Halifax Waterfront Boardwalk.** Running from Casino Nova Scotia to
Fodor'sChoice Marginal Road, this photogenic 1-km (.6-mi) footpath offers back-
★ door access to the Historic Properties and the Marine Museum of the
Atlantic. New landmarks such as **Purdy's Wharf** (site of Halifax's two
grandest skyscrapers) and **Bishop's Landing** (an attractive complex with
condos and shops) are on the route; while others, including the Seaport Farmers' Market, Pier 21, and the cruise ship terminal, are only
a few minutes' walk away. The boardwalk has multiple entry points
and many tourist-friendly amenities. Shops and restaurants line the
section between Sackville Landing and the Historic Properties, and in
peak season, bagpipers, ice-cream peddlers, and street performers do,
too. The water, however, remains the real attraction. To get out on it,
simply take one of the many boat tours that depart from the boardwalk's Cable Wharf.

**Historic Properties.** This series of restored waterfront warehouses dates
from the heady days of yore, when trade and war made Halifax pros-
perous. They were built by such raffish characters as Enos Collins, a
privateer, smuggler, and shipper whose vessels defied Napoléon's block-
ade to bring American supplies to the Duke of Wellington. The buildings have since been taken over by shops, offices, restaurants, and pubs
including those in Privateer's Warehouse. Seven of them, all erected

# Halifax and the Titanic

When the unsinkable *Titanic* sank in 1912, Halifax became, in a sense, the fabled ship's final destination. Being the closest major port, it was the base for rescue and recovery operations, and 150 victims were ultimately buried in city cemeteries.

The year 2012 is the centennial of the *Titanic*'s sinking and public interest is especially strong. Halifax's **Titanic 100** committee (⊕ *www.titanic100. ca*) has scheduled lectures, vigils, a film festival, and more. **The Royal Nova Scotia International Tattoo** (☎ *902/420–1114* or *800/563–1114 wwww.nstattoo.ca*) is paying tribute, too, by adopting a *Titanic* theme for 2012. For visitors eager to see local sites associated with the disaster, **Ambassatours Gray Line** (☎ *902/423–6242* or *800/565–7173* ⊕ *www.ambassatours.com*) is organizing a 75-minute bus excursion (C$27)

that departs twice daily, late-June through mid-October. To cobble together your own DIY tour, pick up the "Voyages Remembered: Titanic" brochure at any tourist office or check out ⊕ *titanic.gov.ns.ca*. Highlights include the **Museum of the Atlantic Line** (*see below*), which is hosting a temporary exhibit to mark the event; and **Fairview Cemetery** (*see below*), where most of the recovered bodies were buried.

Emergency response skills honed in the aftermath of the sinking were put to use five years later when tragedy struck again. In December 1917, two ships collided in Halifax Harbour, one of them loaded with explosives. The event sparked the greatest manmade explosion before Hiroshima, leveling 2 square mi of the city and claiming nearly 2,000 lives.

---

between the late 18th and early 19th century, have been designated as National Historic Sites. ⊠ *Upper Water St.* ☎ *902/429–0530* ⊕ *www. historicproperties.ca*.

♻ ★ **Maritime Museum of the Atlantic.** The exhibits in this waterfront museum, housed partly in a restored chandlery, include small boats once used around the coast, as well as displays describing Nova Scotia's proud sailing heritage. The most memorable ones, though, are devoted to the *Titanic* and the Halifax Explosion. The former has 20-odd artifacts, including the ship's only surviving deck chair. Also on display are a section of wall paneling, a balustrade molding and part of a newel from the dual curving staircase, a mortuary bag, and the log kept by a wireless operator at Cape Race, Newfoundland, on the fateful night. In the explosion exhibit, "Halifax Wrecked," newspaper accounts and quotes from survivors are poignantly paired with everyday objects recovered from the rubble, like a schoolboy's book bag and a broken pocket watch that will forever record the time of impact.

The museum has outdoor attractions, too. On the boardwalk right behind it is a ship-shaped children's playground and, steps away at the wharf, you'll see the hydrographic steamer CSS *Acadia*. After a long life of charting the coasts of Labrador and the Arctic, she's now permanently moored and museum-ticket holders can board her for tours May through September. ⊠ *1675 Lower Water St.* ☎ *902/424–7490*

⊕ *museum.gov.ns.ca/mma* ✉ *May–Oct. C$8.75; Nov.–Apr. C$4.75* ⊙ *May–Oct., Mon. and Wed.–Sat. 9:30–5:30, Tues. 9:30–8; May, Sun. 1–5; June–Oct., Sun. 9:30–5:30; Nov.–Apr., Wed.–Sat. 9:30–5, Tues. 9:30–8, Sun. 1–5.*

**Alexander Keith's Nova Scotia Brewery.** Although Alexander Keith served three terms as mayor of Halifax, his political achievements are overshadowed by another accomplishment: he was colonial Nova Scotia's first certified brewmaster. The brewery building from 1820 that bears his name is a local landmark and on hour-long tours you can see how his India Pale Ale was originally made, then sample a pint or two in the Stag's Head Tavern. (Nonalcoholic beverages are available for teetotalers and underage guests.) Actors in period outfits provide the explanations as well as old-fashioned maritime entertainment. ⊠ *Brewery Market, 1496 Lower Water St.* ☎ *902/455–1474 or 877/612–1820* ⊕ *www.keiths.ca* ✉ *C$15.95* ⊙ *Nov.–May, Fri. 5–8, Sat. noon–8, Sun. noon–5; June–Oct., Mon.–Sat. noon–8, Sun. noon–5.*

OFF THE
BEATEN
PATH

**Fairview Cemetery.** This cemetery is the final resting place of 121 victims of the *Titanic*. The graves are easily found, in a graceful arc of granite tombstones. One—marked J. Dawson—attracts particular attention from visitors. Alas, it's not the fictional artist played by Leonardo DiCaprio in the 1998 film, but James Dawson, a coal trimmer from Ireland. Nineteen other victims are buried in Mount Olivet Catholic Cemetery, 10 in the Baron de Hirsch Jewish Cemetery. The Maritime Museum of the Atlantic has an exhibit about the disaster. ⊠ *3720 Windsor St., 3 km (2 mi) north of downtown.*

**Anna Leonowens Gallery.** Victorian wunderkind Anna Leonowens is famous for the time she spent as a royal governess in Thailand (then Siam), which inspired Rodgers and Hammerstein's musical *The King and I.* But she also spent two decades in Halifax, where she founded the Nova Scotia College of Art and Design; it later returned the favor by opening the Anna Leonowens Gallery. Its three exhibition spaces, which focus on contemporary studio and media art, serve as a showcase for the college faculty and students. The gallery mounts about 125 exhibitions a year. ⊠ *1891 Granville St.* ☎ *902/494–8223* ⊕ *www.nscad.ca* ✉ *Free* ⊙ *Tues.–Fri. 11–5, Sat. noon–4.*

**Government House.** Built between 1799 and 1805 for Sir John Wentworth, the Loyalist governor of New Hampshire, and his racy wife, Fannie (Thomas Raddall's novel *The Governor's Lady* tells their story), this house has since been the official residence of the province's lieutenant governor—the Queen's representative. It's North America's oldest consecutively occupied government residence because the White House, while older, was evacuated and burned during the War of 1812. Its construction of Nova Scotian stone was engineered by a Virginian Loyalist, Isaac Hildrith. The house has been restored to its original elegance and public tours are offered Friday through Monday from 10:15 to 1:15 in July and August; they last about 30 minutes and leave at a quarter after and a quarter to the hour. ⊠ *1451 Barrington St.* ☎ *902/424–7001* ⊕ *www.lt.gov.ns.ca.*

(C) **Halifax Public Gardens.** One of the oldest formal Victorian gardens in North America, this city oasis had its start in 1753 as a private garden. Its layout was completed in 1875 by Richard Power, former gardener to the Duke of Devonshire in Ireland. Gravel paths wind among ponds, trees, and flower beds, revealing an astonishing variety of plants from all over the world. The centerpiece is an ornate gazebo-like band shell erected in 1887 for Queen Victoria's Golden Jubilee: it still stages free Sunday afternoon concerts from 2 to 4, mid-June through mid-September. The gardens are closed in winter, but you can take a pleasant walk along the cast-iron fence of the perimeter. ⊠ *Bounded by Sackville, Summer, and S. Park Sts. and Spring Garden Rd.* ☎ *902/490–3995* ⊕ *www.halifaxpublicgardens.ca* ☑ *Free* ⊙ *May–mid-Nov., daily 8 am–dusk.*

> "The waterfront in Halifax is one of its main draws, and it's easy to see why. There are shops, tours, boats (including the naval shipyard), historical monuments, and museums all along it. . . . The weather was excellent, so we did lots of strolling. There is a casino, and we popped in for a quick look. Las Vegas it ain't. It will give you a gambling fix if you need it, though. . . . People in Halifax in general were just, well, nice, and eager to help out in whatever way they could. —goddessintl

**Mary E. Black Gallery.** Next to Pier 21, the exhibit space for the Nova Scotia Centre for Craft and Design presents rotating shows of innovative, high-end crafts. If the displays of pottery, jewelry, textiles, metalwork, and more inspire you, the NSCCD runs a series of classes for the general public (one- and two-day workshops among them) fall through spring. ⊠ *1061 Marginal Rd.* ☎ *902/492–2522* ⊕ *www.craft-design.ns.ca* ☑ *Gallery free; workshops individually priced* ⊙ *Tues.–Fri. 9–5, weekends 11–4.*

(C) **Nova Scotia Museum of Natural History.** Easily recognized by the massive fiberglass model of a northern spring peeper (a frog) that clings to the southeast side of the building May through October, this is the place to learn about fossils and dinosaurs, as well as the flora and fauna prevalent in Nova Scotia today. The Nature Centre is home to live snakes, frogs, insects, and other creatures, while the Butterfly Pavilion is filled with fluttering species from around the world. The newly spruced-up museum also hosts major traveling exhibits as well as nature talks, walks, and workshops that appeal to all interests and ages. ⊠ *1747 Summer St.* ☎ *902/424–7353* ⊕ *nature.museum.gov.ns.ca* ☑ *C$5.75* ⊙ *Mon., Tues., and Thurs.–Sat. 9–5, Wed. 9–8, Sun. noon–5; Oct.–May, closed Mon.*

**Point Pleasant Park.** Most of the city's former fortifications have been turned into public parks, including this one, which encompasses 186 wooded acres with walking trails and seafront paths. The city originally leased Point Pleasant from the British Crown for a shilling per year. The major military installation here is a massive round tower dating from the late 18th century, but the greatest threat the park ever faced actually came from Mother Nature. In September 2003, Hurricane Juan tore through, uprooting or damaging 75,000 trees (about 75% of them) in a matter of hours, in the process leaving present-day parkgoers the same harbor views that must have inspired its use as a military command post in the first place. Having been nurtured since the storm, Point Pleasant is again immensely popular with strollers, joggers, and dog walkers. It's the perfect vantage point from which to watch ships entering the harbor and is also a summertime stage for Shakespeare by the Sea performances. ⊠ *5718 Point Pleasant Dr., about 12 blocks down S. Park St. from Spring Garden Rd.* ☎ *902/490–4700* ⊕ *www. pointpleasantpark.ca* 🖭 *Free* ⊘ *6 am–midnight.*

**Province House.** Charles Dickens proclaimed this structure, now a National Historic Site, "a gem of Georgian architecture." Erected in 1819 to house Britain's first overseas self-government, the sandstone building still serves as the meeting place for the provincial legislature. The politicos' proceedings are notoriously dull, yet the free tours of the building itself are full of interesting tidbits. ⊠ *1726 Hollis St.* ☎ *902/424–5982* ⊕ *www.nslegislature.ca* 🖭 *Free* ⊘ *July and Aug., weekdays 9–5, weekends 10–4; Sept.–June, weekdays 9–4.*

**OFF THE BEATEN PATH**

**Deadman's Island.** This tiny spit is the final resting place of almost 200 American prisoners of war who died while imprisoned in Halifax during the War of 1812. A new US$10,000 memorial was unveiled by the U.S. Department of Veterans Affairs in 2005 to honor the men, who died of communicable diseases such as smallpox and were buried in mass graves. Over time, the island has become naturally linked to the mainland, so you can walk to it without getting your feet wet. ⊠ *Look for the Deadman's Island sign off Purcell's Cove Rd., 6 km (3.5 mi) northwest of downtown.*

**St. Paul's Church.** Opened in 1750, this is Canada's oldest Protestant church and the burial site of many colonial notables. It also played a pivotal role during the 1917 Halifax Explosion, as the vestry was used as a makeshift hospital. Evidence of the damage done to the building can be seen in the still-broken Explosion Window and debris embedded above the Memorial Doors. Designated as a National Historic Site, St. Paul's remains an active church. A pew is always reserved for Queen Elizabeth at Sunday morning services, and other out-of-town worshippers are welcome as well: Sunday services are at 9 and 11, September through May, and at 10, June through August. ⊠ *1749 Argyle St., on the Grand Parade* ☎ *902/429–2240* ⊕ *www.stpaulshalifax.org* ⊘ *Sept.– May, weekdays 9–4:30; June–Aug., Mon.–Sat. 9–4:30. Sun. services 9 and 11 am Sept.–May; 10 am June–Aug.; Wed. 11 am year-round.*

## WHERE TO EAT

**$$$**
ECLECTIC
★

✕ **Chives Canadian Bistro.** "Canadian" cuisine is broadly defined here (French, German, and Asian influences are all evident) but there is no mistaking the provenance of Chef Craig Flinn's ingredients, which are invariably fresh and local. The menu adapts to whatever is available at the fishmongers' and farmers' market but each meal starts with Chives' signature buttermilk biscuits—and each *should* end with maple crème brûlée. Enjoy them in the main room, where planked-wood floors set a casual tone, or get intimate with a table for four in the former bank building's wine "vault." ✉ *1537 Barrington St.* ☎ *902/420–9626* ⊕ *www.chives.ca* ☯ *No lunch.*

**$$$–$$$$**
ITALIAN
★
✕**Da Maurizio.** This northern Italian restaurant is a classic big-night-out choice. Subdued lighting, elegant furnishings, fresh flowers: all the decor details have been attended to—and ditto for the food, which is at once impressive and satisfying. Excellent seared foie gras is always on the menu, as is veal scaloppine sautéed with lobster and topped with a creamy garlic-and-cognac sauce. Looking for wine to accompany your meal? Prices on the specialty wine list go as high as C$600, but there are also nice bottles for under C$60. ✉ *1496 Lower Water St.* ☎ *902/423–0859* ⊕ *www.damaurizio.ca* ☯ *Closed Sun. No lunch.*

**$$**
JAPANESE
✕**Dharma Sushi.** Tidy sushi, fresh sashimi, and feather-light tempura are artfully presented here; and although the service is fast-paced, the food doesn't suffer as a result. Lunchtime can be especially busy, so if you have trouble choosing from the long-as-your-arm menu, you might opt for a bento box or one of the daily specials. The latter—which can include California rolls, vegetable tempura, miso soup, and a popular chicken teriyaki—are a real deal and ready fast. Seating is available inside this pint-sized eatery and, in summer, on a small street-front patio. ✉ *1576 Argyle St.* ☎ *902/425–7785* ⊕ *www.dharmasushi.com.*

**$–$$**
ECLECTIC
✕**Economy Shoe Shop.** If you're looking for Birkenstocks, you're in the wrong place. But if you're hungry, that's another matter. . . . Variety rules at this chaotic multi-room restaurant-*cum*-club. Start with an imported beer in the Belgian Bar, then head to Backstage to dine among the fake trees and other theatrical decorations before retiring to the private cave in the Diamond for after-dinner coffee. In summer there is also a street-front patio, which is invariably packed with locals. Although food at the "Shoe" isn't haute cuisine, portions are generous and it's very hard to leave. ✉ *1661–1663 Argyle St.* ☎ *902/423–7463* ⊕ *www.economyshoeshop.ca.*

**$–$$**
ECLECTIC
✕**Elephant & Castle.** This affordable eatery doesn't cook or look like a franchise operation, although there are 23 North American locations. You can chalk the former up to the fact that it offers local delicacies, such as steamed mussels and Nova Scotia chowder, along with English-style pub staples. Moreover the heritage building that houses this restaurant is striking inside and out—the ornate 5-meter- (16-foot-) high ceilings are especially lovely. Due to its central location, the Elephant & Castle attracts an eclectic mix of politicos, office workers, and artsy Nova Scotia College of Art and Design students. Sitting mid-hill, it works well for weary tourists, too. ✉ *5171 George St.* ☎ *902/405–8875* ⊕ *www.elephantcastle.com.*

**$$–$$$**
CONTEMPORARY
★
✕**Fid.** This restaurant, a two-minute walk from the main gates of the Halifax Public Gardens, takes its unusual name from a nautical tool used to splice rope. It seems appropriate, then, that chef-owner Dennis Johnston splices together the best of the old and new when designing menus. The casual interior—with its butcher-block tables and a bistro-style blackboard—is the perfect setting for innovative permutations of locally supplied products. You might start with a warm chanterelle tart with Nova Scotia cheddar, and move on to caramelized sea scallops,

line-caught haddock, or the chef's daily "Market Inspiration." ✉ *1569 Dresden Row* ☎ *902/422–9162* ⊕ *www.fidresto.ca* ☾ *Closed Mon.*

**$$$$**
SEAFOOD
✕ **Five Fishermen.** Installed in a heritage building across from the Grand Parade, Five Fisherman is splurge-worthy. Tables are backlit by a wall of stained glass, and the seafood is so good locals keep coming back. Main courses are pricey but each comes with complimentary salad and mussels. The three-course *prix fixe* (a great value at C$42) is an affordable alternative to à la carte choices. Downstairs, the recently opened Five Fishermen Grill ($$–$$$) has a more modest menu and prices to match. It serves dinner and lunch (brunch on weekends) and has an Oyster Happy Hour, daily 4:30–6:30. ✉ *1740 Argyle St.* ☎ *902/422–4421* ⊕ *www.fivefishermen.com* ☾ *No lunch upstairs.*

**$$**
CANADIAN
✕ **Henry House.** Haligonian brewers uphold beer-making tradition dating back to 1754 and you can sample the results at this pub, which was once the house of William Alexander Henry, a prominent Canadian. Henry House serves five unpasteurized English-style ales crafted by Halifax's own Granite Brewery plus special blends like Black Velvet (a cider and stout mix). The food here is impressive, too—especially the fishcakes and homemade bread pudding. Best of all, the kitchen stays open late (till midnight Thursday through Saturday, and till 10 pm on other nights). In winter fireplaces keep the ironstone building toasty, and in summer a tiered-patio gives both afternoon sun, and shelter from wind. ✉ *1222 Barrington St.* ☎ *902/423–5660* ⊕ *www.henryhouse.ca.*

**$$–$$$**
ITALIAN
✕ **Il Mercato Ristorante.** Enter this Italian eatery at your own risk: the gleaming display cases filled with decadent desserts—including the *zuccotto*, a dome of chocolate and cream—are sure to tempt. Il Mercato is owned by Maurizio Bertossi (of local Da Maurizio fame *[see review]*), and tasty pastas are also in plentiful supply at reasonable prices. In the heart of the downtown shopping district, this is an ideal lunch stop. If dinner is your plan, come early, since reservations aren't taken and lines can be long. ✉ *5650 Spring Garden Rd.* ☎ *902/422–2866* ⊕ *www. il-mercato.ca* ⌿ *Reservations not accepted* ☾ *Closed Sun.*

**$$**
CONTEMPORARY
✕ **jane's on the common.** Behind the Halifax citadel is an open green space once used for communal cattle grazing—this is Halifax Common— and jane's, an uncommonly good eatery, is on its northwest corner. It's harder to find than heart-of-the-city spots, but if you come for weekend brunch just look for the line of locals who flock here for the creative comfort food like eggs Benedict served with smoked salmon on a sweet potato biscuit. An adjacent takeout—Jane's Next Door—sells ready-to-eat or reheat options for diners unwilling to wait. ✉ *2394 Robie St.* ☎ *902/431–5683* ⊕ *www.janesonthecommon.com* ⌿ *Reservations not accepted* ☾ *Closed Mon.*

**$$–$$$**
SEAFOOD
✕ **Lower Deck.** History surrounds you in Privateer's Warehouse, where two eateries share old stone walls and hand-hewn beams as well as a few menu items like chicken-and-ribs or fish-and-chips. The main-floor Pub ($–$$) sticks to pub grub, which is served at long trestle tables; the patrons here consider ale an entrée, so order a Keith's and join the fun. Holler "Sociable!" occasionally, and you'll be mistaken for a native in no time. The second-floor Beer Market is less casual and includes more

refined dishes on the menu. ⊠ *Historic Properties, 1869 Upper Water St.* ☎ *902/425–1501* ⊕ *www.lowerdeck.ca.*

**$$–$$$**
SEAFOOD

✕ **McKelvie's.** In a handsome 1906 firehouse across from the Maritime Museum of the Atlantic, McKelvie's is that rare find that hits the sweet spot between upmarket and down-home. Though all the menu mainstays are here, from oysters Rockefeller to surf and turf, the best bets are contemporary twists on seafood classics. Caribbean-inspired calamari, lobster pot stickers, and Thai shrimp pasta are perennial favorites. Although it's been in business for more than 25 years, the look of the restaurant is as fresh as the ingredients it uses, and the service is always friendly. ⊠ *1680 Lower Water St.* ☎ *902/421–6161* ⊕ *www.mckelvies. com* ⊗ *No weekend lunch in July, Aug.*

**$$**
CONTEMPORARY
★

✕ **Morris East.** This casually cool spot stakes its reputation on locally-sourced ingredients, many of which arrive fresh from the Seaport Farmers' Market a few blocks away. Gourmet pizzas—topped with the region's best veggies, cheeses, and charcuterie, are cooked in an oven that burns Annapolis Valley apple wood—are the house specialty. Libations have local flavor, too: artisanal cocktails are made with spirits handcrafted in the province. The room is warm and intimate but they don't accept reservations, so come early and take advantage of the nightly 5–6 pm happy hour. ⊠ *5212 Morris St.* ☎ *902/444–7663* ⊕ *www.morriseast.com* ⊗ *Closed Mon.; no lunch Sun.*

**$$$$**
SEAFOOD
Fodor's Choice
★

✕ **The Press Gang.** Easily one of the hippest upscale establishments in Halifax, the Press Gang prepares fish and meat with equal panache. You can start with crab dumplings or oysters on the half shell, complemented by a glass of muscadet from the well-stocked cellar, then tuck into grilled rib eye with truffled Stilton cream. Adventurous eaters might be interested in the "Drill," four courses of the chef's choice priced at C$150 per couple. Thick, cold stone walls testify to the building's era (1759), but the restaurant is warmed by comfy seating and intimate lighting. ⊠ *5218 Prince St.* ☎ *902/423–8816* ⊕ *www.thepressgang.ca* ⊗ *No lunch; open Sun. Apr.–Oct.*

**$$$–$$$$**
SEAFOOD

✕ **Salty's.** Overlooking Privateer's Wharf and the rest of the harbor, this restaurant wins the prize for best location in Halifax. Steaming bowls of shellfish stew and curried scallops crown a menu that is sure to satisfy any seafood lover, though there are also meat and pasta options. Request a table with a window view and save room for the house dessert, Cadix (chocolate mousse over a praline crust). There is a less expensive Bar & Grill ($$) on the ground level. Salty's serves meals outside on the wharf in summer, but be warned: it can be very windy. ⊠ *Historic Properties, 1869 Upper Water St.* ☎ *902/423–6818* ⊕ *www. saltys.ca* ⤳ *Reservations not accepted for the Bar & Grill.*

**$$–$$$**
ECLECTIC

✕ **The Wooden Monkey.** This fun, funky spot attracts health-conscious diners with its macrobiotic and organic food, locally brewed beer and wines, and fair-trade coffee. Aside from being good for you, though, the food here is also just plain good. Menu mainstays (the vegan dumplings, lentil-based veggie burger, free-range gingered beef, and chocolate tofu pie) are bound to win over skeptics. Don't believe us? Ask Oscar nominee Ellen Page. The *Juno* star is a native Haligonian—and a major

Wooden Monkey fan. ⊠ *1707 Grafton St.* ☎ *902/444–3844* ⊕ *www. thewoodenmonkey.ca.*

## WHERE TO STAY

*For expanded hotel reviews, visit Fodors.com.*

$$$  🏨 **Cambridge Suites Halifax.** Homey comforts are a big selling point at
🕐   this all-suites property. **Pros:** Continental breakfast included; harbor views from some suites and the rooftop deck. **Cons:** the hill up is *steep*; only one-bedroom and junior suites have separate living/sleeping areas. ⊠ *1583 Brunswick St.* ☎ *902/420–0555* or *800/565–1263* ⊕ *www. cambridgesuiteshalifax.com* ⮐ *200 suites* ⅏ *In-room: Wi-Fi. In-hotel: restaurant, room service, bar, gym, parking* ❍ *Some meals.*

$$$–$$$$  🏨 **Delta Halifax.** This business-class hotel—not to be confused with its nearby sister property, the Delta Barrington—has spacious, attractive rooms, but many vacationers choose it specifically for the water views: 126 rooms offer "premium" views and 80 have balconies. **Pros:** pleasant pool area; good location for walkers. **Cons:** awkward location for drivers; add-ons for phone calls, parking, etc. add up. ⊠ *1990 Barrington St.* ☎ *902/425–6700* or *888/890–3222* ⊕ *www.deltahotels. com* ⮐ *279 rooms, 21 suites* ⅏ *In-room: no safe, Internet. In-hotel: restaurant, room service, bar, pool, gym, parking, some pets allowed.*

$$$  🏨 **Halifax Marriott Harbourfront.** Built low to match the neighboring ironstone buildings, this waterfront hotel varies in appearance from others in the chain, and its convenient location in the Historic Properties area contributes to its elegance. **Pros:** only hotel right on the harbor; value-added packages available. **Cons:** most rooms charge for Wi-Fi; parking is pricey. ⊠ *1919 Upper Water St.* ☎ *902/421–1700* or *800/943–6760* ⊕ *www.marriott.com* ⮐ *333 rooms, 19 suites* ⅏ *In-room: no safe (some), Internet, Wi-Fi. In-hotel: restaurant, room service, bar, pool, gym, spa, parking, some pets allowed.*

$$–$$$  🏨 **The Halifax Waverley Inn.** Like Oscar Wilde and P. **Pros:** an urban inn experience; has loads of character. **Cons:** "traditional" category rooms are small; front rooms get street noise. ⊠ *1266 Barrington St.* ☎ *902/423–9346* or *800/565–9346* ⊕ *www.waverleyinn.com* ⮐ *34 rooms* ⅏ *In-room: no safe, Wi-Fi. In-hotel: business center, parking* ❍ *Breakfast.*

$$–$$$  🏨 **The Halliburton.** Three early-19th-century town houses were cleverly combined to create Halifax's original boutique hotel. **Pros:** quality linens; Continental breakfast included. **Cons:** some parking is a block away; all rooms at least one flight of stairs up. ⊠ *5184 Morris St.* ☎ *902/420–0658* or *888/512–3344* ⊕ *www.thehalliburton.com* ⮐ *25 rooms, 4 suites* ⅏ *In-room: no safe, Wi-Fi. In-hotel: restaurant, business center, parking* ❍ *Some meals.*

$$$  🏨 **Prince George Hotel.** Mahogany furnishings, vibrant draperies, and quality linens set the tone for rooms at this business-oriented hotel, while calm prevails in the public areas (garden patios offer a respite from downtown bustle). **Pros:** complimentary Wi-Fi; bathrooms redone in 2010. **Cons:** some find it stuffy; breakfast and parking not always included. ⊠ *1725 Market St.* ☎ *902/425–1986* or *800/565–1567* ⊕ *www.princegeorgehotel.com* ⮐ *189 rooms, 14 suites* ⅏ *In-room: no*

*safe (some), Wi-Fi. In-hotel: restaurant, room service, bar, pool, gym, parking, some pets allowed.*

**$$–$$$** 🕮 **Westin Nova Scotian.** This imposing 1930s hotel sits beside the train station, with the harbor behind and Cornwallis Park in front. **Pros:** half the rooms have harbor views, free downtown shuttle weekdays. **Cons:** on south edge of the action, some bathrooms are cramped. ✉ *1181 Hollis St.* ☎ *902/421–1000 or 877/993–7846* ⊕ *www.westin.ns.ca* ⌂ *310 rooms, 15 suites* ⌂ *In-room: Internet, Wi-Fi. In-hotel: restaurant, room service, bar, tennis court, pool, gym, spa, children's programs, business center, parking, some pets allowed.*

**THE 411 ON NIGHTTIME FUN**

For the 411 on nighttime fun, there are up-to-date entertainment listings in the *Coast* (Halifax's free alternative newspaper); you can also log on to ⊕ *www.thecoast.ca.*

## NIGHTLIFE AND THE ARTS

### NIGHTLIFE

Native Haligonians are, by nature, a convivial lot. Factor in the seafaring types any thriving port attracts and a large contingent of students, and you'll see why this is such a sociable city. Because of the premium put on fun, it can sometimes be difficult to draw the line between dining and entertainment options. For instance, whether the Lower Deck is an eatery masquerading as a watering hole or vice versa remains open to debate. As for the Economy Shoe Shop, it clearly doesn't sell shoes, but whether it functions primarily as a restaurant or club depends on your definition—and the time of day.

BARS **Bearly's House of Blues and Ribs** (✉ *1269 Barrington St.* ☎ *902/423–2526* ⊕ *www.bearlys.ca*) has a bit of a split personality. The dimly-lit tavern's name gives music and food equal billing. But when outstanding blues artists take the stage, it's clear where its true loyalty lies. You can catch an act every evening except Monday and Wednesday. (On the latter killer karaoke is offered instead.)

The **Old Triangle** (✉ *5136 Prince St.* ☎ *902/492–4900* ⊕ *www.oldtriangle. com*), a traditional Irish alehouse, reels in patrons with the promise of better-than-average pub food and pints of Guinness; then keeps them fixated by featuring live Celtic music most nights.

**Reflections Cabaret** (✉ *5184 Sackville St.* ☎ *902/422–2957* ⊕ *www. reflectionscabaret.com*) is an alternative alternative. Though considered a gay bar, it's better described as an "anything goes" bar. Drag queens mingle with throngs of university students who hit the strobe-lit dance floor until 3:30 am.

For late night music the indie crowd gravitates to the **Seahorse Tavern** (✉ *1665 Argyle St.* ☎ *902/423–7200* ⊕ *www.theseahorsetavern.ca*). The dark spot below the Economy Shoe Shop is a top venue for live funk and hip-hop with some Motown thrown in for good measure.

**The Split Crow** (✉ *1855 Granville St.* ☎ *902/422–4366* ⊕ *www.splitcrow. com*) is Halifax's oldest watering hole (its earliest incarnation opened in 1749) and has an old-time ambience with a full menu that's heavy on finger foods and deep-fried seafood. Nevertheless, it is the beer/band combination offered evenings and Saturday afternoons that accounts for the Split Crow's enduring popularity.

If you're of legal drinking age (19 or older here), you can also try your luck at **Casino Nova Scotia** (⊠ *1983 Upper Water St.* ☎ *902/425–7777 or 888/642–6376* ⊕ *www.casinonovascotia.com*). Right on the waterfront, it has a full range of gaming tables and hundreds of slots. There's entertainment, too, mostly provided by tribute bands and C-listers on their way up—or down.

### ARTS

THEATER **Grafton Street Dinner Theatre** (⊠ *1741 Grafton St.* ☎ *902/425–1961* ⊕ *www.graftonstdinnertheatre.com*) stages performances three to six times weekly depending on the season. The **Halifax Feast Company** (⊠ *Maritime Centre, 1505 Barrington St.* ☎ *902/420–1840* ⊕ *www. feastdinnertheatre.com*) specializes in musical comedies; check with the box office for dates. The **Neptune Theatre** (⊠ *1593 Argyle St.* ☎ *902/429–7070 or 800/565–7345* ⊕ *www.neptunetheatre.com*), Canada's oldest professional repertory playhouse, has a main stage and studio theater under one roof. It presents year-round performances ranging from classics to comedy and contemporary Canadian drama. In July and August, **Shakespeare by the Sea** (☎ *902/422–0295* ⊕ *www.shakespearebythesea. ca*) performs the Bard's works every night except Monday at 7 pm, and weekends at 1 pm in Point Pleasant Park's Cambridge Battery, at the southern end of the Halifax peninsula. The natural setting—dark woods, rocky shore, and ruins of fortifications—is a dramatic backdrop. No tickets are required. Just show up and contribute to the bucket (C$15 is suggested). In shoulder months the troupe acts out at the 90-seat Park Place Theatre in the lower parking lot.

### SPORTS AND THE OUTDOORS

CANOEING Some beautiful century-old homes dot the placid Northwest Arm, and the bench of a canoe is definitely the best seat from which to view them. **St. Mary's Boat Club** (⊠ *1641 Fairfield Rd., off Jubilee Rd.* ☎ *902/490–4688* ⊕ *www.halifax.ca/smbc*) rents canoes, weekends only, by the hour for adults 18 years and older and to younger certified canoeists.

GOLF **Glen Arbour** (⊠ *40 Clubhouse Lane, Hammonds Plains* ☎ *902/835–4653 or 877/835–4653* ⊕ *www.glenarbour.com*) has two courses (18 holes and 9 holes) in a residential/golf community that are open to transient players. Greens fees are C$13–$100.

Within an easy drive of downtown Halifax is **Granite Springs Golf Club** (⊠ *4441 Prospect Rd., Bayside* ☎ *902/852–3419* ⊕ *www. granitespringsgolf.com*), an 18-hole, par-72, semiprivate course open to greens-fee play. Rates range from C$27.50 to C$50.50 depending on the date, tee time, and number of holes you play.

HIKING **Point Pleasant Park** (*see above*) is free, easy to reach, and threaded with trails. **Sir Sandford Fleming Park** (⊠ *Dingle Rd.* ☎ *No phone*) is also free and very accessible; it faces Point Pleasant Park from the opposite side of the Northwest Arm. Marked by an impressive stone tower called the Dingle, it's named for the inventor of Standard Time, who summered on the property. **McNab's Island** (☎ *902/861–2560* ⊕ *www. mcnabsisland.ca*), at the mouth of Halifax Harbour, appeals to the more

**1**

adventuresome. Accessible only by boat, it has wooded trails and birding sites, plus a 19th-century fort. Half a dozen companies provide water taxis or tours from different Halifax locations. The trip takes 25 minutes from the boardwalk and costs about C$20.

HORSEBACK RIDING **Hatfield Farms Adventures** (✉ *1840 Hammonds Plains Rd., Hammonds Plains* ☎ *902/835–5676 or 877/835–5676* ⊕ *www.hatfieldfarm. com*) offers a wide variety of riding experiences for all levels, including trail rides, a petting pen, and pony rides.

SEA KAYAKING **Mountain Equipment Co-op** (✉ *1550 Granville St.* ☎ *902/421–2667* ⊕ *www.mec.ca*) in downtown Halifax rents kayaks for $30–$45 a day. **East Coast Outfitters** (✉ *2017 Lower Prospect Rd., Lower Prospect* ☎ *902/852–2567 or 877/852–2567* ⊕ *www.eastcoastoutfitters. net*), based about 30 minutes outside the city off Hwy. 333, offers rental equipment as well as instruction and guided excursions mid-May through mid-September.

> **CRAFTY RESOURCES**
>
> If you're looking specifically for fine arts and crafts, pick up a free copy of the Halifax Art Map or download one at ⊕ *www. halifaxartmap.com.* It lists more than 50 shops and galleries around the city. Looking elsewhere in the province? Try the Nova Scotia Centre for Craft and Design's annual guide (⊕ *www.craft-design. ns.ca/guide*) or Studio Rally's independently prepared Fine Art & Craft Studio Map (⊕ *www. studiorally.ca*).

SURFING *See Surf's Up Down East box in The Eastern Shore and Northern Nova Scotia (page 73).*

SWIMMING Dubious water quality means you shouldn't swim in Halifax Harbour or the Northwest Arm. But, just off the latter, **Chocolate Lake** (✉ *2 Melwood Ave.* ☎ *902/490–5458*) is a popular alternative. For ocean swimming, the closest serviced option is busy **Rainbow Haven Beach Provincial Park** (✉ *2248 Cow Bay Rd., 8 km (5 mi) east of Cow Bay, Cole Harbour* ☎ *No phone* ⊕ *www.novascotiaparks.ca*). Both are free for day use and have lifeguards on duty in July and August.

## SHOPPING

**Spring Garden Road** is by far the liveliest shopping street in town, with an assortment of boutiques spread out along the strip. Along the waterfront are the **Historic Properties** and **Bishop's Landing**, each with shops and boutiques.

SPRING GARDEN ROAD **Jennifer's of Nova Scotia** (✉ *5635 Spring Garden Rd.* ☎ *902/425–3119* ⊕ *www.jennifers.ns.ca*) stocks handmade soaps, hooked mats, ceramics, pewter, and other Nova Scotia–made crafts items.

Yoga fanatics can stock up on togs at Canadian favorite **lululemon** (✉ *5490 Spring Garden Rd.* ☎ *902/422–6641* ⊕ *www.lululemon.com*).

**Mills** (✉ *5486 Spring Garden Rd.* ☎ *902/429–6111 or 800/465–1919* ⊕ *www.millsbrothers.com*), an upscale mini-department store with three floors of fashions, accessories, perfumes, cosmetics, and gifts, is a local institution.

**Park Lane** (✉ *5657 Spring Garden Rd.* ☎ *902/420–0660* ⊕ *www. shopparklane.ca*), the small indoor mall that anchors Spring Garden Road, sells everything from handcrafted clothing to Canadian books.

**Pete's Frootique** (✉ *1515 Dresden Row* ☎ *902/425–5700* ⊕ *www. petesfrootique.com*), also in the Spring Garden area, is the brainchild of British greengrocer (and Canadian TV personality) Pete Luckett. Stop in at the vast gourmet food-and-produce store for a quick bite in the café or a ready-made gourmet sandwich for a picnic at the nearby Public Gardens.

The shops of **Spring Garden Place** (✉ *5640 Spring Garden Rd.* ☎ *902/ 420–0675* ⊕ *www.springgardenplace.ca*) focus on accessories for you and your home.

Just off Spring Garden, look for **Woozles** (✉ *1533 Birmingham St.* ☎ *902/423–7626 or 800/966–0537* ⊕ *www.woozles.com*), a lovely alternative to chain stores and the country's oldest children's book shop. Packed with books—many of them by Canadian and local authors— Woozles somehow manages to shoehorn a slew of toys in alongside the tomes.

WATERFRONT   Boutiques are found throughout **Bishop's Landing** (✉ *1475 Lower Water St.* ☎ *902/422–6412* ⊕ *www.bishopslanding.com*), an attractive complex with shops and condos.

The **Historic Properties** (✉ *Upper Water St.* ☎ *902/429–0530* ⊕ *www. historicproperties.ca*) is a pleasant place to shop and stroll.

Fodor's Choice   Steps from the boardwalk's southern terminus, sits the eye-catching
★   Seaport **Farmers' Market** (✉ *1209 Marginal Rd., Pier 20* ☎ *902/492– 4043* ⊕ *www.halifaxfarmersmarket.com* ☉ *Tues.–Thurs 10–5; Fri. 10–6; Sat 7–4; Sun. 10–5*). Unlike its predecessor—the cramped Brewery Market—this eco-conscious venue is bright, airy, and contemporary. It's open six days a week, too, giving you more opportunity to stock up on edibles and quality crafts or just indulge in the city's best people-watching.

The boardwalk itself is *the* place to see Waterford master-craftsmen blowing glass into graceful decanters and bowls, which can be purchased in the showroom of **Nova Scotian Crystal Ltd.** (✉ *5080 George St.* ☎ *902/492–0416 or 888/977–2797* ⊕ *www.novascotiancrystal.com*).

OFF THE
BEATEN
PATH   The block-long **Hydrostone Market** (✉ *5515–5547 Young St., between Isleville and Gottigen, North End* ☎ *902/454–2000* ⊕ *www. hydrostonemarket.ca*) lures shoppers to the city's North End with all sorts of one-of-a kind items. Flattened by the Halifax Explosion in 1917, the area was rebuilt as a charming garden-style neighborhood using hydrostone—aka concrete. Shops of particular note include **The Bogside Gallery** (☎ *902/453–3063*) for fine crafts; **Lady Luck** for jewelry and accessories (☎ *902/444–3050*); and **Rusty Hinges** (☎ *902/406–1056* ) for household goods, many of them handmade from architectural salvage. After browsing, break for lunch at **Epicurious Morsels** (☎ *902/455–0955*) or grab "gourmet to go" at **Little Europe** (☎ *902/407–7700*).

# SOUTH SHORE AND ANNAPOLIS VALLEY

The South Shore is on the Atlantic side of the narrow Nova Scotia peninsula; the Annapolis Valley on the Bay of Fundy side. So, although they're less than an hour apart by car, the two seem like different worlds. The former, with its rocky coast, island-dotted bays, and historic fishing villages, has launched 1,000 ships—and 1,000 postcards. The latter is most notable for its fertile farmlands, vineyards, and orchards. Highway 103, Highway 3, and various secondary roads form the province's designated Lighthouse Route, which leads southwest from Halifax down the South Shore. It ends in Yarmouth, where the Evangeline Trail begins. This trail winds along St. Mary's Bay through a succession of Francophone communities collectively known as the Acadian Shore. The villages blend into one another for about 50 km (35 mi), each one, it seems, with its own wharf, fish plant, and Catholic church.

> ### THE ACADIANS
>
> The Acadians are descendants of French colonists who settled here in the 1600s. In 1755, they were expelled by the British for refusing to pledge allegiance to the crown. Some eluded capture and slowly crept back, many making new homes in New Brunswick and along this shore of Nova Scotia. Others, however, migrated south to another region held by France at the time: Louisiana, where their name was shortened to Cajun. (Say "Acadian" five times fast and the reason will be apparent!)

The verdant Annapolis Valley runs northeast, sheltered on both sides by the North and South mountains. Occasional roads over the South Mountain lead to the South Shore; short roads over the North Mountain lead to the Fundy Shore. Like the South Shore, the valley has numerous historic sites—some of Canada's oldest among them—and is punctuated by pleasant small towns with a generous supply of Victorian architecture.

## PEGGY'S COVE

*48 km (30 mi) southwest of Halifax.*

Peggy's Cove is the home of Canada's most photographed lighthouse. As you wind along the edge of St. Margaret's Bay, woodlands eventually give way to rugged outcroppings that were deposited when the last glaciers swept through. On one side, massive granite boulders stand semi erect in scrubby fields; on the other, they lie prone, creating the granite shelf on which Peggy's Cove is perched. The hamlet itself consists of little more than a Lilliputian harbor with a tiny wooden church, a cluster of shingled houses, and some salt-bleached jetties. What distinguishes Peggy's Cove, though, is the solitary lighthouse towering over a slab of wave-blasted rock. Just don't be tempted to venture too close to the edge—many an unwary visitor has been swept out to sea by the mighty surf that sometimes breaks here. (Repeat this mantra: dark rocks are wet rocks, and must be avoided.) In addition to navigating the rugged

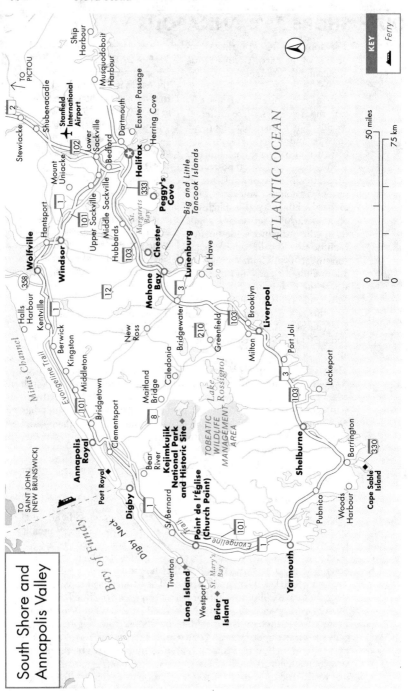

## South Shore and Annapolis Valley

KEY

Ferry

ATLANTIC OCEAN

0    50 miles

0    75 km

TO PICTOU

Ship Harbour

Musquodoboit Harbour

Stewiacke

Shubenacadie

**Stanfield International Airport**

Lower Sackville

Dartmouth

Eastern Passage

Herring Cove

Mount Uniacke

Bedford

**Halifax**

Big and Little Tancook Islands

Hantsport

Upper Sackville

Middle Sackville

Hubbards

St. Margarets Bay

**Peggy's Cove**

**Wolfville**

**Windsor**

**Chester**

**Lunenburg**

**Mahone Bay**

La Have

Halls Harbour

Kentville

Berwick

Kingston

Middleton

New Ross

**Evangeline Trail**

Minas Channel

Bridgetown

Clementsport

Maitland Bridge

Caledonia

Bridgewater

Greenfield

Milton

Brooklyn

**Liverpool**

Port Joli

Lockeport

**Annapolis Royal**

Port Royal

Bear River

**Keimkujik National Park and Historic Site**

St. Bernard

TOBEATIC WILDLIFE MANAGEMENT AREA

Lake Rossignol

**Shelburne**

Barrington

**Cape Sable Island**

TO SAINT JOHN (NEW BRUNSWICK)

**Digby**

Point de l'Église (Church Point)

Pubnico

Woods Harbour

Digby Neck

Bay of Fundy

Tiverton

Westport

**Brier Island**

**Long Island**

St. Mary's Bay

Evangeline Trail

**Yarmouth**

terrain, you'll have to contend with the crowds in summer—750,000 tourists descend annually. To avoid them in July and August, plan to arrive early or late in the day.

**GETTING HERE AND AROUND**

Travelers based in Halifax can reach Peggy's Cove by taking either Exit 2 or Exit 5 from Hwy. 103 onto the 333. The former is mostly inland while the latter runs along St. Margaret's Bay. The ideal scenario, though, is to go via one and return via the other. At Peggy's Cove you can drive almost to the base of the lighthouse, but you'd do better to park in the spacious public lot below and make the three-minute walk up to this Canadian icon.

Peggy's Cove is home to two poignant monuments. The first, at the top of the town itself is the **deGarthe Memorial** (✉ *109 Peggy's Point Rd., off Hwy. 333*), a 30-meter (100-foot) bas-relief carved from local granite by a local artist commemorating the fisherman who lost their lives here. The second, 1.5 km (1 mi) north of the village, is the **Swissair Memorial** (✉ *Hwy. 333*). A tribute to Flight 111, which crashed into the waters off Peggy's Cove in 1998, it honors the 229 casualties and the courageous Nova Scotia fisherfolk who did recovery work and offered comfort to the grieving families.

**WHERE TO EAT AND STAY**

*For expanded hotel reviews, visit Fodors.com.*

**$$–$$$**
SEAFOOD
✕ **Sou'wester Restaurant.** Poised on the rocks near the base of the Peggy's Cove lighthouse, this sprawling 180-seat dining room serves home-style fare, including a wide range of Down East specialties (try the Solomon Gundy, a mélange of marinated herring, onions, and sour cream). It is also a pleasant spot to linger over coffee and warm home-made gingerbread, provided the tour buses that regularly park out back haven't just disgorged hordes of hungry passengers. A large—generally kitschy—souvenir shop is on-site. ✉ *178 Peggy's Point Rd., off Hwy. 333* ☏ *902/823–2561* ⊕ *www.peggys-cove.com*.

**$$**
★
**Oceanstone Inn and Cottages.** Just 3.5 km (2 mi) from Peggy's Cove, Oceanstone is designed to look like an old seaside hamlet. **Pros:** most options have water views; eco-conscious owners. **Cons:** new on-site café (open Tuesday–Sunday from May to November) only serves light fare; one cottage stands alone by the road. ✉ *8650 Peggy's Cove Rd., Indian Harbour* ☏ *902/823–2160 or 866/823–2160* ⊕ *www.oceanstone.ns.ca* ➥ *11 rooms, 8 cottages* ⚒ *In-room: no a/c, kitchen (some), Wi-Fi. In-hotel: restaurant, beach, water sports* ❢❙ *Some meals Apr.–Nov.*

**SPORTS AND THE OUTDOORS**

Boat excursions are available around Peggy's Cove spring through fall.

**Four Winds Boat Charters** (☏ *902/492–0022 or 877/274–8421* ⊕ *www.fourwindscharters.com*), based at the Shining Waters Marina, about a 20-minute drive from Peggy's Corner, runs C$35 high-season tours aboard a Cape Islander that show off native marine life.

**SeaSun Kayak** (☏ *902/850–7732 or 866/775–2925* ⊕ *www.paddlenovascotia.com*) offers an array of paddling tours as well as kayak rentals priced, from C$52 and C$25, respectively. They're based at the nearby Shining Waters Marina.

### SHOPPING

**Beales' Bailiwick** (✉ *124 Peggy's Point Rd.* ☎ *902/823–2099 or 877/823–2099* ⊕ *www.beales.ns.ca*) carries Maritime-designed clothing, pewter, jewelry, and more. The adjoining coffee shop affords one of the best photo ops for Peggy's Cove, and the renovated red schoolhouse next door is a venue for summertime theater and concerts.

## CHESTER

*64 km (40 mi) west of Peggy's Cove.*

Although Chester is a short drive west of Peggy's Cove, you'll be forgiven for thinking you've taken a wrong turn and ended up in Maine or Massachusetts. New England planters settled the site in 1759, and their numbers were later bolstered by Loyalists escaping the American Revolution and Boston Brahmins who simply wanted to escape the city in summer. Thanks to the clapboard saltboxes and Cape Cod–style homes they left behind, Chester still calls to mind a classic New England community. Most visitors are content to explore its tree-shaded lanes or make forays into the surrounding countryside. Yachtsmen invariably stick close to the water.

The area promises some of the best sailing on the Eastern Seaboard and the town itself hosts Canada's largest fixed-keel regatta, **Chester Race Week** (⊕ *www.chesterraceweek.com*), each August.

☺   The **Ross Farm Living Museum of Agriculture,** a restored 19th-century farm,
★   illustrates the evolution of agriculture from 1600 to 1925. The animals are those found on an 1800s farm—draft horses, oxen, and other heritage breeds—and traditional activities such as blacksmithing or spinning are demonstrated. Hands-on programs are regularly scheduled for kids who'd like to help out with the chores. Onsite, the Peddlar's Shop sells items made in the community. ✉ *4568 Hwy. 12, 29 km (18 mi) inland from Chester, New Ross* ☎ *902/689–2210 or 877/689–2210* ⊕ *museum.gov.ns.ca/rfm* 🖼 *C$6* ◷ *May–Oct., daily 9:30–5:30; Nov.–Apr., Wed.–Sun. 9:30–4:30.*

The scenic **Big and Little Tancook islands,** 8 km (5 mi) out in Mahone Bay, have a year-round **passenger-only ferry** (☎ *No phone*) that runs from the dock in Chester. Reflecting its part-German heritage, Big Tancook claims to make the best sauerkraut in Nova Scotia. Exploration of the island is made easy by walking trails. The boat runs four times daily Monday through Thursday, six times on Friday, and twice daily on weekends. The 45-minute ride costs C$5.

### WHERE TO EAT AND STAY

*For expanded hotel reviews, visit Fodors.com.*

¢–$    ✕ **Fo'c'sle Tavern.** This rustic midtown spot feels like a communal living
CANADIAN   room because residents go so regularly. The interior is pine, from the floors and furnishings to the wainscoted walls decorated with local artwork. In the windowed front section you can order hefty servings

of mussels or beer-battered haddock (a wood stove exudes warmth and goodwill on chilly nights). There are pool tables, TVs, and long "drinking tables" at the other end, plus live music many weekends. Though it's a townie hangout, the mood is welcoming and the staff will treat you like kin. ⊠ *42 Queen St.* ☎ *902/275–1408* .

¢–$   ✕ **Julien's Pâtisserie, Bakery & Café.**
CONTINENTAL   The buttery croissants, brioche, and
Fodor's Choice   *pain de campagne* (country bread)
★   here are tasty testaments to Julien's French roots. That's just the beginning, though. Savory homemade soups are also available, as are hefty deli sandwiches (the Knuckle & Claw lobster sandwich is justifiably famous in these parts). A slice of the fruity, brandy-doused tart pays d'Auge, named after an area in Normand, makes a fine finish.

> **THE PLAY'S THE THING**
>
> North America's first play was written, produced, and performed in Nova Scotia in 1606. Community theaters—many of them heritage properties—continue to thrive. Try the **Chester Playhouse** (⊠ *22 Pleasant St.* ☎ *902/275–3933 or 800/363–7529* ⊕ *www.chesterplayhouse.ca*) in Chester, the **Osprey Theatre** (⊠ *107 Water St.* ☎ *902/875–2359* ⊕ *www.ospreyartscentre.com*) in Shelburne, or the **King's Theatre** (⊠ *209 St. George St.* ☎ *902/532–7704* ⊕ *www.kingstheatre.ca*) in Annapolis Royal. Or contact **Theatre Nova Scotia** (☎ *902/425–3876* ⊕ *www.theatrens.ca*).

Load up on lunchables for an impromptu picnic along Chester's scenic waterfront, or pull up a chair in the licensed café section. ⊠ *43 Queen St.* ☎ *902/275–2324* ⊕ *www.juliens.ca* ▤ *AE, MC, V* ⊗ *Closed Mon. mid-Sept.–mid-June.*

$–$$   ☷ **Mecklenburgh Inn.** Nautical touches abound in this heritage B&B at the top of one of Chester's main streets. **Pros:** complimentary gourmet breakfast, claw-foot tubs in three rooms. **Cons:** two blocks from the water, booked a year ahead for Race Week. ⊠ *78 Queen St.* ☎ *902/275–4638 or 866/838–4638* ⊕ *www.mecklenburghinn.ca* ⇆ *4 rooms* ⌂ *In-room: no a/c, no TV, Wi-Fi.* ▤ *MC, V* ⊗ *Jan.–Apr.* ⎆ *Breakfast.*

### SHOPPING

Shops are open daily during the tourist season, which is generally May to October but can change depending on the season.

**Amicus Gallery** (⊠ *20 Pleasant St.* ☎ *902/275–2496* ⊕ *www.amicusgallery.ca*) is an eclectic shop selling everything from jewelry and stained glass crafted by local artisans to the owner's own pottery.

The earthenware pottery at **Jim Smith Fine Studio Pottery** (⊠ *Corner of Duke and Water Sts.* ☎ *902/275–3272* ⊕ *www.jimsmithstudio.ca*) is as cheerful as the bright yellow-and-green building on Chester's front harbor in which it's housed.

**The Warp & Woof** (⊠ *81 Water St.* ☎ *902/275–4795* ⊕ *www.warpandwoof.ca*) is the place to go for locally made hooked rugs, children's sweaters, pewter ware, beach-inspired giftware, and kitchen items.

## MAHONE BAY

*24 km (15 mi) west of Chester.*

Wrapped around a sweeping curve of water, this pastoral town's tranquil tone is set by three vintage churches along the grass-fringed shoreline. Of course, life here wasn't always so serene. Mahone Bay was once a thriving shipbuilding center. Before that, it was popular with pirates and privateers. In fact, Mahone Bay was named for the type of low-lying ship they used: it's a corruption of the French word *mahonne* (a low-lying barge-like boat). Today you can still kayak into the bay's secret coves or around its many islands, including Oak Island, reputedly a favorite haunt of the notorious Captain Kidd. Modern-day treasure hunters are better off perusing the galleries and studios onshore. Although it has a population of just 1,100, Mahone Bay boasts an enviable assortment of craftspeople.

### WHERE TO EAT AND STAY
*For expanded hotel reviews, visit Fodors.com.*

**$–$$**   ✕ **Innlet Café.** This pleasant, chronically cute restaurant at Kedy's Land-
CANADIAN   ing (you'll see it just as you approach town from Exit 10) has a fine view of Mahone Bay and the city's three charming churches. The broad Canadian-style menu has poultry and meats, an understandable emphasis on chowders and seafood, and a few vegetarian options. The Heavenly Chicken (in a white wine and cream sauce) has been a delicious mainstay at the café for years, and the apple strudel (made in-house by the Bavarian-born chef) alone is worth a visit. ✉ *249 Edgewater St.* ☎ *902/624–6363* ⊕ *www.innletcafe.com* ☯ *Closed Jan.–mid-Mar.*

**$**   ✕ **Mug & Anchor Pub.** Take in a view of the bay from inside this old
CANADIAN   British-style alehouse or enjoy waterside dining on the back deck. The menu includes basic pub fare, such as fish-and-chips and hamburgers, but you can also get Lunenburg County favorites like fish cakes. Lunenburg scallops are a specialty, as is the Mug & Anchor meat pie. The pub swells with the sounds of live jazz, blues, and folk music the last Thursday evening of every month. ✉ *643 Main St.* ☎ *902/624–6378* ⊕ *www.themugandanchorpubltd.com.*

**$$**   ⌂ **Amber Rose Inn.** The building dates from 1875 but inside, you'll find creature comforts like a/c, mini fridges, and whirlpool tubs. **Pros:** leafy grounds with a brook in back; quiet location. **Cons:** not on the water; off the main commercial stretch. ✉ *319 Main St.* ☎ *902/624–1060* ⊕ *www.amberroseinn.com* ⇨ *3 suites* ♿ *In-room: Wi-Fi.* ⍟ *Breakfast.*

### SPORTS AND THE OUTDOORS
**South Shore Boat Tours** (✉ *Mahone Bay Civic Marina, 683 Main St.* ☎ *902/527–8544* ⊕ *www.southshoreboattours.com*) runs narrated nature cruises around Mahone Bay three times a day, June through October. Trips last about two hours and cost C$37.

**Sweet Ride Cycling** (✉ *504 Main St.,* ☎ *902/531–3026*) is a new bicycle-slash-candy shop. Half-day rentals are C$20 (a full-day is C$30) and you can buy old-fashioned treats if you need a sugar hit when you finish.

## SHOPPING

**Amos Pewter** (⊠ *589 Main St.* ☎ *902/624–9547 or 800/565–3369* ⊕ *www.amospewter.com*) is a studio in an 1888 seaside building that's been using traditional methods to make pewter since 1974. Jewelry, sculptures, ornaments, and sand dollars are among the items for sale, along with a new original-design Christmas ornament each year. Feeling crafty? Amos's C$5 Hands-On Experience walks you through the process and you can take home what you make. There are interpretive displays and demonstrations for visitors who'd prefer to just watch.

The work of fine Atlantic Canada artists and artisans is sold at **The Moorings Gallery** (⊠ *575 Main St.* ☎ *902/624–6208* ⊕ *www.mooringsgallery. com*). Leave room in your shopping bag for hooked rugs and hand-dyed woolens from **Spruce Top Rug Hooking Studio** (⊠ *255 Main St.* ☎ *902/624–9312 or 888/784–4665* ⊕ *www.sprucetoprughookingstudio.com*).

**Suttles and Seawinds** (⊠ *466 Main St.* ☎ *902/624–8375* ⊕ *www. suttlesandseawinds.com*) has a worldwide reputation for distinctively designed, high-quality quilts, and quilted clothing.

# LUNENBURG

*14 km (9 mi) south of Mahone Bay.*

**Fodor's** Choice ★ This remarkably preserved town has a colorful past and some *very* colorful buildings, a combo that earned it a UNESCO World Heritage Site designation. The British probably had something more staid in mind when they founded Lunenburg in 1753, but the German, Swiss, and French Protestants recruited to settle here put their own stamp on it. The result? Rainbow-hued houses characterized by the "Lunenburg Bump": a detailed dormer over the front door. Naturally, locals didn't spend *all* their time on home improvements. By the 1850s they'd transformed the town into a world-class fishing and shipbuilding center. Today, blacksmiths and dory builders continue to work on the waterfront and, appropriately, the Fisheries Museum of the Atlantic is the top attraction. An in-the-middle-of-it-all location, plus a growing supply of fine lodging, dining, shopping, and touring options makes Lunenburg one of the best bases for a Nova Scotia vacation.

## GETTING HERE AND AROUND

When the Beatles sang about "the long and winding road" they might have had the Lighthouse Route in mind. The curvy back roads that make up most of it hug the South Shore from Halifax to Yarmouth and are undeniably scenic, but if you're looking for a shorter option, you can get to Lunenburg via Highway 103. From 103, you can go to Lunenburg using exit 10 or exit 11; they take about the same amount of time, but exit 11 has nice views around Mahone Bay.

Once you're in town, walking is the way to go provided you're not daunted by the steep hill.

ᐩ **Fodor's** Choice ★ The **Fisheries Museum of the Atlantic,** on the Lunenburg waterfront, gives a comprehensive overview of Nova Scotia's fishing industry. With aquariums devoted to native species, tidal touch tanks, themed films, and exhibits on shipbuilding, whaling, and the like, there's plenty here to keep the whole gang happy. Demonstrations on topics such as sail making, boat building, and dory launching are also offered. Dockside, you can visit a restored Saltbank Schooner and a steel-hulled trawler or hear a few fish tales before dipping back into the museum gift shop.

As if that wasn't enough, the **Bluenose II** (☎ 902/634–4794 or 866/579–4909 ⊕ *www.schoonerbluenose2.ca*), Nova Scotia's sailing ambassador, calls the museum home. She's a faithful replica of the original *Bluenose,* the Lunenburg-built schooner which gained prominence as the fastest vessel in the North Atlantic fleet during the 1920s and 1930s. The ship is expected to emerge from an extensive two-year refit in 2012 and once again be available for tours and sailing trips. But if she's not sitting pretty in port when you arrive, you can still get a glimpse of the famed ship by digging a Canadian dime out of your pocket. The *Bluenose* is pictured on the back. ⊠ *68 Bluenose Dr.* ☎ *902/634–4794 or 866/579–4909* ⊕ *museum.gov.ns.ca/fma* ⊠ *C$10 mid-May–mid-Oct., C$4 mid-Oct.–mid-May* ☉ *Mid-May–mid-Oct., daily 9:30–5:30, until 7 pm Tues.–Sat in July and Aug.; mid Oct.–mid-May, weekdays 9:30–4.*

## WHERE TO EAT

$$$–$$$$
CONTINENTAL
Fodor's Choice
★

✕ **Fleur de Sel.** In-the-know foodies flock to Fleur de Sel, a classy Continental alternative to the South Shore's dime-a-dozen fish joints, tucked into a heritage home on Montague Street. The interior is elegant and airy and the food is superb, from the *tartare de boeuf* through the tuna *niçoise* to the final bite of *fromage*. If you can't snag one of the 35-odd seats at dinner, come for the stellar Sunday brunch, when dishes like lobster eggs Benedict and brioche French toast are served. ⊠ *53 Montague St.* ☎ *902/640–2121 or 877/723–7258* ⊕ *www.fleurdesel.net* ⌂ *Reservations essential* ☉ *Closed Mon.; closed Nov.–Mar. No lunch.*

$$
ECLECTIC
★

✕ **Magnolia's Grill.** Exuberant and unabashedly eccentric, Magnolia's Grill is like the Auntie Mame of Lunenburg restaurants. The booths are close together and the walls cluttered with pictures, yet somehow the decor works and so does the menu, a Nova Scotian–Deep South hybrid featuring fish cakes, creole peanut soup, and pulled pork. Of course, once you see the key lime pie, you might want to skip straight to dessert. The small space fills fast so if you don't have a reservation, be prepared to wait. ⊠ *128 Montague St.* ☎ *902/634–3287* ☉ *Closed Dec.–Feb.*

$$–$$$
SEAFOOD

✕ **Old Fish Factory Restaurant & Ice House Bar.** As you would expect, Lunenburg is riddled with seafood restaurants, but what separates this one from the rest of the pack is its location in a former fish-processing plant at the Fisheries Museum. The eatery overlooks Lunenburg Harbour and offers wharf-side dining in warmer months. Seafood is the order of the day (try the excellent lobster-and-crab-stuffed haddock), but you can also opt for chicken or chops. In summer the adjacent bar has a live jam on Tuesday nights and a ceilidh on Wednesday nights. ⊠ *68 Bluenose Dr.* ☎ *902/634–3333 or 800/533–9336* ⊕ *www.oldfishfactory.com* ☉ *Closed mid-Oct.–mid-May.*

$$–$$$
ITALIAN

✕ **Trattoria della Nonna.** The South Shore's only authentic Italian eatery, this tri-level spot calls to mind the kitchen of an Italian grandmother (nonna) in part because it gets crowded and convivial—some might say noisy, especially in the basement cantina. The decor is welcoming and

## Lodging Alternatives

**1**

Want to pretend that you're lucky enough to live in Nova Scotia? Consider opting for a vacation rental instead of a hotel room. You'll find anything from seaside cottages to UNESCO-protected heritage properties in the heart of town; choices are particularly plentiful on the South Shore and Cape Breton. Web sites like **HomeAway** (⊕ *www.homeaway. com*) and **FlipKey** (⊕ *www.flipkey. com*) are good places to start house hunting. A word to the wise, though: look carefully at a map before committing. Due to complicated coastal topography, neighboring communities can have quite different climates. Lunenburg and Mahone Bay, for example, are generally sunnier than nearby spots that sit on fog-trapping St. Margaret's Bay.

Cost-conscious visitors looking for a class act can book into a college dorm. May through August, local universities—including **Dalhousie** (☎ *902/494–2429* ⊕ *www.dal.ca*), **King's** (☎ *902/422–1271* ⊕ *www. ukings.ns.ca*), **St. Mary's** (☎ *902/420– 5486 or 888/347–5555* ⊕ *www. smu.ca*), and **Mount St. Vincent** (☎ *902/457–6355* ⊕ *www.msvu.ca*)— rent out the no-frills rooms and apartments that students have vacated for the summer. For details, search "Conference Services" on the individual Web sites or call the universities directly. Prices range from C$27–$45 for single rooms, C$70–$145 for apartments, and perks like athletic center privileges are often included.

the food always delicious. The menu leans heavily toward traditional dishes (wood-fired pizza, homemade ravioli, and osso buco) but local veggies and fresh-caught seafood ensures that the dining experience retains a Nova Scotian flavor. ⊠ *9 King St.* ☎ *902/640–3112* ⊕ *www. trattoriadellanonna.ca* ⊗ *Closed Mon. and Jan. No lunch.*

### WHERE TO STAY
*For expanded hotel reviews, visit Fodors.com.*

**$$**  🏠 **Arbor View Inn.** Stained-glass windows, original wood finishes, and handsome antiques enhance this grand early-20th-century house. **Pros:** idyllic grounds; books and board games provide indoor entertainment. **Cons:** no a/c; only two rooms have TVs. ⊠ *216 Dufferin St.* ☎ *902/634– 3658 or 800/890–6650* ⊕ *www.arborview.ca* ⊅ *4 rooms, 2 suites* ⚭ *In-room: no a/c, no safe, no TV (some), Wi-Fi.* ⏺ *Breakfast.*

**$$$**  🏠 **Lunenburg Arms Hotel & Spa.** You seldom find hotel-style amenities in small-town heritage properties, but this place has them . . . and we're not just talking an elevator and ice machine. **Pros:** mid-hill location; complimentary use of spa's steam shower and hot tub. **Cons:** dining deck faces the street; free breakfast off-season only. ⊠ *94 Pelham St.* ☎ *902/640–4040 or 800/679–4950* ⊕ *www.eden.travel* ⊅ *22 rooms, 2 suites* ⚭ *In-room: no safe, Internet, Wi-Fi. In-hotel: restaurant, room service, spa, business center, some pets allowed* ⏺ *Some meals; breakfast Nov.–Apr. only.*

**$$**    🏨 **Lunenburg Inn.** Joseph P. Pros: one suite has a microwave and fridge; both have whirlpool tubs. Cons: street can be noisy; a bit outside the main tourist area. ⊠ *26 Dufferin St.* 🖅 *902/634–3963 or 800/565–3963* 🖷 *902/634–9419* ⊕ *www.lunenburginn.com* ⟲ *5 rooms, 2 suites* ⚭ *In-room: no safe, Wi-Fi. In-hotel: business center, Wi-Fi* ⦿ *Breakfast.*

**$**    🏨 **Pelham House Bed & Breakfast.** Close to downtown, this circa 1906 sea captain's home is decorated in a homey, country fashion and has a friendly golden retriever and three cats who greet guests before returning to their own quarters next door. **Pros:** a sustaining breakfast is included; nice pets. **Cons:** no grounds to speak of; proximity of pets. ⊠ *224 Pelham St.* 🖅 *902/634–7113 or 800/508–0446* ⊕ *www.pelhamhouse.ca* ⟲ *3 rooms, 1 suite* ⚭ *In-room: no a/c, no safe, no TV, Wi-Fi. In-hotel: laundry facilities* ⦿ *Breakfast.*

### SPORTS AND THE OUTDOORS

Two km (1 mi) east of the town center, you can rent cycles from the **Lunenburg Bike Barn** (⊠ *579 Blue Rocks Rd.* 🖅 *902/634–3426* ⊕ *www.bikelunenburg.com*). Prices start at C$25 a day and the friendly advice comes free.

**Lunenburg Ocean Adventures** (🖅 *902/634–4833* ⊕ *www.lunenburgoceanadventures.com*) puts an emphasis on adventure with thrill-seeker activities that run the gamut from deep-sea fishing to shark cage diving. The former costs C$50 per person; the latter C$1,000 for you and five "chums."

Landlubbers might opt for one of the C$15 guided strolls—ghostly ones among them—given year-round by **Lunenburg Town Walking Tours** (🖅 *902/634–3848* ⊕ *www.lunenburgwalkingtours.com*).

Whales, seals, and other marine life are the star attractions of **Lunenburg Whale-Watching Tours** (🖅 *902/527–7175* ⊕ *www.novascotiawhalewatching.com*). The three-hour trips set off four times daily, May through October, from the Fisheries Museum Wharf and cost C$48. You can arrange for bird-watching excursions and tours of Lunenburg Harbour, too.

**Pleasant Paddling** (🖅 *902/541–9233* ⊕ *www.pleasantpaddling.com*) offers kayak rentals priced from C$30 and guided excursions starting at C$50.

June through September, **Star Charters** runs 90-minute daytime and sunset sailing trips (C$24 and C$27, respectively) aboard a 15-meter (48-foot) wooden ketch. (🖅 *902/634–3535 or 877/386–3535* ⊕ *www.novascotiasailing.com*).

Horse-and-carriage tours, available through **Trot in Time,** cost C$20 for 30 minutes and depart from the Fisheries Museum Wharf (🖅 *902/634–8917* ⊕ *www.trotintime.ca*).

### SHOPPING

★   **Black Duck Gallery and Gifts** (⊠ *8 Pelham St.* 🖅 *902/634–3190* ⊕ *www.blackduck.ca*) sells local art and crafts, books, and an imaginative selection of gifts.

The **Houston North Gallery** (✉ *110 Montague St.* ☎ *902/634–8869 or 866/634–8869* ⊕ *www.houston-north-gallery.ns.ca*) represents top-notch Inuit stone carvers and printmakers. December through April, it's generally open by appointment only.

Load up on liquid souvenirs at the new **Ironworks Distillery** (✉ *2 Kempt St.* ☎ *902/640–2424* ⊕ *www.ironworksdistillery.com*). Named for the old blacksmith's shop it occupies, Ironworks produces hand-distilled vodka from Annapolis Valley apples and luscious liqueurs from local berries.

Traditional and contemporary Maritime-made items are sold at the **Out of Hand Craft Gallery** (✉ *135 Montague St.* ☎ *902/634–3499*), seven days a week, June to December.

Next door is **The Spotted Frog** (✉ *125 Montague St.* ☎ *902/634–1976* ⊕ *www.spottedfrog.ca*), a funky gallery that represents some three dozen folk artists from around the province.

Want to help save the earth *and* preserve a piece of Lunenburg's seafaring history? The **Windbag Company of Nova Scotia** (✉ *123 Montague St.* ☎ *902/640–3555* ⊕ *www.windbagcompanyofns.ca*) has terrific totes made from recycled sails.

The **Folk Art Festival** (⊕ *www.nsfolkartfestival.com*), held annually in late July or early August, draws gawkers and shoppers alike to view the fanciful folk art that put Nova Scotia on the artistic map.

**EN ROUTE**  Nearly every town on this storied stretch of coast has a museum or two, and **Bridgewater**, 18 km (11 mi) west of Lunenburg, is no exception. Both the **DesBrisay Museum** (✉ *130 Jubilee Rd.* ☎ *902/543–4033* ⊕ *www.desbrisaymuseum.ca*), which focuses on county history, and the **Wile Carding Mill Museum** ( ✉ *242 Victoria Rd.* ☎ *902/543–8233* ⊕ *museum.gov.ns.ca/wcm*), a restored water-powered wool mill, are worth a quick look. Bridgewater's chief virtue, however, is that it's the "Main Street of the South Shore" and has the region's largest assortment of shops and services. If you're desperate for a Walmart or are jonesing for a multiplex cinema, this is the place to come.

## LIVERPOOL

*69 km (43 mi) southwest of Lunenburg.*

In recent years a paper mill has been this town's economic mainstay, but between the American Revolution and the War of 1812, privateering was the most profitable pursuit. You see, Liverpool was founded in 1759 by New Englanders who turned on their former neighbors with a vengeance. Armed with a "Letter of Marque" from the British crown, they made a booming business out of seizing American ships and the valuable cargo they carried. Such activity was interpreted as political expediency or legalized piracy, depending on which side you were on.

Whatever your opinion, it's still fun to revisit that period in early July during **Privateer Days** (⊕ *www.privateerdays.ca*). The three-day event has themed tours and entertainment, plus an encampment of the King's

Orange Rangers (a group that reenacts the exploits of a pro-British brigade) at Fort Point Lighthouse Park.

Aside from showcasing the work of Sherman Hines and other renowned Canadian photographers, the **Sherman Hines Museum of Photography** traces the history of their chosen art form. Images ranging from daguerreotypes to holograms are on display, as are a broad selection of cameras and related artifacts, such as magic lanterns and film boxes. There's even a mock-up of a Victorian studio. A research center with a good collection of photographic books and a gift shop are also on-site. ⌂ *219 Main St.* ☎ *902/354–2667* ⊕ *www.shermanhinesphotographymuseum.com* ✉ *C$5* ⊙ *Mid-May–mid-Oct., Mon.–Sat. 10–5:30 and Sun., noon–5:30 in July and Aug.*

★  **Rossignol Cultural Centre.** A refurbished high school is now home to this
⏱  eclectic center that contains two galleries and five museums (including one devoted entirely to outhouses). Among the varied displays are a trapper's cabin, an early-20th-century drugstore, 50 stuffed-wildlife exhibits, and a complete wood-paneled drawing room brought over from an English manor house. ⌂ *205 Church St.* ☎ *902/354–3067* ⊕ *www.rossignolculturalcentre.com* ✉ *C$5* ⊙ *Mid-May–mid-Oct., Mon.–Sat. 10–5:30 and Sun., noon–5:30 in July and Aug.*

If you can't time your trip to coincide with Privateer Days, you can still bone up on the backstory by checking out the free Port of the Privateers exhibit inside the titular lighthouse at **Fort Point Lighthouse Park.** ⌂ *21 Fort Point Lane, off Hwy. 103* ☎ *902/354–5741* ✉ *By donation* ⊙ *late May–early Oct., daily 10–6.*

The **Perkins House Museum,** built in 1766, is the historic home of privateer-turned-leading-citizen Simeon Perkins, who kept a detailed diary about colonial life in Liverpool from 1760 until his death in 1812. Built by ships' carpenters, the intriguing structure gives you the illusion of standing in the upside-down hull of a ship. ⌂ *105 Main St.* ☎ *902/354–4058* ⊕ *museum.gov.ns.ca/peh* ✉ *C$4* ⊙ *June–mid-Oct., Mon.–Sat. 9:30–5:30, Sun. 1–5:30.*

★  One of the last untouched tracts of coastline in Atlantic Canada, **Kejimkujik National Park–Seaside** has isolated coves, broad white beaches, and imposing headlands, all of which is managed by Kejimkujik National Park and Historic Site (that's just plain "Keji" to locals or the linguistically challenged). A hike along the adjunct's 6-km (4-mi) trail reveals a pristine coast that's home to harbor seals, eider ducks, and many other species. To protect nesting areas of the endangered piping plover, parts of the St. Catherine's River beach (the main beach) are closed to the public from late April to early August. ⌂ *Off Hwy. 103, 25 km (16 mi) southwest of Liverpool, Port Joli* ☎ *902/682–2772* ⊕ *www.pc.gc.ca* ✉ *C$5.80* ⊙ *Mid-May–mid-Oct., daily 24 hrs.*

The Liverpool area has easy access to some of the South Shore's best sand beaches. Start wading through the list by visiting **Summerville Beach Provincial Park.** ⌂ *7533 Hwy. 3, Summerville Centre* ☎ *No phone* ⊕ *www.novascotiaparks.ca* ✉ *Free* ⊙ *Mid-May–mid-Oct.*

The **Thomas Raddall Provincial Park** is also convenient for beach lovers. ⊠ *529 Raddall Park Rd., East Port l'Hebert* ☎ *902/683–2664* ⊕ *www. novascotiaparks.ca* ☜ *Free* ⊘ *Mid-May–mid-Oct.*

### WHERE TO EAT AND STAY
*For expanded hotel reviews, visit Fodors.com.*

$–$$  ⛫ **Lane's Privateer Inn.** Downtown Liverpool, though long on history, is short on accommodations, so this 200-year-old inn is a fortunate find. **Pros:** pet friendly; rate includes hot breakfast. **Cons:** room sizes vary; some look tired. ⊠ *27 Bristol Ave.* ☎ *902/354–3456 or 800/794–3332* ⊕ *www.lanesprivateerinn.com* ➺ *27 rooms* ⚥ *In-room: no safe, Wi-Fi. In-hotel: restaurant, bar* ⑩ *Breakfast.*

$$$–$$$$  ⛫ **Quarterdeck Beachside Villas & Grill.** Built just above the high-water mark, these quality villas make you feel like you're staying on a houseboat. Propane fireplaces keep them cozy and, since many have full kitchens, they're practical as well. Two smaller, more secluded cottages are also available. The lawns leading down to the water are perfect for lounging, and the long sandy beach is a launch pad for sea kayakers and body surfers. The resort's landmark grill ($$–$$$) is known for its seafood dishes, especially lobster tails stuffed with scallops and shrimp. **Pros:** terrific beach; some units have whirlpool tubs. **Cons:** restaurant closed off-season; dining reservations essential. ⊠ *7499 Hwy. 3, Summerville Centre, 15 km (10 mi) west of Liverpool* ☎ *902/683–2998 or 800/565–1119* ⊕ *www.quarterdeck.ns.ca* ➺ *13 villas, 2 cottages* ⚥ *In-room: no a/c, no safe, kitchen (some), Wi-Fi. In-hotel: restaurant, room service, beach.*

### SPORTS AND THE OUTDOORS
The **Mersey River** and its affiliated lakes attract anglers during the freshwater fishing seasons (April through September). Trout, salmon, pickerel, and perch swim in these waters, and bass can be found here, too. The **South Shore Bassmasters Club** (☎ *No phone* ⊕ *www.ssbassmasters. com*) invites nonmembers to compete in summertime tournaments.

**Rossignol Surf Shop** (☎ *902/354–7100* ⊕ *www.surfnovascotia.com*) offers two-hour surfing clinics for C$65, all equipment included, daily in July and August, as well as on weekends mid-May through June, and September through October. Board rentals and guided kayak excursions are also available.

## KEJIMKUJIK NATIONAL PARK AND HISTORIC SITE

*67 km (42 mi) northwest of Liverpool; 45 km (28 mi) southeast of Annapolis Royal.*

★ You'll have to veer inland to see this 381-square-km (147-square-mi) park, which is about halfway between the Atlantic and Fundy coasts. Its gentle waterways were used by the Mi'Kmaq for thousands of years, a fact made plain by the ancient petroglyphs carved into rocks along the shore. Today their former routes and woodsy park trails attract campers, canoeists, hikers, birdwatchers, and cyclists. You can explore Keji on your own or take a guided interpretive hike (perhaps spying white-tailed deer, beaver, owls, loons, and other wildlife along the way). Guided paddles and children's programs are also available daily in summer. Because the park is open year-round, leaf peepers can see the deciduous forests blaze with color in autumn, and cross-country skiers can hit the trails in winter. Further proving that this is a stellar attraction, the Royal Astronomical Society of Canada designated Keji as the province's first Dark Sky Preserve in 2010 and the park has initiated nighttime programs for stargazers. ⊠ *Off Hwy. 8 (Kejimkujik Dr.), Maitland Bridge* ☎ *902/682–2772* ⊕ *www.pc.gc.ca* ✉ *C$5.80* ☿ *Visitor Reception Center open Mid-June to Labor Day, 8:30–8; Labor Day to mid-June, 8:30–4:30.*

## WHERE TO STAY

*For expanded hotel reviews, visit Fodors.com.*

**$$**  ⚅ **Mersey River Chalets.** Swimming, paddling, hiking, and bedtime bon-
**★**  fires fill the agenda at this 375-acre wilderness resort 5 km (3 mi) north of Keji. **Pros:** pets welcome; snowshoeing and cross-country skiing offered in winter. **Cons:** on-site restaurant ($$) doesn't serve lunch in-season and closes October through April. ⊠ *RR #2, off Hwy. 8, Caledonia* ☎ *902/682–2443 or 877/667–2583* ⊕ *www.merseyriverchalets. com* ⇆ *9 chalet rooms, 4 lodge rooms, 3 tents* ⚲ *In-room: no a/c, no safe, kitchen (some), no TV. In-hotel: restaurant, tennis court, water sports, some pets allowed.*

**¢–$**  ⚅ **Whitman Inn.** You can go wild without sacrificing creature comforts at this friendly inn. **Pros:** pairs a B&B's intimacy with extra amenities; snow sports offered off-season. **Cons:** breakfast not included; no a/c. ⊠ *12389 Hwy. 8, Kempt* ☎ *902/682–2226 or 800/830–3855* ⊕ *www. whitmaninn.com* ⇆ *8 rooms, 1 apartment* ⚲ *In-room: no a/c, no safe, kitchen (some), no TV. In-hotel: restaurant, pool.*

## SPORTS AND THE OUTDOORS

**Jakes Landing** (☎ *902/682–5253* ⊕ *www.liverpooladventureoutfitters. com*), inside Kejimkujik Park, rents bicycles, rowboats, kayaks, and canoes from mid-May through mid-October. Prices for both bikes and boats start at C$7 per hour, C$25 per day.

# SHELBURNE

*67 km (42 mi) southwest of Liverpool.*

Shelburne, about two-thirds of the way down the Lighthouse Route, has a real frozen-in-time look that many travelers love. It was settled after the American Revolution, when 10,000 Loyalists briefly made it one of the largest locales in North America—bigger than either Halifax or Montréal at the time. Another temporary influx of Americans (albeit a smaller one) changed the face of Shelburne again in 1994 when moviemakers arrived to shoot Roland Joffe's version of *The Scarlet Letter*. The film, starring Demi Moore, was an unequivocal mess, but the producers did help tidy up this frozen-in-time town and raise awareness about its rich architectural heritage. Today the waterfront district looks much like it did when it was laid out in the 1780s, and a surprising number of its buildings—some of the best of which have been turned into museums—date from that period.

Shelburne's big-ticket attraction, the **Shelburne Museum Complex,** includes three properties, all of which are operated by the Shelburne Historical Society (☎ *902/875–3141* ⊕ *www.historicshelburne.com*). There is the **Ross-Thomson House & Store Museum** (⊠ *9 Charlotte La.* ⊙ *June–mid-Oct., daily 9:30–5:30*), reputedly the oldest surviving (and from the looks of it, best stocked) general store in North America; the **Dory Shop Museum** (⊠ *11 Dock St.* ⊙ *June–Sept., daily 9:30–5:30*), where boats are still crafted the old-fashioned way; and, rounding out the trio, the **Shelburne County Museum** (⊠ *20 Dock St.* ☎ *902/875–3219* ⊙ *June–mid-Oct., daily 9:30–5:30; mid-Oct.–May, weekdays 9:30–noon and 1:30–4:30*), which provides an overview of area history. Admission to these venues costs C\$3 each, or C\$8 with a combined Shelburne Museum Complex ticket.

When Shelburne's population exploded after the Revolutionary War, Black Loyalists were relegated to land 7 km (4.5 mi) northwest of town. The community they created—Birchtown (named for the British general who oversaw their evacuation from New York)—became the biggest free settlement of African Americans in the world. Birchtown's virtually forgotten story was told in Lawrence Hill's award-winning novel *The Book of Negroes,* and its founders are now honored at the **Black Loyalist Heritage Site,** which includes a national historic monument, a 1.5 km (1 mi) interpretive trail, and a small museum. ⊠ *104 Old Birchtown Rd., Birchtown* ☎ *902/875–1310* ⊕ *www.blackloyalist.com* 🎟 *Monument and trail free; museum C\$3* ⊙ *Monument and trail daily year-round; museum June–Oct., Tues–Sun 11–5.*

## AROUND SHELBOURNE

**Cape Sable Island**—not to be confused with Sable Island, *waaaaay* out in the Atlantic—is a sleepy spot just off the beaten path. Located 48 km (35 mi) south of Shelburne and accessed via a short causeway, it's Nova Scotia's southernmost point. You'll find colorful fishing boats afloat in Clark's Harbour as well as fine sandy beaches, one of which, Hawk Beach, offers excellent bird-watching and views of the 1861 Cape Sable Island Lighthouse. Actual "sites" are hard to come by around here, but the **Archelaus Smith Museum** (⊠ *915 Hwy. 330* ☎ *902/745–2642* ⊕ *www.archelaus.org* 🎟 *By donation* ⊙ *July–Aug., Mon.–Sat. 10–4:30, Sun. 1:30–4:30*), named for an early New England settler, is worth a gander. It recaptures late-1700s life with household items such as quilts and toys, plus fishing gear and information about shipwrecks and sea captains.

Barrington, on the mainland side of the causeway, also has several old buildings worth visiting when looping back along the island's 21-km (13-mi) road. Choices here include the self-explanatory **Barrington Woolen Mill Museum** (⊠ *2368 Hwy. 3* ☎ *902/637–2185* ⊕ *museum. gov.ns.ca/bwm*) and **Old Meeting House Museum** (⊠ *2408 Hwy. 3* ☎ *902/637–2185* ⊕ *museum.gov.ns.ca/omh*). Both are open on the same seasonal schedule (June–September, Monday–Saturday 9:30–5:30, Sunday 1–5:30) and charge C\$3 admission.

## WHERE TO EAT AND STAY

*For expanded hotel reviews, visit Fodors.com.*

**$$–$$$**
CONTINENTAL
**Fodor's**Choice
★

✕ **Charlotte Lane Café.** Chef-owner Roland Glauser whips up creative seafood, meat, and pasta dishes in this restored building, which started out as a butcher shop in the mid-1800s. The chowder is generous enough for a noon repast, while the rack of lamb with port wine-orange sauce and sun-dried berries is ideal at dinner, especially when capped with a refreshing lemon panna cotta. The café has a pleasant garden patio (a big plus as there are only about 25 seats inside) plus a shop selling quality crafts. Reservations aren't accepted at lunch but highly recommended at dinner due to the combination of good food and good value. ✉ *13 Charlotte La.* ☎ *902/875-3314* ⊕ *www.charlottelane.ca* ⊘ *Closed Sun. and Mon. and late Dec.–early May.*

**$$–$$$**
CONTINENTAL

✕ **Lothar's Café.** This small eatery pays homage to its chef-owner's homeland by featuring plenty of Germanic specialties on the menu, including schnitzel, spatzle, sauerbraten, and a divine Black Forest cake. Indeed, the café is billed as "A Taste of Germany on the South Shore." Nevertheless, regional ingredients are a mainstay and twists on favorite regional dishes—such as scallop cakes or a maple-dressed spinach salad—appear as well. Like the place as a whole, Lothar Mayer is warm and unpretentious, so don't be surprised if he pops up tableside to greet you. ✉ *149 Water St.* ☎ *902/875-3697* ⊕ *www.lothars-cafe.com* ⊘ *Closed Tues. and Wed.; closed Oct.–June except for most major holidays.*

**$–$$**

🏠 **Cooper's Inn.** Shelburne's historic waterfront was the site of a major Loyalist landing in 1783, and a year later the structure that now houses this inn went up. **Pros:** lovely location with water-view garden; some rooms have massage chairs. **Cons:** only breakfast is served on-site; no a/c. ✉ *36 Dock St.* ☎ *902/875-4656 or 800/688-2011* ⊕ *www.thecoopersinn.com* 🛏 *7 rooms, 1 suite* ⌂ *In-room: no a/c, no safe, kitchen (some), Wi-Fi* ⊘ *Closed mid-Oct.–Apr.* ❢⃝ *Breakfast.*

### SPORTS AND THE OUTDOORS

Shelburne has a beautiful natural harbor, and **Shelburne Harbour Boat Tours** (✉ *107 Water St.* ☎ *902/875-6521 or 875-4439* ⊕ *www.shelburneharbourboattours.com*) will take you out to explore it aboard a 13-meter (44-foot) trawler. Tours start at C$25 and operate thrice daily, June through September. If wearing hiking boots makes you happy, morning tours can drop you off on McNutt's Island to hoof it up to the Cape Roseway Lighthouse.

# YARMOUTH

*98 km (61 mi) west of Shelburne.*

Yarmouth's status as a large port and its proximity to New England accounted for its early prosperity and today the town's shipping heritage is still reflected in its fine harbor, marinas, and museums. Since the discontinuation of ferry service from Maine, this isn't such an obvious destination for U.S. travelers. However, handsome Victorian architecture and a pleasantly old-fashioned main street make it worth a visit. Since the Evangeline Trail and Lighthouse Trail converge here, Yarmouth also allows easy access to the Acadian villages to the north or the Loyalist communities to the south.

## EXPLORING

**The Art Gallery of Nova Scotia (Western Branch)** is the AGNS's only satellite location. Like the larger original in Halifax, this one is housed in a heritage building and has a broad mandate, yet it's at its best when foregrounding the work of regional artists. Permanent and rotating exhibitions as well as educational programs (including occasional family Sundays and children's workshops) are offered. ⊠ *341 Main St.* ☎ *902/749–2248* ⊕ *www.artgalleryofnovascotia.ca* ▣ *By donation* ⊙ *Thurs.–Sun. noon–5.*

The **Yarmouth County Museum & Archives** has one of the largest collections of ship paintings in Canada, along with exhibits of household items, musical instruments (including rare mechanical pianos and music boxes), and other items that richly evoke centuries past. The museum has a preservation wing and an archival research area, where local history and genealogy are documented. Next door is the **Pelton-Fuller House,** summer home of the original Fuller Brush Man, which is maintained and furnished much as the family left it. The museum also offers guided tours of a third building in high season: the **Killam Brothers Shipping Office.** Located at 90 Water Street, it recalls a long-standing family business that was established here in 1788. ⊠ *22 Collins St.* ☎ *902/742–5539* ⊕ *yarmouthcountymuseum.ednet.ns.ca* ▣ *Museum C$3, museum and Pelton-Fuller House C$5, archives C$5, Killam Brothers Shipping Office by donation* ⊙ *Museum: June–mid-Oct., Mon.–Sat. 9–5; mid-Oct.–June, Tues.–Sat. 2–5. Pelton-Fuller House: June–mid-Oct., Mon.–Sat. 9–5. Killam Brothers Shipping Office mid-June–Aug., Mon.–Sat. 10–4.*

The **Cape Forchu Lighthouse** isn't the South Shore's most photogenic—the one at Peggy's Cove wins that award—but it comes a close second, scoring points for its dramatic vistas. (The dearth of other camera-clutching tourists helps, too.) Erected in 1962 on the site of an earlier lighthouse, the concrete structure rises 23 meters (75 feet) above the entrance to Yarmouth Harbour. The adjacent keeper's quarters houses a small museum, a tearoom serving local treats, and a gift shop. ⊠ *1856 Cape Forchu Rd., off Hwy. 304, Cape Forchu* ☎ *902/742–4522* ⊕ *www. capeforchulight.com* ▣ *Donations accepted* ⊙ *May–Oct., daily 11–5.*

ↂ The **Firefighters' Museum of Nova Scotia** is a good rainy-day destination. It recounts the history of fire-fighting in the province through photographs, uniforms, and other artifacts, including vintage hose wagons, ladder trucks, and an 1863 Amoskeag Steamer. Kids with a fireman fetish will especially enjoy this spot. After checking out the toy engines, they can don a fire helmet and take the wheel of a 1933 Bickle Pumper. ⊠ *451 Main St.* ☎ *902/742–5525* ⊕ *museum.gov.ns.ca/fm* ▣ *C$3* ⊙ *June–Sept., Mon.–Sat. 9–5, Sun. 10–5; Oct.–May, weekdays 9–4, Sat. 1–5.*

## WHERE TO EAT AND STAY

*For expanded hotel reviews, visit Fodors.com.*

**$-$$**　✕ **JoAnne's Quick 'n Tasty.** Laminated tables, vinyl banquettes, and bright
CANADIAN　lights greet you at this retro diner that still looks much as it did circa
1960. Options include fresh seafood and no-nonsense standbys like
turkey burgers and club sandwiches. Devotees, however, swear by the
hot lobster sandwich. Indeed, Haligonians have been known to make
the three-hour trek just to dine on the creamed crustacean concoction
that was supposedly invented here. ⊠ *Hwy. 1, 4 km (2 mi) northeast of
Yarmouth, Dayton* ☎ *902/742–6606* ☉ *Closed Nov.–Apr.*

**$$**　✕ **Rudder's Seafood Restaurant and Brew Pub.** As its name implies this hop-
SEAFOOD　ping waterfront spot serves the expected fish dishes and a few surprises
(anyone for lobster poutine?) along with pub grub, all of which can
be washed down with hand-crafted ales. Seating is inside a converted
warehouse supported by 18th-century beams or, in fine weather, at pic-
nic tables on the wraparound deck. Since Rudder's doubles as a micro-
brewery, you can also buy beer to go. Live entertainment on Wednesday,
Friday, and Saturday evenings is good reason to linger. ⊠ *96 Water St.*
☎ *902/742–7311* ⊕ *www.ruddersbrewpub.com.*

**$$**　🛏 **Harbour's Edge Bed & Breakfast.** The rooms in this 1864 home (all
named for women who resided here) are especially attractive because
the owners opted for an uncluttered look rather than floral overload. **Pros:** exemplary hosts; terrific French toast at breakfast. **Cons:**
road outside can be busy; private bath for the "Clara Caie" room is
down the hall (the other three rooms have en suite bathrooms). ⊠ *12
Vancouver St.* ☎ *902/742–2387* ⊕ *www.harboursedge.ns.ca* ⇥ *4 rooms*
⌂ *In-room: no a/c, no safe, no TV, Wi-Fi* ⦿ *Breakast.*

**$$$**　🛏 **Trout Point Lodge.** "If you build they will come" seems to have been the
Fodor's Choice　philosophy behind this eco-resort on the fringe of a protected wilderness,
★　40 km (25 mi) northeast of Yarmouth. **Pros:** Relais & Chateaux property;
hot tub, sauna, and in-room massages available. **Cons:** dinner reserva-
tions required; secluded. ⊠ *189 Trout Point Rd. (off the East Branch
Rd. & Hwy. 203), East Kemptville* ☎ *902/761–2142* ⊕ *www.troutpoint.
com* ⇥ *10 rooms, 2 cottages* ⌂ *In-room: no a/c, no safe, no TV (some).
In-hotel: 2 restaurants, 2 bars, beach, water sports* ⦿ *Some meals.*

## SHOPPING

Tired of craft shows, professional potters Michael and Frances Morris
opened a shop called **At the Sign of the Whale** (⊠ *543 Hwy. 1, R.R. 1,
Dayton* ☎ *902/742–8895* ⊕ *www.signofthewhaleonline.com*) in their
home on the outskirts of Yarmouth: the antique furniture forms a hand-
some backdrop for the work of 150 craftspeople. Wood, textiles, pew-
ter, clothing, paintings, and the Morrises' own excellent stoneware are
for sale.

Goodies on sale at **Hands On Crafts** (⊠ *314 Main St.* ☎ *902/742–3515*
⊕ *www.handsoncrafts.ca*), a downtown artisan's co-op, include cool
jewels and birch-bark soap.

Whether you're looking for a gift or something to keep you warm on
chilly Nova Scotian evenings, **The Yarmouth Wool Shoppe** (⊠ *352 Main
St.* ☎ *902/742–2255*) has you covered. A local institution since 1883,

it stocks duffle coats, mohair throws, cashmere shawls, Guernsey fisherman-knit sweaters, and tartan robes.

## POINT DE L'ÉGLISE (CHURCH POINT)

*70 km (43 mi) north of Yarmouth.*

Small as they are, you still can't miss the communities that collectively make up the Acadian Shore. Each one on this stretch, beginning roughly in Beaver River and ending in St. Bernard, seems to have a surplus of Stella Maris flags, a disproportionately large Catholic church, and a French-speaking populace with an abiding passion for *rappie* pie (a hearty chicken stew with shredded potatoes). Church Point, called Point de l'Église by Francophones, tops the rest on all three counts.

The Acadian flags (picture France's tricolor with a gold star in the upper left-hand corner) are most prominently displayed in late July when the village hosts the two-week **Festival Acadien de Clare** (⊕ *www. festivalacadiendeclare.ca*), the Atlantic Provinces' oldest Acadian celebration.

### EXPLORING

**Université Ste-Anne** (✉ *1695 Hwy. 1* ☎ *902/769–2114 or 888/338–8337* ⊕ *www.usainteanne.ca*) is the only French-language institution among Nova Scotia's 17 degree-granting colleges and universities. Founded in 1891, this small university off Highway 1 is a focus of Acadian studies and culture in the province.

**The Rendez-vous de la Baie Cultural and Interpretive Centre** (☎ *902/ 769–1234* ⊕ *www.rendezvousdelabaie.com* ✑ *C$5 for exhibit halls, other areas free* ⊙ *Sept.–June, daily 7–4:30; July–Aug. daily 7 am– 8 pm*), which opened on the campus in 2010, offers an overview for visitors. It includes Acadian-themed exhibits, an art gallery, a theater space, and a boutique as well as a utilitarian Internet café (¢).

**St. Mary's Church (Église Ste-Marie),** the *église* for which this village is named, stands proudly on the main road overshadowing everything around it. That's hardly surprising given that it is the largest wooden church in North America. Completed in 1905, St. Mary's is 58 meters (190 feet) long by 56 meters (185 feet) high, and the steeple, which requires 40 tons of rock ballast to keep it steady when ocean winds blow, can be seen for miles. The church is a registered museum with a stunning interior, two exhibit rooms housing a collection of vestments, and a souvenir shop that sells religious articles. Bilingual guides give tours regularly in summer, and off-season by appointment. ✉ *1713 Hwy.1* ☎ *902/769–2832* ⊕ *www.museeeglisesaintemariemuseum.ca* ✑ *C$2 recommended donation* ⊙ *Mid-May–mid-Oct., daily 9–5.*

### WHERE TO EAT

**$$$**
CANADIAN
★

✕**Chez Christophe.** Right up the road from Church Point in Grosses Coques (French for "Big Clams"), this homey restaurant specializes in classic Acadian cuisine, so *rappie* pie—along with fish chowder and the stewlike *fricot* with dumplings—is always on the menu. Chez Christophe also holds musical "kitchen parties" in summer as part of the region-wide *Musique de la Baie* program (⊕ *www.musiquedelabaie.ca*), which means diners get to enjoy free entertainment in addition to hearty food. If you can't bear to leave, Chez Christophe rents out rooms in an adjacent guesthouse (¢–$, breakfast included). ⊠ *2655 Hwy. 1, Grosses-Coques* ☎ *902/837–5817* ⊕ *www.chezchristophe.ca* ⊗ *Closed Mon.*

¢    ✕ **Râpure Acadienne.** Just as you can't judge a book by its cover, you can't
CANADIAN    judge an eatery by its exterior. Take Râpure Acadienne: though it's little more than a village take-out shack, the *rappie* pie here—picnic-ready and sold to go—is hard to beat. The traditional dish (properly called pâté à la rapure) is made of beef, chicken, and sometimes clams mixed with grated potatoes from which much of the starch has been removed, and most restaurants along the shore serve it. ⊠ *1443 Hwy. 1, Church Point* ☎ *902/769–2172* ⊟ *No credit cards.*

▌**THAT
SOUNDS
HEAVENLY!**    If Acadian fiddlers and spoon players aren't your style, try catching one of the classical concerts at St. Bernard Church, a few miles north of Church Point. The neo-Gothic stone structure is famous for its acoustics, and on select summer Sundays at 4 pm acclaimed artists from Canada and beyond perform here under the **Musique Saint-Bernard** banner. The church seats 1,000, and tickets are available at the door. ⊠ *Hwy. 1, St. Bernard* ☎ *902/665–5103* ⊕ *www.musiquesaintbernard.ca* ⊠ *C$15.*

# DIGBY

*35 km (22 mi) northeast of Church Point/Point de l'Église.*

Digby is underappreciated: people tend to race to or from the ferry connecting it with Saint John, New Brunswick. Yet there is quite a bit to the town, including a rich history that dates to the 1783 arrival of Loyalists from New England. Then, of course, there are the legendary Digby scallops. The world's largest inshore scallop fleet calls the harbor here home, and the plump, sweet "fruits of the sea" they unload are deemed to be delicacies everywhere. There *are* other fish in the sea, though, and while walking along the waterfront, you can buy ultra-fresh halibut, cod, and lobster—some merchants will even cook them up for you on the spot. You can also sample Digby chicks (aka salty smoked herring) in local pubs or buy them from fish markets.

Knowing a good thing when they see it, townspeople honor the magnificent mollusk during **Digby Scallop Days** (⊕ *www.digbyscallopdays. com*), a five-day festival in early August replete with parades, fireworks, and food.

### GETTING HERE AND AROUND

Bay Ferries Ltd. sails the *Princess of Acadia* between Saint John, New Brunswick, and Digby year-round. There is at least one round-trip per day—two in summer—and the crossing takes about three hours. The town itself is easily explored on foot.

### EXPLORING

The **Admiral Digby Museum**, which relates the history of Digby County through interesting collections of furnishings, artifacts, paintings, and maps, will get you up to speed on the town's past. ⊠ *95 Montague Row* ☎ *902/245–6322* ⊕ *www.admuseum.ns.ca* ⊠ *By donation*

⊗ *Mid-June–Aug., Mon.–Sat. 9–5; Sept. Tues.–Fri. 9–noon and 1–4:30; Oct.–mid-June, Wed. and Fri. 9–noon and 1–4:30.*

## WHERE TO STAY

*For expanded hotel reviews, visit Fodors.com.*

$$-$$$ ⊡ **Digby Pines Golf Resort and Spa.** Complete with walking trails, lavish gardens, and Annapolis Basin views, this casually elegant 300-acre property offers myriad comforts. **Pros:** kids under seven eat free; no charge for Digby shuttle service. **Cons:** nearest beach is small, rocky, and across the road. ⊠ *103 Shore Rd.* ☎ *902/245–2511 or 800/667– 4637* ⊕ *www.digbypines.ca* ⊃ *84 rooms, 6 suites, 31 cottages* ⚭ *In-room: no safe. In-hotel: restaurant, room service, bar, golf course, tennis courts, pool, gym, spa* ⫩*Some meals* ⊗ *Closed mid-Oct.–May.*

### SPORTS AND THE OUTDOORS

Looking for something out of the ordinary? Contact **Fundy Adventures** (⊠ *679 Gulliver's Cove Rd., off Hwy. 217* ☎ *902/245–4388* ⊕ *www. fundyadventures.com*), located in Gulliver's Cove about 15 minutes from the town of Digby. The owners organize tasty activities like clam digging and dulse harvesting. Tours cost C$66–C$110.

If you want to get out on the water, drop by the **Fundy Complex** (⊠ *34 Water St.* ☎ *902/245–4950 or 866/445–4950* ⊕ *www.fundyrestaurant. com*) to rent a kayak or board a whale-watching boat.

# LONG ISLAND AND BRIER ISLAND

*About 46 km (40 mi) southwest of Digby.*

You don't just stumble across these islands—reaching them requires a commitment. Maybe Nova Scotian nature lovers are betting on that so they can keep this place all to themselves. You see, Long Island and Brier Island are surrounded by water rich in plankton, which attracts a variety of whales along with harbor porpoises, seals, and abundant sea birds.

### GETTING HERE AND AROUND

First, follow Highway 217 down to the end of Digby Neck, a narrow peninsula separating St. Mary's Bay and the Bay of Fundy, to the hamlet of East Ferry. From there hop a five-minute ferry for Tiverton, Long Island. If you're carrying on to Brier Island, take a second, eight-minute ferry ride onward from Freeport, Long Island, to Westport. Brier Island Ferry links the two islands. Ferries must scuttle sideways to fight the ferocious Fundy tidal streams coursing through the narrow gaps. They operate hourly, year-round, at a cost of C$5 return trip for car and passengers.

### ESSENTIALS

Ferry Contacts **Brier Island Ferry** ☎ *902/839–2302.*

### WHERE TO EAT AND STAY

*For expanded hotel reviews, visit Fodors.com.*

$–$$ ⊡ **Brier Island Lodge and Restaurant.** Atop a bluff at Nova Scotia's most western point, this three-building complex commands a panoramic view of the Bay of Fundy. **Pros:** have their own whale-watching tours;

on-site gift shop. **Cons:** motel-quality decor, main lodge rooms lack ocean views. ✉ *557 Water St., Westport* ☎ *902/839–2300 or 800/662–8355* ⊕ *www.brierisland.com* 🛏 *40 rooms* ♿ *In-room: no a/c, no safe. In-hotel: restaurant, bar* ⊘ *Closed Nov.–Apr.*

### SPORTS AND THE OUTDOORS

WHALE-
WATCHING
Of the half-dozen or so operators running seasonal boat tours, **Brier Island Whale and Seabird Cruises** (☎ *902/839–2995 or 800/656–3660* ⊕ *www.brierislandwhalewatch.com*) is best. On thrice-daily trips, from early June until mid-October, you travel out of Westport with researchers who collect data for international organizations. The fare is C$49, a portion of which funds further research. The same company also offers adrenaline-fueled C$58 Zodiac excursions five times daily mid-May through mid-October.

**Mariner Cruises Whale & Seabird Tours** (☎ *902/839–2346 or 800/239–2189* ⊕ *www.novascotiawhalewatching.ca*), which boasts narration by an onboard naturalist, is a solid choice. Its two- to four-hour cruises (C$49) leave Westport daily from mid-June to mid-October.

**Ocean Explorations Whale Cruises** (☎ *902/839–2417 or 877/654–2341* ⊕ *www.oceanexplorations.ca*) operates fast-paced Zodiac trips out of Tiverton. Led by a biologist, they're priced at C$59.

## ANNAPOLIS ROYAL

*37 km (23 mi) northeast of Digby.*

★ Annapolis Royal's history spans nearly four centuries, and the town's bucolic appearance today belies its turbulent past. One of Canada's oldest settlements, it was founded by the French in 1605, destroyed by the British in 1613, rebuilt by the French as the main town of Acadia, and then fought over for the better part of a century. Finally, in 1710, New England colonists claimed the town and renamed it in honor of Queen Anne. There are approximately 150 historic sites and heritage buildings here, including the privately owned DeGannes-Cosby House, the oldest wooden house in Canada (built in 1708), which happens to sit on St. George, Canada's oldest street.

As if it didn't have enough history on its own, Annapolis Royal is also the ideal starting point for excursions to Port Royal, the place where Canada began.

Because the town flip-flopped between the French and English so many times, the past here is a complicated affair, but the members of the **Historical Association of Annapolis Royal** (☎ *902/532–3035* ⊕ *www. tourannapolisroyal.com*) are happy to walk you through it. They've developed a series of high-season strolls led by guides dressed in typical 18th-century fashion. This is an entertaining way to learn more about the historic significance and cultural heritage of the region, and, at only C$7, it's a bargain. Options include tours of the National Historic District and sites associated with the Acadian Experience. Want to really get into the spirit of things? Candlelight tours of Canada's oldest English graveyard are available early June through mid-October. The association has also put together a pamphlet outlining a self-guided walk for visitors who'd rather wander independently.

Like everything else in this town, the plants are a blast from the past—at least at the **Annapolis Royal Historic Gardens.** Its 17 heritage-themed acres represent different eras and include a glorious Victorian garden, a knot garden, a typical Acadian house garden, and a 2,000-bush rose collection. ⊠ *441 St. George St.* ☎ *902/532–7018* ⊕ *www.historicgardens. com* ⊠ *C$7.75* ⊗ *May–June and Sept.–Oct., daily 9–5; July, daily 8–9; Aug., daily 8–8.*

★ Gazing over the grassy knolls, it's hard to believe that **Fort Anne National Historic Site** qualifies as the "most attacked spot in Canadian history" or that those knolls are actually 300-year-old earthwork ramparts built up, in part, with rubble and blood. First fortified in 1629, the site preserves what is left of the fourth military edifice to be erected here, an early-18th-century gunpowder magazine and officers' quarters. The latter now houses a small museum, and anyone who believes a picture is worth 1,000 words should be sure to see the massive Heritage Tapestry displayed inside. Its four meticulously detailed panels depict four centuries of local history and as many local cultures. ⊠ *323 St. George St.* ☎ *902/532–2397 or 902/532–2321* ⊕ *www.pc.gc.ca* ⊠ *Grounds free, museum C$3.90* ⊗ *Mid-May–June, daily 9–5:30; July and Aug., daily 9–6; Sept.–mid-Oct., daily 9–5:30; mid-Oct.–mid-May, by appointment.*

☾ Downriver from Annapolis Royal is the **Port Royal National Historic Site,**
Fodor'sChoice a reconstruction of Sieur de Monts and Samuel de Champlain's fur-
★ trading post. The French set up shop here in 1605—two years before the English established Jamestown—making this the first permanent European settlement north of Florida. Port Royal also set other New World records, claiming the first tended crops, the first staged play, the first social club, and the first water mill. Unfortunately, it didn't have the first fire department: the original fortress burnt down within a decade. At this suitably weathered replica, ringed by a log palisade, you're free to poke around the forge, inspect the trading post, pull up a chair at the dining table, or simply watch costumed interpreters perform traditional tasks in the courtyard. Children can play dress-up, too, donning period outfits and wooden sabot shoes. ⊠ *Hwy. 1 to Granville Ferry, then left 10.5 km (6.5 mi) on Port Royal Rd.* ☎ *902/532–2898 or 902/532–2321* ⊕ *www.pc.gc.ca* ⊠ *C$3.90* ⊗ *July and Aug., daily 9–6; mid-May–June and Sept.–mid-Oct., daily 9–5:30.*

**Farmers' Market.** On Saturday mornings, mid-May through mid-October or Wednesday afternoons in July and August, the best place to stock up on picnic supplies is the Farmers' Market, which sets up on lower St. George Street next to Ye Olde Towne Pub. Expect artisanal bread, cured meats, homemade sweets, and preserves, plus fresh Annapolis Valley veggies and fruit. Local craftsmen attend, too. Most booths are cash only. ⊠ *St. George St.* ☎ *902/245–4824.*

☾ Apple orchards, green lawns, and beautiful trees cover **Upper Clements Park,** which has 50-odd rides and attractions, many of which are kiddy classics. Mini planes and trains, an old-fashioned carousel; the list goes on. More action-oriented guests can brave the Tree Topper Roller Coaster (the highest ride in Atlantic Canada) or zoom above the property on a 91-meter (300-foot) zip line, then splash out on the park's 70-meter (230-foot) waterslide. Want more? The park embarked on a million-dollar expansion in 2011 with new options like horseback-riding trails, a BMX bike course, and a canopy-style aerial adventure zone set to open in phases. ⊠ *Exit 22 off Hwy. 101* ☎ *902/532–7557 or 888/248–4567* ⊕ *www.upperclementsparks.com* ▣ *C$10 for entry, rides extra* ⊘ *Mid-June–mid-Sept., daily 11–7.*

## WHERE TO EAT AND STAY
*For expanded hotel reviews, visit Fodors.com.*

$
CANADIAN ✕ **Ye Olde Towne Pub.** Any eatery that puts the words "ye olde" in front of its name makes gourmets understandably suspicious, but this place isn't aimed at them anyway. The substantial lunches and dinners served at this merry, low-key pub are a hit with locals who appreciate the good homemade fare, including the always excellent apple crisp. Diners sometimes spill out of the 1884 brick building and onto the patio, which is adjacent to a square where the farmers' market takes place. In a town short on nightlife, it's also a good place for post-dinner lounging. ⊠ *9–11 Church St.* ☎ *902/532–2244.*

$$ ▦ **The Bailey House.** This blissful B&B in an immaculately restored
★ Georgian-style home does everything right. **Pros:** only B&B in town on the water; comfy feather-topped beds. **Cons:** 4 pm check-in; no a/c. ⊠ *150 St. George St.* ☎ *902/532–1285 or 877/532–1285* ⊕ *www. baileyhouse.ca* ⇆ *4 rooms, 1 suite* ⌂ *In-room: no a/c, no safe, no TV, Wi-Fi* ¶⊙ *Breakfast.*

$–$$ ▦ **Bread and Roses Inn.** This interesting inn resulted from the rivalry
★ between a doctor and a dentist: in 1880, the former built a new house and the latter, in the spirit of competition, set out to build a better one nearby, which is now the Bread and Roses. **Pros:** stunning public areas; some rooms are über romantic. **Cons:** room sizes vary; third floor has only 2.5-meter (8-foot) ceilings. ⊠ *82 Victoria St.* ☎ *902/532–5727 or 888/899–0551* ⊕ *www.breadandroses.ns.ca* ⇆ *9 rooms* ⌂ *In-room: no safe, Wi-Fi* ¶⊙ *Breakfast.*

$–$$ ▦ **Hillsdale House Inn.** Princes, kings, and prime ministers have all visited this historic 1859 property, which is surrounded by 12 acres of manicured lawns and gardens (the former seem tailor-made for games of croquet or bocce). **Pros:** pet-friendly; impeccably clean. **Cons:** room quality varies; a/c in third floor and some second floor rooms only. ⊠ *519 George St.* ☎ *902/532–2345 or 877/839–2821* ⊕ *www. hillsdalehouseinn.ca* ⇆ *13 rooms* ⌂ *In-room: no a/c (some), no safe, Wi-Fi. In hotel: business center, some pets allowed* ¶⊙ *Breakfast.*

$$–$$$ ▦ **Queen Anne Inn.** Like Annapolis Royal's best inns, the Queen Anne occupies a beautiful Victorian building that's rimmed with gardens. **Pros:** in-room extras include fluffy bathrobes. **Cons:** dinner served Wednesday to Sunday only; inn closed off-season. ⊠ *494 St. George St.* ☎ *902/532–7850 or 877/536–0403* ⊕ *www.queenanneinn.ns.ca* ⇆ *12 rooms* ⌂ *In-room: no safe, Wi-Fi. In-hotel: restaurant* ⊘ *Closed Dec.–Apr.* ¶⊙ *Breakfast.*

## SHOPPING

**Catfish Moon Studio** (✉ *170 St. George St.* ☎ *902/532–3055 or 888/378–3899* ⊕ *www.catfishmoon.com*) sells its own whimsical earthenware as well as fun local crafts and folk art.

**Lucky Rabbit Pottery** (✉ *15 Church St.* ☎ *902/532–0928* ⊕ *www. luckyrabbitpottery.ca*) specializes in classic porcelain pieces.

**Traditional Marine Outfitters** (✉ *360 St. George St.* ☎ *902/532–7634 or 800/363–2628* ⊕ *www.traditionalmarine.com*) has a huge cache of marine-themed memorabilia, from vintage buoys, jigs, and floats to carved figureheads.

**The Highland Lace Company** (✉ *360 St. George St.* ☎ *902/532–7800 or 800/465–5223* ⊕ *www.highland-lace.com*) has fine lace and repurposed textiles.

# WOLFVILLE

*114 km (71 mi) east of Annapolis Royal.*

Settled in the 1760s by New Englanders, Wolfville is a fetching college town with ornate Victorian homes (some of which have been converted into B&Bs), a lively arts scene, and several fine restaurants. The natural setting is impressive, too: after all, the fields here are fertile enough to support a thriving wine industry. That's due partly to a mild microclimate and partly to an elaborate system of dikes built by the Acadians in the early 1700s to reclaim arable land from the unusually high tides. They can still be viewed along many of the area's back roads. The original Acadians didn't get to enjoy the fruits of their labor, but their legacy lives on at nearby Grand-Pré.

★ The **Grand Pré National Historic Site** commemorates the expulsion of the Acadians by the British in 1755 and a community effort has been launched to have it certified as Nova Scotia's third UNESCO World Heritage Site. The tragic story is retold at the visitor center through artifacts and an innovative multimedia presentation that depicts *Le Grand Dérangement* from both a civilian and military perspective. The latter is shown in a wrap-around theater that's modeled on a ship's interior. A bronze statue of Evangeline, the title character of Longfellow's tearjerking epic poem, stands outside a memorial stone church that contains Acadian genealogical records. The manicured grounds have a garden, a duck pond, and, appropriately enough, French weeping willows. ✉ *Hwy. 1, 5 km (3 mi) east of Wolfville, Grand Pré* ☎ *902/542–3631 or 866/542–3631* ⊕ *www.pc.gc.ca* ▣ *C$7.80* ⊙ *Mid-May–mid-Oct., daily 9–6; grounds open year-round.*

**Acadia University** (✉ *University Ave.* ☎ *902/542–2201 or 902/585–2201* ⊕ *www.acadiau.ca*) is now Wolfville's raison d'être. Size-wise, its student body rivals the resident population, and its handsome hillside campus (established in 1838) dominates the town. Two sites on it are of particular interest to travelers.

The **Acadia University Art Gallery** (✉ *Beveridge Arts Centre* ☎ *902/ 585–1373* ⊕ *gallery.acadiau.ca* ▣ *Free* ⊙ *Tues.–Sun., noon–4*) mounts temporary exhibitions devoted to established and up-and-coming artists.

**The Harriet Irving Botanical Gardens** (✉ *Entry through the K. C. Irving Environmental Science Center* ☎ *902/585–5242* ∰ *botanicalgardens. acadiau.ca* ✍ *Free* ☉ *Daily 8–dusk, weather permitting*) consists of 6 acres devoted mainly to indigenous plants from the Acadian Forest Region.

**Fodor's Choice**
★

With award-winning vintages and sigh-inducing Fundy views, **Domaine de Grand Pré** will fulfill any oenophile's grape expectations. Vineyard tours and tastings are offered three times daily, May through October. They take about 45 minutes, but you'll likely want to linger on this picturesque 10-acre property, so plan to have a meal at Le Caveau Restaurant ($$$), sip a glass of wine under the pergola, or choose a bottle to take home from the on-site shop. ✉ *11611 Hwy. 1, 3 km (2 mi) east of Wolfville* ☎ *902/542–1753 or 866/479–4637* ∰ *www. grandprewines.com* ✍ *Tour and tasting $7* ☉ *Wine shop open early Jan.–Apr., Sat.–Sun. noon–5; May–Oct., Mon.–Sat. 10–6, Sun. 11–6; Nov.–Dec., Wed.–Sun. 11–5. Restaurant open for lunch and dinner Mar.–Oct.; dinner only Tues.–Sat., Nov. and Dec.*

**▌OFF THE BEATEN PATH**

You'll see one of the best natural harbors on the upper Bay of Fundy and some of the highest tides *anywhere* in **Hall's Harbour** (☎ *902/678– 7001* ∰ *www.hallsharbour.org*), 16 km (10 mi) north of Kentville via Highway 359. Go for a walk on a gravel beach bordered by cliffs, try sea kayaking, or seek out the artisans whose studios open here during summer months.

While you're in the neighborhood, be sure to sample the eponymous specialty at **Hall's Harbour Lobster Pound & Restaurant** (✉ *1157 West Halls Harbour Rd.* ☎ *902/679–5299* ∰ *www.hallsharbourlobster.com* ☉ *Closed mid-Oct.–mid-May*).

## WHERE TO EAT AND STAY

*For expanded hotel reviews, visit Fodors.com.*

**$$–$$$**
CONTEMPORARY

✕ **Acton's Grill & Café.** Although it sits smack-dab on Wolfville's main drag, Acton's feels like a tranquil retreat thanks to an appealing fireplace, wood floors, and attractively set tables. Modern art compliments the updated look, and service is top-notch. Stand-out dishes include salmon with roasted vegetable risotto, coriander-crusted Digby scallops, and duck breast wrapped in prosciutto. Portions are filling but try to save room for dessert, many of which feature Annapolis Valley fruit. A terrace is available for alfresco dining in summer months. ✉ *406 Main St.* ☎ *902/542–7525* ∰ *www.actons.ca* ☉ *Closed Sun. No lunch Mon. or Sat., Dec.–Mar.*

**$$–$$$**
CONTEMPORARY
**Fodor's Choice**
★

✕ **Tempest World Cuisine.** With a menu that encompasses dishes like pad Thai and buenuelos (Mexican-style fritters made with Belgian chocolate) you could liken dining at Tempest to a whirlwind world tour, save for the fact that there's nothing hurried about this place. Chef Michael Howell, Nova Scotia's Slow Food guru, masterfully prepares local fare with international flair—the signature chowder, with *finnan haddie* (smoked haddock) and chorizo sausage replacing the usual seafood

CLOSE UP

# For the Birds

1

Many Wolfvillians will tell you that the best show in town is watching swifts—aerobatic birds that fly in spectacular formation—descend on the oversized chimney at the **Robie Tufts Nature Centre** (✉ *Off Front St.* ☎ *No phone*) on summer evenings at dusk. The venue is named in honor of the late ornithologist and long-time resident who wrote *Birds of Nova Scotia* in 1961. Tufts's illustrated tome is still considered the bible for birders in the province, and he had lots of material to work with because Nova Scotia, being strategically located on the Atlantic flyway, is an important staging point for migratory species. Birders can tick several off their "must see" list without straying too far from Wolfville. Each summer as many as half a million sandpipers and plovers flock to Evangeline Beach near Grand Pré to gorge on the Minas Basin's nutrient-rich mudflats before continuing nonstop to South America. Winter, meanwhile, brings hundreds of regal bald eagles to Sheffield Mills, northeast of Kentville. For more information on birding in the province contact the **Nova Scotia Bird Society** (☎ *902/885–2970* ⊕ *nsbs. chebucto.org*).

suspects, is a prime example. Moreover, the results are meant to be savored. The dining room, though upscale, never feels fussy and a patio is open when the weather's fine. ✉ *117 Front St.* ☎ *902/542–0588 or 866/542–0588* ⊕ *www.tempest.ca* ⚠ *Reservations essential on summer weekends* ☉ *Closed Mon. No lunch Tues. or Wed.*

**\$\$** 🏨 **Blomidon Inn.** Teak and mahogany furnishings, marble fireplaces, and a painted ceiling mural all add to the ambience at this 1887 inn. **Pros:** 14 rooms have Jacuzzis and propane fireplaces; the stand-alone Perth Cottage offers maximum privacy. **Cons:** dinner reservations recommended even for guests; room sizes vary. ✉ *195 Main St.* ☎ *902/542–2291 or 800/565–2291* ⊕ *www.blomidon.ns.ca* 🛏 *28 rooms, 1 cottage, 4 apartments* ⚙ *In-room: no safe, Internet, Wi-Fi. In-hotel: restaurant, tennis court, business center* ⱺ *Some meals.*

**\$–\$\$** 🏨 **Farmhouse Inn Bed and Breakfast.** This 1860 B&B has cozy rooms, many of which are equipped with a two-person whirlpool tub and/ or a propane fireplace. **Pros:** well-positioned for outdoor enthusiasts; open year-round. **Cons:** removed from Wolfville's restaurants; two-night minimum on weekends July through September. ✉ *9757 Main St., 15 km (10 mi) north of Wolfville, Canning* ☎ *902/582–7900 or 800/928–4346* ⊕ *www.farmhouseinn.ca* 🛏 *2 rooms, 4 suites* ⚙ *In-room: no safe, Wi-Fi* ⱺ *Breakfast.*

**\$\$** 🏨 **Victoria's Historic Inn & Carriage House.** A 2.5-meter (8-foot) stained-★ glass window imported from Britain more than a century ago sets the decorative mood at this fine 1893 mansion. **Pros:** some rooms have fireplaces and/or balconies; friendly, efficient staff. **Cons:** no restaurant; a few rooms are stuffed with stuff. ✉ *600 Main St.* ☎ *902/542–5744 or 800/556–5744* ⊕ *www.victoriashistoricinn.com* 🛏 *15 rooms, 1 suite* ⚙ *In-room: no safe, Wi-Fi (some)* ⱺ *Breakfast.*

### SPORTS AND THE OUTDOORS

Energetic types can head to **Blomidon Provincial Park** (✉ *3138 Pereau Rd., Cape Blomidon* ☎ *902/582–7319* ⊕ *www.novascotiaparks.ca* 🎫 *No charge for day use* ☉ *Mid-May–early Sept.*), off Highway 101, 20 km (12.5 mi) from Wolfville on the shores of the Minas Basin. It has four main trails that collectively cover 14 km (9 mi). The Lookoff Trail offers especially good cliff-top vistas.

The 1.5-km (1-mi) woodland trail at **Harriet Irving Botanical Gardens** *(see above)* on the Acadia campus is a relatively easy trek.

# WINDSOR

*25 km (16 mi) southeast of Wolfville.*

Windsor has much in common with Bridgewater on the South Shore in that both are historic towns that have evolved into regional service centers. The countryside around Windsor is also pretty, particularly in autumn, and residents of Halifax often make the 66-km (41-mi) drive to the "Gateway of the Annapolis Valley" to take in two fall events.

The **Hants County Exhibition** (☎ *902/798–0000 or 902/798–1559* ⊕ *www.hantscountyex.com*) takes place over six days in September. Staged annually since 1765, the continent's oldest agricultural fair is still an old-fashioned affair complete with ox pulls, horse shows, horticultural exhibits, craft displays, and entertainment.

In early October, the one-day **Pumpkin Festival** (☎ *902/798–2728* ⊕ *www.worldsbiggestpumpkins.com*), part of a larger region-wide celebration, starts with a giant pumpkin weigh-in (some are over 800 pounds) and culminates in a regatta involving supersized pumpkins that are carved into boats and raced across Lake Pizzquid.

Despite a devastating fire in 1897, some evidence of Windsor's earliest days remains at **Fort Edward** (✉ *Fort Edward St.* ☎ *902/532–2321 or 902/798–4706* ⊕ *www.pc.gc.ca*), which, dating from 1750, is the oldest blockhouse in Canada.

**King's-Edgehill School** (✉ *33 King's-Edgehill La.* ☎ *902/798–2278* ⊕ *www.kes.ns.ca*), founded in 1788, is the oldest independent school in the British Commonwealth.

♻ The **Mermaid Theatre of Nova Scotia** uses puppets and performers to retell traditional and contemporary children's classics. The troupe's home base is the 400-seat MIPAC (Mermaid Imperial Performing Arts Centre) adjacent to its Gerrish Street headquarters, but catching a show can be tricky because of the hectic worldwide touring schedule. If you can't time your trip to coincide with a play date, you can still marvel at Mermaid's props and puppets, as several floors filled with them are open for public viewing. ✉ *132 Gerrish St.* ☎ *902/798–5841* ⊕ *www.mermaidtheatre.ns.ca* 🎫 *By donation* ☉ *Year-round, weekdays 9–4.*

The **Haliburton House Museum** was once home to Judge Thomas Chandler Haliburton (1796–1865), a lawyer, politician, historian, and, above all, humorist. Hugely popular in his own day, Haliburton inspired Mark

Twain and put Nova Scotia on the literary map with *The Clockmaker,* a book that used a fictional Yankee clock peddler named Sam Slick to poke fun at provincial foibles. Although you may not be familiar with Haliburton's name, you surely know some of the phrases he coined. The Windsor wordsmith gave us expressions like "quick as a wink," "it's raining cats and dogs," and "the early bird gets the worm." Themed programs and events are offered throughout the summer.

Haliburton is also remembered for making the first recorded reference to hockey—the sport that was "born" here in the early 1800s. Fittingly, antique skates, hand-carved sticks, wooden pucks, and other artifacts from the collection of the **Windsor Hockey Heritage Centre** (formerly on view in a small museum downtown) are now displayed in the house as well. ⊠ *414 Clifton Ave.* ☎ *902/798–2915* ⊕ *museum.gov.ns.ca/hh* 🖅 *C$3.60* ⊗ *June–mid-Oct., Mon.–Sat. 10–5, Sun. 1–5.*

Visits to the family-owned **Sainte Famille Winery** in Falmouth, 5 km (3 mi) west of Windsor, combine ecological history with the intricacies of growing grapes and aging wine. Tasting is done in the gift shop, where bottles are sold at bargain prices. The winery gives tours twice daily, at 10 and 2, May through October, but the best time to come is at the end of the season when Sainte Famille hosts its annual Harvest Wine Fest. The one-day event features food, entertainment, and a competitive Grape Stomp. Even the kids' category is hotly contested. ⊠ *Dyke Rd. and Dudley Park La.* ☎ *902/798–8311 or 800/565–0993* ⊕ *www.st-famille.com* 🖅 *Tours and tastings C$3.50–C$11.50* ⊗ *Shop open Apr.–Dec., Mon.–Sat. 9–5, Sun. noon–5; Jan.–Mar., Mon.–Sat. 9–5.*

**OFF THE BEATEN PATH** **Uniacke Estate Museum Park.** This country mansion was built in about 1815 for Richard John Uniacke, attorney general and advocate general to the Admiralty court during the War of 1812. Now a provincial museum, the Georgian-style house is preserved in its original condition, right down to the antique furnishings. Seven walking trails wend through the large lakeside property. There are picnic tables and a small tearoom on-site. ⊠ *758 Hwy. 1, 30 km (19 mi) east of Windsor, Mount Uniacke* ☎ *902/866–0032* 🖅 *C$3.60* ⊕ *museum.gov.ns.ca/uemp* ⊗ *Museum June–mid-Oct., Mon.–Sat. 9:30–5:30, Sun. 11–5:30.*

## WHERE TO EAT

**$$$**
ECLECTIC

✕ **Cocoa Pesto Bistro.** Since Windsor is a hockey town, it's probably not surprising that the ubiquitous coffee shop chain founded by pro player Tim Horton was long considered the culinary gold standard here. Then Cocoa Pesto debuted in 2006. The menu includes assorted pastas, pecan-crusted salmon, and sweet- and dry-rub pork ribs straight from an apple-wood smoker. The bistro's three licensed rooms have a minimalist look that nicely balances the heritage building's original architectural features, and a patio provides outside dining in summer. Cocoa Pesto is part of the **Woodshire Inn** ($$), so exhausted eaters can bed down in one of two suites upstairs. ⊠ *494 King St.* ☎ *902/472–3300* ⊕ *www.cocoapesto.com* ⊗ *No lunch Mon.–Tues.*

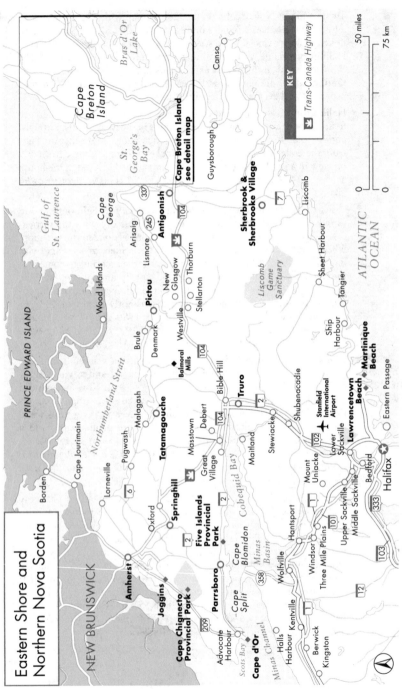

## Eastern Shore and Northern Nova Scotia

**KEY**

✈ *Trans-Canada Highway*

50 miles

75 km

PRINCE EDWARD ISLAND

NEW BRUNSWICK

*Gulf of St. Lawrence*

ATLANTIC OCEAN

*Bras d'Or Lake*

*Cape Breton Island*

*St. George's Bay*

**Cape Breton Island see detail map**

Canso

Guysborough

Liscomb

**Sherbrook & Sherbrooke Village**

7

Sheet Harbour

Tangier

Ship Harbour

**Martinique Beach**

Eastern Passage

**Lawrencetown Beach**

Bedford

Halifax

333

103

12

Middle Sackville

Upper Sackville

Lower Sackville

101

Mount Uniacke

1

Three Mile Plains

Windsor

Hantsport

Wolfville

Kentville

Halls Harbour

Berwick

Kingston

358

*Cape Split*

*Cape Blomidon*

*Minas Basin*

*Minas Channel*

*Scots Bay*

**Cape d'Or**

Advocate Harbour

209

**Joggins**

**Cape Chignecto Provincial Park**

**Amherst**

**Parrsboro**

**Five Islands Provincial Park**

2

Oxford

Lorneville

6

Pugwash

Malagash

*Northumberland Strait*

Wood Islands

Borden

Cape Jourimain

**Springhill**

**Tatamagouche**

Masstown

Debert

Great Village

104

Maitland

*Cobequid Bay*

Stewiacke

Shubenacadie

Stanfield International Airport

102

**Truro**

2

Bible Hill

Balmoral Mills

Denmark

Brule

**Pictou**

Westville

Stellarton

Thorburn

New Glasgow

Lismore

Arisaig

245

337

*Cape George*

**Antigonish**

104

**Liscomb Game Sanctuary**

## CLOSE UP

## Surf's Up Down East

Being sparsely developed, the Eastern Shore—which starts on the fringes of Halifax and covers more than 200 km (125 mi) of coast—has few residents and even fewer tourist attractions. But, oh, boy, does it have beaches! Two of the best are **Lawrencetown** (⊠ 4348 Lawrencetown Rd., Lawrencetown ☎ No phone ⊕ parks.gov.ns.ca) and **Martinique** (⊠ 2389 Petpeswick Rd., East Petpeswick ☎ No phone ⊕ parks.gov.ns.ca).

Located about 25 and 45 minutes respectively from downtown Halifax, both strands are designated provincial parks and have lifeguards on duty in season to supervise swimming. Yet it's not so much dog-paddlers as surfers that these beautiful, wave-blasted beaches attract. Summer is prime time here (especially when north-tracking hurricanes churn the Atlantic up), so if you've already got surf gear all you have to do before hitting the water is check the local surf forecast at ⊕ www.magicseaweed.com. Otherwise there are several outfitters who rent or sell boards and wetsuits (you'll want the latter because the water is cold).

**Happy Dudes Surf Emporium** (☎ 902/827–4962 ⊕ www.happydudes.ca) has two rental locations—one serving Martinique Beach (⊠ 2137 E. Petpeswick Rd., East Petpeswick ) and another 3 km (2 mi) east of Lawrencetown Beach (⊠ 4891 Hwy. 207, Three Fathom Harbour)—as well as a mobile outlet that's typically parked right at Lawrencetown when the surf is up. It offers instruction at both beaches. Groups of three or more can get 3½-hour lessons for C$30, plus equipment rental. Private lessons are C$100.

**Kannon Beach Surf Shop** (☎ 902/471–0025 ⊕ www.kannonbeach.com) is based at Lawrencetown. Lessons with equipment included start at C$75.

For girls harboring Blue Crush fantasies, **One Life Surf School** (☎ 902/880–7873 ⊕ www.onelifesurf.com) is operated by women at Lawrencetown Beach, but classes are open to both sexes. Lessons, with equipment included, start at C$70.

For more information and event listings, click the Web site for the Surfing Association of Nova Scotia (⊕ www.surfns.com).

# THE EASTERN SHORE AND NORTHERN NOVA SCOTIA

From the rugged Atlantic coastline to the wave-ravaged rim of the Bay of Fundy and the gentle shores of Northumberland Strait, the area east and north of Halifax is characterized by contrasts. The road toward Cape Breton meanders past thinly populated fishing villages and thick forests, whereas Northumberland Strait is bordered by attractive towns and sandy beaches. The Fundy Shore, meanwhile, scores points for dramatic scenery—expect steep cliffs harboring prehistoric fossils and intense tides that draw back to reveal the muddy sea floor.

This region has three excellent driving routes. The 316-km (196-mi) Sunrise Trail wends its way along Northumberland Strait, from the wild Tantramar Marsh in Amherst (on the New Brunswick border) to the thriving college town of Antigonish. The 315-km (195-mi) Marine Drive travels through romantic seaside villages and the living-history museum in Sherbrooke. Highlights on the 365-km (226-mi) Glooscap Trail include a majestic lighthouse at Cape D'Or and the notable fossil finds in Joggins. Any one leg could be done comfortably in two days from Halifax with a single overnight along the way.

## SHERBROOKE AND SHERBROOKE VILLAGE

*243 (151 mi) northeast of Halifax.*

★    Most visitors come to Sherbrooke to see Sherbrooke Village: a living-history museum set within the contemporary town of Sherbrooke. It contains more than two dozen restored buildings (including an operating water-powered sawmill) that re-create life during the town's heyday. Between 1860 and 1914, this was a prime shipbuilding, lumbering, and gold-rush center. Now costumed interpreters and artisans recapture the bustle by demonstrating blacksmithing, weaving, wood turning, soap making and similar skills. Special events, such as old-fashioned Christmas and courthouse concerts, are held throughout the year. ⊠ *42 Main St., Hwy. 7, Sherbrooke* ☎ *902/522–2400 or 888/743–7845* ⊕ *www. sherbrookevillage.ca* ☜ *C$10.75* ☉ *June–mid-Oct., daily 9:30–5; Christmas celebrations the last weekend in Nov.*

**OFF THE BEATEN PATH**

**Port Bickerton Lighthouse Beach Park.** Two lighthouses share a lofty bluff about 20 km (12 mi) east of Sherbrooke on Highway 211. One is still working; the other, built in the early 1920s, houses the Nova Scotia Lighthouse Interpretive Centre, which recounts the history, lore, and vital importance of the province's lifesaving lights. Hiking trails and a boardwalk lead to a sandy beach. ⊠ *640 Lighthouse Rd., Port Bickerton* ☎ *902/364–2000* ⊕ *www.novascotiaheritage.ca* ☜ *C$2.50* ☉ *June 15–Sept. 15, daily 9–5.*

### WHERE TO STAY

*For expanded hotel reviews, visit Fodors.com.*

$$–$$$    **Liscombe Lodge Resort.** Just 27 km (17 mi) west of Sherbrooke on Highway 7, this sister property of the Keltic Lodge in Cape Breton and Digby Pines on the Bay of Fundy has choices ranging from lodge rooms to cottages and chalets (most boasting fireplaces and verandas), all in a superb natural setting. In this case, it's the Liscomb River, which promises boating, beaches, and bird-watching. Some 16 km (15 mi) of wooded and riverside trails lace the property, plus there are activities such as tennis, biking, and horseshoes on-site. Once you've worked up an appetite, the Riverside Dining Room ($$–$$$) serves everything from standard pub fare to excellent planked salmon. **Pros:** fun packages and free experiential programs; complimentary use of boats. **Cons:** rooms could use a redo; better suited to families than singles. ⊠ *2884 Hwy. 7, Liscomb Mills* ☎ *902/779–2307 or 800/665–6343* ⊕ *www. signatureresorts.com* ☜ *29 rooms, 1 suite, 38 cottages* ☒ *In-room: no a/c, no safe, Wi-Fi. In-hotel: restaurant, room service, bar, tennis court,*

*pool, gym, water sports, children's programs, laundry facilities* |◎| *Some meals* ⊙ *Closed mid-Oct.–May.*

# ANTIGONISH

*61 km (38 mi) north of Sherbrooke, 55 km (34 mi) west of the Canso Causeway.*

Pretty Antigonish, on the main route to Cape Breton Island, is home to St. Francis Xavier University, a center for Gaelic studies and the first coeducational Catholic institution to graduate women. The campus also has lots of cultural attractions.

The campus **Art Gallery** (⊠ *West St., off Hwy. 104* ☎ *902/863–3300* ⊕ *www.stfx.ca*) has changing exhibits year-round. The **Immaculata Auditorium** hosts a performance series that brings touring artists to town.

During the school year, **The Bauer Theatre** (⊠ *West St., off Hwy. 104* ☎ *902/867–3333* ⊕ *www.mystfx.ca/theatre-antigonish*) on the St. Francis Xavier campus is home to Theatre Antigonish, a nonprofit community company. In summer it sets the stage for **Festival Antigonish** (☎ *902/867–3333 or 800/563–7529* ⊕ *www.festivalantigonish.com*), which has matinees geared to kids and evening performances for adults.

The biggest and oldest **Highland Games** (☎ *902/863–4275* ⊕ *www.antigonishhighlandgames.ca*) outside of Scotland are held in Antigonish each July. The energetic weeklong event includes caber tossing and hammer throwing. Pipe-band concerts, highland dance competitions, and ceilidhs round out the schedule.

## WHERE TO EAT AND STAY

*For expanded hotel reviews, visit Fodors.com.*

**$$–$$$** ╳**Gabrieau's Bistro.** Gabrieau's has earned a place in Antigonish hearts
ECLECTIC with its pleasant interior and an epicurean (yet affordable) menu that includes seafood, pasta, gourmet pizzas, and a variety of vegetarian dishes. There are luscious desserts and an impressive wine list, too. If the weather is nice, take a seat on the sunny patio and watch the town go by. If you want to learn how to duplicate your favorite dish, the restaurant offers public cooking classes in the separate open-kitchen Hawthorne room. ⊠ *350 Main St.* ☎ *902/863–1925* ⊕ *www.gabrieaus. com* ⊙ *No lunch Sat. Closed Sun.*

**$$–$$$** ╳**Lobster Treat Restaurant.** This cozily decorated restaurant on High-
SEAFOOD way 104, a few blocks west of the Antigonish town exit, was once
Ⓒ a two-room schoolhouse. As you'll guess from the name, lobster is the specialty—boiled lobster in particular—though the menu also has chicken, pastas, and stir-fries. Breads and pies are baked on the premises. Traveling with kids? Lobster Treat is popular with families because of the children's menu and friendly, relaxed atmosphere. ⊠ *241 Post Rd. (Hwy. 104)* ☎ *902/863–5465* ⊙ *Closed mid-Oct.–mid-Apr.*

**$$** ⊞ **Antigonish Victorian Inn.** Turn-of-the-century Victorian style reigns at this lovely B&B. The turreted mansion has been restored to its former glory days, when it hosted a bishop, parliamentarian and other esteemed guests. Those joining their ranks now will note that every immaculately kept room has attractive period touches as well as modern amenities like a/c, Wi-Fi, and, in some rooms, fully-equipped kitchens. There are nearly five acres of delightful grounds for strolling, though the center of town is just a short walk away. **Pros:** open year round; delicious hot breakfast. **Cons:** not all options have en suite bathrooms; room size varies widely. ☒ *149 Main St.* ☎ *902/863–1103 or 800/706–5558* ⊕ *www. antigonishvictorianinn.ca* ⤴ *10 rooms, 2 apartments* ⚿ *In-room: no safe, kitchen (some), Wi-Fi* ⫮*Breakfast.*

### SPORTS AND THE OUTDOORS
A 4.8-km (3-mi) **walking trail** along the shoreline of Antigonish Harbour borders a large tidal marsh teeming with ospreys, bald eagles, and other birds.

### SHOPPING
**Lyncharm Pottery** (☒ *9 Pottery La.* ☎ *902/863–6970* ⊕ *www.lyncharm. com*) produces handsome, functional stoneware that's sold in the shop and exported worldwide.

The **Lyghtesome Gallery** (☒ *166 Main St.* ☎ *902/863–5804 or 902/863–8122* ⊕ *www.lyghtesome.ns.ca*) has a good variety of Nova Scotian art at reasonable prices.

For the town's most comprehensive selection of crafts and incredible edibles drop by the self-explanatory **The Made in Nova Scotia Store** (☒ *324 Main St.* ☎ *902/867–2642* ⊕ *www.themadeinnovascotiastore.com*).

# PICTOU

*74 km (46 mi) northwest of Antigonish*

Many people come to Pictou for the sole purpose of catching the ferry onward to PEI (it departs from Caribou, just minutes away) but that's too bad because the town itself is a lovely one with a revitalized waterfront centered on a very different vessel. In 1773 an aging cargo ship named the Hector arrived here carrying the initial load of Scottish Highlanders, making Pictou "The Birthplace of New Scotland."

Each year in mid-August, the quay is the focal point for the weekend-long **Hector Festival**, which celebrates the Scots' arrival. There are concerts, reenactments, and other themed activities.

The descendents of many the Scots who arrived in Pictou went into the lobster fishing business, which inspires the raucous **Pictou Lobster Carnival** (☎ *902/485–5150* ⊕ *www.pictoulobstercarnival.ca*). Held in early July to mark the close of this region's fishing season, it features lobster-boat races, trap-hauling contests, and, of course, tasty crustaceans.

### EXPLORING
The **Hector Heritage Quay,** where a 34-meter (110-foot) fully-rigged replica of the *Hector* is moored, recounts the story of the first hardy pioneers (33 families plus 25 unmarried men) and the flood of Scots who followed them. It has working blacksmith, rigger, and carpentry shops, along with a handsome post-and-beam interpretive center. ☒ *33 Caladh Ave.* ☎ *902/485–4371* ⊕ *shiphector.com* ⬛*C$6* ⊙ *Mid-May–June and mid-Sept.–mid-Oct., daily 9–5; July–mid-Sept. daily 9–8.*

Your own job may be the last thing you want to think about while vacationing, but if you're curious about those the industrious locals have traditionally held, Stellarton, just 20 km (12 mi) from Pictou, is worth a detour for the **Nova Scotia Museum of Industry** (Atlantic Canada's largest museum), which brings our industrial heritage to life. Like factory and mine workers of old, visitors can punch in with a time card; then get straight to work. Hands-on exhibits will show you how to hook a rag mat, print a bookmark, operate a steam engine, or work an assembly line. Interactive computer exhibits explore multimedia as a tool of industry and some 30,000 industrial artifacts are on display, including Canada's oldest steam locomotives. ⊠ *147 N. Foord St., Exit 24 off Hwy. 104* ☎ *902/755–5425* ⊕ *www.industry.museum.gov.ns.ca* ⊠ *C$8.15* ⊙ *Year-round, weekdays 9–5; May–Oct., Sat. 9–5; May–June, Sun. 1–5; July–Oct., Sun. 10–5.*

## WHERE TO STAY

*For expanded hotel reviews, visit Fodors.com.*

$–$$   **Auberge Walker Inn.** A registered Heritage Property built in the 1860s, this centrally located inn is a block from the waterfront. **Pros:** some rooms have water views; suite has kitchenette and private entry. **Cons:** lots of stairs but no elevator; only a cold breakfast buffet included. ⊠ *78 Coleraine St.* ☎ *902/485–1433 or 800/370–5553* ⊕ *www.walkerinn. com* ↪ *10 rooms, 1 suite* ⚄ *In-room: no a/c (some), no safe, Wi-Fi* ☉ *Some meals.*

$–$$   **Stonehame Lodge & Chalets.** Handmade quilts and other country accoutrements await at this peaceful spot comprised of log chalets and lodge rooms on Fitzpatrick Mountain. **Pros:** some rooms have whirlpool tubs. **Cons:** conventional room decor; off the beaten path with no on-site restaurant. ⊠ *R.R. 3, 12 km (7½ mi) west of Pictou, Exit 19 or 21 off TCH 104, Scotsburn* ☎ *902/485–3468 or 877/646–3468* ⊕ *www.stonehamechalets.com* ↪ *15 rooms, 10 chalets* ⚄ *In-room: no a/c (some), no safe, kitchen (some). In-hotel: pool, laundry facilities, some pets allowed.*

## NIGHTLIFE AND THE ARTS

The **DeCoste Entertainment Centre** (⊠ *85 Water St.* ☎ *902/485–8848 or 800/353–5338* ⊕ *www.decostecentre.ca*) presents a summer-long program of concerts, pipe bands, Highland dancing, and ceilidhs with Gaelic music and dance.

## SHOPPING

You can see handcrafted **Grohmann Knives** (⊠ *116 Water St.,* ☎ *902/485–4224 or 888/756–4837* ⊕ *www.grohmannknives.com*) displayed at the Museum of Modern Art in New York—and you can buy them at the factory outlet store here. Prices are discounted and free factory tours are usually available Monday to Friday, 9–3:30.

Quality craftspeople set up at the lively **Pictou County Weekend Market** (⊠ *66 Caladh Ave.* ☎ *902/485–6329* ⊕ *www.pictouweekendmarket. com*), held on the waterfront each Saturday and Sunday from 10 to 5, mid-June through mid-September.

The artisans' co-op **Water Street Studios** (✉ *110 Water St.* ☎ *902/485–8398*) sells hand-dyed and natural yarns, felted woolen items, and knits, along with weaving, blankets, pottery, stained glass, jewelry, and woodwork.

### SPORTS AND THE OUTDOORS

The **Jitney Trail** (☎ *No phone* ⊕ *www.trails.gov.ns.ca*) is a 5-km (3-mi) water's edge route around Pictou Harbour that puts you in sight of marine life and working wharves. It's frequented by hikers and bikers.

Popular **Melmerby Beach** (☎ *No phone* ⊕ *www.trails.gov.ns.ca*) has a boardwalk, lifeguards, and some of the province's warmest water. It's about 23 km (14 mi) east of Pictou—follow the shore road from Highway 104.

**Pictou Island Charters** (☎ *902/921–1033* ⊕ *www.pictouislandcharters. ca*) offers transportation to and tip-to-tip tours of the eponymous little island in the middle of Northumberland Strait. Priced at C$50, the six-hour outing runs Thursday and Friday in July and August.

---

> ### THE GIANT ANNA SWAN
>
> Anna Swan, born near Tatamagouche in 1846, weighed 18 pounds and was 27 inches long at birth, was 4 feet 6 inches when she was four years old, and 6 feet 2 inches by the time she was 10. The supersized Swan joined P. T. Barnum's museum when she was 7 feet 2 inches, but continued to grow for several more years until she reached her full height of 7 feet 5½ inches. She married another famously tall person: Martin Van Buren Bates, who is believed to have been at least 7 feet 9 inches.

---

# TATAMAGOUCHE

*50 km (31 mi) west of Pictou.*

Though it only has about 1,000 residents, tiny Tatamagouche is a force to be reckoned with. Canada's second-largest Oktoberfest (☎ *800/895–1177* ⊕ *www.nsoktoberfest.ca*)—a boisterous event complete with sausages, schnitzel, and frothy steins of beer—is held here each fall. Summer brings strawberry and blueberry festivals, lobster, and chowder suppers.

★ **Creamery Square** is the hub of activity in Tatamagouche. The newly developed waterfront attraction, centered on a former dairy facility, includes an eclectic Heritage Centre. Inside it, the **Sunrise Trail Museum** traces Tatamagouche's Mi'Kmaq, Acadian, French, and Scottish roots through interactive displays. Galleries relating to local giantess Anna Swan and the 290-million-year-old Brule fossil tracks (discovered nearby in 1994) are housed here as well. Demonstrations on boatbuilding and butter making are regularly staged. Creamery Square is also the site of a Saturday morning farmers' market (February through December, 8 am to noon) where crafts are sold alongside produce and baked goods. ✉ *39 Creamery Rd.* ☎ *902/657–3449* ⊕ *www.creamerysquare. ca* 🎟 *C$5* 🕓 *Late May–mid-Oct., Sun.–Fri. 10–6, Sat. 9–6.*

CLOSE UP

## Milling Around

Within a 10-minute drive of Tatamagouche you have the opportunity to visit two historic mills.

**Balmoral Grist Mill**, built in 1874 and one of the few water-powered mills still operating in Nova Scotia, serves as the centerpiece of a small museum. You can observe flour-milling demonstrations and walk the site's 1-km (½-mi) trail. ✉ *660 Matheson Brook Rd., Balmoral Mills* ☎ *902/657–3016* 🌐 *www.museum.gov.ns.ca* 🎫 *C$3.60* 🕒 *June–mid-Oct., Tues.–Sat. 10–5, Sun. 1–5.*

**The Sutherland Steam Mill Museum**, dating from 1894, produced useful items ranging from carriages and sleds to old-time wooden bathtubs. Demos and hands-on activities are offered in July and August. ✉ *3169 Denmark Rd., off Hwy. 326, Denmark* ☎ *902/657–3365* 🌐 *www.museum.gov.ns.ca* 🎫 *C$3.60* 🕒 *June–mid-Oct., Tues.–Sat. 10–5, Sun. 1–5.*

If you're crushing on grapes, put **Jost Vineyards** on your itinerary. Located in Malagash, 17 km (11 mi) west of Tatamagouche, the vineyard produces a surprisingly wide range of wines, including a notable ice wine (a sweet wine made after frost has iced the grapes). Jost offers complimentary tastings year-round and complimentary tours from mid-June to mid-September. There is also a well-stocked shop. ✉ *48 Vintage La., Hwy. 6 off Hwy. 104* ☎ *902/257–2636 or 800/565–4567* 🌐 *www.jostwine.com* 🕒 *Mid-June–mid-Sept., daily 9–6; mid-Sept.–mid-June, daily 9–5; closed Sun. Dec. 23–Apr. 30; tours offered mid-June–mid-Sept., daily noon and 3.*

### WHERE TO EAT AND STAY

*For expanded hotel reviews, visit Fodors.com.*

$$ ★ **Train Station Inn.** Guests at this ingeniously restored inn can sleep in an 1887 train station or one of seven cabooses parked on the tracks outside. **Pros:** complimentary tea, coffee, muffins, and scones at breakfast; memorable gift shop. **Cons:** a/c in railcars only; often booked well in advance. ✉ *21 Station Rd.* ☎ *902/657–3222 or 888/724–5233* 🌐 *www.trainstation.ca* *3 rooms, 7 suites* *In-room: no a/c (some), no safe, Wi-Fi. In-hotel: business center* *Some meals* 🕒 *Closed Nov.–Apr.*

### SHOPPING

At **Sara Bonnyman Pottery** (✉ *Hwy. 246, RR 2, 1½ km [1 mi] uphill from post office* ☎ *902/657–3215* 🌐 *www.sarabonnymanpottery.com*) you can watch the potter herself at work. The studio is open Monday through Saturday, 10 to 4 in July and August, and by appointment off-season.

Maritime crafts sold at **The Sunflower** (✉ *249 Main St.* ☎ *902/657–3276 or 902/657–2495*) include pewter, baskets, wrought iron, quilts, candles, and stoneware by noted local potter Sara Bonnyman.

**SPORTS AND THE OUTDOOR**

**The Butter Trail** (⊕ *www.trails.gov.ns.ca*), named for the creamery it backs onto, is part of the TransCanada Trail System. The 26-km (16-mi) multiuse path follows the reclaimed rail bed that the Train Station Inn's cabooses once traversed.

# SPRINGHILL

*57 km (35 mi) west of Tatamagouche.*

If you're not going to be visiting Cape Breton, Springhill (on Highway 2) is worth a stop since it gives you a second chance to sample Nova Scotia's music-and-mining combo. This town was both the birthplace of acclaimed songstress Anne Murray and, before that, home to the ill-fated coal mine immortalized in "The Ballad of Springhill" by Peggy Seeger and Ewen McColl.

## EXPLORING

Anne Murray's long, illustrious career is celebrated at the **Anne Murray Centre.** Costumes, gold records, and more are on display. Die-hard fans can record a virtual duet with Murray. ⊠ *36 Main St.* ☎ *902/597–8614* ⊕ *www.annemurraycentre.com* ⊠ *C$6* ⊙ *Mid-May–mid-Oct., daily 9–4:30.*

Site of several tragedies, the Springhill coalfield gained international attention in 1958 when a "bump" trapped 174 miners underground. Today you can descend under safer circumstances at the **Springhill Miners Museum.** Some of the guides are retired miners who offer firsthand accounts of their working days. ⊠ *145 Black River Rd., off Hwy. 2* ☎ *902/597–3449* ⊠ *C$5.25* ⊙ *Mid-May–mid-Oct., daily 9–5.*

# AMHERST

*33 km (21 mi) northwest of Springhill.*

Today, Amherst is a quaint, quiet town with a central location, though from the mid-1800s to the early 1900s it was a bustling center of industry and influence—four of Canada's Fathers of Confederation hailed from Amherst, including Sir Charles Tupper, who later became prime minister.

From Amherst, Nova Scotia's Sunrise Trail heads toward Northumberland Strait, while the Glooscap Trail runs west through fossil country. For motorists traveling between provinces, Amherst is a mere 7 km (4 mi) from the New Brunswick border and 55 km (34 mi) from the Confederation Bridge, which connects the Maritime mainland to Prince Edward Island.

## EXPLORING

In contrast with tame Amherst is the **Tantramar Marsh,** alive with incredible birds and wildlife. It was originally called Tintamarre (in French, literally "din") because of the racket made by vast flocks of wildfowl. Said to be the world's largest marsh, the Tantramar is a migratory route for hundreds of thousands of birds and a breeding ground for more than 100 species.

Joggins—on the Glooscap Trail, 35 km (22 mi) southwest of Amherst and 70 km (43 mi) northeast of Cape Chignecto—is famous for Coal Age fossils that were embedded in sandstone, then uncovered through erosion caused by Fundy's surging tides. You can spy them outside, in the sea cliffs, or inside the **Joggins Fossil Centre.** Opened in 2008 (the same year Joggins was named a UNESCO World Heritage Site), this striking C$9-million museum has a large, well-curated collection of specimens dating back some 300-million years, along with interesting displays outlining the region's geological and archaeological history. Half-hour (C$5) and two-hour (C$12) guided tours of the cliffs run daily in peak months; an in-depth four-hour tour (C$55) runs monthly by reservation only. If you're traveling as a family, try to come on a Friday in July or August, when children are admitted free to the museum and activities aimed specifically at them are offered. ⊠ *100 Main St.* ☎ *902/251–2727 or 888/932–9766* ⊕ *www.jogginsfossilcliffs.net* ☒ *C$8* ⊘ *Late Apr.– May and early Sept.–Oct., weekdays 11–4, weekends 9:30–5:30; June– early Sept., daily 9:30–6:30; off-season by appointment.*

### WHERE TO EAT AND STAY
*For expanded hotel reviews, visit Fodors.com.*

$–$$  **Amherst Shore Country Inn.** This seaside establishment has a 183-meter (600-foot) private beach and 20 acres of lawns and gardens overlooking Northumberland Strait. **Pros:** tranquil location; outstanding dining. **Cons:** most accommodations are situated away from the actual inn at varying distances; breakfast is not included. ⊠ *Hwy. 366, 32 km (20 mi) northeast of Amherst, Lorneville* ☎ *902/661–4800 or 800/661–2724* ⊕ *www.ascinn.ns.ca* ↩ *4 rooms, 4 suites, 3 cottages* ⌂ *In-room: no safe, kitchen (some), Wi-Fi. In-hotel: restaurant, beach, business center* ⊘ *Closed weekdays Nov.–May.*

$$  **The Regent Bed & Breakfast.** Set peacefully back from the street, this picturesque 1898 Georgian house stands out for its grandeur. **Pros:** open year-round; luxurious linens. **Cons:** innkeepers will take guests sightseeing upon request, though in Amherst there's not that much to see. ⊠ *175 East Victoria St.* ☎ *902/667–7676 or 866/661–2861* ⊕ *www.theregent. ca* ↩ *4 rooms* ⌂ *In-room: no safe, refrigerator, Wi-Fi* ⦿ *Breakfast.*

## CAPE CHIGNECTO AND CAPE D'OR

*105 km (65 mi) southwest of Amherst.*

Two imposing promontories—Cape Chignecto and Cape d'Or—reach into the Bay of Fundy near Chignecto Bay.

### EXPLORING
Cape Chignecto is home to **Cape Chignecto Provincial Park,** which includes miles of untouched coastline; over 10,000 acres of old-growth forest harboring deer, moose, and eagles; and a variety of unique geological features. Nova Scotia's largest provincial park, it's circumnavigated by a 51-km (31-mi) hiking trail along rugged cliffs that rise 185 meters (600 feet) above the bay. Wilderness cabins and campsites are available. ⊠ *1108 West Advocate Rd., off Hwy. 209, Advocate Harbour* ☎ *902/*

*392–2085* ⊕ *www.capechignecto. net* ✉ *C$5.10* ⊙ *mid-May–Oct., daily 8–4:30.*

**Fodor's** Choice ★ South of Cape Chignecto, **Cape d'Or** *(Cape of Gold)* was poetically but inaccurately named by explorer Samuel de Champlain: there's copper in them thar hills, not gold. The region was actively mined a century ago, and at nearby Horseshoe Cove you may still find nuggets of almost pure copper on the beach as well as amethysts and other semiprecious stones. Cape d'Or's hiking trails border the cliff edge above the Dory Rips, a turbulent meeting of currents from the Minas Basin and the Bay of Fundy punctuated by a fine lighthouse.

> ### THE MYSTERY OF THE MARY CELESTE
>
> The *Mary Celeste*, originally christened the *Amazon*, was built on Spencer's Island in 1861. Its first captain died on the ship's maiden voyage and the boat was renamed. In 1872 the ship set sail for Europe carrying a cargo of wine and liquor. Less than a month later it was discovered abandoned at sea, all sails set and undamaged but without a trace of the crew and passengers. A cairn at Spencer's Island Beach (across from the Beach House Restaurant on Highway 209) commemorates the vessel.

A delightful beach walk at **Advocate Harbour** follows the top of an Acadian dike that was built by settlers in the 1700s to reclaim farmland from the sea. Advocate Beach, noted for its monumental supply of tide-cast driftwood, stretches for about 5 km (3 mi) east from Cape Chignecto.

The **Age of Sail Museum Heritage Centre** traces the history of the area's shipbuilding and lumbering industries. You can also see a restored Methodist church, a blacksmith shop, a boathouse, and a lighthouse. A cute café serves light meals like chowder, lobster rolls, and sandwiches. ✉ *8334 Hwy. 209, Port Greville* ☎ *902/348–2030* ⊕ *www. ageofsailmuseum.ca* ✉ *C$3* ⊙ *June, Thurs.–Mon. 10–6; July–mid-Oct., daily 10–6.*

### WHERE TO EAT AND STAY

*For expanded hotel reviews, visit Fodors.com.*

**$$–$$$**
CANADIAN
★
✕ **Wild Caraway Restaurant & Café.** The young proprietors of this eatery are enthusiastic about using local products in their menus. Casual but quality options like lobster rolls, fish cakes, quiche, and a daily pasta are served at lunch; dinner offerings are more sophisticated and may include pan-fried haddock, local scallops, and a 12-ounce rib eye. The 1860s building has windows that overlook the wharf. There are also two basic guest rooms ($, breakfast included) on the top floor, with a shared bathroom, for overnight stays. ✉ *3721 Hwy. 209, Advocate Harbour* ☎ *902/392–2889* ⊕ *www.wildcaraway.com* ⊙ *Closed Tues. May–Sept.; call for off-season hours.*

**$$**
🏠 **Driftwood Park Retreat.** Five modern chalets face the Fundy shore at this eco-friendly property. **Pros:** rates are discounted off-season. **Cons:** there's not much else around; TVs are free but must be specially requested. ✉ *47 Driftwood La., Advocate Harbour* ☎ *902/392–2008 or 866/810–0110* ⊕ *www.driftwoodparkretreat.com* 🛏 *5 cottages*

&#9832; *In-room: no a/c, no safe, kitchen. In-hotel: beach, business center, some pets allowed* &#9737; *Closed Jan.–Mar.*

**$**
**★** &#9787; **The Lighthouse on Cape d'Or.** Before automation, two lighthouse keepers manned the light on rocky Cape d'Or, and their cottages have been transformed into an excellent restaurant ($$; closed Wednesday) and a small inn with unparalleled views of the Minas Basin. **Pros:** cool concept; warm hosts. **Cons:** difficult access; no credit cards accepted. &#8862; *Cape d'Or off Hwy. 209* &#9775; *Box 122, Advocate B0M 1A0* &#9742; *902/670–0534* &#9728; *www.capedor.ca* &#8617; *4 rooms* &#9832; *In-room: no a/c, no safe, no TV. In-hotel: restaurant* &#9473; *No credit cards* &#9737; *Closed Nov.–Apr.*

**$–$$** &#9787; **Reid's Century Farm Tourist Home.** Nestled between Cape d'Or and Cape Chignecto, this is a working cattle farm where you can enjoy the bucolic pleasures of country life or take a short drive to the Fundy shore. **Pros:** in-room coffee; cottage has a washer, dryer, and dishwasher. **Cons:** remote location; farm setting might irritate allergies. &#8862; *1391 W. Advocate Rd., West Advocate* &#9742; *902/392–2592* &#9728; *www.reidstouristhome. ca* &#8617; *3 rooms, 1 cottage* &#9832; *In-room: no a/c, no safe, kitchen (some)* &#9737; *Closed Oct.–May.*

### SPORTS AND THE OUTDOORS

**NovaShores Adventures** (&#8862; *37 School La., Advocate Harbour* &#9742; *902/392–276 or 866/638–4118* &#9728; *www.novashores.com*) organizes kayak tours that explore the unspoiled coast of Cape Chignecto daily from mid-May through September. A beach picnic is included in the C$85 fee. Overnight options are also available.

# PARRSBORO

*55 km (34 mi) east of Cape d'Or.*

Parrsboro, the main town on the north shore of the Minas Basin, is a hot spot for rock hounds and fossil hunters.

The cliffs that rim the **Minas Basin** are washed by the world's highest tides twice daily: the result is a wealth of plant and animal fossils revealed in the rocks or carried down to the shore.

Semiprecious stones such as amethyst, quartz, and stilbite can be found at **Partridge Island,** 1 km (½ mi) offshore and connected to the mainland by an isthmus.

The combination of fossils and semiprecious stones makes Parrsboro a natural place to hold the **Nova Scotia Gem and Mineral Show** during the third weekend of August. In addition to dozens of exhibitors, the show includes themed demonstrations and geological field trips. There are even experts on hand to identify any treasures you turn up.

&#9786; The **Fundy Geological Museum** isn't far from the Minas Basin, where some of the oldest dinosaur fossils in Canada have been found. Two-hundred-million-year-old specimens are showcased here alongside other mineral, plant, and animal relics. The opportunity to peer into a working geology lab and see bright new interactive exhibits (like the Bay of Fundy Time Machine) give this museum real kid appeal. On Fridays and Saturdays in July and August, the curator leads three- to five-hour field trips through the surrounding area. Note that these interpretative walking tours are free but you need your own transportation since most don't start at the museum. ⊠ *162 Two Island Rd.* ☎ *902/254–3814* ⊕ *www.fundygeo.museum.gov.ns.ca* ☒ *$7.50* ☉ *Late May–early Oct., daily 9:30–5:30; mid-Oct.–May, Tues.–Sat.; hrs vary, call ahead.*

☾ The world's smallest dinosaur footprints, along with rare minerals, rocks, and fossils, are displayed at Eldon George's **Parrsboro Rock and Mineral Shop and Museum.** George, a goldsmith, lapidary, and woodcarver, sells his work in his shop and hosts tours for fossil and mineral collectors. ⊠ *349 Whitehall Rd.* ☎ *902/254–2981* ☒ *Donations accepted* ☉ *May–Oct., daily 10–6.*

Although fossils have become Parrsboro's claim to fame, this harbor town was also a major shipping and shipbuilding port, and its history is described at the **Ottawa House-by-the-Sea Museum.** The house, which overlooks the Bay of Fundy, is the only surviving building from a 1700s settlement. It was later the summer home of Sir Charles Tupper (1821–1915), a former premier of Nova Scotia who was briefly prime minister of Canada. Those with roots in Nova Scotia can research their ancestors in the genealogical archives. ⊠ *1155 Whitehall Rd., 3 km (2 mi) east of downtown* ☎ *902/254–2376* ☒ *C$2* ☉ *Mid-May–mid-Sept., daily 10–6.*

## WHERE TO EAT AND STAY
*For expanded hotel reviews, visit Fodors.com.*

**$$$**
CONTEMPORARY
★
☾

✕ **Bare Bones Bistro.** "Foodie destination" isn't the first phrase that comes to mind when describing Parrsboro, so Bare Bones is something of an epicurean oasis. Organic ingredients supplied by local farmers and fishermen strike the keynote on a menu that is deceptively simple—you might find, for example, fresh flounder with julienned summer vegetables, followed by warm blueberry cake served with brown sugar sauce and Chantilly cream. A children's menu in the main dining room and hand-tossed pies made in the adjacent Bare Bones Pizzeria ($) ensure that no one leaves the premises hungry. ⊠ *121 Main St.* ☎ *902/254–2270* ⊕ *www.barebonesbistro.com* ☉ *Closed Mon.*

**$–$$**

▦ **Gillespie House Inn.** Colorful gardens border the driveway leading up to this gracious 1890 home. **Pros:** impeccable rooms; customized packages available. **Cons:** complimentary Continental breakfast is the only meal served; no elevator. ⊠ *358 Main St.* ☎ *902/254–3196 or 877/901–3196* ⊕ *www.gillespiehouseinn.com* ⇆ *7 rooms* ⚹ *In-room: no a/c, no safe, no TV, Wi-Fi. In-hotel: some pets allowed* ☉ *Closed Nov.–Apr.* ⑩ *Breakfast.*

**$–$$**

▦ **Maple Inn, Parrsboro.** Local residents often reserve Room 1 in this Italianate-style home built in 1893 because many of them were born here when the building was a hospital and this was the delivery room. **Pros:** full breakfast included; RBC Rewards points can be redeemed. **Cons:** no elevator; potential wallpaper overload. ⊠ *2358 Western Ave.* ☎ *902/254–3735 or 877/627–5346* ⊕ *www.mapleinn.ca* ⇆ *6 rooms, 2 suites* ⚹ *In-room: no a/c, no safe, Wi-Fi* ☉ *Closed Nov.–Apr.* ⑩ *Breakfast.*

**$–$$** 🏨 **Parrsboro Mansion Inn.** Although this 1880 home, set far back on a 4-acre lawn, presents an imposing face, it's bright and modern inside. **Pros:** massages are available in a separate treatment room; heated pool. **Cons:** no elevator to suite; only some a/c. ✉ *3196 Eastern Ave.* ☎ *902/254–2585 or 866/354–2585* ⊕ *www.parrsboromansion.com* 🛏 *3 rooms, 1 suite* ⚬ *In-room: a/c (some), no safe, Wi-Fi. In-hotel: pool, spa, laundry facilities, business center* ⊙ *Closed mid-Oct.–mid-June* ⦿ *Breakfast.*

## NIGHTLIFE AND THE ARTS

**Ship's Company Theatre** (✉ *18 Lower Main St.* ☎ *902/254–2003 or 800/ 565–7469* ⊕ *www.shipscompany.com*) presents top-notch plays, comedy, and a concert series at its unique facility, July through September. The *Kipawo*, a former Minas Basin ferry, was moved from the beach and has been integrated into the lobby.

## SPORTS AND THE OUTDOORS

If you'd like to see the water from a different perspective, consider going for an aerial view with Pegasus Paragliding (☎ *902/254–2972* ⊕ *www. pegasusparagliding.com*). Based in nearby Diligent River, they offer tandem flights for C$115.

**EN ROUTE** Located between Parrsboro and Truro (about 15 miles east of Parrsboro), Five Islands is one of the most scenic areas along Highway 2. According to Mi'Kmaq legend, these islands were created when the god Glooscap threw handfuls of sod at Beaver, who had mocked and betrayed him.

**Five Islands Provincial Park,** on the shore of Minas Basin, has a campground (C$24 a night), plus a beach for combing, trails for hiking, and mud flats for clam digging. Interpretive displays reveal the area's interesting geology (semiprecious stones, Jurassic-period dinosaur bones, and fossils can all be found within the park's 1,500 acres). Better still, complimentary programs covering topics like astronomy, rock hounding, and tidal pool exploration are offered during high season (check the Web site). Due to towering tides you can walk on the ocean floor here at ebb times, when the water recedes nearly 1 mile, though you'll literally have to run back in mighty fast when the tide turns. That's precisely the goal of participants in the **Not Since Moses 10K Race** (⊕ *www.notsincemoses.com*): an event of biblical proportions staged each summer. ✉ *618 Bentley Rd., Hwy. 2* ☎ *902/254–2980* ⊕ *parks. gov.ns.ca* 🎫 *Free* ⊙ *mid-May–Sept., daily dawn–dusk.*

**Cobequid Interpretation Centre** highlights the geology, history, and culture of the Five Island area with pictures, videos, and interpretive panels. Get a sweeping view of the countryside and the impressive tides from the World War II observation tower. The center is home base for the **Kenomee Hiking and Walking Trails,** which allow you to explore varied landscapes ranging from the coast, cliffs, and waterfalls, to forested valleys. ✉ *3248 Hwy. 2, Economy* ☎ *902/647–2600* 🎫 *By donation* ⊙ *June and Sept.–mid-Oct., daily 9–5; July and Aug., daily 9–6.*

## TRURO

*91 km (57 mi) east of Parrsboro.*

Truro's central location places it on many travelers' routes: this is rightly called "The Hub of Nova Scotia" because if you're driving down the TransCanada Highway you'll have to pass by whether you're headed for Halifax, Cape Breton, and either the PEI or Newfoundland ferry. Within Truro itself, watch for the Tree Sculptures, a creative tribute to trees killed by the dreaded Dutch elm disease. Artists have been transforming the dead trees into handsome sculptures of historical figures, wildlife, and cultural icons.

Truro, surrounded by rich agricultural land and home to the province's agricultural college, shows its roots at a large farmers' market every Saturday from mid-May to the end of October.

### EXPLORING

For up-close appreciation of where some of the local produce comes from, visit **River Breeze Farm** (⊠ *660 Onslow Rd., exit 14A off Hwy. 102* ☎ *902/895–5138*). They have pick-your-own-strawberry fields in summer and Atlantic Canada's largest corn maze in the fall.

Truro's least-known asset is also its biggest—the 400-acre **Victoria Park** is where, right at the edge of downtown, you'll find wooded hiking trails, a winding stream, two waterfalls, public tennis courts, and an outdoor pool that becomes a skating rink in the winter. Even if you don't intend to stay in Truro, this park is a good pit stop for car-weary travelers: kids especially will enjoy the picnic pavilion and playground. ⊠ *Corner of Court and Prince Sts.* ☎ *902/893–6078* 🖃 *Free* ☉ *Daily dawn–dusk.*

### WHERE TO EAT AND STAY

*For expanded hotel reviews, visit Fodors.com.*

**$$**

**CONTEMPORARY**

✕ **Bistro 22.** Truro is fringed with rich farmland and chef Dennis Pierce knows how to make the most of the fabulous produce grown around here. His 32-seat eatery has an upscale-casual ambience and a small but mighty menu. Salads, sandwiches, and whole-grain pizzas topped with fresh ingredients dominate at lunch while the meatier offerings at dinner include pork stuffed with locally made Gouda and served with seasonal vegetables. Dessert choices change daily but are always made in-house and are generously portioned. ⊠ *16 Inglis Pl.* ☎ *902/843–4123* ⊕ *www.bistro22.ca* ☉ *Closed Sun. and Mon., no dinner Tues. and Wed.*

**$–$$**

**🖰 Holiday Inn Hotel & Conference Centre.** Because Truro is more of a place to pause for a night rather than one to thoroughly peruse, the Holiday Inn is a reliable choice. It has the kind of clean, comfy rooms you'd expect from the chain, as well as bonuses like a heated indoor pool, a fitness center, and free in-room Wi-Fi. Parents will appreciate the bunk-bedded suites and the fact that kids under 13 eat free in the hotel restaurant ($$–$$$). **Pros:** downtown location; appeals to families and pet owners. **Cons:** standard, rather charmless rooms; breakfast not included. ⊠ *437 Prince St.* ☎ *902/895–1651 or 866/863–3351* ⊕ *www.hitrurohotel.com* 🛏 *114 rooms* ⚼ *In-room: no safe, Wi-Fi. In-hotel: restaurant, room service, pool, gym, laundry facilities, business center, parking, some pets allowed.*

$ ⊞ **Suncatcher Bed and Breakfast.** Rooms at this modest B&B are cheerful and bright: ditto for the owners, who know the province stem-to-stern and will happily advise you on itineraries and attractions. **Pros:** knowledgeable hosts; two-day stained glass workshops available by reservation. **Cons:** 10 minutes outside of Truro; can be difficult to find. ⊠ *25 Wile Crest Ave.* ☎ *902/893–7169 or 877/203–6032* ⊕ *www. suncatcherbnb.com* ⇆ *2 rooms* ⚷ *In-room: no a/c, no safe, Wi-Fi* ⦿ *Breakfast.*

## SPORTS AND THE OUTDOORS

**Shubenacadie River Adventure Tours** (☎ *902/261–2222 or 888/878–8687* ⊕ *www.shubie.com*) is an outfit that runs white-water tours.

Fodor'sChoice Don't be misled by the whole "bore" thing. Riding the white water
★ churned up as the Fundy Tidal Bore rushes into Nova Scotia's largest river is an adventure you won't soon forget. With **Shubenacadie River Runners** (⊠ *8681 Hwy. 215, Maitland* ☎ *902/261–2770 or 800/856–5061* ⊕ *www.tidalborerafting.com*) you can confront the waves head-on in a self-bailing Zodiac. Tide conditions and time of day let you choose mildly turbulent or ultrawild rides. A 3½-hour excursion costs C$80–$85 (with a barbecue), and a two-hour trip is C$60–$65 (with hot drinks).

**The Tidal Bore Rafting Park** (☎ *902/758–4032 or 800/565–7238* ⊕ *www. tidalboreraftingpark.com*) is a white-water tour company.

## SHOPPING

**Saltscapes** (⊠ *Exit 13A off Hwy. 102, Millbrook* ☎ *902/843–6700* ⊕ *www.saltscapes.com*), Atlantic Canada's lifestyle magazine, opened this eponymous retail outlet on Highway 102 just outside Truro (if you're Halifax bound, you can't miss it). Maple syrup, maritime music CDs, and other regional products share shelf space at this pseudo general store. A 170-seat dining room ($$) that focuses on East Coast comfort food is also on-site.

**Thrown Together Pottery and Art** (⊠ *37 King St.* ☎ *902/895–9309* ⊕ *www. throwntogetherpottery.com*) sells the owner's clay creations as well as works by many other local artisans.

Fodor'sChoice **Sugar Moon Farm Maple Products & Pancake House.** This sugar camp and
★ pancake house in the Cobequid Mountains, about 30 km (19 mi) north
☺ of Truro off Highway 311, is Nova Scotia's only year-round maple destination. From 9 to 5 daily in the summer and on weekends the rest of the year—plus Fridays in September—you can tour the working facility and hike the sugar woods. In spring, when the sap is running, you can also watch demonstrations. Afterward, tuck into whole-grain buttermilk pancakes and waffles, maple syrup, local sausage, fresh biscuits, maple baked beans, and organic coffee ($) at the lodge. Multiple times per year, a guest chef also prepares a gourmet dinner menu that cleverly incorporates maple products (C$69). You can buy your own sweet souvenirs (maple syrup, maple cream, maple candy, maple butter, and more) before departing. ⊠ *221 Alex MacDonald Rd., Earltown* ☎ *902/657–3348 or 866/816–2753* ⊕ *www.sugarmoon.ca* ⊟ *MC, V* ☺ *Closed weekdays Sept.–June.*

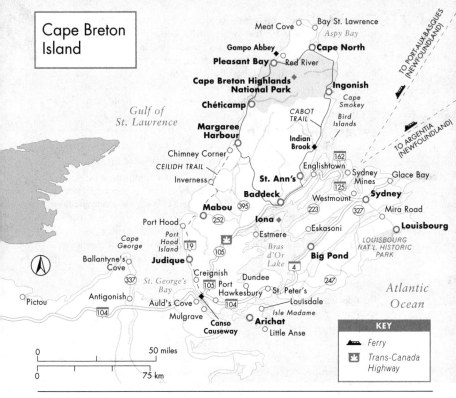

Cape Breton Island

KEY

⚓ Ferry

🍁 Trans-Canada Highway

0 ___ 50 miles
0 ___ 75 km

# CAPE BRETON ISLAND

**Fodor's Choice ★**  There isn't much new in the northeastern corner of Nova Scotia and that's precisely the point; Cape Breton Island's reputation rests on simple pleasures and heartfelt hospitality. Spectacular scenery doesn't hurt either, and the very best of it is found on the Cabot Trail, a scenic 298-km (185-mi) stretch of road, winding along precipitous ocean-side cliffs, that is routinely counted among the world's most magnificent driving routes. This rugged terrain made the Highland Scots, who settled here in the 18th century, feel right at home and their influence remains obvious: North America's first single-malt whiskey distillery is on Cape Breton, as is its only college devoted to Gaelic language, arts, and culture.

Elsewhere on the coast you'll find Francophone villages full of Acadian joie de vivre, plus historic attractions like the mighty Fortress at Louisbourg, which bear witness to the area's long-standing French presence. Bras d'Or Lake—a vast, almost landlocked inlet of the sea occupying the entire center of Cape Breton—is still home to ancient Mi'Kmaq communities, yet it appeals equally to an international contingent of boaters who come to cruise the lake's unspoiled coves and islands.

# The Music of Cape Breton

**1**

Weaned on old-time Scottish tunes, Cape Breton Island musicians are among the world's finest, and in summer you can hear them play at festivals, concerts, and, of course, ceilidhs (pronounced KAY-lees). The word, Gaelic for "visit," derives from the days when folks would gather in a neighbor's kitchen for music, stories, and step dancing. Today ceilidhs have evolved into public events that visitors are welcome to join. Bulletin boards, newspapers, and visitor information centers are a good source for listings. Inverness Country, which encompasses the Ceilidh Trail and is the epicenter of activity, has its own ceilidh lineup online at ⊕ www.invernessco. com. Any night of the week in peak season you'll also be able to attend a square dance somewhere in Inverness County. Propelled by virtuoso fiddling, locals of every age whirl through taxing "square sets," shaking the floor and rattling the rafters in the process.

Come autumn, the nine-day **Celtic Colours International Festival** (☎ 902/562–6700 or 877/285–2321 ⊕ www.celtic-colours.com) showcases the very best Celtic musicians and dancers. International artists and homegrown talent shine in performances staged in more than three dozen island communities. Workshops and seminars covering all aspects of Gaelic language, lore, history, crafts, and culture complement the joyful noise.

**GETTING HERE AND AROUND**

To reach Cape Breton, you can drive from mainland Nova Scotia via the Canso Causeway; take a Marine Atlantic ferry from Newfoundland; or fly into Sydney's J.A. Douglas McCurdy Airport. The island itself has five convenient, camera-ready driving routes—and since these collectively cover about 710 km (440 mi), you should allow five days to explore. For an upfront blast of Caper culture, enter by way of the causeway on Highway 104. Turning left at the rotary, take Highway 19 (the Ceilidh Trail), which winds along the hillside through fields and glens for 107 km (67 mi) before meeting the west end of the fabled Cabot Trail. As a bonus, this stretch of coast facing the Gulf of St. Lawrence is famous for sandy beaches, warm water, and sublime sunsets. Alternately, from the causeway you could follow the Bras d'Or Lakes Scenic Drive, which loops along lesser known roads of central Cape Breton and around the massive lake that lent the route its name; or veer east on the linked Fleur-de-Lis/Marconi Trail, which takes you to the must-see Fortress of Louisbourg and then onward to Sydney (Cape Breton's main city). Following either of these latter options will allow you to access the Cabot Trail from the east. Note that driving in this direction also puts your vehicle on the waterside for most of the trail making it easier to pull over for photo ops.

# JUDIQUE

*30 km (18 mi) north of the Canso Causeway on Hwy. 19; 75 km (47 mi) northeast of Antigonish.*

Like so many Cape Breton communities, Judique is only a little clutch of buildings with Highway 19 running straight through as the main street. Nevertheless, the presence of the **Celtic Music Interpretive Centre** makes Judique an essential destination for anyone interested in the island music scene.

## EXPLORING

**Celtic Music Interpretive Centre.** Packed with exhibits detailing the fine points of fiddling, the center also has an archive with classic recordings and oral history interviews. Visitors eager to pick up a bow can play along to a video tutorial. (The adjacent Buddy McMaster School of Fiddling also offers week-long courses for serious contenders during October's Celtic Colours International Festival.) If you'd rather just get an earful, that's no problem. Monday through Saturday, there are musical demos (C$12, exhibits included) about a dozen times daily. During the same months, the center's dining room hosts ceilidhs Monday through Saturday at lunch (free) and on Sunday afternoons 3–6:30 (C$8). Wednesday evening ceilidhs (C$6) run from July through mid-October. ✉ *5741 Hwy. 19* ☎ *902/787–2708* ⊕ *www.celticmusiccentre.com* ✂ *C$6* ☼ *Late May–mid-Oct., Mon.–Sat. 9–5, Sun. 11–6:30.*

## SPORTS AND THE OUTDOORS

Need some fresh air before getting back in the car and continuing up the Ceilidh Trail? The coastal area around Judique is good for hiking (a portion of the TransCanada Trail threads through) as well as swimming. For an offshore experience, consider taking a tour out of Little Judique Harbour.

# MABOU

*28 km (17 mi) northeast of Judique.*

The village of Mabou is very Scottish (Gaelic-language signs attest to it), and the residents' respect for tradition is apparent in everything from the down-home meals they serve to the music they so exuberantly play; arguably the best place to sample both of the above is at the Red Shoe. The area around Mabou is riddled with hiking trails.

## WHERE TO EAT AND STAY

*For expanded hotel reviews, visit Fodors.com.*

$$
CANADIAN

✕ **Mull Café & Deli.** It's doubtful you'll drive by this informal restaurant on Mabou's main thoroughfare without seeing a parking lot full of cars. Owned by the proprietors of the Duncreigan Country Inn, it's a popular hangout for Cape Bretoners but also draws "come from away" diners thanks to its hearty salads, creamy chowders, deep-fried seafood plates, and homemade desserts—so at peak times, having a reservation helps. There is local artwork on display, making this a pleasant place to linger, though if you're in a rush there's a take-out deli counter too. ✉ *11630 Hwy. 19* ☎ *902/945–2244* ⊕ *www.mullcafe.com.*

**1**

**$$** ✕ **Red Shoe.** More than a mere pub, this Cape Breton institution has
**Fodor's Choice** become an attraction in its own right. Once a general store stocking dry
★ goods and groceries, the "Shoe" is a magnet for the finest fiddlers and
CANADIAN step dancers. You might even see one of the Rankins (Canada's most cel-
ebrated singing siblings) take the stage since the venue is owned by four
Rankin sisters, all of whom grew up in the village. There's music here
every night: Monday to Wednesday 5–7 pm, Thursday through Satur-
day 10 pm–1 am, and a Sunday ceilidh from 4–7 pm. ⊠ *11573 Hwy.
19* ☎ *902/945–2996* ⊕ *www.redshoepub.com* ☉ *Closed mid-Oct.–May.*

**$$** ⊞ **Duncreigan Country Inn.** Though erected in the 1990s, this inn on the
shore of Mabou Harbour calls to mind the early 1900s in design and
furnishing: indeed, architectural details from an earlier incarnation were
integrated into the main building. **Pros:** full buffet breakfast included;
open year round. **Cons:** no restaurant on-site; trees block some harbor
views. ⊠ *11409 Hwy. 19* ☎ *902/945–2207, 800/840–2207 for reservations* ⊕ *www.duncreigan.ca* ↩ *7 rooms, 1 suite* ♿ *In-room: no safe,
Wi-Fi.*

**$$–$$$** ⊞ **Glenora Inn & Distillery.** North America's first single-malt whiskey dis-
tillery adjoins this whitewashed inn north of Mabou, so don't miss the
opportunity to sample a wee dram of Glenora's own Glen Breton Rare.
**Pros:** unique atmosphere; sylvan property bisected by a brook. **Cons:**
inn rooms could use a refresh; road to chalets is tricky to negotiate
at night. ⊠ *13727 Hwy. 19 Glenville* ☎ *902/258–2262 or 800/839–
0491* ⊕ *www.glenoradistillery.com* ↩ *9 rooms, 6 chalets* ♿ *In-room:
a/c (some), no safe, kitchen (some), Wi-Fi. In-hotel: restaurant, bar*
☉ *Closed Nov.–mid-May.*

## NIGHTLIFE

If the Red Shoe leaves you longing for more music, you can frequently
catch concert-style shows at Mabou's performing arts center, **Strathspey
Place** (⊠ *11156 Hwy. 19* ☎ *902/945–5300* ⊕ *www.strathspeyplace.
com*).

Fun family square dances are held Saturday nights year-round from 10
pm to 1 am, at the **West Mabou Sports Club** (⊠ *2399 West Mabou Rd.,
West Mabou* ☎ *902/945–2816* 🎫 *C$8*).

## SPORTS AND THE OUTDOORS

★ The **Mabou Highlands** mountain range has 14 nature trails, measuring
over 35 km (21 mi) in total, which are maintained by the Cape Mabou
Trail Club. Some of the latter follow old cart tracks that connected
pioneer settlements. Gaelic-speaking immigrants from Scotland settled
this region of plunging cliffs, isolated beaches, rising mountains, glens,
meadows, and hardwood forests. Today it is so hauntingly quiet that
you might halfway expect to meet the sidhe, the Scottish fairies, caper-
ing on the hillsides. Trail maps can be purchased from local retailers or
online at ⊕ *www.trails.com/activity.aspx?area=12055.*

**West Mabou Beach Provincial Park.** There is a 12-km (7.5-mi) network of
hiking trails in this park. ⊠ *Little Mabou Rd., off Rte. 19.*

EN ROUTE **Golfers now have another reason to swing over to Cape Breton. Cabot Links (☎ 902/258-4653 or 855/652-2268 🌐 www.cabotlinks.com)—which is already being billed as "Canada's next great golf course"—debuted 10 of its 18 holes in the summer of 2011. Once completed, the Rod Whitman-designed course will extend from the town of Inverness (about halfway between Mabou and Margaree Harbour) straight to the sea providing both challenging play and panoramic water views. The walking-only course is slated to officially open in the spring of 2012.**

## MARGAREE HARBOUR

*53 km (33 mi) north of Mabou.*

Aside from pleasant pastimes like hillside hiking and saltwater swimming (Whale Cove and Chimney Corner are the local's top picks for the latter), the Margaree area promises world-class fly-fishing. Margaree Harbour not only marks the point where the Ceilidh Trail joins the Cabot Trail, it also sits at the mouth of the Margaree River: a designated Canadian Heritage River known for legendary salmon runs.

### EXPLORING

Exhibits at the unassuming **Margaree Salmon Museum** are proudly old-school, which seems fitting since they're housed in a former one-room schoolhouse. On display are all manner of fishing tackle, photographs, hand-tied flies, and other memorabilia related to salmon angling on the Margaree. Visitors can watch videos, study models of the river, and peek into the fish tank. ✉ *60 East Big Intervale Rd., Northeast Margaree* ☎ *902/248-2848* 🎟 *C$2* ⏲ *Mid-June–mid-Oct., daily 9–5.*

### WHERE TO EAT AND STAY

*For expanded hotel reviews, visit Fodors.com.*

**$$–$$$** 🏨 **Normaway Inn and Cabins.** Set on 500 acres in the Margaree Valley this inn has vintage rooms and cabins, many with woodstoves and private screened porches. **Pros:** bucolic site; centrally located on island touring loops. **Cons:** isn't luxurious (and doesn't aspire to be); lodgings vary in size and quality. ✉ *691 Egypt Rd., Margaree Valley* ☎ *902/248-2987 or 800/565-9463* 🌐 *www.thenormawayinn.com* 🛏 *11 rooms, 3 suites, 14 cabins* t *In-room: a/c (some), no safe, no TV. In-hotel: restaurant, tennis court, business center, some pets allowed* ⏲ *Closed Nov.–May; cabins may be booked off-season by arrangement* 🍽 *Some meals.*

### SPORTS AND THE OUTDOORS

The Margaree has two fishing seasons: the early summer run (opens annually on June 1) and the fall run (which goes from mid-September through October, coinciding with the peak foliage period). Gear and licenses are readily available, as are guides who'll typically charge C$125–$150 per day to help you land a trophy-sized salmon. For details, contact the **Margaree Salmon Association** (☎ *902/248-2578* 🌐 *www.margareesalmon.org*).

# CHÉTICAMP

*25 km (16 mi) north of Margaree Harbour.*

In Chéticamp, an Acadian enclave for more than 200 years, Franco-phone culture and traditions are still very much alive. That's why the Gaelic-inflected lilt in locals' voices is replaced by a distinct French accent. (You might be greeted in French but can respond in English—most residents are bilingual.) Size is another distinguishing factor because, with population of about 4,000, Chéticamp feels like a major metropolis compared to other western shore communities. The land-scape is different, too. Poised between mountains and sea, Chéticamp stands exposed on a wide lip of flat land below a range of bald green hills, behind which lies the high plateau of the Cape Breton Highlands. Commercial fishing is the town's raison d'être but rug hooking is its main claim to fame: a fact reflected in local attractions and shops. So pause to peruse them before racing into the adjacent national park.

## EXPLORING

**Les Trois Pignons Cultural Center,** which contains the Elizabeth LeFort Gallery, displays samples of the rugs, tapestries, and related artifacts that helped make Chéticamp the World Rug Hooking Capital. Born in 1914, LeFort created more than 300 tapestries, some of which have hung in the Vatican, the White House, and Buckingham Palace. (One standout depicting U.S. presidents is made from seven miles of yarn!) Les Trois Pignons is also an Acadian cultural and genealogical information center. ⊠ *15584 Cabot Trail Rd.* ☎ *902/224–2642* ⊕ *www.lestroispignons. com* ⊠ *C$5* ⊙ *July and Aug., daily 9–7; mid-May–June, Sept.–mid Oct., daily 9–5.*

## WHERE TO EAT AND STAY

*For expanded hotel reviews, visit Fodors.com.*

$$ ✕ **Le Gabriel Restaurant and Lounge.** You can't miss Le Gabriel's large
CANADIAN lighthouse entranceway. The casual 125-seat dining room offers simple but substantial fare that includes North American standards and traditional Acadian favorites—think *poutine* (french fries covered with cheese curds and gravy) or *fricot* (a hearty stew with potatoes, pork bits, chives, and beef or chicken). Fresh fish dishes are popular, too, with snow crab and lobster available in season. The lounge has billiard tables, and there's live music most Saturday nights. ⊠ *15424 Cabot Trail Rd.* ☎ *902/224–3685* ⊕ *www.legabriel.com.*

$$–$$$ ⌂ **Cabot Trail Sea & Golf Chalets.** Beside Le Portage Golf Club, these ocean-side chalets work well for golfers and anyone wanting more than a mere hotel room. **Pros:** discounted weekly rates; great golfing. **Cons:** books quickly; no meals available. ⊠ *71 Fraser Doucet La.* ☎ *902/224–1777 or 877/224–1777* ⊕ *www.seagolfchalets.com* ⇥ *12 chalets, 1 suite* ⌂ *In-room: no a/c, no safe, kitchen, Wi-Fi. In-hotel: golf course* ⊙ *Closed mid-Oct.–mid-May.*

$ ⌂ **Chéticamp Outfitters' Inn Bed & Breakfast.** Clean, cozy rooms overlook the ocean, mountains, and valley at this inn, and there's a top-floor patio along the length of the cedar house, taking full advantage of the view. **Pros:** walking distance to beach; breakfast includes memorable blueberry muffins. **Cons:** three rooms have shared bathrooms; most lack televisions. ⊠ *13938 Cabot Trail Rd.* P*902/224–2776* ⊕ *www. cheticampns.com/cheticampoutfitters* ⇆ *6 rooms, 1 chalet* ♿ *In-room: no a/c, no safe, no TV (some)* ⊗ *Closed Dec.–Apr. 15* ⧄ *Breakfast.*

### SPORTS AND THE OUTDOORS

On whale-watch cruises departing from Chéticamp's government wharf, you can see minkes, humpbacks, and finbacks in their natural environment.

**Captain Zodiac Whale Cruise** (☎ *902/224–1088 or 877/232–2522* ⊕ *www. novascotiawhales.com*) goes out five times a day and guarantees sightings on its two-hour junket (C$39).

**Whale Cruisers Ltd.** (☎ *902/224–3376 or 800/813–3376*) runs tours aboard a 13-meter (42-ft) vessel twice or thrice daily, May 15 through October 15 (C$30). These take about three hours.

The par-72 **Le Portage Golf Club** (⊠ *15580 Cabot Trail Rd.* ☎ *902/224– 3338 or 888/618–5558* ⊕ *www.leportagegolfclub.com*), one of Cape Breton's "Fabulous Foursome," has 18 holes overlooking the Gulf of St. Lawrence. Greens fees are C$51-$59.

**Little Pond Stables** (☎ *902/224–3858 or 888/250–6799* ⊕ *www. horsebackcapebreton.com*) organizes daily horseback rides on wooded trails, beaches, and foothill paths. Tours (C$25–$90) last 30 minutes to three hours.

### SHOPPING

Supplied by nearly 75 happy hookers, **Chéticamp Hooked Rugs Coopérative Artisanale** (⊠ *15067 Cabot Trail Rd.* ☎ *902/224–2170* ⊕ *www. cheticamphookedrugs.com*) has been the go-to spot for handmade rugs since 1963. They also sell small items like hooked coasters in case you're traveling light.

## CAPE BRETON HIGHLANDS NATIONAL PARK

*5 km (3 mi) north of Chéticamp; 108 km (67 mi) north of Ingonish.*

Fodor'sChoice
★

A 950-square-km (366-square-mi) wilderness of wooded valleys, barren plateaus, and steep cliffs, this park stretches across northern Cape Breton from the gulf shore to the Atlantic. The highway that runs through it (the renowned Cabot Trail) is magnificent, rising to the tops of the coastal mountains and descending through scenic switchbacks to the sea. In fact, the road has been compared to a 106-km (66-mi) roller-coaster ride, stretching from Chéticamp to Ingonish, so good brakes are imperative. Pull-offs provide photo opportunities, and exhibits explain the land and its history.

High-altitude bogs here are home to wild orchids and other unique flora. For animal lovers there's much to see as well, including moose, eagles, deer, bears, foxes, bobcats, and coyotes. Your chances of spotting wildlife naturally improve if you venture off the main road and hike one of the 25 trails at dusk or dawn. Be advised, though, that it's illegal to feed or approach any animal in the park and all should be observed from a safe distance.

⚠ In the fall of 2009, a solo hiker was tragically killed by coyotes on the park's Skyline Trail. Exercise caution and never hike isolated trails alone. Even motorists must remain alert—particularly when driving in moose zones (these are marked by highway signs). Since moose sometimes claim the road as their own, things won't end well if you hit an animal weighing 1,200 pounds. A permit or pass is required for entering sections of the Cabot Trail within the national park and for use of the facilities such as exhibits, hiking trails, and picnic areas; there are additional fees for camping, fishing, and golf. Full details are available at the gateway information centers. ⊠ *Entrances on Cabot Trail near Chéticamp and Ingonish* ☎ *902/224–2306, 902/224–3814 bookstore* ⊕ *www.parkscanada.ca* ⊠ *C$7.80* ⊙ *Year-round, daily dawn–dusk.*

## PLEASANT BAY

*41 km (26 mi) north of Chéticamp.*

Pleasant Bay is, well, pleasant, and because it's located about halfway around the Cabot Trail, it's a convenient place to stop. Local fishermen catch lobster in spring and snow crab in summer. The water yields much bigger creatures, too, and it could be said that whales here outnumber people. Of course, that isn't hard considering the population is just about 350.

☾ Visitors who like to stay on dry land while observing sea life should stop by the **Whale Interpretive Centre.** Using zoom scopes on the whale-spotting deck, you may catch a close-up glimpse of the many different species that often frolic just offshore. Inside the modern structure, exhibits and models explain the unique world of whales. ⊠ *104 Harbour Rd., Pleasant Bay* ☎ *902/224–1411* ⊠ *C$4* ⊙ *June–mid-Oct., daily 9–5.*

**OFF THE BEATEN PATH**

**Gampo Abbey.** Strangely enough, Nova Scotia is a center of Shambhala Buddhism (Shambala International is actually headquartered in Halifax) and this abbey is its spiritual heart. Finding the zenlike site high above the sea, however, requires more than soul searching. From Pleasant Bay, a spur road creeps along the cliffs to Red River; beyond that a gravel road twists and turns for some 3 km (2 mi) before reaching the broad, flat bench of land upon which the monastery sits. In July and August, tours are usually conducted on weekdays between 1:30 and 3:30. You can also wander through some of the abbey's 230 acres to visit a small shrine and grotto. If the abbey is closed for a retreat, continue down the road for about ½ km (¼ mi) to see the Stupa of Enlightenment, a large and elaborate shrine dedicated to world peace. ⊠ *Red River Rd., Pleasant Bay* ☎ *902/224–2752* ⊕ *www.gampoabbey.org.*

### SPORTS AND THE OUTDOORS

**WHALE-WATCHING**  **Captain Mark's Whale & Seal Cruise** (☎ *902/224–1316 or 888/754–5112* ⊕ *www.whaleandsealcruise.com*) guarantees sightings on both zodiac (C$39) and cabin cruiser (C$30) tours, available May through mid-September.

**Fiddlin' Whale Tours** (☎ *902/383–2340 or 866/688–2424* ⊕ *www. fiddlinwhaletours.com*) adds music to the mix, so you can enjoy live traditional Cape Breton fiddling on their C$40 cruises; sightings guaranteed. This may seem like a bizarre pairing but apparently whales respond to the pitch and sometimes contribute their own songs. An onboard hydrophone helps you hear them.

**Wesley's Whale Watching** (☎ 902/224–1919 or 866/999–4253 ⊕ www. novascotiawhales.com) leads two-hour trips (C$25) in Cape Island boats May 15 through October 15 to see whales, dolphins, seals, and scenery.

# CAPE NORTH

*30 km (19 mi) east of Pleasant Bay.*

At the northernmost point on the Cabot Trail, just outside the boundaries of the national park, this is where explorer Giovanni Caboto (aka John Cabot) allegedly made land in 1497. Not only does Cape North still feel like a new discovery, it also provides access to locales that are even more remote, like Bay St. Lawrence and Meat Cove.

### EXPLORING

**Cabot's Landing Provincial Park** (⊠ 1904 Bay St. Lawrence Rd., 2 km (1 mi) north of Four Mile Beach Inn ☎ No phone ⊕ parks.gov.ns.ca) has a cairn commemorating Cabot's arrival, plus a long sandy beach and jaw-dropping picnic spots overlooking Aspy Bay. Admission is free daily, mid-May through mid-October.

### WHERE TO STAY

*For expanded hotel reviews, visit Fodors.com.*

$-$$ ⛺ **Four Mile Beach Inn.** Views of Aspy Bay and the ridge of the high-land mountains are fantastic from this large 19th-century house near Cabot's Landing. **Pros:** breakfast buffet included; knowledgeable hosts. **Cons:** smallish rooms; two have shared bathrooms. ⊠ 1528 Bay St Lawrence Rd., Cape North ☎ 902/383–2282 or 888/602–3737 ⊕ www. fourmilebeachinn.com ⌐ 8 rooms, 5 suites ⌂ In-room: a/c (some), no safe, kitchen (some), no TV, Wi-Fi. In-hotel: water sports, some pets allowed ⊙ Closed Nov.–mid-June (season varies) ⑩ Breakfast.

### SPORTS AND THE OUTDOORS

**Captain Cox's Whale Watch** (☎ 902/383–2981 or 888/346–5556 ⊕ www. whalewatching-novascotia.com) gives several tours (C$45) daily in season from the Bay St. Lawrence Wharf. If you don't see a whale, you get another trip for free.

Based in Dingwall, which neighbors Cape North, **Eagle North** (☎ 902/ 383–2552 or 888/616–1689 ⊕ www.kayakingcapebreton.ca) offers kayak tours (from C$45) as well as boat and bike rentals (from C$15 and C$10 per hour respectively), May through October.

**Oshan Whale Watch** (☎ 902/383–2883 or 877/383–2883 ⊕ www.oshan. ca) charges C$30 and guarantees sightings or you get another trip.

# INGONISH

*35 km (22 mi) southeast of Cape North.*

Ingonish—western gateway to the Cabot Trail—is one of the leading vacation destinations on Cape Breton, largely because it's home to the much-touted Keltic Lodge Resort and adjacent Highland Links golf course. The spot is actually comprised of five villages—Ingonish proper, Ingonish Centre, Ingonish Beach, Ingonish Harbour, and Ingonish Ferry. Poised on two bays and divided by a long narrow peninsula, all together they cover about 16 km (10 mi).

## WHERE TO EAT AND STAY

*For expanded hotel reviews, visit Fodors.com.*

$$$–$$$$
★
☁
**Keltic Lodge Resort and Spa.** Spread across the sea cliffs, the Keltic Lodge has glorious views of Cape Smokey and the surrounding highlands. **Pros:** breakfast is included; lots to do. **Cons:** rooms vary in size; rooms at Inn at Keltic could use a makeover. ⊠ *383 Keltic Inn Rd., Ingonish Beach* ☎ *902/285–2880 or 800/565–0444* ⊕ *www.signatureresorts.com* ➦ *72 rooms, 2 suites, 10 cottages* ⌂ *In-room: a/c (some), Wi-Fi. In-hotel: 2 restaurants, bar, golf course, tennis courts, pool, spa, beachfront, children's programs, some pets allowed* ⊘ *Closed late Oct.–mid-May* ⦿ *Some meals.*

$$–$$$
★
**Lantern Hill & Hollow.** Hearing the surf is no problem at this intimate property because the six cottages are just steps from a private 3-km (2-mi) beach that is ideal for quick dips and nightly bonfires; firewood and beach toys are supplied. **Pros:** gorgeous property; convenient location. **Cons:** no breakfast; self-catering has only light housekeeping. ⊠ *36845 Cabot Trail Rd., Ingonish Beach* ☎ *902/285–2010 or 888/663–0225* ⊕ *www.lanternhillandhollow.com* ➦ *3 suites, 6 cottages* ⌂ *In-room: no a/c, no safe, kitchen (some), Wi-Fi. In-hotel: beach, business center* ⊘ *Closed Mid-Oct.–late May.*

## SPORTS AND THE OUTDOORS

**Cape Smokey Provincial Park** (⊠ *40301 Cabot Trail Rd., Ingonish Ferry* ☎ *No phone* ⊕ *parks.gov.ns.ca* ⊡ *Free* ⊘ *Daily, mid-May–early Oct.*), which caps the eponymous 300-meter (984-foot) peak, has a challenging coastal trail that is breathtaking in more ways than one. Hiking it takes about four hours.

Perennially ranked as one of Canada's top courses, **Highlands Links** (⊠ *Cape Breton Highlands National Park* ☎ *902/285–2600 or 800/441–1118* ⊕ *www.highlandslinksgolf.com*) was designed by Stanley Thompson, who dubbed it "the mountains and ocean" course. It's open daily, dawn to dusk, from May through October. Playing 18 holes will cost you C$49–$103 depending on the date and tee time.

---

# ST. ANN'S BAY AND AROUND

*Extends for 65 km (40 mi) from Ingonish south to St. Ann's.*

Continuing down the Cabot Trail down from Ingonish, you'll skirt St. Ann's Bay where communities are of the blink-and-you'll-miss-it variety.

Indeed, if you didn't read their names on a map, you'd barely know they were communities at all. So, with the exception of the Gaelic College of Arts and Crafts (North America's only Gaelic college), there are few actual attractions around here. What you will find—during tourist season, at least—are fun outdoor opportunities and some of Atlantic Canada's most distinctive shops.

Being home to direct descendants of the Gaelic pioneers, St. Ann's Bay is a logical site for the **Gaelic College of Celtic Arts and Crafts.** The facility was established in 1938 with a mission to promote and preserve the settlers' heritage. And mission accomplished because today the campus offers a crash course in Gaelic culture. For instance, after learning about Scottish history in the Great Hall of Clans (particularly the Highland Clearances which sparked a mass exodus of Scots to the New World during the 18th century), you can view a short Gaelic-language film, then discover traditional disciplines like weaving and dancing at interactive stations. Not surprisingly, music at the college is especially noteworthy. Week-long summer school courses—as well as occasional weekend workshops—focus on topics such as bagpiping and fiddling. The college also hosts a Wednesday evening ceilidh in summer and in fall is a key site for Celtic Colours. ⊠ *51779 Cabot Trail Rd., St. Ann's* ☎ *902/295-3411* ⊕ *www.gaeliccollege.edu* ⊠ *C$7* ⊘ *June and Sept., weekdays 9–5; July–Aug., daily 9–5.*

**OFF THE BEATEN PATH**

When you reach the Barachois River Bridge, you can stay on the Cabot Trail as it turns inland or choose a coastal route (the 312) that goes onward to Jersey Cove. From there you can take a ferry across St. Ann's Bay to Englishtown; then follow Highway 105 into Baddeck. Weather permitting, the ferry operates 24/7 year-round. Although you save minimal driving time (about 15 minutes) the two-minute trip is pretty and the one-way fare a mere C$5 per car.

## WHERE TO EAT AND STAY

*For expanded hotel reviews, visit Fodors.com.*

$$–$$$ ★ ⛺ **Chanterelle Country Inn & Cottages.** You don't have to be a fan of the namesake mushroom to fall for the Chanterelle. **Pros:** natural soaps that are made especially for the inn; activity-based packages are offered, including golfing, kayaking, and things like mushroom-picking. **Cons:** three-day minimum stay in cottages; TVs and phones for inn rooms must be requested. ⊠ *48678 Cabot Trail Rd., North River Bridge* ☎ *902/929–2263 or 866/277–0577* ⊕ *www.chanterelleinn.com* ⤴ *8 rooms, 1 suite, 3 cottages* ⚐ *In-room: no a/c, no safe, kitchen (some), no TV (some), Wi-Fi (some). In-hotel: restaurant, bar, water sports* ⊘ *Inn open May–Oct., cottages year-round* ⏽⭕⏽ *Breakfast.*

$$–$$$ ★ ⛺ **English Country Garden Bed & Breakfast.** This B&B is well positioned for those wishing to explore the bay area, and the 37-acre lakefront property is itself ideal for strolling, though at the end of the day there's a lot to draw you indoors. **Pros:** reduced rates for extended stays; romance packages. **Cons:** spotty satellite TV coverage; very rural. ⊠ *45478 Cabot Trail Rd., Indian Brook* ☎ *866/929–2721* ⊕ *www.capebretongarden.*

*com* ⌂ *5 suites, 1 cottage* ⛄ *In-room: no a/c, no safe, Wi-Fi, business center* ⦿ *Breakfast.*

## SPORTS AND THE OUTDOORS

**North River Kayak Tours.** Half- (C$64) and full-day (C$104) guided excursions are available from mid-May to mid-October. Overnight packages and basic rentals are available as well. ⊠ *644 Murray Rd., North River Bridge* ☎ *902/929–2628 or 888/865–2925* ⊕ *www.northriverkayak.com.*

## SHOPPING

The **Gaelic College of Celtic Arts and Crafts Gift Shop** (⊠ *51779 Cabot Trail Rd., St. Ann's* ☎ *902/295–3411* ⊕ *www.gaeliccollege.edu*) is filled with Celtic and clan-related items and has a custom kilt maker on-site.

Gorgeous glassware—be it stained, painted, blown, or fused—is sold at **Glass Artisans Studio & Gallery** (⊠ *45054 Cabot Trail Rd., North Shore* ☎ *902/929–2585 or 888/262–6435* ⊕ *www.glassartisans.ca*).

Sculptors forge ahead at **IronArt** (⊠ *48084 Cabot Trail Rd., Tarbot* ☎ *902/929–2821* ⊕ *www.ironart.ca*).

Purses, pet collars, and even old-fashioned leather fire buckets are the specialty at **Leatherworks** (⊠ *45808 Cabot Trail Rd., Indian Brook* ☎ *902/929–2414* ⊕ *www.leather-works.ca*).

**Piper Pewter** (⊠ *46112 Cabot Trail Rd., Indian Brook* ☎ *902/929–2227* ⊕ *www.piperpewter.com*) produces lead-free pewter giftware, much of it inspired by Celtic designs.

Ready for some retail therapy? Theatrical, handmade hats in almost every imaginable style and fabric are sold at **Sew Inclined** (⊠ *41819 Cabot Trail Rd., Wreck Cove* ☎ *902/929–2259* ⊕ *www.sewinclined.ca*).

**Singing Pebbles Pottery** (⊠ *42164 Cabot Trail Rd., Wreck Cove* ☎ *902/ 929–2399* ⊕ *www.singingpebbles.ca* ⊗ *Mon. and Fri. or by appointment*) sells teapots, mugs, and other pieces of fine, functional pottery that are made on-site.

**Wildfire Pottery** (⊠ *44429 Cabot Trail Rd., North Shore* ☎ *902/929– 2315* ⊕ *www.wildfirepottery.ca*) specializes in cool clay creations, many of them in the shape of area animals. Hours are sporadic.

Wooden bowls, boxes, toys and trinkets are made on-site at the **Woodsmiths Studio** (⊠ *44556 Cabot Trail Rd., Englishtown* ☎ *902/929–2111* ⊕ *www.woodsmithsstudio.com*).

# BADDECK

*20 km (12 mi) southwest of St. Ann's.*

Baddeck has enough down-to-earth amenities (grocery store etc.) to make it a service center, and enough charm to make it a tourist destination. The population is only about 1,000 residents but its larger than usual concentration of lodgings, restaurants, and shops attracts motorists who are ending (or starting) a Cabot Trail trek. Boaters also come to explore Bras d'Or Lake. The most competitive among them raise anchor during Regatta Week, Baddeck's main event, which begins the first Sunday in August at the Bras d'Or Yacht Club (☎ *902/295–2107* ⊕ *www.brasdoryachtclub.ca).*

☼ The **Alexander Graham Bell National Historic Site of Canada** pays hom-
★ age to Bell's many inventions and humanitarian work. Inside the main
building, films, photos, artifacts, and models provide a window into
his ideas for creating telephones, man-carrying kites, airplanes, and a
record-setting hydrofoil boat (a full scale replica of which dominates
one exhibit hall). A kid's corner hosts demos and hands-on activities
for aspiring young inventors. Bell spent large blocks of time, from 1886
until his death in 1922, at his Baddeck estate—Beinn Bhreagh, Gaelic
for "beautiful mountain." In fact, Bell so loved the region he once wrote
"I have travelled the globe. I have seen the Canadian and American
Rockies, the Andes and the Alps and the highlands of Scotland, but for
simple beauty, Cape Breton outrivals them all." His home (which is still
owned by the family) can be seen from the roof of the National Historic
Site that bears his name. ✉ *559 Chebucto St.* ☎ *902/295–2069* ⊕ *www.
parkscanada.ca* 🎟 *C$7.80* ☽ *May and late Oct., daily 9–5; June, daily
9–6; July–mid-Oct., daily 8:30–6; Nov.–Apr., by appointment.*

**Bras d'Or Lakes Interpretive Centre.** Occupying a former post office, this
small interpretive center takes an ecological look at the body of water—
some 965 km (600 mi) around—that cuts Cape Breton in two. ✉ *532
Chebucto St.* ☎ *902/295–1675* ⊕ *www.brasdorpreserveation.ca* 🎟 *By
donation* ☽ *Daily 9–7, June–mid-Oct.*

**Usige Bàn Falls Provincial Park** ( ✉ *715 North Branch Rd., Baddeck Forks*
☎ *No phone* ⊕ *parks.gov.ns.ca*), 14.5 km (9 mi) north of Baddeck,
has a forested trail that culminates in a much-photographed waterfall.
Admission is free daily, mid-May through mid-October.

The **Wagmatcook Culture & Heritage Centre** spotlights the ancient history and rich traditions of the native Mi'Kmaq people, with aboriginal guides providing interpretations and cultural entertainment. The
center's restaurant serves traditional foods (such as moose and eel) as
well as more contemporary fare, and a crafts shop sells items made by
members of this First Nation community. ✉ *10765 Hwy. 105, 16 km
(10 mi) west of Baddeck* ☎ *902/295–1542 or 866/295–2999* ⊕ *www.
wagmatcook.com* 🎟 *Free (fees for some services)* ☽ *Year-round daily,
11–4 (hours are flexible, so check first).*

## WHERE TO EAT AND STAY

*For expanded hotel reviews, visit Fodors.com.*

**$$$**
SEAFOOD

✗ **Baddeck Lobster Suppers.** For superfresh seafood, try this casual res-
taurant in a former lake-side legion hall. It's open daily from mid-June
to mid-October, from 4 to 9, and can seat 100 diners but during busy
times (or when a tour bus unloads), you may have to wait for a table.
Options include lobster, plank salmon, and, for landlubbers, grilled
steak—each served with unlimited mussels, chowder, dessert, a bev-
erage, and homemade buns and biscuits. Unlike some similar spots,
this one is fully licensed so you can wash all that down with a cold
brew. ✉ *17 Ross St.* ☎ *902/295–3307* ⊕ *www.baddecklobstersuppers.
ca* ☽ *Closed mid-Oct.–mid-June.*

$ 🏠 **Baddeck Heritage House.** Since town sites are within walking distance, this 1860s B&B serves as a good base for touring. **Pros:** attentive, eco-conscious owners. **Cons:** small-ish rooms; the friendly family cat may make allergies flare. ✉ *121 Twining St.* ☎ *902/295–3219 or 877/223–1112* ⊕ *www.baddeckheritagehouse.ca* 🛏 *4 rooms* ⚘ *In-room: no a/c, no safe, Wi-Fi* ⊙ *Closed late Oct.–early May* ⊙| *Breakfast.*

$$$–$$$$ 🏠 **Castle Moffett.** Though not a historic property (it was erected in 1992), ★ this "castle" is enticingly regal. **Pros:** the property is stunning in fall; suites are spacious. **Cons:** pricey; dining room has only one 7 pm sitting. ✉ *11980 Hwy. 105, Bucklaw* ☎ *902/756–9070 or 888/756–9070* ⊕ *www.castlemoffett.com* 🛏 *6 rooms, 3 suites* ⚘ *In-room: no safe, Wi-Fi. In-hotel: restaurant, room service, bar, gym, spa, business center* ⊙ *Closed Nov.–Apr.*

$$ 🏠 **Inverary Resort.** This lakeside lodging has idyllic views, lots of sporting opportunities, and a range of rooms, including cottages, suites, and some modern hotel units on the 11-acre property or rooms in the 1850 lodge. **Pros:** very family friendly; walking distance to town. **Cons:** breakfast not included; though open year-round, there are reduced services November through May. ✉ *368 Shore Rd.* ☎ *902/295–3500 or 800/565–5660* ⊕ 🛏 *129 rooms, 9 cottages* ⚘ *In-room: no safe, kitchen (some), Wi-Fi. In-hotel: 2 restaurants, bar, tennis courts, pool, gym, spa, water sports, children's programs, business center, some pets allowed.*

## NIGHTLIFE AND THE ARTS

**The Baddeck Gathering** (✉ *480 Chebucto St.* ☎ *902/295–0971* ⊕ *www.baddeckgathering.com*) hosts ceilidhs at St. Michael's Parish Hall every evening in July and August, starting at 7:30. The cost is C$10.

## SPORTS AND THE OUTDOORS

### GOLF

In addition to panoramic views from almost all of its 18 holes, the **Bell Bay Golf Club** (✉ *761 Hwy. 205* ☎ *902/295–1333 or 800/565–3077* ⊕ *www.bellbay.ca*) has a highly regarded golf school and one of the largest practice facilities in Eastern Canada. Greens fee are C$65–$79.

### BOAT TOURS

**Amoeba Sailing Tours** (☎ *902/295–2481* ⊕ *www.amoebasailingtours.com*) takes you out to view bald eagles and the Bell Estate aboard a sleek schooner (C$25).

The Bird Islands, 2 km (1 mi) off the entrance to the Bras d'Or Lake, are the breeding grounds for Atlantic puffins, as well as other seabirds and gray seals. To see them, sign on with **Donelda's Puffin Boat Tours** (✉ *1099 Hwy. 312, just before the Englishtown Ferry, Englishtown* ☎ *902/929–2563 or 877/278–3346* ⊕ *www.puffinboattours.com*), which offers narrated nature cruises (C$34.50) daily from mid-May to October. Boats depart about 20 minutes east of Baddeck.

**Paddle Dog** (☎ *902/929–2628 or 888/865–2925* ⊕ *www.paddledog.ca*) operates easy 90-minute kayak tours in July and August (C$44).

**OFF THE BEATEN PATH**

Iona, 77 km (48 mi) south of Baddeck, is admittedly off the beaten path. To reach Iona from Baddeck, follow Highway 105 to Exit 6, which leads to Little Narrows, then board a cable ferry for the two-minute ride to the Iona Peninsula (C$5; 24 hours a day, year-round). If you're big on Gaelic culture, a visit to the living history museum there will be ample reward.

**Fodor's** Choice    The 43-acre **Highland Village Museum** is set high on a mountainside with
★    a spectacular view of Bras d'Or Lake and narrow Barra Strait. Its 11 historical buildings (among them a forge, a school, a church, and a barn filled with heritage breeds of livestock) were assembled from all over the province to depict the Highland Scots' way of life, from their origins in the Hebrides to the present day. Costumed animators who tackle daily chores lend the village a further touch of authenticity and are always on the ready to give an impromptu Gaelic lesson. There's a gift shop on site as well as a Genealogy and Family History Center (open by appointment) that may be of interest to anyone with Cape Breton blood in their veins. ⊠ *4119 Hwy. 223* ☎ *902/725–2272 or 866/442–3542* ⊕ *www.highlandvillage.museum.gov.ns.ca* ⊠ *C$9* ⊘ *June–mid-Oct., daily 9:30–5:30.*

# SYDNEY

*62 km (39 mi) northeast of Iona, 77 km (48 mi) east of Baddeck.*

If you come directly to Cape Breton via plane, ferry, or cruise ship, Sydney is where you'll land. If you're seeking anything resembling an urban experience, it's also where you'll want to stay: after all, this is the island's sole city. Admittedly, it is not the booming center it was a century ago when the continent's largest steel plant was located here (that era is evoked in Fall on Your Knees, an Oprah Book Club pick penned by Cape Bretoner Anne-Marie MacDonald). However, Sydney has a revitalized waterfront and smattering of Loyalist-era building that appeal to visitors. Moreover, it offers convenient access to popular attractions in the region—like the Miner's Museum in nearby Glace Bay (named for the *glace*, or ice, that filled its harbor in winter), the Fortress at Louisbourg, and beautiful Bras d'Or Lake.

### GETTING HERE AND AROUND

Sydney is a major arrival/departure point for Cape Breton because it's on the Marconi Trail, one of the province's driving routes, and it has Cape Breton's only real airport. There are year-round air connections via Halifax on Air Canada/Jazz and seasonal ones via Toronto on West-Jet. Scheduled flights to the French-held islands of St-Pierre and Mique-lon also take off from Sydney Airport.

Marine Atlantic operates ferries between Newfoundland and North Sydney year-round. There are also as many as 50 cruise ships making port in Sydney Harbour annually from late April until late October.

### TOURS

**The Old Sydney Society** which operates Cossit House as well as a trio of other restored building-cum-museums (Jost House, St. Patrick's Church, and the Cape Breton Centre for Heritage and Science) orga-nizes 90-minute Ghost Walks through the historic North End on Tues-day and Wednesday evenings in July and August. Tours cost C$10 (refreshments included) and start at 7 pm, reservations required.

## ESSENTIALS

**Old Sydney Society** (✉ *225 George St.* ☎ *902/539–1572* ⊕ *www.oldsydney.com*).

## EXPLORING

★ The **Cape Breton Miners' Museum** details the difficult lives of the local men whose job it was to extract coal from undersea collieries. After perusing the exhibits, you can don a hardhat and descend into the damp, claustrophobic recesses of a shaft beneath the museum with a retired miner who'll recount his own experiences toiling in the bowels of the earth. The 15-acre property also includes a replica village that gives you a sense of workers' home life, plus a theater where the Men of the Deeps (a renowned choir made up of miners) perform in summer. Glace Bay is just 19 km (12 mi) east of Sydney. ✉ *17 Museum St., Quarry Point, Glace Bay* ☎ *902/849–4522* ⊕ *www.minersmuseum.com* 🖻 *Museum C$6, museum and mine tour C$12* ⊘ *June–Aug., daily 10–6, until 7 on Tues.; Sept. and Oct., daily 9–6; Nov.–May, weekdays 9–4.*

**Cossit House.** Built in 1787, this unpretentious wood building was originally home to Reverend Ranna Cossit—Cape Breton's first protestant minister—his wife Thankful, and their 10 children. Now faithfully restored and occupied by costumed interpreters, the North End residence is furnished with period pieces based on Cossit's own inventory. ✉ *75 Charlotte St.* ☎ *902/539–7973* ⊕ *www.cossit.museum.gov.ns.ca* 🖻 *C$2* ⊘ *June–mid-Oct., Mon.–Sat. 10–5, Sun. 1–5.*

The **Marconi National Historic Site of Canada** in nearby Glace Bay commemorates the spot at Table Head where, in 1902, Guglielmo Marconi built four tall wooden towers and beamed the first official wireless messages across the Atlantic Ocean. An interpretive trail leads to the foundations of the original towers and transmitter buildings. The visitor center has large models of the towers as well as artifacts and photographs chronicling the radio pioneer's life and work. ✉ *Timmerman St. (Hwy. 255)* ☎ *902/295–2069* ⊕ *www.pc.gc.ca* 🖻 *Free* ⊘ *Open June–mid-Sept., daily 10–6.*

**Sydney Mines Heritage Museum and Fossil Centre.** Across the harbor from Sydney proper, a vintage train station has been converted into a small museum that explores the area's coal-mining connection. Displays include 300-million-year-old fossil specimens from the Sydney Coal Fields. The curator leads two-tour fossil field trips, by reservation, on Tuesdays and Thursdays at 10 am (you'll need your own transportation to get to the start of the fieldtrip). ✉ *159 Legatto St., Sydney Mines* ☎ *902/544—0992* ⊕ *www.cbfossil.org* 🖻 *Museum C$5, field trip C$10 (entry included, car required)* ⊘ *June–Sept., Tues.–Sat. 9–5.*

## WHERE TO EAT AND STAY

*For expanded hotel reviews, visit Fodors.com.*

**$$–$$$**
CONTEMPORARY

✕ **Flavor.** In a city where deep fryers reign supreme, this small bistro-style eatery is a welcome addition. The haddock is poached, the scallops seared, the prawns tossed in pesto sauce—and the absence of greasy batter means Flavor's flavors shine through. The menu is a broad one:

homemade pastas are popular, as are the inventive sandwiches and all-day breakfast items. There are several gluten-free, vegan, and vegetarian options, too (a rarity in these parts). You can eat outside on the patio in summer months. ✉ *16 Pitt St.,* ☎ *902/562–6611* ⊕ *www.cbflavor. com* ☾ *Closed Sun.*

$$ ✗**Governor's Pub and Eatery.** Sydney's first mayor, Walter Crowe, once
CONTEMPORARY lived in this Victorian home, built in the late 1800s. The restaurant, with hardwood floors, a fireplace, and high ceilings, is known for fresh seafood and hand-cut steaks, though there are lighter options like salads, wraps, and burgers, as well. Both the restaurant and the pub upstairs have large patios that overlook Sydney Harbour. Most nights the atmosphere is bustling and lively, with locals and travelers alike mixing over a pint. Desserts are homemade. ✉ *233 Esplanade* ☎ *902/562–7646* ⊕ *www.governorseatery.com.*

$$–$$$ 🏨**Cambridge Suites Hotel.** If you're looking to take a break from the little inns and rural B&Bs so prevalent in Cape Breton, put yourself in the center of the action on the Sydney waterfront by staying at this comfortable all-suites hotel. Each room has a separate living room area, and some of the spacious one-bedroom and studio options directly overlook the harbor—even better views can be enjoyed from the rooftop deck. **Pros:** free Continental breakfast buffet; pet friendly. **Cons:** other people's pets are sometimes audible; conventional room decor. ✉ *380 Esplanade* ☎ *902/562–6500 or 800/565–9466* ⊕ *www.cambridgesuitessydney.com* ⇥ *147 rooms* ⚄ *In-room: no safe, kitchen, Internet, Wi-Fi. In-hotel: restaurant, room service, gym, laundry facilities, business center, parking, some pets allowed* ❑ *Some meals.*

$$–$$$ 🏨**Delta Sydney.** On the harbor close to the center of town, the Delta ☾ has many perks, including a sauna and exercise room, and an indoor pool with a 17-meter (55-foot) waterslide. **Pros:** rooms in the Premier, Deluxe, and Jr. Suite category have been renovated; children under 17 stay free and those under six eat free. **Cons:** unrenovated rooms look tired; pub can be noisy. ✉ *300 Esplanade* ☎ *902/562–7500 or 800/565–1001* 🖷 *902/562–3023* ⊕ *www.deltahotels.com* ⇥ *152 rooms* ⚄ *In-room: no safe, Wi-Fi. In-hotel: restaurant, room service, bar, pool, gym, parking, some pets allowed.*

## NIGHTLIFE AND THE ARTS

**Cape Breton University** (✉ *1250 Grand Lake Rd.* ☎ *902/539–5300 or 888/959–9995* ⊕ *www.cbu.ca*) is the area's leading cultural institution. On campus, visitors are drawn to the 337-seat Boardmore Playhouse and the CBU Art Gallery (the only public gallery on the island).

More than just a port for the 70,000-odd passengers who dock here each year, the **Joan Harriss Cruise Pavilion** (✉ *74 Esplanade* ☎ *902/564–9775* ⊕ *www.portofsydney.ca*) is a popular entertainment venue, too. Its main stage and lighthouse stage host many musical acts, especially during events like Sydney's mid-summer **Action Week** (⊕ *www.actionweek. com*) and the province-wide **Celtic Colours International Festival** (⊕ *www. celtic-colours.com*). Even if you're not arriving by ship, the pavilion is easy enough to find: just look for the 18-meter (60-foot) fiddle that towers outside it.

At **Casino Nova Scotia** (✉ *525 George St.* ☎ *902/563–7777 or 866/334–1114* ⊕ *www.casinonovascotia.com*), you can try your luck at slot machines, test your skill at gaming tables, or simply settle in to enjoy the live entertainment—assuming you're at least 19 years old (the legal drinking age in Nova Scotia).

### SPORTS AND THE OUTDOORS

**Peterfield Provincial Park.** Take a hike through history at this park, poised on the south arm of Sydney Harbour. Initially developed as the private domain of David Matthews, a onetime mayor of New York City who remained loyal to the crown during the War of Independence, today its 56-acres are is laced with trails. ✉ *1126 Westmount Rd. (off Rte. 239), Westmount* ☎ *No phone* ⊕ *parks.gov.ns.ca* ⊟ *Free* ☉ *Daily, mid-May–mid-Oct.)*

### SHOPPING

**The Cape Breton Centre for Craft and Design** (✉ *322 Charlotte St.,* ☎ *902/270-7491* ⊕ *www.capebretoncraft.com*) showcases the work of both classic and cutting-edge Cape Breton artisans in its airy second-floor gallery. The center, which houses on-site studios for pottery, weaving, and glass- and jewelry-making, also hosts hands-on workshops that are open to craft aficionados.

Top island retailers—among them Hattie's Heirlooms, the Cape Breton Curiosity Shop, Man of War Gallery, and Tastes of Cape Breton—are represented at **Harbourside Boutiques** ( ✉ *74 Esplanade* ☎ *902/564-9775* ⊕ *www.harboursideboutiques.ca*) in the Joan Harriss Cruise Pavilion. The caveat is that they're only open seasonally: sometimes daily in high season, sometimes just when cruise ships are in port.

## LOUISBOURG

*53 km (33 mi) south of Glace Bay.*

Though best known as the home of the largest historical reconstruction in North America, Louisbourg is also an important fishing community with a lovely harborfront. There are a number of good places to stay here, too.

The **Fortress of Louisbourg National Historic Site of Canada** may be Cape Breton's most remarkable attraction. After the French were forced out of mainland Nova Scotia in 1713, they established their headquarters here in a walled, fortified town on a low point of land at the mouth of Louisbourg Harbour. The fortress was captured twice (once by New Englanders in 1745, once by the British in 1758) and after the second attack the formidable military complex was razed. Its demise was critical in ending France's dream of a North American empire . . . but in the 1960s, archaeologists took up where the imperialists left off, rebuilding a fifth of the fortress to look just as it did before the initial siege. June through mid-October, costumed interpreters convincingly re-create the activities of the original inhabitants, so you can watch a military drill, see nails and lace being made, or dine on food prepared from 18th-century recipes in the town's three inns. Free guided tours are given in

Fodor's Choice ★

high season and events available at extra cost—including themed dinner theaters and archeological programs—make a visit here even more memorable. Whenever you come, plan on spending a full day. Bring a warm sweater or jacket, too, because Louisbourg tends to be chilly at any time of the year. ☒ *259 Parks Service Rd.* ☎ *902/733–2280* ⊕ *www. pc.gc.ca* ☒ *C$17.60* ⊘ *mid-May–Oct., daily 9:30–5; Nov.–mid-May limited access to site by pre-arrangement.*

## WHERE TO EAT AND STAY
*For expanded hotel reviews, visit Fodors.com.*

$$ ✕ **Grubstake Restaurant.** *Coquilles St. Jacques* (scallops with mushrooms
CANADIAN in a white wine–cream sauce), seafood pasta, and shrimp-and-scallop flambé are popular menu items at this 120-seat restaurant where elegant, family, and country cuisine are all wrapped into one. Although seafood is the specialty, the baked Chicken Royale with mushrooms and the country-style barbecue pork are also excellent. The cocktail lounge is a great place to relax with a drink and meet some locals. Service is friendly and laid back—though this sometimes translates into slow. Desserts are made on-site. ☒ *7499 Main St.* ☎ *902/733–2308* ⊕ *www. grubstake.ca* ⊘ *Closed Nov.–June.*

$–$$ ⊡ **Cranberry Cove Inn.** This cranberry-hued house, built in 1904, is a
★ short drive from the Fortress of Louisbourg. **Pros:** cooked breakfast included; impeccable rooms. **Cons:** no elevator for three-story building; Wi-Fi is spotty in some rooms. ☒ *12 Wolfe St.* ☎ *902/733–2171 or 800/929–0222* ⊕ *www.cranberrycoveinn.com* ⇨ *7 rooms* ⌂ *In-room: no a/c, no safe, Wi-Fi. In-hotel: business center* ⊘ *Closed Nov.–Apr.* ⦿| *Breakfast.*

$–$$ ⊡ **Louisbourg Harbour Inn Bed & Breakfast.** The central location of this B&B makes it just a few minutes walk to the Louisbourg Playhouse, Main Street, and the harbor. **Pros:** cooked breakfast included. **Cons:** no elevator for three-story building; several rooms are small. ☒ *9 Lower Warren St.,* ☎ *902/733–3222 or 888/888–8466* ⊕ *www.louisbourgharbourinn. com* ⇨ *7 rooms* ⌂ *In-room: no a/c, no safe, Wi-Fi. In-hotel: business center* ⊘ *Closed early Oct.–early June* ⦿| *Breakfast.*

$$–$$$ ⊡ **Point of View Suites.** This modern hotel, built to resemble an oversized beach house, is the closest property to the Fortress of Louisbourg and the only one on the water. **Pros:** private pebble beach; knowledgeable owners who grew up in the area. **Cons:** non-oceanview units overlook an RV lot; limited restaurant menu off-season. ☒ *15 Commercial St. Ext.* ☎ *902/733–2080 or 888/374–8439* ⊕ *www.louisbourgpointofview.com* ⇨ *19 rooms* ⌂ *In-room: no safe, kitchen (some), Wi-Fi. In-hotel: restaurant, beach, business center* ⊘ *Closed mid-Oct.–mid-May.*

## NIGHTLIFE AND THE ARTS
You can take in traditional Cape Breton music and other entertainments nightly at the **Louisbourg Playhouse**, a 17th-century-style theater that was modeled after Shakespeare's Globe. Originally constructed as part of the Disney movie set for *Squanto: A Warrior's Tale,* the venue was donated to the community in 1994 after filming wrapped. ☒ *11 Aberdeen St.*

☎ *902/733–2996 or 888/733–2787* ⊕ *www.louisbourgplayhouse.com* ⊗ *mid-June–mid-Oct., nightly at 8.*

## SPORTS AND THE OUTDOORS

### HIKING

The sprawling **Fortress of Louisbourg property** (✉ *259 Parks Service Rd., Louisbourg* ☎ *902/733–2280* ⊕ *www.pc.gc.ca*) has a series of free hiking trails that lead to a lighthouse, redoubts, and a swimmable beach at Kennington Cove where the conquering New Englanders and Brits both came ashore.

### BOATING

Kayaker can dip into the past at **Rising Tide Expeditions** (✉ *8806 Gabarus Highway, Gabarus* ☎ *902/884–2884 or 877/884–2884* ⊕ *www.risingtideexpeditions.ca*), which runs a full-day kayaking excursion called "Fortress of Louisbourg: Paddle Through Time" for C$135 June to September.

# BIG POND

*50 km (31 mi) west of Louisbourg.*

This tiny community consists of a few houses dotted along the highway, but most people come to see one in particular: the former home of singer-songwriter Rita MacNeil, now operated as **Rita's Tea Room.** Originally a one-room schoolhouse where Rita lived with her children, the building has been expanded to accommodate the multitude of visitors who arrive to sample Rita's Tea Room Blend Tea, which is served along with light meals and tasty baked goods. You can visit a display room of Rita's awards and photographs and browse the gift shop. On Sunday afternoons in summer, the lady herself typically appears to greet guests between 1 and 2. ✉ *8077 Hwy. 4* ☎ *902/828–2667* ⊕ *www.ritamacneil.com* ⊗ *Gift shop, June–mid Oct., daily 10–5; Tea room, end of June–mid-Oct., daily 10–5.*

# ARICHAT

*62 km (38 mi) southwest of Big Pond.*

Arichat is the principal village on Isle Madame: the largest island in a 44-square-km (17-square-mi) archipelago of the same name, which sits at Cape Breton's southernmost tip. Known today for its friendly Acadian culture and many secluded coves and inlets, Arichat has a deep harbor that made it an important fishing, shipbuilding, and trading center during the 19th century. Some fine old buildings from that period still remain, including Notre Dame de l'Assomption Church and the LeNoir Forge Museum. The two cannons overlooking the harbor were installed after the village was sacked by John Paul Jones during the American Revolution.

### GETTING HERE AND AROUND

To get here from Big Pond, take Route 4 to Highway 320, which leads through Poulamon and D'Escousse before bridging Lennox Passage. Highway 206 meanders through the low hills to a maze of land and water at West Arichat. Together, the two routes encircle the island, meeting at Arichat.

One of the best ways to experience Isle Madame is by foot. Try Cape Auguet Eco-Trail, an 8.5-km (5-mi) hiking trail that extends from Boudreauville to Mackerel Cove and follows the rocky coastline overlooking Chedabucto Bay. Another good half-day hike leads to Gros Nez, the "large nose" that juts into the sea. The island also lends itself to biking, as most roads glide gently along the shore.

### EXPLORING

Arichat was once the seat of the local Catholic diocese. **Notre Dame de l'Assomption** church, built in 1837, still retains the grandeur of its former cathedral status. Its bishop's palace is now a law office. ⊠ *2316 High Road, Hwy. 206* ☎ *902/226–2109* ⊠ *Free* ☉ *Dawn–dusk. Mass, year-round Sun. 9:15 am.*

**LeNoir Forge Museum** (⊠ *Hwy. 206, off Hwy. 4 via Exit 46 to Isle Madame* ☎ *902/226–9364*) is a restored 18th-century French blacksmith shop. The handsome stone structure is open June through August, daily 10 to 5, and admission is free.

# New Brunswick

**WORD OF MOUTH**

"I believe one of the best places to walk the floor in the Bay of Fundy is at Fundy National Park/Alma which is about 1.5 hour drive from Saint John. Some would recommend Hopewell Rocks which is about 45 minutes farther. Remember to check the tide tables in order to time your trip around low tide (which would likely be limited by the timing available to you from your cruise ship)."

—mat54

# WELCOME TO NEW BRUNSWICK

## TOP REASONS TO GO

★ **Go whale-watching:** There are licensed tour operators throughout the province.

★ **Experience Acadian culture:** Visit attractions such as Le Pays de la Sagouine or Acadian Historical Village on the Acadian Coastal Drive.

★ **Eat well:** Enjoy freshly caught salmon, scallops, and lobster, fresh-picked fiddlehead ferns and dulse (seaweed), Acadian poutine (a potato dumpling with pork filling, quite unlike the Québecois dish of the same name), and buffalo steaks.

★ **Take a hike:** New Brunswick's provincial and national parks have amazing hiking trails and plenty of great spots to catch your breath and contemplate the gorgeous scenery or watch birds from an ocean cliff.

★ **Go for a swim:** New Brunswick, like the rest of Atlantic Canada, is blessed with beaches, rivers, and lakes; you can choose from water that's cold or warm, fresh or salty, in expansive spaces or intimate coves.

**1 Saint John.** The port city of Saint John has become a vibrant urban destination, with a revitalized waterfront, an eclectic restaurant scene, lively nightlife and festivals, fun street art, and one of Canada's loveliest city parks. There's plenty of history too, from first-class museums and historic sites to streets lined with 19th-century homes.

**2 The Fundy Coast.**
Boasting some of the highest tides in the world, the Bay of Fundy is a diverse region with dramatic coastlines, tiny fishing villages, charming islands, and rocky beaches perfect for treasure hunting. Time seems to stand still here, and life is laid-back and informal yet rich in intriguing experiences like whale-watching.

The city of Moncton, billed as the "crossroads of the Maritimes" or "Hub City," is an increasingly vibrant place to visit, with fun attractions for the kids.

**3 The Acadian Coast & St John River Valley.**
A highlight of this region is the French Acadian culture with its distinct foods, music, and festivals. Unlike the Bay of Fundy, the water on the Acadian Coast is downright balmy, and the selection of beaches can be mind-boggling. Much of the St. John River—more than 500 km (310 mi) of it—meanders through cities, townships, and charming villages. Pastoral farmland and the blue sweep of the water accompany you most of the way.

# GETTING ORIENTED

New Brunswick has it all: a mighty river (and many other impressive waterways), coastal waters with dramatically high tides on the Fundy shore, forests that sweep for miles, and mountain ranges perfect for activities like hiking and skiing. Most of all, this province has a people who are exceptionally friendly. You'll find activities and attractions to suit every age and taste and then some.

**4 Fredericton.** A gracious, small city on the gentle slopes of the St. John River Valley, Fredericton is the capital of New Brunswick and home to two fine universities. It has a historic core, arts and culture, and great shopping.

Updated by Penny Phenix

Stunning scenery, vast forests, and world-class attractions characterize New Brunswick. Topping the list is the Bay of Fundy, shortlisted to be one of the "New 7 Wonders of Nature," with the highest tides in the world, marine life that includes several species of whales, stretches of wilderness coastline, and charming harbor villages.

Add to this national and international historic sites, national parks teeming with wildlife, great beaches, vibrant towns and cities, and a thriving diversity of cultures, and you might wonder how the population can remain so utterly laid-back, but that's just another facet of New Brunswick's charm. The province is an old place in New World terms, and the remains of a turbulent past are still evident in some of its quiet nooks. Near Moncton, for instance, wild strawberries perfume the air of the grassy slopes of Fort Beauséjour, where, in 1755, one of the last battles for possession of Acadia took place, with the English finally overcoming the French. Other areas of the province were settled by the British; by Loyalists, American colonists who chose to live under British rule after the American Revolution; and by Irish immigrants, many seeking to avoid the famine in their home country. If you stay in both Acadian and Loyalist regions, a trip to New Brunswick can seem like two vacations in one.

For every gesture in the provincial landscape as grand as the giant rock formations carved by the Bay of Fundy tides at Hopewell Hill, there is one as subtle as the gifted touch of a sculptor in a studio. For every experience as colorful as salmon and fiddleheads served at a church supper, there is another as low-key as the gentle waves of the Baie des Chaleurs. New Brunswick is the luxury of an inn with five stars and the tranquillity of camping under a million.

At the heart of New Brunswick is the forest, which covers 85 percent of the province—nearly all its interior. The forest contributes to the economy, defines the landscape, and delights hikers, anglers, campers, and bird-watchers, but New Brunswick's soul is the sea. The biggest of Canada's three Maritime provinces, New Brunswick is largely surrounded by coastline. The warm waters of the Baie des Chaleurs, Gulf of St. Lawrence, and Northumberland Strait lure swimmers to their sandy beaches, and the chilly Bay of Fundy, with its monumental tides, draws breaching whales, whale-watchers, and kayakers.

## PLANNING

### DRIVING TIPS

Watch out for moose, deer, porcupines, and raccoons, especially at night. Although major highways have moose and deer fences, many of the secondary roads do not, and twilight is an especially dangerous time for wildlife entering the roads. Reduce speed at night.

## FESTIVAL FUN

New Brunswick's festival season starts with winter carnivals and snow fests from January to April.

Early July is the **Irish Festival** (⊕ *www.canadasirishfest.com*) in Miramichi. Later in the month are the **New Brunswick Highland Games & Scottish Festival** (⊕ *www.highlandgames.ca*) in Fredericton; the **Shediac Lobster Festival** (⊕ *www.lobsterfestival.nb.ca*); Edmundston's **Foire Brayonne** (⊕ *www.foirebrayonne.com*); Sackville's theater and music celebration, the **Festival by the Marsh** (⊕ *www.festivalbythemarsh.ca*); and Saint John's **Buskers on the Boardwalk** (⊕ *www.marketsquaresj.com*), which is about as entertaining as they come.

August means the **Acadian Festival** (⊕ *www.festivalacadiencaraquet.com*) at Caraquet and St. Stephen's **Chocolate Festival** (⊕ *www.town.ststephen.nb.ca*), which is popular for the whole family. The **Miramichi Folksong Festival** (⊕ *www.miramichifolksongfestival.com*) and **Miramichi Scottish Festival** (⊕ *www.miramichiscottishfestival.com*) are also held in August, as is Fredericton's **Summer Music Festival** (⊕ *nbsummermusicfestival.ca*), featuring mostly classical musicians.

In September Fredericton hosts the **Harvest Jazz and Blues Festival** (⊕ *www.harvestjazzandblues.com*), one of the province's top events.

## GETTING HERE AND AROUND
### BY BOAT AND FERRY

Bay Ferries Ltd. runs from Saint John, New Brunswick, to Digby, Nova Scotia, and back once or twice a day, depending on the season. Passenger fares are C$41 per adult, C$82 for a car, plus a C$20 fuel surcharge for the three-hour, one-way trip July through September. Off-season rates are cheaper.

East Coast Ferries Ltd. runs services from Deer Island, New Brunswick, to Campobello, New Brunswick, and Eastport, Maine, from late June to mid-September. On the Campobello route, the fares are C$16 for a car and driver, C$3 for each adult passenger. The crossing takes about 40 minutes. On the Eastport route, the fares are C$13 for a car and driver and C$3 for each adult passenger. On both routes a fuel surcharge of C$4 is also applied.

The year-round 20-minute ferry crossing from Letete, on mainland New Brunswick, to Deer Island is a free service operated by the government of New Brunswick.

Coastal Transport has up to seven crossings per day from Blacks Harbour to Grand Manan July through mid-September and four crossings per day the rest of the year. Round-trip fares, payable on the Grand Manan side, are C$32.55 for a car and C$10.90 for an adult. A one-way crossing takes about 1½ hours.

**Contacts** **Bay Ferries Ltd.** ☎ *506/694–7777, 877/882–8686* ⊕ *www.nfl-bay.com.*

**East Coast Ferries Ltd.** ☎ *506/747–2159, 877/747–2159* ⊕ *www.eastcoastferriesltd.com.*

**Coastal Transport** ☎ *506/662–3724* ⊕ *www.coastaltransport.ca.*

### BY AIR

New Brunswick has three major airports: Saint John Airport, about 15 minutes east of downtown Saint John; Greater Moncton International Airport, about 10 minutes east of downtown Moncton; and Fredericton Airport, 10 minutes east of that city's downtown.

### BY CAR

New Brunswick is the largest of the Atlantic provinces, covering nearly 78,000 square km (30,000 square mi): around 320 km (200 mi) north to south and 240 km (150 mi) east to west. Unless you plan to fly into one of the hubs and stay there for your visit, you'd be wise to have a car. There's a good selection of car-rental agencies (book early for July and August); call or visit the Web sites to search for pick-up and drop-off locations throughout the province (bear in mind that rentals from airports carry a surcharge).

From Québec, the Trans-Canada Highway (Route 2) enters New Brunswick at St-Jacques and follows the St. John River through Fredericton and on to Moncton and the Nova Scotia border. From Maine, Interstate 95 crosses at Houlton to Woodstock, New Brunswick, where it connects with the Trans-Canada Highway. Those traveling up the coast of Maine on Route 1 cross at Calais to St. Stephen, New Brunswick. New Brunswick's Route 1 extends through Saint John and Sussex to join the Trans-Canada Highway near Moncton.

New Brunswick has an excellent highway system with numerous facilities. The Trans-Canada Highway, marked by a maple leaf, is the same as Route 2. Route 7 joins Saint John and Fredericton. Fredericton is connected to Miramichi City by Route 8. Route 15 links Moncton to the eastern coast and to Route 11, which follows the coast to Miramichi, around the Acadian Peninsula, and up to Campbellton.

### BY TRAIN

Train travel options in New Brunswick are limited: VIA Rail offers passenger service every day but Tuesday from Campbellton, Miramichi, and Moncton to Montréal and Halifax—there is no train service to the main cities of Saint John or Fredericton.

## MAKING THE MOST OF YOUR TIME

A good way to tour New Brunswick is to follow one of the five scenic drives into which the province is divided: The River Valley Scenic Drive follows more than 500 km (310 mi) of road along the St. John River; the Fundy Coastal Drive has potential views of whales and wildlife in the region of the Bay of Fundy; the Acadian Coastal Drive offers sandy beaches, picturesque villages, and vibrant culture; the Miramichi River Route is home to salmon fishing and folk festivals; and the Appalachian Range Route has serene mountain vistas and beautiful bays. The Fundy Coastal is a popular route and many prefer to spend less time in Saint John, rather than more: Overnight in Alma, the town that services Fundy National Park, or in Moncton, which has some fun amusements for children.

## OUTDOOR ACTIVITIES AND TOURS

Whale-watching, sea kayaking, bird-watching, scuba diving, garden touring, river cruising, golfing, fishing, and snowmobiling are just a few of New Brunswick's alluring experiences. Tourism New Brunswick, as well as several other provincial and commercial companies, has details and can provide information on day adventures, scenic driving routes, and accommodations.

Bicycling in particular is a favorite way to tour New Brunswick. Two favorite biking areas in the province are the 33 km (20 mi) of country roads on Grand Manan Island (you can rent bikes from Adventure High; *see the Grand Manan listings*) and the Quoddy Loop, which goes around Passamaquoddy Bay and the western mouth of the Bay of Fundy.

Baymount Outdoor Adventures operates bicycle tours for large groups along the Fundy shore near Hopewell Cape. B&Bs frequently have bicycles for rent, and Tourism New Brunswick has listings and free cycling maps.

**Contacts Adventure High** ☎ *800/732–5492, 506/662–3563* ⊕ *www. adventurehigh.com.*

**Baymount Outdoor Adventures** ☎ *506/734–2660* ⊕ *www. baymountadventures.com.*

**Golf New Brunswick** ☎ *877/833–4662* ⊕ *www.golfnb.com.*

**New Brunswick Trails Council** ☎ *506/459–1931, 800/526–7070* ⊕ *www. sentiernbtrail.com.*

**Quoddy Loop Tourism** ⊕ *www.quoddyloop.com.*

**Tourism New Brunswick** ☎ *800/561–0123* ⊕ *www.tourismnewbrunswick.ca.*

## TASTES OF NEW BRUNSWICK

A spring delicacy is fiddleheads—emerging ferns that look like the curl at the end of a violin neck. These emerald gems are picked along riverbanks, then boiled and sprinkled with lemon juice, butter, salt, and pepper. Seafood is plentiful all year (lobsters, oysters, crabs, mussels, clams, scallops, and salmon) and prepared in as many ways as there are chefs. Cast your line just about anywhere in New Brunswick and you'll find some kind of fish-and-chips. Try snacking on dulse, a dried purple seaweed as salty as potato chips and as compelling as peanuts.

The beers of choice are Moosehead, brewed in Saint John, and, of course, the various Molson brews. A number of local breweries and wineries are also popular, so ask what's available in stores and restaurants.

New Brunswick's maple products are sought the world over, and chocolates made by Ganong Brothers of St. Stephen, who have been in the candy business for a century and a quarter, are a popular treat.

### WHAT IT COSTS

| | **IN CANADIAN DOLLARS** | | | | |
|---|---|---|---|---|---|
| | ¢ | $ | $$ | $$$ | $$$$ |
| Restaurants | under C$8 | C$8–C$12 | C$13–C$20 | C$21–C$30 | over C$30 |
| Hotels | under C$75 | C$75–C$125 | C$126–C$175 | C$176–C$250 | over C$250 |

Restaurant prices are per person for a main course at dinner. Hotel prices are for two people in a standard double room in high season, excluding 14% harmonized sales tax (HST).

### WHEN TO GO

Each season brings unique reasons to travel to New Brunswick. Winter means skiing, snowmobiling, skating on public rinks, and cozy dinners. Spring is the time for canoeing the inland rivers, fishing, picking fiddleheads, and watching the province come alive.

Summer is peak tourist season, and Parlee Beach attracts thousands of sun-lovers. The resort towns of Fundy, including Alma, St. Andrews, and St. George, get busy, too. It's a good time to trek up to the lighthouse at Cape Enrage. Summer festivals abound, and the province's two national parks, Fundy and Kouchibouguac, are filled with nature lovers.

Fall means country fairs, harvest suppers, and incredibly beautiful scenic drives to enjoy autumn foliage. Fall colors are at their peak from late September through mid- to late October. The Autumn Foliage Colours Line (☎ *800/268–3255*) provides daily updates on which drives are best.

## EXPLORING NEW BRUNSWICK

A well-designed, well-marked system of provincial scenic drives takes you to most of the places in New Brunswick that you'd want to go. Begin in the south, on the phenomenal Fundy Coastal Drive (watch for the lighthouse-on-a-cliff logo). At the upper end of the bay it connects with the Acadian Coastal Drive (the logo is a white starfish on a red background), which hugs the gentle eastern shore. In the middle of the Acadian Drive is a bit of a detour for the Miramichi River Route (a jumping salmon logo). The Acadian Drive eventually meets the Appalachian Range Route (mountains logo), which takes you across the rugged northern part of the province, where the hardwood ridges ignite in a blaze of color in fall, and then connects with the River Valley Scenic Drive (a fiddlehead logo), which runs down the entire western side of the province and back to Saint John, on the Fundy Coastal Drive.

# SAINT JOHN

Like any seaport worth its salt, Saint John is a welcoming place, but, more than that, it is fast transforming into a sophisticated urban destination worthy of the many cruise ships that dock on its revitalized waterfront. All the comings and goings over the centuries have exposed Saint Johners to a wide variety of cultures and ideas, creating

# GREAT ITINERARIES

### IF YOU HAVE 4 DAYS

If you have a short time, concentrate on one region, such as the Fundy Coast, where North America's first global geopark, the Stonehammer, covers 2,500 sq. km (965 sq. mi) of geological heritage. You can start in Saint John, steeped in English and Irish traditions and rich in history and art. The resort town of **St. Andrews by-the-Sea** is an hour's drive west and has plenty of art, crafts, history, nature, and seafood. Whale-watching tours leave from the wharf, and the outstanding **Kingsbrae Horticultural Garden** invites lingering. Spend a day and a night, then backtrack through Saint John, taking Route 1 past Sussex to Route 114 and **Fundy National Park**. Route 915, east of the park, hugs the coast. At **Cape Enrage** you can visit a working lighthouse and enjoy a cup of seafood chowder. There is lots to do around **Hopewell Cape**, where the Fundy tides have sculpted gigantic rocks into flowerpot formations that turn into islands at high tide. Finish the trip with **Moncton**, a microcosm of New Brunswick culture and just an hour's drive from Fundy National Park.

### IF YOU HAVE 7 DAYS

Add an Acadian Coast experience to the four-day tour *above*. Head north from **Moncton** and explore the area around **Shediac**, famous for its lobsters and Parlee Beach. Just beyond is **Bouctouche**, where visitors can walk for free for miles on a boardwalk over the dunes, and the make-believe land of Le Pays de la Sagouine, which pays tribute to Acadian author Antonine Maillet and La Sagouine, the charwoman character she created. Another 50 km (31 mi) north is **Kouchibouguac National Park**, with protected beaches, forests, and peat bogs. The coastal drive from the park to **Miramichi City**, about 75 km (47 mi), passes through several bustling fishing villages. Most of the communities are Acadian, but as you approach Miramichi City, English dominates again. A stopover here positions you perfectly to begin your exploration of the Acadian Peninsula. It's only about 120 km (74 mi) from Miramichi City to **Caraquet,** where the Acadian Historical Village is a careful re-creation of traditional Acadian way of life.

### IF YOU HAVE 10 DAYS

Follow the 7-day itinerary *above*. From **Caraquet** plan at least half a day to drive across the top of New Brunswick (Route 134 along the coast and Route 17 inland through the forest) to the St. John River valley. Begin your explorations among the flowers and the music of the New Brunswick Botanical Gardens in St-Jacques, outside **Edmundston**. The drive from here to Fredericton is about 275 km (171 mi) of panoramic pastoral and river scenery, including a dramatic gorge and waterfall at **Grand Falls**, the longest covered bridge in the world at Hartland, and historic Woodstock, New Brunswick's first town. **Kings Landing Historical Settlement**, near Fredericton, is a faithful depiction of life on the river in the 19th century. With its Gothic cathedral, Victorian architecture, museums, and riverfront pathways, **Fredericton** is a great stopping place and the seat of the province's government. The drive from Fredericton back to Saint John on Route 102 is just over 100 km (62 mi).

a characterful Maritime city with a vibrant artistic community. Visitors will discover rich and diverse cultural products in its urban core, including a plethora of art galleries and antiques shops in uptown.

Industry and salt air have combined to give parts of Saint John a weather-beaten quality, but you'll also find lovingly restored 19th-century wooden and redbrick homes as well as modern office buildings, hotels, and shops.

The natives welcomed the French explorers Samuel de Champlain and Sieur de Mons when they landed here on St. John the Baptist Day in 1604. Then, nearly two centuries later, in May 1783, 3,000 British Loyalists fleeing the aftermath of the American Revolutionary War poured off a fleet of ships to make a home amid the rocks and forests. Two years later the city of Saint John became the first in Canada to be incorporated.

Although most of the Loyalists were English, there were some Irish among them. After the Napoleonic Wars in 1815, thousands more Irish workers found their way to Saint John. It was the Irish potato famine of 1845 to 1852, though, that spawned the largest influx of Irish immigrants, and today a 20-foot Celtic cross on Partridge Island at the entrance to St. John Harbour stands as a reminder of the hardships and suffering they endured. Their descendants make Saint John Canada's most Irish city, a fact that's celebrated in grand style each March with a weeklong St. Patrick's celebration.

The St. John River, its Reversing Rapids, and St. John Harbour divide Saint John into eastern and western districts. The historic downtown area is on the east side, where an ambitious urban-renewal program started in the early 1980s continues to transform the downtown waterfront. Older properties have been converted into trendy restaurants and shops, while glittering new apartment and condo buildings will take full advantage of the spectacular view across the bay.

Harbour Passage, a redbrick walking and cycling path with benches and lots of interpretive information, begins downtown at Market Square and winds along the waterfront all the way to the Reversing Rapids. A shuttle boat between Market Square and the falls means you have to walk only one way.

On the lower west side, painted-wood homes with flat roofs—characteristic of Atlantic Canadian seaports—slope to the harbor. Industrial activity is prominent on the west side, which has stately older homes on huge lots.

Regardless of the weather, Saint John is a delightful city to explore, as so many of its key downtown attractions are linked by enclosed overhead pedways known as the "Inside Connection."

### GETTING HERE AND AROUND

If you arrive in the downtown area by car, park and proceed on foot for full enjoyment. Additionally, Saint John Transit offers sight-seeing bus tours of historic areas from June to early October, with three departures daily at 9:30 am, 11:15 am, and 1 pm from Barbour's General Store *(see below)* in the downtown waterfront area. The tour lasts about one and a half hours, and passengers on the first two tours can hop off at any of the stops and re-board a later bus to continue. Tickets, which can be purchased from the driver, cost C$20 for adults.

To get to sites farther afield, like the Rockwood Park and the Cherry Brook Zoo or Irving Nature Park, you're best off with a car.

Rockwood Park Stables has a four-passenger horse-drawn carriage (C$80/hour) and four 14-passenger trollies (C$105/hour within the park or C$226/hour for city tours) for rent and offers rides anywhere in the city, with sleigh rides in winter.

**ESSENTIALS**

**Tour Information Rockwood Park Stables** ☎ 506/633–7659 ⊕ www. horsesinsaintjohn.com. **Saint John Transit** ☎ 506/658–4700 ⊕ www. saintjohntransit.com.

**Visitor Information Cape Enrage Interpretive Center** ⊠ 650 Cape Enrage Rd., Waterside, New Brunswick, Canada ☎ 506/887–2273, 888/423–5454 ⊕ www.capeenrage.ca.

**Tourism Saint John** ☎ 506/658–2990, 866/463–8639 ⊕ www.tourismsaintjohn. com.

**Visitor Information Center** ⊠ 424 Main St. (in the lighthouse at the harbor), St. Martins, New Brunswick, Canada ☎ 506/833–2006 ⊕ www.stmartinscanada. com ⊙ June–Sept.

## TOP ATTRACTIONS

**Cherry Brook Zoo.** Snow leopards, Siberian tigers, and other exotic species are highlights of this small zoo with pleasant woodland trails, a waterfowl habitat with a boardwalk and floating gazebo, and an Aboriginal Medicine Wheel and Garden. There's an Awareness and Discover Center, where displays highlight the ongoing problem of poaching of endangered species and show more than 100 items seized by Canadian officials. The zoo also has a monkey house, a miniature golf course, and the Vanished Kingdom Park, a display that focuses on extinct animals. ⊠ 901 Foster Thurston Dr., Saint John, New Brunswick, Canada ☎ 506/634–1440 ⊕ www.cherrybrookzoo.com ☜ C$10.50 ⊙ Daily 10–9 summer, 10–5 winter (closing times may vary).

**Irving Nature Park.** The ecosystems of the southern New Brunswick coast are preserved in this lovely 600-acre park on a peninsula close to downtown. Roads and eight walking trails (up to several miles long) make bird- and nature-watching easy. Many shorebirds breed here, and it's a staging site on the flight path of shorebirds migrating to and from the Arctic and South America. Stop at the information kiosk just inside the entrance for a naturalist's notebook, a guide to what you'll find in the park, season by season. Tours are available, and it's an excellent spot for picnicking. ⊠ Sand Cove Rd., Saint John, New Brunswick, Canada ⊹ From downtown take Rte. 1 west to Exit 119A (Catherwood Rd.) south; follow Sand Cove Rd. 4½ km (3 mi) ☎ 506/653–7367 ☜ Free ⊙ May–mid-Nov., daily dawn–dusk; vehicles permitted 8–8.

**Loyalist Burial Ground.** The Old Loyalist Burial Ground was established on this site soon after the United Empire Loyalists arrived in 1783. It

Barbour's General Store ........... **4**

Carleton Martello Tower ......... **17**

Cherry Brook Zoo ....... **7**

Irving Nature Park ........... **16**

King Street .... **14**

King's Square ........ **11**

Loyalist Burial Ground .......... **9**

Loyalist House ........... **5**

Market Slip ..... **2**

New Brunswick Museum ........ **3**

Old Courthouse ... **10**

Prince William Street ......... **15**

Reversing Rapids ............ **1**

Rockwood Park .............. **8**

Saint John City Market ... **13**

Stone Church ........... **6**

Trinity Church ........ **12**

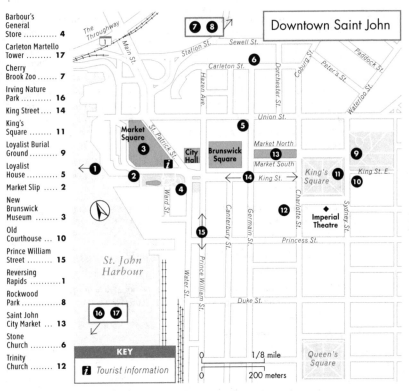

**Downtown Saint John**

**KEY**

*i* *Tourist information*

closed as a cemetery in 1848, however, and fell into disrepair. In 1994, the Irving family restored it as a gift to the people of Saint John. Brick and granite walkways were constructed, memorial gates were specially carved, and hundreds of trees and thousands of flowers were planted. A highlight of the grounds is a magnificent beaver-pond fountain created to depict the hard work and tenacious spirit of the city's founders and those who followed them. ⊠ *Sydney St., between King and E. Union Sts., Saint John, New Brunswick, Canada* ⊡ *Free* ☉ *Daily 24 hrs.*

**Market Slip.** The waterfront area at the foot of King Street is where the Loyalists landed in 1783. Today it's the site of Market Square, the Hilton Saint John Hotel, and restaurants, but it still conveys a sense of the city's Maritime heritage. A floating wharf accommodates boating visitors to the city and those waiting for the tides to sail up the St. John River. ⊠ *Saint John, New Brunswick, Canada.*

**New Brunswick Museum.** Imaginative and engaging in its approach, the provincial museum has fascinating displays covering the history, geology, and culture of New Brunswick. The popular whale exhibit includes Delilah, a full-size young right whale skeleton, suspended from the ceiling. You can also watch the phenomenal Bay of Fundy tides rise and fall in a glass tidal tube connected to the harbor and find out why the Stonehammer Geopark has global importance. There is a large and

## Walking Tour of Downtown Saint John

Saint John is a city on hills, and **King Street**, its main street, slopes steeply to the harbor. A system of escalators, elevators, and skywalks inside buildings allows you to climb to the top and take in some of the more memorable spots without effort, though you can also walk outside. A year-round information center is located about halfway in the Shoppes of City Hall.

Start at the foot of King, at **Market Slip**. This is where the Loyalists landed in 1783 and is the site of **Barbour's General Store** and the Little Red Schoolhouse. At Market Square, restored waterfront buildings house historical exhibits, shops, restaurants, and cafés. Also here are the Saint John Regional Library, a year-round visitor information center, a replica of the *Marco Polo* ship, and the fine **New Brunswick Museum**.

From the second level of Market Square a skywalk crosses St. Patrick Street and an escalator takes you up into the City Hall shopping concourse. Here, you can branch off to Harbour Station, with its busy schedule of concerts, sporting events, and trade shows. Once you're through City Hall, another skywalk takes you across Chipman Hill and into the Brunswick Square complex of shops and offices, adjoining the city's largest hotel, the Delta Brunswick. To visit historic **Loyalist House**, exit onto Germain Street and turn left; it's on the corner at the top of the hill. Continue on for a block to see the venerable **Stone Church**. In the flavorful **Saint John City Market**, across from Brunswick Square, make sure to look up at the ceiling, which resembles the inverted hull of a ship. The oldest market in North America, constructed in 1875–76, it's also a great place to stop for lunch. When you leave by the door at the top of the market, you're near the head of King Street and right across Charlotte Street from **King's Square**. Take a walk through the square, past the statues and bandstand, to Sydney Street. Notice the walkways in the shape of the Union Jack Flag. Cross Sydney and you're in the **Loyalist Burial Ground**. Make your way back to Sydney Street and then cross King Street East to the **Old Courthouse** with its spiral staircase made from cantilevered stones. Head south on Sydney, and turn right on King's Square South, where you can catch a glimpse of the handsome Imperial Theatre. Follow King's Square South and cross Charlotte Street to reach the back door of historic **Trinity Church**.

Finally, make your way back to King Street and walk down the hill toward the water. **Prince William Street** is at the foot of the hill, just steps from where you began at Market Slip. Turn left for antiques shops, galleries, and historic architecture.

**TIMING:** Allow the better part of a day for this walk if you include a few hours for the New Brunswick Museum and some time for shopping. On Sunday the indoor walkways are open but the City Market is closed.

outstanding collection of artwork in the galleries, and the Family Discovery Gallery has fun and educational games for all ages. ✉ *1 Market Sq., Saint John, New Brunswick, Canada* ☎ *506/643–2300, 888/268–9595* ⊕ *www.nbm-mnb.ca* ✆ *C$8* ⊙ *Weekdays 9–5, Thurs. 9–9, Sat. 10–5, Sun. noon–5. Closed Mon. mid-Nov.–mid-May.*

**Reversing Rapids.** The strong Fundy tides rise higher than the water level of the river, so twice daily, at the Reversing Rapids, the tidewater pushes the river water back upstream. When the tide ebbs, the river once again pours over the rock ledges and the rapids appear to reverse themselves. To learn more about the phenomenon, watch the film shown at the Reversing Rapids Visitor Information Center. Jet-boat tours provide a wild ride as well as a closer (and wetter) look, or you can get an overhead view from a zip-line tour. A pulp mill on the bank is not so scenic, but multimillion-dollar upgrades to pollution controls have eliminated any unpleasant odors. ■TIP➔ **It takes time to appreciate the Reversing Rapids fully; you need to visit at high, slack, and low tides. Check with any visitor information office for these times to help you plan.** ✉ *200 Bridge Rd., Saint John, New Brunswick, Canada* ☎ *506/658–2937* ✆ *Free* ⊙ *Daily dawn–dusk; Visitor Center late May–late Oct., daily 9 am–7 pm; jet-boat tours June–early Oct., daily 10 am–dusk.*

☾ **Rockwood Park.** Encompassing 2,200 acres, this is one of the largest in-city parks in Canada. There are hiking trails through the forest, 13 lakes, several sandy beaches, a campground, a golf course with an aquatic driving range, the Cherry Brook Zoo, horseback riding, events, concerts, and a unique play park for people of all ages. ✉ *Main entrance off Crown St., Saint John, New Brunswick, Canada* ☎ *506/658–2883* ⊕ *rockwoodpark.ca* ✆ *Free* ⊙ *Daily 8 am–dusk.*

★ **Saint John City Market.** The inverted ship's hull ceiling of this handsome market—the oldest continuously operating market in North America (1876)—occupies a city block between Germain and Charlotte streets. Its temptations include live and fresh-cooked lobsters, great cheeses, dulse, and tasty, inexpensive snacks, along with plenty of souvenir and crafts items. ✉ *47 Charlotte St., Saint John, New Brunswick, Canada* ☎ *506/658–2820* ⊕ *www.sjcitymarket.ca* ⊙ *Weekdays 7:30–6, Sat. 7:30–5.*

## WORTH NOTING

**Barbour's General Store.** This authentic 19th-century country shop was established in 1967 as a museum commemorating the local family business that became Canada's leading producer of tea, spices, and nut butter. In 2011 it reopened as a retail outlet and tea room in addition to displaying some 2,000 artifacts dating back to the 1860s. ✉ *10 Market Sq., Saint John, New Brunswick, Canada* ☎ *506/642–2242* ✆ *Free* ⊙ *Mid-June–mid-Sept., daily 10–6.*

**Carleton Martello Tower.** The tower, a great place from which to survey the harbor and Partridge Island, was built during the War of 1812 as a precaution against an American attack. Guides tell you about the spartan life of a soldier living in the stone fort, and an audiovisual presentation outlines its role in the defense of Saint John during World War II. ✉ *454*

*Whipple St., Saint John, New Brunswick, Canada* ☎ *506/636–4011*
⊕ *www.pc.gc.ca* 🖃 *C$3.90* ⊙ *June–early Oct., daily 10–5:30.*

**King Street.** The steepest, shortest main street in Canada, lined with solid Victorian redbrick buildings, is filled with a variety of shops, eateries, and businesses. ⊠ *Saint John, New Brunswick, Canada.*

**King's Square.** Laid out in a Union Jack pattern, this green refuge has a two-story bandstand and a number of monuments. The mass of metal on the ground in the northeast corner is actually a great lump of melted tools from a neighboring hardware store that burned down in Saint John's Great Fire of 1877, in which hundreds of buildings were destroyed. ⊠ *Between Charlotte and Sydney Sts., Saint John, New Brunswick, Canada.*

**Loyalist House.** David Daniel Merritt, a wealthy Loyalist merchant, built this imposing Georgian structure in 1810. It's distinguished by its authentic period furniture and eight fireplaces. July through August the mayor sponsors a tea party here each Wednesday afternoon, during which admission to the house is free. ⊠ *120 Union St., Saint John, New Brunswick, Canada* ☎ *506/652–3590* 🖃 *C$5* ⊙ *Mid-May–mid-Sept., Mon.–Sat. 9 am–5 pm; rest of year, by appointment.*

**Old Courthouse.** This 1829 neoclassical building has a three-story spiral staircase built from tons of unsupported stones. The staircase can be seen year-round during business hours, except when court is in session. Hours sometimes vary. ⊠ *King St. E and Sydney St., Saint John, New Brunswick, Canada* 🖃 *Free* ⊙ *Weekdays 9–5.*

**Prince William Street.** South of King Street near Market Slip, this street is full of historic bank and business buildings that now hold shops, galleries, and restaurants; it's emerging as a dining destination. The lamp known as the Three Sisters, at the foot of Prince William Street, was erected in 1848 to guide ships into the harbor. Next to it is a replica of the Celtic cross on nearby Partridge Island, where many immigrants landed and were quarantined. ⊠ *Saint John, New Brunswick, Canada.*

**Stone Church.** The first stone church in the city was built for the garrison posted at nearby Fort Howe of stone brought from England as ships' ballast. ⊠ *87 Carleton St., Saint John, New Brunswick, Canada* ☎ *506/634–1474* 🖃 *By donation* ⊙ *July and Aug., Tues., Wed., and Fri. 8:30–3:30.*

**Trinity Church.** The present church dates from 1880, when it was rebuilt after the Great Fire. Inside, over the west door, is a coat of arms—a symbol of the monarchy—rescued from the council chamber in Boston by a British colonel during the American Revolution. It was deemed a worthy refugee and given a place of honor in the church. ⊠ *115 Charlotte St., Saint John, New Brunswick, Canada* ☎ *506/693–8558* 🖃 *Free* ⊙ *June–Aug., weekdays 8:30 am–5 pm; other times call ahead.*

## WHERE TO EAT

$$$$ ✕ **Billy's Seafood Company.** It's a restaurant, it's an oyster bar, it's a fish
SEAFOOD market, and it's lots of fun, too, with jazzy background music and amusing fish paintings on the walls. The fresh fish selection is impressive, and

everything is cooked to perfection. The huge pesto scallops are always a hit, as is the grilled halibut with blueberry balsamic vinegar. Local lore says that this is where cedar-planked salmon originated, and it's delicious. Dining outside is a treat, and you can get live and cooked lobsters packed to go. ⊠ *Saint John City Market, Charlotte St. entrance, Downtown, Saint John, New Brunswick, Canada* ☎ *506/672–3474, 888/933–3474.*

**$$**  ✕ **Lemongrass Thai Fare.** Phad Yum, a traditional red curry with seafood
THAI and lime leaves, is the house specialty, but you could make a meal of appetizers such as satay *gai* (chicken, beef, or pork), *hoy op* (mussels), and *tod mun pla* (fish cakes). At this intimate restaurant in an old building with lots of character as well as a heated outdoor patio, you call the shots when it comes to the spices, so your meal is as hot (or not) as you like. There's also a limited "un-Thai'ed" menu if you're in the mood for something else. The lunch menu is a great value. ⊠ *4 Market Sq., Downtown, Saint John, New Brunswick, Canada* ☎ *506/657–8424.*

**$$**  ✕ **Opera Bistro.** Guests get celebrity treatment at this hip restaurant with
INTERNATIONAL an upbeat atmosphere, excellent service, and food that features local ingredients with international flavor. There are several tempting small, medium-, and entrée-size options and a selection of daily bistro specials. The menu changes weekly; you might choose between the "Bay of Fundy cupcake" (a seafood soufflé) or the "Opera Crust" (a flatbread with a cheese and herb filling). In summer, you can purchase a picnic to go, which may include lobster and potato salad, rosemary lamb chops, and chocolate truffles. Desserts are housemade. ⊠ *60 Prince William St., Downtown, Saint John, New Brunswick, Canada* ☎ *506/642–2822.*

**$$$**  ✕ **Saint John Ale House.** The gastro-pub concept has been fully embraced
BRITISH here, and it couldn't be in a better location, with a great patio overlooking the downtown waterfront. Drawing on supplies from local farmers, fishermen, and food producers, the menu presents "progressive pub food." This might include soy citrus roasted Atlantic salmon fillet, chicken breast with a beer-based curry sauce, or a tender, 30-day dry-aged porterhouse steak, and even the more basic options, like fish-and-chips and cheeseburgers, have the gourmet touch. There's a mind-boggling beer menu, too, including brews from local microbreweries. ⊠ *1 Market Sq., Saint John, New Brunswick, Canada* ☎ *506/657–2337* ⊕ *www.saintjohnalehouse.com.*

**$**  ✕ **Taco Pica.** This modest restaurant is a slice of home for the former
LATIN AMERICAN Guatemalan refugees, now proud Canadian citizens, who run it as a worker's co-op. The atmosphere is colorful—ornamental parrots rule in the dining room—and the recipes are authentically seasoned with garlic, mint, coriander seeds, and cilantro. The *pepian* (beef stew) and the garlic shrimp are standout options. A guitarist often entertains on Friday and Saturday evenings. ⊠ *96 Germain St., Downtown, Saint John, New Brunswick, Canada* ☎ *506/633–8492* ☉ *Closed Sun.*

**$**  ✕ **Urban Deli.** Cool yet pleasingly unpretentious, this downtown eatery
DELI has been getting rave reviews since it opened in 2009, attracting an eclectic mix of businesspeople, shoppers, students, and city visitors. The menu features classic deli fare, including sandwiches piled high with meat smoked on the premises, hearty soups, imaginative salads, and

such comfort food as mac and cheese and ribs. There's a great weekend breakfast menu, too, including champagne or vodka cocktails. This is not a late-night spot—it's only open until 3 pm early in the week—so plan to eat early, and if you have to stand in line, be assured it's worth the wait. ⊠ *68 King St., Downtown, Saint John, New Brunswick, Canada* ☎ *506/652–3354* ⊕ *www.urbandeli.ca* ⊗ *No dinner Sun.–Tues.*

## WHERE TO STAY

*For expanded hotel reviews, visit Fodors.com.*

**\$\$** **Delta Brunswick Hotel.** Part of Brunswick Square with its many shops and services, the Delta Brunswick has the efficient service one would expect from a venerable chain. **Pros:** friendly and helpful staff; near all downtown attractions. **Cons:** long-term roadworks, continuing into 2012, are hampering access to the parking garage so call for directions. ⊠ *39 King St., Saint John, New Brunswick, Canada* ☎ *506/648–1981* ⊕ *www.deltahotels.ca* ↗ *254 rooms* ⟡ *In-room: a/c, Wi-Fi. In-hotel: restaurant, bar, pool, gym, laundry facilities, parking, some pets allowed.*

**\$** **Hilton Saint John.** In this Hilton, furnished in a traditional Loyalist manner, guest rooms overlook the harbor or the town. **Pros:** close to Harbour Station; spacious and tasteful rooms, many with harbor views. **Cons:** atmosphere affected when conventioneers are accommodated. ⊠ *1 Market Sq., Saint John, New Brunswick, Canada* ☎ *506/693–8484, 800/561–8282 in Canada* ⊕ *www.hilton.com* ↗ *197 rooms* ⟡ *In-room: Internet. In-hotel: restaurant, bar, pool, gym, parking, some pets allowed.*

**\$** **Homeport Historic Bed & Breakfast Inn.** Graceful arches, fine antiques, Italian marble fireplaces, Oriental carpets, and a Maritime theme are some of the features in these twin mansions built in 1858 by twin brothers of a prominent Saint John shipbuilding family. **Pros:** hospitable owners; great sense of history; close to downtown and the Reversing Rapids. **Cons:** the amazing view is sometimes obscured by fog. ⊠ *80 Douglas Ave., Saint John, New Brunswick, Canada* ☎ *506/672–7255, 888/678–7678* ⊕ *www.homeport.nb.ca* ↗ *6 rooms, 4 suites* ⟡ *In-room: a/c, Wi-Fi. In-hotel: parking, some pets allowed* ⍥ *Breakfast.*

**\$\$** **Inn on the Cove & Spa.** With its back lawn terraced down to the ocean, this inn near Irving Nature Park has as much character as its owners, who used to tape their delightful cooking show in the kitchen. **Pros:** close to Irving Nature Park; owners are TV chefs and cookbook authors Ross and Willa Mavis and their full cooked breakfast is a treat, as is dinner. **Cons:** proximity to the Bay of Fundy shore means sudden and unexpected temperature changes; out of easy walking distance from the historic downtown. ⊠ *1371 Sand Cove Rd., Saint John, New Brunswick, Canada* ☎ *506/672–7799, 877/257–8080* ⊕ *www.innonthecove.com* ↗ *8 rooms, 1 apartment* ⟡ *In-room: Wi-Fi. In-hotel: spa, parking, some pets allowed* ⍥ *Breakfast.*

**\$** **Shadow Lawn Inn.** In an affluent suburb with tree-lined streets, pala-
★ tial homes, tennis, golf, and a yacht club, this inn fits right in with its clapboards, columns, and antiques. **Pros:** great food; hospitable

service. **Cons:** the location just outside of Saint John means a ride into town if you want to go out at night. ⊠ *3180 Rothesay Rd., 12 km (7 mi) northeast of Saint John, Rothesay, New Brunswick, Canada* ☎ *506/847–7539, 800/561–4166* ⊕ *www.shadowlawninn.com* ➟ *9 rooms, 2 suites* ⚬ *In-room: Wi-Fi. In-hotel: restaurant, parking, some pets allowed* ⏐◯⏐ *Breakfast.*

## NIGHTLIFE AND THE ARTS

### THE ARTS

★ **Saint John Arts Centre.** Saint John Arts Centre has several galleries displaying the work of local artists and artisans. ⊠ *20 Hazen Ave., Saint John, New Brunswick, Canada* ☎ *506/633–4870* ⊕ *www.saintjohnartscentre. com.*

**Imperial Theatre.** Saint John's theater, opera, ballet, and symphony productions take place at the Imperial Theatre, a beautifully restored 1913 vaudeville arena. Tours (C$2) are available in July and August. ⊠ *24 King's Square S, Saint John, New Brunswick, Canada* ☎ *506/674–4100* ⊕ *www.imperialtheatre.nb.ca.*

### NIGHTLIFE

★ **Harbour Station.** Musical and other types of performances take place at the Harbour Station hockey arena. ⊠ *99 Station St., Saint John, New Brunswick, Canada* ☎ *506/657–1234, 800/267–2800* ⊕ *www. harbourstation.ca.*

**O'Leary's Pub.** O'Leary's Pub, in the downtown historic district, specializes in old-time Irish fun complete with Celtic performers on off-season Tuesdays; on Wednesday, Brent Mason, a well-known neofolk artist, starts the evening and then turns the mike over to the audience, and Thursday to Saturday it's mostly live classic rock bands. ⊠ *46 Princess St., Saint John, New Brunswick, Canada* ☎ *506/634–7135* ⊕ *www. olearyspub.com.*

## SPORTS AND THE OUTDOORS

**Reversing Falls Jet Boat.** The Reversing Falls Jet Boat has 20-minute thrill rides in the heart of the Reversing Rapids (C$41.95). Be prepared for a wild ride and don't think for a second that the yellow slickers they supply will keep you dry—having a change of clothes in your car is an excellent idea. Size restrictions apply to the jet boat and bubble, and times depend on the tides. The company also offers more sedate one-hour sightseeing tours (C$41.95) along the rapids and up the river (departing instead from Market Square when there's a cruise ship in dock) June to mid-October, 10 am to dusk. ⊠ *100 Fallsview Ave., Saint John, New Brunswick, Canada* ☎ *506/634–8987, 888/634–8987* ⊕ *www.jetboatrides.com* ☉ *June–mid-Oct.*

**Saint John Adventures.** This is the place to go for zip-lining across the Reversing Rapids. ⊠ *50 Fallsview Ave., Saint John, New Brunswick, Canada* ☎ *506/634–9477, 877/634–9477* ⊕ *www.saintjohnadventures. ca* ☉ *Late May–Oct., daily 9–dusk.*

## SHOPPING

★ **Brunswick Square.** Brunswick Square, a large mall connected to the city's "Inside Connection" covered walkway, has many top-quality boutiques. ⊠ *King and Germain Sts., Saint John, New Brunswick, Canada* ☎ *506/658–1000.*

**Handworks Gallery.** Handworks Gallery carries the best professional crafts and fine art made in New Brunswick. ⊠ *12 King St., Saint John, New Brunswick, Canada* ☎ *506/652–9787* ⊕ *www.handworks.ca.*

**Peter Buckland Gallery.** Peter Buckland Gallery, open Tuesday through Saturday or by appointment, is an exceptional gallery that carries prints, photos, paintings, drawings, and sculpture by Canadian artists. ⊠ *80 Prince William St., Saint John, New Brunswick, Canada* ☎ *506/693–9721.*

**Trinity Galleries.** Trinity Galleries represents fine Maritime and Canadian artists. ⊠ *128 Germain St., Saint John, New Brunswick, Canada* ☎ *506/634–1611.*

**EN ROUTE**

**New River Beach.** Unlike most Bay of Fundy beaches, New River Beach is sandy and great for swimming, especially if you wait until the tide is coming in. The sun warms the sand at low tide, and the sand warms the water as it comes in. It's part of the New River Beach Provincial Park (C$8 vehicle entrance fee) that also offers interpretive programs, hiking trails, and kayak rentals. ⊠ *Off Hwy. 1, 50 km (30 mi) west of Saint John, Saint John, New Brunswick, Canada.*

# THE FUNDY COAST

Bordering the chilly and powerful tidal Bay of Fundy, where the world's most extreme tides rise and fall twice daily, is some of New Brunswick's most dramatic coastline. This area extends from the border town of St. Stephen and the lovely resort village of St. Andrews, past tiny fishing villages and rocky coves, through Saint John, and on through Fundy National Park and beyond. A vast area, encompassing inland areas and the coastline, is now designated the Stonehammer Geopark, with a dozen specific sites illustrating remarkable geological features formed over billions of years. The Fundy Isles—Grand Manan Island, Deer Island, and Campobello—are havens of peace that have lured harried mainlanders for generations. Some of the impressive 50-km (31-mi) stretch of coastline between St. Martins and Fundy National Park can be viewed from the Fundy Trail Parkway.

**Fundy Trail Parkway.** The Fundy Trail Parkway (⊕ *www.fundytrailparkway.com*) is 16 km (10 mi) of coastal roadway with a 16-km (10-mi) network of walking, hiking, and biking trails that lead to an interpretive center and suspension bridge at Big Salmon River. On the other side of the bridge is the 41-km (24-mi) Fundy Footpath for serious hikers. ⊠ *New Brunswick, Canada* ☎ *506/833–2019, 866/386–3987* 🎫 *C$5* ⊗ *Mid-May–mid-Oct.*

# ST. STEPHEN

*107 km (66 mi) west of Saint John.*

The elegant Ganong factory-outlet chocolate and candy store dominates the main street of St. Stephen, across the St. Croix River from Calais, Maine, and the small town is a mecca for chocoholics. Indeed, St. Stephen is known as "Chocolate Town." The Ganong brothers first opened a small grocery store in 1873 but soon began specializing in chocolate and candy making. Over the years, many chocolate-related innovations occurred here, including the production of the first chocolate candy bar with nuts in North America and the introduction of the heart-shaped box of chocolates (originally produced for Christmas but now a long-standing symbol of Valentine's Day). In early August "choctails," chocolate puddings, cakes, and all things chocolate are served during the Chocolate Festival, when you might see the "Chocolate Mousse" about town.

### GETTING HERE AND AROUND

St. Stephen is 114 km (71 mi) west of Saint John via Route 1, right up against the U.S. border at Calais, Maine.

### ESSENTIALS

**Visitor Information Town of St. Stephen** ⊠ *5 King St., corner Milltown Blvd., St. Stephen, New Brunswick, Canada* ☏ *506/466–7930* ⊕ *www.chocolatetown. ca.*

### EXPLORING

♺ **Chocolate Museum.** The Chocolate Museum, behind Ganong Chocolatier, explores the sweet history of candy making with hand-dipping videos and hands-on exhibits. ⊠ *73 Milltown Blvd., St. Stephen, New Brunswick, Canada* ☏ *506/466–7848* ⊕ *www.chocolatemuseum.ca* ⊟ *C$7.90* ⊙ *Mar.–Apr., weekdays 10–4; May–June, weekdays 10–4, Sat. 11–3; July–Aug., Mon.–Sat. 9:30–6:30, Sun. 11–3; Sept., Mon.–Sat. 10–4; Oct. and Nov., weekdays 10–4.*

**Ganong Chocolatier.** Ganong's famed hand-dipped chocolates and other candies are available at this factory store. ⊠ *73 Milltown Blvd., St. Stephen, New Brunswick, Canada* ☏ *506/465–5611* ⊙ *June–Aug., weekdays 8–7, Sat. 9–5, Sun. 10–5; Sept.–May, Mon.–Sat. 9–5.*

▌EN
ROUTE
**St. Croix Island.** St. Croix Island, an International Historic Site where explorers Samuel de Champlain and Sieur de Monts spent their first harsh winter in North America in 1604, can be seen from an interpretive park on Route 127, between St. Stephen and St. Andrews. ⊠ *St. Stephen, New Brunswick, Canada.*

# ST. ANDREWS BY-THE-SEA

*29 km (18 mi) southeast of St. Stephen.*

St. Andrews by-the-Sea, a designated National Historic District on Passamaquoddy Bay, is one of North America's prettiest resort towns. It has long been a summer retreat of the affluent, and mansions ring the town. Of the town's 550 buildings, 280 were erected before 1880, and 14 of those have survived from the 1700s. Some Loyalists even brought their

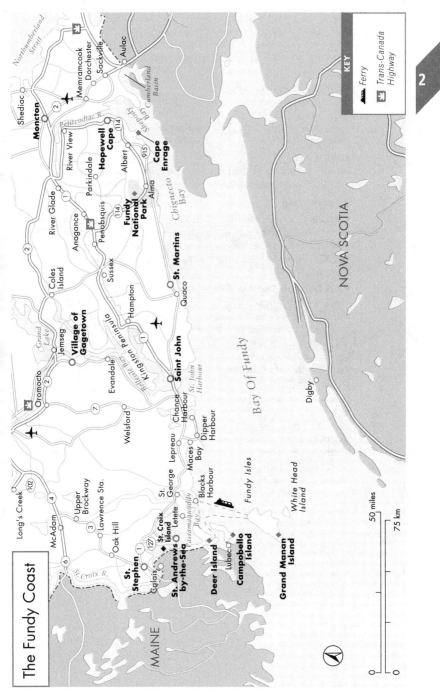

# The Fundy Coast

**KEY**

🚢 Ferry
🛫 Trans-Canada Highway

NOVA SCOTIA

Bay Of Fundy

Digby

Northumberland Strait

Shediac

Moncton

Memramcook
Dorchester
Sackville
Aulac

Petitcodiac R.

Cumberland Basin

River View

Hopewell Cape

Cape Enrage

River Glade

Parkindale

Albert

Alma

Anagance

Penobsquis

Fundy National Park

Chignecto Bay

Coles Island

Sussex

Hampton

St. Martins

Quaco

Village of Gagetown

Jemseg

Grand Lake

Evandale

Saint John

St. John Harbour

Oromocto

Welsford

Chance Harbour

Dipper Harbour

Lepreau

Maces Bay

Blacks Harbour

Fundy Isles

White Head Island

Long's Creek

McAdam

Upper Brockway

Lawrence Sta.

Oak Hill

St. George

Letete

St. Croix Island

St. Stephen

Calais

St. Andrews by-the-Sea

Deer Island

Lubec

Campobello Island

Grand Manan Island

St. Croix R.

MAINE

50 miles

75 km

homes with them piece by piece from Castine, Maine, across the bay, when the American Revolution didn't go their way. Pick up a walking-tour map at the visitor information center and follow it through the pleasant streets. Water Street, by the harbor, has eateries, gift and crafts shops, and artists' studios.

**GETTING HERE AND AROUND**

St. Andrews by-the-Sea is about 100 km (60 mi) west of Saint John via Highway 1 then Route 127. Once there, the Water Street and harbor area is delightfully walkable, but a car would be needed to get to some of the attractions.

**ESSENTIALS**

**Visitor Information St. Andrews** ⊠ *24 Reed Ave., in the arena, St. Andrews, New Brunswick, Canada* ☎ *506/529–3556, 800/563–7397.*

**EXPLORING**

**Charlotte County Courthouse.** A particular gem is the Charlotte County Courthouse, active since 1840 and a National Historic Site since 1983. Free tours are available during summer; check-in at the Old Gaol. ⊠ *123 Frederick St., St. Andrews by-the-Sea, New Brunswick, Canada* ☎ *506/529–4248.*

☼ **Fundy Discovery Aquarium.** In a superb new building that opened in 2011, this excellent aquarium is at the Huntsman Ocean Sciences Center, established more than a century ago. Marine exhibits include a huge tidal exhibit, teeming touch tanks, rare lobsters, sturgeon, and some very entertaining harbor seals fed at 11 and 4 daily, as well as free movies and slide shows. ⊠ *1 Lower Campus Rd., St. Andrews by-the-Sea, New Brunswick, Canada* ☎ *506/529–1200* ⊕ *www.huntsmanmarine. ca* ☜ *C$14* ☼ *Daily 10–5.*

**Greenock Church.** Greenock Church owes its existence to a remark made at an 1822 dinner party about the "poor" Presbyterians not having a church of their own. Captain Christopher Scott, who took exception to the slur, spared no expense on the building, which is decorated with a carving of a green oak tree in honor of Scott's birthplace, Greenock, Scotland. ⊠ *146 Montague St., St. Andrews by-the-Sea, New Brunswick, Canada* ☎ *No phone.*

**Fodor's Choice**
★
☼
**Kingsbrae Horticultural Garden.** Nearly 2,500 varieties of trees, shrubs, and plants cover the 27 acres of woodland trails and many theme gardens at the Kingsbrae Horticultural Garden and earned it a place among the "Top Five North American Gardens Worth Travelling For" in 2011. It is certainly one of Canada's most spectacular public gardens, including a garden specially designed for touch and smell, a rose garden, a bird and butterfly garden, and a gravel garden. A children's fantasy garden offers child-centered activities, and there are daily programs for kids under 12 (1:30 in July and August). Canada's first Wollemi pine, named Pericles, is a big attraction, as is the opportunity to participate in a ladybug release program every morning at 10:30. A Sculpture Garden features works by Don Pell and from the Beaverbrook collection, and Kingsbrae also has an art gallery and a café. ⊠ *220 King St., St. Andrews by-the-Sea, New Brunswick, Canada* ☎ *506/529–3335, 866/566–8687* ⊕ *www. kingsbraegarden.com* ☜ *C$14* ☼ *Mid-May–mid-Oct., daily 9–6.*

**Ministers Island.** This huge island estate, once completely self-sufficient, was the summer home of Sir William Van Horne, chairman of the Canadian Pacific Railway from 1899 to 1915. In summer, you can access the island by car, by bike, or on foot at low tide and by shuttle boat at high tide. Tours of the property include Covenhoven, Sir William's 50-room summer home; a tidal swimming pool; a livestock barn; a cottage; an old windmill; and the 1790 Minister's House from which the island takes its name. ■ TIP→ If you drive, walk, or bike over, be sure to leave the island before the tide comes in or you will be stuck for another six hours. Check the tide schedule in the paper or call ahead. ⊠ *Bar Rd. off Rte. 127, 5 km (3 mi) north of St. Andrews, St. Andrews by-the-Sea, New Brunswick, Canada* ☎ *506/529–5081 for tour information* ⊕ *www. ministersisland.com* ⊠ *C$15, includes boat and guided tour* ⊙ *Mid-May–mid-Oct., daily; times vary according to tides.*

**Old Gaol.** Directly adjacent to the courthouse, the stone-walled Old Gaol functioned as the town jail from 1834 to 1979. Today it houses the Charlotte County archives. Tours are available. ⊠ *123 Frederick St., St. Andrews by-the-Sea, New Brunswick, Canada* ☎ *506/529–4248* ⊠ *Free* ⊙ *May–June, weekdays 9–5; July–Aug., Mon.–Sat. 9–5.*

**Ross Memorial Museum.** The Ross Memorial Museum was established by an American couple who had a summer home in St. Andrews for 40 years. The Rosses donated the trappings of that home and an extensive collection of 19th-century New Brunswick furniture and decorative artwork to the town and purchased this 1824 Georgian mansion to house them. ⊠ *188 Montague St., St. Andrews by-the-Sea, New Brunswick, Canada* ☎ *506/529–5124* ⊠ *Donations accepted* ⊙ *Early June–mid-Oct., Mon.–Sat. 10–4:30.*

## WHERE TO EAT

$$$
SEAFOOD
**Fodor's**Choice
★

✕ **The Gables.** A relaxing, surprisingly affordable meal on the outdoor deck of the Gables is the perfect way to end a day of whale-watching or craft shopping. The lobster club sandwich is a favorite, but you won't be disappointed by the steaks, salmon, or lobster dinners at this casual harborside eatery. The hearty seafood chowder will warm the heart and soul on a foggy Fundy night, and homemade desserts top off the meal. The outdoor patio and deck offer breathtaking views of the harbor, and if you want to linger into the evening, when the winds come up, there are clean, warm fleece blankets available. The owner's art decorates the walls, and guests keep returning for the down-home, friendly service. ⊠ *143 Water St., St. Andrews by-the-Sea, New Brunswick, Canada* ☎ *506/529–3440.*

$$$
MODERN
CANADIAN

✕ **Niger Reef Tea House.** Overlooking the bay, with seating inside or out on a rustic deck, this 1926 former meeting house (of the Imperial Order of the Daughters of the Empire) is where red-seal chef David Peterson works his magic with locally sourced ingredients. Everything is top quality, from the simple but expertly produced lunchtime options— seafood chowder, sandwiches, frittata—to a select menu of imaginative offerings on the evening blackboard menu. These might include traditional cedar-planked salmon with a ginger glaze, or lamb shanks braised in tomato and red wine. While waiting for your meal, take a look at the splendid restored mural, painted by New York artist

Lucille Douglass (1877–1935)—once the food arrives it will have your full attention. Arrive early for dinner; the Tea House closes at 8 pm. ⊠ *1 Joes Point Rd., St. Andrews by-the-Sea, New Brunswick, Canada* ☎ *506/529–8005* ⊕ *www.nigerreefteahouse.com.*

$$$$ ✕ **Savour the Restaurant.** Accomplished young chef Alex Haun and his MODERN wife have transformed a modest house on the edge of town into a stylish CANADIAN restaurant in which to present his creative cuisine. Haun offers fixed-price three-course (C$38) and six-course (C$60) meals, based on what's market-fresh each day, and the fun part is that you show up and eat what he has chosen to cook that day. Typically, this will include nicely balanced dishes of some complexity, such as seared Fundy yellow-fin tuna with herb risotto, beet gastrique, buttered zucchini, sugar snap peas, cauliflower smear, savory foam, and beet powder. Local and organic ingredients and fair-trade imports reflect Haun's commitment to environmental issues. Savour's popularity is such that reservations need to be made at least 48 hours in advance, and might need two weeks in high season. ⊠ *4442 Rte. 127, Chamcook, St. Andrews by-the-Sea, New Brunswick, Canada* ☎ *506/529–4055* ⊕ *www.chefalexhaun.com* ⌂ *Reservations essential* ⊗ *No lunch; no dinner Mon. and Tues. Closed weekdays in winter.*

### WHERE TO STAY
*For expanded hotel reviews, visit Fodors.com.*

$ ⊡ **Fairmont Algonquin.** This grand old resort, where the bellhops wear ★ kilts and dinner is served on the wraparound veranda in fine weather, presides on a hill above town like an elegant dowager. **Pros:** personal service; luxurious surroundings; right on the golf course. **Cons:** some of the rooms in the older section are small. ⊠ *184 Adolphus St., St. Andrews by-the-Sea, New Brunswick, Canada* ☎ *506/529–8823* ⊕ *www.fairmont.com/algonquin* ⟳ *234 rooms* ⌂ *In-room: Wi-Fi. In-hotel: restaurant, bar, golf course, pool, tennis court, gym, spa, beach, children's programs, parking, some pets allowed.*

$$$ ⊡ **Kingsbrae Arms.** Expect excellent service from the hosts and staff at Fodor's Choice this restored 1897 estate, where eclectic antiques fill the rooms, and ★ pampering touches include plush robes and daily afternoon tea. **Pros:** lovely grounds, close to Kingsbrae Horticultural Garden; delicious local food prepared by creative chef. **Cons:** in winter the only meal offered is breakfast. ⊠ *219 King St., St. Andrews by-the-Sea, New Brunswick, Canada* ☎ *506/529–1897* ⊕ *www.kingsbrae.com* ⟳ *8 suites, 2 rooms* ⌂ *In-room: a/c, Internet. In-hotel: restaurant, pool, some pets allowed* ⫟ *Some meals.*

$ ⊡ **Montague Rose B&B.** In a good location, just two blocks back from the harbor, this lovely French empire–style home offers a warm welcome and individually styled, comfortable bedrooms. **Pros:** friendly hosts; good location close to all downtown attractions. **Cons:** bathrooms have either a shower or a tub, so specify which you would prefer; rooms vary in size. ⊠ *258 Montague St., St. Andrews by-the-Sea, New Brunswick, Canada* ☎ *506/529–8963, 888/529–8963* ⊕ *www.themontaguerose. com* ⟳ *4 rooms* ⌂ *In-room: no a/c, Wi-Fi* ⫟ *Breakfast.*

**2**

**$** ⛱ **Rossmount Inn Hotel Restaurant & Bar.** "Hospitality plus" easily defines this inn set on 87 acres at the base of Chamcook Mountain and the attitude of its charming owners. **Pros:** impeccable surroundings and details; fresh bay air is perfect for working up an appetite for the amazing dinners served on-site. **Cons:** some rooms are very small; stairways steep. ⊠ *4599 Rte. 127, St. Andrews by-the-Sea, New Brunswick, Canada* ☎ *506/529–3351* ⊕ *www.rossmountinn.com* ⤳ *18 rooms* ⚭ *In-room: no a/c, no TV, Wi-Fi. In-hotel: restaurant, bar, pool* ⊙ *Closed Jan.–Easter.*

**$$** ⛱ **Treadwell Inn.** This is one of the best locations in St. **Pros:** lovely views; good value; spacious rooms. **Cons:** fills up fast. ⊠ *129 Water St., St. Andrews by-the-Sea, New Brunswick, Canada* ☎ *506/529–1011, 888/529–1011* ⊕ *www.treadwellinn.com* ⤳ *7 rooms* ⚭ *In-room: a/c, kitchen, Wi-Fi* ⦿*Breakfast.*

## SPORTS AND THE OUTDOORS

**Sunbury Shores Arts & Nature Centre.** The Sunbury Shores Arts & Nature Centre offers art workshops in drawing, etching, painting, pottery, and many other media in conjunction with environmental excursions. ⊠ *139 Water St., St. Andrews by-the-Sea, New Brunswick, Canada* ☎ *506/529–3386.*

GOLF **Algonquin Golf Club.** The Algonquin Golf Club has a beautifully landscaped 18-hole, par-71 signature course designed by Thomas McBroom. The holes on the back 9—especially the 12th—have beautiful views of Passamaquoddy Bay, as does the Clubhouse Grill. ⊠ *Off Rte. 127, St. Andrews by-the-Sea, New Brunswick, Canada* ☎ *506/529–8165.*

WATER SPORTS Whale and nature cruises and kayak tours all begin at the town wharf.

**Eastern Outdoors.** Eastern Outdoors has single and double kayaks and mountain bikes for rent, as well as lessons, tours around Navy Island, and white-water kayaking. ⊠ *St. Andrews by-the-Sea, New Brunswick, Canada* ☎ *506/529–4662, 800/565–2925* ⊕ *www.easternoutdoors. com.*

**Fundy Tide Runners.** Fundy Tide Runners will take you out on their 24-foot Zodiacs to search for whales, seals, and marine birds. ⊠ *St. Andrews by-the-Sea, New Brunswick, Canada* ☎ *506/529–4481* ⊕ *www.fundytiderunners.com.*

**Quoddy Link Marine.** Quoddy Link Marine offers whale and wildlife tours for up to 47 passengers on a powered catamaran. ⊠ *St. Andrews by-the-Sea, New Brunswick, Canada* ☎ *506/529–2600* ⊕ *www. quoddylinkmarine.com.*

**Seascape Kayak Tours.** Seascape Kayak Tours provides instruction as well as trips around the area from a half day to a week. ⊠ *St. Andrews by-the-Sea, New Brunswick, Canada* ☎ *506/747–1884, 866/747–1884* ⊕ *www.seascapekayaktours.com.*

**Tall Ship Whale Adventures.** Tall Ship Whale Adventures operates the *Jolly Breeze,* an elegant vessel for whale-watching. ⊠ *St. Andrews by-the-Sea, New Brunswick, Canada* ☎ *506/529–8116.*

## SHOPPING

**Crocker Hill Store/Steven Smith Designs.** The Crocker Hill Store/Steven Smith Designs has art and other items for those who love gardens, birds, and dogs. ⊠ *45 King St., St. Andrews by-the-Sea, New Brunswick, Canada* ☏ *506/529–4303.*

**Garden by the Sea.** Garden by the Sea is an aromatic shop with fabulous flowers, soaps, and teas that specializes in all-natural body products including Bay of Fundy sea salts and ecoflowers. ⊠ *217 Water St., St. Andrews by-the-Sea, New Brunswick, Canada* ☏ *506/529–8905.*

**Naturally for Life: The Eco Store.** The name of the store gives a big clue to what's inside: an interesting range of eco-friendly cleaning materials, personal care, natural remedies, books, kids' stuff, bags, stationery, and teas. ⊠ *154 Water St., St. Andrews by-the-Sea, New Brunswick, Canada* ☏ *506/848–0044* ◷ *Jan.–Apr.*

**Oven Head Salmon Smokers.** You can observe the smoking process of some of New Brunswick's best salmon at Oven Head Salmon Smokers, where you can buy the finished product at the on-site store—you'll also see it for sale in local grocery stores and on the menu at many regional restaurants. ⊠ *101 Oven Head Rd., off Hwy. 1, Bethel, New Brunswick, Canada* ☏ *506/755–2507, 877/955–2507* ⊕ *www.ovenheadsmokers.com.*

**Serendipin' Art and the Little Big Art Gallery.** Serendipin' Art sells hand-blown glass, hand-painted silks, jewelry, and other crafts by New Brunswick artists. A second gallery next door has large works of original fine art, small furniture, and sculpture. In all, around 100 New Brunswick artists are represented. ⊠ *168–170 Water St., St. Andrews by-the-Sea, New Brunswick, Canada* ☏ *506/529–3327, 866/470–5500* ⊕ *www.serendipinart.ca.*

**Toose's.** Owner Pam Vincent's sense of style is reflected in the artsy, sometimes quirky, range of gifts, jewelry, greetings cards, homewares, and irresistible chocolate truffles in this upscale boutique. There's another one just like it in the town of Quispamsis. ⊠ *147 Water St., St. Andrews by-the-Sea, New Brunswick, Canada* ☏ *506/529–4040* ◷ *Jan.–May.*

# GRAND MANAN ISLAND

*35 km (22 mi) east of St. Andrews by-the-Sea to Blacks Harbour, 1½ hrs by car ferry from Blacks Harbour.*

Grand Manan, the largest of the three Fundy Islands, is also the farthest from the mainland. You might see whales, seals, or the occasional puffin on the way over. Circular herring weirs dot the island's coastal waters, and fish sheds and smokehouses lie beside long wharfs that reach out to bobbing fishing boats. Place names are evocative: Swallowtail, Southern Head, Seven Days Work, and Dark Harbour. It's easy to get around; only about 32 km (20 mi) of road lead from the lighthouse at Southern Head to the one at North Head. John James Audubon, that human encyclopedia of birds, visited the island in 1831, attracted by the more than 240 species of seabirds that nest here. The puffin may be the island's symbol, but whales are the stars. Giant finbacks, right whales, minkes, and humpbacks feed in the rich waters. With only

2,700 residents, it may seem remote and quiet, but there is plenty to do including birding, kayaking, whale-watching, and beachcombing. You can visit lighthouses, hike a heritage trail, visit the Whale and Seabird Research Station, or just hang around the busy wharves and chat with the fishermen. A day trip is possible, but you'll wish you had planned to stay at least one night.

### GETTING HERE AND AROUND

Ferry service to Grand Manan is provided by **Coastal Transport,** which leaves the mainland from Blacks Harbour, off Route 1, and docks at North Head on Grand Manan Island. Plan to be at the ferry early as it operates on a first-come, first-served basis. Cars are C$32.55, excluding the driver, payable on return passage from Grand Manan; adults are C$10.90.

**Adventure High** offers bike rentals and sea-kayak tours around the island.

### ESSENTIALS

**Kayak Tours Adventure High** ☎ 800/732–5492, 506/662-3563 ⊕ www. adventurehigh.com.

**Ferry Contact Coastal Transport** ☎ 506/662-3724 ⊕ www.coastaltransport.ca.

### WHERE TO STAY

*For expanded hotel reviews, visit Fodors.com.*

$ 🍽 **Compass Rose.** Two charming small homes on the water combine to give this lovely English-style country inn a cottage atmosphere. **Pros:** gorgeous views; comfortable beds; good location; close to the ferry terminal and whale-watching boats. **Cons:** traffic to/from the ferry can be noisy. ⊠ 65 Rte. 776, Grand Manan, New Brunswick, Canada ☎☎ 506/662–8570 ⊕ www.compassroseinn.com ➪ 6 rooms ⌂ In-room: no a/c. In-hotel: restaurant, parking, some age restrictions ❚⊙❚ Breakfast.

$ 🍽 **Inn at Whale Cove.** The main inn building here dates back to 1816 and has three guest rooms and a shared living room with a fireplace and library. **Pros:** great rustic feel; lovely property for wandering. **Cons:** restaurant not open all year. ⊠ 26 Whale Cottage Rd., off Whistle Rd., Grand Manan, New Brunswick, Canada ☎ 506/662–3181 ⊕ www. whalecovecottages.ca ➪ 3 rooms, 4 cottages, 2 apartments ⌂ In-room: no a/c, Wi-Fi. In-hotel: beach, some pets allowed.

$ 🍽 **Marathon Inn.** This mansion built by a sea captain sits on a hill overlooking the harbor and has lovely views. **Pros:** good food; pleasant hosts. **Cons:** rooms vary in size. ⊠ 19 Marathon La., Grand Manan, New Brunswick, Canada ☎ 506/662–8488 ⊕ www.marathoninn.com ➪ 24 rooms ⌂ In-room: a/c, no TV, Wi-Fi. In-hotel: restaurant, bar, pool, tennis court, parking, some pets allowed.

### SPORTS AND THE OUTDOORS

WHALE-WATCHING A whale-watching cruise from Grand Manan takes you well out into the bay. Dress warmly, but some boats have winter jackets, hats, and mittens on board for those who don't heed this advice.

**Sea Watch Tours.** Interpreters on Sea Watch Tours are very knowledgeable about the birds you might encounter on your cruise, as well as about the whales. Trips (C$63–$90) are four to five hours, late June through September. ✉ *New Brunswick, Canada* ☎ *877/662–8552* ⊕ *www. seawatchtours.com.*

**Seascape Kayak Tours.** Seascape Kayak Tours in St. Andrews-by-the-Sea provides visitors with high quality sea-kayaking experiences and responsible adventure tourism. Seascape has received international recognition for its sustainable tourism practices. ✉ *New Brunswick, Canada* ☎ *506/747–1884, 866/747–1884* ⊕ *www.seascapekayaktours.com.*

**Tourism New Brunswick.** For complete information on bird-watching, nature photography, hiking, cycling, horseback riding, sea kayaking, and whale-watching, contact Tourism New Brunswick. ⬢ *Box 12345, Fredericton, New Brunswick, Canada E3B 5C3* ☎ *800/561–0123* ⊕ *www.tourismnewbrunswick.ca.*

**Whales-n-Sails Adventures.** Whales-n-Sails Adventures uses a 60-foot sailboat to visit the whales. Trips (C$73.45, including tax, fish chowder, and hot drinks) are four to five hours, mid-June through mid-September. ✉ *New Brunswick, Canada* ☎ *506/662–1999, 888/994–4044* ⊕ *www. whales-n-sails.com.*

# DEER ISLAND

*50 km (31 mi) east of St. Andrews by-the-Sea to Letete, 30 min by free ferry from Letete.*

One of the pleasures of Deer Island is walking around the fishing wharves like those at Chocolate Cove. Exploring the island takes only a few hours; it's a mere 12 km (7 mi) long, varying in width from almost 5 km (3 mi) to a few hundred feet at some points.

### GETTING HERE AND AROUND

From Saint John travel west on Highway 1 and take the Saint George exit, then take Route 172 south, a total distance of about 85 km (53 mi). The ferry runs every 30 minutes from 6:30 am to 5 pm, then hourly, with the last one back to the mainland leaving at 10 pm. There is no bike rental on the island, so all but avid hikers will need a car.

### EXPLORING

**Deer Point.** At Deer Point, walk through a small nature park while waiting for the ferry to Campobello Island. Just a few feet offshore in the Western Passage, the **Old Sow**, the second-largest whirlpool in the world, is visible, but its intensity depends on the state of the tide. The water is always highly active, though, and porpoises can often be seen. ✉ *New Brunswick, Canada.*

### WHERE TO EAT AND STAY

*For expanded hotel reviews, visit Fodors.com.*

$$
CANADIAN
✗ **45th Parallel Restaurant.** Seafood is an integral part of home cooking on the island, especially at this motel restaurant. The lobster roll is renowned but you won't go wrong with other country diner options like fresh panfried haddock or scallops. Old-fashioned chicken dinners—baked chicken, stuffing, real gravy, mashed potatoes, veggies, and cranberry sauce—are served here, too. Flowers surround this casual

and friendly place, and a newly enlarged dining terrace overlooks Passamaquoddy Bay. ✉ *941 Hwy. 772, Fairhaven, New Brunswick, Canada* ☎ *506/747–2222 year-round, 506/747–2231 May–Oct.* ☉ *Closed weekdays Nov.–Mar.*

$    **Sunset Beach Cottage & Suites.** A modern property surrounded by natural beauty, this complex is right above a secluded cove. **Pros:** peaceful and relaxing. **Cons:** a bit of a slope up the path from the beach. ✉ *21 Cedar Grove Rd., Fairhaven, New Brunswick, Canada* ☎ *506/747–2972, 888/576–9990* ⊕ *www.cottageandsuites.com* ↪ *5 suites, 1 cottage* ⚒ *In-room: no a/c. In-hotel: pool.*

### SPORTS AND THE OUTDOORS

**Seascape Kayak Tours.** Two-hour, half-day, and full-day tours are available, and usually include sightings of wildlife, including seals, porpoises, whales, and bald eagles. ✉ *40 NW Harbour Branch Rd., Richardson, Deer Island, New Brunswick, Canada* ☎ *506/747–1884, 866/747–1884* ⊕ *www.seascapekayaktours.com.*

## CAMPOBELLO ISLAND

★ *40 mins by ferry (June to September) from Deer Island; 90 km (56 mi) southeast of St. Stephen via bridge from Lubec, Maine.*

Neatly manicured, preening itself in the bay, Campobello Island has always had a special appeal for the wealthy and the famous.

### GETTING HERE AND AROUND

From Saint John, follow the directions for Deer Island (above). Once on Deer Island, drive 12 km (7 mi) to its southern tip for the East Coast Ferries service to Campobello (C$16 for car and driver, C$3 for each adult passenger, and C$4 fuel surcharge), a journey of around 30 minutes. Ferries from Deer Island run hourly from 8:30 am to 6:30 pm. The company also runs a ferry from Eastport, Maine, to Campobello (C$13 for car and driver, C$3 for each adult passenger, and a C$4 fuel surcharge). Once there, a car is essential.

The ferry from Campobello to Deer Island departs on the hour, every hour, until 7 pm.

### EXPLORING

**Herring Cove Provincial Park.** The island's Herring Cove Provincial Park has camping facilities, a restaurant, a 9-hole, par-36 Geoffrey Cornish golf course, a sandy beach, and miles of hiking trails. ✉ *Welshpool, New Brunswick, Canada* ☎ *506/752–7010.*

**Roosevelt Campobello International Park.** The 34-room rustic summer cottage of the family of President Franklin Delano Roosevelt is now part of a nature preserve, Roosevelt Campobello International Park, a joint project of the Canadian and U.S. governments. The miles of trails here make for pleasant strolling. Roosevelt's boyhood summer home was also the setting for the 1960 movie *Sunrise at Campobello.* To drive here from St. Stephen (a trip of about 80 km [50 mi]), cross the border into Maine, drive down Route 1, and take Route 189 to Lubec, Maine, then cross the bridge to the island. ✉ *Roosevelt Park Rd., New Brunswick,*

*Canada* ☎ *506/752–2922* ✉ *Free* ☉ *House late May–mid-Oct., daily 10–5:45; grounds daily year-round.*

## WHERE TO STAY

*For expanded hotel reviews, visit Fodors.com.*

$ 🖭 **An Island Chalet.** With stunning coastal views from their windows and front porches, and beds for four people, these log cottages (in spite of the singular name, there are five of them) offer great value. **Pros:** close to the FDR Bridge and Roosevelt-Campobello International Park; plenty of space for the price, and a real bargain for a party of four. **Con:** cell phone reception can be unreliable; beach rather difficult to reach. ✉ *115 Narrows Rd., Welshpool, New Brunswick, Canada* ☎ *506/752–2971* ⊕ *anislandchalet.com* ⮌ *5 cottages* ⚲ *In-room: no a/c, kitchen, Wi-Fi.*

$ 🖭 **The Owen House.** Owned by artist Joyce Morrell, this lovely house, dating from 1835, retains many original features and is furnished with antiques. **Pros:** a really peaceful haven, free of everyday distractions; if you have to stay connected, the library next door has Wi-Fi. **Cons:** the only TV, in the sunroom, is only set up for video. ✉ *11 Welshpool St., Welshpool, New Brunswick, Canada* ☎ *506/752–2977* ⊕ *www. owenhouse.ca* ⮌ *9 rooms* ⚲ *In-room: no a/c, no TV. In-hotel: some age restrictions.*

# ST. MARTINS

*45 km (28 mi) east of Saint John.*

The fishing village of St. Martins has a rich shipbuilding heritage, whispering caves, miles of lovely beaches, spectacular tides, and a cluster of covered bridges, as well as several heritage inns and a couple of restaurants right on the beach. It's also the gateway to the spectacular Fundy Trail Parkway.

## GETTING HERE AND AROUND

From Saint John go north on Route 1, then head east on Route 111, past the airport, following signs for St. Martins. Coming from the Trans-Canada Highway (Route 2), exit onto Route 1 or Route 10; both will get you to Route 111, signposted St. Martins.

## EXPLORING

**Fundy Trail Parkway.** The scenic drive portion of the Fundy Trail Parkway extends to an interpretive center at Salmon River, and by 2013 will go all the way to the Fundy National Park. The road closely parallels the cycling-walking Fundy Trail along the shore. There are lots of places to park and many accessible scenic lookouts. The 41-km (24-mi) Fundy Footpath, for expert hikers, already continues through to the national park. The parkway portion operates mid-May through mid-October. ✉ *St. Martins, New Brunswick, Canada* ☎ *506/833–2019* ⊕ *www. fundytrailparkway.com* ✉ *C$5.*

## WHERE TO EAT AND STAY

*For expanded hotel reviews, visit Fodors.com.*

$ 🖭 **St. Martins Country Inn.** High on a hill overlooking the Bay of Fundy, this restored sea captain's home is furnished with Victorian antiques, including old-fashioned wallpaper and quilts. **Pros:** charming decor;

good food. **Cons:** some rooms are small. ⊠ *303 Main St., St. Martins, New Brunswick, Canada* ☎ *506/833–4534, 800/565–5257* ⊕ *www. stmartinscountryinn.com* ⇆ *16 rooms* ♿ *In-room: a/c. In-hotel: restaurant, bar.*

$ 🏨 **Tidal Watch Inn.** This luxurious property is situated just where the highest tides in the world sweep in and out each day, a mere 150 feet away! **Pros:** comfortable decor and atmosphere; good food. **Cons:** rooms vary in size; not all rooms have good views; Wi-Fi not reliable in some rooms. ⊠ *16 Beach St., St. Martins, New Brunswick, Canada* ☎ *506/833–4772* ⊕ *www.tidalwatchinn.ca* ⇆ *15 rooms* ♿ *In-room: Wi-Fi. In-hotel: restaurant, parking.*

$ 🏨 **Weslan Inn.** Fireplaces, antiques, and lots of floral prints give the rooms and the suite in this former sea captain's home an English country feel. **Pros:** true country charm in decor and service. **Cons:** watch out for mosquitoes on the lawn in the evenings. ⊠ *45 Main St., St. Martins, New Brunswick, Canada* ☎ *506/833–2351* ⊕ *www.weslaninn.com* ⇆ *3 rooms, 1 suite* ♿ *In-hotel: restaurant* �“❘*Breakfast.*

### SPORTS AND THE OUTDOORS

SKIING **Poley Mountain Resort.** Poley Mountain Resort has more than 100 skiable acres with a 660-foot vertical drop from a 910-foot summit, and five ski lifts. There are more than 30 trails, a snowboard park, and night skiing is also available. ⊠ *69 Poley Mountain Rd., Waterford, 10 km (6 mi) southeast of Sussex, St. Martins, New Brunswick, Canada* ☎ *506/433–7653* ⊕ *www.poleymountain.com.*

# FUNDY NATIONAL PARK

*135 km (84 mi) northeast of Saint John.*

### GETTING HERE AND AROUND

Fundy National Park is bisected by Route 114, which loops down along the coast from Moncton, via Riverview, enters the park at Alma, and continues back up to Sussex. From the Trans-Canada Highway (Route 2), exit onto Route 10 to Sussex, take Route 1 east for a short distance (signposted Moncton) before exiting onto Route 114 south. There are a number of parking places within the park.

### EXPLORING

**Alma.** The small seaside town of Alma services Fundy National Park with motels, restaurants that serve good lobster, and a bakery that sells sublime sticky buns. There's plenty to do around here—from birdwatching and kayaking to horseback riding. ⊠ *Alma, New Brunswick, Canada.*

Fodor'sChoice **Fundy National Park.** Fundy National Park is an incredible 206-square-
★ km (80-square-mi) microcosm of New Brunswick's inland and coastal climates. Park naturalists offer several programs each day, including beach walks and hikes to explore the park's unique climatic conditions and the fascinating evolution evident in the forests. The park has 100 km (60 mi) of varied hiking and mountain-biking trails, year-round camping, golf, tennis, a heated Bay of Fundy saltwater pool, and a playground. Among the most scenic of the trails is Laverty Falls, a 2.5-km

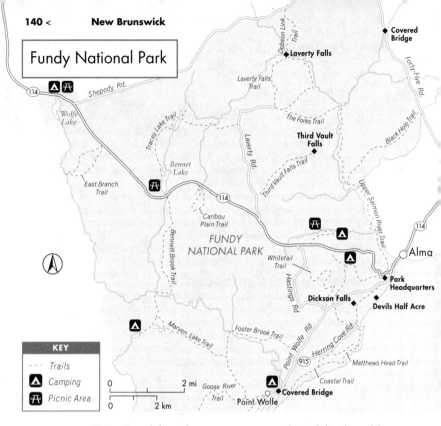

**Fundy National Park**

Covered Bridge

Laverty Falls

Laverty Falls Trail

The Forks Trail

Third Vault Falls

Shepody Rd.

Tracey Lake Trail

Wolfe Lake

Bennet Lake

East Branch Trail

Caribou Plain Trail

FUNDY NATIONAL PARK

Bennett Brook Trail

Laverty Rd.

Third Vault Falls Trail

Dobson Link Trail

Forty-Five Rd.

Black Hole Trail

Upper Salmon River Trail

Alma

Whitetail Trail

Hastings Rd.

Dickson Falls

Park Headquarters

Devils Half Acre

Marven Lake Trail

Foster Brook Trail

Point Wolfe Rd.

Herring Cove Rd.

Matthews Head Trail

Coastal Trail

Goose River Trail

Point Wolfe

Covered Bridge

**KEY**
- - - *Trails*
▲ *Camping*
🛆 *Picnic Area*

0      2 mi
0      2 km

(1.5-mi) trail that takes you on an ascent through hardwood forests to the beautiful Laverty waterfall and arrives at the old Shepody Road. At Third Vault Falls, a 3.7-km (2.3-mi) trail starting from the Laverty Auto Trail Parking Lot, hikers emerge at the falls and can take a refreshing dip in the pool. On the way to the Coppermine Trail, a hike to an abandoned mine at Point Wolfe, visitors wind around a steep curve and through a bright-red covered bridge, a favorite spot for photographers. In the evening there are interactive programs in the amphitheater and campfires. The more than 600 campsites range from full-service to wilderness. ✉ *Rte. 114, Alma, New Brunswick, Canada* ☎ *506/887–6000* ⊕ *www.pc.gc.ca* 🖃 *C$7.80.*

## WHERE TO STAY
*For expanded hotel reviews, visit Fodors.com.*

$ 🏨 **Falcon Ridge Inn.** Perched high above the village and the ocean, every window (and there are many) in this modern property affords a spectacular view and eliminates any need for air-conditioning. **Pros:** amazing view of the fishing boats of Alma and shale cliffs of Fundy. **Cons:** Fundy fog can unexpectedly block the vista; if you're walking down to the village, note that the property is on a steep slope. ✉ *24 Falcon Ridge Dr., Alma, New Brunswick, Canada* ☎ *506/887–1110, 888/321–9090*

⊕ *www.falconridgeinn.nb.ca* ⇥ *4 rooms* ⌂ *In-room: Wi-Fi. In-hotel: parking* ⦿ *Breakfast.*

$ ⊞ **Parkland Village Inn.** Right on the water yet in the heart of the bustling village, this long-established inn was given a C$100,000 makeover in 2010. **Pros:** view of the Bay of Fundy is extraordinary; nine of the guest rooms overlook the bay. **Cons:** can be hard to get a room in peak season; restaurant can be crowded in the peak tourist months of July and August. ⊠ *8601 Main St., Alma, New Brunswick, Canada* ☎ *506/887–2313* ⊕ *www.parklandvillageinn.com* ⇥ *10 rooms, 5 suites* ⌂ *In-room: no a/c, Wi-Fi. In-hotel: restaurant, bar, beach* ⊘ *Closed Nov.–Apr.* ⦿ *Breakfast.*

## SPORTS AND THE OUTDOORS

BIRD-WATCHING **Mary's Point.** Every summer the bit of shoreline at Mary's Point draws tens of thousands of migrating birds, including semipalmated sandpipers and other shorebirds. The area, now a bird sanctuary and interpretive center, is near Riverside-Albert. ⊠ *Follow signs off Rte. 915, Alma, New Brunswick, Canada.*

GOLF **Fundy National Park Golf Club.** The Fundy National Park Golf Club, one of the province's most beautiful and challenging 9-hole courses, is near cliffs overlooking the restless Bay of Fundy. ⊠ *Fundy National Park near the Alma entrance, Alma, New Brunswick, Canada* ☎ *506/887–2970.*

HORSEBACK RIDING **Broadleaf Guest Ranch.** Broadleaf Guest Ranch arranges trail rides through lowland marshes or along the beach, as well as overnight adventures in the forest. The Ranch Restaurant has themed evenings—for example, line dancing or roping instruction—and reservations are essential. There are also two-bedroom log cottages to rent, with all the comforts of home for C$150 (five people or less) to C$200 (six to eight people) a night. ⊠ *5526 Rte. 114, Hopewell Hill, New Brunswick, Canada* ☎ *506/882–2349, 800/226–5405* ⊕ *www.broadleafranch.com.*

SEA KAYAKING **Baymount Outdoor Adventures.** Baymount Outdoor Adventures offers sea kayaking around the Hopewell Rocks, as well as hiking and biking. ⊠ *Hopewell Rocks, Hopewell Cape, New Brunswick, Canada* ☎ *506/734–2660.*

**FreshAir Adventure.** FreshAir Adventure conducts Bay of Fundy sea-kayaking excursions that last from two hours to three days. Guides, instruction, and equipment are provided. ⊠ *16 Fundy View Dr., Alma, New Brunswick, Canada* ☎ *506/887–2249, 800/545–0020* ⊕ *www. freshairadventure.com.*

EN ROUTE Along routes 915 and 114 from Alma to Moncton are dozens of talented artists and craftspeople, many of whom open their studios and galleries to visitors. Visitor information centers have more information and maps.

**Kindred Spirits Stained Glass Studio.** Diana Winchester creates unique patterns with glass carefully chosen for its color and texture at this studio. ⊠ *2831 Main St., Hillsborough, New Brunswick, Canada* ☎ *506/734–2342.*

**Samphire Casuals.** In a large converted community hall Judy Tait makes pottery from local clay. ⊠ *902 Albert Mines Rd., off Rte. 114 near Hopewell, Alma, New Brunswick, Canada* ☎ *506/734–2851.*

**Studio on the Marsh.** Studio on the Marsh is the perfect setting for wildlife art. ⊠ *Marys Point Rd. off Rte. 915, Alma, New Brunswick, Canada* ☎ *506/882–2917.*

**Tim Isaac and Karin Bach's.** Many of owner Karin Bach's wildlife clay sculptures are on display in a lovely organic garden outside, and the gallery contains more of her pottery and paintings, along with works by other local artists and artisans. ⊠ *Rte. 915 between Alma and Riverside-Albert, Alma, New Brunswick, Canada* ☎ *506/882–2166.*

**Wendy Johnston's Pottery.** Wendy Johnston's Pottery sells contemporary, functional, brightly colored pieces with abstract designs. The new location also features the Art Effects Fine Craft Gallery, representing more than 45 Maritimes artists, and two bed-and-breakfast suites. ⊠ *3923 Rte. 114, Hopewell Cape, New Brunswick, Canada* ☎ *506/734–2046.*

## CAPE ENRAGE

*15 km (9 mi) east of Alma.*

Cape Enrage juts more than 7 km (4 ½ mi) out into the bay, with a 6-km (4-mi) driftwood-cluttered beach, a lighthouse, and spectacular views, as well as an adventure center with a restaurant.

### GETTING HERE AND AROUND

Just east of Alma, Route 915 branches right off Route 114, following a scenic route through Waterside. Look for a right turn on a minor road to Cape Enrage. Coming from the Hopewell Rocks end of the bay, Route 915 forks left off Route 114 at Riverside-Albert, and the Cape Enrage road is a left turn. There is an admission charge of C$4.50 mid-May–mid-October.

### ESSENTIALS

**Cape Enrage Interpretive Centre** ⊠ *650 Cape Enrage Road, Waterside* ☎ *506/887-2273 or 888/423-5454;* ⊕ *www.capeenrage.ca.*

### SPORTS AND THE OUTDOORS

**Cape Enrage Adventures.** Cape Enrage Adventures has rappelling and rock-climbing (C$78 for 2 hours), zip-lining (C$43), an obstacle course, beach hiking, guided tours of the lighthouse and beach (C$5 each), and more. Prices include the C$4.50 admission to the cape. Make reservations. A restaurant and a gift shop are on-site. ⊠ *650 Cape Enrage Rd., off Rte. 915, Cape Enrage, New Brunswick, Canada* ☎ *506/887–2273, 888/423-5454* ⊕ *www.capeenrage.ca.*

## HOPEWELL CAPE

*40 km (25 mi) northeast of Alma.*

The coastal road (Route 114) from Alma to Moncton winds through covered bridges and along rocky coasts.

2

#### GETTING HERE AND AROUND

Hopewell Cape is about 47 km (29 mi) south of Moncton, via Riverview, on Route 114. It is 190 km (118 mi) from Saint John, via Route 1 toward Moncton. Just beyond Sussex, take exit 211 onto Route 114 and continue through Fundy National Park, Alma, and Riverside-Albert.

### EXPLORING

Fodor's Choice ★ **Hopewell Rocks.** Hopewell Rocks is home to the famous Giant Flowerpots—rock formations carved by the Bay of Fundy tides. They're topped with vegetation and form tiny islands at high tide, while low tide reveals the entire columns and you can descend to the exposed seabed for closer study. There are also trails, an interactive visitor center, sea-kayaking tours, a café-restaurant, a gift shop, and a children's play area. It's quite a long walk from the visitor center to the rocks, but a shuttle service (C$2 each way) is available. Be careful. The tide comes in very quickly, so check tide tables, keep an eye on your watch, and exit the beach with time to spare. ✉ *131 Discovery Rd., Hopewell Cape, New Brunswick, Canada* ☎ *877/734–3429* 🌐 *www.thehopewellrocks.ca* *C$9* ⊙ *May–Oct., daily 9–7; closing hrs vary slightly, so call ahead.*

### WHERE TO STAY

*For expanded hotel reviews, visit Fodors.com.*

$ **Florentine Manor Heritage Inn.** With silver candlesticks on the dining-room table and handmade quilts on the beds, this restored shipbuilder's house is a haven for honeymooners and romantics. **Pros:** comfortably decorated, but not overstuffed rooms; abundant bird life; good food. **Cons:** corkage fee charged for bring-your-own wine. ✉ *356 Rte. 915, Harvey on the Bay, New Brunswick, Canada* ☎ *506/882–2271, 800/665–2271* 🌐 *www.florentinemanor.com* *9 rooms* *In-room: no a/c, Internet. In-hotel: parking, some age restrictions* *Breakfast.*

$ **Innisfree Bed and Breakfast.** An 1847 farmhouse just minutes from Hopewell Rocks now provides stylish and comfortable accommodations in rooms furnished with antiques and quilts. **Pros:** closest bed-and-breakfast to Hopewell Rocks; friendly, helpful hosts; mountain bikes for rent. **Cons:** watch out for mosquitoes in summer. ✉ *4270 Hwy. 114, Hopewell Cape, New Brunswick, Canada* ☎ *506/734–3510* 🌐 *www.innisfreebandb.com* *5 rooms* *In-room: no a/c, Wi-Fi. In-hotel: some age restrictions* *Breakfast.*

### SHOPPING

**Farm Life Studio.** Normand Brandford's paintings and prints reflect his affinity with farm animals—some living examples of the subject matter look on from the surrounding pastures—as well as local wildlife, landscapes, and nostalgic scenes. ✉ *474 Albert Mines Rd., Albert Mines, Hopewell Cape, New Brunswick, Canada* ☎ *506/734–3493* ⊙ *Oct.–May.*

## MONCTON

*80 km (50 mi) northeast of Alma.*

Metro Moncton—the second largest city in Atlantic Canada (after Halifax, Nova Scotia)—is an attractive, welcoming city, with several family-friendly attractions. There is an ongoing calendar of festivals throughout the year. The World Wine and Food Expo and the annual Santa Claus Parade of Lights draw more than 100,000 people in November, as do the HubCap Comedy Festival in February and the Northrop Frye Festival, the largest bilingual literary festival in Canada, in April. The annual outdoor summer concert at Magnetic Hill, by the likes of U2, The Rolling Stones, and The Eagles, is especially popular, while year-round entertainment is provided at the historic Capitol Theatre, the new casino's concert hall, and smaller venues.

An agreeable, lively place, and home to two universities, Moncton is often called the Gateway to Acadia because of its equal mix of English and French and its proximity to the Acadian shore, though it also has a large Irish population and a growing Korean community. Moncton has a renovated downtown with unique shops and restaurants and such beautiful flowers that it has won national "Communities in Bloom" awards. It is also beginning to make the most of its downtown riverside, with a park and boardwalk.

The twin cities of Moncton and Dieppe—the join is almost imperceptible—are considered the shopping mecca of Atlantic Canada. Moncton's big chain stores are mostly strung out along Mountain Road and the Trinity Power Centre, while Dieppe is home to the Champlain Place shopping mall, a good Saturday farmers' market, and other retail opportunities.

This city has long touted two natural attractions: the Tidal Bore and the Magnetic Hill, though you might be disappointed if you've read too much about either of them. Nevertheless, it's worth experiencing Magnetic Hill, and the city has a program underway to restore the Tidal Bore to its former glory, diminished over the years by riverbank erosion.

### GETTING HERE AND AROUND

Moncton is one of the few places in the province accessible by rail, on VIA Rail's Montréal—Halifax route known as "The Ocean." It also has one of the province's major airports. By road, the Trans-Canada Highway (Route 2) loops around the city, with several exit points.

Moncton has an excellent bus system, operated by Codiac Transit; the fare is C$2, or you can buy a 10-trip pass for C$18 or a 20-day pass for C$34.50, available from the bus station at 140 Millennium Boulevard or Shoppers Drug Marts (⊠ 535 Edinburgh Dr. or 860 Mountain Rd.). Free transfers are available from the driver if you need to change buses to get to a single destination. Buses are equipped with bike racks, so you can bike and ride to different destinations. Acadian Lines provides intercity and interprovincial bus service.

Roads to Sea offers day tours of the city and of some of the province's natural wonders.

### ESSENTIALS

Bus Information **Acadian Lines** ☎ 800/567-5151 ⊕ www.acadianbus.com. **Codiac Transit** ☎ 506/857-2008 ⊕ www.codiactranspo.ca.

Tour Information **Roads to Sea** ☎ 506/850-7623 ⊕ www.roadstosea.com.

Visitor Information **Go Moncton** ☎ 800/363-4558 ⊕ www.tourism.moncton.ca.

## TOP ATTRACTIONS

☺ **Crystal Palace.** A stop here is virtually guaranteed to win beleaguered parents adoring looks from their children. With more than a dozen indoor rides and attractions, including miniature golf, laser tag, a climbing wall, and an arcade, this is a popular vacation spot for families and especially convenient if you stay at the adjacent Ramada *(see below)*. Rides include a wave swinger and a low-rise bullet roller coaster. ⊠ *499 Paul St., across from Champlain Place, Dieppe, Moncton, New Brunswick, Canada* ☎ *506/859–4386, 877/856–4386* ⊕ *www.crystalpalace. ca* ✇ *C$74.60 pass for a family of four for one day* ⊙ *End of June–early Sept., daily 10–9; Sept.–June, Mon.–Thurs. noon–8, Fri. noon–9, Sat. 10–9, Sun. 10–8.*

☺ **Magnetic Hill Zoo.** The Magnetic Hill Zoo, the largest zoo in Atlantic Canada, has no shortage of exotic species, including lemurs, lions and other big cats, zebras, and ostrich. A tropical house has reptiles, amphibians, birds, and primates, and at Old MacDonald's Barnyard, children can pet domestic animals or ride a pony in summer. ⊠ *125 Magic Mountain Rd., off Trans-Canada Hwy. Exit 450 on the outskirts of Moncton, Moncton, New Brunswick, Canada* ☎ *506/877–7718* ✇ *C$6.50, C$9.74, or C$1.25, depending on season* ⊙ *Apr.–late May, daily 10–4; late May–early Sept., daily 9–7; early Sept.–late Oct., weekdays 10–6, weekends 9–6.*

☺ **Magic Mountain Water Park.** An excellent water theme park, Magic Mountain Water Park is adjacent to Magnetic Hill. It includes thrill-ride body slides as well as gentler fun. ⊠ *Off Trans-Canada Hwy. Exit 450 on the outskirts of Moncton, Moncton, New Brunswick, Canada* ☎ *506/857–9283, 800/331–9283 in Canada* ⊕ *www.magicmountain. ca* ✇ *C$25.50* ⊙ *Mid–late June and mid-Aug.–early Sept., daily 10–6; July–mid-Aug., daily 10–7.*

☺ **Magnetic Hill.** Magnetic Hill creates a bizarre optical illusion. If you park your car in neutral at the designated spot, you seem to be coasting uphill without power. Don't be tempted to turn the vehicle around; the effect is most pronounced when you are going backwards. Shops, a restaurant, the largest water park in Atlantic Canada, an award-winning zoo, a golf course, and a small railroad are part of the larger complex here (there are extra charges for the attractions). ⊠ *North of Moncton off Trans-Canada Hwy. Exit 450; watch for signs, Moncton, New Brunswick, Canada* ☎ *506/384–9527* ⊕ *www.magnetichill.com* ✇ *C$5* ⊙ *May–early Sept., daily 8–7.*

★ **Riverfront Park.** The 5 km (3.1 mi) of multiuse trail along the banks of the Petitcodiac River are a delight for walkers, joggers, and bicyclers. Bore Park is a good place from which to view the Tidal Bore. ⊠ *Assomption Blvd., Moncton, New Brunswick, Canada.*

**Tidal Bore.** A multimillion-dollar restoration program, due for completion in 2013, is working to restore one of Moncton's prime natural attractions. In days gone by, before the Petitcodiac River's flow was reduced by construction of a causeway and the harbor mouth filled with silt, the Tidal Bore was an incredible sight, a high wall of water that surged in through the narrow opening of the river to fill red mud banks to the brim. It still moves up the river and is worth seeing, but when the project is completed it will once again be a raging torrent. Riverfront Park on Main Street is the best vantage point; viewing times are posted. At low tide the muddy river bottom is often visible, but within an hour of the arrival of the Bore, the water level rises about 7½ meters (roughly 25 feet) and fills the river to its banks. ⊠ *Moncton, New Brunswick, Canada.*

## WORTH NOTING

**Aberdeen Cultural Centre.** The halls of the Aberdeen Cultural Centre, a converted schoolhouse home to theater and dance companies, a framing shop, artists' ateliers, and several galleries, ring with music and chatter. **Galerie 12** represents leading contemporary Acadian artists. **Galerie Sans Nom** is an artist-run co-op supporting avant-garde artists from throughout Canada. The artist-run **IMAGO Inc.** is the only print-production shop in the province. Guided tours are available by appointment. ⊠ *140 Botsford St., Moncton, New Brunswick, Canada* ☎ *506/857–9597* ✉ *Free* ⊘ *Weekdays 10–4.*

**Acadian Museum.** The Acadian Museum, at the University of Moncton, has a remarkable collection of artifacts reflecting 300 years of Acadian life in the Maritimes. There's also a fine gallery showcasing contemporary art by local and national artists. ⊠ *Clement Cormier Bldg., Université Ave, Moncton, New Brunswick, Canada* ☎ *506/858–4088* ✉ *C$4* ⊘ *Open weekdays 9–5, weekends 1–5; winter hours may differ, call to check.*

**Lutz Mountain Heritage Museum.** At Lutz Mountain Heritage Museum you'll find genealogical records of the area's non-Acadian pioneer settlers from as far back as 1766. With more than 3,000 artifacts, there's plenty to see at this hands-on museum. ⊠ *3143 Mountain Rd., Moncton, New Brunswick, Canada* ☎ *506/384–7719* ⊕ *www.lutzmtnheritage.ca* ✉ *C$2 donation suggested* ⊘ *Mid-June–mid-Sept., Mon.–Sat. 9:30–5:30; rest of year by appointment.*

**Moncton Museum.** Comprehensive exhibits trace the city's history from the days of the Mi'Kmaq people to the present at the Moncton Museum. ⊠ *20 Mountain Rd., Moncton, New Brunswick, Canada* ☎ *506/856–4383* ✉ *By donation* ⊘ *Mon.–Sat. 9–4:30, Sun. 1–5.*

## WHERE TO EAT

$$$
CANADIAN
★

✕ **Little Louis' Oyster Bar.** Some of the best food in Canada can be experienced at this out-of-the-way location on a predominantly industrial street. Oysters are, of course, a highlight, but there is much more to Chef Pierre Richard's Modern French menu, in creations such as lamb loin chops crusted with dried grapes with curry shank ravioli, cucumber yogurt, tomato tuille, kalamata emulsion, and pea shoots, or arctic char with air-dried chorizo, quinoa tabbouleh, mango, kumquat, fresh mint, and endive marmalade sauce. Desserts to leave you speechless, an award-winning wine list, and impeccable service complete the experience. ⊠ *245 Collishaw St., Moncton, New Brunswick, Canada* ☎ *506/855–2022* ⊕ *www.littlelouis.ca* ⊘ *No lunch.*

$$
ITALIAN

✕ **Pastalli Italian Cucina.** Seafood, steaks, lamb, and veal share the menu with pasta and pizzas at this upbeat Italian resto where Old World flavors are showcased in a friendly New World setting. The portions are large, and the bread bar is almost as popular as the World Wine Cellar, where wine is sold by weight so you can try different kinds with different courses. ✉ *611 Main St., Moncton, New Brunswick, Canada* ☎ *506/383–1050* ⊕ *www.pastalli.com.*

**$$$** ✕ **Pisces by Gaston.** Seafood of all types is the obvious star on the creative menu—local seafood goes into dishes such as hazelnut halibut, lobster linguine, and baked stuffed lobster, for example—but there are turf options, like proscuitto chicken, to go with your surf. Casual elegance is the theme. ✉ *300 Main St., Moncton, New Brunswick, Canada* ☎ *506/854–0444* ⊕ *www.piscesbygaston.com.*

SEAFOOD

**$$$** ✕ **St James' Gate.** Named after the Guinness brewery in Dublin, this is by no means the standard idea of an Irish-theme pub. It is as authentic a re-creation of an ancient vaulted stone cellar as you will find, providing an atmospheric location to enjoy the accomplished cooking of head chef Emanuel Brison. The menu is strong on local seafood, such as halibut baked with a pistachio crust and curry maple glaze. Meat dishes are equally delicious, and the menu includes snacks, lighter meals, and pub favorites. There's a central, dark-wood bar, a street-side patio, and live music five nights a week. Upstairs is a chic 10-room boutique hotel. ✉ *14 Church St., Moncton, New Brunswick, Canada* ☎ *506/388–4283* ⊕ *www.stjamesmoncton.com/stjamesgate* ⊗ *No dinner Sun.*

ECLECTIC

**$$** ✕ **Tide and Boar.** The name is not only a reference to the seafood and boar on the menu, it also hints at this classy modern gastro-pub's proximity to Moncton's tidal bore. With main floor, basement, and patio seating, you can choose from a well-constructed menu that includes upscale pub favorites and inventive combinations of flavors. The drinks menu is long, focusing mainly on draught and bottled craft beers. There's live music on Saturdays. ✉ *700 Main St., Moncton, New Brunswick, Canada* ☎ *506/857–9118* ⊕ *www.tideandboar.com.*

ECLECTIC

## WHERE TO STAY

*For expanded hotel reviews, visit Fodors.com.*

**$** 🏨 **Casino Hotel.** Opened in the summer of 2010, this five-story hotel is part of the Casino New Brunswick complex and is linked to the gaming rooms and entertainment center via an interior walkway. **Pros:** friendly and helpful staff; very good value, even without the regular special offers on room prices. **Cons:** food service is in the casino (age limit 19 years), so the only option for younger guests is room service or a summer-only Continental breakfast room; it's quite a walk to the restaurant. ✉ *21 Casino Dr., off Rte. 2 (Trans-Canada Hwy.), exit 450, Moncton, New Brunswick, Canada* ☎ *506/859–7770 859–7775* ⊕ *www.casinonb.ca* ⤴ *95 rooms, 31 suites* ⚐ *In-room: a/c, kitchen, Wi-Fi. In-hotel: pool, gym, spa, parking* ⦿ *No meals.*

**$$** 🏨 **Château Moncton Hotel & Suites.** This modern re-roofed châteaulike hotel stretches along the Petitcodiac River, with an extensive riverfront walking trail right out back, and is close to downtown businesses, large shopping malls, restaurants, and theaters. **Pros:** convenient location; pleasant atmosphere. **Cons:** geared to business travelers; no restaurant on-site. ✉ *100 Main St., Moncton, New Brunswick,*

*Canada* ☎ *506/870–4444, 800/576–4040* ⊕ *www.chateau-moncton. nb.ca* ⤴ *106 rooms, 12 suites* ♿ *In-room: a/c, Internet. In-hotel: bar, gym, parking* ⦿ *Breakfast.*

$

★ ▦ **Delta Beauséjour.** In a great downtown location, this is one of Moncton's finest and friendliest hotels, catering not only to business travelers, but also to families—particularly since its 38-meter (125-foot) indoor waterslide was added to the pool area. **Pros:** right in the hub of downtown shopping, restaurants, and businesses. **Cons:** some rooms are still to be refurbished in the ongoing program of improvements. ⊠ *750 Main St., Moncton, New Brunswick, Canada* ☎ *506/854–4344, 888/351–7666* ⊕ *www.deltahotels.com* ⤴ *298 rooms, 6 suites* ♿ *In-room: a/c, Internet. In-hotel: restaurant, pool, gym, spa, business center, parking, some pets allowed.*

$$

☾ ▦ **Ramada Plaza Crystal Palace.** Part of the Crystal Palace indoor amusement complex, this hotel has a sunny, tropical-look indoor pool at its heart, with pool-side rooms with patios, pool-view rooms, theme rooms (nautical, rock and roll, Victorian, library), and suites with Jacuzzis. **Pros:** excellent service and indoor access to the amusement park make this a great place for families. **Cons:** can feel overrun with children; themed rooms are cute, but some are not particularly spacious. ⊠ *499 Paul St., Dieppe, New Brunswick, Canada* ☎ *506/858–8584, 800/561–7108* ⊕ *www.crystalpalacehotel.com* ⤴ *115 rooms, 21 suites* ♿ *In-room: a/c, Wi-Fi. In-hotel: restaurant, pool, gym, children's programs.*

## NIGHTLIFE AND THE ARTS

**Casino New Brunswick.** Opened in 2010, the casino offers gaming tables and slots, an adjacent hotel, a restaurant, a pub, and a large, state-of-the-art concert hall with a lineup that ranges from George Thorogood and the Destroyers to Glen Campbell. ⊠ *21 Casino Dr., Moncton, New Brunswick, Canada* ☎ *506/859–7770, 877/859–7775.*

**iRock.** A young crowd comes for DJs playing loud dance music into the early hours. Friday is Ladies Night. ⊠ *415 Elmwood Dr., Moncton, New Brunswick, Canada* ☎ *506/384–4324.*

**Navigators Pub.** An antidote to the trendy Rouge next door, Navigators Pub is a no-frills downtown watering hole offering live jazz on Sundays, folk and blues on Mondays, and rock on Wednesdays. ⊠ *191 Robinson Crt., Moncton, New Brunswick, Canada* ☎ *506/854–8427.*

**The Old Triangle Irish Alehouse.** The Old Triangle Irish Alehouse is a good re-creation of the quintessential Dublin pub, with a buzzing atmosphere, good food, and live music Wednesday through Sunday—some Irish, some easy listening. ⊠ *751 Main St., Moncton, New Brunswick, Canada* ☎ *506/384–7474* ⊕ *www.oldtriangle.com.*

**Pump House Brewery.** In addition to the house brews at the Pump House Brewery, you can enjoy live music Saturday nights; the pub is a venue for the HubCap Comedy Festival in February. ⊠ *5 Orange La., Moncton, New Brunswick, Canada* ☎ *506/855–2337.*

## SPORTS AND THE OUTDOORS

The Moncton area is home to two of New Brunswick's four signat golf courses.

**Fox Creek Golf Club.** Fox Creek Golf Club offers an exceptional 6,065-yard course and a 9,000-square-foot clubhouse with a restaurant and pro-shop. It's fast becoming famous for its architectural and natural beauty. Club and cart rentals available. ⊠ *200 Golf St., Dieppe, Moncton, New Brunswick, Canada* ☎ *506/859–4653* ⊕ *www.foxcreekgolfclub.ca.*

**Royal Oaks Golf Club.** Royal Oaks Golf Club is an 18-hole, par-72 PGA Championship course, the first Canadian course designed by the American golf course architect Rees Jones. ⊠ *1746 Elmwood Dr., Moncton, New Brunswick, Canada* ☎ *506/388–6257, 866/769–6257 in Canada* ⊕ *www.royaloaks.ca.*

**TreeGO Moncton.** Children and adults can clamber through the treetops of Centennial Park, negotiating swinging rope-suspended logs, rope ladders, and zip lines, all while safely harnessed. Parents can watch their kids' progress from the ground. Adults embark on four courses, each more challenging than the last. Reservations required. Allow at least three hours, as there are many other things to do in the 230-acre park, including a SplashPark for children. ⊠ *Centennial Park, 811 St. George Blvd., Moncton, New Brunswick, Canada* ☎ *506/388–4646, 877/707–4646* ⊕ *www.treegomoncton.com* ☑ *C$34* ☉ *May–mid-Oct., 9:30–5.*

## SHOPPING

Dieppe's Champlain Mall and Moncton downtown boutiques make the twin cities one of New Brunswick's major shopping destinations. There's also quite a network of secondhand clothing stores—the Frenchy's chain is outstanding—with some amazing designer bargains. Farmers' markets in both cities and Moncton's new Artisan Village focus on quality foods, arts, and crafts from local producers.

**Artisan Village.** Downtown Moncton's new Artisan Village is an ambitious and exciting transformation of a former bus depot/car dealership into an open-concept community of artists and craftspeople, the only one of its kind in the Maritimes. Metal artist Shane Myers is the visionary at the forefront of the project, which will eventually include up to a dozen ateliers, a gallery and an upscale boutique, a café-bar and a "world-cuisine village," a lecture hall, and plenty of opportunities for the public to interact with some of the province's finest artisans. ⊠ *465 Main St., Moncton, New Brunswick, Canada* ☎ *506/532–0091.*

**Champlain Place.** Champlain Place is a huge mall with more than 150 shops. ⊠ *477 Paul St., Dieppe, New Brunswick, Canada* ☎ *506/855–6255* ⊕ *www.champlainplace.com.*

**Dieppe Market.** Every Saturday, the Dieppe Market brims with fresh produce, baked goods, ethnic cuisine, crafts, and music from 7 am to 1:30 pm. ⊠ *333 Acadie Ave., Dieppe, Moncton, New Brunswick, Canada* ⊕ *www.marchedieppemarket.com.*

**Marché Moncton Market.** The Marché Moncton Market buzzes on Saturdays from 7 to 2, and vendors serve delicious ethnic lunches Monday through Saturday. ⊠ *120 Westmorland St., Moncton, New Brunswick, Canada* ☎ *506/389-5969* ⊕ *www.marchemonctonmarket.ca.*

# THE ACADIAN COAST AND ST. JOHN RIVER VALLEY

History and nature meet on the Tantramar salt marshes east of Moncton. Bounded by the upper reaches of the Bay of Fundy, the province of Nova Scotia, and the Northumberland Strait, the region is rich in history and culture. The inspiration for Canadian artists such as Alex Colville and of poets from Sir Charles G. D. Roberts to Douglas Lochhead, the marshes provide a highly productive wetland habitat, and the region is among North America's major migratory bird routes.

The white sands and gentle tides of the Northumberland Strait and Baie des Chaleurs are in stunning contrast to the rocky cliffs and powerful tides of the Bay of Fundy. Along the Acadian Coast the water is warm, the sand is fine, and the food delicious. Many people here find their livelihood in the forests, in the mines, and on the sea, and along the Acadian Peninsula working wharves are an attraction within themselves.

## DORCHESTER AND MEMRAMCOOK

*Memramcook is 24 km (15 mi) southeast of Moncton. Dorchester is 14 km (9 mi) south of Memramcook.*

Memramcook and Dorchester are on opposite sides of a marsh, each surrounded by the gentle, rolling landscape filled with colorful native grasses. Acadian roots run deep in Memramcook, while Dorchester was a center of British culture and industry long before the Loyalists landed and is home to some of the province's oldest buildings.

### GETTING HERE AND AROUND

Memramcook and Dorchester are 24 km (15 mi) and 38 km (24 mi) southeast of Moncton via Route 106 through Dieppe. From the Trans-Canada Highway (Route 2), take exit 488 for Memramcook and exit 482 (Renaissance Street) for Dorchester. Route 106 (Royal Road) links the two towns.

### ESSENTIALS

**Visitor Information Center** ⊠ *4984 Main St., Dorchester, New Brunswick, Canada* ☎ *506/379-3030* ☉ *June–Aug. Mon.–Sat. 9–5, Sun. noon–5; Sept.–May Mon.–Fri. 8:30–1.*

**Visitor Information Center** ⊠ *480 Centrale St., Memramcook, New Brunswick, Canada* ☎ *506/758-9808* ☉ *Daily 9–5.*

### EXPLORING

**Keillor House, Coach House Museum, and St. James Church.** Keillor House, Coach House Museum, and St. James Church are all museums. Keillor House is an early Regency stone house containing thousands of artifacts relating to mid-18th-century life; guides are in costume. A minute away

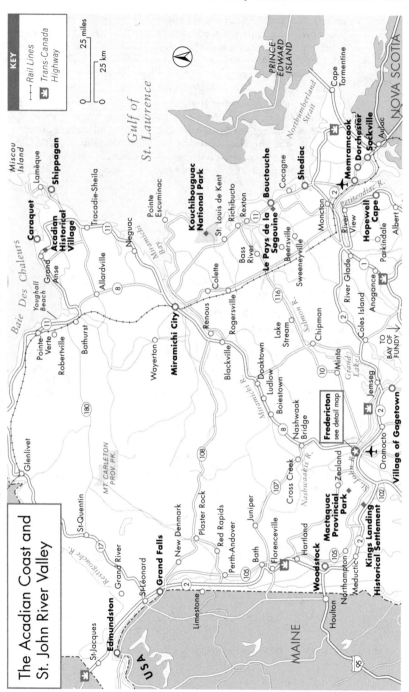

The Acadian Coast and St. John River Valley

on foot, St. James Church is also known as St. James Textile Museum. The Coach House, part of the Keillor property, contains a fascinating collection of artifacts from the Dorchester Penitentiary. ✉ *4974 Main St., Dorchester, New Brunswick, Canada* ☎ *506/379–6633* ⊕ *www. keillorhousemuseum.com* 🖾 *C$3 Keillor House, C$2 St. James Church* ⊙ *June–mid-Sept., Tues.–Sat. 10–5, Sun. noon–5.*

**Monument Lefebvre National Historic Site.** The Monument Lefebvre National Historic Site, in Memramcook, is in the original home of St. Joseph's College, the first degree-granting French-language institution in Atlantic Canada, founded by Camille Lefebvre in 1864. ✉ *480 Central St., Memramcook, New Brunswick, Canada* ☎ *506/758–9808* ⊕ *www.pc.gc.ca* 🖾 *C$3.90* ⊙ *June–mid-Oct., daily 9–5; mid-Oct.– May, by appointment.*

### WHERE TO EAT

$     ✕ **Bell Inn Restaurant.** This restaurant on the village square in Dorchester
CANADIAN  was built in 1811 as a stagecoach stop and is reputed to be the oldest stone structure in New Brunswick. Wander through the three dining rooms while you wait for an old-fashioned, delicious roast turkey dinner; the homemade desserts are particularly delectable. ✉ *3515 Cape Rd., off Rte. 106, Dorchester, New Brunswick, Canada* ☎ *506/379– 2580* ⊙ *Closed Mon. and Tues.*

### SPORTS AND THE OUTDOORS

**Johnson's Mills Shorebird Reserve.** The beaches at Johnson's Mills Shorebird Reserve are an internationally recognized staging area for migratory shorebirds such as semipalmated sandpipers. Their numbers are most impressive in July and August, when a Nature Conservancy interpretive center is open to coincide with high tides. ✉ *Rte. 935, about 8 km [5 mi] south of Dorchester, New Brunswick, Canada* ☎ *506/379– 6347 (July and Aug. only).*

# SACKVILLE

*22 km (14 mi) southeast of Dorchester and Memramcook.*

Sackville is an idyllic university town complete with a swan-filled pond. Its stately homes and ivy-clad university buildings are shaded by venerable trees, and there's a waterfowl park right in town. With a program of high-profile festivals and events, it all makes for a rich blend of history, culture, and nature.

### GETTING HERE AND AROUND

Sackville has two exits (504 and 506) of the TransCanada Highway (Rte. 2), about 50 km (31 mi) south of Moncton and 17 km (10½ mi) north of Amherst, Nova Scotia.

### ESSENTIALS

**Visitor Information Center** ✉ *34 Mallard Dr., Sackville, New Brunswick, Canada* ☎ *506/364–4967* ⊙ *May and Oct. Mon.–Sat. 9–5; June and Sept. 9–6; July–Aug. 9–8; Nov.–Dec. Mon.–Sat. 10–5.*

## EXPLORING

**Fort Beauséjour National Historic Site.** Near the Nova Scotia border in Aulac and 12 km (7 mi) east of Sackville, the Fort Beauséjour National Historic Site holds the ruins of a star-shaped fort that played a part in the 18th-century struggle between the French and British. The Deportation of the Acadians began here. The fort has fine views of the marshes at the head of the Bay of Fundy, and the Visitor Center has a fascinating collection of artifacts and interpretive exhibits. ☒ *111 Fort Beauséjour Rd., Aulac, Sackville, New Brunswick, Canada* ☎ *506/364–5080 June–mid-Oct., 506/876–2443 mid-Oct.–May* ⊕ *www.pc.gc.ca/beausejour* ☜ *C$3.90* ◉ *June–mid-Oct., daily 9–5.*

**Owens Art Gallery.** The Owens Art Gallery, the oldest art gallery in Canada, is on the Mount Allison University campus. It houses 3,200 works of 19th- and 20th-century European, American, and Canadian artwork in its permanent collection, and there are usually rotating exhibits as well. ☒ *61 York St., Sackville, New Brunswick, Canada* ☎ *506/364–2574* ⊕ *www.mta.ca/owens* ☜ *Free* ◉ *Weekdays 10–5, weekends 1–5.*

★ **Sackville Waterfowl Park.** The Sackville Waterfowl Park, in the heart of the town, has more than 3 km (2 mi) of boardwalk and trails through 55 acres of wetlands. Throughout the marsh, viewing areas and interpretive signs reveal the rare waterfowl species that nest here. There's an interpretive center, and guided tours (C$6, including a snack at the end) are available in French and English mid-June through mid-September. ☒ *34 Mallard Dr., Sackville, New Brunswick, Canada* ☎ *506/364–4967 June–Aug.* ⊕ *www.sackville.com/visit/attractions/waterfowl* ☜ *Free* ◉ *May–Aug., daily 9–5.*

## WHERE TO STAY

*For expanded hotel reviews, visit Fodors.com.*

$$ **Marshlands Inn.** A list of celebrity guests is displayed in the entrance
★ hall of this grand and elegant inn, including Queen Elizabeth II, who stopped in for afternoon tea and left the signed portrait on the upstairs landing. **Pros:** good food; friendly owners. **Cons:** one room has a nice claw-foot bath, but the encircling shower curtain tends to cling. ☒ *55 Bridge St., Sackville, New Brunswick, Canada* ☎ *506/536–0170, 800/561–1266* ⊕ *www.marshlands.nb.ca* ⬅ *18 rooms* ⚑ *In-room: a/c, no TV, Wi-Fi. In-hotel: restaurant, parking, some pets allowed* ⎛⎞ *No meals.*

## SPORTS AND THE OUTDOORS

**Canadian Wildlife Service.** Without a doubt, bird-watching is the pastime of choice in this region. For information, contact the Canadian Wildlife Service. ☒ *17 Waterfowl La., Sackville, New Brunswick, Canada* ☎ *506/364–5044.*

**Cape Jourimain Nature Centre.** Cape Jourimain Nature Centre, at the Cape Jourimain National Wildlife Area, covers 1,800 acres of salt and brackish marshes. Large numbers of waterfowl, shorebirds, and other species can be seen here. The outstanding interpretive center includes a restaurant specializing in local fare and a boutique with nature art and fine crafts. You will also find a viewing tower, 13 km (8 mi) of trails, and daily programs. ■ TIP→ **This is the best location to photograph**

the striking architecture of the 12.9-km (8-mi) Confederation Bridge that links New Brunswick to Prince Edward Island. ⊠ *Exit 51 off Rte. 16 at the foot of Confederation Bridge, Bayfield, New Brunswick, Canada* ☎ *866/538–2220, 506/538–2220* ⊕ *www.capejourimain.ca* ✉ *Free (donations welcome); programs C$3* ⊗ *Mid-May–mid-June and late Aug.–mid-Oct., daily 9–6; mid-June–late Aug., daily 8–7.*

## SHOPPING

**Fog Forest Gallery.** Fog Forest Gallery is a small, friendly, and reputable commercial gallery representing Atlantic Canadian artists. ⊠ *14 Bridge St., Sackville, New Brunswick, Canada* ☎ *506/536–9000* ⊕ *www. fogforestgallery.ca.*

**Sackville Harness Shop.** The Sackville Harness Shop still makes harnesses for horses and is the only place in North America that makes horse collars by hand. It also makes fine leather belts, wallets, bags, and jewelry. ⊠ *39 Main St., Sackville, New Brunswick, Canada* ☎ *506/536–0642, 800/386–4888* ⊕ *www.sackvilleharness.com.*

# SHEDIAC

*25 km (16 mi) northeast of Moncton.*

Shediac is the self-proclaimed Lobster Capital of the World, and it has a giant lobster sculpture to prove it. Beautiful Parlee Beach also draws people to this fishing village/resort town.

## GETTING HERE AND AROUND

From Moncton, take Route 15 east to exit 31B onto Route 11, then almost immediately exit onto Route 133 and follow signs into the town. The town is great for strolling, but a car is necessary to get to the beaches.

## ESSENTIALS

**Visitor Information Center** ⊠ *229 Main St., Shediac, New Brunswick, Canada* ☎ *506/532–7788* ⊗ *mid-May–end Sept.*

## EXPLORING

⟳ ★ **Parlee Beach.** A 3-km (2-mi) stretch of glistening sand, Parlee Beach has been named the best beach in Canada by several surveys. It is a popular vacation spot for families and plays host to beach-volleyball and touch-football tournaments; an annual sand-sculpture contest and a triathlon are held here as well. Services include canteens and a restaurant, changing rooms, and showers. ⊠ *Exit 37 off Rte. 133, Shediac, New Brunswick, Canada* ☎ *506/533–3363* ✉ *C$11 per vehicle* ⊗ *Mid-May–mid-Sept., daily 7 am–9 pm.*

**Parc de l'Aboiteau.** Parc de l'Aboiteau, on the western end of Cap-Pelé, has a fine, sandy beach as well as a boardwalk that runs through salt marshes where waterfowl nest. The beach complex includes a restaurant and lounge with live music in the evening. Cottages are available for rent year-round. ⊠ *Exit 53 off Rte. 15, Shediac, New Brunswick, Canada* ☎ *506/577–2080 for cottage information, 506/577–2030 off season* ✉ *C$4 per vehicle* ⊗ *Beach June–Sept., daily dawn–dusk.*

CLOSE UP

## Acadian Culture

Culture is often defined by geographical boundaries, but Acadian culture defines Acadia because it isn't so much a place as it is an enduring French society. In New Brunswick it abides (although not exclusively) above an imaginary diagonal line drawn from Edmundston to Moncton. In the heartland you hear remnants of Norman-French (a dialect of old French), while around Moncton you're just as apt to hear a melodious Acadian dialect called Chiac, a tweedy kind of French with bits of English.

French settlers arrived in the early 1600s and brought with them an efficient system of dikes called *aboiteaux* that allowed them to farm the salt marshes around the head of the Bay of Fundy. In the 1700s they were joined by Jesuit missionaries who brought the music of Bach, Vivaldi, and Scarlatti, along with their zeal. In 1713 England took possession of the region, and authorities demanded that Acadians swear an oath to the English crown. Some did; others didn't. By 1755 it didn't seem to matter: only those who fled into the forests escaped Le Grand Dérangement—the Expulsion of the Acadians, mostly during the Seven Years' War—which dispersed them to Québec, the eastern seaboard, Louisiana (where they became known as Cajuns), France, and even as far as the Falkland Islands. It was a devastating event that probably should have eradicated French language and culture in the Maritimes, but it didn't. It did, however, profoundly affect Acadian expression—mobility remains a pervasive theme in the art, literature, and music of Acadian people.

Whether they were hiding deep in Maritime forests or living in exile, Acadians clung tenaciously to their language and traditions. Within 10 years of their deportation, they began to return, building new communities along coasts and waterways in the northeastern part of the province, remote from English settlement. In the 1850s Acadians began to think "nationally." By 1884 there was an Acadian national anthem and a flag.

The Acadian national holiday, on August 15, provides an official reason to celebrate Acadian culture. Le Festival Acadien de Caraquet stretches the celebration out for the two preceding weeks, with music and cultural events.

The earliest Acadian settlers made pine furniture that was elegant in its simplicity. Modern Acadian artisans continue to make functional things, such as pottery and baskets, beautiful. Handmade wooden spoons are doubly beautiful—in pairs they keep time for the music at kitchen parties, where Acadian families have traditionally sung their history around the kitchen fire. But it isn't necessary to have a party to enjoy "music de cuisine." Today, folk singer Edith Butler of Paquetville takes some of that history back to her French cousins in Paris.

Clearly, the love of music endures: it rings clear in churches; the cotillion and quadrille are danced at Saturday-night soirees; Acadian sopranos and jazz artists enjoy international renown; and a world-class Baroque-music festival in Lamèque still celebrates Bach, Vivaldi, and Scarlatti.

—Ana Watts

## WHERE TO EAT AND STAY

*For expanded hotel reviews, visit Fodors.com.*

**$$**
**SEAFOOD**
✕ **The Green House on Main Restaurant.** Loaded with charm, artwork, and antiques, this upbeat restaurant is trendy despite its 19th-century building. You can eat outside on the heated patio or upstairs in the intimate dining room. The tiger prawns and Thai shrimp are faultless. ⊠ *406 Main St., Shediac, New Brunswick, Canada* ☎ *506/533–7003* ⊕ *greenhouseonmain.ca.*

**$$$**
**SEAFOOD**
✕ **Paturel Shore House Restaurant.** This big "cottage" on the beach is quite cozy, and the chef has a way with salmon, sole, and lobster. ⊠ *46 Cap Bimet, at Legere St., Shediac, New Brunswick, Canada* ☎ *506/532–4774* ☽ *No lunch. Closed mid-Sept.–May.*

**$**
⌂ **Auberge Inn Thyme.** This elegant Heritage Inn was built in 1911 and has been carefully restored and furnished with lovely period furniture; it was the home of Shediac's first dentist, and later a provincial premier lived here. **Pros:** lovely country inn feel; gracious hosts; spacious front porch. **Cons:** Room 7 on the first floor can be noisy. ⊠ *310 Main St., Shediac, New Brunswick, Canada* ☎ *506/532–6098, 877/466–8496* ⊕ *www.innthyme.com* ⇆ *7 rooms* ☍ *In-room: a/c, no TV, Wi-Fi. In-hotel: parking* ☽ *Closed Dec. and Jan.* ⦿| *Breakfast.*

**$**
⌂ **La Louisianne.** Owned and run by two sisters from Alberta who fell in love with the Maritimes, this 1914 home has been lovingly converted to feature individually styled bedrooms, some with antique furnishings and original features. **Pros:** generous breakfasts include seasonal specialties. **Cons:** two rooms share a bathroom; about a half-mile walk from downtown. ⊠ *427 Main St., Shediac, New Brunswick, Canada* ☎ *506/351–0505* ⊕ *www.lalouisianne.ca* ⇆ *5 rooms* ☍ *In-room: a/c, Wi-Fi. In-hotel: some pets allowed* ⦿| *Breakfast.*

**$$$**
⌂ **Tait House.** Built in 1911, this elegant and stately historic mansion right in the middle of town has rooms with fireplaces, canopy beds, and Jacuzzis. **Pros:** good food; good combination of modern amenities and antiques; reduction on room rate for evening diners. **Cons:** some areas a bit dark; only a Continental breakfast is included in the price. ⊠ *293 Main St., Shediac, New Brunswick, Canada* ☎ *506/532–4233* ⊕ *www. maisontaithouse.com* ⇆ *9 rooms* ☍ *In-room: a/c, Wi-Fi. In-hotel: restaurant, parking* ⦿| *Breakfast.*

# BOUCTOUCHE

*35 km (22 mi) north of Shediac.*

This idyllic, bustling town on the sandy shores of Bouctouche Bay is famous for pristine beauty and for Le Pays de la Sagouine, a theme park based on an Acadian novel. The 12-km (7½-mi) dune of Bouctouche is one of the few remaining on the east coast of North America and is bordered by a 2-km (1¼-mi) boardwalk along the Irving Eco-Centre.

## GETTING HERE AND AROUND

Bouctouche is 58 km (36 mi) northeast of Moncton via Route 15 east. From Route 15 take exit 31B onto Route 11 north, then take exit 32B for Bouctouche. A car is essential to reach all of the attractions.

## ESSENTIALS

**Visitor Information Center** ✉ *4 Acadie St., Bouctouche, New Brunswick, Canada* ☎ *506/743–8811* ⊙ *June–Sept. 9–9.*

## EXPLORING

**Irving Eco-Centre: La Dune de Bouctouche.** Irving Eco-Centre: La Dune de Bouctouche is a superb example of a coastal ecosystem that protects the exceptionally fertile oyster beds in Bouctouche Bay. Hiking trails and boardwalks to the beach make it possible to explore sensitive areas without disrupting the environment of one of the few remaining great dunes on the northwest coast of the Atlantic Ocean. An outstanding interpretive center puts the ecosystem in perspective with nature exhibits, a film presentation, and a saltwater aquarium. The staff regularly conducts guided walks. Swimming is allowed. ✉ *1932 Rte. 475, Bouctouche, New Brunswick, Canada* ☎ *888/640–3300, 506/743–2600* ⊕ *www.irvingecocentre.com* ☒ *Free* ⊙ *Hiking trails and boardwalk daily dawn–dusk. Visitor center July and Aug., daily 10–8; May, June, and Sept., daily 10–5 or 6.*

**Le Pays de la Sagouine.** Le Pays de la Sagouine is an Acadian culture theme park, with a make-believe island community that comes to life in French in daylong musical and theatrical performances and dinner theater/musical evenings July through September, with an English version on Sunday, mid-July through August. Tours are available in English and French, and the Friday-night jam sessions are accessible to English-speaking visitors, too. La Sagouine is an old charwoman-philosopher created by celebrated Acadian author Antonine Maillet. ✉ *Exit 32 off Hwy. 11, Bouctouche, New Brunswick, Canada* ☎ *506/743–1400, 800/561–9188* ⊕ *www.sagouine.com* ☒ *C$16* ⊙ *Open late June–mid-Sept., daily 10–5:30.*

**The Olivier Soapery.** About 10 km (6 mi) up the coast from Bouctouche in Ste.-Anne-de-Kent is the Olivier Soapery. There's a skin-care art gallery, featuring paintings commissioned for soap labels throughout the years, and, naturally, plenty of soap is for sale. By far the best attraction, however, is the soap-making demonstration, six times a day. ✉ *831 Rte. 505, Ste.-Anne-de-Kent, Bouctouche, New Brunswick, Canada* ☎ *506/743–8938, 800/775–5550* ⊕ *www.oliviersoaps.com* ☒ *Free* ⊙ *Daily 9–8.*

## WHERE TO STAY

*For expanded hotel reviews, visit Fodors.com.*

$ **Auberge le Vieux Presbytère de Bouctouche.** Near the water, this lovely inn was formerly a rectory and then a retreat house complete with chapel (now a conference room). **Pros:** friendly staff; lovely grounds. **Cons:** rooms are rather old-fashioned; the inn is sometimes busy with weddings and conferences. ✉ *157 chemin du Couvent, Bouctouche, New Brunswick, Canada* ☎ *506/743–5568* ⊕ *www.vieuxpresbytere. nb.ca* ⇆ *11 rooms, 5 suites* ⚹ *In-room: a/c, kitchen, Wi-Fi. In-hotel: restaurant, parking* ⊙ *Closed Oct.–May* ⧖ *Breakfast.*

## KOUCHIBOUGUAC NATIONAL PARK

*40 km (25 mi) north of Bouctouche, 100 km (62 mi) north of Moncton.*

**GETTING HERE AND AROUND**

Kouchibouguac National Park is off Route 11. Take exit 75 onto Route 117 and follow the signs. An alternative route is on the scenic Acadian Coastal Drive, following the starfish road signs.

**EXPLORING**

★ **Kouchibouguac National Park.** The word Kouchibouguac (Kou-she-boo-gwack) means "river of the long tides" in the Mi'kmaq language, and this natural wilderness park consists of dunes, bogs, salt marshes, lagoons, and freshwater, and is home to an abundance of birds. A new visitor center opened in 2011, and features information and interpretive exhibits. Kellys Beach is supervised and has facilities. There are more than 60 km (38 mi) of trails that are also used for biking and hiking, and, in winter, for cross-country skiing, snowshoeing, snow walking, and kick sledding. The forests and peat bogs can be explored along 10 nature trails, each of which has a parking lot. There are lots of nature-interpretation programs, and you can canoe, kayak, and picnic or rent bikes and boats. Reserve ahead for one of the 311 campsites. ✉ *186 Rte. 117, Kouchibouguac, New Brunswick, Canada* ☎ *506/876–2443* ⊕ *www.pc.gc.ca/kouchibouguac* ✉ *C$7.80 late May–mid-Sept.; C$6.90 mid-Sept.–late May.*

## MIRAMICHI

*40 km (25 mi) north of Kouchibouguac, 150 km (93 mi) north of Moncton.*

Celebrated for salmon rivers that reach into some of the province's richest forests, and the ebullient nature of its residents (Scottish, English, Irish, and a smattering of First Nations and French), this is a land of lumber kings, ghost stories, folklore, and festivals—celebrating the Irish in July, and folk songs and the Scottish in August. Sturdy wood homes dot the banks of Miramichi Bay. The city of Miramichi incorporates the former towns of Chatham and Newcastle and several small villages and is where the politician and British media mogul Lord Beaverbrook grew up and is buried.

Miramichi is 175 km (109 mi) northeast of Fredericton via Route 8 (also designated the scenic "Miramichi River Route"). From Moncton take Route 15 east then Route 11 north. A car is necessary to see all the attractions.

**ESSENTIALS**

**Visitor Information Center** ✉ *199 King St., Miramichi City, New Brunswick, Canada* ☎ *506/778-8444* ⊙ *June–end Aug.*

**EXPLORING**

**Atlantic Salmon Museum.** The Atlantic Salmon Museum provides a look at the endangered Atlantic salmon and at life in noted fishing camps along the rivers. It has an aquarium, displays of fishing equipment, and works of art. ✉ *263 Main St., 80 km (50 mi) southwest of Miramichi*

City, Doaktown, New Brunswick, Canada ☎506/365–7787 ⊕ www. atlanticsalmonmuseum.com ⊒ C$5 ⊙ mid-Apr.–mid-Oct., Mon.–Sat. 9–5, Sun. 1–5; may be closed Sun. early and late in the season.

**Beaubears Island.** Formerly a thriving shipbuilding center, this is one of Miramichi's most interesting outdoor spots. Start at the museum-style interpretive center, with interactive audio-visual displays. A short boat trip will then take you to the island to see two historic sites, staffed by characters who love to share their colorful island stories and adventures. There are also trips around the island in a 26-foot traditional canoe. ⊠ 35 St. Patrick's Dr., Nelson, Miramichi City, New Brunswick, Canada ☎ 506/622–8526 ⊕ www.beaubearsisland.ca ⊒ Interpretive center C$5; tours C$23, canoe trip C$25 ⊙ Mid-May–late June and late Aug.–early Oct., Mon.–Sat. 10–4, Sun noon–4; late June–late Aug., Mon.–Sat. 10–8, Sun. noon–8.

🔄 **Central New Brunswick Woodmen's Museum.** This 15-acre site has a 100-year-old trapper's cabin, a blacksmith shop, wheelwright shop, cookhouse/bunkhouse, and other exhibits pertaining to the woodman's way of life. A popular 10-passenger amusement train (C$3) winds along 1½ km (1 mi) of woodland track. ⊠ 6342 Rte. 8, 110 km (68 mi) southwest of Miramichi City, Boiestown, New Brunswick, Canada ☎ 506/369–7214 ⊕ www.woodmensmuseum.com ⊒ C$6 ⊙ May–mid-Oct., daily 9–5.

🔄 **Ritchie Wharf Park.** Ritchie Wharf Park is a waterside public park with a nautical-theme playground complete with a "Splash Pad" that sprays water from below and dumps it from buckets above. Shops sell local crafts, and there are several restaurants and docking facilities. An amphitheater showcases local entertainers on Sunday afternoons in summer. ⊠ Norton's La., Newcastle waterfront off King George Hwy., Miramichi City, New Brunswick, Canada ⊒ Free ⊙ Park daily dawn–dusk. Shops mid-May–early Sept., daily 11–10.

## WHERE TO EAT AND STAY
*For expanded hotel reviews, visit Fodors.com.*

$$ ✕ **Cunard Restaurant.** With its Irish accent and lumberjack history,
CHINESE   Miramichi is an unlikely place to find a great Chinese restaurant. The Cunard, however, has what it takes to make it anywhere. It is renowned for its Szechuan chicken and hot orange beef, and steaks and seafood are on the menu, too. ⊠ 32 Cunard St., Miramichi City, New Brunswick, Canada ☎ 506/773–7107.

$   ⊡ **King George B&B.** In a listed historic building in the former town of Newcastle, a stylish blend of antique and modern furnishings provides upscale accommodations. **Pros:** within walking distance of the Ritchie Wharf boardwalk; evening meal can be arranged for late arrivals. **Cons:** rooms vary in size, the Princess Room being quite compact. ⊠ 561 King George Hwy., Miramichi City, New Brunswick, Canada ☎ 506/352–0557 ⊕ kinggeorgebandb.com ⊃4 rooms ⊂ In-room: Internet, Wi-Fi ⊺⊘ Breakfast.

$$ ⊡ **Pond's Resort.** This property near the water offers a traditional fishing-camp experience with a few added luxuries. **Pros:** a fisherman's paradise and a haven from the modern world. **Cons:** a bit too rustic for some;

the six lodge rooms share two bathrooms. ✉ *91 Porter Cove Rd., 100 km (62 mi) southwest of Miramichi City; follow signs on Rte. 8, Ludlow, New Brunswick, Canada* ☎ *506/369–2612* ⊕ *www.pondsresort. com* ⬭ *6 rooms, 15 cabins* ⚒ *In-room: no a/c. In-hotel: restaurant, bar, some pets allowed* ⊘ *Closed mid-Oct.–mid-Apr.*

$$ ⚇ **Rodd Miramichi River.** This grand riverside hotel, with warm natural wood and earth-tone interiors, feels like a traditional inn, despite its size. **Pros:** conveniently located for lots of outdoor activities, but not too far from major towns; good fishing opportunities. **Cons:** sometimes taken over by business conventions. ✉ *1809 Water St., Miramichi City, New Brunswick, Canada* ☎ *506/773–3111* ⊕ *www.rodd-hotels.ca* ⬭ *76 rooms, 4 suites* ⚒ *In-room: a/c, Wi-Fi. In-hotel: restaurant, bar, pool, gym, some pets allowed.*

# SHIPPAGAN

*37 km (23 mi) north of Tracadie-Sheila.*

Shippagan is an important fishing and marine education center as well as a bustling town with lots of amenities and the gateway to the idyllic islands of Lamèque and Miscou.

### GETTING HERE AND AROUND
Shippagan is about 110 km (68 mi) northeast of Miramichi via Route 11, taking exit 217 onto Route 113 for the final 12 km (7½ mi). The town is very walkable, but a car is necessary to get to the islands.

### ESSENTIALS
**Visitor Information Center** ✉ *200 Hôtel-de-ville Ave., Shippagan, New Brunswick, Canada* ☎ *506/336–3993* ⊘ *mid-June–late Aug.*

### EXPLORING
⚇ **Aquarium and Marine Centre.** The wonderful Aquarium and Marine Centre has a serious side and a fun side. The labs here are the backbone of marine research in the province, while the marine museum houses more than 3,000 specimens. A tidal tank lets you watch how the marine life deal with the changing tides, a family of seals in the aquarium puts on a great show in the pool at feeding time, and there's a fascinating jellyfish tank. There's a wheelhouse where you can check all the electronic fish-finding devices and then steer the boat right to the fish, and a touch tank for making the acquaintance of various sea creatures. ✉ *100 rue de l'Aquarium, Shippagan, New Brunswick, Canada* ☎ *506/336–3013* ⊕ *www.gnb.ca/aquarium* ⊡ *C$8.50* ⊘ *May–Sept., daily 10–6.*

**Île Miscou (Miscou Island).** Île Miscou (Miscou Island), accessible by bridge from Île Lamèque, has white sandy beaches. The dunes and lagoons are good places to see migrating bird species. ✉ *Shippagan, New Brunswick, Canada.*

**Ste-Cécile Church.** Across a causeway from Shippagan is Île Lamèque and Ste-Cécile Church. Although the church is plain on the outside, every inch of it is decorated on the inside. Each July, the International Festival of Baroque Music takes place here. **International Festival of Baroque Music.** Each July, the International Festival of Baroque Music takes place here. ⊠ *Shippagan, New Brunswick, Canada* ☎ *506/344–5846, 877/377–8003* ⊠ *Rte. 113 at Petite-Rivière-de-l'Île, Shippagan, New Brunswick, Canada.*

## CARAQUET

*40 km (25 mi) west of Shippagan.*

Perched on Caraquet Bay, along the beautiful Baie des Chaleurs, with Québec's Gaspé Peninsula beckoning across the inlet, Caraquet is rich in French flavor and is the acknowledged Acadian cultural capital. Its beaches are also a draw.

### GETTING HERE AND AROUND
Caraquet is 113 km (70 mi) north of Miramichi on Route 11. A car is necessary to get around its scattered attractions.

### ESSENTIALS
**Visitor Information Center** ⊠ *39 St.-Pierre Blvd. W, Caraquet, New Brunswick, Canada* ☎ *506/726-2676* ⊕ *www.caraquet.ca* ☉ *late May–late Sept.*

### EXPLORING
**Acadian Festival.** Celebrating its 50th year in 2012, the two-week Acadian Festival is held here in the first two weeks of August. In the Tintamarre, costumed participants parade noisily through the streets; the Blessing of the Fleet, a colorful and moving ceremony that's usually held on the first Sunday of the festival, eloquently expresses the importance of fishing to the Acadian economy and way of life. ⊠ *Caraquet, New Brunswick, Canada* ☎ *506/727-2787* ⊕ *www.festivalacadien.ca.*

⟳ ★ **Acadian Historical Village.** A highlight of the Acadian Peninsula is the Acadian Historical Village. The more than 40 restored buildings re-create Acadian communities between 1770 and 1949. There are modest homes, a church, a school, and a village shop, as well as an industrial area that includes a working hotel, a bar and restaurant, a lobster hatchery, a cooper, and a tinsmith shop. The bilingual staff tells fascinating stories. The demonstrations are great fun, and visitors are invited to take part. ⊠ *14311 Rte. 11, 10 km (6 mi) west of Caraquet, Rivière-du-Nord, New Brunswick, Canada* ☎ *506/726-2600, 877/721-2200* ⊕ *www.villagehistoriqueacadien.com* 🎟 *C$16* ☉ *Early June–mid-Sept., daily 10–6; mid-Sept.–late Sept., daily 10–5, with reduced operations.*

**Pope's Museum.** The Pope's Museum, 7 km (4 mi) outside Caraquet, is the only museum in North America dedicated to papal history. It celebrates the church's artistic and spiritual heritage with models of buildings such as St. Peter's Basilica and the cathedral in Florence. ⊠ *184 Acadie St., Grand-Anse, New Brunswick, Canada* ☎ *506/732-3003* 🎟 *C$8* ☉ *Mid-June–Aug., Wed.–Sun. 10–6 (last tour at 5).*

### WHERE TO EAT AND STAY
*For expanded hotel reviews, visit Fodors.com.*

**$$$$**
EUROPEAN
✕ **La Fine Grobe Sur Mer.** North of Bathurst in Nigadoo, about 80 km (50 mi) outside of Caraquet, is one of New Brunswick's finest restaurants. The French cuisine, seafood, and wine are outstanding, largely due to

the chef-owner's dedication to quality. He grows his own herbs and greens and bakes his baguettes in an outdoor oven. Lobster, lamb, and *lapin* (domestic rabbit) are all on the menu. The dining room is small but has a cozy fireplace and three walls of windows overlooking the ocean. Dinner is served each evening; lunch can be arranged. There are two bedrooms on the second floor for overnight stays. ⊠ *289 rue Principal, Nigadoo, New Brunswick, Canada* ☎ *506/783–3138* ⊕ *www. finegrobe.com* ⊙ *Lunch by special arrangement only.*

**$$$** ⛆ **Hotel Paulin.** Caraquet is famous not only for lobsters, oysters, artisans,
★ and festivals, but also for Hotel Paulin. **Pros:** personal service; excellent food. **Cons:** atmosphere can feel a bit stuffy. ⊠ *143 blvd. St-Pierre W, Caraquet, New Brunswick, Canada* ☎ *506/727–9981, 866/727–9981* ⊕ *www.hotelpaulin.com* ⇆ *6 rooms, 6 suites* ⚲ *In-room: Wi-Fi. In-hotel: restaurant, spa, beach, parking, some pets allowed* ⦿ *Breakfast.*

### SPORTS AND THE OUTDOORS

☾ **Sugarloaf Provincial Park.** The eight trails on the 507-foot drop at Sugarloaf Provincial Park accommodate skiers and snowboarders of all levels in winter and mountain bikers in summer; a chairlift operates in both seasons. There are also 25 km (16 mi) of cross-country ski trails, hiking trails, a summer alpine slide, and other recreational amenities. Instruction and equipment rentals are available, there's a summer welcome center, and the lodge operates a lounge and restaurant year-round. ⊠ *596 Val d'Amour Rd., 180 km (112 mi) northwest of Caraquet, Atholville, New Brunswick, Canada* ☎ *506/789–2366, 506/753–6825 for ski/snowboard rentals* ⊕ *www.sugarloafpark.ca.*

# ST. JOHN RIVER VALLEY

The St. John River valley scenery is panoramic—gently rolling hills and sweeping forests, with just enough rocky gorges to keep it interesting. The native peoples (First Nations, French, English, Scots, and Danes) who live along the river ensure that its culture is equally intriguing. The St. John River forms 120 km (74 mi) of the border with Maine, then swings inland, eventually cutting through the heart of Fredericton and rolling down to the city of Saint John. Gentle hills of rich farmland and the blue sweep of the water make this a lovely area for driving. In the early 1800s the narrow wedge of land at the northern end of the valley was coveted by Québec, New Brunswick, and the United States. To settle the issue, New Brunswick governor Sir Thomas Carleton rolled dice with the governor of British North America at Québec. Sir Thomas won—by one point. Settling the border with the Americans was more difficult; even the lumberjacks engaged in combat. Finally, in 1842, the British flag was hoisted over Madawaska County. One old-timer, tired of being asked to which country he belonged, replied, "I am a citizen of the Republic of Madawaska." So began the mythical republic, which exists today with its own flag (an eagle on a field of white) and a coat of arms.

# EDMUNDSTON

*275 km (171 mi) northwest of Fredericton.*

Edmundston, the unofficial capital of Madawaska County, has always depended on the wealth of the deep forest around it—the legend of Paul Bunyan was born in these woods. Even today the town looks to the pulp mills of the Twin Rivers Paper Company (formerly Fraser Papers) as the major source of employment.

### GETTING HERE AND AROUND

Edmundston is on the Trans-Canada Highway (Route 2) about 16 km (10 mi) southeast of the Québec border—exit 18 is best for downtown—and just across the river from Madawaska, Maine. A car is necessary to visit the Botanical Garden, on the northern edge of the city.

### ESSENTIALS

**Visitor Information Edmundston–Madawaska Tourism** ⊠ *121 Victoria St., Edmundston, New Brunswick, Canada* ☎ *506/735–1850, 866/737–6766* ⊕ *http://tourismedmundston.com.*

**Woodstock Visitor Information Center** ⊠ *220 King St., Edmundston, New Brunswick, Canada* ☎ *506/325–9094* ⊕ *www.gwcc.ca.*

### EXPLORING

**Connell House.** A fine example of Greek Revival architecture, this beautiful former home of politician, the Hon. Charles Connell (1810–73) has been partially restored, with work continuing as funds become available. It is home to the Carleton County Historical Society and contains fine furniture, artifacts, and musical instruments, with temporary exhibitions and occasional concerts as added attractions. ⊠ *128 Connell St., Edmundston, New Brunswick, Canada* ☎ *506/328–9706* ⊕ *www.cchs-nb.ca* ⌑ *C$5* ⊙ *July–Aug., Tues.–Fri. 9–6, Sat. 10–6, Sun. and Mon. by appointment; Sept.–June Tues.–Fri. 9–5.*

**Foire Brayonne.** The annual Foire Brayonne, held in Edmundston over the long weekend surrounding New Brunswick Day (beginning on the Wednesday before the first Monday in August), is one of the largest Francophone festivals outside of Québec. It's also one of the liveliest and most vibrant cultural events in New Brunswick, with concerts by acclaimed artists as well as local musicians and entertainers. ⊠ *Edmundston, New Brunswick, Canada* ☎ *506/739–6608* ⊕ *www.foirebrayonne.com.*

**New Brunswick Botanical Garden.** At the New Brunswick Botanical Garden, in the Edmunston suburb of St-Jacques, roses, rhododendrons, alpine flowers, and dozens of other annuals and perennials bloom in 10 gardens. Khronos, the newest garden, has an astronomical theme. The music of Mozart, Handel, Bach, and Vivaldi often plays in the background. Two arboretums have coniferous and deciduous trees and shrubs. Mosaiculture plantings on metal frames placed throughout the gardens illustrate legends and cultural themes. Children enjoy the living butterfly exhibit. ⊠ *15 Main St., St.-Jacques, Edmundston, New Brunswick, Canada* ☎ *506/737–4444* ⊕ *www.jardinnbgarden.com*

🎟 *C$14* 🕙 *May, June, and Sept., daily 9–6; July and Aug., daily 9–8; also for special events for Halloween and Christmas.*

**Old County Court House.** Dating from 1833, this splendid galleried former court house has been restored after years of neglect and misuse and was opened to the public by H.R.H. Princess Anne in 1986. Guided tours are available in summer and occasional special events include an annual Christmas concert. ✉ *19 Court St., Upper Woodstock, Edmundston, New Brunswick, Canada* ☎ *506/328–9706* ⊕ *www.cchs-nb.ca* 🎟 *C$2 donation requested* 🕙 *July–Aug., Tues.–Sat. 10–6, Sun. and Mon. by appointment.*

## WHERE TO STAY

*For expanded hotel reviews, visit Fodors.com.*

$ 🏨 **Auberge les Jardins Inn and Motel Brayon & Chalets.** Fine French cuisine ($$–$$$$) is the major attraction at this inn, although the guest rooms, decorated with woodland themes with maple, cedar, aspen, oak, and pine, are pleasant as well. **Pros:** good food; peaceful despite the highway. **Cons:** not much else to do here; some distance from downtown Edmundston. ✉ *60 rue Principal, St-Jacques, New Brunswick, Canada* ☎ *506/739–5514, 800/630–8011* ⊕ *www.lesjardinsinn.com* 🛏 *30 rooms, 10 cottages* ♿ *In-room: a/c, Internet. In-hotel: restaurant, pool, laundry facilities, parking.*

$$ 🏨 **Best Western Woodstock.** Recently renovated and expanded this modern hotel is just off the TransCanada Highway on the edge of town. **Pros:** convenient for the highway. **Cons:** no restaurant; out of walking distance to downtown. ✉ *123 Gallop Ct., St-Jacques, New Brunswick, Canada* ☎ *506/328–2378, 888/580–1188 reservations* ⊕ *www. bestwesternwoodstock.com* 🛏 *86 rooms, 18 suites* ♿ *In-room: a/c, Wi-Fi. In-hotel: pool, gym, some pets allowed* 🍴 *Breakfast.*

¢ 🏨 **Covered Bridge B&B.** High above the St. **Pros:** friendly and helpful owners; children welcome; special rates for longer off-season stays. **Cons:** a few unexpected steps to watch out for; one bathroom, though private, is not en suite. ✉ *2651 Rte. 103, Somerville, New Brunswick, Canada* ✛ *20 km (12 mi) north of Woodstock via Hwy. 2 then Rte. 590* ☎ *506/324–0939* ⊕ *www.coveredbridgebandb.ca* 🛏 *5 rooms* ♿ *In-room: a/c, Wi-Fi. In-hotel: some pets allowed* 🍴 *Breakfast.*

## SPORTS AND THE OUTDOORS

**Mont Farlagne.** Mont Farlagne has 21 trails for downhill skiing on a vertical drop of 600 feet. Its four lifts can handle 4,000 skiers per hour, and there's night skiing on eight trails. Snowboarding, tube sliding, and a snow park with jumps and modules add to the fun. Equipment rentals and lessons are available, and there are a pro-shop, a cafeteria and a bar. ✉ *360 Mont Farlagne Rd., St-Jacques, New Brunswick, Canada* ☎ *506/739–7669* ⊕ *www.montfarlagne.com.*

# GRAND FALLS

*65 km (40 mi) southeast of Edmundston.*

The St. John River rushes over a high cliff, squeezes through a narrow rocky gorge, and emerges as a wider river at the town of Grand Falls. The result is a magnificent cascade whose force has worn strange round wells in the rocky bed, some as large as 5 meters (16 feet) in circumference and 9 meters (30 feet) deep. ⊠ *Grand Falls, New Brunswick, Canada.*

### GETTING HERE AND AROUND

Grand Falls is just off the Trans-Canada Highway (Route 2), exit 77 or 79. From Edmundston an alternative (and about the same distance) is on Route 144, the River Valley Scenic Drive. There's not much to see in town, other than the falls and gorge, but it's an easy walk across the bridge along Broadway Boulevard to cafés and restaurants.

### ESSENTIALS

**Visitor Information Town of Grand Falls** ⊠ *25 Madawaska Rd., Grand Falls, New Brunswick, Canada* ☎ *506/475–7788* ⊕ *www.grandfalls.com* ⊙ *mid-May– June, daily 10–6; July–Aug., daily 9–9; Sept.–mid-Oct., daily 10–5.*

### EXPLORING

**Grand Falls Museum.** The Grand Falls Museum has pioneer and early Victorian artifacts as well as the balance beam used by daredevil Van Morrell, who crossed the falls on a tightrope in 1904. ⊠ *68 Madawaska Rd., Ste. 100, Grand Falls, New Brunswick, Canada* ☎ *506/473–5265* ⊠ *Free; donations accepted* ⊙ *July and Aug., weekdays 9–5.*

**longest covered bridge.** The River Valley Scenic Drive heads south through typical small communities, one of which, Hartland—about 20 km (12 mi) south of Florenceville—has the longest covered bridge in the world (391 meters [1,282 feet] long). It's still used by traffic crossing the river between Routes 103 and 105. ⊠ *Grand Falls, New Brunswick, Canada.*

**Malabeam Tourist Information Center.** The Gorge Walk, which starts at the Malabeam Tourist Information Center and covers the full length of the gorge, is dotted with interpretive panels and monuments. There's no charge for the walk, unless you descend the 250 steps to the wells (C$5), holes worn in the rocks by the swirling water. Guided walking tours (C$4 or $8, depending on the length of the tour) are also available. According to native legend, a young maiden named Malabeam led her Mohawk captors to their deaths over the foaming cataract rather than guide them to her village. The bodies of the Mohawks were found the following day, but Malabeam was not found. The view overlooking the gorge and out from the center is breathtaking. ⊠ *25 Madawaska Rd., Grand Falls, New Brunswick, Canada* ☎ *506/475–7788 information center* ⊠ *Free* ⊙ *Daily dawn–dusk.*

**pontoon boat.** This outfitter operates a pontoon boat at the lower end of the gorge, offering a fascinating perspective of the cliffs and wells, from May through October; rides are C$25. Zip-lining, repelling, and kayaking are also offered.

**La Rochelle Tourist Information Centre.** Boat tickets are available at the La Rochelle Tourist Information Centre. ✉ *1 Chapel St., Grand Falls, New Brunswick, Canada* ☎ *877/475–7769, 506/475–7766* ⊕ *www. grandfalls.com* ✉ *16087 Rte. 105, Grand Falls, New Brunswick, Canada* ☎ *506/473–4803, 506/477–9799* ⊕ *www.openskyadventures.com.*

EN
ROUTE
**Andrew and Laura McCain Gallery.** About 75 km (47 mi) south of Grand Falls, stop in Florenceville for a look at the Andrew and Laura McCain Gallery. It hosts a lively and eclectic series of exhibitions each year, showcasing Atlantic Canadian artists working in traditional and experimental media, as well as art and craft workshops, seasonal festivals, and children's events. ✉ *8 McCain St., Florenceville, New Brunswick, Canada* ☎ *506/392–6769* ⊕ *mccainartgallery.com* ⊙ *Tues., Wed., and Fri., 10:30–5, Thurs. noon–8.*

## WOODSTOCK

New Brunswick's first incorporated town (in 1856), Woodstock still preserves many fine old buildings on its leafy streets, and a self-guiding walking-tour leaflet is available from the visitor information center. A focal point of the town is the meeting of its two rivers, the St. John and the Meduxnekeag, with riverside walks, a nature reserve, a floating dock in summer, and a small marina. The big celebrations are Old Home Week and the Dooryard Arts Festival, both in August. Other than that, it's a laid-back town with a kind of understated charm.

### GETTING HERE AND AROUND

Woodstock is off the Trans-Canada Highway (Route 2) at exits 188 and 185. Coming from the U.S., Interstate 95 becomes Route 95 as it crosses the U.S. border at Houlton, Maine, and continues the short distance to Woodstock. Downtown is easily explored on foot, but a car is necessary to visit the Old Court House in Upper Woodstock.

## KINGS LANDING HISTORICAL SETTLEMENT

*210 km (130 mi) south of Grand Falls, 30 km (19 mi) west of Fredericton.*

### GETTING HERE AND AROUND

King's Landing is about 68 km (42 mi) southeast of Woodstock via the Trans-Canada Highway (Route 2) or the River Valley Scenic Drive, and is well signposted from both.

### EXPLORING

Fodor's Choice ★

**Kings Landing Historical Settlement.** The Kings Landing Historical Settlement came into being as a consequence of the 1960s Mactaquac Dam project—the original settlements were going to be destroyed, so the historically important buildings were moved to a new shore, then restored and furnished to create a living-history museum. To best appreciate the museum, plan to spend at least a half day. Route 102 passes through some spectacular river and hill scenery on the way, including by the Mactaquac Dam—turn off here if you want to visit Mactaquac Provincial Park.

Today, Kings Landing evokes the sights, sounds, and society of rural New Brunswick between 1790 and 1900. The winding country lanes and meticulously restored homes pull you back more than a century, and various "Heritage Workshops" are available to let you try 19th-century trades, process wool "from sheep to shawl," prepare herbal remedies from the plants in the lanes and gardens, and more. There are daily productions in the theater, barn dances, and strolling minstrels. See how the wealthy owner of the sawmill lived and how different things were for the immigrant farmer. Hearty meals are served at the Kings Head Inn. Each week throughout the summer, children ages 9 to 15 can take part in the Visiting Cousins & Family Kin program, where they dress in period costume, attend the one-room schoolhouse, and learn the chores, games, and mannerisms of 19th-century youth. ✉ *5804 Rte. 102, Exit 253 off Trans-Canada Hwy., Prince William, New Brunswick, Canada* ☎ *506/363–4999* ⊕ *www.kingslanding.nb.ca* ✉ *C$15.50* ⊙ *Late May–mid-Oct., daily 10–5.*

## MACTAQUAC PROVINCIAL PARK

*25 km (16 mi) west of Fredericton.*

### GETTING HERE AND AROUND

The park is on Route 105, west of Fredericton and off the Trans-Canada Highway (Route 2) at exit 258, via Routes 102 then 105. There are two main entrances: on the northern edge opposite the intersection of Routes 105 and 615, and midway down the western side off Route 105 near the golf course. A third, southern entrance only leads to Walinaik Cove marina.

### EXPLORING

**Mactaquac Provincial Park.** Surrounding the giant pond created by the Mactaquac Hydroelectric Dam on the St. John River is Mactaquac Provincial Park. Its facilities include an 18-hole championship golf course, two beaches, two marinas (one for powerboats and one for sailboats), supervised crafts activities, myriad nature and hiking trails, and a restaurant. There are also guided walks on summer Wednesdays through a nature reserve to beaver ponds. Reservations are advised for the 300 campsites in summer, but winter is fun, too; there are lots of trails for cross-country skiing and snowshoeing, and sleigh rides are available by appointment. The toboggan hills and skating/ice hockey ponds are even lighted in the evening. ✉ *1265 Rte. 105, Mactaquac, New Brunswick, Canada* ☎ *506/363–4747* ✉ *C$8 per vehicle, mid-May–mid-Oct.; no entrance fee in winter* ⊙ *Daily 8 am–dusk; overnight camping mid-May–mid-Oct.*

EN ROUTE

**Camp Gagetown Military Museum.** Oromocto, along Route 102 from Mactaquac Provincial Park, is the site of the Canadian Armed Forces base Camp Gagetown, the largest military base in Canada (not to be confused with the pretty Village of Gagetown farther downriver), which has an interesting military museum. Prince Charles completed his helicopter training here. ✉ *Bldg. A5, off Walnut St., Camp Gagetown, New Brunswick, Canada* ☎ *506/422–1304* ✉ *Free* ⊙ *Weekdays 8–4.*

# FREDERICTON

The small inland city of Fredericton, on a broad point of land jutting into the St. John River, is a gracious and beautiful place that feels more like a large village. It's especially interesting to visit if history is your passion.

Fredericton's predecessor, the early French settlement of Ste. Anne's Point, was established in 1642 during the reign of the French governor Joseph Robineau de Villebon, who made his headquarters at the junction of the Nashwaak and St. John rivers. Settled by Loyalists and named for Frederick, second son of George III, the city serves as the seat of government for New Brunswick's 754,000 residents. Wealthy and scholarly Loyalists set out to create a gracious and beautiful place, and even before the establishment of the University of New Brunswick, in 1785, the town served as a center for liberal arts and sciences.

Fredericton was the first city in Canada to offer free Wi-Fi throughout downtown. To learn more check out ⊕ *www.fred-ezone.ca.*

### GETTING HERE AND AROUND

Fredericton is a little way north of the Trans-Canada Highway (Route 2), with four exits to choose from. Coming from the west, exit 280 onto Route 8 is best; from the east take exit 294 onto Route 7. Fredericton has an excellent bus service, operating Monday to Saturday; fares are C$2 or 10 for C$18, exact change required.

Downtown Queen Street runs parallel to the river and has several historic sights and attractions. Most major sights are within walking distance of one another.

The downtown Lighthouse on the Green, on the St. John River at the foot of Regent Street, is a great place to get information or tickets for day adventures, craft workshops, cultural tours, and ghost walks. It's opens at 10:30 am, closing at 9:30 pm in peak season and 6 or 7 pm in June and September. Bike rentals are available and there are bike tours Wednesday through Sunday at 9:30 am and 2:30 pm for C$13.50 per person, including wheels. The rental desk is open late May to mid-September, but hours vary, so call first. The Lighthouse also has a "Play & Learn" exhibit that children will enjoy.

Dressed in 18th-century costume, actors from the Calithumpians Theater Company conduct free historical walks three times a day, from Canada Day (July 1) to Labor Day. The tours start at City Hall at 10 am, 2:30 pm, and 5 pm and last about an hour. After dark, actors lead a Haunted Hike (C$13) through historic neighborhoods and ghostly graveyards. Check at the City Hall Visitor Information Centre for details.

### ESSENTIALS

Bike rentals **Lighthouse on the Green** ☎ *506/460–2939.* **Radical Edge** ✉ *129 Westmorland St., Fredericton, New Brunswick, Canada* ☎ *506/459–1448.* **Savage's** ✉ *441 King St., Fredericton, New Brunswick, Canada* ☎ *506/457–7452* ⊕ *www.sbcoutlet.com.*

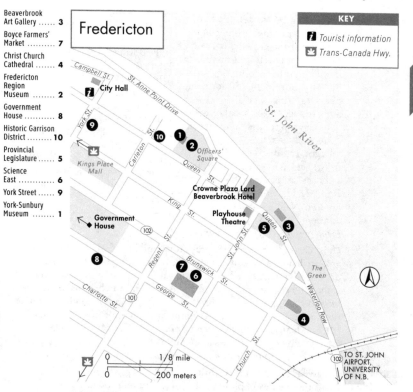

Beaverbrook
Art Gallery ...... **3**

Boyce Farmers'
Market ......... **7**

Christ Church
Cathedral ....... **4**

Fredericton
Region
Museum ........ **2**

Government
House .......... **8**

Historic Garrison
District ......... **10**

Provincial
Legislature ...... **5**

Science
East ............. **6**

York Street ..... **9**

York-Sunbury
Museum ........ **1**

**Tour Information** **Calithumpians Theater Company** ☎ *506/457–1975* ⊕ *www.calithumpians.com.*

**Visitor Information** **City Hall Visitor Information Centre** ✉ *397 Queen St., Fredericton, New Brunswick, Canada* ☎ *506/460–2129* ⊕ *www. tourismfredericton.ca.* **Fredericton Tourism** ✉ *11 Carleton St., Fredericton, New Brunswick, Canada* ☎ *506/460–2041, 888/888–4768* ⊕ *www.tourismfredericton. ca.* **Visitor Information Center** ✉ *Tilley House, 69 Front St., Village of Gagetown, New Brunswick, Canada* ☎ *506/488–2966.*

## EXPLORING

★ **Beaverbrook Art Gallery.** A lasting gift of the late Lord Beaverbrook, this gallery could hold its head high in the company of some of the smaller European galleries, and holds a significant collection of Canadian, American, and British masterworks that rivals many major Canadian galleries. Salvador Dalí's gigantic painting *Santiago el Grande* has always been the star, but a rotation of avant-garde Canadian paintings now shares pride of place. The McCain "gallery-within-a-gallery" is devoted to the finest Atlantic Canadian artists. ✉ *703 Queen St., Fredericton, New Brunswick, Canada* ☎ *506/458–8545* ⊕ *www. beaverbrookartgallery.org* 🖺 *C$5* ⊙ *Fri.–Wed. 9–5:30, Thurs. 9–9.*

**Boyce Farmers' Market.** It's hard to miss this Saturday-morning market because of the crowds. It's one of the finest markets in Canada, the building and surrounding space housing more than 250 local suppliers offering lots of local meat and produce, cheeses, baked goods, maple syrup, crafts, and seasonal items such as wreaths. The market sells good ready-to-eat food as well, from German sausages to tasty samosas. ⊠ *Bounded by Regent, Brunswick, and George Sts., Fredericton, New Brunswick, Canada* ☏ *506/451–1815* ⊕ *frederictonfarmersmarket.ca* ☉ *Sat. 6 am–1 pm.*

---

### FREDERICTON ARTS

The **Downtown Fredericton Culture Crawl** takes place the first Thursday of every month, from June to September. During the festival, you can visit around 15 of the art galleries, craft studios, and shops in the downtown area, all within walking distance of each other, and all stay open until 8 pm. It's free, and maps are available at City Hall Visitor Information Centre.

---

★ **Christ Church Cathedral.** This gray stone building, completed in 1853, is an excellent example of decorated neo-Gothic architecture. The cathedral's design was based on a medieval prototype in England, and the cathedral became a model for many American churches. Inside is a clock known as "Big Ben's little brother," the test run for London's famous timepiece, designed by Lord Grimthorpe, and some fine carved marble. ⊠ *Church St., Fredericton, New Brunswick, Canada* ☏ *506/450–8500* ⊠ *Free* ☉ *Self-guided tours weekdays 9–6, Sat. 10–6, Sun. between services. Guided tours July and Aug., weekdays 9–6, Sat. 10–6, Sun. 1–5.*

**OFF THE BEATEN PATH**

**Marysville.** A National Historic District, Marysville is one of Canada's best-preserved examples of a 19th-century mill town. Its architecture and social history are amazing and can be appreciated with the help of a self-guided walking-tour booklet available at the Fredericton Regional Museum and at Westminster Books on King Street. Marysville itself is on the north side of the St. John River, about 10 km (6 mi) from downtown Fredericton via Route 8.

**Knobb Hill Gallery.** Knobb Hill Gallery, home of the Catherine Karns Munn Collection and one of the stops on the Marysville walking tour, has paintings and crafts depicting the local area and Victorian scenes. ⊠ *285 Canada St., Fredericton, New Brunswick, Canada* ☏ *506/450–1986* ⊠ *Fredericton, New Brunswick, Canada.*

☘ **Fredericton Region Museum.** The Officers' Quarters in the Historic Garrison District house a museum that presents a living picture of the community from the time when only First Nations peoples inhabited the area through the Acadian and Loyalist days to the immediate past. Its World War I trench puts you in the thick of battle, and the shellacked remains of the giant Coleman Frog, a Fredericton legend, still inspire controversy. ⊠ *Officers' Sq., 571 Queen St., Fredericton, New Brunswick, Canada* ☏ *506/455–6041* ⊕ *www.frederictonregionmuseum.com* ⊠ *C$5* ☉ *July–Aug., daily 10–5; Apr.–June and Sept.–Nov., Sun. and Mon. 1–4 or by appt; Dec.–Mar. by appt.*

**Government House.** This imposing 1828 Palladian mansion has been restored as the official residence and office for New Brunswick's lieutenant governor. A hands-on interpretive center spans 12,000 years of history. Guided tours take in elegantly restored state rooms and art galleries. The 11-acre grounds include a 17th-century Acadian settlement and border an early Maliseet burial ground. ✉ *51 Woodstock Rd., Fredericton, New Brunswick, Canada* ☎ *506/453–2505* 💲 *Free* ⊙ *Weekdays, 10 am–5 pm; tours mid-May–Aug., Mon.–Sat. 10 am–4 pm, Sun. noon–4 pm.*

**Historic Garrison District.** The restored buildings of this British and Canadian post, which extends two blocks along Queen Street, include soldiers' barracks, a guardhouse, and a cellblock. This is a National Historic Site and one of New Brunswick's top attractions. Local artisans operate studios in the casemates below the soldiers' barracks in Barracks Square. In July and August free guided tours run throughout the day, and there are outdoor concerts in **Officers' Square** Tuesday and Thursday evenings. Redcoat soldiers have long stood guard in Officers' Square, and a formal changing-of-the-guard ceremony takes place July and August at 11 am and 4 pm daily, with an additional ceremony at 7 pm on Tuesday and Thursday. It's even possible for children to live a soldier's life for a while: each summer afternoon at 1:30, would-be redcoats get their own uniforms, practice drilling, and take part in a "mission" (C$8 per person). At 12:15 pm on weekdays and 2 pm on weekends and holidays the Caliathumpians offer songs and stories of the guardhouse. Sunday evenings in July and August, free classic movies are shown under the stars in Barracks Square at dusk. ✉ *Queen St. at Carleton St., Fredericton, New Brunswick, Canada* ☎ *506/460–2129* 💲 *Free* ⊙ *Daily 24 hrs.*

**Provincial Legislature.** The interior chamber of the legislature, where the premier and elected members govern the province, reflects the taste of the late Victorians. The chandeliers are brass, and some of the prisms are Waterford. Replicas of portraits by Sir Joshua Reynolds of King George III and Queen Charlotte hang here. There's a freestanding circular staircase, and the library owns a complete four-volume set of Audubon's *Birds of America*, which will be back on view once a new display case has been completed. Call ahead to arrange a tour. ✉ *706 Queen St., Fredericton, New Brunswick, Canada* ☎ *506/453–2527* 💲 *Free* ⊙ *Legislature tours 1st Mon. in June–mid-Aug., weekdays 8:30 am–4:30 pm; mid-Aug.–June, weekdays 9–4. Library weekdays 8:15–5.*

**Science East.** This hands-on science center, in the former York County Jail, is all about family fun, with more than 100 hands-on exhibits. You can test your reflexes in the Batak Reaction Tester, have fun with flying machines in the wind tunnel, set off the rocket launcher, walk into a giant kaleidoscope, create a mini-tornado, and explore the museum in the dungeon. There's a giant pirate ship in the outdoor playground. ✉ *668 Brunswick St., Fredericton, New Brunswick, Canada* ☎ *506/457–2340* ⊕ *www.scienceeast.nb.ca* 💲 *C$8* ⊙ *June–Aug., Mon.–Sat. 10–5, Sun. noon–4; Sept.–May, weekdays noon–5, Sat. 10–5.*

**York Street.** This is the city's high-fashion block, with designer shops, an incense boutique, a general store with an eclectic assortment of gifts and housewares, and a newsstand/cigar store. At the middle of the upriver side of the block is Mazucca's Alley, the gateway to more shops and the pubs and restaurants in Piper's Lane. King and Queen streets, at either end of the block, have some fun shops, too. ⊠ *Fredericton, New Brunswick, Canada.*

## WHERE TO EAT

$$$   ✕ **The Blue Door.** The concept is upscale global cuisine with a Thai bent,
ECLECTIC   and the food is inventive and consistently good, served in an intimate setting with superior service. Blue doors in unlikely places, colorful bar stools, and an extensive martini menu do the trick. There's seafood with a twist, too, such as maple-chili salmon and Athenian haddock. Lots of local fine art for sale adds a nice touch. ⊠ *100 Regent St., at King St., Fredericton, New Brunswick, Canada* ☎ *506/455–2583* ⊕ *www. thebluedoor.ca.*

$$$   ✕ **Brewbaker's.** With an old-world Italian atmosphere, California and
ECLECTIC   eclectic cuisine, and a rooftop garden patio, Brewbaker's is downtown's most popular casual lunch and dinner spot. Dishes include fabulous salads, authentic pastas, and thin-crust pizzas. Steak and seafood are also hot menu items. The duck and goat cheese pizza is superb. ⊠ *546 King St., Fredericton, New Brunswick, Canada* ☎ *506/459–0067.*

$$   ✕ **El Burrito Loco.** This perennial favorite was so popular that it expanded
MEXICAN   to the second floor of its building. The recipes are authentic Mexican. Everything is made on the spot, and you can get huevos rancheros for breakfast and burritos, tacos, and guacamole later in the day. Steak and lobster are on the menu, too, and there's a large patio and outdoor margarita bar in summer. ⊠ *304 King St., Fredericton, New Brunswick, Canada* ☎ *506/459–5626.*

$$   ✕ **Fusion Bistro.** This is the smartest eatery in town, featuring an eclectic
ECLECTIC   daily-changing menu that might include seafood linguine, Thai chicken stir-fry, and penne primavera, plus delectable desserts such as a triple-chocolate cheesecake. There are gluten-free and vegetarian options too. Events include wine-tastings, guest-chef evenings, and weekly live music from local and touring performers. ⊠ *610 Main St., Fredericton, New Brunswick, Canada* ☎ *506/328–6942* ⊕ *www.fusioncoffeeco.com* ⊗ *Mon.–Thurs. 7 am–10 pm, Fri. 7 am–11 pm, Sat. 8 am–11 pm, Sun. 10 am–7 pm.*

$$   ✕ **Heino's German Cuisine.** Renowned across the Maritimes and across
GERMAN   the border, this authentic German restaurant is in the rather unlikely setting of an out-of-town motel, the John Gyles Motor Inn. Heino has been running both since 1971, and serves up satisfying portions of dishes such as sauerbraten (succulent marinated beef), German-style pot roast with herb gravy, various schnitzels, and seven kinds of sausage. The Heino Platter, in two sizes (neither of them small), is a good option, offering tastings of several main course dishes. There are also "Canadian" steak, burger, and seafood choices and delectable desserts. Reservations recommended. ⊠ *1182 Rte. 165, Fredericton, New Brunswick, Canada* ⊕ *15 km (9 mi) south of Woodstock via Rte. 165, or just off exit 200 of Hwy. 2* ☎ *506/328–6622, 866/381–8800* ⊕ *www. johngylesmotorinnltd.ca* ⊗ *Mon.–Sat. 5–9, Sun. 5–8.*

$$$ ✕**The Palate Restaurant & Café.** Artwork by local artists enhances the
MEDITERRANEAN colorful decor here, and the open kitchen gives a view of the enthusias-
★ tic red-seal chefs in action. The menu leans toward Mediterranean and
Western European, adding a few exotic touches and interesting combi-
nations of flavors, as in a Thai coconut chicken soup, a richly flavored
pork tenderloin with smoked paprika, and lemon meringue salmon,
with lemon, Parmesan and chive aioli. The vegetarian option might be
a tofu "meat loaf" with baked sweet potato and roasted onion sauce.
The lunch menu focuses on creative sandwiches, panini, stir-fries, and
salads and is significantly less expensive than dinner. ⊠ *462 Queen St.,
Fredericton, New Brunswick, Canada* ☎ *506/450–7911* ⊘ *Closed Sun.*

¢ ✕**Trinitea's Cup.** Superb lunches, light dinners of hearty soups and sand-
CAFÉ wiches, and an astonishing array of tea—more than 50 varieties, includ-
ing bubble tea—are available, and there's live music on Saturday night
in the winter. High tea (by reservation) includes finger sandwiches,
savories, assorted fruit, fancy squares, and scones. ⊠ *87 Regent St.,
Fredericton, New Brunswick, Canada* ☎ *506/458–8327.*

# WHERE TO STAY

*For expanded hotel reviews, visit Fodors.com.*

$ ▥**Carriage House Inn.** Originally the 1875 home of Fredericton's mayor,
this lovely Victorian-style mansion has beautifully decorated bedrooms
furnished with Victorian antiques. **Pros:** excellent location near every-
thing; fabulous breakfast; accommodating and friendly hosts. **Cons:**
decor might feel a bit overstuffed to some. ⊠ *230 University Ave., Fred-
ericton, New Brunswick, Canada* ☎ *506/452–9924, 800/267–6068*
⊕ *www.carriagehouse-inn.net* ⇆ *11 rooms* ⚲ *In-room: a/c, Wi-Fi. In-
hotel: parking* ⦿ *Breakfast.*

$$ ▥**Crowne Plaza Lord Beaverbrook Hotel.** This downtown waterfront
property is in the midst of the city's most important landmarks and
historic sites. **Pros:** has the comfort and amenities you'd expect from a
large chain hotel; convenient location. **Cons:** some rooms small. ⊠ *659
Queen St., Fredericton, New Brunswick, Canada* ☎ *506/455–3371,
866/444–1946* ⊕ *www.cpfredericton.com* ⇆ *155 rooms, 13 suites* ⚲ *In-
room: Wi-Fi. In-hotel: restaurant, bar, pool, gym, some pets allowed.*

$$$ ▥**Delta Fredericton Hotel.** This stately riverside property is a pleasant
walk from downtown, and the elegant decor is almost as delightful as
the sunset views over the river from the patio restaurant and many of
the modern rooms. **Pros:** comfort and amenities you'd expect from Can-
ada's leading hotel chain. **Cons:** pricey. ⊠ *225 Woodstock Rd., Freder-
icton, New Brunswick, Canada* ☎ *506/457–7000* ⊕ *www.deltahotels.
com* ⇆ *222 rooms, 14 suites* ⚲ *In-room: Wi-Fi. In-hotel: restaurant,
bar, pool, gym, spa, business center, parking, some pets allowed.*

$ ▥**Riverside Resort and Conference Centre.** Overlooking the Mactaquac
☾ Headpond, this modern hotel has a luxurious look but a relaxed,
country atmosphere. **Pros:** comfortable, affordable family accommo-
dations; lovely property. **Cons:** a few minutes outside of Fredericton.
⊠ *35 Mactaquac Rd., off Rte. 102, 20 km (12 mi) west of Fredericton,
Fredericton, New Brunswick, Canada* ☎ *506/363–5111, 800/561–5111*

⊕ *www.riversidefredericton.com* ⟳ *82 rooms, 4 suites, 6 cottages* ♿ *In-room: Internet. In-hotel: bar, pool, tennis court, gym, laundry facilities, some pets allowed.*

$  ▦ **The Very Best: A Victorian B&B.** This elegant and luxurious home, with its fine antiques and original artwork, is in the downtown Heritage Preservation Area. **Pros:** great central location in downtown Fredericton. **Cons:** lovely rooms, but sizes vary. ⊠ *806 George St., Fredericton, New Brunswick, Canada* ☎ *506/451–1499* ⊕ *www.bbcanada.com/2330.html* ⟳ *5 rooms* ♿ *In-room: Wi-Fi. In-hotel: pool, laundry facilities* ⎢◎⎢ *Breakfast.*

## NIGHTLIFE AND THE ARTS

### THE ARTS

**Calithumpians Theatre Company.** The Calithumpians Theatre Company has free outdoor performances daily in summer (12:15 weekdays, 2 weekends) in Officers' Square, and an evening Haunted Hike (C$13; Mon.–Sat. 9:15 pm) ambles through a historic neighborhood and ghostly graveyards. ⊠ *Fredericton, New Brunswick, Canada* ☎ *506/457–1975.*

**Harvest Jazz and Blues Festival.** The annual Harvest Jazz and Blues Festival takes place in mid-September, with venues all over downtown. ⊠ *81 Regent St., Fredericton, New Brunswick, Canada* ☎ *506/455–4523, 888/622–5837* ⊕ *www.harvestjazzandblues.com.*

**Playhouse.** The Playhouse is a performing arts venue for a wide range of entertainment, from comedy and concerts to theater and most other cultural performances, including Symphony New Brunswick, Theatre New Brunswick, and traveling ballet and dance companies. ⊠ *686 Queen St., Fredericton, New Brunswick, Canada* ☎ *506/458–8344.*

### NIGHTLIFE

★ Fredericton has a lively nightlife, with lots of live music in downtown pubs, especially on weekends. King Street and Piper's Lane, off the 300 block of King Street, have a number of spots.

**The Capital.** An eclectic collection of live bands, covering all genres, plays at the Capital Bar. It forms part of the Capital Complex, which also has a dance club and pub. ⊠ *362 Queen St., Fredericton, New Brunswick, Canada* ☎ *506/459–3558.*

**Dolan's Pub.** Dolan's Pub, owned by drummer Barry Hughes, has live rock and blues bands from all over Eastern Canada on Thursday, Friday, and Saturday nights, and a first-rate rock/blues open mic session on Wednesdays. ⊠ *349 King St., Fredericton, New Brunswick, Canada* ☎ *506/454–7474* ⊕ *www.dolanspub.ca.*

**F Studio.** Tucked away behind the King Street/Piper's Lane parking lot, up a metal staircase, this artsy bar features live rock, jazz, and blues bands, open mic (Tuesday), and karaoke (Wednesday), and there's soon to be a dance club and lounge on the second floor. ⊠ *377 King St., Fredericton, New Brunswick, Canada* ☎ *506/206–3266.*

**Isaac's Way.** Isaac's Way is a place to relax and enjoy comfort food with a twist. ⊠ *73 Carleton St., Fredericton, New Brunswick, Canada* ☎ *506/472–7937.*

**Lunar Rogue.** The Lunar Rogue has an Old World pub atmosphere, a globally ranked whiskey bar, and live music Saturday night except in summer. ⊠ *625 King St., Fredericton, New Brunswick, Canada* ☎ *506/450–2065* ⊕ *www.lunarrogue.com.*

**The Snooty Fox.** Live acoustic, folk, and easy-listening acts perform at this cozy downtown pub on Monday nights. ⊠ *66 Regent St., Fredericton, New Brunswick, Canada* ☎ *506/474–1199.*

## SPORTS AND THE OUTDOORS

### CANOEING AND KAYAKING

**Small Craft Aquatic Center.** Shells, canoes, and kayaks can be rented by the hour or day at the Small Craft Aquatic Center, which also arranges guided tours and instruction. ⊠ *Behind Victoria Health Centre where Brunswick St. becomes Woodstock Rd., Fredericton, New Brunswick, Canada* ☎ *506/460–2260.*

### GOLF

**Kingswood Park.** The Kingswood Park features an 18-hole, par-72 championship course and a 9-hole executive course designed by Cooke-Huxham International. ⊠ *31 Kingswood Park, Fredericton, New Brunswick, Canada* ☎ *506/443–3333, 800/423–5969* ⊕ *www.kingswoodpark.com.*

### SKIING

Many of Fredericton's 70 km (44 mi) of walking trails, especially those along the river and in Odell and Wilmot parks, are groomed for cross-country skiing.

**Ski Crabbe Mountain.** Ski Crabbe Mountain has 18 trails, a vertical drop of 263 meters (853 feet), snowboard and ski rentals, a ski shop, instruction, a skating pond, cross-country skiing, babysitting, and a lounge and restaurant. ⊠ *50 Crabbe Mountain Rd., 55 km [34 mi] west of Fredericton, Central Hainesville, New Brunswick, Canada* ☎ *506/463–8311 select 300 for Snow Phone* ⊕ *www.crabbemountain.com.*

### WALKING

Fredericton has a fine network of walking trails, one of which follows the river from the Green past the Victorian mansions on Waterloo Row, behind the Beaverbrook Art Gallery, and along the riverbank to the Sheraton.

**Visitor Information Center.** The visitor information center has a trail map. ⊠ *City Hall, Queen St. at York St., Fredericton, New Brunswick, Canada* ☎ *506/460–2129.*

## SHOPPING

Mammoth indoor crafts markets are held in the fall, and a Labor Day–weekend outdoor crafts fair (the New Brunswick Fine Crafts Festival) is held in Officers' Square. You can find pottery, blown glass, pressed flowers, turned wood, leather, and other items, all made by members of the New Brunswick Craft Council.

★ **Aitkens Pewter.** Aitkens Pewter designs, produces, and sells pewter goblets, belt buckles, candlesticks and other home decor pieces, and jewelry. ⊠ *408 Queen St., Fredericton, New Brunswick, Canada* ☎ *506/ 453–9474.*

**Bejewel.** Bejewel sparkles with wearable works of art. You can often see the jewelers working in the studio. ⊠ *540 Queen St., Fredericton, New Brunswick, Canada* ☎ *506/450–7305.*

**Botinicals.** Botinicals sells crafts by Maritime artisans. ⊠ *610 Queen St., Fredericton, New Brunswick, Canada* ☎ *506/454–6101.*

**Carrington & Co.** Carrington & Co. in the Delta is a gem for crafts and clothes, especially Tilley Endurables. ⊠ *225 Woodstock Rd., Fredericton, New Brunswick, Canada* ☎ *506/450–8415.*

**Eloise.** Eloise carries women's fashions, specializing in Canadian clothing lines. ⊠ *83 York St., Fredericton, New Brunswick, Canada* ☎ *506/453–7715.*

**Endeavours and Think Play.** Artistic endeavors are catered to here, with all kinds of art and crafts supplies and stationery, funky toys, and games that appeal to all ages. ⊠ *412 Queen St., Fredericton, New Brunswick, Canada* ☎ *506/455–4278, 506/472–7529* ⊕ *www.pendeavours.com, www.thinkplay.ca.*

**Gallery 78.** Gallery 78 has original works by Atlantic Canadian artists. ⊠ *976 Queen St., Fredericton, New Brunswick, Canada* ☎ *506/ 454–5192.*

**River Valley Crafts and Artist Studios.** At River Valley Crafts and Artist Studios you'll find pottery, jewelry, paintings, and other crafts. ⊠ *Soldiers' Barracks in the Historic Garrison District, Barracks Sq., 485 Queen St., Fredericton, New Brunswick, Canada* ☎ *506/460–2837.*

**Urban Almanac General Store.** The Urban Almanac General Store sells an eclectic collection of household gifts, furniture, loose-leaf teas, gadgets, and gizmos of exemplary design. ⊠ *75 York St., Fredericton, New Brunswick, Canada* ☎ *506/450–4334* ⊕ *www.urbanalmanac.com.*

## VILLAGE OF GAGETOWN

*50 km (31 mi) southeast of Fredericton.*

The historic riverside Village of Gagetown—not to be confused with the Gagetown military base at Oromocto—bustles in summer, when artists welcome visitors, many of whom arrive by boat and tie up at the marina, to their studios and galleries. It also has several small restaurants with interesting menus.

### GETTING HERE AND AROUND

If you're driving from Fredericton, the Trans-Canada Highway (Route 2) is fast and direct, leaving at exit 330, signposted "Village of/de Gagetown"(do not follow the earlier signs for "Gagetown," which lead to the military base). Route 102 from Fredericton is the scenic option. Once there, the village is great for strolling.

## EXPLORING

**Queens County Museum.** The Queens County Museum is growing by leaps and bounds. Its original building, **Tilley House** (a National Historic Site), was the birthplace of Sir Leonard Tilley, one of the Fathers of Confederation. It displays Loyalist and First Nations artifacts, early-20th-century medical equipment, Victorian glassware, and more.

**Queens County Courthouse.** The nearby Queens County Courthouse is part of the museum and has archival material and courthouse furniture as well as changing exhibits. ⊠ *16 Courthouse Rd., Gagetown, New Brunswick, Canada* ☎ *506/488–2483* ⊠ *69 Front St., Gagetown, New Brunswick, Canada* ☎ *506/488–2483* ⊕ *www.queenscountyheritage. com* 🖻 *C$3 for both buildings* ☉ *Mid-June–mid-Sept., daily 10–5.*

## WHERE TO STAY

*For expanded hotel reviews, visit Fodors.com.*

$ 🛏 **Step-Aside B&B.** In the heart of the village, this waterfront heritage B&B overlooks the marina. **Pros:** delicious breakfast; friendly and knowledgeable owners. **Cons:** bathrooms in the original house are private but not en suite. ⊠ *58 Front St., Gagetown, New Brunswick, Canada* ☎ *506/488–1808* ⊕ *www.bbcanada.com/6860.html* 🛏 *4 rooms* ♿ *In-room: a/c* ☉ *Closed Jan.–Apr.* ⦿| *Breakfast.*

## SHOPPING

**Grieg's Pottery.** Grieg's Pottery carries superior pottery made on the premises. ⊠ *36 Front St., Gagetown, New Brunswick, Canada* ☎ *506/488–2074.*

**Grimross Crafts.** Grimross Crafts represents 25 area craftspeople. ⊠ *64 Front St., Gagetown, New Brunswick, Canada* ☎ *506/488–2832.*

**Juggler's Cove.** Juggler's Cove is a studio-gallery featuring pottery and paintings. ⊠ *27 Front St., Gagetown, New Brunswick, Canada* ☎ *506/488–2574.*

# Prince Edward Island

**WORD OF MOUTH**

"To my mind the central fact of PEI is the strong color everywhere. The red soil, the incredibly green grass and trees and the blue skies punctuated by the glorious wildflowers (pink, white, blue) and the roses/peonies are just simply breathtaking. It is a calm beauty not one of stark or dramatic sights. The Gentle Island is a fitting nickname for PEI. . . . Dalvay by the Sea . . . is beyond wonderful."

—cmcfong

# WELCOME TO PRINCE EDWARD ISLAND

Yeo House, Green Park Provincial Park

## TOP REASONS TO GO

★ **Overdose on Anne:** The orphan nobody wanted has been adopted by the world. She's everywhere on the Island, but Cavendish's Green Gables farmhouse is ground zero.

★ **Get Beached:** Been there? Dune this. The most jaded, jet-setting beach bum will still be dazzled by the parabolic dunes at Prince Edward Island National Park in Greenwich.

★ **Go Golfing:** A concentration of championship courses—among them The Links at Crowbush Cove, Dundarave, and Brudenell River—make PEI a top choice for golfers.

★ **Cycle the Confederation Trail:** Even "I haven't ridden a bike in ages" types can cover the stunning 10-km (6-mi) waterside stretch between Morell and St. Peter's Bay.

★ **Sup on Fresh Seafood:** Forget the frozen fish sticks of your childhood. The local seafood here—whether served in a classy restaurant or community hall—is sensational.

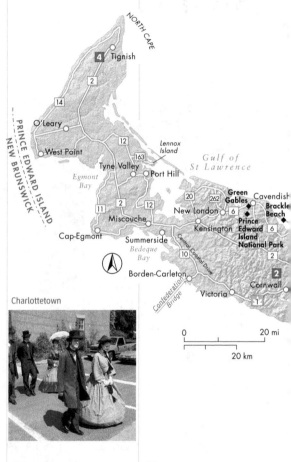

Charlottetown

**1 Charlottetown.** PEI's historic capital city has urban amenities and a small-town vibe. Centrally located, it makes an excellent base for exploring the Island.

**2 Central Coastal Drive.** This 198-km (123-mi) circuit encompasses Green Gables, Prince Edward Island National Park, and the less-touristed Red Sands Shore.

endish

QUEBEC

3

## GETTING ORIENTED

Erosion and time have gnawed Prince Edward Island into a ragged crescent, with deep inlets and tidal streams that divide the province into three nearly equal parts, known locally by their county names (from east to west) of Kings, Queens, and Prince. The Island is 195 km (121 mi) long and ranges in width from 6 km (4 mi) to 61¼ km (38 mi). Despite the gentle hills in the eastern and central regions of Prince Edward Island, the land never rises to a height of more than 152 meters (500 feet) above sea level. To the west, from Summerside to North Cape, the terrain is flatter.

**3** **Points East Coastal Drive.** Lovely lighthouses and great golf courses plus fishing ports, hidden coves, singing sands, and fun festivals are all highlights here.

**4** **North Cape Coastal Drive.** Anchored by Summerside (the Island's second largest city), this region includes a distinctive coastline and farm-filled interior.

Updated
by Susan
MacCallum-
Whitcomb

Prince Edward Island is a unique landmass marked by verdant patchwork fields that stretch out beneath an endless cobalt sky to meet sandy white beaches and the surrounding sea. At just 195 km (121 mi) long and 61¼ km (38 mi) wide, its accessible size is part of the Island's appeal. Warm hospitality welcomes you, and the laid-back, slow-paced Island lifestyle entices visitors to return year after year.

Colonized by France in 1603, Prince Edward Island (or Île Saint-Jean, as it was then called) was handed over to Britain under the Treaty of Paris in 1763. Tensions steadily increased as absentee British governors and proprietors failed to take an active interest in the area's growth; nevertheless, the development of fisheries and agriculture in the early 19th century strengthened the local economy. Soon settlement increased, and those willing to take a chance on the Island prospered.

As relations between emboldened tenants and their distant landlords continued to worsen, heated talk about uniting with other colonies in British North America began. (The Civil War, then raging in the United States, made the idea of forging a peaceable alliance all the more appealing.) So in 1864, the Island's capital city hosted the Charlottetown Conference, a milestone in this nation's history, which ultimately led to the creation of the Dominion of Canada in 1867.

Despite this political alliance, it took another 130 years—and almost 13 km (8 mi) of concrete—for Prince Edward Island to be *physically* linked with the rest of the country. When the Confederation Bridge opened between Borden-Carleton and Cape Jourimain, New Brunswick, in 1997, traditionalists feared it would destroy PEI's tranquillity. (As you explore the villages and fishing ports, it's easy to see why they cherish it so.) Yet outside the tourist mecca of Cavendish, the Island still seems like an oasis of peace in an increasingly busy world.

## PLANNING

### THE CONFEDERATION TRAIL

In the 1980s, new life was given to the ground once covered by the Prince Edward Island Railway when the abandoned track was converted into a recreational route. Today the Confederation Trail (part of the larger Trans-Canada Trail system) extends almost the complete length of the Island, from Tignish to Elmira. Gorgeous, well groomed, and generally flat, its 357 km (222 mi) are ideal for hiking and, above all, biking. Cyclists can race through it in 17 hours. But most opt for a more leisurely pace that allows them to stop and smell the lupines. Companies like Eastwind Cycle and Freewheeling Adventures help you do this in style by providing multiday inn-to-inn trips complete with luggage transfers and van support. No law, however, states that the trail has to be covered in its entirety. If you're short on time, rent a bike from any cycle shop and just do a single section. Plum-colored access gates are located near roadways at many points, and food and lodging are available at villages along the way. Tourism PEI (⊕ *www. tourismpei.com*) provides details on rental locations and touring tips, plus a free "Confederation Trail Cycling Guide" that includes maps and itinerary highlights.

Plan to actually arrive using pedal power? A round-trip ferry ride will set cyclists back C$20. You won't be permitted to bike across the Confederation Bridge, but a shuttle that operates 24/7 on a load-and-go will carry you and your bike across for C$8. Just a final heads-up: helmets are compulsory in PEI for drivers and passengers, regardless of age.

### DEALS AND DISCOUNTS

The PEI Heritage Passport allows you up to 35% savings on admission to three of the seven provincial museums (from west to east, the Green Park Shipbuilding Museum, Acadian Museum, Eptek Art & Culture Centre, Beaconsfield Historic House, Orwell Corner Historic Village, Basin Head Fisheries Museum, and Elmira Railway Museum). Prices are C$9.95 for adults and C$29.95 for a family of two adults and two children. For further information, see ⊕ *www.peimuseum.com* or call ☏ *902/368–6600*.

### EXPERIENCE REQUIRED

Prince Edward Island may be a Lilliputian place with a laid-back atmosphere but it has a very sophisticated tourism sector that is constantly coming up with new ways to engage visitors. The provincial tourism board has bundled the best of them together under the Authentic PEI Experiences banner. Eager to haul a lobster trap or tour a potato farm? No problem. Prefer to paint a watercolor or turn PEI's signature red clay into a piece of pottery? Consider it done. How about trying your hand at fiddling or deep-sea fishing? Those too can be arranged. Click ⊕ *www.tourismpei.com/pei-experiences* for complete listings.

### FESTIVALS

June through mid-October, the calendar is crowded with events—many of them arts-oriented. The spotlight shines brightest on the Charlottetown Festival (☏ *902/628–1864* ⊕ *charlottetownfestival.com*), where *Anne of Green Gables—The Musical* takes center stage. But Summerside, Georgetown, and Victoria-by-the-Sea each host their own summer theater festival. Different musical genres are represented, too. In June, the province-wide Island Fusion Festival (☏ *800/463–4734* ⊕ *www. tourismpei.com/fusion*) celebrates multicultural music. Cavendish goes a little bit country during July's Cavendish Beach Music Festival (*No phone* ⊕ *www.cavendishbeachmusic.com*)—make that a lot country: Brad Paisley and Reba McEntire are past headliners—and the Souris area counters with festivals devoted to bluegrass and fiddling the same month. The capital, meanwhile, gets jazzed up in August for the PEI Jazz & Blues Festival (☏ *902/894–8364* ⊕ *www.jazzandblues.ca*).

Sporting events are also prevalent, among them Old Home Week (☏ *902/629–6623* ⊕ *www.oldhomeweekpei.com*), which is centered on harness racing, and the PEI Marathon (☏ *902/629–6609* ⊕ *www. princeedwardislandmarathon.com*). These are held in Charlottetown during August and October respectively. If you think eating is an extreme sport, there are numerous over-the-top seafood festivals too *(see the "Enjoying Shellfish" box for specifics)*.

## GETTING HERE AND AROUND

### BY AIR

Scheduled air service operates in and out of Charlottetown Airport (YYG), 5 km (3 mi) north of the capital. Air Canada runs direct service year-round from Halifax, Montreal, Ottawa, and Toronto. WestJet provides year-round service from Toronto. Delta has non-stop flights to Charlottetown, but only from mid-June to mid-September. At the airport you can rent a car or grab a cab for the C$11 drive into town.

**Air Canada** ☏ *888/247–2262* ⊕ *www.aircanada.ca.*

**Charlottetown Airport** ☏ *902/566–7997* ⊕ *www.flypei.com.*

**Delta Airlines** ☏ *800/221–1212, 800/241–4141* ⊕ *www.delta.com.*

**WestJet** ☏ *888/937–8538* ⊕ *www.westjet.com.*

### BY BIKE

**Eastwind Cycle** ☏ *902/471–4424* ⊕ *www.eastwindcycle.com.*

**Freewheeling Adventures** ☏ *902/857–3600, 800/672—0775* ⊕ *www. freewheeling.ca.*

### BY BUS

Acadian Lines offers daily scheduled service, via Moncton, to Borden-Carleton, Charlottetown, and Summerside. Mini-bus service to Borden-Carleton, Charlottetown, and Summerside is available from Halifax through PEI Express Shuttle or Advanced Shuttle Service.

**Acadian Lines** ☏ *800/567–515* ⊕ *www.acadianbus.com.*

**Advanced Shuttle Service** ☏ *902/888–3353, 877/886–3322* ⊕ *www. advancedshuttleservice.ca.*

**PEI Express Shuttle** ☏ *902/462–8177, 877/877–1771* ⊕ *www.peishuttle.com.*

### BY CAR OR MOTORCYCLE

Due to limited public transport, having your own wheels is almost a necessity on the Island. Motorists can come via the 13-km (8-mi) Confederation Bridge, which connects Cape Jourimain, New Brunswick, with Borden-Carleton, PEI. The crossing takes about 10 minutes, and the toll is C$27.25 for motorcycles, C$43.25 for cars and, for larger vehicles, C$7 per each additional axle. On the island, there are more than 3,700 km (2,300 mi) of paved road, including three scenic drives: North Cape Coastal Drive, Central Coastal Drive, and Points East Coastal Drive. Designated Heritage Roads offer an old-fashioned alternative. Surfaced with red clay (the local soil base) and often arched with a canopy of trees, they meander through rural, undeveloped areas where you're likely to see lots of wildflowers and birds. A four-wheel-drive vehicle isn't necessary, but in spring and inclement weather the mud can get quite deep, making narrow, unpaved roads impassable. A highway map of the province is available from Tourism PEI and at visitor centers on the Island. Specific info for motorcyclists is also available online through Motorcycle Prince Edward Island.

■TIP→ Don't get too excited about crossing over to the Island without purchasing a ferry ticket or paying the bridge toll. Fares are only collected when you leave PEI—giving you further incentive to stay.

**Confederation Bridge** ☎ 902/437–7300, 888/437-6565 ⊕ www. confederationbridge.com.

**Motorcycle Prince Edward Island** ⊕ www.motorcyclepei.com.

### BY FERRY

Weather permitting, Northumberland Ferries sails between Wood Islands, PEI, and Caribou, Nova Scotia, from May to late December. The crossing takes about 75 minutes, and there are three to nine per day depending on the season. Round-trip rates vary with the length of vehicle; those up to 6 meters (20 feet) long cost C$65 and those up to 15.25 meters (50 feet) long cost C$105. Foot passengers are charged C$16, cyclists C$20, and motorcyclists C$40. Fuel surcharges (C$5 per passenger vehicle at the time of writing) must also be added in.

**Northumberland Ferries** ☎ 888/249–7245 ⊕ www.nfl-bay.com.

### LOCAL DINING

As in many other parts of Atlantic Canada, local ingredients are key. So when you see lobster, mussels, and oysters on the menu, they're likely from the neighborhood; ditto for organic produce and PEI's renowned potatoes. The island's dining scene has grown in recent years as innovative restaurants have opened, primarily in Charlottetown. You can eat Italian, French, Lebanese, Asian, or Canadian with a contemporary twist, yet the ambience remains relaxed even in the finest places. If dining is your true raison d'être be sure to investigate the PEI Flavours' Culinary Trail (⊕ www.peiflavours.com). Not only does it pinpoint restaurants, farmers' markets, fishmongers, and related festivals, it also tells you where to experience cool culinary adventures like clam digging or Cows Creamery tours. Aspiring amateur chefs will also find info on cooking "boot camps."

### LODGING

Full-service resorts, posh boutique hotels, modest motels, and cute country cottages are just some of your lodging options on PEI. If you're planning to arrive in July or August, it's wise to book three to six months in advance—either directly or through the province's online reservation system (⊕ www.tourismpei.com/pei-online-reservations). Note that all accommodations here are nonsmoking and precious few have elevators. Due to the sandy composition of the land, it's too expensive to lay the necessary foundations for them (we note *in this chapter* only when a hotel *does* have an elevator). But staff are always ready to help lift luggage. Since so many of the lodgings here are still family owned and operated, friendly service is pretty much guaranteed.

## WHAT IT COSTS

| | ¢ | $ | $$ | $$$ | $$$$ |
|---|---|---|---|---|---|
| **WHAT IT COSTS IN CANADIAN DOLLARS** | | | | | |
| Restaurants | under C$8 | C$8–C$12 | C$13–C$20 | C$21–C$30 | over C$30 |
| Hotels | under C$75 | C$75–C$125 | C$126–C$175 | C$176–C$250 | over C$250 |

Restaurant prices are per person for a main course at dinner. Hotel prices are for two people in a standard double room in high season.

### WHEN TO GO?

PEI is generally considered a summer destination—in July and August the beaches have the warmest water north of the Carolinas—but don't overlook the shoulder seasons. May, June, September, and October usually have fine weather and few visitors. In late spring those famous farm fields look especially green, and bright wildflowers blanket the roadsides. Autumn, too, is multihued thanks to the changing fall foliage. If white is your color, come in winter for cross-country skiing, snow-mobiling, and ice skating. Bear in mind that many sights and services outside the cities do close in mid-October; however, you won't have any problem finding food, lodging, and fun things to do year-round in Charlottetown or Summerside.

# CHARLOTTETOWN

Designated as the Island capital in 1765, Charlottetown is both PEI's oldest and largest urban center. However, since the whole "metropolitan" area only has a population of about 60,000, a pleasing small-town atmosphere remains. The city is a winner appearance-wise as well. Peppered with gingerbread-clad homes, converted warehouses, striking churches, and monumental government buildings, Charlottetown's core seems relatively unchanged from its 19th-century heyday when it hosted the conference that led to the formation of Canada. The city is understandably proud of its role as the "Birthplace of Confederation" and, in summer, downtown streets are dotted with people dressed as personages from the past who'll regale you with tales about the Confederation debate. Regular residents are equally friendly. So whether you've come to see the sites, browse the shops, or dine in one of the top-notch restaurants, a warm greeting awaits.

### GETTING HERE AND AROUND

The city center is compact, so walking is the way to go. If you drive in for a day of sightseeing, you can park at an on-street meter or in garages like those on Pownal, Queen, and Fitzroy streets. Alternately, you can rent a bike at **Smooth Cycle, Go Wheelin Bike Rentals,** or **MacQueen's Bike Shop.** Rentals start around C$25 per day. **Trius Transit** also operates trolley-style buses as part of a public-private partnership (some cover the surrounding communities of Cornwall and Stratford, too). Most have their hub downtown at the Confederation Centre of the Arts, and the fare is C$2 in exact change. Prefer a guided tour? **Founders'**

# PEI ITINERARIES

### IF YOU HAVE 3 DAYS

Begin your Island escape by crossing the Confederation Bridge from the mainland to Borden-Carleton. The PEI section of the TransCanada Highway begins here and continues through Charlottetown to the Wood Islands Ferry Terminal. Following it, make your first stop 22 km (14 mi) east in **Victoria**, one of the Island's quaintest little communities. Proceeding on to **Charlottetown**, you'll have time to see key city sights and catch a performance of *Anne of Green Gables—The Musical* at the Confederation Centre before bedtime. On Day 2 make the 39-km (24-mi) cross-Island drive to **The Green Gables Shore**—aka northern Queens County—for the quintessential PEI sun-and-sand experience. Landing in **Cavendish**, you can lounge on the beach (or take advantage of the educational programming) in Prince Edward Island National Park; make a pilgrimage to the Green Gables farmhouse (Anne's fictional home); then indulge in some cheesy but fun amusements along the Route 6 strip. On Day 3, veer 91 km (57 mi) east to **Georgetown** in Kings County. Take a stroll through this classic waterside town, then sign on for one of the up-close seafood encounters run locally by Tranquility Cove Adventures. From Georgetown, it's a 41-km (26-mi) drive south to **Wood Islands**, where you can catch a ferry back to the mainland. Just bear in mind that May through mid-November, the last one leaves at 8 pm. Note that this route can essentially be done in reverse if you're entering the Island by way of the Northumberland Strait boat.

### IF YOU HAVE 5 DAYS

Stick to the above itinerary but leave an extra day to pursue your passion in both Queens County and Kings County. In the former that might mean investigating more Anne-related sites or sussing out PEI's other famous export—oysters. In the latter, it might mean looking at lighthouses or cycling an especially nice section of the Confederation Trail. Beach bumming and golfing opportunities also abound in each.

### IF YOU HAVE 7 DAYS

Since PEI is so small, you can see it all. Travelers who want comprehensive coverage can spend their additional two days exploring Prince County to the west: **Summerside** (the Island's second city) and windy **North Cape** are well worth a look, as is the rich, agricultural area inland. An alternative, though, is to stop driving and just drink it all in. Prince Edward Island is an ideal place to decompress. So simply park yourself somewhere—anywhere—and give yourself permission to genuinely relax.

**Hall** organizes C$12.50 walks led by costumed interpreters at 11 am, mid-June through August. A ghostly evening version is also available. The amphibious **Harbour Hippo** offers hour-long land-and-sea tours (C$20) through town, June through September, from its headquarters at Prince Street Wharf, near Founders' Hall. **Abegweit Tours,** meanwhile, runs one-hour double-decker bus tours of the city ($11), as well as full-day tours to the North Shore (C$80) and "Anne's Land" (C$65).

**ESSENTIALS**

**Abegweit Tours** ☎ *902/894–9966*
⊕ *www.abegweittours.ca.*

**Founders' Hall Walking Tours**
✉ *Charlottetown, Prince Edward Island,
Canada* ☎ *902/368–1864* ⊕ *www.
foundershall.ca.*

**Go Wheelin Bike Rentals** ✉ *6 Prince
St., Charlottetown, Prince Edward Island,
Canada* ☎ *902/566–5259, 877/286–
6532* ⊕ *www.gowheelinpei.com.*

**Harbour Hippo** ☎ *902/628–8687*
⊕ *www.harbourhippo.com.*

**MacQueen's Bike Shop** ✉ *430 Queen
St., Charlottetown, Prince Edward Island,
Canada* ☎ *902/368–2453, 800/969–
2822* ⊕ *www.macqueens.com.*

**Smooth Cycle** ✉ *330 University
Ave., Charlottetown, Prince Edward Island, Canada* ☎ *902/569–5690* ⊕ *www.
smoothcycle.com.*

**Trius Transit** ☎ *902/566–9962* ⊕ *www.triustransit.ca.*

> ## WHAT'S IN A NAME?
>
> Prince Edward Island was named for the fourth son of King George III (the monarch who lost America in the War of Independence). A rather run-of-the-mill royal, Edward seemed destined to be little more than an historical footnote until he was saved from obscurity by Britain's convoluted rules of succession. Because none of Edward's older siblings had living heirs (at least not legitimate ones), his daughter took the throne by default when she was just 18 years old. Her name? Victoria.

## TOP ATTRACTIONS

☾ **Beaconsfield Historic House.** Designed by W.C. Harris in 1877 for shipbuilder James Peake Jr., this gracious mansion-*cum*-museum near the entrance to Victoria Park is one of the Island's finest historic homes. The 11 furnished rooms have rich architectural details and accents (imagine ornate plaster moldings and imported chandeliers)—little wonder the once-wealthy Peake went bankrupt soon after his house was completed. Having taken a tour of the first and second floors, pause to enjoy a view of Charlottetown Harbour from the veranda. An on-site bookstore has a variety of Island publications, and special events (such as musical performances and history-themed lectures) are held year-round. A carriage house on the grounds also hosts a children's festival on weekday mornings, mid-July through late-August. ✉ *2 Kent St., Charlottetown, Prince Edward Island, Canada* ☎ *902/368–6603* ⊕ *www.peimuseum. com* 🎫 *C$4.50* ☾ *July–late Aug., daily 10–5; late Aug.–Oct., weekdays noon–4; Nov.–June, call for hrs.*

**Boardwalk.** Charlottetown's boardwalk extends from Confederation Landing to Victoria Park, wending its way along the water past historic sites and leafy picnic spots, providing views of sailboats and cruise ships enroute. As an added bonus, it's lit at night for romantic strolls. ✉ *Charlottetown, Prince Edward Island, Canada.*

☾
★ **Confederation Centre of the Arts.** With a 1,100-seat main stage theater, a 1,000-seat outdoor amphitheater, and several studio stages, this block-long building—opened in 1964 to mark the centennial of the Charlottetown Conference—is the Island's leading cultural venue. Each year, from

## A Good Walk

Start your walk at the **Confederation Centre of the Arts** on Richmond Street, in the heart of downtown. Housing the provincial art gallery and a public library, it's also home to the **Charlottetown Festival**. Next door, the **Province House National Historic Site** is where the first meeting to discuss federal union took place. Turn onto Great George Street, dipping into **St. Dunstan's Basilica**, a Roman Catholic Church notable for its twin Gothic spires. Then continue down Great George to the water, where you can enjoy lunch at a wharf-side restaurant or a picnic in **Confederation Landing Park**. Next, follow the boardwalk to **Founders' Hall**. After going

inside for a crash course in Canadian history, head back to Province House and explore the shops of **Victoria Row** before investigating what Queen Street has to offer in the way of pubs and restaurants. Many visitors will be happy to call it a day there. But if you have the time (and attention span) for one further sight, venture west to visit one of the finest 19th-century residential buildings in the city: **Beaconsfield Historic House**.

**TIMING:** The downtown area can be explored on foot in a few hours, but the wealth of sights and harbor views warrants a full day.

mid-June through September, it hosts the famous **Charlottetown Festival** (☎ 902/628–1864 or 800/565–0278 ⊕ www.charlottetownfestival. com), which includes *Anne of Green Gables—The Musical,* plus concerts, comedy acts, and other theatrical productions. Weather permitting, the festival offers free lunchtime performances in the amphitheater and on the plaza. Off-season, a dynamic mix of touring and local productions, choral concerts, and special events is also scheduled. Visitors planning to take advantage of any of these will find that the Centre's bar and bistro, Mavor's ($$$), makes a convenient spot for pre-show dining. Also on-site: a provincial art gallery and public library. The former (which has over 15,000 works in its collection) holds year-round exhibits showcasing Canadian art. The latter, being cool and quiet, offers a welcome break from vacation craziness. ⊠ *145 Richmond St., Charlottetown, Prince Edward Island, Canada* ☎ *902/566–1267, 800/565–0278* ⊕ *www. confederationcentre.com* ☉ *Gallery: mid-May–mid-Oct., daily 9–5; mid-Oct.–mid-May, Wed.–Sat. 11–5, Sun. 1–5. Library: Mon., Fri., and Sat. 10–5, Tues.–Thurs. 10–9 (10–8 in summer), Sun. 1–5.*

☉ **Founders' Hall–Canada's Birthplace Pavilion.** The state-of-the-art exhibits and multimedia displays at this 21,000-square-foot interpretive center on the Historic Charlottetown Waterfront merge high tech with history. A case in point: the "Time Travel Tunnel," which transports visitors back to the Charlottetown Conference of 1864, eventually returning them to the present day with a greater understanding of how Canada came together as a country. In addition to its own inviting gift shop, Founders' Hall has a civic visitor information center and a TicketPro location on-site, so you can pick up maps, brochures, and advice, purchase theater tickets, and more. ⊠ *Historic Charlottetown Waterfront,*

Beaconsfield
Historic
House ......... 10

Boardwalk ...... 5

Confederation
Centre
of the Arts ...... 1

Confederation
Landing
Park ............. 6

Founders'
Hall-Canada's
Birthplace
Pavilion ......... 7

Port-La-Joye—
Fort Amherst
Historic Site ... 12

Province
House
National
Historic Site .... 2

Red Shores
Racetrack and
Casino ........ 13

St. Dunstan's
Basilica ......... 4

St. Paul's Anglican
Church .......... 3

St. Peter's
Cathedral ..... 11

Victoria Park .... 9

Victoria Row .... 8

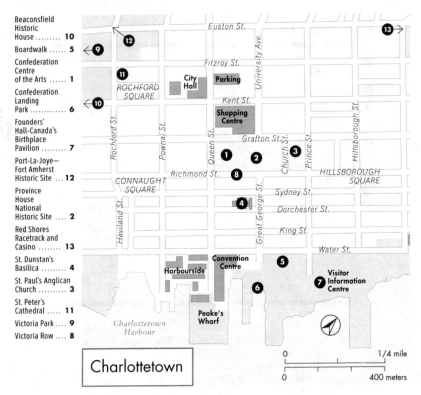

Charlottetown

*6 Price St., Charlottetown, Prince Edward Island, Canada* ☎ *902/368–1864, 800/955–1864* ⊕ *www.foundershall.ca* ✉ *C$9.50* ⊗ *May, daily 9–4; June, daily 9–6; July–Aug., daily 8:30–8; Sept.–Oct., daily 9–4:30; Nov.–April, weekdays 9–3:30.*

**Port-La-Joye–Fort Amherst National Historic Site.** History buffs can delve deeper into PEI's past by driving 20 minutes west of town to the Port-La-Joye-Fort Amherst National Historic Site. Today's verdant grounds hide a tale of colonial intrigue. Ownership of the land seesawed between England and France until 1758, when the British used Fort Amherst (as they called it) as a base from which to expel Acadians. You can stroll along the wooded trails and over the original earthworks or just enjoy the panoramic views of Charlottetown Harbour. Guided 45-minute tours are given several times daily in July and August. ⊠ *191 Hache Gallant La., off Rte. 19, Rocky Point, Prince Edward Island, Canada* ☎ *902/566–7626* ⊕ *www.pc.gc.ca/eng/lhn-nhs/pe/amherst/index.aspx* ✉ *C$3.90* ⊗ *June–Oct., daily 9–5.*

★ **Province House National Historic Site.** This three-story neoclassical sandstone structure, completed in 1847 to house the colonial government, is a designated National Historic Site and remains the seat of the Provincial Legislature. Period rooms, now restored to their 1860s appearance, include the Confederation Chamber where representatives of the

19th-century British colonies originally gathered. A short film explains the significance of their meeting; and, in summer, there are themed interpretive programs available weekdays from 9 to 5. July through September, starting at 9:30 pm, the PEI Sound and Light Show (which focuses on Confederation and the Island) is projected onto the front of the building as well. Visitors more interested in the "hot potato" topics of today are welcome to watch from a public gallery as local politicos debate during the Spring and Fall legislative sessions. ⊠ *165 Richmond St., Charlottetown, Prince Edward Island, Canada* ☎ *902/566–7626* ⊕ *www.assembly.pe.ca* ✉ *By donation* ◷ *Mid-Oct.–May, weekdays 9–5; June–mid-Oct., daily 9–5.*

**3**

**NEED A BREAK?**

**Cows Ice Cream.** Cows Ice Cream is the most famous frozen treat on the Island. Using a family recipe, fresh milk from Prince Edward Island cows is carefully combined with other fine, natural ingredients to create more than 32 flavors of premium ice cream that should be slowly savored (ideally in a handmade waffle cone). Cows sells humorously captioned T-shirts plus "udder stuff" embellished with their cartoonish cow logo as well.

Ice cream aficionados will also find Cows outlets open seasonally on Route 6 in Cavendish, in Gateway Village at the approach to the Confederation Bridge, and on board the PEI–Nova Scotia passenger ferry, *The Confederation.* ⊠ 150 Queen St., Charlottetown, Prince Edward Island, Canada ☎ 902/892–6969 ⊕ www.cows.ca ✉ Peake's Wharf, Charlottetown, Prince Edward Island, Canada ☎ 902/566–4886.

**Cows Creamery Factory.** Just outside of Charlottetown, the Cows Creamery Factory offers 30-minute tours that teach you everything you need to know about ice cream production. Following a film (shown in the "Milky Whey Theater"), you can watch staff make waffle cones, whimsical T-shirts, cheddar cheese, and, of course, that award-winning ice cream. Happily, lick-worthy samples are included. ⊠ 397 Capital Dr., Charlottetown, Prince Edward Island, Canada ☎ 902/370–3155 ✉ C$6 ◷ Tours daily (on the half hr) 10–4.

**Victoria Row.** The section of Richmond Street between Queen and Great George streets is home to a variety of shops (Island crafts, art, handmade paper, hand-knitted sweaters, chocolates, antiques, and glassware are just some of what you'll find inside), together with eateries, cafés, and a dance club. This vibrant, compact stretch of road really comes alive in summer, when traffic is blocked off and you'll frequently see musicians perform at lunchtime or in the evenings. For more shopping, head around the corner to Queen Street or Water Street. ⊠ *Charlottetown, Prince Edward Island, Canada.*

## WORTH NOTING

**Confederation Landing Park.** This waterfront recreation area at the bottom of Great George Street occupies the site where the Fathers of Confederation famously landed in 1864. Walkways and park benches offer plenty of opportunities to survey the activity of the harbor, with the added attraction of banks and banks of wild rose bushes behind. During summer, performers in period costume stroll about the area re-creating the events that led up to Canadian Confederation. Occasionally, the park also doubles as a venue for Canadian acts like Nickelback or Cirque du Soleil. **Peake's Wharf,** right next to it, has casual restaurants and bars, souvenir and crafts shops, and a marina where boat tours can be arranged. It hosts its own outdoor concert series in peak months. Featuring local talent, the free shows start at 2:30 and 6:30 daily. ⊠ *Water St. between Queen and Hillsborough Sts., Charlottetown, Prince Edward Island, Canada* 🎫 *Free* ⊙ *Daily dawn–dusk.*

**Red Shores Racetrack and Casino.** Since 1880 this track at the eastern end of the city has been the home of a sport dear to islanders—harness racing. (No, they don't race harnesses. They race horses harnessed to tippy, two-wheeled carriages called sulkies). An on-site theater simulcasts racing from other tracks, while slot machines and Texas Hold'em provide further gambling options. If you'd rather save your dollars for dinner, there is excellent dining at the Top of the Park Dining Room ($$–$$$) too. In August, during **Old Home Week** (☎ *902/629–6623* ⊕ *www.oldhomeweekpei.com*), Eastern Canada's best harness horses converge here for 15 races in nine days. Old Home Week also brings the provincial agricultural exhibition and a family-friendly midway to Red Shores. ⊠ *21 Exhibition Dr., Charlottetown, Prince Edward Island, Canada* ☎ *902/620–4222, 877/620–4222* ⊕ *www.redshores.ca* 🎫 *Free* ⊙ *Mon.–Thurs., 11 am–midnight; Fri. and Sat., 11 am–2 am; Sun., noon–midnight; races Apr.–Jan., schedule varies.*

**St. Dunstan's Basilica.** One of Canada's largest churches, St. Dunstan's, is the seat of the Roman Catholic diocese on the Island. The church is known for its fine Italian carvings and twin Gothic spires. ⊠ *45 Great George St., Charlottetown, Prince Edward Island, Canada* ☎ *902/894–3486* ⊕ *www.stdunstans.pe.ca* ⊙ *Weekdays 9–5; Services weekdays at noon, Sat. at 9 and 5, Sun. at 10:30 and 5.*

**St. Paul's Anglican Church.** Erected in 1896, this is actually the third church building on the same site. The first was erected in 1769, making this parish the Island's oldest. Large sandstone blocks give it a heavy exterior. However, the interior seems to soar heavenward, largely because of the vaulted ceilings: a common architectural feature of churches designed by W.C. "Willy" Harris. It seats only 450 but appears much larger. Harris is reputed to be the Island's finest architect, and St. Paul's will give you an idea why. Some of the stained glass dates back to the 19th century. ⊠ *101 Prince St., Charlottetown, Prince Edward Island, Canada* ☎ *902/892–1691* ⊕ *www.stpaulschurch.ca* ⊙ *Weekdays 9–5; Sun. services at 8 and 10 am.*

**St. Peter's Cathedral.** The glorious murals adorning this Anglican edifice's **All Souls' Chapel** were painted by artist Robert Harris, and the chapel itself was designed in 1888 by his brother W.C. Harris, the most celebrated Island architect. (It is attached to the side of the cathedral. If it isn't open, just ask.) Within the main sanctuary, free summer organ recitals are given Thursdays at noon. ⊠ *Rochford Square, All Souls'*

*Lane and Rochford St., Charlottetown, Prince Edward Island, Canada* ☎ *902/566–2102* ⊕ *www.stpeter.org/cathedra.html* ⊙ *Weekdays 9–5; Sun. morning services at 8 and 10:30 (10 in summer).*

⟲ **Victoria Park.** At the southern tip of the city, overlooking Charlottetown Harbour, sit 40 serene acres that provide the perfect place to stroll, picnic, or cool off on a hot day. Next to the park, on a hill between groves of white birches, is the white Georgian-style **Government House.** Built in 1834 as the official residence for Lieutenant Governors (the Queen's provincial representatives), it's open weekdays in July and August from 10 to 4 for free guided tours. The collection of antique cannons that still "guard" the city's waterfront is a play area for children, though there is also an actual playground, a pool open daily in summer from 11 to 8, and a water-play area at the northwest entrance to the park. Runners and walkers can take advantage of woodland trails and a boardwalk that edges the harbor. ⊠ *Lower Kent St., Charlottetown, Prince Edward Island, Canada* ☎ *902/368–1025* ⊙ *Daily sunrise–sunset.*

## WHERE TO EAT

¢ ✕ **Beanz Espresso Bar.** This hip-with-a-heart café is an excellent spot
CAFÉ for hearty sandwiches, plus soups, salads, and, of course, coffee. Just remember to save room for the sweets: Beanz' inexpensive squares, bars and cakes taste like they came right out of an *Anne of Green Gables* church social. (Bakers who can prepare these old-school recipes are a dying breed!) Come daily for breakfast, lunch, or a *very* early dinner. The cafe closes at 6 Monday to Saturday, 4 on Sunday. ⊠ *38 University Ave., Charlottetown, Prince Edward Island, Canada* ☎ *902/892–8797* ⊕ *www.beanzespressobar.com.*

$$$ ✕ **Claddagh Oyster House.** Urban decor meets rural delicacies at this
SEAFOOD upscale restaurant, which occupies a handsome brick building downtown. Not surprisingly, given the name and location, seafood is a specialty here—the local oysters, mussels, and lobsters are all memorable. But there are alternatives for meat-loving locavores (think lamb lollipops or grilled PEI striploin served with roasted PEI potatoes). It's a popular spot for tourists and residents alike, and the service is friendly. Upstairs, the Olde Dublin Pub ($) makes Irish eyes smile. It has pub grub, ample ale, and live music on the Guinness Stage seven nights a week from mid-June to mid-September. ⊠ *131 Sydney St., Charlottetown, Prince Edward Island, Canada* ☎ *902/902/892–9661* ⊕ *www. claddaghoysterhouse.com.*

$$$ ✕ **Daniel-Brenan Brickhouse.** Opened in 2011 in a converted warehouse
ECLECTIC downtown, this is the sort of place that could pull a trendy crowd based soley on its urban decor and novel menu. Food-wise, however, Chef Ilona Daniel's open kitchen really delivers. Prime local ingredients are used to create dishes with United Nations appeal (think Korean-style beef cheeks served on a kimchi pancake, or organic falafel with edamame hummus). The restaurant has an extensive wine list for vino lovers, and playful desserts like gourmet s'mores and whoopie pies for sweet-toothed diners. Dietary purists, meanwhile, will be pleased by the number of vegan, vegetarian, and gluten-free offerings. ⊠ *125 Sydney*

*St., Charlottetown, Prince Edward Island, Canada* ☏ *902/566–4620* ⊕ *danielbrenanbrickhouse.com.*

**$$**
SEAFOOD

✕ **Fishbones Oyster Bar & Seafood Grill.** Fishbones, on pedestrianized Victoria Row right behind the Confederation Centre of the Arts, is a good choice for pre- or post-theater dining. Although focused on fish, the menu is broad enough to include quality options for non–seafood fans (the baby back ribs are highly recommended), and the service is at once efficient and friendly. Prices are reasonable, too. But the setting—whether under the giant faux tree inside or on the patio outside, where diners are often serenaded by live jazz music—will still make you feel like you're having a proper night out. ⊠ *136 Richmond St., Charlottetown, Prince Edward Island, Canada* ☏ *902/628–6569* ⊕ *www.fishbones.ca* ⊗ *late Sept.–late May.*

**$**
SEAFOOD
★

✕ **The Gahan House Pub & Brewery.** PEI's only microbrewery, housed in an 1880 brick building downtown, clearly takes pride in its products. Seven handcrafted ales (and one wickedly good root beer) are prominently displayed on the upstairs menu, and tours of the downstairs brewing operation (C$8, samples included) are given twice daily in summer. Beer reappears in several dishes as well, including the signature brown-bag fish-and-chips with honey wheat ale–battered haddock and pulled pork sandwiches accented with IPA barbeque sauce. But even teetotalers will appreciate that the food here is always tasty, affordable, and well presented. ⊠ *126 Sydney St., Charlottetown, Prince Edward Island, Canada* ☏ *902/626–2337* ⊕ *www.gahan.ca* ⊗ *Tours in July and Aug. only, Mon.–Sat. at 5 and 7.*

**¢**
GERMAN

✕ **Leonhard's.** Alexandra and Axel Leonhard have gone from humble beginnings selling homemade bread at a local farmers' market to running a full-fledged café where food is made from scratch without additives, preservatives, or artifical flavorings. The room is bright and cheerful, and the devoted clientele keeps coming back for breakfast, casseroles, hearty gluten-free soups, sandwiches, and delicious desserts. Organic teas and freshly roasted European-style coffee are served as well. With only six tables inside (and a couple more on the street in summer), you may have to wait for a seat or grab something to go. In any case, come early: Leonhard's closes at 5. ⊠ *42 University Ave., Charlottetown, Prince Edward Island, Canada* ☏ *902/367–3621* ⊕ *www.leonhards.ca* ⊗ *Closed Sun. No dinner.*

**$$$**
CONTEMPORARY
★

✕ **Lot 30.** Acclaimed chef Gordon Bailey has one basic agenda at his restaurant—to serve stand-out meals inspired by quality produce, meat, and seafood from PEI and Maritime sources. He tailors his menu to what's available that day, but notable dishes have included a lobster salad appetizer with citrus vanilla vinaigrette and mains such as duck breast with potato gnocchi, organic shepherd's pie, and pan-roasted salmon with Thai black rice. The sophisticated dining room is spacious yet spare, and the atmosphere is lively. ⊠ *151 Kent St., Charlottetown, Prince Edward Island, Canada* ☏ *902/629–3030* ⊕ *www.lot30restaurant.ca* ⊗ *No lunch. Closed Mon.*

**$$$**
CANADIAN

✕ **The Lucy Maud Dining Room.** Chefs at this restaurant, part of the acclaimed Culinary Institute of Canada, are second-year students working under the supervision of master-chef instructors and service is provided by hospitality students. It's an opportunity to enjoy ambitious dishes that combine local ingredients with international influences. The institute's dining room could use some freshening up, but nothing can detract from the view of the water out its large windows. Although dinner is served year-round, lunch is offered only October through April. The Montgomery Room, a self-serve cafeteria on the first floor, is another spot to sample the students' creations. ⊠ *4 Sydney St., Charlottetown, Prince Edward Island, Canada* ☎ *902/894–6868* ⊕ *www. hollandc.pe.ca/culinary_institute_of_canada/lucy_maud_dining_room. php* ⚱ *Reservations essential* ☉ *Closed last wk of July. Closed Sun., Mon., and holidays.*

$$

CANADIAN

✕ **Merchantman Pub.** In an 1850s building with original brickwork and open-beam ceilings, this popular spot has a pub menu ($) that lists fish and chips, wings, burgers, and such as well as a more substantial mains menu ($$$) that includes lobster linguini, pan-seared scallops, and an artichoke-stuffed pork tenderloin. Everything is made with fresh Island products, and local draft beer complements the imported on-tap options. The waterfront walking path near Confederation Landing Park is only steps away, which is great if you want to whet your appetite or work off a hearty meal. ⊠ *23 Queen St., Charlottetown, Prince Edward Island, Canada* ☎ *902/892–9150* ⊕ *www.merchantmanpub. com* ☉ *Closed Sun.*

$$

CANADIAN

✕ **The Pilot House.** In the 19th-century Roger's Hardware building, this restaurant has both fine dining and casual fare. Old wooden beams, brick columns, and a unique bar top made of black granite inlaid with bird's-eye maple make the place cozy. A sandwich-centric pub menu ($) offers twists on traditional favorites (picture a lobster BLT or Moroccan chicken club), while AAA Island Certified Black Angus beef and fresh seafood dominate the creative dinner menu ($$$). ⊠ *70 Grafton St., Charlottetown, Prince Edward Island, Canada* ☎ *902/894–4800* ⊕ *www.thepilothouse.ca* ☉ *Closed Sun.*

$$$$

STEAKHOUSE

✕ **Sims Corner Steakhouse and Oyster Bar.** Ross Munro's farm-to-plate focus helped him earn PEI's peer-selected Chef of the Year Award in 2011, while the choice, custom-cut, Island-raised beef he prepares (it's aged 45 days for richer taste) has helped him earn kudos from patrons. Seafood selections start with a wide range of oysters at the raw bar, and divine desserts are made in-house. All can be washed down with an award-winning selection of Old and New World wines. Earthy colors, brick walls, exposed beams, and plush booths encourage you to linger indoors, but there is also a pleasant patio for warm-weather dining. ⊠ *86 Queen St., Charlottetown, Prince Edward Island, Canada* ☎ *902/894– 7467* ⊕ *www.simscorner.ca* ☉ *No lunch mid-Sept.–mid-June.*

$$

ITALIAN

★

✕ **Sirenella Ristorante.** Northern Italian cuisine and unfailingly good service make Sirenella one of Charlotteville's top restaurant choices. The menu, which changes twice a year, has something for everyone. Owner Italo Marzari handpicks the Italian wines on the list, and noteworthy mains—like the excellent *vitello pizzaiola* (veal in a sauce of white wine, capers, garlic, and oregano, topped with *bocconcini* cheese and tomato sauce)—are complemented by a range of handmade pastas. As for ambience, it's intimate enough for date night, but a children's menu means

## CLOSE UP

## Enjoying Shellfish

Prince Edward Island shellfish has a reputation for being among the world's best. Mollusks and crustaceans are harvested all along the coast, so you can spot fishermen in shallow boats scooping up oysters with what look like giant salad servers. Moreover, you can see rows of buoys in bays and estuaries holding up lines covered with mussels, plus solo buoys securing the lobster traps that wait to be hauled offshore. Obviously, you'll see shellfish on almost every Island menu too—as well as on many activity rosters now that tour operators are taking increasing numbers of visitors out to trap, haul, tong, and shuck. Shellfish also pops up on festival calendars.

Summerside holds a weeklong Lobster Carnival in July (☎ *902/724–4925* ⊕ *www.summersidelobstercarnival.ca*), while Tyne Valley, an attractive Prince County community, hosts an Oyster Festival (☎ *902/831–3294* ⊕ *www. tynevalleyoysterfestival.ca*) in August complete with fried oyster suppers and oyster chowder competitions. Democratic as always, Charlottetown plays no favorites during the PEI International Shellfish Festival in September (☎ *866/955–2003* ⊕ *www. peishellfish.com*). It promises seafood galore (some of it prepared by guest chefs like Curtis Stone) along with fishing excursions, cooking demos, and other themed events.

it's family-friendly too. ⊠ *83 Water St., Charlottetown, Prince Edward Island, Canada* ☎ *902/628–2271* ⊕ *www.sirenella.ca* ☉ *Closed Sun.*

## WHERE TO STAY

*For expanded hotel reviews, visit Fodors.com.*

**$$$** 🏨 **Delta Prince Edward.** Location, location, location—that's the main draw at this high-rise hotel. **Pros:** elevator; all rooms have minifridges; most have harbor views. **Cons:** lobby and some rooms could use revamping; a new convention center (slated for completion in early 2013) is going up adjacent to the hotel, so construction-related issues may arise. ⊠ *18 Queen St., Charlottetown, Prince Edward Island, Canada* ☎ *902/566–2222, 866/894–1203* ⊕ *www.deltaprinceedward.com* ⇱*202 rooms, 8 suites* ⑃ *In-room: kitchen, Internet. In-hotel: restaurant, bar, pool, gym, spa, laundry facilities, business center, parking, some pets allowed.*

**$$$** 🏨 **Dundee Arms Inn.** A 1903 Queen Anne mansion and modern annex (actually a surprisingly stylish 1960s motel) make up this attractive inn just minutes from downtown. **Pros:** relaxed setting; in-room perks include fluffy robes and AVEDA bath products. **Cons:** rooms vary widely in size and quality. ⊠ *200 Pownal St., Charlottetown, Prince Edward Island, Canada* ☎ *902/892–2496, 877/638–6333* ⊕ *www.eden.travel/ dundee* ⇱*18 rooms, 4 suites* ⑃ *In-room: Wi-Fi. In-hotel: restaurant, bar, parking.*

**$$$** 🏨 **Elmwood Heritage Inn.** Tranquil is the key term to describe this 1889 ★ inn, which sits at the end of a tree-lined lane in a residential neighborhood. **Pros:** an acre of grounds; in-room mod cons like iPod docks and flat-screen TVs. **Cons:** rather flowery for some tastes; a 15-minute walk to downtown. ✉ *121 N. River Rd., Charlottetown, Prince Edward Island, Canada* ☎ *902/368–3310, 877/933–3310* ⊕ *www.elmwoodinn.pe.ca* ⛵ *5 rooms, 3 suites* ⟁ *In-room: kitchen, Wi-Fi. In-hotel: parking* ⧑ *Breakfast.*

$$$ ▦ **Fairholm National Historic Inn.** The

Fodor'sChoice Fairholm, a designated National
★ Historic Site, is the primo Maritime example of the architectural Picturesque movement. **Pros:** lovely gardens; attractive packages and specials offered. **Cons:** lots of wallpaper; not for those seeking big-hotel amenities. ✉ *230 Prince St., Charlottetown, Prince Edward Island, Canada* ☎ *902/892–5022, 888/573–5022* ⊕ *www.fairholminn.com* ⛵ *7 rooms* ⟁ *In-room: Wi-Fi. In-hotel: business center, parking* ⧑ *Breakfast.*

$$$ ▦ **The Great George.** This centrally located boutique hotel is fashioned

Fodor'sChoice out of 15 heritage buildings. **Pros:** excellent staff; comfy beds topped
★ with duvets and premium linens. **Cons:** street noise is sometimes audible on the Great George side. ✉ *58 Great George St., Charlottetown, Prince Edward Island, Canada* ☎ *902/892–0606, 800/361–1118* ⊕ *www.thegreatgeorge.com* ⛵ *34 rooms, 22 suites, 4 condos* ⟁ *In-room: kitchen, Wi-Fi. In-hotel: gym, business center, parking* ⧑ *Breakfast.*

$$$$ ▦ **The Holman Grand Hotel.** Downtown Charlottetown's first newly built hotel in 25 years officially opened in late 2011. **Pros:** some suites have kitchenettes; all rooms have mini-fridges and Keurig coffeemakers. **Cons:** standard rooms have spa-worthy showers but no tubs; comparatively pricey. ✉ *123 Grafton Street., Charlottetown, Prince Edward Island, Canada* ☎ *902/367–7777, 877/455–4726* ⊕ *theholmangrand.com* ⛵ *62 rooms, 18 suites* ⟁ *In-room: kitchen, Wi-Fi. In-hotel: restaurant, pool, gym, laundry facilities, business center, parking, some pets allowed.*

$$ ▦ **The Hotel on Pownal.** Affordability and urban style combine to make
★ this newcomer on the Charlottetown lodging scene an instant favorite. **Pros:** free parking, Wi-Fi, and buffet breakfast; free coffee, tea, and home-baked treats available 24/7. **Cons:** no elevator; no views. ✉ *146 Pownal St., Charlottetown, Prince Edward Island, Canada* ☎ *902/892–1217, 800/268–6261* ⊕ *thehotelonpownal.com* ⛵ *40 rooms, 5 suites* ⟁ *In-room: Wi-Fi. In-hotel: laundry facilities, business center, parking* ⧑ *Breakfast.*

$$ ▦ **Shipwright Inn B&B.** The name of this cottage-y 1860s inn is a nod to the first owner's occupation, and its charming accommodations further attest to his seafaring ways (the Captain's Quarters, the Navigator's Retreat . . . you get the picture). **Pros:** downtown location with pretty garden; some rooms have balconies and fireplaces. **Cons:** minimalists may find the number of knickknacks disconcerting; five rooms are in a 1996 addition. ✉ *51 Fitzroy St., Charlottetown, Prince Edward Island,*

---

CROSSROADS

The intersection of Richmond Street and Great George Street is frequently—although you can never predict when—the place to see all manner of old and new conveyances: modern buses, elegant horse-drawn carriages, trolleys, double-decker tour buses, and "The Hippo" amphibious vehicles are all used to get around this historic city.

3

*Canada* ☎ *902/368–1905, 888/306–9966* ⊕ *www.shipwrightinn.com* ⇥ *8 rooms, 1 apartment* ⚬ *In-room: kitchen, Wi-Fi. In-hotel: business center, parking* ◎ *Breakfast.*

## NIGHTLIFE AND THE ARTS

For complete and current listings of entertainment events check *The Buzz*; you can pick up a free copy at most hotels, restaurants, and newsstands or view it online at ⊕ *www.buzzon.com.*

### NIGHTLIFE

**Globe World Flavours.** Prim Anne fans may not approve. But after hours, Wednesday through Saturday, Globe World Flavours (a Victoria Row eatery) morphs into a dance club. ⊠ *132 Richmond St., Charlottetown, Prince Edward Island, Canada* ☎ *902/370–4040* ⊕ *www. dinedrinkdance.ca.*

**St. James Gate Pub.** Live music makes the St. James Gate Pub another good place to eat, drink, and be merry. ⊠ *129 Kent St., Charlottetown, Prince Edward Island, Canada* ☎ *902/892–4283.*

### THE ARTS

**Benevolent Irish Society Hall.** The Benevolent Irish Society Hall stages Friday night ceilidhs with Celtic dancing, fiddling, and a few stories thrown in for good measure, mid-May through October. ⊠ *582 N. River Rd., Charlottetown, Prince Edward Island, Canada* ☎ *902/892–2367.*

**Feast Dinner Theatre.** Atlantic Canada's longest-running dinner theater specializes in fun, fluffy musicals. Watch lively shows while chowing down on a four-course meal from mid-June through August. ⊠ *Rodd Charlottetown Hotel, 75 Kent St., Charlottetown, Prince Edward Island, Canada* ☎ *902/629–2321* ⊕ *www.roddvacations.com/feast.*

**The Guild.** The Guild, one of Charlottetown's major cultural centers, hosts plays, performances, and a variety of exhibits throughout the year. ⊠ *111 Queen St., Charlottetown, Prince Edward Island, Canada* ☎ *902/620–3333, 866/774–0717* ⊕ *www.theguildpei.com.*

**St. Mary's Church.** Built in 1902 by Island architect W. H. Harris, this church hosts performances by visiting artists in July and August as part of the Indian River Festival of Music. The church has very good acoustics and a beautiful pastoral setting, and the concerts here are often broadcast nationally by the Canadian Broadcasting Corporation. ⊠ *Rte. 104, 6 km (3.5 mi) south of Malpeque, 1374 Hamilton Rd., Indian River, Prince Edward Island, Canada* ☎ *902/836–4933, 866/856–3733* ⊕ *www.indianriverfestival.com* ▭ *C$24–$32.*

## SPORTS AND THE OUTDOORS

### GOLF

**Clyde River Golf and Country Club.** The club is a 27-hole facility with linked 9- and 18-hole courses, located about 10 minutes west of Charlottetown. Part of the scenery includes pretty farmland and the Clyde River itself. The club, its pro shop, and restaurant are open May through October. ⊠ *384 Clyde River Rd., Rte. 247, RR #2, Clyde River, Prince*

*Edward Island, Canada* ☎ *902/675–2585, 902/394–2728 off-season* ⊕ *www.clyderivergolf.ca.*

**Fox Meadow Golf and Country Club.** This 18-hole club is a mere five minutes southeast of the city. Its challenging par-72 championship course, designed by Rob Heaslip, overlooks Charlottetown Harbour and the community of Stratford. ⊠ *167 Kinlock Rd., Stratford, Prince Edward Island, Canada* ☎ *902/569–4653, 877/569–8337* ⊕ *www.foxmeadow. pe.ca.*

### WATER SPORTS

**Mark's Charters.** Mark's Charters offers fun, informative lobster fishing excursions for C$45 (C$80 with a lobster dinner included) from July through mid-September. ⊠ *2 Prince St., Charlottetown, Prince Edward Island, Canada* ☎ *902/626–6689* ⊕ *www.markscharters.com.*

**Peake's Wharf Boat Tours.** June to mid-September, Peake's Wharf Boat Tours operates assorted cruises—sunset and seal-watching ones among them—aboard a 13-meter (42-foot) vessel. Prices start at C$25 for a 70-minute trip. ⊠ *1 Great George St., Peake's Wharf, Charlottetown, Prince Edward Island, Canada* ☎ *902/566–4458* ⊕ *www. peakeswharfboattours.com.*

**Saga Sailing Adventures.** During high season, you can sail away on a sloop courtesy of Saga Sailing Adventures. The 2½-hour outings are priced at C$60. Charter tours are also available. ⊠ *Charlottetown Yacht Club, 1 Pownal St., Charlottetown, Prince Edward Island, Canada* ☎ *902/672–1222* ⊕ *www.sagasailing.com.*

## SHOPPING

The most interesting shops in Charlottetown are on Peake's Wharf, in Confederation Court Mall (off Queen Street), along Victoria Row (the section of Richmond Street between Queen and Great George streets), and on Water Street. There are also factory outlet stores along the Trans-Canada Highway at North River Causeway near the western entrance to the city, next to Cows Creamery.

**Anne of Green Gables Chocolates.** This local chocolatier fittingly sells old-fashioned chocolates, peanut brittle, and assorted candy—all made here. (For a double dose of local flavor, try chocolate-coated PEI potato chips.) Sweet treats for those who can't get enough of the Island's sweetest fictional orphan are available at this location year-round. Other outlets in Avonlea Village, Gateway Village and on the Cavendish Boardwalk open seasonally. ⊠ *100 Queen St., Charlottetown, Prince Edward Island, Canada* ☎ *902/368–3131* ⊕ *www.annechocolates.com.*

**Charlottetown Farmers' Market.** Along with the expected array of local produce, artisanal cheeses, organic meats and tasty baked goods, you'll find a fine array of Island-made crafts. The market runs from 9 until 2 on Saturdays year-round as well as on Wednesdays, July through early October. ⊠ *100 Belvedere Ave., Charlottetown, Prince Edward Island, Canada* ☎ *902/626–3733* ⊕ *charlottetownfarmersmarket.weebly.com.*

**Moonsnail Soapworks and Aromatherapy.** The vegetable-based soaps sold here are handcrafted and scented with essential oils. The expanding inventory also includes sublime bath and body-care products, plus a new pet-care line. ✉ *85 Water St., Charlottetown, Prince Edward Island, Canada* ☎ *902/ 892–7627, 888/771-7627* ⊕ *www. moonsnailsoapworks.com.*

**Northern Watters Knitwear.** This shop carries its own line of chill-chasing knitted sweaters and a wide range of other Island-made products. ✉ *150 Richmond St., Charlottetown, Prince Edward Island, Canada* ☎ *902/566–5850, 800/565–9665* ⊕ *www.nwknitwear.com.*

**Pilar Shephard Art Gallery.** This gallery has earned a name for quality Maritime, Canadian, Inuit, and international art. Antiques and Canadian-designed jewelry are also sold on-site. ✉ *82 Great George St., Charlottetown, Prince Edward Island, Canada* ☎ *902/892–1953* ⊕ *www.pilarshephard.com.*

# CENTRAL COASTAL DRIVE

The 198 km (123 mi) Central Coastal Drive heads northeast on Route 2 out of Charlottetown and continues, with a left turn onto Route 6, to the north shore. Route 6 takes you by classic fishing communities and the striking strands of Prince Edward Island National Park before depositing you in *Anne of Green Gables* country. (The section around Cavendish is cluttered with commercial tourist tat. If you look beyond the fast-food outlets and tacky gift shops, however, you can still find unspoiled beauty.) This beach-blessed section alone—newly christened the Green Gables Shore—has enough in the way of attraction, amusements, and outdoor opportunities to satisfy many vacationers. Yet it's worth traveling south, too, following the coast to the quieter Red Sands Shore on the other side of the Island, passing rolling farmland and oyster-filled Malpeque Bay en route. Considering that visitors who come to the Island via the Confederation Bridge land smack in the middle of this shore, it seems ironic that its red headlands remain relatively undiscovered. Historic sites, villages harking back to Victorian days, and a distinctive sandstone coastline are there to explore.

## PRINCE EDWARD ISLAND NATIONAL PARK

**Fodor's**Choice *24 km (15 mi) north of Charlottetown.*
★	**Prince Edward Island National Park.** Prince Edward Island National Park has been touched with nature's boldest brushstrokes—sky and sea meet red sandstone cliffs, woodlands, wetlands, rolling dunes, and long stretches of sand. The original portion, a narrow strip of protected coast, extends for 40 km (25 mi) along the north shore of the Island

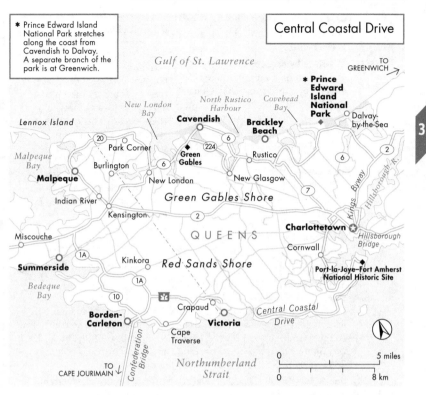

✷ Prince Edward Island National Park stretches along the coast from Cavendish to Dalvay. A separate branch of the park is at Greenwich.

from Cavendish to Dalvay. A separate adjunct sits about 24 km (15 mi) farther east on the Greenwich Peninsula. (⇨ *For details on the latter, see Greenwich section.*)

There are several entrances to the park system off routes 6, 13, and 313. Start your visit at Cavendish Grove, which occupies the former site of a 16-hectare amusement park off Route 6. Pull in at the Welcome Centre; then take a pleasant 1-km (.6-mi) stroll to Cavendish Beach. The beach itself is supervised in summer, and the way down to it is lined with maple trees, which seems fitting here in the "Cradle of Confederation." A relaxing alternative is to picnic in the titular grove, accompanied by a soundtrack of songbirds and honking Canada geese who call the nearby pond home. A full slate of cultural and ecological interpretive programs aimed at all ages is also available. More active types can bike, hike, or (in winter) cross-country ski on the park's scenic trails. If you'd rather be out on the water, **Outside Expeditions** (☎ *902/963–3366 or 800/207–3899, ⊕ www.getoutside.com*) rents kayaks and runs area paddling tours. Deep-sea fishing is offered by a handful of operators as well; these include **Richard's Deep-Sea Fishing** (☎ *902/672–2376*) and **Salty Seas** (☎ *902/672–3246*). ✉ *Charlottetown, Prince Edward Island, Canada* ☎ *902/672–6350* ⊕ *www.pc.gc.ca* 🖭 *C$7.80* ☺ *Daily dawn–dusk; full services July and Aug. only.*

## WHERE TO STAY

*For expanded hotel reviews, visit Fodors.com.*

$$$$ ⊡ **Dalvay-by-the-Sea.** Built in 1895 as the summer retreat for a U.S. oil tycoon, this sprawling Queen Anne Revival "cottage" is on the east edge of Prince Edward Island National Park. **Pros:** vintage vibe; 100 meters (328 feet) from the beach. **Cons:** cottages don't have kitchens; too early to tell how it will fare under new owners. ⊠ *Rte. 6, near Dalvay Beach, Stanhope, Prince Edward Island, Canada* ☎ *902/672–2048, 888/366–2955* ⊕ *www.dalvaybythesea.com* ⌨ 26 rooms, 8 cottages ⌨ In-room: no a/c, no TV. In-hotel: restaurant, bar, tennis court, water sports, laundry facilities ☉ Closed mid-Oct.–May.

> **DEJA VIEW**
>
> Dalvay-by-the-Sea received international press coverage when the Duke and Duchess of Cambridge came to visit on their first official trip together in the summer of 2011. That is not the first time it's made a big splash on the small screen, though. The Victorian showstopper appeared as The White Sands Hotel in the *Anne of Green Gables* miniseries and long-running *Road to Avonlea* TV program.

## SPORTS AND THE OUTDOORS

GOLF **Stanhope Golf and Country Club.** The 18 holes of the links-style, par-72 course at Stanhope Golf and Country Club are among the most challenging and scenic on the Island. Ocean breezes help. The course is a couple of miles west of Dalvay, along Covehead Bay. ⊠ *Off Rte. 6, 2961 Bay Shore Rd., Stanhope, Prince Edward Island, Canada* ☎ *902/672–2842, 888/672–2842* ⊕ *www.stanhopegolfclub.com.*

**Dalvay Bike Rentals.** The resort Dalvay-by-the-Sea rents bikes suitable for all members of the family to guests and nonguests alike. Rates are C$9 per hour, C$26 per day. ⊠ *Rte. 6, near Dalvay Beach, Stanhope, Prince Edward Island, Canada* ☎ *902/672–2048* ⊕ *www.dalvaybythesea.com.*

# BRACKLEY BEACH

*15 km (9 mi) north of Charlottetown.*

Brackley Beach (on Route 15, just north of Route 6) abuts Prince Edward Island National Park, so park access is easy and sand is in ample supply. Because this is more a chunk of coastline than an actual community, Brackley Beach offers considerably fewer amenities than neighboring Cavendish. Activities here are refreshingly simple. Water sports, for example, tend to be the non-motorized kind, and gentle pursuits like bird-watching are popular (area waterways attract many migratory species). Nevertheless, lodgings such as Shaw's have been in business for generations, so clearly there is enough here to warrant guests' return.

## WHERE TO EAT AND STAY

*For expanded hotel reviews, visit Fodors.com.*

**$$$**  ✕**The Dunes Café.** Sharing a property with the Dunes Studio Gallery
CANADIAN  (⇨ *see under Shopping below*), this café has wood ceilings that soar
**Fodor's**Choice  above the indoor dining room and a deck overlooking the dunes and
★  marshlands of Covehead Bay. Like the view, the food is amazing. Chef
Emily Wells and her team dish out local ingredients with an interna-
tional twist. Your main, for example, might be a Mediterranean rack of
lamb, scallops Provençal, or lobster pad thai. The eclectic menu is also
offered in the lounge and on a patio that sits above vibrant gardens.
✉ *Rte. 15, 1 km (½ mi) south of the national park, Brackley Beach,
Prince Edward Island, Canada* ☎ *902/672–1883* ⊕ *www.dunesgallery.
com* ☉ *Closed Oct.–May.*

**$$$**  🏨**Barachois Inn.** Rustico, just below Brackley Beach, is one of the old-
est communities on the Island—and this 1880 inn's Victorian elegance
lets it blend right into the historic surroundings. **Pros:** themed packages
available; thoughtful hosts can arrange almost anything (including a
masseuse who makes house calls). **Cons:** pretty far from civilization;
gable ceilings not great for tall guests. ✉ *2193 Church Rd., Rte. 243,
off Rte. 6, 8 km (5 mi) west of Brackley Beach, Rustico, Prince Edward
Island, Canada* ☎ *902/963–2194, 800/963–2194* ⊕ *www.barachoisinn.
com* ➬ *4 rooms, 4 suites* ♿ *In-room: Wi-Fi. In-hotel: gym* ⦿ *Breakfast.*

**$$**  🏨**Shaw's Hotel and Cottages.** Canada's oldest family-operated inn has
☾  won a faithful following since opening in 1860. **Pros:** next to the
★  national park; free kayaks and canoes. **Cons:** there may be mosquitoes
in the air or jellyfish in the water. ✉ *99 Apple Tree Rd., Rte. 15, Brack-
ley Beach, Prince Edward Island, Canada* ☎ *902/672–2022* ⊕ *www.
shawshotel.ca* ➬ *14 rooms, 3 suites, 25 cottages* ♿ *In-room: no a/c,
kitchen, Internet. In-hotel: restaurant, bar, beach, water sports, chil-
dren's programs, laundry facilities, some pets allowed* ☉ *Closed early
Oct.–May; some winterized cottages open year-round* ⦿ *Breakfast.*

## NIGHTLIFE AND THE ARTS

**Brackley Drive-In Theatre.** Brackley Drive-In Theatre gives visitors in this
neck of the woods a reason to stay up past dark. It shows a pair of
first-run flicks nightly in high season. Onion rings and other classic
snacks from the canteen complement the experience. ✉ *3164 Brackley
Point Rd., Rte. 15, Brackley Beach, Prince Edward Island, Canada*
☎ *902/672–3333* ⊕ *drivein.ca.*

**Howes Hall Gallery.** Howes Hall Gallery specializes in original paintings
and primitive hooked mats. There is an exhibit space in back, and the
artist/owners give occaional summer classes that allow artsy vacationers
to hone their own skills. ✉ *3421 Brackley Point Rd., Rte. 15, Brack-
ley Beach, Prince Edward Island, Canada* ☎ *902/672–4111* ⊕ *www.
howeshallgallery.com* ☉ *Oct.–mid-June.*

## SPORTS AND THE OUTDOORS

**Northshore Rentals.** This shop can equip you with kayaks, canoes, and
bicycles. Per hour rates are C$12, C$11, and C$6.50 respectively.
✉ *Rte. 15 at Shaw's Hotel, Brackley Beach, Prince Edward Island,
Canada* ☎ *902/672–2022.*

## SHOPPING

**The Dunes Studio Gallery.** This gallery sells an array of cool Canadian-made goods. Choose between pottery (you can watch it being crafted on-site), Island art, clothing with an unmistakable Indonesian influence, funky furniture, fine jewelry, contemporary glassware and other one-of-a-kind items. ⊠ *Rte. 15, 1 km (½ mi) south of the national park, Brackley Beach, Prince Edward Island, Canada* ☎ *902/672–2586* ⊕ *www.dunesgallery.com* ⊗ *closed Nov.–Apr.*

**The Great Canadian Soap Co.** Time to come clean! The Great Canadian Soap Co. produces dozens of types of goat's milk soap at its home base in Brackley Beach. (That explains the gamboling goats you'll encounter near the shop). Other all-natural bath and beauty products are available as well. ⊠ *4224 Portage Rd., Rte. 6, Brackley Beach, Prince Edward Island, Canada* ☎ *800/793–1644* ⊕ *www.greatcanadiansoap.com.*

# CAVENDISH

*21 km (13 mi) west of Brackley Beach.*

Cavendish is the most visited Island community outside Charlottetown. The proximity of Prince Edward Island National Park, with its promise of summertime sun and sand, is one reason for the heavy influx of vacationers. The crop of amusement park–style attractions that has sprung up on Route 6 as a counterpoint to the pristine park is another *(see the "Cavendish with Kids" box).* However, it all began with *Anne of Green Gables.* Thousands of Anne-ites flock to the Cavendish area every year to visit the homes associated with Lucy Maud Montgomery, who was born and buried in the area, and to explore the places so lovingly described in her books.

## GETTING HERE AND AROUND

Most visitors drive themselves to Cavendish. But Prince Edward Tours does provide a shuttle service, departing twice daily from Founders' Hall in Charlottetown, mid-June to late September. The cost is C$15 for a one-way ticket, C$25 for same-day return (☎ *902/566–5466 or 877/286–6532* ⊕ *princeedwardtours.com*). Once there, you can take advantage of the old-style Cavendish Beach Trolley, which connects popular sites along the Route 6 corridor. In peak season, it runs hourly (Thursday–Tuesday 10–5, Wednesday noon–5). Hop on–hop off tickets cost C$5 per day.

## EXPLORING

**Gardens of Hope.** Need a break from those Cavendish crowds? Gardens of Hope, part of the PEI Preserve Company property, is located about 8 km (5 mi) south of town beside the Island's most beautiful river valley. The garden itself covers more than 12 acres. With 2 km (1 mi) of walking trails that thread past fountains and groomed flower beds, then through natural woodland, it provides ample opportunity for quiet contemplation. ⊠ *2841 New Glasgow Rd., off Rte. 13, New Glasgow, Prince Edward Island, Canada* ☎ *902/964–4300, 800/565–5267* ⊕ *gardensofhope.ca* 🖃 *By donation* ⊗ *Dawn to dusk.*

## Who is Anne, anyway?

In Lucy Maud Montgomery's 1908 novel, Marilla Cuthbert and her brother Matthew live on a PEI farm. Getting on in years, the pair decides to adopt an orphan boy to help out with the chores. It's with some surprise, then, that Matthew comes back from the train station with a feisty, 11-year-old, redheaded *girl*. But it's not long before Anne—and her adventures and mishaps and friends—becomes an essential part of Marilla and Mathew's lives. An immediate hit, the book made Anne an essential part of *readers'* lives as well. Even Mark Twain, who called her "the dearest and most lovable child in fiction since the immortal Alice [in Wonderland]," was smitten.

Montgomery went on to write a total of eight volumes in the series. In 1985, the original was made into a two-part TV movie, which was a huge success, airing first on the CBC in Canada and then on PBS in the United States. That was followed by a series that ran from 1990 to 1996. Anne has also become a stage staple thanks to theatrical productions like *Anne of Green Gables—The Musical* (a must-see at the Confederation Centre in Charlottetown) and *Anne and Gilbert* (a melodious sequel that debuted in 2005). Of course, for the millions of modern-day Anne fans, Cavendish is hallowed ground because the top Green Gables sites and experiences are all in the area. These include **Green Gables,** the **Site of Lucy Maud Montgomery's Cavendish Home, Avonlea—Village of Anne of Green Gables,** the **Lucy Maud Montgomery Birthplace,** and the **Anne of Green Gables Museum at Silver Bush.**

🕐 ★ **Green Gables.** Green Gables, ½ km (¼ mi) west of Lucy Maud Montgomery's Cavendish Home, is the green-and-white 19th-century farmhouse that served as the inspiration for the Cuthbert place in *Anne of Green Gables*. The house, outbuildings, and grounds, all of which belonged to cousins of the author's grandfather, re-create some of the settings found in the book. The same goes for short walking trails dubbed the Haunted Wood and Lovers Lane/Balsam Hollow. If you're well acquainted with the novel you'll spy lots of evocative details on-site (say, a broken slate or amethyst brooch). If not, watching an introductory film in the Visitor Centre will help you get up to speed. An audiovisual presentation on Montgomery's life shares space with a café in the barn nearby. This National Historic Site has been part of Prince Edward Island National Park since 1937 and hosts daily events throughout July and August such as guided tours, puppet shows, and old-fashioned games. ✉ *8619 Rte. 6, Cavendish, Prince Edward Island, Canada* ☎ *902/963–7874* ⊕ *www.pc.gc.ca/lhn-nhs/pe/greengables/index.aspx* 💳 *C$7.80* 🕐 *May–Oct., daily 9–5.*

**Lucy Maud Montgomery Birthplace.** The Lucy Maud Montgomery Birthplace is a cottage-y white house with green trim overlooking New London Harbour, 11 km (7 mi) southwest of Cavendish. The *Anne* author was born here in 1874, and the interior has been furnished with antiques to conjure up that era. Among memorabilia on display are a replica of Montgomery's wedding gown and personal scrapbooks filled with many of her poems and stories. ⊠ *Junction of Rtes. 6 and 20, Cavendish, Prince Edward Island, Canada* ☎ *902/886–2099* ⌨ *C$3* ⊙ *late May–early Oct., daily 9–5.*

**Site of Lucy Maud Montgomery's Cavendish Home.** The Site of Lucy Maud Montgomery's Cavendish Home is where the writer lived with her maternal grandparents after the untimely death of her mother. Though the foundation of the house where Montgomery wrote *Anne of Green Gables* is all that remains, the homestead's fields and old apple-tree gardens are lovely walking grounds. A bookstore and museum are also on the property, which is operated by descendants of the family and is a National Historic Site of Canada. ⊠ *8521 Rte. 6, Cavendish, Prince Edward Island, Canada* ☎ *902/963–2231* ⊕ *www.peisland.com/lmm* ⌨ *C$3* ⊙ *Mid-May–June and Sept.–mid-Oct., daily 9–5; July-Aug., daily 9–6.*

## WHERE TO EAT

$$

CANADIAN

✕ **Café on the Clyde at Prince Edward Island Preserve Company.** One of the best spots on the Island to stop for a bite, this café has wonderful desserts and an extensive tea list. The dining room, with a soaring ceiling and two walls of windows looking over the Clyde River, opens for breakfast, lunch, and dinner. Everything served is noted for freshness—even the ice cream is homemade. Particularly praiseworthy items include the savory potato pie with maple-bacon cream and not-too-sweet raspberry cream cheese pie. A popular shop sells gourmet products and preserves made on-site. ⊠ *2841 New Glasgow Rd., off Rte. 13, New Glasgow, Prince Edward Island, Canada* ☎ *902/964–4300, 800/565–5267* ⊕ *www.preservecompany.com* ⊙ *Closed mid-Oct.–late May.*

$$$

SEAFOOD

☾

★

✕ **New Glasgow Lobster Suppers.** Established in 1958, New Glasgow Lobster Suppers brings fresh lobster direct from a pound on the premises to your plate. Scallops, roast beef, salmon, chicken, ham, even a vegetarian dish are other choices if you've already had your fill of crustaceans. All come with fresh rolls, steamed mussels, seafood chowder, salads, homemade desserts, and beverages. Whew . . . Bar service is available, as is a children's menu, too. The bustling dining area can seat up to 500 guests at one time, and it often fills up. But because turnover is fast, there isn't usually a long wait. ⊠ *604 Rte. 258, off Rte. 13, New Glasgow, Prince Edward Island, Canada* ☎ *902/964–2870* ⊕ *www.peilobstersuppers. com* ⊙ *No lunch. Closed mid-Oct.–late May.*

## WHERE TO STAY

Accommodations in the Cavendish area are often booked a year in advance for July and most of August. If you're late in planning, don't despair—hotels in Charlottetown and elsewhere in the central region are still within easy driving distance of "Anne's Land."

*For expanded hotel reviews, visit Fodors.com.*

$

☾

🏨 **Bay Vista Motel and Cottage.** This straightforward, spotlessly clean motel caters mainly to families. **Pros:** friendly staff; picnic area with shared use barbecues. **Cons:** looks like a motel inside and out. ⊠ *9517 Rte. 6, Cavendish, Prince Edward Island, Canada* ☎ *902/963–2225,*

*800/846–0601* ⊕ *www.bayvista.ca* ⛵ *31 rooms, 2 suites, 1 cottage* ⬧ *In-room: kitchen, Internet, Wi-Fi. In-hotel: pool, laundry facilities, some pets allowed* ⊘ *Closed late Sept.–early June* ⦿ *Breakfast.*

**$$** ⬚ **Cavendish Country Inn and Cottages.** The family atmosphere of this
⟲ 9-acre cottage complex is a big draw for some folks; there are several playgrounds on-site, as well as a pair of pools, fire pits, and outdoor games (complimentary movies help on rainy days). **Pros:** choice of accommodations for the budget-conscious; lots for kids to do. **Cons:** dated decor; if you want a quieter holiday, this isn't the place. ⊠ *8405 Cavendish Rd., Rte. 6, Cavendish, Prince Edward Island, Canada* ☎ *902/963–2181, 800/454–4853* ⊕ *www.cavendishpei.com* ⛵ *11 rooms, 35 cottages* ⬧ *In-room: no a/c, kitchen, Wi-Fi. In-hotel: pool, laundry facilities, some pets allowed* ⊘ *Closed late Oct.–mid-May.*

**$$** ⬚ **Kindred Spirits Country Inn and Cottages.** Named in a nod to Anne, this lovely 6-acre property is just a short walk from Green Gables. **Pros:** helpful staff; National Park passes provided. **Cons:** decor a bit twee for some tastes; breakfast not included for cottagers. ⊠ *Memory La. off Rte. 6, Cavendish, Prince Edward Island, Canada* ☎ *902/963–2434, 800/461–1755* ⊕ *www.kindredspirits.ca* ⛵ *25 rooms, 20 cottages* ⬧ *In-room: kitchen, Wi-Fi. In-hotel: pool, gym, laundry facilities* ⊘ *Closed late Oct.–mid-May* ⦿ *Breakfast.*

## SPORTS AND THE OUTDOORS

GOLF  **Green Gables Golf Course.** This classic Stanley Thompson–designed course was restored by Thomas McBroom in 2007. The result reflects many of Thompson's original features. With great views and ocean breezes tickling your shot, it's a good choice for both aspiring and avid golfers. The clubhouse lounge serves refreshments and light meals. The 18-hole, par-72 course opens for play May through October. ⊠ *8727 Rte. 6, Cavendish, Prince Edward Island, Canada* ☎ *902/963–4653, 888/870–5454* ⊕ *www.greengablesgolf.com.*

⟲ **Avonlea—Village of Anne of Green Gables.** At Avonlea, purpose-built structures have been combined with heritage ones—among them a schoolhouse where L.M. Montgomery once taught—to convincingly re-create Anne's fictional hometown. Blissed-out devotees can sip raspberry cordial and take in the scene as strolling actors bring favorite scenes to life. For everyone else, activities like spoon-playing lessons, wagon rides, and old-fashioned sack races still ensure a fun day out. ⊠ *8779 Rte. 6, Cavendish, Prince Edward Island, Canada* ☎ *902/963–3050* ⊕ *www. avonlea.ca* ▣ *C$19.05; C$6 in Sept. for limited program* ⊘ *mid-June–Aug., daily 10–5; first weeks of Sept., daily 10–4.*

**Andersons Creek Golf Club.** The 18-hole, par-72 Andersons Creek Golf Club, just southwest of Cavendish, was designed by Graham Cooke. Proud of the game's Scottish roots, the championship course employs its own bagpiper. ⊠ *68 Rte. 240, Stanley Bridge, Prince Edward Island, Canada* ☎ *902/886–2222, 866/886–4422* ⊕ *www.andersonscreek.com.*

**Eagles Glenn Golf Course.** Graham Cooke was the designer behind the par-72 Eagles Glenn Golf Course, which celebrates its 10th anniversary in 2012. It has 18 walkable holes, plus a stunning setting. This championship course, along with its practice facility and clubhouse, is

## CAVENDISH WITH KIDS

Cavendish holds obvious appeal for beach babies and budding biblio-philes. Yet it also delivers for kids who love kitsch. Topping the list of irresistibly cheesy amusements operating seasonally along the Route 6 tourist corridor is **Shining Waters Family Fun Park** (☎ 877/963–3939 ⊕ www.shiningwaterspei.com). Open from mid-June to early September, it has waterslides, a kiddy splash pool, pseudo–pirate ship, petting zoo, and more. **Sandspit** (☎ 902/963–2626 ⊕ www.sandspit.com) kicks things

up a notch with midway rides appealing to tots and tweens alike. On rainy days, spots like Ripley's Believe It or Not! (☎ 902/963–2242 ⊕ www.ripleyspei.com), Wax World (☎ 902/963–3444 ⊕ www.waxworldpei.com), and **Black Magic Indoor Blacklight Mini Golf** (☎ 902/963–2889 ⊕ www.cavendishsavings.com) exert their own magnetic pull.

open May through October. ⊠ *374 Eagles Glenn Blvd., Rte. 6, Cavendish, Prince Edward Island, Canada* ☎ *902/963–3600, 866/963–3600* ⊕ *www.eaglesglenn.com.*

**Glasgow Hills Resort and Golf Club.** The 18-hole, par-72 Glasgow Hills Resort and Golf Club, about five minutes southeast of Cavendish, wins high praise for its challenging Les Furber–designed layout and killer clubhouse views. ⊠ *98 Glasgow Hills Dr., New Glasgow, Prince Edward Island, Canada* ☎ *866/621–2200* ⊕ *www.glasgowhills.com.*

**Inn at the Pier.** Inn at the Pier lets you splash out in rented kayaks or Jet Skis. Parasailing rides and kiteboarding lessons can also be arranged. ⊠ *9796 Rte. 6, Cavendish, Prince Edward Island, Canada* ☎ *902/886–3126, 877/886–7437* ⊕ *www.innatthepier.com/watersports.*

## MALPEQUE

*Malpeque is 32 km (20 mi) west of Cavendish.*

There are two good reasons why motorists veer off Rte. 6 at New London onto Rte. 20. Some do it to cram in one last Anne shrine—specifically Silver Bush at Park Corner. Others continue westward to stuff themselves full of oysters. Named for the bay from which many are drawn, the Malpeque variety has had a huge cachet since earning the "best in show" title at the 1900 Paris World's Fair. Eating them is a time-honored tradition. The same goes for harvesting them: traditional methods are still employed (tongs are used, not dredgers) despite the fact that Prince Edward Island sells about 300,000 tons of oysters annually.

**EN ROUTE**

Just north of Darnley (on Rte. 20, about halfway between Park Corner and Malpeque) lies a long beach with a number of sandstone caves at the end. Darnley Beach does not have developed facilities and is often almost entirely deserted except for the seabirds—so it's perfect for those seeking a "castaway" experience.

## EXPLORING

**Cabot Beach Provincial Park.** In addition to a popular campground, 360-acre Cabot Beach Provincial Park has fine day-use facilities—particularly for families. In summer, the sandy beach is supervised, plus there's a playground and children's programming. Naturalist-led walks are also available. ⊠ *449 King St., Rte. 20, Malpeque, Prince Edward Island, Canada* ☎ *902/836–8945* ⌂ *Free for day use* ☉ *June–Sept., daily dawn–dusk.*

**Anne of Green Gables Museum at Silver Bush.** The Anne of Green Gables Museum at Silver Bush was once home to Lucy Maud Montgomery's aunt and uncle. The writer also lived here for a time and was married in the parlor in 1911—in fact, that room serves as a wedding venue for modern-day couples. Inside the house, which is still owned by Montgomery descendants, are mementos such as photographs and a quilt Montgomery worked on. The site includes a gift shop jam-packed with licensed Anne of Green Gables goodies, and there is a Matthew Cuthbert look-alike on hand to take visitors on buggy rides around the pastoral 110-acre property. Trip lengths vary with rates starting at C$4. ⊠ *Rte. 20, Park Corner, Prince Edward Island, Canada* ☎ *902/886–2884, 800/665–2663* ⊕ *www.annemuseum.com* ⌂ *C$5* ☉ *May and Oct., daily 11–4; June and Sept., daily 10–4; July and Aug., daily 9–5; off-season by appt.*

## WHERE TO EAT AND STAY

*For expanded hotel reviews, visit Fodors.com.*

**$$** ╳ **Malpeque Oyster Barn.** If it's oysters you're after, here's where to get
SEAFOOD 'em! You'll be hard pressed to find fresher bivalves; after all, you can see their beds right outside the window of this casual wharf-side eatery. Nor will you find plumper, sweeter ones. Oysters can be prepared several ways, but purists should just order a dozen unadorned (with a cold beer as an accompaniment), then slurp away. Chowder, steamed mussels, lobster rolls, and similiar fare appear on the menu as well, and there is a retail outlet in case you want to take some seafood home. ⊠ *Malpeque Wharf Rd., Rte. 20, Malpeque, Prince Edward Island, Canada* ☎ *902/836–3999* ☉ *Sept.–June.*

**$$** ⌂ **Noble House.** Staying at this cheery yellow heritage farmhouse with its welcoming front porch and gingerbread trim, you might feel like you have stepped into a Norman Rockwell painting—save for the fact that, back in the day, guests wouldn't have been able to book into well-equipped rooms that pair period charm with contemporary amenities like Jacuzzi tubs, cable TV, and high-speed Internet. **Pros:** close to Cabot Beach and Indian River Festival concerts; off-season rates available mid-September to mid-June. **Cons:** no a/c; resident pets may not appeal to those with allergies. ⊠ *187 Taylor Rd., RR #1, Malpeque, Prince Edward Island, Canada* ☎ *902/836–4380* ⊕ *www.bbcanada.com/5051. html* ⌂ *3 rooms* ♿ *In-room: no a/c, Internet* ♜ *Breakfast.*

## SPORTS AND THE OUTDOORS

**Dale's Deep Sea Adventures.** Daily fishing trips leave from Malpeque Harbour (beside Cabot Beach Provincial Park) from July to early September. The C$40 price includes all equipment, and Dale will clean

## A Bridge Too Far?

Gephyrophobiacs (people with an extreme fear of bridges) had best avoid the Confederation Bridge. Linking Borden-Carleton to Cape Jourimain, New Brunswick, it is the longest in the world spanning ice-covered water. But for anyone else intent on driving to or from PEI, the so-called "fixed link" is the way to go. Even if you're merely passing by while doing the Central Coastal circuit, this 13-km (8-mi) engineering marvel is worth a look. To construct it, massive concrete pillars—each 65 feet across and 180 feet high—were sunk into waters

more than 110 feet deep. The cost? A cool billion.

First-time traversers invariably want to stop on the bridge itself to take a picture. Don't—it's illegal. You must maintain a speed of 80 kmph (50 mph). The best angles are from the Prince Edward Island side anyway. For an up-close perspective, pull into Gateway Village at the foot of the bridge. In addition to a 3-acre park where you can take in the bridge view, it has a plethora of souvenir shops where you can buy postcards of said view.

what you catch. ⊠ *Rte. 20, Malpeque, Prince Edward Island, Canada* ☎ *902/836–3393.*

**Malpeque Bay Kayak Tours.** Malpeque is a French corruption of the Mi'kmaq word for "big water." You can go out and explore it in summer with Malpeque Bay Kayak Tours. Informative, half-day interpretive trips cost C$50. The company also rents kayaks and—for on-shore adventures—bicycles. ⊠ *Rte. 20, Malpeque, Prince Edward Island, Canada* ☎ *902/836–3784, 866/582–3383* ⊕ *www.peikayak.ca.*

## VICTORIA

*22 km (14 mi) east of Borden-Carleton.*

Cross country from the Green Gables Shore is the Red Sands Shore where charming, understated villages await. The jewel in this coastal crown is Victoria, just off the TransCanada Highway 22 km (14 mi) east of the Confederation Bridge. Known locally as Victoria-by-the-Sea, it is, well, Victorian . . . and by the sea. It's also peaceful, lovingly preserved, and popular with artsy types who come to escape the hectic pace of modern life. To fully appreciate Victoria, park by the wharf and set out on foot. Browse the shops. Watch the fishing boats. Admire the architecture. It's only two blocks wide and two blocks long, so you won't get lost.

### EXPLORING

**Victoria Provincial Park.** The usually uncrowded Victoria Provincial Park is just outside the village. Here beach lovers enjoy the warm, calm waters of the Northumberland Strait. You can walk on the sand flats at low tide, and if you're lucky enough to be in town when there's an electrical storm, the display over the water is quite something. ⊠ *Victoria, Prince Edward Island, Canada.*

## WHERE TO EAT AND STAY

*For expanded hotel reviews, visit Fodors.com.*

$ ✕ **Landmark Café.** This quirky, memorabilia-filled eatery has soups, sal-
CAFÉ ads, sandwiches, and a killer daily quiche. But it's the fresh seafood that
★ really stands out. Try Eugene's Cajun-style shrimp and scallops, or go
back to basics with what may be the Island's best chowder. You can
count on friendly service, too. Like so many places on PEI, this one is
family owned and operated—and it shows. The caveat is that the little
Landmark fills up quickly, so having reservations (or patience) helps.
✉ *12 Main St., Victoria, Prince Edward Island, Canada* ☎ *902/658–
2286* ⊕ *www.landmarkcafe.ca* ☉ *Closed Oct.–May.*

$ ⛫ **Victoria Village Inn and Restaurant.** Guest rooms in this three-story Vic-
torian—built for a sea captain in the 1880s—are rather basic in terms
of decor. **Pros:** common living room with TV and board games; open
year-round. **Cons:** some rooms are small; no TVs. ✉ *22 Howard St.,
Victoria, Prince Edward Island, Canada* ☎ *902/658–2483, 866/658–
2483* ⊕ *www.victoriavillageinn.com* ⇗ *3 rooms, 1 suite* ⚭ *In-room: no
a/c, no TV, Wi-Fi. In-hotel: restaurant, some pets allowed* ⧉ *Breakfast.*

## NIGHTLIFE AND THE ARTS

**Victoria Playhouse.** Offering a renowned professional program that celebrates Canadian theater and music, this place may only have 150 seats
but it has big talent and huge heart. From late June through September,
the circa-1914 venue opens nightly, mounting four plays plus a Monday night Musical Showcase Series. ✉ *Howard and Main Sts., Victoria, Prince Edward Island, Canada* ☎ *902/658–2025, 800/925–2025*
⊕ *www.victoriaplayhouse.com.*

## SHOPPING

**Island Chocolates.** A family-run chocolate factory in a 19th-century store,
Island Chocolates sells sweets handmade with Belgian chocolate, fresh
fruit, nuts, and liqueurs. Espresso, teas, and other decadent desserts
are also available, and there is a nice deck to sit on while you munch.
Willy Wonka wannabes will enjoy the chocolate-making workshops
(C$35) held on Wednesdays and Sundays. ✉ *7 Main St., Victoria, Prince
Edward Island, Canada* ☎ *902/658–2320* ⊕ *www.islandchocolates.ca*
☉ *Closed mid-Sept.–mid-June.*

## SPORTS AND THE OUTDOORS

**By the Sea Kayaking.** June through September, By the Sea Kayaking runs
paddle tours—among them ones with clam-digging included. Kayaks
as well as bicycles are also available for rent. ✉ *Victoria Wharf, Victoria, Prince Edward Island, Canada* ☎ *902/658–2572, 877/879–2572*
⊕ *www.bytheseakayaking.ca.*

# POINTS EAST COASTAL DRIVE

For 375 km (233 mi), the Points East Coastal Drive traces the coastline of tranquil Kings County on the east end of PEI. The route passes
forests, farms, fishing villages, and (in early summer, at least) fields of
blue, white, pink, and purple lupines that slope down to red cliffs and
blue sea. Championship golf courses are also in abundant supply. Ditto

for lighthouses and long, uncrowded beaches; among these, Basin Head and the Greenwich section of Prince Edward Island National Park stand out. Accessible by car from other parts of the province, the Points East Coastal Drive can also be reached via ferry from Nova Scotia.

## GEORGETOWN

*52 km (32 mi) northeast of Charlottetown.*

The pint-sized capital of Kings County, at the tip of a peninsula jutting into Cardigan Bay, was a major shipbuilding center in the 19th century. Thanks to its location—and early settlers' vocation—the town has both wraparound sea views and a collection of charming, Victorian-era buildings. Georgetown is also a mere five minutes from Brudenell River Provincial Park (the county's largest such facility). To get here from Charlottetown or the Wood Islands Ferry, follow the signs for the well-marked Points East Coastal Drive. Alternately, you can save time by cutting cross-country from Charlottetown on Route 3.

### WHERE TO EAT AND STAY

*For expanded hotel reviews, visit Fodors.com.*

**$$$**
SEAFOOD
✕ **Clamdiggers Beach House and Restaurant.** In theory you could come here and just gorge on the waterfront restaurant's namesake bivalves: imagine starting with soft-shell steamers before moving on to a generous platter of whole, hand-breaded fried clams served with PEI fries and house-made coleslaw. But if you did you'd miss out on the fresh crab cakes . . . and the seafood stew . . . and the seared halibut. There are lots of options for meat lovers too. All of the above can be enjoyed either inside the bright, beach house–style dining room or outside on a deck that sits a mere 8 m (26 ft) from Cardigan Bay. ⊠ *7 West St., Georgetown, Prince Edward Island, Canada* ☎ *902/652–2466* ⊕ *www. clamdiggers.ca* ⊘ *Oct.–May.*

**$**
⌂ **Georgetown Inn.** The mantra for guests at the Georgetown Inn could be "eat, sleep, repeat" because it offers both quiet, country-style accommodations and exceptional dining experiences. **Pros:** peacefulness personified; convenient location. **Cons:** dinner reservations essential; sloped ceilings reduce headroom in third-floor lodgings. ⊠ *62 Richmond St., Georgetown, Prince Edward Island, Canada* ☎ *902/652–2511, 877/641–2414* ⊕ *peigeorgetownhistoricinn.com* ↙ *8 rooms* ⌂ *In-room: Wi-Fi. In-hotel: restaurant* ❙◎❙ *Breakfast.*

**$$$**
⌂ **Rodd Brudenell River—A Rodd Signature Resort.** If you've come to eastern PEI to golf, this resort is *the* place to stay because the provincial park that shares its name is home to (count 'em) two 18-hole championship courses plus a 9-hole executive course. **Pros:** many rooms and all cottages have private decks or balconies; half the cottages have fireplaces and full kitchens. **Cons:** tired decor; fine dining available late June to mid-September only. ⊠ *86 Dewars Ln., Brudenell River Provincial Park, Georgetown, Prince Edward Island, Canada* ☎ *902/652–2332, 800/565–7633* ⊕ *www.roddvacations.com* ↙ *67 rooms, 32 hotel suites, 32 cottage suites* ⌂ *In-room: kitchen, Wi-Fi. In-hotel: restaurant, bar, golf course, pool, tennis court, gym, spa, business center, some pets allowed* ⊘ *Closed Nov.–Apr.*

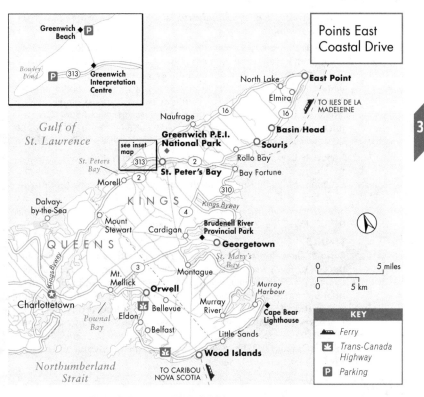

## NIGHTLIFE AND THE ARTS

**Kings Playhouse.** In summer months, the Kings Playhouse stages light-hearted comedies on Sunday and Wednesday evenings. On Tuesdays, the venue is turned over to fiddlers and dancers during the weekly ceilidh. ✉ *65 Grafton St., Georgetown, Prince Edward Island, Canada* ☎ *902/652–2053, 888/346–5666* ⊕ *www.kingsplayhouse.com.*

## SPORTS AND THE OUTDOORS

**Brudenell River Golf Course.** The 18-hole, par-72 Brudenell River Golf Course is one of the best in the country and arguably the most popular on the Island. ✉ *283 Brudenell Island Blvd., Rte 3, Brudenell River Provincial Park, Georgetown, Prince Edward Island, Canada* ☎ *800/235–8909* ⊕ *www.golflinkspei.com.*

**Brudenell River Provincial Park.** In July and August, the park promises interpretative programs, plus a wealth of outdoor opportunities—including boating, hiking, and supervised swimming. Two championship golf courses (Brudenell River and Dundarave) are the icing on its proverbial cake. ✉ *283 Brudenell Island Blvd., Rte. 3, Georgetown, Prince Edward Island, Canada* ☎ *902/652–8966.*

**Dundarave Golf Course.** With its striking red sandstone bunkers, the 18-hole Dundarave Golf Course is Brudenell River's beautiful younger sister. ✉ *283 Brudenell Island Blvd., Rte. 3, Brudenell River Provincial*

*Park, Georgetown, Prince Edward Island, Canada* ☎ *800/235–8909* ⊕ *www.golflinkspei.com.*

**Outside Expeditions.** July through early September, Outside Expeditions offers both kayak rentals and kayak tours at its Brudenell River Provincial Park location. The latter includes everything from easy 90-minute paddles (C$39) appropriate for any level of expertise to six-hour seal-watching excursions (C$120). Multiday trips are also available. ⊠ *283 Brudenell Island Blvd., Rte. 3, Brudenell River Provincial Park, Georgetown, Prince Edward Island, Canada* ☎ *902/963–3366, 800/207–3899* ⊕ *www.getoutside.com.*

**Tranquility Cove Adventures.** One way to experience PEI like a native is to sign up with Tranquility Cove Adventures for a few hours of lobster catching (May and June), clam digging, or deep-sea fishing (both July– September). The fun, informative outings cost C$49–$89. ⊠ *1 Kent St., Georgetown Wharf, Georgetown, Prince Edward Island, Canada* ☎ *902/969–7184* ⊕ *tranquilitycoveadventures.com.*

### TOURS

⟳ **Roma at Three Rivers.** This National Historic Site, about 2 km (1 mi) outside of Georgetown, commemorates the trading post French merchant Jean Pierre Roma established here in 1732. Costumed staffers offer interpretive programs and guided tours daily (there are trails with informational panels if you'd prefer to explore independently). Heritage lunches with sustaining soup and brick-oven bread are also served onsite. ⊠ *505 Roma Point Rd., off Rte. 319, Brudenell Pt., Prince Edward Island, Canada* ☎ *902/838–3413* ⊕ *www.roma3rivers.com* ⧉ *By donation* ☉ *Late June–early Sept., daily 10–6.*

## SOURIS

*Souris is 46 km (29 mi) northeast of Georgetown.*

A pretty town perched on the water, Souris (pronounced "Surrey") gives easy access to PEI's essential sights and sounds. The seascape includes harbors, lighthouses, and bountiful beaches. There's music in the salt air too. Souris stages a Music in the Park series and holds Tuesday evening ceilidhs in summer (see ⊕ *www.sourispei.com* for details). Rollo Bay, five minutes away, has ceilidhs on Thursday evenings. Plus it hosts the PEI Bluegrass and Old Time Music Festival (☎ *902/566–2641* ⊕ *bluegrasspei.com*) in early July and the Rollo Bay Fiddle Festival midmonth (☎ *902/687–2584* ⊕ *www.rollobayfiddlefest.ca*).

### GETTING HERE AND AROUND

The East Connection Shuttle (☎ *902/393–5132 or 902/892–6760*) carries passengers on request from Charlottetown to Souris and other Kings County communities. The fare is approximately C$80 one way. You'll want your own vehicle, however, to properly see outlying areas. To drive yours here from Georgetown, follow signs for the Points East Coastal Drive; or veer a little inland to Rte. 4, which merges with Rte. 2 near Fortune.

## EXPLORING

Ↄ **Basin Head Provincial Park.** Located 13 km (8 mi) east of Souris, this park is noted for an expanse of exquisite silvery sand that's backed by grassy dunes. The beach (accessible via a boardwalk and supervised in peak months) no longer qualifies as a secret. But it's still well worth visiting—and not only because it's one of the Island's most beautiful. If you scuff your feet in the sand here, you can hear it squeak and squawk. The so-called "singing sand" is a rare phenomenon produced by the sand's high silica content.

On a beach-top bluff inside the park, you'll also find the small **Basin Head Fisheries Museum** (☎ *902/357–7233* ⊕ *www.peimuseum.com* ▭ *C$4* ☉ *Early June–Oct., daily 9–5*), which depicts the ever-changing nature of PEI's inshore fishing industry through artifacts, exhibits, and dioramas. If the museum's emphasis on ocean edibles leaves you hankering for seafood, **Skallywags Patio Restaurant** (☎ *902/357–2211*) serves fish and chips, scallop burgers, and similar fishy fare nearby. It's open daily, 11–7, June to September. ⊠ *336 Basin Head Rd., off Rte. 16, Souris, Prince Edward Island, Canada* ☎ *902/357–7230* ⊕ *www. tourismpei.com/provincial-park/basin-head.*

**Myriad View Artisan Distillery.** The Myriad View Artisan Distillery in Rollo Bay, just west of Souris, handcrafts spirited spirits—like Strait Vodka and Dandelion 'Shine. Complimentary tours and tastings are offered May through September and products can be purchased on-site. ⊠ *1336 Rte. 2, Rollo Bay, Prince Edward Island, Canada* ☎ *902/687– 1281* ⊕ *www.straitshine.com.*

**Prince Edward Distillery.** A must-see for tippling tourists is the Prince Edward Distillery, north of Souris. Its premium vodka proves that more than french fries and chips can be made from those famous PEI potatoes. Take a tour, then buy some liquid souvenirs to take home. ⊠ *9984 Rte. 16, Hermanville, Prince Edward Island, Canada* ☎ *902/687–2586, 877/510–9669* ⊕ *www.princeedwarddistillery.com.*

## WHERE TO EAT AND STAY

*For expanded hotel reviews, visit Fodors.com.*

¢ ✕ **Sheltered Harbour Café.** Cheerfully decorated in a nautical theme, this
CANADIAN roadside family restaurant is frequented mostly by locals. It's a handy place to stop during a drive along the shore; the basic fare—clams, scallops, and other seafood, burgers, salads, sweet potato fries, liver and onions—is served in large portions at reasonable prices. The café is open year-round, but finding it is tricky. En route to Souris, look for Abel's Corner Ultramar. ⊠ *2065 Rte. 2, junction of Rtes. 2 and 340, Fortune, Prince Edward Island, Canada* ☎ *902/687–1997.*

$$$ 🏨 **Inn at Bay Fortune.** This 1910 inn was built by Elmer Blaney Har-
★ ris (whose play *Johnny Belinda* was inspired by PEI events) and later owned by actress Colleen Dewhurst (who played Marilla in the *Anne of Green Gables* series). **Pros:** bikes and kayaks on-site; many rooms have fireplaces and some have balconies. **Cons:** mosquitoes can be bothersome; not directly on the beach. ⊠ *758 Rte. 310, off Rte. 2, 10 minutes west of Souris, Bay Fortune, Prince Edward Island, Canada* ☎ *902/687–3745, 888/687–3745* ⊕ *www.innatbayfortune.com* ⤺ *11*

*rooms, 6 suites, 2 cottages* ⚑ *In-room: Wi-Fi. In-hotel: restaurant* ⊙ *Closed early Oct.–late May* |⊙| *Breakfast.*

$$$   ⛩ **Inn at Spry Point.** Inn at Bay Fortune's sister property hugs the end of a 110-acre peninsula a few kilometers east, so you benefit from both an attractive shoreline and a 1-km (½-mi) sandy beach. **Pros:** ocean sounds lull you to sleep; comfy beds. **Cons:** relatively remote; no lunch option on-site. ⊠ *Spry Point Rd., off Rte. 310, Little Pond, Prince Edward Island, Canada* ☎ *902/583–2400, 888/687–3745* ⊕ *www. innatsprypoint.com* ⟿ *15 rooms* ⚑ *In-room: no TV, Wi-Fi. In-hotel: restaurant* ⊙ *Closed early Oct.–mid-June* |⊙| *Breakfast.*

### SPORTS AND THE OUTDOORS

**Paradise on the Sea Adventures.** This outfitter will lead you on a seafood hunt. Snorkel for bar clams or oysters, with a little mackerel fishing and a lot of eating thrown in for good measure. Full-day tours cost C$89 and C$99 respectively. Bluefin tuna charters and relaxing sunset cruises are offered as well. ⊠ *118 Breakwater St., Souris Marina, Souris, Prince Edward Island, Canada* ☎ *902/969–7727* ⊕ *www. paradiseontheseaadventures.com.*

## ST. PETER'S BAY

*28 km (17 mi) northwest of Souris.*

St. Peter's Bay won the location lottery—as least that's what folks who love quiet, outdoorsy destinations think. The nearby Greenwich portion of Prince Edward Island National Park has dunes that draw beachgoers, hikers, and birdwatchers too: so many avian species flock here that the park runs themed programs. If you'd rather pursue a different kind of birdie, the Links at Crowbush Cove are a short drive west. St. Peter's Bay, meanwhile, provides a sublime backdrop for cycling. On the waterside leg of the Confederation Trail between the village and Morell, you pedal past idyllic coves dotted with boats and buoys.

### GETTING HERE AND AROUND

Driving independently is the best way to get here. From Souris continue along the Points East Coastal Drive or take a cross-country shortcut on Rte. 2. Alternately, the East Connection Shuttle (☎ *902/393–5132 or 902/892–6760*) will bring you here from Charlottetown; expect to pay about C$65 one-way.

### EXPLORING

**Greenwich (P.E.I. National Park).** The west end of the Greenwich peninsula, known for its superior beach and shifting sand dunes, was federally protected in 1998 when a 6-km (3.5-mi) section was incorporated into Prince Edward Island National Park. Because the dunes are still moving, gradually burying the nearby woods, here and there bleached tree bits thrust up through the sand like wooden skeletons. The road in ends at an interpretive center (open early June to early September) where displays, hands-on activities, and themed programs teach visitors about the ecology of this unique land formation. Walking trails let you follow the progression from forest to dune to beach, and include a photogenic boardwalk over Bowley Pond. Due to the delicate nature of the dune system, you're required to stay on designated paths and refrain from touching flora. Changing facilities and a picnic area can be found at the beach itself, which is supervised from July to mid-August. ⊠ *Rte. 313, 6 km (4 mi) west of St. Peters Bay, Greenwich, Prince Edward Island, Canada* ☎ *902/672–6350* ⊕ *www.pc.gc.ca* ⊠ *C$7.80* ☉ *Daily dawn–dusk.*

## WHERE TO EAT AND STAY

*For expanded hotel reviews, visit Fodors.com.*

$ ✕ **Rick's Fish 'n' Chips and Seafood House.** Rick's french fries are fresh-cut,
SEAFOOD his haddock fresh-caught—and together they make one of the Island's top fish-and-chip platters. Also on the menu at this spartan spot: deep-fried clams, scallop burgers, steamed mussels, and oysters on the half-shell. The standard burger and wings selection is available for those who aren't seafood fans. Service is friendly, but you might have to wait a bit during peak hours for a seat inside or a picnic table outside. ⊠ *5544 Rte. 2, St. Peters, Prince Edward Island, Canada* ☎ *902/961–3438* ⊕ *www. ricksfishnchips.com* ⚠ *Reservations not accepted* ☉ *Closed Oct.–May.*

$$$ ⊞ **The Inn at St. Peters.** One of the province's best-positioned inns occu-
★ pies 13 idyllic acres minutes from the Greenwich park. **Pros:** attentive service; rooms' perks include sofas, fireplaces, DVD players, and mini-fridges. **Cons:** relatively pricey; restructured rates no longer include dinner. ⊠ *1668 Greenwich Rd., off Rte. 313, St. Peters Bay, Prince Edward Island, Canada* ☎ *902/961–2135, 800/818–0925* ⊕ *www. innatstpeters.com* ⏏ *16 suites* ⚐ *In-room: Wi-Fi. In-hotel: restaurant, some pets allowed* ☉ *Open late May–early Oct.* ⊙ *Breakfast.*

## NIGHTLIFE AND THE ARTS

**St. Peters Courthouse Theatre.** In summer, local musical acts perform and amateur actors mount plays several times per week at the St. Peters Courthouse Theatre. Logically enough, the venue is a restored courthouse that dates back to 1874. ⊠ *5697 Rte. 2, St. Peters, Prince Edward Island, Canada* ☎ *902/961–3636, 902/961–3004* ⊕ *www. courthousetheatre.com.*

## SPORTS AND THE OUTDOORS

**The Links at Crowbush Cove.** Talk about a sand trap. Designed by Thomas McBroom, the Links at Crowbush Cove is an 18-hole, par-72 Scottish-style course with dune views. ⊠ *710 Canavoy Rd., Rte. 350, between West St. Peters and Morell, Lakeside, Prince Edward Island, Canada* ⊕ *golflinkspei.com.*

**Plover Bike Rentals.** Plover Bike Rentals has cycles and accessories, including tag-along kid carriers. Open May through October (daily in peak season, weekdays only in shoulder season), its rates start at C$25 for a half-day. ⊠ *15465 Northside Rd., junction of Rte. 2 and Rte. 16, St. Peters, Prince Edward Island, Canada* ☎ *902/961–3223* ⊕ *www. stpetersbay.com/rentals.*

**Turret Bell.** Turret Bell organizes walking tours and geo-caching adventures in the St. Peters Bay area from June to September. Off-season outings are available on request. ⊠ *5599 Rte. 2, St. Peters, Prince Edward Island, Canada* ☎ *902/961–1070, 902/961–3273* ⊕ *www.turretbell.com.*

**East Point Lighthouse.** Ships from many nations have been wrecked on the reef running northeast from East Point Lighthouse. Guided tours of the towering 1867 edifice are offered mid-June through Labor Day. Books about life at sea, as well as local crafts, are available at the on-site gift shop. Because of the erosion, caution should be used when approaching the high cliffs overlooking the ocean here. ⊠ *Lighthouse Rd., off Rte. 16, East Point, Prince Edward Island, Canada* ☎ *902/357–2106* ⊕ *www.eastpointlighthouse.com* ☜ *C$4.*

# NORTH CAPE COASTAL DRIVE

Prince County's 350-km (217-mi) North Cape Coastal Drive winds along the west coast of the Island, through very old, very small villages that still adhere to a traditional way of life. Fishermen plowing boats through choppy seas and farmers driving tractors through fields of rich, red soil are common sights. (The potatoes the latter grow prove Anne and oysters aren't the Island's only major exports!) You may be tempted to stay on the straight, flat Route 2 most of the way. But to see all that "Up West" has to offer take Route 14 to West Point and continue north along Northumberland Strait, returning along the Gulf of St. Lawrence via Route 12.

## SUMMERSIDE

*71 km (44 mi) west of Charlottetown.*

Summerside, the second-largest city on PEI, has an attractive waterfront with a beach and boardwalk in the west end. It has a fine collection of heritage homes, too, many of them erected around the turn of the 20th century when Summerside was the headquarters of a virtual gold rush based on silver fox ranching (a small municipal museum tells that tale). Today fishing and potato processing are more profitable enterprises—though good fish and chips spots are curiously in short supply. Happily, lobster is plentiful in early July during the 10-day Summerside Lobster Carnival (☎ *902/724–4925* ⊕ *www.summersidelobstercarnival.ca*).

### GETTING HERE AND AROUND

Summerside can be accessed by car, bus, or shuttle. Once there, you're best off exploring on foot. Biking is another option: the Confederation Trail passes through the city, and the former railway station makes an excellent starting point for cycling excursions.

### EXPLORING

**Acadian Museum** (*Musée Acadien*). Many descendants of PEI's first French settlers still live in the Miscouche area, 10 km (6 mi) northwest of Summerside, and the Acadian Museum commemorates their history. This National Historic Site includes a permanent exhibition on Acadian life as well as an audiovisual presentation outlining the story of Island Acadians from the early 1700s onward. A genealogical center, heritage walking trail, and themed gift shop are also on-site. ⊠ *23 Main Dr. E, Rte. 2, Miscouche, Prince Edward Island, Canada* ☎ *902/432–2880*

CLOSE UP

# Lighthouses of Eastern PEI

The Points East Coastal area is nirvana for lighthouse lovers. PEI has over 50 of the navigational aids, but many of the highlights (literally) are right here. Aside from the East Point Light, top picks—from north to south—include the following:

**Panmure Head Lighthouse:** Marking the entrance to Georgetown Harbour, it stands more than 18.5 meters (60 feet) tall. After ascending to the top, catch your breath browsing the on-site gift shop (*62 Lighthouse Rd., Rte. 347, Panmure Island* ☎ *902/838–3568*).

**Cape Bear Lighthouse:** It was a wireless operator here who received the initial distress call from the sinking Titanic in 1912. A museum annex houses a replica of the original Marconi Station. (*Cape Bear Rd., off Rte. 18, Cape Bear* ☎ *902/962–2917*).

**Wood Islands Lighthouse:** This one, by the ferry terminal, has exhibits on local history and marine lore—like the Phantom Ship of Northumberland Strait. (*173 Lighthouse Rd., Rte. 1, Wood Islands* ☎ *902/962–3110* ⊕ *www.woodislandslighthouse.com*).

**Point Prim Lighthouse:** Erected in 1845, it is PEI's oldest light. Daily tours run from late June to late September (*2147 Point Prim Rd., Rte. 209, 11 km [7.5 mi] west of Belfast* ☎ *902/659–2768 or 902/659–2407* ⊕ *www.pointprimlighthouse.com*).

All are open to the public in July and August, and they charge about C$5 admission each. For further details, grab a copy of the themed brochure produced by the PEI Lighthouse Society.

---

⊕ *www.peimuseum.com* ✉ *C$4.50* ⊙ *July and Aug., daily 9:30–7; Sept.–June, weekdays 9:30–5, Sun. 1–4.*

**Bishop's Foundry.** The Bishop's Foundry is an old-fashioned machine shop, where you can see an interesting collection of tools and gadgets. ✉ *101 Water St., Summerside, Prince Edward Island, Canada* ☎ *902/432–1296* ⊕ *www.wyattheritage.com* ✉ *By donation* ⊙ *Mid-June–Sept., Mon.–Sat., 10–4; off-season by appointment.*

**Eptek Art and Culture Centre.** On the waterfront, Eptek Art and Culture Centre has rotating exhibits of PEI history and fine arts on display in the main gallery: the variety of the exhibitions is one of the center's hallmarks. The same complex houses the Harbourfront Theatre and PEI Sports Hall of Fame.

**Harbourfront Theatre.** ✉ *124 Harbour Dr., Summerside, Prince Edward Island, Canada* ☎ *902/888–2500, 800/708–6505* ⊕ *www. harbourfronttheatre.com* ⊙ *Open year-round.*

**PEI Sports Hall of Fame.** ✉ *124 Harbour Dr., Waterfront Properties, Summerside, Prince Edward Island, Canada* ☎ *902/436–0423* ✉ *By donation* ⊙ *Days and hrs vary; call ahead* ✉ *130 Harbour Dr., Summerside, Prince Edward Island, Canada* ☎ *902/888–8373* ⊕ *www. peimuseum.com* ✉ *By donation* ⊙ *June and Sept., weekdays 9–4,*

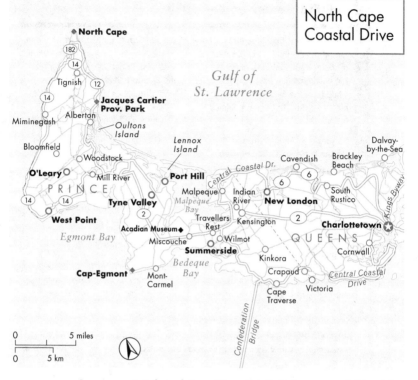

**North Cape Coastal Drive**

*Sun. noon–4; July and Aug., Mon.–Sat. 9–5, Sun. noon–5; Oct.–May, Tues.–Fri. 10–4, Sun. noon–4.*

**International Fox Museum and Hall of Fame.** Housed in a 1911 armory, the International Fox Museum and Hall of Fame recounts the days when fox fur was the height of fashion—and fox "farming" was a thriving Summerside industry. ✉ *33 Summer St., Summerside, Prince Edward Island, Canada* ☎ *902/432–1296* 🎟 *Donation* ☾ *mid-June–Sept., Mon.–Sat. 10–4.*

**Spinnakers' Landing.** Spinnakers' Landing, the cornerstone of Summerside's waterfront revitalization project, is a collection of cheery little structures that are linked by a boardwalk and designed to evoke a seaside fishing village. The development offers a good blend of shopping, history, and entertainment; plus you can climb a lighthouse lookout for panoramic views of Bedeque Bay and the city. In summer, weather permitting, there's often free weekend entertainment (usually starting at 6 pm) on the outdoor stage over the water. ✉ *150 Harbour Dr., Summerside, Prince Edward Island, Canada* ☎ *902/436–2264* ⊕ *www.spinnakerslanding.com* ☾ *Mid-June–mid-Sept.*

**Summerside Lobster Carnival.** During the third week of July, all of Summerside celebrates the eight-day Summerside Lobster Carnival, with livestock exhibitions, harness racing, fiddling contests, and, of course, lobster suppers. ⌨ *Summerside, Prince Edward Island, Canada* ☎ *902/724–4925* ⊕ *www.summersidelobstercarnival.ca.*

**Wyatt House Museum.** Built in 1867 (the year Canada was "born"), the restored, heirloom-filled home of a prominent local family feels like a Summerside time capsule. Guided interpretive tours last about 45 minutes. The entry fee also admits you to a pair of other Wyatt Heritage Properties: the Macnaught History Centre & Archives (at 75 Spring St.) and the Lefurgey Cultural Centre (at 205 Prince St.). ⌨ *85 Spring St., Summerside, Prince Edward Island, Canada* ☎ *902/432–1327* ⊕ *www.wyattheritage.com* ⌨ *C$7* ☾ *June–Sept., Mon.–Sat.10–5; Oct.–May, Tues.–Fri. by appointment.*

## WHERE TO EAT AND STAY

*For expanded hotel reviews, visit Fodors.com.*

**$$**

**CANADIAN**

✕**The Deckhouse Pub & Eatery.** Summerside hardly qualifies as a foodie haven, so your best picks are places that keep it simple. The Deckhouse delivers on that front. Generous portions of traditional pub grub are supplemented by a range of tasty seafood dishes (try the chowder). Being located right at Spinnakers' Landing, water views are one added bonus. Live music, performed on Friday and Saturday evenings, is another. The downside is that it's only open in the summer months. ⌨ *150 Harbour Dr., Summerside, Prince Edward Island, Canada* ☎ *902/436–0660* ☾ *Early Sept.–late June.*

**¢**

⌂ **Clark's Sunny Isle Motel.** PEI may be one of the last places in Canada where motels are plentiful and worth recommending. **Pros:** well-tended 20-acre property includes a walking trail to the water; each room has a mini-fridge and high-def LCD TV. **Cons:** free Continental breakfast only served in May and October; basic decor. ⌨ *720 Water St. E, Summerside, Prince Edward Island, Canada* ☎ *902/436–5665, 877/682–6824* ⊕ *www.sunnyislemotel.com* ⇥ *21 rooms* ⏃ *In-room: Internet, Wi-Fi. In-hotel: business center, parking* ☾ *Nov.–Apr.* ⊘*Breakfast.*

**$$**

⌂ **Silver Fox Inn.** This Queen Anne Revival home—a designated historic property designed by celebrated PEI architect W. **Pros:** on a quiet street; knowledgeable hosts. **Cons:** rooms vary in size and quality; sloping ceilings on third floor. ⌨ *61 Granville St., Summerside, Prince Edward Island, Canada* ☎ *902/436–1664, 800/565–4033* ⊕ *www.silverfoxinn. net* ⇥ *6 rooms* ⏃ *In-room: Wi-Fi. In-hotel: laundry facilities, parking, some age restrictions* ⊘*Breakfast.*

## NIGHTLIFE AND THE ARTS

**College of Piping and Celtic Performing Arts of Canada.** The College of Piping and Celtic Performing Arts of Canada hosts an energetic revue in July and August. More than 30 bagpipers, Highland dancers, step dancers, and fiddlers perform Tuesday through Thursday evening. Mini-concerts also run three times daily in July and August. The C$5 tab can be credited towards the price of evening show tickets. ⌨ *619 Water St. E, Summerside, Prince Edward Island, Canada* ☎ *902/436–5377, 877/224–7473* ⊕ *www.collegeofpiping.com.*

**Feast Dinner Theatre.** At Feast Dinner Theatre, musical comedy is served up with a four-course seafood or chicken meal Tuesday through Saturday, from mid-June to early September. ⊠ *Brothers 2 Restaurant, 618 Water St., Summerside, Prince Edward Island, Canada* ☎ *902/436–7674* ⊕ *www.brothers2.ca.*

**Harbourfront Theatre.** The 527-seat Harbourfront Theatre stages dramatic and musical productions year-round. Touring musicians routinely drop by, too. ⊠ *124 Harbour Dr., Summerside, Prince Edward Island, Canada* ☎ *902/888–2500, 800/708–6505* ⊕ *www.harbourfronttheatre.com.*

### SPORTS AND THE OUTDOORS

**PEI Segway Tours.** PEI Segway Tours puts a different spin on two-wheeling fun. Tours (30 and 90 minutes, C$39 and C$69 respectively) depart four times daily from the Spinnakers' Landing Lighthouse. ⊠ *150 Harbor Dr., Summerside, Prince Edward Island, Canada* ☎ *902/436–8184* ⊕ *www.peisegway.com.*

## O'LEARY

*37 km (23 mi) northwest of Summerside.*

Central Prince County is composed of a loose network of small communities set amidst green fields. In the tradition of their forebears, most residents are farmers, and those in O'Leary are no exception. In terms of preferred crops, the potato is big here—literally. A giant fiberglass one that looms outside the PEI Potato Museum is the town's distinguishing feature. After eating potatoes prepared every possible way, you can work off the calories in nearby Mill River Provincial Park with golfing and other outdoor activities. To reach O'Leary from Summerside, follow Rte. 2 west, then transfer onto Rte. 142.

### EXPLORING

**PEI Potato Museum.** The potato is one terrific tuber: that's the message delivered by the PEI Potato Museum. Earnest and intriguing, it has exhibits devoted to "The Amazing Potato," displays of antique potato-farming equipment, a Potato Hall of Fame, even a gift shop selling potato-themed goods. The museum also runs fun add-on tours, which include a guided spin through the facility, plus a trip out to a potato farm, a potato fudge-making lesson, and a lunch of (you guessed it) potato-based dishes. ⊠ *1 Dewar Ln., O'Leary, Prince Edward Island, Canada* ☎ *902/859–2039, 800/565–3457* ⊕ *www.peipotatomuseum.com* ⊠ *C$6 for museum, C$49 for tours* ☉ *mid-May–mid-Oct.; Mon.–Sat. 9–5, Sun. 1–5.*

### WHERE TO STAY

*For expanded hotel reviews, visit Fodors.com.*

**$$** 🏨 **Rodd Mill River—A Rodd Signature Resort.** Since full-blown resorts are so rare in this portion of the province, Rodd Mill River provides a welcome change of pace. **Pros:** good base for exploring western PEI; golf packages are frequently available. **Cons:** uninspired furnishings, some public areas could be refreshed. ⊠ *Rte. 136, 5 km (3 mi) east of*

# Club Hopping—Island Style

Great golf clubs are par for the course on PEI, where green gables and green fields are complemented by challenging golf greens. There are more than 30 9- and 18-hole courses open to the public from May through October; and counted among that number are 10 of Canada's Top 100. The hit list, from west to east, includes: Mill River, Andersons Creek, Eagles Glenn, Green, Glasgow Hills, Stanhope, Fox Meadow, Links at Crowbush Cove, Brudenell

River, and Dundarave. All are within a 45-minute drive of one another—which means ambitious golfers can play 27 or 36 holes a day. Contact Golf PEI (☎ 866/465–3734 ⊕ www. golfpei.ca) for details on courses, events and play-and-stay packages or to book tee times.

*O'Leary, 180 Mill River Resort Rd., Woodstock, Prince Edward Island, Canada* ☎ *902/859–3555, 800/565–7633* ⊕ *www.roddvacations.com* 🛏 *90 rooms, 10 suites* ♻ *In-room: Wi-Fi. In-hotel: restaurant, bar, golf course, pool, tennis court, gym, spa, business center, some pets allowed* ☉ *Closed Nov.–Jan. and Apr.*

## SPORTS AND THE OUTDOORS

**Mill River Golf Course.** The 18-hole, par-72 Mill River Golf Course is among the most scenic and challenging in eastern Canada. It has been the site of several championship tournaments, and a season of the golf reality show *The Big Break* was filmed here. Book in advance. ⊠ *180 Mill River Resort Rd., off Rte. 2, Mill River Provincial Park, Woodstock, Prince Edward Island, Canada* ☎ *800/235–8909* ⊕ *www. golflinkspei.com* ☉ *Closed late Oct.–early May.*

## SHOPPING

**MacAusland's Woollen Mills.** The MacAusland's Woollen Mills, 5 km (3 mi) west of O'Leary, has been producing its famous MacAusland 100% pure virgin wool blankets since 1932. ⊠ *Rte. 2, Bloomfield, Prince Edward Island, Canada* ☎ *902/859–3005, 877/859–3005* ⊕ *www. macauslandswoollenmills.com.*

# WEST POINT

*24 km (15 mi) south of O'Leary.*

West Point, on the south tip of the west shore, seems made for lighthouse fans. Because it is so small (there are only about 700 residents) and so accessible by car from O'Leary via Rte. 14, the tiny community could easily constitute a day trip. Yet the presence of PEI's tallest functioning navigational aid makes it a destination in its own right. After admiring the lighthouse—or better yet, overnighting inside it—you can stroll the new 1,500-meter (4,921-foot) beachfront boardwalk; then cool off with a swim at Cedar Dunes Provincial Park.

### EXPLORING

**Fodor's Choice** ★ ☾ **West Point Lighthouse Museum.** Built in 1875, lit in 1876, manned until 1963, and still operating today, the West Point Lighthouse is a certifiable PEI icon. A gracefully tapered shape and eye-popping black-and-white stripes make the 21-meter (69-foot) structure very photogenic. Inside, displays and assorted artifacts relating to lighthouses province-wide make it educational too. Be sure to climb the 72 steps to the top for panoramic views. Beautiful any time of day, they are especially glorious at sunset because the lighthouse faces west. ⊠ *364 Cedar Dunes Park Rd., Rte. 14, West Point, Prince Edward Island, Canada* ☎ *902/859–3605, 800/764–6854* ⊕ *www.westpointlighthouse.com* ⊠ *C$3.50* ☾ *Daily, late May–late Sept., 9–9.*

### WHERE TO EAT AND STAY

*For expanded hotel reviews, visit Fodors.com.*

$$ ✕ **Sandals Restaurant.** As part of the West Point Lighthouse Inn and MODERN Museum overhaul, the restaurant formerly located on-site has moved CANADIAN into attractive new digs about 1 km (.6 mi) away at the West Point Harbourside Centre. The menu at the two-level waterview eatery, however, retains its regional focus, with most items—from fish to fruit—being sourced from the surrounding area. Expect fine dining in a casual setting. ⊠ *West Point Harbourside Centre, 159 Cedar Dunes Park Rd., Rte. 14, West Point, Prince Edward Island, Canada* ☎ *902/859–3330* ☾ *mid-Sept.–late May.*

$$ ▥ **West Point Lighthouse Inn.** Few people can say they've spent the night **Fodor's Choice** in a lighthouse—or at least in a guest room adjacent to one—so take ★ the opportunity when you're here. **Pros:** annex rooms have all new furnishings and fixtures; original rooms are full of character. **Cons:** the inn books up quickly; lighthouse equals bright flashing light. ⊠ *364 Cedar Dunes Park Rd., Rte. 14, West Point, Prince Edward Island, Canada* ☎ *902/859–3605, 800/764–6854* ⊕ *www.westpointlighthouse.com* ⇥ *13 rooms* ⚭ *In-room: Internet. In-hotel: beach, some pets allowed* ☾ *Closed early Oct.–late May* ▯⊙▯ *Breakfast.*

### SPORTS AND THE OUTDOORS

**Cedar Dunes Provincial Park.** Cedar Dunes Provincial Park, which encompasses the lighthouse site, boasts blissful beaches and supervised swimming in summer. Recreational programs—included guided walks of the park's nature trails—are also available seasonally. ⊠ *265 Cedar Dunes Park Rd., Rte. 14, West Point, Prince Edward Island, Canada* ☎ *902/859–8785.*

## NORTH CAPE

*47 km (29 mi) north of O'Leary.*

★ Mother Nature meets modern technology at PEI's northwest tip. The Gulf of St. Lawrence and Northumberland Strait converge at North Cape's reef (the longest rock reef in North America) creating a popular hangout for seals, seabirds, and other forms of marine life. But it's the wind sweeping over the water that makes this place really stand out. Scores of windmills—some of them 80 meters (262 feet) high—dot the site. Part of the Atlantic Wind Test Site and Wind Farm, they were built to make the "Gentle Island" even greener. To reach North Cape, take Rte. 14 along the Strait or Rte. 12 along the Gulf.

**EN ROUTE**

Wonder why you see horses pulling low, cart-like contraptions at the water's edge? Well the folks with them are gathering Irish moss. The fan-shaped red alga, found in abundance on this coast, is the source of carrageenan, a natural thickener used in processing ice cream and many other foods. In the tiny village of Miminegash—20 km (12 mi) south of North Cape—an equally tiny Irish Moss Interpretive Centre (☎ 902/882–4313 ✉ C$2) tells all about it. You can get a taste of it there, too, by ordering a slice of savory "seaweed pie" at the adjacent café. If you would like to try collecting the moss yourself, round the Cape to Seacow Pond and sign on for the hands-on Mossing Experience (☎ 902/882–3134 ⊕ *www.tignish.com/experiences/experiences/mossing.htm* ✉ *C$35–$75 depending on number of participants*). Ice cream will never seem the same.

3

## EXPLORING

**Interpretive Centre and Aquarium.** The North Cape Wind Energy Interpretive Centre has exhibits that explain how turbine technology channels wind power to produce "clean" electricity for Islanders. It also includes a few displays pertaining to local history and a touch tank with lobster, crabs, and starfish that kids will enjoy. (A staff member will lift one out so you can get a real feel for these aquatic creatures.) ✉ *21817 Rte. 12, North Cape, Prince Edward Island, Canada* ☎ *902/882–2991* ⊕ *www. northcape.ca* ✉ *C$5.25* ☉ *July and Aug., daily 9–8; May–June and Sept.–Oct., daily 10–6.*

## WHERE TO EAT AND STAY

*For expanded hotel reviews, visit Fodors.com.*

**$$**
**SEAFOOD**
✕ **The Boat Shop Steak & Seafood Restaurant.** This attractive spot occupies a converted boat builder's workshop—which explains not only its waterfront location but its oversized windows and soaring ceiling. Fine, fresh seafood, not surprisingly, dominates the menu. (Time your visit right and you may be able to see fishermen unloading the catch of the day or graceful blue herons angling for their own dinner.) Traditional homemade desserts like blueberry bread pudding and sticky date cake are another highlight. Patio seating is available on fine days. ✉ *296 Rte. 152, 33 km (21 mi) south of North Cape, Northport, Prince Edward Island, Canada* ☎ *902/853–4510* ⊕ *www.northportpier.ca* ☉ *Closed mid-Sept.–May.*

**$$**
**SEAFOOD**
✕ **Wind & Reef Restaurant.** Dining options are few and far between in this remote corner of PEI, so it's a blessing that the airy eatery above the North Cape Wind Energy Interpretative Centre offers more than mere sustenance. The Island seafood—including oysters, mussels, and lobster—is fresh and well prepared. Ditto for the beef and chicken dishes. Service is unfailingly friendly too. The restaurant's panoramic windows, providing views of the water and (at low tide) the reef, are an added bonus. ✉ *21817 Rte. 12, North Cape, Prince Edward Island, Canada* ☎ *902/882–3535* ☉ *Closed Oct.–May.*

**$**
🛏 **Hunter House Inn.** In the midst of so much agricultural land, staying at a farmhouse B&B seems particularly appropriate, and this one is a beauty.

**Pros:** friendly owners will provide shuttle service to area restaurants. **Cons:** no a/c; about a 25-minute drive to North Cape. ⊠ *1013 Rte.152, Alberton, Prince Edward Island, Canada* ☎ *902/853–4027, 888/853–4027* ⊕ *www.bbcanada. com/hunterhouse* ⇆ *3 rooms* ⑂ *In-room: no a/c, Wi-Fi. In-hotel: laundry facilities* ☉ *Nov.–late May* ⑂⊙⑂ *Breakfast.*

$$ 🏨 **Northport Pier Inn.** Conveniences like a/c and Wi-Fi set this spot a notch above many rural inns, but it's the view that guests really rave about. **Pros:** a restaurant and marina are next door; roomy kitchenette suites work well for families. **Cons:** decor is basic; during lobster season (May and June) early morning harbor traffic might waken light sleepers. ⊠ *298 Rte. 152, 33 km (21 mi) south of North Cape, Northport, Prince Edward Island, Canada* ☎ *902/853–4520, 866/887–4520* ⊕ *www.northportpier.ca* ⇆ *12 rooms, 2 suites* ⑂ *In-room: Wi-Fi. In-hotel: laundry facilities* ☉ *Closed Oct.–May* ⑂⊙⑂ *Breakfast.*

## SPORTS AND THE OUTDOORS

**Black Marsh Nature Trail.** One of the best ways to see North Cape's natural and manmade assets is by hiking the Black Marsh Nature Trail. The 5.5-km (3.5-mi) return path extends past tidal pools, whirring windmills, and the Cape's 1908 lighthouse to a pretty bog crossed via a boardwalk. ⊠ *21817 Rte. 12, North Cape, Prince Edward Island, Canada.*

**Jacques Cartier Provincial Park.** Jacques Cartier Provincial Park, south of North Cape, was named for the famed French explorer who came ashore nearby in 1534. In July and August, you can take naturalist-led hikes on park trails or swim on the supervised Gulf of St. Lawrence beach. ⊠ *16448 Rte. 12, Kildare Capes, Prince Edward Island, Canada* ☎ *902/853–8632.*

**Matthews Deep Sea Fishing & Ocean Adventures.** Matthews Deep Sea Fishing and Ocean Adventures offers fishing trips and scenic boat cruises (complete with complimentary steamed mussels) out of Northport from July to mid-September. ⊠ *Rte. 152, Northport, Prince Edward Island, Canada* ☎ *902/853–7943, 902/853–2688* ⊕ *www. matthewsdeepseafishing.ca.*

---

**SEA OF LOVE**

The 2011 arrival of Will and Kate, the royal "It Couple," underscored PEI's romantic potential. But the Island is more than just a magical locale for a post-wedding vacation. Many prospective brides and grooms choose it as a destination wedding venue. Tourism PEI (www.tourismpei.com/pei-wedding-destination) has helpful info for lovebirds.

# Newfoundland and Labrador

**WORD OF MOUTH**

"God, make me an honorary Newfie, for I loved the place. . . . Never have I met friendlier people than in Newfoundland, nor viewed as many spectacular and just plain beautiful vistas."

—Happyfella

# WELCOME TO NEWFOUNDLAND AND LABRADOR

## TOP REASONS TO GO

★ **Appreciate the rugged beauty of Gros Morne National Park:** Magnificent mountains, fine hiking, sweeping vistas, quaint lighthouses, hidden fjords, and the deep blue sea are just some of the reasons people flock to this park.

★ **Meet the people:** You'll never get lost here because the people go out of their way to help visitors. These are some of the nicest, friendliest folks you're likely to meet.

★ **See the wildlife:** Whales, puffins, caribou, and moose. Whale-watching boat tours. Bird sanctuaries and ecological reserves. Thirty-three million seabirds can't be wrong.

★ **Spot Icebergs:** Newfoundland is one of the easiest places to see these 10,000-year-old beauties of the ocean. See them from St. Anthony to St. John's.

★ **Eat amazing fish dishes:** Crab cakes, seafood chowder, lobster, shrimp, and cod, cod, cod: au gratin, panfried, or in the traditional Newfoundland dish of fish and *brewis* (pronounced "bruise"), a meal of cod and hardtack (hard bread).

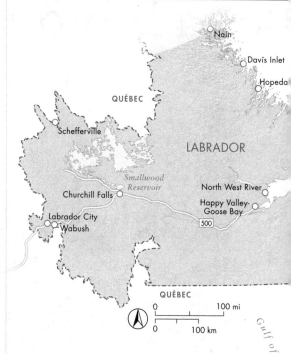

**1** **St John's.** The capital of Newfoundland is usually the starting point for visits to the province.

**2** **Avalon Peninsula.** This picturesque region is home to about half of Newfoundland's population. Cape Spear National Historic Site is the easternmost point in North America.

**3** **Eastern Newfoundland.** The Bonavista Peninsula has history and archaeological artifacts; the Burin Peninsula is more about stark landscapes. Clarenville, halfway between the two, is a good base for exploring, though not much of a destination in itself. Terra Nova was Newfoundland's first National Park.

**4** **Gander and around.**
Gander is known for its
airport and aviation history;
it's mostly a good base for
exploring fishing villages like
Twillingate as well as Fogo
Island, which is becoming
known for its international
artist studios.

**5** **Western Newfound-
land.** The wild and rugged
Great North Peninsula is
home to two UNESCO World
Heritage Sites (Gros Morne
National Park and L'Anse
aux Meadows), and the
west coast is famed for its
Atlantic salmon fishing, Long
Range Mountains, winter
sports, and the hub of the
west coast: Corner Brook.

## GETTING
## ORIENTED

The province includes the
island of Newfoundland
and Labrador; the latter is
on the mainland, border-
ing Québec. Most airlines
fly in to the provincial
capital of St. John's (not
to be confused with the
city of Saint John, in New
Brunswick), on the Avalon
Peninsula, making it the
logical starting point for
visitors to Newfoundland.
Farther west is the Burin
Peninsula, and to the
north are the Bonavista
Peninsula and Notre
Dame Bay. On the west
side of Newfoundland,
the Northern Peninsula
stretches up toward
Labrador; Corner Brook is
a good starting point for
exploring the mountains. In
Newfoundland, you'll do
much of your driving on
Route 1, the Trans-Canada
Highway, which goes
east–west from St. John's
to Port aux Basques.

Updated by
Keith Nicol

Magnificent mountains, sweeping vistas, wooden houses perched on rocky sea cliffs, hidden fjords, and the deep blue sea. Newfoundland, or "the Rock" as the island is sometimes affectionately called, lures visitors with the promise of dramatic landscapes, incredible hiking and outdoor experiences, and the warmth of the people. Canada starts here, from the east, on the island of Newfoundland in the North Atlantic. Labrador, to the northwest, is on the mainland bordering Québec. Along the province's nearly 17,699 km (11,000 mi) of coastline, humpback whales feed near shore, millions of seabirds nest, and 10,000-year-old icebergs drift by fishing villages.

On the east coast of Canada, the province of Newfoundland and Labrador, as it is officially called, is a bit of a contradiction in terms: it's the youngest province—it joined the Confederation in 1949—but its European timeline stretches back to AD 1000, when Vikings made first landfall on the Great Northern Peninsula. They assembled a sod hut village at what is now a National Historic Site at L'Anse aux Meadows, calling their new home Vinland. They stayed less than 10 years and then disappeared into the mists of history. As early as the Vikings were, they were actually preceded by the Maritime Archaic people who lived in the region as long ago as 6,000 years. L'Anse Amour, a 7,500-year-old burial ground in southern Labrador, is the oldest-known cemetery in North America.

When explorer John Cabot arrived at Bonavista from England in 1497, he reported an ocean so full of fish they could be caught in a basket lowered over the side of a boat. Within a decade, St. John's had become a crowded harbor. Soon, fishing boats from France, England, Spain, and Portugal vied for a chance to catch Newfoundland's lucrative cod, which would shape the province's history.

At one time, 700 outports dotted Newfoundland's coast, devoted to the world's most plentiful fish. Today, only about 400 of these settlements survive. By 1992, cod had become so scarce from overfishing that the federal government called a moratorium, throwing thousands out of work. The cod have not yet returned, forcing generations of people to retrain for other industries or leave, and the fishing industry has since diversified into other species, mainly shrimp and crab. The development of one of the world's richest and largest nickel deposits at Voisey's Bay in northern Labrador, near Nain, holds hope for new prosperity, as does the growing offshore oil and gas industry.

Despite its more than 50 years as a Canadian province, the people here are still very independent and maintain a unique language and lifestyle. E. Annie Proulx's Pulitzer Prize–winning novel *The Shipping News* (1993) brought the province to the attention of the world, and Newfoundland writers such as Wayne Johnston (*The Colony of Unrequited Dreams, The Navigator of New York*), Michael Crummey (*River Thieves, Galore*), and Lisa Moore (*February*) continue to introduce international audiences to the province.

Visitors to Newfoundland find themselves straddling the centuries. Old Irish, French, and English accents and customs still exist in small towns and outports despite television and the Internet, but the cities of St. John's in the east and Corner Brook to the west are very much part of the 21st century. Wherever you travel in the province, you're sure to meet some of the warmest, wittiest people in North America. Strangers have always been welcome in Newfoundland.

## PLANNING

### FESTIVALS

Newfoundlanders love a party, and from the cities to the smallest towns they celebrate their history and unique culture with festivals and events throughout the summer. "Soirees" and "times"—big parties and small parties—offer a combination of traditional music, recitation, comedy, and local food.

**Newfoundland and Labrador Folk Festival.** The Newfoundland and Labrador Folk Festival, the first weekend in August in St. John's, is the province's biggest traditional music festival. ☎ *709/576–8508, 866/576–8508 ⊕ www.nlfolk.com.*

### FISHING

Fishing the unpolluted waters of Newfoundland is an angler's dream. Eureka Outdoors has a salmon fishing lodge on the Humber River in Newfoundland, and Tuckamore Lodge in Main Brook offers guided fishing trips.

**Outfitters Eureka Outdoors** ☎ *709/638–8098 ⊕ www.eurekaoutdoors.nf.ca.*

### GETTING HERE AND AROUND

#### BY AIR

The province's main airport is St. John's International Airport, though another international airport is at Gander, farther west. Domestic airports in Newfoundland are at Stephenville, Deer Lake, and St. Anthony.

#### BY BOAT AND FERRY

Marine Atlantic operates a car ferry from North Sydney, Nova Scotia, to Port aux Basques, Newfoundland (crossing time is six hours), and, from June through September, from North Sydney to Argentia (crossing time 12 to 14 hours). The province also runs several smaller ferries to island or otherwise inaccessible communities along the northeast and south coasts of the Island.

**Contacts Marine Atlantic** ☎ *902/794–5254, 800/341–7981 ⊕ www.marine-atlantic.ca.*

### BY CAR

In winter, some highways close during and after severe snowstorms. The Government of Newfoundland and Labrador's Web site has up-to-date information on road conditions and closures. Newfoundland and Labrador Tourism can help with any travel-related problems.

Newfoundland has an excellent highway system, and all but a handful of secondary roads are paved. Travel time along the Trans-Canada Highway (Route 1) from Port aux Basques to St. John's is about 11 hours, with time out for a meal. The trip from Corner Brook to St. Anthony, at the northernmost tip of the island, is about five hours. The drive from St. John's to Grand Bank, on the Burin Peninsula, takes about four hours. If you're heading for the southern coast of the Avalon Peninsula, pick up Route 10 just south of St. John's and follow it toward Trepassey.

**Contacts** **Newfoundland and Labrador Tourism** ☎ 709/729–2830, 800/563–6353 in North America ⊕ www.newfoundlandlabrador.com. **Department of Transportation & Works** ☎ 709/635–4100 in Deer Lake, 709/292–4300 in Grand Falls–Windsor and Central Newfoundland, 709/466–4132 in Clarenville, 709/729–2382 in St. John's ⊕ www.roads.gov.nl.ca.

## HIKING

Newfoundland is a hiker's paradise. Many provincial parks and both of the national parks have hiking and nature trails, and coastal and forest trails radiate out from most small communities. The East Coast Trail on the Avalon Peninsula covers 540 km (336 mi) of coastline; it passes through two dozen communities and along cliff tops that provide ideal lookouts for icebergs and seabirds. The East Coast Trail Association helps hikers navigate the 540 km (336 mi) of East Coast Trails. Gros Morne Adventures runs guided day and multiday hikes in Gros Morne National Park.

**Outfitters** **East Coast Trail Association** ☎ 709/738–4453 ⊕ www.eastcoasttrail.com.

**Gros Morne Adventures** ☎ 709/458–2722 ⊕ www.grosmorneadventures.com.

## LOCAL FLAVOR

Seafood is an excellent value in Newfoundland and Labrador. Cod can be found panfried, baked, or poached; cold-water shrimp, snow crab, and lobster are also good choices. Many restaurants offer seasonal specialties with a wide variety of traditional wild and cultured species, such as steelhead trout, salmon, mussels, and sea scallops.

In July and August, Newfoundland's wild berries ripen. Partridgeberries, also called mountain cranberries, cowberries, and lingonberries (among other names), are used for pies, jams, cakes, pancakes, and in a delicious sauce for meats. The province's most unusual berry is the bakeapple. Also known as cloudberries, they look like yellow raspberries and grow on low plants in bogs. Pickers often sell them by the side of the road in jars. If the ones you buy are hard, wait a few days and they'll ripen into rich-tasting fruit. The berries are great on ice cream, cheesecake, or spread on bread. Blueberries are also common.

## LODGING

Try to stay at least one night in a bed-and-breakfast. You'll get a chance to experience Newfoundland's world-renowned hospitality. You may just want a place to lay your head, but you'll be treated to a wonderful home-cooked breakfast and you'll probably leave feeling like family.

## MOOSE WARNING

Newfoundland is home to more than 110,000 moose, and most highways run through their habitat. If possible, avoid night driving, as most moose-related vehicle accidents (about 700 a year) happen between dusk and dawn. Watch for vehicles that slow down or stop on the sides of roads: drivers may have spotted a moose. And pay attention to the caution signs, which are placed in areas where moose are known to cross frequently.

## PACKING TIPS

It's all about layers in Newfoundland. You'll need shorts and short-sleeve shirts for when it's warm and sunny. Pack a fleece jacket or a hoodie in case the temperature drops. A windbreaker might be the most important piece of clothing; you'll need it to keep the chill out when the winds are up. To top off your ensemble, you'll need rain gear, like a slicker. Throw in a pair of gloves, too. May the sun shine on your holidays, but if it doesn't, you'll be dressed for it.

## TOURS

Local operators offer sea kayaking, ocean diving, canoeing, wildlife viewing, mountain biking, white-water rafting, hiking, and interpretive walks in summer. In winter, snowmobiling expeditions are popular. In spring and early summer, a favored activity is iceberg-watching. Maxxim Vacations in St. John's organizes packaged adventure and cultural tours. Tuckamore Lodge, in Main Brook, uses its luxurious lodge on the Great Northern Peninsula as a base for viewing caribou, seabird colonies, whales, and icebergs and for winter snowmobile excursions. Wildland Tours in St. John's has three week-long guided tours that view wildlife and visit historically and culturally significant sites across Newfoundland.

McCarthy's Party in St. John's has guided bus tours across Newfoundland, learning vacations, and charter services.

**Contacts Maxxim Vacations** ☎ 709/754–6666, 800/567–6666 ⊕ www.maxximvacations.com.

**McCarthy's Party** ☎ 709/579–4444, 888/660–6060 ⊕ www.mccarthysparty.com.

**Newfoundland and Labrador Tourism** ☎ 709/729–2830, 800/563–6353 in North America ⊕ www.newfoundlandlabrador.com

**Tuckamore Lodge** ☎ 709/865–6361, 888/865–6361 ⊕ www.tuckamorelodge.com.

**Wildland Tours** ☎ 709/722–3123, 888/615–8279 ⊕ www.wildlands.com.

### UNIQUE TIME

Newfoundland has its own time zone: Newfoundland Standard Time, a half hour ahead of the rest of Labrador and the other Atlantic provinces. When time zones were established, the Dominion of Newfoundland was an independent country with its own time zone. The government tried to make the province conform to Atlantic Standard Time in 1963, but the measure was quashed by public outcry.

### WHAT IT COSTS

| WHAT IT COSTS IN CANADIAN DOLLARS | | | | |
|---|---|---|---|---|
| | ¢ | $ | $$ | $$$ | $$$$ |
| Restaurants | under C$8 | C$8–C$12 | C$13–C$20 | C$21–C$30 | over C$30 |
| Hotels | under C$75 | C$75–C$125 | C$126–C$175 | C$176–C$250 | over C$250 |

Restaurant prices are per person for a main course at dinner. Hotel prices are for two people in a standard double room in high season.

### WHEN TO GO

Seasons vary dramatically in Newfoundland and Labrador. Most tourists visit between June and September, when the bogs and meadows turn into a colorful riot of wildflowers and greenery and the province is alive with festivals, fairs, and concerts. Daytime temperatures hover between 20°C (68°F) and 25°C (77°F). In spring, icebergs float down from the north, and in late spring, whales arrive to hunt for food along the coast, staying until August. Fall is also popular: the weather is usually fine, hills and meadows are loaded with berries, and the woods are alive with moose, caribou, partridge, and rabbits. In winter, ski hills attract downhillers and snowboarders, forest trails hum with snowmobiles, and cross-country ski trails in various communities, provincial and national parks are oases of quiet.

This rocky island perched on the edge of the cold North Atlantic Ocean might be the only place in the world where you can have four seasons in one day and where the saying "If you don't like the weather out your front door, go look out the back door" rings true. St. John's is a weather champion in Canada. It holds the distinctions of being the foggiest, snowiest, wettest, windiest, and cloudiest of all major Canadian cities.

# ST. JOHN'S, NEWFOUNDLAND

Old meets new in the province's capital (population just under 200,000), with modern office buildings surrounded by heritage shops and colorful row houses. St. John's mixes English and Irish influences, Victorian architecture and modern convenience, and traditional music and rock and roll into a heady brew. The arts scene is lively, but overall the city has a relaxed pace.

For centuries, Newfoundland was the largest supplier of salt cod in the world, and St. John's Harbour was the center of the trade. As early as 1627, the merchants of Water Street—then known as the Lower Path—

# GREAT ITINERARIES

### IF YOU HAVE 3 DAYS

Pick either the west or east coast of Newfoundland. On the west coast, after arriving by ferry at **Port aux Basques,** drive through the Codroy Valley, heading north to **Gros Morne National Park** and overnight in nearby Rocky Harbour or Woody Point. The next day, visit **L'Anse aux Meadows National Historic Site,** where the Vikings built a village a thousand years ago. Spend the night in **St. Anthony** or nearby.

On the east coast, the ferry docks at Argentia. Explore the Avalon Peninsula, beginning in **St. John's,** where you should spend your first night. The next day visit **Cape Spear,** the most easterly point in North America, and the **Witless Bay Ecological Reserve,** where you can see whales, seabirds, and icebergs. Drive through **Placentia** and spend Day 3 at **Cape St. Mary's Ecological Reserve,** known for its gannets and dramatic coastal scenery.

### IF YOU HAVE 6 DAYS

In addition to spending a couple of days each in Gros Morne National Park and the St. Anthony area, spend a day in Corner Brook exploring the scenic Bay of Islands. The next day, travel west of **Stephenville** to Port au Port Peninsula, home of Newfoundland's French-speaking population.

On the east coast add **Trinity** to your must-see list, and spend the night there or in **Clarenville.** The north shore of Conception Bay is home to many picturesque villages, including **Cupids** and **Harbour Grace.** Several half-day, full-day, and two-day excursions are possible from St. John's: in each direction a different personality of the region unfolds.

### IF YOU HAVE 9 DAYS

In addition to the places already mentioned on the west coast, take a drive into central Newfoundland and visit the lovely villages of Notre Dame Bay. Overnight in **Twillingate.** Catch a ferry to **Fogo** or the **Change Islands.**

On the east coast add the Burin Peninsula and a trip to France—yes, France—to your itinerary. You can reach the French territory of **St-Pierre and Miquelon** by passenger ferry from Fortune. Explore romantic **Grand Bank,** named for the famous fishing area just offshore, and climb Cook's Lookout in **Burin,** where Captain James Cook kept watch for smugglers from St-Pierre. You could cover St. John's, Gros Morne, and L'anse aux Meadows in a nine-day trip, which would involve lots of car time. Instead consider a fly-and-drive to Deer Lake from St. John's (or vice versa); see the best of both coasts with less driving.

**4**

were doing a thriving business buying fish, selling goods, and supplying alcohol to soldiers and sailors.

## EXPLORING ST. JOHN'S

The city of St. John's encircles St. John's Harbour, expanding past the hilly, narrow streets of old St. John's. Downtown has the most history and character. The city was destroyed by fire many times, and much of the row housing dates back to the last major blaze, known as the Great Fire, in 1892. Heritage houses on Waterford Bridge Road, winding west from the harbor along the Waterford River, and on Rennies Mill Road and Circular Road to the east (backing onto Bannerman Park) were originally the homes of sea captains and merchants. Duckworth Street and Water Street, which run parallel to the harbor, are where to find the shops and restaurants, but take a trip down the narrow lanes and paths as you get farther from the harbor to get the best sense of the city's history.

Signal Hill in the east end, with its distinctive Cabot Tower, is the city's most prominent landmark. The hill rises up from The Narrows, the appropriately named entrance to St. John's Harbour. Standing at Cape Spear and looking back towards St. John's you will see Cabot Tower (and Signal Hill) but you'll scarcely believe there's a city there, because the entrance to the port is narrow and almost hidden.

### GETTING HERE AND AROUND

A walk downtown takes in many historic buildings, but you'll want a car to explore farther afield.

On the St. John's Haunted Hike, the Reverend Thomas Wickam Jarvis (actor Dale Jarvis) leads several different and very popular walking tours of the city's haunted sites and urban legends on summer evenings; tours begin at the west entrance of the Anglican Cathedral on Church Hill. Look for the crowd of people standing in the dark.

### ESSENTIALS

**Walking Tours** St. John's Haunted Hike ☎ 709/685-3444 ⊕ *www. hauntedhike.com.*

## TOP ATTRACTIONS

**Basilica Cathedral of St. John the Baptist.** This 1855 Roman Catholic cathedral in the Romanesque style has a commanding position above Military Road, overlooking the older section of the city and the harbor. The church is rich in stained-glass windows, side altars, and statuary. The centerpiece of the sanctuary is The Dead Christ, made of Carrara marble in the mid-19th century by the Irish sculptor John Hogan. A museum with vestments and religious objects is next door in the Bishop's Palace, where a harp recital takes place on Thursdays, July–September at 1 (C\$5). ⊠ *200 Military Rd., St. John's, Newfoundland and Labrador, Canada* ☎ *709/726-3660* ⊕ *www.thebasilica.ca* ✉ *Museum C\$2* ☉ *Museum mid-June–Aug., Mon.–Sat. 10–4, Sun. 1–4; Sept.–mid-June 8–3.*

**Colonial Building.** This columned building (erected 1847–50) was the seat of the Newfoundland government from the 1850s until 1960, when the legislature moved to its current home, the Confederation Building, in the north end of the city. The limestone for the building was imported from Cork, Ireland. It is closed for renovations until 2014. ⊠ *Military and Bannerman Rds., St. John's, Newfoundland and Labrador, Canada.*

**Court House.** The late-19th-century courthouse has an eccentric appearance: each of its four turrets is in a different style. ⊠ *Duckworth St. at bottom of Church Hill, St. John's, Newfoundland and Labrador, Canada.*

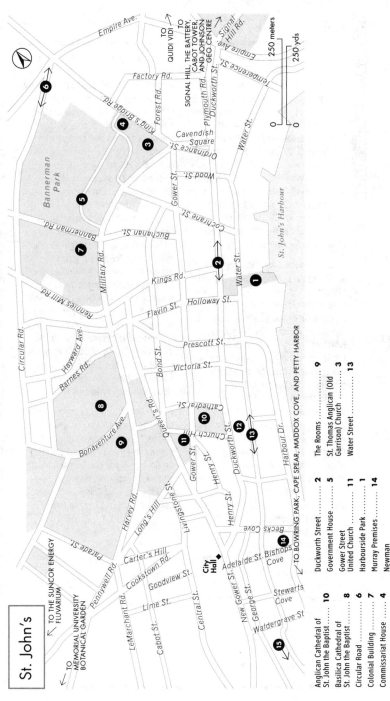

St. John's

TO THE SUNCOR ENERGY FLUVARIUM

TO MEMORIAL UNIVERSITY BOTANICAL GARDEN

Empire Ave.

TO QUIDI VIDI

TO SIGNAL HILL, THE BATTERY, CABOT TOWER, AND JOHNSON GEO CENTRE

Factory Rd.

Forest Rd.

King's Bridge Rd.

Cavendish Square

Ordnance St.

Plymouth Rd.

Duckworth St.

Signal Hill Rd.

Empire Ave.

Temperence St.

Wood St.

Gower St.

Cochrane St.

Water St.

St. John's Harbour

Bannerman Park

Bannerman Rd.

Buchanan St.

Military Rd.

Rennies Mill Rd.

Kings Rd.

Flavin St.

Holloway St.

Prescott St.

Bond St.

Victoria St.

Cathedral St.

Church Hill

Gower St.

Henry St.

Duckworth St.

Harbour Dr.

Circular Rd.

Hayward Ave.

Barnes Rd.

Bonaventure Ave.

Queen's Rd.

Harvey Rd.

Long's Hill

Livingstone St.

Henry St.

Becks Cove

TO BOWRING PARK, CAPE SPEAR, MADDOX COVE, AND PETTY HARBOR

Parade St.

Carter's Hill

Cookstown Rd.

Goodview St.

Lime St.

Central St.

Cabot St.

LeMarchant Rd.

Pennywell Rd.

City Hall

Adelaide St.

Bishops Cove

Stewarts Cove

New Gower St.

George St.

Waldergrave St.

250 meters

250 yds

Anglican Cathedral of St. John the Baptist ....... **10**
Basilica Cathedral of St. John the Baptist ....... **8**
Circular Road ............... **6**
Colonial Building .......... **7**
Commissariat House ...... **4**
Court House ................. **12**
Duckworth Street .......... **2**
Government House ......... **5**
Gower Street United Church .............. **11**
Harbourside Park ........... **1**
Murray Premises ........... **14**
Newman Wine Vaults ..... **15**
The Rooms .................. **9**
St. Thomas Anglican (Old Garrison) Church ......... **3**
Water Street ................ **13**

# A Good Walk

Begin at **Harbourside Park**, on Water Street, where Gilbert planted the staff of England and claimed Newfoundland. When you leave, turn left on Water Street, right on Holloway Street, and then right onto **Duckworth Street**. The east end of this street is full of crafts shops and other stores. After walking east for five blocks, turn left onto Ordnance Street, just one of several streets that recall St. John's military past. Cross Military Road to **St. Thomas Anglican (Old Garrison) Church**, built in the 1830s as a place of worship for British soldiers.

Turn left as you leave St. Thomas and walk up King's Bridge Road. The first building on the left is **Commissariat House**, an officer's house restored to the style of the 1830s and one of the oldest buildings in the province. North of here, a shady lane on the left leads to the gardens of **Government House. Circular Road**, where the business elite moved after a fire destroyed much of the town in 1846, is across from the gardens in front of the house. Back on Military Road, cross Bannerman Road to the **Colonial Building**, the former seat of government. Walk west on Military Road. The Roman Catholic **Basilica Cathedral of St. John the Baptist**, finished in 1855, is on the right; the Basilica Museum in the Bishop's Palace is just west of the Basilica. Cross Bonaventure Avenue as you leave the Basilica to visit **The Rooms**, the province's one-stop shop for arts, culture, and heritage and the home of the provincial archives, museum, and art gallery. As you leave the Rooms, turn right down Garrison Hill, so named because it once led to Fort Townshend, now home to fire and police stations. Cross Queen's Road

and walk down Cathedral Street to Gower Street and the Gothic Revival **Anglican Cathedral of St. John the Baptist**. The entrance is on the west side on Church Hill. **Gower Street United Church** is directly across from the cathedral on the west side of Church Hill. Continue to the bottom of Church Hill to see the Duckworth Street **Court House**, with its four different turrets. Exit the courthouse and turn right; then go down the long set of steps to **Water Street**, one of the oldest commercial streets in North America. Turn right to reach the **Murray Premises**, a restored mercantile complex with boutiques, a science center, offices, restaurants, a coffee bar, and a wine cellar. Exit Murray Premises, take a left on Water Street, and continue to the last stop, the historic **Newman Wine Vaults**, at 436 Water Street, just west of the corner of Water and Springdale streets, where for 200 years the legendary Newman's Port has been aged.

Downtown St. John's is compact but hilly. The walk avoids major uphill climbs. Expect to spend up to a full day visiting these sights, depending on how long you stay at each location and the number of stores you take in along the way. This walk is best undertaken from spring to fall.

**Duckworth Street.** Once called the Upper Path, this has been the "second street" of St. John's for centuries (Water Street is the main street). Stretching from the bottom of Signal Hill in the east to near City Hall in the west, Duckworth Street has restaurants, bars, antiques and crafts shops, and lawyers' offices. Lanes and stairways lead down to Water Street and up to higher elevations. ⊠ *St. John's, Newfoundland and Labrador, Canada.*

**Government House.** This is the residence of the lieutenant governor—the queen's representative in Newfoundland. Myth has it that the moat around Government House was designed to keep out snakes, though Newfoundland is one of a handful of regions in the world (along with Ireland and New Zealand) where there are none. The 1830s house, so the story goes, was originally intended for the governor from a warmer colony, where serpents might be a problem. The truth of the matter is that the moat was designed to allow more light into the basement rooms. Tours of the house can be arranged in advance by appointment; the marvelous garden you can explore on your own. ⊠ *50 Military Rd., St. John's, Newfoundland and Labrador, Canada* ☏ *709/729–4494* ⊕ *www.govhouse.nl.ca* ⊠ *Free* ☉ *Weekdays 8:30–5, garden open daily.*

**Gower Street United Church.** This 1896 church has a redbrick facade, green turrets, 50 stained-glass windows, and a massive pipe organ. The church itself is on a sort of concrete island, the lone occupant of a small tract of land surrounded by four streets. ⊠ *99 Queen's Rd., at Gower St., St. John's, Newfoundland and Labrador, Canada* ☏ *709/753–7286* ⊕ *www.gowerunited.ca* ⊠ *Free* ☉ *Sept.–May, weekdays 9–4; July and Aug., weekdays 9–noon; tours available year-round during office hours or by appointment.*

**Harbourside Park.** This is the spot where Sir Humphrey Gilbert claimed Newfoundland for Britain in 1583, much to the amusement of the French, Spanish, and Portuguese fishermen in port at the time. They thought him a fool, a judgment borne out a few days later when he ran his ship aground and drowned. The small park is a good vantage point to watch the boats come and go and a nice spot to stop for a rest, but the larger parks have more green space and are better for picnics. The area down here where the harbor-pilot boat is docked is known as the Queen's Wharf. ⊠ *Water St. E, St. John's, Newfoundland and Labrador, Canada.*

Fodor's Choice ★ **The Rooms.** The provincial archives, museum, art gallery, and a multilevel atrium are all part of this cultural space, which opened in 2005. The design of the Rooms was inspired by traditional "fishing rooms," tracts of land by the waterside where fishing activities took place, and the views over St. John's from the third and fourth levels of this industrial space are awe inspiring. The two floors of galleries hold a collection of more than 7,000 contemporary works of art. On the fourth floor, the Rooms Café ($–$$) serves tasty seafood dishes including Newfoundland seafood chowder and desserts like sticky toffee pudding with crème anglaise; on Wednesday nights it's open for dinner, and it's a great place to watch the sun set or the fog creep in over the city. ⊠ *9 Bonaventure Ave., St. John's, Newfoundland and Labrador,*

*Canada* 🕾 *709/757–8000* ⊕ *www.therooms.ca* 📧 *C$7.50, free Wed. 6–9 pm and first Sat. of each month (Nov.–May); special exhibits extra* ☉ *June–mid-Oct., Mon., Tues., and Thurs.–Sat. 10–5, Wed. 10–9, Sun. noon–5; mid-Oct.–May, Tues. and Thurs.–Sat. 10–5, Wed. 10–9, Sun. noon–5. Archives closed Sun. year-round.*

**Water Street.** Originally called the Lower Path, Water Street has been the site of businesses since at least the 1620s. The older architecture resembles that of seaports in southwest England and Ireland. ⊠ *St. John's, Newfoundland and Labrador, Canada.*

## WORTH NOTING

**Anglican Cathedral of St. John the Baptist.** A fine example of Gothic Revival architecture designed by Sir George Gilbert Scott, this church was first completed in the mid-1800s; it was rebuilt after the 1892 fire. There are free lunchtime organ recitals on Wednesdays from 1:15 to 1:45. Women of the parish operate a tearoom in the crypt in July and August from 2:30 to 4:30 Monday, Tuesday, Thursday, Friday, and from 2 pm on Wednesday. Drop down for a cuppa with homemade scones, tea biscuits, and cookies (C$8). There are daily church services. ⊠ *16 Church Hill, St. John's, Newfoundland and Labrador, Canada* 🕾 *709/726–5677* ⊕ *www.stjohnsanglicancathedral.org* 📧 *Free* ☉ *Tours July and Aug., weekdays 10–noon, 2–4; Sat. 10–noon; Sun. after 11 am service.*

**Circular Road.** After the devastating fire of 1846, the business elite of St. John's moved to Circular Road. The street contains some very fine Victorian houses and shade trees. ⊠ *St. John's, Newfoundland and Labrador, Canada.*

**Commissariat House.** The residence and office of the British garrison's supply officer in the 1830s has been restored to reflect that era. Interpreters sometimes dress in period costume. ⊠ *King's Bridge Rd. and Military Rd., St. John's, Newfoundland and Labrador, Canada* 🕾 *709/729–6730, 709/729–0592* ⊕ *www.seethesites.ca* 📧 *C$3* ☉ *Mid-May–mid-Oct., daily 10–5:30.*

**Murray Premises.** One of the oldest buildings in St. John's, the Murray Premises dates from only 1846; the last (and worst) time the city was destroyed by fire was in 1892. This restored warehouse now houses shops, offices, and restaurants. ⊠ *5 Beck's Cove, St. John's, Newfoundland and Labrador, Canada.*

**Newman Wine Vaults.** This 200-year-old building with stone barrel vaults is where the renowned Newman's Port was aged. According to legend, a Newman and Company vessel loaded with port wine was driven off course by pirates in 1679 and forced to winter in St. John's. Upon its return to London, the cargo was found to have improved in flavor, and after that the company continued to send port to be matured in these wine cellars. The vaults are now a provincial historic site with guides who interpret the province's long and unique association with port. You can purchase more than 20 different brands of port on-site. Guided tours are available. ⊠ *436 Water St., St. John's, Newfoundland and Labrador, Canada* 🕾 *709/739–7870* ⊕ *www.historictrust.ca* 📧 *C$3, or C$5 per family (max 4 people)* ☉ *June–Aug., daily 10–5:30 or by appointment.*

**St. Thomas Anglican (Old Garrison) Church.** English soldiers used to worship at this black-wood church, the oldest in the city, during the early and mid-1800s. ⊠ *8 Military Rd., St. John's, Newfoundland and Labrador, Canada* ☎ *709/576–6632, 709/576-6641* 🖃 *Free* ☉ *June–Aug., weekdays 9–2; call for off-season hrs.*

# GREATER ST. JOHN'S

A number of must-see attractions can be found a short drive from the downtown core of St. John's. When you stand with your back to the ocean at Cape Spear National Historic Site—the easternmost point of North America—the entire population of the continent is to your west. Cape Spear and the historic property with Hill National Historic Site are excellent places to see icebergs and whales in spring and early summer. Plan to spend a full day exploring Greater St. John's to give yourself some time at each spot.

**4**

## TOP ATTRACTIONS

**The Battery.** This tiny fishing village perches precariously at the base of steep cliffs between Signal Hill and St. John's Harbour. Narrow lanes snake around the houses so it's a good place to get out of the car and walk. ⊠ *St. John's, Newfoundland and Labrador, Canada.*

**Cabot Tower.** This tower at the summit of Signal Hill was constructed in 1897 to commemorate the 400th anniversary of explorer John Cabot's landing in Newfoundland. The drive here up along Signal Hill Road affords fine harbor, ocean, and city views, as does the tower itself. ⊠ *Signal Hill Rd., St. John's, Newfoundland and Labrador, Canada* ☎ *709/772–5367* ⊕ *www.pc.gc.ca* 🖃 *Free* ☉ *Mid-April–May and Labor Day–mid-Jan., daily 9–5; June–Labor Day, daily 8:30 am–9 pm.*

★ **Cape Spear National Historic Site.** At the easternmost point of land on the continent, songbirds begin chirping in the dim light of dawn, and whales (in early summer) feed directly below the cliffs, providing an unforgettable start to the day. From April through July, you might see icebergs floating by. **Cape Spear Lighthouse,** Newfoundland's oldest such beacon, has been lovingly restored to its original form and furnishings. There's a small, well-stocked souvenir kiosk in the parking lot for those who don't want to or are unable to climb the path to the main gift shop. ⊠ *Rte. 11, St. John's, Newfoundland and Labrador, Canada* ☎ *709/772–5367* ⊕ *www.pc.gc.ca* 🖃 *Site free, lighthouse C$3.90, C$6.30 for same-day access with Signal Hill* ☉ *Site daily dawn–dusk; lighthouse mid-May–mid-June, Wed.–Sun. 9–5; mid-June–Sept., daily 10–6; Sept.–mid-Oct., Wed.–Sun. 9–5. Visitor Interpretation Centre and Heritage Gift Shop mid-May–late June, daily 10–6; late June–mid-Oct, daily 8:30–8:30.*

☾ **Johnson GEO CENTRE.** Built deep into the earth with only the entryway protruding aboveground, this geological shrine is literally embedded in Signal Hill, itself made up of 550-million-year-old rocks. (The province's oldest rocks date back 3.87 billion years.) There are exhibts about how Earth was made and on the solar system. An exhibit called "The Titanic Story" displays some artifacts and submersible footage of the wreck site. Step on an oil platform in the ExxonMobil Oil & Gas Gallery and learn about how oil and gas are formed. Kids 5 and up love the 3D Earth and Space Theatre. ⊠ *175 Signal Hill Rd., St. John's, Newfoundland and Labrador, Canada* ☎ *709/737–7880, 866/868–7625* ⊕ *www.geocentre. ca* ⊠ *C$11.50* ⊙ *Mon.–Sat. 9:30–5, Sun. noon–5.*

★ **Memorial University Botanical Garden.** The gardens at this 110-acre natural area include rock gardens, a Newfoundland historic-plants bed, peat and woodland beds, an alpine house, a medicinal garden, a native plant collection, a vegetable garden, a crevice garden, a shade garden, a dried flower garden, and a compost demonstration garden. There are also five pleasant walking trails. You can see scores of varieties of rhododendron here, as well as many kinds of butterflies and the rare hummingbird hawkmoth. Guided walks are available with advance notice for groups of 10 or more. The nature trails and gardens are closed to the public from November through April, but the gift shop remains open. ⊠ *C.A. Pippy Park, Oxen Pond, 306 Mt. Scio Rd., St. John's, Newfoundland and Labrador, Canada* ☎ *709/864–8590* ⊕ *www.mun.ca/botgarden* ⊠ *C$6* ⊙ *May, daily 10–4; June–Oct., daily 10–5; Oct. and Nov., 10–4.*

**NEED A BREAK?**

**The Garden Cafe.** The Garden Cafe is on the grounds of the MUN Botanical Garden. There are many teas to choose from, along with fresh-baked scones, soups, salads, and sandwiches. The menu changes daily and offers vegetarian and vegan choices, and the restaurant packs picnic lunches. ⊠ *St. John's, Newfoundland and Labrador, Canada* ☎ *709/753–0173* ⊙ *May–Oct., daily 10:30–4:30.*

**Quidi Vidi.** No one knows the origin of the name of this fishing village, one of the oldest parts of St. John's. The town is best explored on foot, as the roads are narrow and make driving difficult. The inlet, known as the Gut, is a traditional outport in the middle of a modern city, making it a contrast worth seeing. It's also a good place to catch sea-run brown trout in the spring. ⊠ *Take the first right off Kings Bridge Rd. (at the Sheraton Hotel Newfoundland) onto Forest Rd., which heads into the village, St. John's, Newfoundland and Labrador, Canada.*

☾ **Signal Hill National Historic Site.** In spite of its height, Signal Hill was dif-
**Fodor's Choice** ficult to defend: throughout the 1600s and 1700s it changed hands with
★ every attacking French, English, and Dutch force. In 1762, this was the site of the final battle between the French and British in the Seven Years' War (usually called the French and Indian War in the United States). A wooden palisade encircles the summit of the hill, indicating the boundaries of the old fortifications. In July and August, cadets in 19th-century British uniform perform a tattoo of military drills and music. En route to the hill is the **Visitor Center,** with exhibits describing the history of St. John's. In 1901 Guglielmo Marconi received the first transatlantic-wire transmission near **Cabot Tower,** at the top of Signal Hill, and today you can visit the Marconi exhibit on the top floor. From the top of the hill it's a 500-foot drop to the narrow harbor entrance below; views are excellent. Walking trails take you to the base of the hill and closer to the ocean. Dress warmly; it's always windy. ⊠ *Signal Hill Rd., St. John's, Newfoundland and Labrador, Canada* ☎ *709/772–5367* ⊕ *www.pc.gc.ca* ⊠ *Site free; visitor center C$3.90, C$6.30 pass*

*on same-day visit with Cape Spear* ☉ *Site daily dawn–dusk. Visitor center mid-May–mid-Oct., daily 10–6; mid-Oct.–mid-May, weekdays 8:30–4:30.*

## WORTH NOTING

**Bowring Park.** An expansive Victorian park west of downtown, Bowring resembles the famous city parks of London, after which it was modeled. Dotting the grounds are ponds and rustic bridges; the statue of Peter Pan just inside the east gate was cast from the same mold as the one in Kensington Park in London. The wealthy Bowring family donated the park to the city in 1911. ⊠ *Waterford Bridge Rd., St. John's, Newfoundland and Labrador, Canada* 🖼 ⊕ *www. bowringpark.com* 🖼 *Free* ☉ *Daily dawn–dusk.*

---

### DAY AT THE RACES

If you're in St. John's on the first Wednesday of August, head down to Quidi Vidi Lake and experience the Royal St. John's Regatta (⊕ www.stjohnsregatta.org), the oldest continuous sporting event in North America. The fixed-seat rowing shells hold a crew of six and the coxswain. The town shuts down for this garden party/reunion/sporting event that draws more than 30,000 people. If the winds are high, the holiday's off, shops open, and the regatta moves to Thursday, Friday, or whenever the weather clears.

---

**Maddox Cove and Petty Harbour.** These neighboring fishing villages lie along the coast between Cape Spear and Route 10. The wharves and sturdy seaside sheds, especially those in Petty Harbour, hearken back to a time not long ago when the fishery was paramount in the economy and lives of the residents. ⊠ *St. John's, Newfoundland and Labrador, Canada.*

**The Suncor Energy Fluvarium.** A tributary of a nearby river was diverted here so visitors could see the life that inhabits it from under water. See into the river through nine large windows at the only public facility of its kind in North America. In season you can observe spawning brown and brook trout in their natural habitat. Feeding time for the fish, frogs, and eels is 4 pm daily. ⊠ *5 Nagle's Pl., C.A. Pippy Park, St. John's, Newfoundland and Labrador, Canada* 🖼 *709/754–3474* ⊕ *www.fluvarium. ca* 🖼 *C$7* ☉ *June–Aug., daily 9–5; Sept.–May, weekdays 9–4:30, weekends noon–4:30.*

---

## WHERE TO EAT

**$$$**  ╳ **Bacalao.** The hands-on owners chose a clever, tasty link between local
**CANADIAN** cuisine and culture. Bacalao (pronounced "back-allow") is salt cod, a staple for Newfoundlanders and the Mediterraneans who came to fish here, and a variation of it is featured every night. Other nouvelle Newfoundland menu options include caribou (as a starter or entrée) and mussels served in locally brewed ale or in Newfoundland's Iceberg vodka. All the dishes here, including desserts, are prepared from scratch and, when possible, using local ingredients—down to the soap in the washroom. In addition to global wines, local wines, port, ales, and Lady of the Woods (a wine made from birch sap) are available, many by the glass. The four rooms of this old house in St. John's have been

converted into cozy dining rooms, all with fireplaces. ⊠ *65 LeMerchant Rd., St. John's, Newfoundland and Labrador, Canada* ☎ *709/579–6565* ⊕ *www.bacalaocuisine.ca* ⌕ *Reservations essential* ⊘ *Closed Mon.*

**$$$$**
SEAFOOD
Fodor's Choice
★

✕ **Bianca.** Bianca is known for its fine wines and its unique approach to the wine list: simply walk up to the racks and choose the one you want; prices are on the labels. If you don't know what you want, Bianca herself might be around to help. The spacious restaurant, painted purple and brightened by a few well-chosen pieces of art, fronts Water Street, and panels of a light, sheer purple hang in the windows, giving privacy by day and offering an attractive, hazy surrealist view of passers-by at night. Soups, including snow crab bisque, are a specialty, and snow crab also turns up in crab cakes and in a crab ravioli served with panko-crusted salmon. ⊠ *171 Water St., St. John's, Newfoundland and Labrador, Canada* ☎ *709/726–9016* ⊕ *www.biancas.net* ⌕ *Reservations essential* ⊘ *No lunch weekends.*

**$$$**
SEAFOOD

✕ **Blue on Water.** The trendy restaurant in the hotel of the same name makes organic synonymous with simple, tasty, and fresh. A hint of strawberry and maple complement the foie gras. Specials include whatever fresh seafood has come this way, such as oysters, mussels, or salmon. In the bar area, floor-length windows open onto Water Street, making the space both airy and intimate. ⊠ *319 Water St., St. John's, Newfoundland and Labrador, Canada* ☎ *709/754–2583* ⊕ *www. blueonwater.com.*

**$$$**
MEDITERRANEAN

✕ **The Casbah.** A bright red exterior welcomes you into this stylish, tropical-looking spot. By day, large windows let in lots of sun, and, in the evening, red fairy lights illuminate the open balcony. The seasonal menu includes soups, salads, and paninis, as well as more cosmopolitan mains and seafood, all made with fresh, local organic produce. The weekend brunch is popular, which is almost guaranteed to fill you up if you opt for the steak and eggs, potatoes, grilled vegetables, baked beans, and home-style toast. ⊠ *2 Cathedral St., St. John's, Newfoundland and Labrador, Canada* ☎ *709/738–5293.*

**$$$$**
EUROPEAN

✕ **The Cellar.** Named for its original basement premises in Baird's Cove, the Cellar has moved aboveground and around the corner into a place of prominence on Water Street, one of the oldest streets in North America. Menu options focus on steak and seafood, with a few creative twists in the appetizer selections. The clubby atmosphere complements the fine dining experience. ⊠ *189 Water St., St. John's, Newfoundland and Labrador, Canada* ☎ *709/579–8900* ⊕ *www.thecellarrestaurant. ca* ⊘ *No lunch.*

**$**
SEAFOOD
Fodor's Choice
★

✕ **Ches's.** Since the 1950s, this restaurant has been serving fish-and-chips to a steady stream of customers from noon until after midnight. They come from all walks of life to sample the flaky fish fried in a batter whose recipe the owner keeps under lock and key (literally). It's strictly laminated tabletops and plastic chairs, but the fish is hot, fresh, and delicious, and there are wings and chicken for those who are looking for something different. ⊠ *9 Freshwater Rd., St. John's, Newfoundland and Labrador, Canada* ☎ *709/722–4083* ⊕ *www.chessfishandchips. ca* ⊠ *655 Topsail Rd., St. John's, Newfoundland and Labrador, Canada* ☎ *709/368–9473* ⊠ *29–33 Commonwealth Ave., St. John's,*

*Newfoundland and Labrador, Canada* ☎ *709/364–6837* ✉ *8 Highland Dr., St. John's, Newfoundland and Labrador, Canada* ☎ *709/738–5022.*

**$$** ✕ **India Gate.** Consistency and quality in service and food make this one
INDIAN of the busiest restaurants in St. John's for evening dining, takeout, or
Fodor's Choice the popular weekday lunch buffet. Lunch turnover is high, and the buf-
★ fet steamers are continuously replenished with steaming "rice pillow,"
mulligatawny soup, lamb, and vegetable korma. In the evening, you can
choose a five-course dinner for two (C$50–$60) or share options such
as butter chicken or the exceptional prawns nilgiri (prawns in a rich
sauce of spices and cashews). The presence of the owner on-site and the
(recorded) sitar music add to the inviting atmosphere. Regulars have
been known to spend an entire meal speculating on the secret behind the
perfect rice. ✉ *286 Duckworth St., Downtown, St. John's, Newfound-
land and Labrador, Canada* ☎ *709/753–6006* ⊕ *www.indiagate.250x.
com* ⊙ *No lunch weekends.*

**$** ✕ **International Flavours.** This restaurant at the foot of Signal Hill may
INDIAN not look like much, but the home-style curry dishes are delicious. It's
easy to miss, as there's almost no storefront, but worth persevering to
find. There's only street parking, so the best idea is to combine your
visit with a stroll through the Battery or reward yourself after a hike
up to Cabot Tower. ✉ *4 Quidi Vidi Rd., St. John's, Newfoundland and
Labrador, Canada* ☎ *709/738–4636* ⊙ *Closed Sun. and Mon.*

**$** ✕ **Magic Wok Eatery.** In operation for 20 years, this popular family-run
CHINESE eatery has grown to its present quarters: a stand-alone, spacious struc-
ture with containers of flowers and shrubs brightening the sidewalk
out front. The menu offers more than 100 traditional Chinese dishes
in the Hong Kong style, plus "North American–style Chinese dishes"
for the less adventurous. Prices are very reasonable, and it's a popular
local spot for couples, families, and groups of office workers or friends,
who come for the beef, duck, and seafood, often flambéed at the table.
Try Har Gaw (like a light, crispy wonton) for a crunchy starter, and
sizzling shrimp in black bean sauce. An added bonus is that Magic Wok
Eatery, near the Delta and the Mile One entertainment complex, is one
of the few downtown restaurants that offers free parking. ✉ *402–408
Water St., West End, St. John's, Newfoundland and Labrador, Canada*
☎ *709/753–6907* ⊕ *www.magicwok.ca* ⊙ *Closed Mon. No weekend
lunch.*

**$** ✕ **The Sprout.** Local artists and craftspeople display their art on the walls
VEGETARIAN here, but the real works of genius arrive at your table in the form of
salads, soups (like the Me-So Hungry Miso Soup), and sandwiches (the
Bravocado is cheese, avocado, and sprouts on homemade whole-grain
bread). This is excellent vegetarian fare: choose between a lentil burger,
a tofu burger, the chickpea "Give Peas a Chance" burger, or Thai One
On (pad thai). The vegan chocolate mousse is decadent. You can sit at
tables or in one of the four booths. ✉ *364 Duckworth St., St. John's,
Newfoundland and Labrador, Canada* ☎ *709/579–5485* ⌦ *Reserva-
tions not accepted* ⊙ *Closed Mon. No lunch Sun.*

**$** ✕ **Sun Sushi and Bubble Tea Restaurant.** This is the place to enjoy squid
JAPANESE if you love it or to try it for the first time: the panfried delicacy with a
light soy glaze is tender and will forever separate the words "rubbery"

and "squid" in your mind. The dark wood tables are overlaid with glass tops, and everything is spotless and bright. Most tables front Duckworth Street, but you can also sit by the open kitchen area and observe the concentration of cooks preparing an eel roll. Sun Sushi is especially popular with a young crowd, who enjoy the affordable tuna, octopus, and battered shrimp with a sweet tempura sauce. There's only one white and one red wine available, but each is carefully chosen and fairly priced. ⊠ *186 Duckworth St., Downtown, St. John's, Newfoundland and Labrador, Canada* ☎ *709/726–8688* ⊕ *www.sunsushi. com* ⊙ *Closed Sun.*

**$$**
CANADIAN
✕ **Velma's Place.** Many "townies" home on vacation head here for traditional Newfoundland fare such as fish and *brewis* (bread and fish soaked in water and boiled) and Jigg's dinner (boiled salted meat served with potatoes, carrots, cabbage, and turnips). Prices have risen as the tourists have found Velma's, but it's still pretty reasonable if it's down-home food rather than fancy decor you're after. ⊠ *264 Water St., St. John's, Newfoundland and Labrador, Canada* ☎ *709/576–2264.*

## WHERE TO STAY

*For expanded hotel reviews, visit Fodors.com.*

**$$**
🏨 **Blue on Water.** A modern 12-room boutique hotel with stylish contemporary decor, Blue on Water is the essence of its name: a calm, comfortable lodging with a whiff of the Atlantic when the windows are open. **Pros:** spacious bathrooms; great restaurant and bar downstairs. **Cons:** there's sometimes noise from George Street. ⊠ *319 Water St., St. John's, Newfoundland and Labrador, Canada* ☎ *709/754–2583* ⊕ *www.blueonwater.com* ⤵ *12 rooms* ᐊ *In-room: Wi-Fi. In-hotel: restaurant, bar.*

**$$$**
🏨 **Holiday Inn—Government Centre.** The surprise at this chain hotel is the location: walking trails meander around small lakes and link with the Grand Concourse hiking trails. **Pros:** outdoor heated pool in summer; easy to find from airport or Trans-Canada Highway. **Cons:** a long walk to downtown; rooms are fine but nothing special. ⊠ *180 Portugal Cove Rd., St. John's, Newfoundland and Labrador, Canada* ☎ *709/722–0506, 800/933–0506* ⊕ *www.holidayinn.com* ⤵ *252 rooms* ᐊ *In-room: Wi-Fi. In-hotel: restaurant, bar, pool, gym, parking, some pets allowed.*

**$$**
🏨 **McCoubrey Manor.** This Queen Anne–style heritage home was built in 1904 for Henry T. **Pros:** two suites have full kitchens; fireplaces in some rooms; evening snack. **Cons:** truck traffic passes nearby; some parking is on street. ⊠ *6–8 Ordnance St., St. John's, Newfoundland and Labrador, Canada* ☎ *709/722–7577, 888/753–7577* ⊕ *www.mccoubrey.com* ⤵ *4 rooms, 2 suites* ᐊ *In-room: a/c, kitchen, Wi-Fi. In-hotel: laundry facilities, parking* ⦿| *Breakfast.*

**$$$**
B&B/INN
🏨 **Park House Inn, Bed and Breakfast.** Three Newfoundland prime ministers have lived at this house built in the late 1870s. **Pros:** central location; private on-site parking; property backs on a park. **Cons:** near a busy intersection; no elevator; rooms in front may get street noise. ⊠ *112 Military Rd., St. John's, Newfoundland and Labrador, Canada* ☎ *709/576–2265, 866/303–0565* ⊕ *www.newfoundlandbedandbreakfast.nl.ca*

CLOSE UP

# Newfoundland English

Newfoundland English is full of words brought to this rocky land centuries ago, when the fertile fishing grounds lured sailors and settlers from all over Europe and the British Isles. In the late 16th century, colonies of people came here with very little—except, of course, for their culture, in the form of words, sayings, and songs. Because of the province's relative isolation, accents remained strong and the archaic words took root to become Newfoundland English.

Listen for Newfoundland expressions for everything, from food terms like *scoff* (a big meal), *touton* (fried bread dough), and *duff* (a pudding), to words to describe the fickle weather, such as *leeward* (a threatening storm), *air-some* (bracing cold), and *mauzy* (foggy and damp). "The sun is splitting the rocks!" is something you might hear on a fine day.

There are also a plethora of terms that relate to the fishing industry: a *flake* is where you dry fish, perhaps after having caught them on your *dory*, a small rowboat. A *bedlamer* is a young seal. And, of course, there are plenty of words to describe all manner of people: a *gatcher* is a show-off and a *cuffer* tells tall tales.

A *drung* is a narrow road, a *scuff* is a dance, to *coopy* means to crouch down, and if you're going for a *twack*, you're window-shopping. If you're from *Upalong*, that means you're not from here.

To help develop an ear for the provincial dialects, pick up a copy of the *Dictionary of Newfoundland English* (⊕ www.heritage.nf.ca/dictionary), first published in 1982; it's now in its second edition and has more than 5,000 words.

**2 Streels.** This St. John's–based company preserves old Newfoundland words by printing them on T-shirts in their Twackwear line. ☎ 709/579–4761 ⊕ www.twackwear.com.

⤴4 *rooms* ⬧ *In-room: a/c, Wi-Fi. In-hotel: laundry facilities, parking* ⦿*Breakfast.*

**$$$** ⊞ **Sheraton Hotel Newfoundland.** Charming rooms overlook the harbor at
★ this nine-story hotel where uniformed bellhops sometimes meet you at the door. **Pros:** heritage neighborhood; walking distance to Signal Hill and the Battery; spa and hair salon on-site. **Cons:** no indoor parking garage; on-site restaurants overpriced. ⊠ *115 Cavendish Sq., St. John's, Newfoundland and Labrador, Canada* ☎*709/726–4980* ⊕*www. sheraton.com/newfoundland* ⤴*301 rooms* ⬧ *In-room: a/c, Wi-Fi. In-hotel: restaurant, bar, pool, gym, spa, laundry facilities, parking.*

## NIGHTLIFE AND THE ARTS

St. John's has tremendous variety and vitality considering its small population. Celtic-inspired traditional music and classic rock are the city's best-known music genres, although there's also a vibrant blues and alternative-rock scene. For theater, venues include traditional spaces, courtyards, and parks.

## THE ARTS

**The Arts and Culture Centre.** The Arts and Culture Centre has a 1,000-seat main theater and the St. John's Public Library. It's the site of musical and theatrical events from September through June. ⊠ *95 Allandale Rd., St. John's, Newfoundland and Labrador, Canada* ☎ *709/729–3650* ⊕ *www.artsandculturecentre.com.*

**Resource Centre for the Arts.** An innovative theater with professional main-stage and experimental second-space productions year-round, the Resource Centre for the Arts has been the launching pad for the province's best-known and most successful theatrical exports. ⊠ *LSPU Hall, 3 Victoria St., St. John's, Newfoundland and Labrador, Canada* ☎ *709/753–4531* ⊕ *www.rca.nf.ca.*

**Ship Pub.** The Ship Pub traditionally served as the local arts watering hole. Folk night is Wednesday, and there's live music Wednesday through Saturday year-round. Pub food is served noon–4 daily, noon–8 Wednesday to Friday. ⊠ *Solomon's La. between Duckworth and Water Sts., 265 Duckworth St., St. John's, Newfoundland and Labrador, Canada* ☎ *709/753–3870.*

## NIGHTLIFE

The well-deserved reputation of St. John's as a party town has been several hundred years in the making.

**George Street.** Downtown George Street is the city's most famous street, with more bars per capita than any other street in North America. The short cobblestone street has dozens of pubs and restaurants. Seasonal open-air concerts, which close off the street, are held here as well. ⊠ *St. John's, Newfoundland and Labrador, Canada.*

**O'Reilly's Pub.** When Russell Crowe comes to town, he jams at O'Reilly's Pub, famous for its nightly live Irish and Newfoundland music. Start times vary, but shows typically start late. O'Reilly's also has a full pub-grub menu; the fish-and-chips is excellent. ⊠ *13 George St., St. John's, Newfoundland and Labrador, Canada* ☎ *709/722–3735, 866/307–3735* ⊕ *www.oreillyspub.com.*

# SPORTS AND THE OUTDOORS

## HIKING

**Grand Concourse.** A well-developed, marked trail system, the Grand Concourse, crosses St. John's, Mount Pearl and Paradise, covering more than 120 km (75 mi). Some trails traverse river valleys, parks, and other open areas; others are sidewalk routes. Well-maintained trails encircle several lakes, including Long Pond and Quidi Vidi Lake, both of which are great for bird-watching. Detailed maps are available at tourist information centers and many hotels. ⊠ *St. John's, Newfoundland and Labrador, Canada* ☎ *709/737–1077* ⊕ *www.grandconcourse.ca.*

## SCUBA DIVING

The ocean around Newfoundland and Labrador rivals the Caribbean in clarity but certainly not in temperature. There are thousands of known shipwreck sites. One, a sunken whaling ship, is only several feet from the shore of the Conception Bay community of Conception Harbour.

The wrecked ship and a wealth of sea life can be explored with a snorkel and wet suit.

**Ocean Quest.** Ocean Quest offers a wide range of classes, from beginners to experts, and leads ocean tours aboard Zodiacs and a 38-foot custom boat to popular scuba-diving sites, including the WWII shipwrecks off Bell Island and the Conception Bay whaling wrecks. They also organize tours from Gros Morne National Park and Terra Nova National Park and seasonal Close Encounters tours with icebergs, whales and caves. Tours start from the Foxtrap Marina. ⊠ *17 Stanley's Rd., Conception Bay South, Newfoundland and Labrador, Canada* ☎ *709/834–7234, 866/623–2664* ⊕ *www.oceanquestadventures.com.*

### SEA KAYAKING

One of the best ways to explore the coastline is by kayak, which lets you visit sea caves and otherwise inaccessible beaches. There's also a very good chance you'll see whales, icebergs, and seabirds.

**O'Brien's Whale & Bird Tours Inc.** O'Brien's Whale & Bird Tours Inc, about 30 minutes outside St. John's, conducts tours to view whales, puffins, seabirds, and icebergs. ⊠ *Bay Bulls, Newfoundland and Labrador, Canada* ☎ *709/753–4850* ⊕ *www.obriensboattours.com.*

**Stan Cook Sea Kayak Adventures.** Stan Cook Sea Kayak Adventures offers excursions leaving from Cape Broyle through world-famous sanctuaries, under waterfalls, and inside caves. In season, paddle with whales and icebergs. They also run guided hiking tours of the East Coast Trail. ⊠ *67 Circular Rd., St. John's, Newfoundland and Labrador, Canada* ☎ *709/579–6353, 888/747–6353* ⊕ *www.wildnfld.ca.*

### WHALE-WATCHING

The east coast of Newfoundland, including the area around St. John's, provides spectacular whale-watching opportunities with 22 species of dolphins and whales visible along the coast. Huge humpback whales weighing up to 30 tons come close to shore to feed in late spring and early summer. You may be able to spot icebergs and large flocks of nesting seabirds in addition to whales on many boat tours. For tour times and rates, visit the tour company booths at harborside near Pier 7 in summer, or inquire at your hotel.

**Iceberg Quest Ocean Tours.** Iceberg Quest Ocean Tours has daily sailings of its two-hour fully narrated tour (C$55), which leaves from Pier 6 on Harbour Drive, at 9:30, 1, 4, and 7. You'll be entertained with traditional and local music aboard, as the boat heads out through the narrows of the harbor between Signal Hill and Fort Amherst to Cape Spear. Keep your eyes open for whales and icebergs and the beautiful scenery of the most easterly points in North America. There are snacks and full bar service and Screechins' on request. Private charters and special packages available. ⊠ *135 Harbour Dr., Pier 6, St. John's, Newfoundland and Labrador, Canada* ☎ *709/722–1888, 866/720–1888* ⊕ *www.icebergquest.com.*

## SHOPPING

**Christina Parker Gallery.** Christina Parker Gallery carries the work of local artists in all media, including painting, sculpture, drawing, and prints. ⊠ *50 Water St., St. John's, Newfoundland and Labrador, Canada* ☎ *709/753–0580* ⊕ *www.christinaparkergallery.com.*

**Devon House Craft Centre.** The Devon House Craft Centre displays local work, showcases innovative designs, and serves as headquarters of the Craft Council of Newfoundland and Labrador. Check out the exhibits upstairs. ⊠ *59 Duckworth St., St. John's, Newfoundland and Labrador, Canada* ☎ *709/753–2749* ⊕ *www.craftcouncil.nl.ca.*

★ **Downhome Shoppe and Gallery.** With more than 5,000 items, each written, sung, or produced by a Newfoundlander or Labradorian, the Downhome Shoppe and Gallery is the best overall place in town to look for souvenirs. Its large selection of local books, crafts, art, and souvenirs are housed in two buildings from the late 1850s. ⊠ *303 Water St., St. John's, Newfoundland and Labrador, Canada* ☎ *709/722–2970, 888/588–6353* ⊕ *www.shopdownhome.com.*

**Eastern Edge Gallery.** This contemporary artist-run center has everything from paintings and drawings to performance and video art from emerging artists. ⊠ *72 Harbour Dr., between Clift's-Baird's Cove and Prescott St., St. John's, Newfoundland and Labrador, Canada* ☎ *709/739–1882* ⊕ *www.easternedge.ca.*

**Emma Butler Gallery.** Emma Butler Gallery represents some of the more prominent established artists in the province. ⊠ *111 George St. W, St. John's, Newfoundland and Labrador, Canada* ☎ *709/739–7111* ⊕ *www.emmabutler.com.*

**Fred's Records.** Fred's Records has the best selection of local recordings—about 1,000 individual titles—as well as other music. ⊠ *198 Duckworth St., St. John's, Newfoundland and Labrador, Canada* ☎ *709/753–9191* ⊕ *www.freds.nf.ca.*

**The Lane Gallery.** The Lane Gallery has seascapes, landscapes, icebergs and other works by Newfoundland photographer Don Lane. ⊠ *Sheraton Hotel Newfoundland, 115 Cavendish Sq., main lobby, St. John's, Newfoundland and Labrador, Canada* ☎ *709/753–8946, 877/366–5263* ⊕ *www.lanegallery.com.*

---

### PINK, WHITE, AND GREEN

You won't be in St. John's long before you'll ask what's with the pink, white, and green? The tricolor flag flies from houses and buildings, and in souvenir shops the cheerful bands of color show up on rings, earrings, fleece, windbreakers, mittens, and aprons. To quote the song "The Flag of Newfoundland": "The pink the rose of England shows, the green St. Patrick's emblem bright, while in between a spotless sheen of Andrew's cross displays the white." The 19th-century flag has gained popularity in recent years as an affectionate symbol of the "secret nation."

**Living Planet.** Living Planet specializes in eco-friendly T-shirts designed by local artists. ⊠ *197 Water St., St. John's, Newfoundland and Labrador, Canada* ☏ *709/754–9300* ⊕ *www.livingplanet.ca.*

**Newfoundland Weavery.** The Newfoundland Weavery sells throws, prints, lamps, books, crafts, and other gift items. ⊠ *177 Water St., St. John's, Newfoundland and Labrador, Canada* ☏ *709/753–0496.*

**NONIA** (*Newfoundland Outport Nursing and Industrial Association*). NONIA was founded in 1920 to raise money for public health services: the proceeds from the sale of the homespun, hand-knit clothes was used to hire public nurses. Today this nonprofit shop sells a variety of knits for all ages. ⊠ *286 Water St., St. John's, Newfoundland and Labrador, Canada* ☏ *709/753–8062, 877/753–8062* ⊕ *www.nonia.com.*

**O'Brien's Music Store.** O'Brien's Music Store is the oldest store on the oldest street in the oldest city in North America. Behind the counter, Gord O'Brien will make you feel at home; it's worth a visit just to look at the accordions, tin whistles, fiddles, ukulele, and ugly sticks, traditional Newfoundland instruments made from discarded tools and household items. ⊠ *278 Water St., St. John's, Newfoundland and Labrador, Canada* ☏ *709/753–8135* ⊕ *www.obriensmusic.com.*

**Wild Things.** Wild Things sells Newfoundlandia crafts and jewelry, Labradorite jewelry, and tea dolls (traditional toys made from caribou hide and stuffed with loose tea). ⊠ *124 Water St., St. John's, Newfoundland and Labrador, Canada* ☏ *709/722–3123.*

# AVALON PENINSULA

On the southern half of the Newfoundland peninsula, small Irish hamlets are separated by large tracts of wilderness. You can travel part of the peninsula's southern coast in one or two days, depending on how much time you have. Quaint towns line Route 10, and the natural sights are beautiful. La Manche and Chance Cove, both abandoned communities–turned–provincial parks, attest to the region's bounty of natural resources. At the intersection of routes 90 and 91 in Salmonier, you can head west and then south to Route 100 to Cape St. Mary's Ecological Reserve, or north toward Salmonier Nature Park and on to the towns on Conception Bay. Each of these routes takes about three hours. On the latter, Harbour Grace is a good place to stop; if you plan to travel on to Bay de Verde, at the northern tip of the peninsula, and down the other side of the peninsula on Route 80 along Trinity Bay, consider overnighting in the Harbour Grace–Carbonear area. Otherwise turn around and retrace your steps to Route 1.

## WITLESS BAY ECOLOGICAL RESERVE

*29 km (18 mi) south of St. John's.*

Four small islands and the water surrounding them make up the Witless Bay Ecological Reserve, the summer home of millions of seabirds—puffins, murres, kittiwakes, razorbills, and guillemots. The birds and the humpback and minke whales that linger here before moving north to

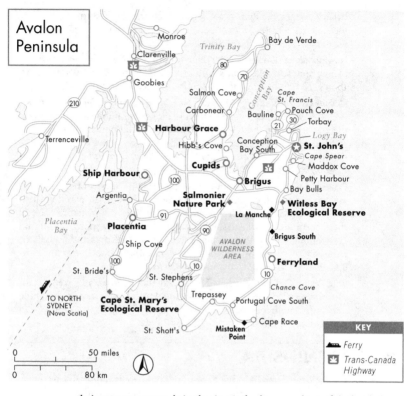

**Avalon Peninsula**

their summer grounds in the Arctic feed on capelin (a fish that belongs to the smelt family) that swarm inshore to spawn.

This is an excellent place to see icebergs in late spring and early summer, which can remain in Newfoundland waters into June and sometimes July, cooling the water temperature before falling victim to the milder climate. The loud crack as an iceberg breaks apart can be heard from shore, but a boat gets you a closer look at these natural ice sculptures. Icebergs have spawned a lucrative business in Newfoundland beyond tourism. Iceberg water and iceberg vodka are now on the market, made from ice chipped from the 10,000-year-old bergs as they float by. The best views of birds and icebergs are from the tour boats that operate here and are the only way to visit the reserve. ⊠ *Rte. 10; take Pitts Memorial Dr. (Rte. 2) from downtown St. John's and turn right onto Goulds off-ramp, then left onto Rte. 10, Newfoundland and Labrador, Canada.*

## SPORTS AND THE OUTDOORS

**Gatherall's Puffin and Whale Watch.** From May 1 to the end of September Gatherall's Puffin and Whale Watch leads six 90-minute trips per day into the reserve on a high-speed catamaran. The catamaran is quite stable in rough seas, so if you get queasy it might be the way to go. Shuttle service is available from hotels in St. John's. ⊠ *Newfoundland*

and Labrador, Canada ☎709/
334–2887, 800/419–4253 ⊕www.
gatheralls.com.

**O'Brien's Whale and Bird Tours.**
O'Brien's Whale and Bird Tours
offers two-hour excursions in a
100-passenger boat to view whales,
icebergs, and seabirds, as well as
90-minute tours in 12-passenger
boats. Dress warmly. ✉ Newfoundland and Labrador, Canada
☎709/753–4850, 877/639–4253
⊕ www.obriensboattours.com.

**EN
ROUTE** Although there are many pretty
hamlets along the way from Witless Bay to Ferryland on Route 10,
**La Manche,** accessible only on foot,

> ## THE IRISH LOOP
>
> The Irish Loop (Route 10) goes
> around the southern shore of the
> Avalon Peninsula below St. John's.
> The highway hugs the coastline
> and takes you into the heart of
> Irish Newfoundland—to Bay Bulls,
> Witless Bay, Ferryland, Aquaforte,
> Fermeuse, Portugal Cove South,
> Trepassey, and Salmonier. It's a
> world filled with whales, caribou,
> and seabirds. If you keep follow-
> ing the loop around you'll end up
> back in St. John's.

and **Brigus South** have especially attractive settings. La Manche is an
abandoned fishing community between Tors Cove and Cape Broyle.
The former residents moved to other towns after a storm destroyed part
of the community in 1966; a suspension bridge washed away by the
storm's tides has since been rebuilt and is worth a visit. Brigus South is
a fishing village with a strong traditional flavor whose name is derived
from an old French word for "intrigue."

# FERRYLAND

*43½ km (27 mi) south of Witless Bay Ecological Reserve.*

The main road into Ferryland hugs the coastline, where tiny bay houses
dot the steep hills. Ferryland is one of the oldest European settlements
in North America: the Englishman Lord Baltimore, Sir George Calvert, settled it in 1620. Calvert didn't stay long on this cold windswept
shore—he left for a warmer destination and is more commonly cred-
ited with founding Maryland. In the summer this is a great spot to
whale-watch.

## EXPLORING

**Colony of Avalon.** The major ongoing Colony of Avalon archaeological dig at Ferryland has uncovered the early-17th-century colony of
Lord Baltimore. The site includes an archaeology laboratory, exhibit
center, gift shop, and museum, period gardens, and a reconstructed
17th-century kitchen. Guided tours are available. ✉ Rte. 10, Ferryland,
Newfoundland and Labrador, Canada ☎709/432–3200, 877/326–
5669 ⊕ www.colonyofavalon.ca ☑ C$9.50 includes tour ⊙ Mid-May–
early Oct., daily 10–6.

**Ferryland Lighthouse.** This historic lighthouse, built in 1871, now sig-
nals the spot for breathtaking views, worry-free picnics, and great
food like smoked salmon and ice shrimp sandwiches, green salads,
and gooseberry fools. You bring the appetite, and the lighthouse staff
packs everything else—even the blanket. Bread is baked daily in the

lighthouse; in fact everything is made on-site down to the desserts and freshly squeezed lemonade. There must be romance in the shadow of the lighthouse, because it has become a popular destination for engagement proposals. Check the Web site for menus. Picnics start at C$23 per person and reservations are required. ✉ *Rte. 10, Ferryland, Newfoundland and Labrador, Canada* ☎ *709/363–7456* ⊕ *www.lighthousepicnics.ca* ⊙ *late May–late Sept., Tues.–Sun. 11:30–4:30.*

**OFF THE BEATEN PATH**

**Mistaken Point Ecological Reserve.** At 565 million years old, this is one of the most significant fossil sites in the world. Fossils of more than 20 species of ancient organisms are found in the mudstones here, and almost all of them represent extinct groups unknown in our modern world. Mistaken Point is 145 km (90 mi) south on Route 10 from downtown St. John's. Access to the fossils is by guided hike only. Tours are offered daily at 1 pm (May to mid-October) and begin at the Edge of Avalon Interpretive Centre in Portugal Cove South. Tours generally take 3½–4 hours and include a 3-km (1.8-mi) one-way hike across the barrens towards the ocean to the fossil site.

■ TIP → While you're here, travel 5 km (3 mi) farther along the road to the Cape Race Lighthouse, the northeasternmost point in North America and most famous for receiving one of the first SOS messages from the *Titanic*. ✉ *Off Rte. 10, Portugal Cove South, Newfoundland and Labrador, Canada* ☎ *709/438–1012, 709/438–1100 Call ahead to ensure availability and to check weather conditions* ⊕ *www.env.gov.nl.ca* ⊠ *Free* ⊙ *May–mid-Oct.*

### SPORTS AND THE OUTDOORS

**Stan Cook Sea Kayak Adventures.** Kayaking excursions with Stan Cook Sea Kayak Adventures leave from the old General Store on Harbour Road in Cape Broyle. They offer 2½- and 4-hour kayak trips as well as the "Go and Tow," a kayak trip out onto the ocean with return trip by motorized towboat. During whale season this is a great way to get up close and personal with humpbacks and minkes. They also run guided hiking tours of the East Coast Trail. ✉ *67 Circular Rd., St. John's, Newfoundland and Labrador, Canada* ☎ *709/579–6353, 888/747–6353, 709/432–3332* ⊕ *www.wildnfld.ca.*

## SALMONIER NATURE PARK

*88 km (55 mi) northwest of Ferryland, 14½ km (9 mi) north of the intersection of Rtes. 90 and 91.*

**Salmonier Nature Park.** Many indigenous animal species, including moose, caribou, lynx, and otters, can be seen at this 3,460-acre wilderness reserve area. An enclosed 100-acre exhibit allows up-close viewing. ✉ *Salmonier Line, Rte. 90, Ferryland, Newfoundland and Labrador, Canada* ☎ *709/229–7888* ⊕ *www.gov.nl.ca/snp* ⊠ *Free* ⊙ *Early June–early Sept., daily 10–6; early Sept.–mid-Oct., weekdays 10–4.*

**EN ROUTE**

**Hawke Hills.** From Salmonier Nature Park to Brigus, take Route 90, which passes through the scenic Hawke Hills before meeting up with the Trans-Canada Highway (Route 1). This reserve is the best representative of alpine barrens in Canada east of the Rockies. Turn off at Holyrood Junction (Route 62) and follow Route 70, which skirts Conception Bay, to get there. ⊠ *Ferryland, Newfoundland and Labrador, Canada.*

## BRIGUS

*19 km (12 mi) north of intersection of Rtes. 1 and 70.*

This compact historic village on Conception Bay is wonderfully walkable, with a lovely public garden, winding lanes, and a teahouse. Brigus is best known as the birthplace of Captain Bob Bartlett, the famed Arctic explorer who accompanied Admiral Robert Peary on polar expeditions during the first decade of the 20th century.

### EXPLORING

**Hawthorne Cottage.** Captain Bartlett's home is one of the few surviving examples of picturesque cottage style, with a veranda decorated with ornamental wooden fretwork. It dates from 1830 and is a National Historic Site. During July and August (daily at 3 pm) look for the Live! On the Lawn Theatre, a series of 25-minute vignettes about historic Brigus and Bartlett's adventures. ⊠ *South St. and Irishtown Rd., Brigus, Newfoundland and Labrador, Canada* ☎ *709/528–4004 May–Oct.* ⊕ *www.historicsites.ca* ⊠ *C$5 (theatre and tour of house)* ⊙ *May–Oct., daily 10–6.*

### WHERE TO STAY

*For expanded hotel reviews, visit Fodors.com.*

$ **Brittoner Bed & Breakfast.** This 1842-year-old restored home is in the
B&B/INN  heart of Brigus, near Hawthorne Cottage and hiking trails. **Pros:** on a pond; harbor view from some rooms; full hot breakfast. **Cons:** no credit cards accepted. ⊠ *12 Water St., Box 163, Brigus, Newfoundland and Labrador, Canada* ☎ *709/528–3412, 709/579–5995 Nov.–Apr.* ⊕ *www. bbcanada.com* ➷ *3 rooms* ⌂ *In-room: no a/c, no TV, Wi-Fi. In-hotel: laundry facilities, business center, parking, some pets allowed* ▤ *No credit cards* ⊙ *Closed Nov.–Apr.* ⦿ *Breakfast.*

$ **Brookdale Manor.** This farmhouse is in a quiet, country setting on the
B&B/INN  outskirts of town. **Pros:** open year-round; quiet area. **Cons:** furnishings don't reflect Brigus heritage and grandeur; 1-km (½-mi) walk to town center. ⊠ *26 Farm Rd., Brigus, Newfoundland and Labrador, Canada* ⌑ *Box 121, Brigus, Newfoundland and Labrador, Canada A0A 1K0* ☎⌸ *709/528–4544, 888/528–4544* ⊕ *www.bbcanada.com* ➷ *4 rooms* ⌂ *In-room: no a/c, no TV, Wi-Fi* ⦿ *Breakfast.*

## CUPIDS

*5 km (3 mi) northwest of Brigus.*

Cupids is the oldest English colony in Canada, founded in 1610 by John Guy, to whom the town erected a monument in 1910. Nearby is a reproduction of the enormous Union Jack that flew during that 300th-anniversary celebration. When the wind snaps the flag, you can hear it half a mile away. Cupids recently celebrated its 400th anniversary, and the new Cupids Legacy Centre was built to house the many artifacts that have been found related to the archaeology of John Guy's settlement.

### EXPLORING

**Cupids Legacy Centre & Museum.** With interactive displays, interpretive tours, a shop, and an archaeological lab, the Cupids Legacy Centre & Museum is a good place to get a glimpse of the early English settlement. Visit the dig nearby at the original plantation site. Recovered artifacts on view include the oldest coin found in Canada and trade beads. ⊠ *368 Seaforest Dr., Cupids, Newfoundland and Labrador, Canada* ☎ *709/528–3500* ⊕ *www.cupidslegacycentre.ca* ⊠ *C$11 plantation and museum* ⊘ *June–Oct., daily 10–5, off season by appt.*

> ## ROUTE 100: THE CAPE SHORE
>
> The Cape Shore area, which includes Cape St. Mary's north to Argentia, is culturally and historically rich: the French settlers had their capital here in Placentia, and Irish influence is also strong in music and manner. Birders come to view the fabulous seabird colony at Cape St. Mary's. You can reach the Cape Shore, on the western side of the Avalon Peninsula, from Route 1 at its intersection with Route 100. The ferry from Nova Scotia docks in Argentia, near Placentia.

### WHERE TO STAY

*For expanded hotel reviews, visit Fodors.com.*

$

B&B/INN

**Skipper Ben's.** This 1891 heritage home has been restored to its original character, with wood ceilings and antique furnishings. **Pros:** ocean views from deck and rooms; the sound of the sea will lull you to sleep at night; smoke-free. **Cons:** no a/c; road runs between B&B and water. ⊠ *408 Seaforest Dr., Cupids, Newfoundland and Labrador, Canada* ⌂ *Box 137, Cupids, Newfoundland and Labrador, Canada A0A 2B0* ☎ *877/528–4436* ☎ *709/528–4436* ⊕ *www.skipperbens.com* ⇆ *3 rooms with shared bath* ⌂ *In-room: no a/c, Wi-Fi. In-hotel: restaurant, laundry facilities, parking* ⍾ *Breakfast.*

## HARBOUR GRACE

*21 km (13 mi) north of Cupids.*

Harbour Grace, once the headquarters of 17th-century pirate Peter Easton, was a major commercial town in the 18th and 19th centuries. Beginning in 1919, the town was the departure point for many attempts to fly the Atlantic. Amelia Earhart left Harbour Grace in 1932 to become the first woman to fly solo across the Atlantic. The town has two fine churches and several registered historic houses.

### WHERE TO STAY

*For expanded hotel reviews, visit Fodors.com.*

$

B&B/INN

**Rothesay House Inn Bed & Breakfast.** This provincial heritage structure was built in 1855 in Brigus, then dismantled, transported, and reconstructed in the Queen Anne style in Harbour Grace in 1905. **Pros:** local seasonal produce and seafood; engaging and helpful hosts. **Cons:** no a/c; two resident dogs. ⊠ *34 Water St., Box 577, Harbour Grace,*

*Newfoundland and Labrador, Canada* ☎ *709/596–2268, 877/596-2268* ⊕ *www.rothesay.com* ➪ *4 rooms* ⬧ *In-room: no a/c, no TV, Wi-Fi* ⦾ *Breakfast.*

## PLACENTIA

*48 km (30 mi) south of Rte. 1.*

Placentia was first settled by 16th-century Basque fishermen and was Newfoundland's French capital in the 1600s. The remains of an old fort built on a hill look out over Placentia and beyond, to the placid waters and wooded, steep hillsides of the inlet.

### EXPLORING

**Castle Hill National Historic Site.** Just north of town, Castle Hill is what remains of the French fortifications. The visitor center has a "Life at Plaisance" exhibit that shows the hardships endured by early English and French settlers. Performances of *Faces of Fort Royal,* a play about the French era, take place mid-July to mid-August (call for times). There are hiking trails from the forts and many lookouts on-site as well as a gift shop. ✉ *Off Rte. 100, Placentia, Newfoundland and Labrador, Canada* ☎ *709/227–2401* 🖃 *Site C$3.90, play by donation* ☉ *Site and visitor center mid-May–mid-Oct., daily 10–6.*

### WHERE TO STAY

*For expanded hotel reviews, visit Fodors.com.*

$  🏨 **Harold Hotel.** Five kilometers (3 mi) from the Argentia–Nova Scotia Ferry, the Harold Hotel is in the very heart of Placentia and a two-minute walk from the boardwalk and the ocean. **Pros:** smoke-free; minutes to ferry terminal; dining room is air-conditioned. **Cons:** no a/c in guest rooms. ✉ *Main St., Placentia, Newfoundland and Labrador, Canada* ✉ *Box 142, Placentia, Newfoundland and Labrador, Canada A0B 2Y0* ☎ *709/227–2107, 877/227–2107* 🖷 *709/227–7700* ⊕ *www. haroldhotel.com* ➪ *19 rooms* ⬧ *In-room: no a/c, Wi-Fi. In-hotel: restaurant, bar, laundry facilities.*

$  🏨 **Rosedale Manor Bed & Breakfast.** You'll wake up to the smell of home-
B&B/INN  baked bread and pastries prepared by the chef/host of this 1893 water-
**Fodor's**Choice  front heritage home in the Second Empire style. **Pros:** 1 km (½ mi)
★  from Argentia Ferry, 50 km (31 mi) from Cape St. Mary's, and 1½ hours from St. John's; cordless phones available with free long distance. **Cons:** no elevator. ✉ *40 Orcan Dr., Box 329, Placentia, Newfoundland and Labrador, Canada* ☎ *709/227–3613, 877/999–3613* ⊕ *www.rosedalemanor.ca* ➪ *6 rooms* ⬧ *In-room: no a/c, no TV, Wi-Fi* ⦾ *Breakfast.*

## SHIP HARBOUR

*34 km (21 mi) north of Placentia.*

The historic significance of this isolated place is that in 1941, on a ship in these waters, Franklin Roosevelt and Winston Churchill signed the Atlantic Charter and formally announced the "Four Freedoms," which still shape the politics of the world's most successful democracies:

freedom of speech, freedom of worship, freedom from want, and freedom from fear. Off Route 102, amid the splendor of Placentia Bay, an unpaved road leads to an Atlantic Charter monument.

## CAPE ST. MARY'S ECOLOGICAL RESERVE

★  *65 km (40 mi) south of Placentia.*

**Cape St. Mary's Ecological Reserve.** Cape St. Mary's Ecological Reserve is the third-largest nesting colony of gannets in North America and the most accessible seabird colony on the continent. A paved road takes you within a mile of the colony. You can visit the interpretation center—guides are on-site in summer—and then walk to within 100 feet of nesting gannets, murres, black-billed kittiwakes, and razorbills. Most birds visit March through August. Call the weather line to check on conditions before heading out. The reserve has some of the most dramatic coastal scenery in Newfoundland and is a good place to spot whales. From July through September the interpretation center has performances of traditional music by local artists; call for information and times. ⊠ *Off Rte. 100, Cape St. Mary's, Newfoundland and Labrador, Canada* ☎ *709/277–1666 cell phone, 709/337–2473* ⊕ *www.env.gov. nl.ca* ⊠ *Free* ☉ *Mid-May–June and Sept.–mid-Oct., daily 9–5; July and Aug., daily 8–7.*

### WHERE TO STAY

*For expanded hotel reviews, visit Fodors.com.*

$       📺 **Bird Island Resort.** The landscape around this lodging a half-hour drive
B&B/INN    from Cape St. **Pros:** efficency units have decks. **Cons:** no restaurant; no a/c. ⊠ *Off Rte. 100, St. Bride's, Newfoundland and Labrador, Canada* ☎ *709/337–2450, 888/337–2450 NL only* ⊕ *www.birdislandresort. com* ➾ *5 rooms, 15 efficiency units* ⟁ *In-room: no a/c, kitchen. In-hotel: gym, laundry facilities, parking.*

$       📺 **Capeway Motel & Efficiency Units.** This former convent is about a 15-minute drive from the seabird sanctuary at Cape St. **Pros:** well-equipped one- and two-bedroom efficiencies; guest rooms have in-room tea/coffee. **Cons:** no elevator. ⊠ *Main St., St. Bride's, Newfoundland and Labrador, Canada* ☎ *709/337–2163, 866/337–2163* ⊕ *www. thecapeway.ca* ➾ *2 rooms, 5 efficiency units* ⟁ *In-room: no a/c, kitchen, Wi-Fi. In-hotel: laundry facilities, parking.*

# EASTERN NEWFOUNDLAND

Eastern Newfoundland has plenty of history and fabulous natural landscapes. The Bonavista Peninsula has archaeological artifacts; the Burin Peninsula is more about stark landscapes. Clarenville, halfway between the two, is a good base for exploring, though not much of a destination in itself. Terra Nova was Newfoundland's first National Park.

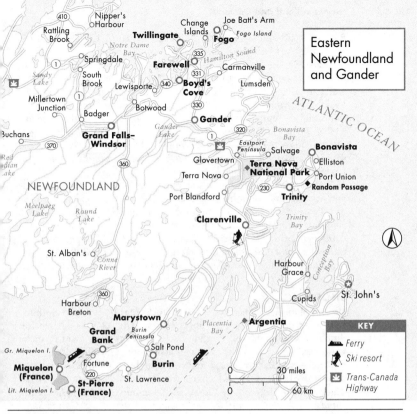

## CLARENVILLE

*189 km (117 mi) northwest of St. John's.*

Clarenville, about two hours northwest of St. John's via the Trans-Canada Highway (Route 1), is the departure point for several different excursions: the Bonavista Peninsula with its Discovery Trail and the twin communities of Trinity and Bonavista; Terra Nova National Park; and the Burin Peninsula.

### EXPLORING

★ **Discovery Trail.** If history and quaint towns appeal to you, follow the Discovery Trail, which begins in Clarenville on Route 230A. The trail includes two gems: the old town of Trinity, famed for its architecture and theater festival, and Bonavista, one of John Cabot's reputed landing spots. Clarenville itself is largely a departure point for these more attractive destinations. ⊠ *Clarenville, Newfoundland and Labrador, Canada.*

### WHERE TO EAT AND STAY

*For expanded hotel reviews, visit Fodors.com.*

$ × **Clarenville Circle K & Restaurant.** Service may be slow but the all-day
CANADIAN breakfast is worth the stop. In addition to inexpensive home-cooked food and clean washrooms, this pit stop has a great view of Trinity

Bay and Random Island. ⊠ *398 Trans-Canada Hwy., Clarenville, Newfoundland and Labrador, Canada* ☎ *709/466–2073.*

$   ⊞ **Clarenville Inn.** This hotel on the Trans-Canada Highway won't win any design awards, but the rooms are comfortable and have wall-to-wall carpeting; rooms on the top floor are brighter, and the ones in the back have a view of Clarenville and Random Sound. **Pros:** heated outdoor pool in summer; lounge with a patio. **Cons:** right on the highway. ⊠ *134 Trans-Canada Hwy., Clarenville, Newfoundland and Labrador, Canada* ☎ *709/466–7911, 877/466–7911* ⊕ *www.clarenvilleinn.ca* ⇆ *62 rooms, 1 suite* ⚥ *In-room: Wi-Fi. In-hotel: restaurant, bar, pool, parking, some pets allowed.*

$   ⊞ **St. Jude Hotel.** The rooms at this popular modern hotel are spacious and comfortable; ones fronting the highway have a good view of the bay. **Pros:** friendly staff; restaurant has outdoor patio; elevator. **Cons:** smoking permitted in eight rooms; road construction company parks equipment behind hotel. ⊠ *247 Trans-Canada Hwy., Clarenville, Newfoundland and Labrador, Canada* ☎ *709/466–1717, 800/563–7800* ⊕ *www.stjudehotel.com* ⇆ *60 rooms, 3 suites* ⚥ *In-room: a/c, Wi-Fi. In-hotel: restaurant, bar, some pets allowed.*

### SHOPPING

**Mercer's Marine.** This family-run store stocks marine gear and clothing, rain wear, outdoor apparel, rubber boots, warm clothes in case you didn't pack enough, and knitting material in case you want to make your own. The shop, which also sells just about everything else, including kitchenware, is worth a stop if you're in the neighborhood, but you can also order a catalog, which features staff as models, and shop from home. ⊠ *210 Marine Dr., Clarenville, Newfoundland and Labrador, Canada* ☎ *709/466–7430* ⊕ *www.mercersmarine.com* ⊙ *Closed Sun.*

## TERRA NOVA NATIONAL PARK

⟳   *24 km (15 mi) north of Clarenville.*

Terra Nova, established in 1957, was Newfoundland's first national park. On Bonavista Bay, it has natural beauty, dramatic coastline, and rugged woods. Moose, black bear, and other wildlife move about freely in the forests and marshy bogs, while pods of whales play within sight of the shores and many species of birds inhabit the cliffs and shores encompassed by the 400-square-km (154-square-mi) park.

Golf, sea kayaking, fishing, and camping are some of the draws here, and you can book summer marine tours and seasonal fishing through **Coastal Connections** (☎ *709/533–2196 or 709/640–0814 off season* ⊕ *www.coastalconnections.ca*). The visitor center leads guided walks and has exhibits, a small shop, and a small but decent snack bar/cafeteria. Eight backcountry camping areas are accessible by trail or canoe. ⊠ *Trans-Canada Hwy., Glovertown, Newfoundland and Labrador, Canada* ☎ *709/533–2801 National Parks, 709/533–2942 Terra Nova National Park* ⊕ *www.pc.gc.ca* 🎫 *C$5.80* ⊙ *Daily dawn–dusk; visitor center mid-May–June and Sept.–mid-Oct., daily 10–5; July and Aug., daily 9–7.*

**GETTING HERE AND AROUND**

There is no charge to simply driving through Terra Nova National Park, located along the Trans Canada Highway. However, if you plan to use any facilities you need to purchase a daily pass. There are park entrances near Glovertown to the west and near Port Blandford to the east. The visitor center in the middle of the park is the place to stop if you want hiking or other information.

**WHERE TO STAY**

*For expanded hotel reviews, visit Fodors.com.*

**$$$** ☷ **Terra Nova Resort and Golf Community.** This 220-acre oceanfront prop-
☾ erty at Port Blandford has some of the most beautiful golf courses in Canada. **Pros:** heated indoor/outdoor pool year round; dining room overlooks Clode Sound; Mulligan's Pub serves a full menu. **Cons:** some rooms not air-conditioned; some rooms could use some renovations. ✉ *Rte. 1, Box 160, Port Blandford, Newfoundland and Labrador, Canada* ☎ *709/543–2525, 709/543–2626 golf reservations, 877/546-2525* ⊕ *www.terranovagolf.com* ⇨ *73 rooms, 7 suites, 7 chalets* ⚭ *In-room: a/c, Wi-Fi. In-hotel: restaurant, bar, golf course, pool, tennis court, gym, spa, business center, some pets allowed.*

**OFF THE BEATEN PATH**

**The Eastport Peninsula.** A short, pretty drive from Terra Nova National Park, part of it on a thin strip of road between two bodies of water, will take you to the Eastport Peninsula; take Route 310, at the northern boundary of the national park. There are two beautiful, sandy beaches—at Eastport and at Sandy Cove—and either is perfect to laze away an afternoon, or you can sightsee. The very old outport of Salvage and the small port of Happy Adventure are charming. B&Bs and cabins dot this agricultural peninsula, and the schedule of musical and literary festivals (⊕ *www.beachesheritagecentre.ca*) might convince you to stay a night or two. At Burnside, you can visit an archaeology center with Beothuk artifacts or take a boat ride to The Beaches, once the largest Beothuk settlement in Bonavista Bay (⊕ *www.burnsideheritage.ca*).

# TRINITY

*71 km (44 mi) northeast of Clarenville.*

★ Trinity is one of the jewels of Newfoundland. The village's ocean views, winding lanes, and snug houses are the main attractions, and several homes have been turned into museums and inns. In the 1700s, Trinity competed with St. John's as a center of culture and wealth. Its more contemporary claim to fame, however, is that its intricate harbor was a favorite anchorage for the British navy. The smallpox vaccine was introduced to North America here by a local rector. On West Street an information center with costumed interpreters is open daily mid-June through October.

**GETTING HERE**

To get here from Clarenville, take Route 230 to Route 239.

## EXPLORING

**Lester-Garland Premises Mercantile Building.** This provincial historic site takes you back more than a century to when merchant families ruled tiny communities. Next door the counting house has been restored to the 1820s and the retail store to the 1900s. An interpretation center traces the history of the town, once a mercantile center. ⊠ *West St., Trinity, Newfoundland and Labrador, Canada* ☎ *709/464–2042* ⊕ *www. seethesites.ca* 🖅 *C$3* ⊙ *Mid-May–mid-Oct., daily 10–5:30.*

**Skerwink Trail.** About 9,000 people a year come to hike the Skerwink Trail, a cliff walk with panoramic views of Trinity and the ocean. Along this historic footpath, you'll see sandy beaches, sea stacks (giant protruding rocks that have slowly eroded over time), and seabirds, and, in season, whales, icebergs, and bald eagles. This 6-km (3.7-mi) walk, which begins across the harbor in Port Rexton–Trinity East, is not for the faint of heart. It takes about two hours and can be steep in places. Maps are available at the Visitor's Information Center in Southern Bay. ⊠ *Off Rte. 230, Port Rexton, Newfoundland and Labrador, Canada* ☎ *709/466–3845* ⊕ *www.theskerwinktrail.com.*

## WHERE TO EAT AND STAY

*For expanded hotel reviews, visit Fodors.com.*

**$$** ✕ **Dock Restaurant.** Right on the wharf, this restaurant is in a restored
SEAFOOD　300-year-old fish merchant's headquarters. The menu includes tradi-
★　tional Newfoundland meals and seafood as well as the standard Canadian fare: burgers, chicken, and steak. Upstairs is an art gallery and crafts shop. ⊠ *Trinity Waterfront, Trinity, Newfoundland and Labrador, Canada* ☎ *709/464–2133* ⊙ *Closed early Oct.–Apr.*

**$$$** 🏨 **Artisan Inn.** Owner Tineke Gow oversees accommodations in six
B&B/INN　houses in the heart of Trinity. ⊠ *49 High St., Trinity, Newfoundland and Labrador, Canada* ☎ *709/464–3377, 877/464–7700* ⊕ *www. trinityvacations.com* 🛏 *5 rooms, 1 suite, 4 vacation homes* 🖢 *In-room: no a/c, kitchen, Wi-Fi. In-hotel: restaurant, parking* ⊙ *Closed Nov.–Apr.* ⍩ *Breakfast.*

**$** 🏨 **Eriksen Premises.** This two-story mansard-style building, built in the
B&B/INN　late 1800s as a general store and tearoom, has been restored to its original elegance and character. **Pros:** good location; common room has a TV, fridge, and tea and coffee. **Cons:** no elevator; no a/c; dining room very busy pretheater. ⊠ *West St., Trinity Bay, Newfoundland and Labrador, Canada* ⍐ *Box 58, Trinity Bay, Newfoundland and Labrador, Canada A0C 2S0* ☎ *709/464–3698, 877/464–3698* ⊕ *www. trinityexperience.com* 🛏 *7 rooms* 🖢 *In-room: no a/c, no TV, Wi-Fi. In-hotel: restaurant, parking* ⊙ *Closed mid-Oct.–Apr.* ⍩ *Breakfast.*

**$$** 🏨 **Fishers' Loft Inn.** Whales sometimes swim among the small fishing
B&B/INN　boats in the harbor within sight of the several 19th-century buildings
Fodor's Choice　that make up this spectacular hillside property, and icebergs drift by
★　farther out in the bay. **Pros:** colorful kitchen gardens enrich dining experience; gift shop with juried crafts; main floor wheelchair-accessible rooms. **Cons:** no a/c; one dining option only (breakfast C$16 and dinner four courses C$55); no elevator. ⊠ *Mill Rd., 15 km (9 mi) northeast of Trinity, Port Rexton, Newfoundland and Labrador, Canada* ⍐ *Box 36, Port Rexton, Newfoundland and Labrador, Canada A0C*

2H0 ☎ 877/464–3240 ⊕ *www.fishersloft.com* ⇄ *14 rooms, 7 suites* ♿ *In-room: no a/c. In-hotel: restaurant, parking* ⊘ *Closed Nov.–Apr.*

$ 📺 **Sherwood Suites.** These affordable efficiencies are spacious and have living rooms and private patios: they're not particularly stylish, but rooms are large and bright with private entrances. **Pros:** near Skerwink Trail; beautiful 20-acre property; several restaurants within a 10-minute drive. **Cons:** no restaurant on-site; no phone; no a/c. ⊠ *Rocky Hill Rd., Port Rexton, Newfoundland and Labrador, Canada* 🏣 *Box 2, Port Rexton, Newfoundland and Labrador, Canada A0C 2H0* ☎ 709/464–2130, 877/464–2133 ⊕ *www.sherwoodsuites.com* ⇄ *4 rooms, 12 suites* ♿ *In-room: no a/c, kitchen, Wi-Fi. In-hotel: laundry facilities, parking, some pets allowed* ⊘ *Closed Oct.–late May.*

## NIGHTLIFE AND THE ARTS

**Rising Tide Theatre.** Dinner theater, local dramas, comedies, and newly commissioned plays are performed from mid-June to mid-October as part of the Bight Festival at the Rising Tide Theatre. Check the Web site for show dates and times. The theater, on the waterfront, is styled like an old mercantile warehouse. The theater company also offers the New-Founde-Land Trinity Pageant and walking tours of the lanes, roads, and sites of the town (Wednesday and Saturday at 2), which are more theater than tour, with actors in period costume. ⊠ *Rte. 230 to Rte. 239, then left onto road into Trinity, Trinity, Newfoundland and Labrador, Canada* ☎ *709/464–3232, 888/464–3377* ⊕ *www.risingtidetheatre.com.*

## SPORTS AND THE OUTDOORS

**Atlantic Adventures Charters and Tours.** Sail on a 46-foot motorized sailboat for whale-watching or just cruising Trinity Bay. The boat departs daily at 10 am and 2 pm, depending on the weather and on charter bookings. Tours are two hours and cost about C$60 per person plus tax. Group charters (2½-hour tour) with a meal are available. The vessel departs from the Dockside Marina. ⊠ *Trinity, Newfoundland and Labrador, Canada* ☎ *709/464–2133, 709/781–2255 off-season* ⊕ *www.atlanticadventures.com.*

**Rugged Beauty Boat Tours.** Rugged Beauty Boat Tours operates a 27-foot open boat that can accommodate 12 guests. The boat departs daily at 10 am and 2 pm from May to October next to the Random Passage Site for a three-hour tour that visits the resettled communities of Kerley's Harbour, Ireland's Eye, and British Harbour. Special charters are available. The cost is C$70 for adults and C$50 for children. ⊠ *Rte. 239 at New Bonaventure, off Rte. 230, Trinity, Newfoundland and Labrador, Canada* ☎ *709/464–3856* ⊕ *www.ruggedbeautyboattours.net.*

**OFF THE BEATEN PATH**

**Random Passage.** Drive along Route 239, until the end of the road at New Bonaventure, about 14 km (8½ mi) from Trinity, then walk a short ways, and you'll reach the breathtaking cove now known as Random Passage. Bernice Morgan's novel of that name, set in early 19th-century Newfoundland, captured the imagination of readers, and in 2000, an internationally televised miniseries based on the book was filmed here at this constructed site. You can roam the church, a schoolroom, houses, and a fishing stage and flakes (where the fish is dried), or sit near the vegetable garden and enjoy the quiet beauty of the cove's meadows and pastures. There are guided one-hour site tours. From July to September, there's a Sunday afternoon reading/concert (Random Passage Series) with writers and musicians. The Old Schoolhouse tearoom (open 9:30–4:30) offers homemade fish cakes, pea soup, and light lunches. ⊠ *On Rte. 239 at New Bonaventure, off Rte. 230, Trinity, Newfoundland and Labrador, Canada* ☎ *709/464–2233* ⊕ *www.randompassagesite. com* ⊠ *C\$8* ⊙ *Mid-May–mid-Oct. 9:30–5:30.*

# BONAVISTA

*28 km (17 mi) north of Trinity.*

No one knows exactly where explorer John Cabot landed when he came to Atlantic Canada in 1497, but many believe, based on his descriptions of the newfound land, it was at Bonavista.

## EXPLORING

**Cape Bonavista Lighthouse.** The Cape Bonavista Lighthouse is a Provincial Historic Site on the point, about 1 km (½ mi) outside town. Built in 1843, it has been restored to the way it looked in 1870. Admission includes entry to the Mockbeggar Plantation. ⊠ *Bonavista, Newfoundland and Labrador, Canada* ☎ *709/468–7444* ⊕ *www.seethesites.ca* ⊠ *C\$3; free Sun.* ⊙ *Mid-May–early Oct., daily 10–5:30.*

Ⓒ **Mockbeggar Plantation.** Learn about the life of an outport merchant in the years immediately before Confederation. Interpreters lead you through an early 18th-century fish store, carpentry shop, and cod-liver-oil factory. The Bradley house on-site has been restored to its 1939 appearance. Admission includes entry to the Cape Bonavista Lighthouse. ⊠ *Off Rte. 230, Bonavista, Newfoundland and Labrador, Canada* ☎ *709/468–7300* ⊕ *www.seethesites.ca* ⊠ *C\$3; free Sun.* ⊙ *Mid-May–early Oct., daily 10–5:30.*

**Ryan Premises National Historic Site.** The Ryan Premises National Historic Site on the waterfront depicts the 500-year history of the commercial cod fishery in a restored fish merchant's property. ⊠ *Off Rte. 230 on Rte. 235, Bonavista, Newfoundland and Labrador, Canada* ☎ *709/468–1600* ⊕ *www.pc.gc.ca* ⊠ *C\$3.90* ⊙ *Mid-May–mid-Oct., daily 10–6.*

## WHERE TO STAY

*For expanded hotel reviews, visit Fodors.com.*

\$\$\$   ▦ **The Harbour Quarters.** Built in the 1920s as a general store overlooking
B&B/INN   Bonavista Harbour, the Harbour Quarters is now a fabulous place to drop anchor for the night. **Pros:** easy walk to everything; sunset view from restaurant with new patio; smoke-free; elevator. **Cons:** located right on the main road; restaurant closed until 4 in off-season. ⊠ *42 Campbell St., Box 399, Bonavista, Newfoundland and Labrador, Canada* ☎ *709/468–7982, 866/468–7982* ⊕ *www.harbourquarters. com* ⇱ *11 rooms* ⚲ *In-room: Internet. In-hotel: restaurant, bar, parking* ⚑ *Breakfast.*

# MARYSTOWN

*283 km (175 mi) southwest of Bonavista; 171 km (107 mi) from Clarenville; 306 km (191 mi) from St. John's.*

Marystown, on the Burin Peninsula, is built around beautiful Mortier Bay, which is so big it was considered large enough for the entire British fleet during the early days of World War II. Shipbuilding is still the main industry, although it's certainly declined. Of note is the 20-foot statue of the Virgin Mary that looks out over the bay.

## WHERE TO STAY

*For expanded hotel reviews, visit Fodors.com.*

$ 🏨 **Marystown Hotel and Convention Center.** The Burin Peninsula's largest hotel has standard but comfortable rooms; those on the upper floors are a bit brighter. **Pros:** in the center of town; walking distance to fitness center. **Cons:** only some rooms have a/c; hotel attracts weddings and conventions; some smoking rooms. ⊠ *76 Ville Marie Dr., Marystown, Newfoundland and Labrador, Canada* ☎ *709/279–1600, 866/612–6800* ⊕ *www.marystownhotel.com* ⇱ *133 rooms* ☖ *In-room: a/c, kitchen, Wi-Fi. In-hotel: restaurant, bar, some pets allowed.*

# BURIN

*17 km (11 mi) south of Marystown.*

A community built amid intricate cliffs and coves, Burin was an ideal setting for pirates and privateers, who used to lure ships into the rocky, dead-end areas to plunder them. When Captain James Cook was stationed here to chart the coast in the 1760s, one of his duties was to watch from the hill now named Cook's Lookout for smugglers bringing in rum from the island of St-Pierre. Smuggling continues to this day.

## EXPLORING

**Bank of Nova Scotia Museum.** Bank of Nova Scotia Museum is considered one of the best community museums in Newfoundland. It has a display of the 1929 tidal wave that struck Burin and the surrounding coastal communities and information on the famous gangster Al Capone, who helped raise money for the local cottage hospital and arts center when he ran rum through the Burin Peninsula during prohibition. The museum is part of Burin's Heritage Square, along with the Burin Heritage House, or the Reddy House, which gives you a sense of what life used to be like in this fishing community. Heritage Square also inclues a craft shop and café. ⊠ *33 Seaview Dr., off Rte. 221, Burin, Newfoundland and Labrador, Canada* ☎ *709/891–2217* ⊕ *www.townofburin.com/tourism.htm* ⊠ *Free* ☉ *Apr.–Sept., weekdays 8:30–5; July and Aug., also weekends 9–7.*

**OFF THE BEATEN PATH**

**Cashel's Cove Crafts.** Tucked away in the woods overlooking Mortier Bay is this little treasure of a store filled with only 100% Newfoundland-made products: there are traditional outport hooked and poked rugs, locally made quilts, pottery, homespun knits, jewelry, native juniper-wood turnings, walking sticks, and Screech tea (screech is rum). The owner encourages visitors to walk down the footpaths to the woodlands along the shoreline or to the beach. ✉ *Take Rte. 210 (Burin Peninsula) at Goobies, make an immediate right turn as you enter Spanish Room, and follow signs to Cashel's Cove, Burin, Newfoundland and Labrador, Canada* ✆ *Box 665, Marystown, Newfoundland and Labrador, Canada* ☎ *709/279–1846* ⊕ *www.cashelscovecrafts.com* ☉ *Daily 9–9.*

# GRAND BANK

*62 km (38 mi) west of Burin.*

One of the loveliest communities in Newfoundland, Grand Bank has a fascinating history as an important fishing center. Because of trading patterns, the architecture here was influenced more by Halifax, Boston, and Bar Harbor, Maine, than by the rest of Newfoundland.

### EXPLORING

**Provincial Seamen's Museum.** A sail-shaped building holds the Provincial Seamen's Museum. The museum's exhibits display items used to live and work on land and on the sea from the 1800s to the present. ✉ *54 Marine Dr., Grand Bank, Newfoundland and Labrador, Canada* ☎ *709/832–1484* ⊕ *www.therooms.ca/museum/prov_museums.asp* 💷 *C$2.50* ☉ *Mid April–early Oct., Mon.–Sat. 9–4:45, Sun. noon–4:45.*

### WHERE TO STAY

*For expanded hotel reviews, visit Fodors.com.*

$   ⌂ **Granny's Motor Inn.** Guest rooms here may be small and not exactly cutting edge in design, but they're clean and cozy and the owners are friendly. **Pros:** helpful hosts; 5 km (3 mi) to St-Pierre ferry; home-cooked meals. **Cons:** no bar; secondhand smoke can drift in through open window. ✉ *33 Grandview Blvd., Grand Bank, Newfoundland and Labrador, Canada* ☎ *709/832–2355, 888/275–1098* ⊕ *www. grannysmotorinn.ca* ⥿ *10 rooms* ⚒ *In-room: no a/c, Wi-Fi. In-hotel: restaurant, parking.*

# ST-PIERRE AND MIQUELON

*70-min ferry ride from Fortune, which is 10 km (6 mi) south of Grand Bank.*

The islands of St-Pierre and Miquelon, France's only territory in North America, are a ferry ride away if you crave French cuisine or a bottle of perfume. Shopping and eating are both popular pastimes here. The bakeries open early, so there's always piping-hot fresh bread for breakfast, and bargain hunters can find reasonably priced wines from all over France. An interesting side trip via boat takes you to see seals, seabirds, and other wildlife, plus the huge sandbar (formed on the bones of shipwrecks) that now connects formerly separate Great and Little Miquelon.

### GETTING HERE AND AROUND

You can fly to St-Pierre from St. John's with Air Saint Pierre or take a ferry from Fortune. Once you arrive in St-Pierre everything is within a short taxi drive or walking distance.

## EXPLORING

**Air Saint-Pierre.** Air Saint-Pierre offers international flight service between St. John's and the French island of Saint-Pierre as well as domestic service between the islands of Miquelon and Saint-Pierre. ⌂ *BP 4225, Saint-Pierre and Miquelon, France F-97500* ☎ *877/277–7765* ⊕ *www. airsaintpierre.com.*

Visitors to the islands must carry proof of citizenship—even U.S. citizens must have a passport, and Canadians should have a passport or a government-issued photo ID. Because of the ferry schedule, a trip to St-Pierre means an overnight stay in a hotel or a pension, the French equivalent of a B&B. Note that St-Pierre time is a half hour ahead of Newfoundland, so make sure you adjust your watch for the ferry schedule.

**St-Pierre and Miquelon Tourist Board.** Contact the St-Pierre and Miquelon Tourist Board for accommodations and additional information about traveling to these French islands. ⌂ *BP 4274, Saint-Pierre and Miquelon, France 97500* ☎ *508/410–200* ⊕ *www.tourisme-saint-pierre-et-miquelon.com.*

**St-Pierre Tours.** A passenger ferry operated by St-Pierre Tours leaves Fortune (south of Grand Bank) daily from April to June and twice a day in July and August; the crossing takes 90 minutes. Call for schedule and rates. ⊠ *Grand Bank, Newfoundland and Labrador, Canada* ☎ *709/832–2006, 800/563–2006* ⊕ *www.spmtours.com.*

## WHERE TO STAY

*For expanded hotel reviews, visit Fodors.com.*

$$$ ⌂ **Hotel Robert.** Gangster Al Capone stayed in a wing of this place when he ran rum through St-Pierre during prohibition, and you can see his hat in the mini Prohibition-era museum on-site. **Pros:** on the waterfront, a five-minute walk from ferry; ocean views from breakfast room. **Cons:** no elevator; no room service. ⊠ *Rue du 11 Novembre, Saint-Pierre and Miquelon, France* ☎ *508/412–419,* ⬦ *43 rooms* ⌂ *In-room: no a/c, Wi-Fi. In-hotel: restaurant, laundry facilities* ⦿ *Breakfast.*

# GANDER AND AROUND

Gander, in east-central Newfoundland, is known for its airport and its aviation history. North of it is Notre Dame Bay, an area of rugged coastline and equally rugged islands that was once the domain of the now extinct Beothuk tribe. Only the larger islands are currently inhabited. Before English settlers moved into the area in the late 18th and early 19th centuries, it was seasonally occupied by French fisherfolk. Local dialects preserve centuries-old words that have vanished elsewhere. The bay is swept by the cool Labrador Current, which carries icebergs south through Iceberg Alley; the coast is also a good whale-watching area.

# GANDER

*367 km (228 mi) north of Grand Bank; 331 km (207 mi) west of St. John's; 149 km (93 mi) west of Clarenville.*

Gander, a busy town of 9,500 people, is notable for its aviation history. It also has a variety of lodging options and is a good base for travel in this part of the province. After September 11, 2001, Gander gained international attention for having sheltered thousands of airline passengers whose planes were rerouted here.

## GETTING HERE AND AROUND

Gander's airport is just east of town and most visitor services are conveniently located along the Trans-Canada Highway. Gander is also a jumping-off point for popular Twillingate and surrounding area. Highway 330 leads north, eventually connecting to Highway 340 to Twillingate. Alternately travelers wanting to visit Change Islands and Fogo Island will branch off on Highway 335. Causeways now allow you to drive to Twillingate but you will need to get the ferry schedule to travel to Change and Fogo Islands (⊕ *www.tw.gov.nl.ca/ferryservices/ schedules/c_fogo.html*). With its airport, Gander also makes for a possible fly and drive option for those visitors with limited time.

## EXPLORING

**Gander International Airport.** During World War II, Gander International Airport was chosen by the Canadian and U.S. air forces as a major strategic air base because of its favorable weather and secure location. After the war, the airport became an international hub for civilian travel; today it's a major air-traffic control center. ⊠ *1000 James Blvd., Gander, Newfoundland and Labrador, Canada* ☎ *709/256–6666* ⊕ *www. ganderairport.com.*

Ⓒ **North Atlantic Aviation Museum.** The North Atlantic Aviation Museum gives an expansive view of Gander's and Newfoundland's roles in aviation. In addition to viewing models (including a World War II Lockheed Hudson and a Voodoo fighter jet) and photographs, you can climb into the cockpit of a real DC-3. There's also a unique aviation gift shop. ⊠ *135 Trans-Canada Hwy.(Rte. 1), between hospital and visitor information center, Gander, Newfoundland and Labrador, Canada* ☎ *709/256–2923* ⊕ *www.naam.ca* ✉ *C$5* ☉ *May–mid-June, weekdays 9–5; mid-June–Labor Day, daily 9–8; Labor Day–Sept., weekdays 9–6; Oct.–Nov., weekdays 9–5.*

**Silent Witness Memorial.** The Silent Witness Memorial marks the spot where, on December 12, 1985, an Arrow Air DC-8 carrying the 101st Airborne Division home for Christmas crashed, killing 256 American soldiers and civilian flight crew. The memorial, eastbound on the Trans-Canada Highway 4 km (2½ mi) from Gander, is two or three minutes off the highway on a rough gravel road, but it's a must-see. The site, a clearing in the woods overlooking the grandeur of Gander Lake, is moving, and the sculpture itself, of a boy and girl holding the hands of a peacekeeper, is quite poignant. ⊠ *Gander, Newfoundland and Labrador, Canada.*

**OFF THE
BEATEN
PATH**

**Change Islands and Fogo Island.** Modernity arrived late here, and old expressions and accents still survive, so these outposts feel frozen in time. Change Islands (⊕ *www.changeislands.ca*), a town with outbuildings built on rock outcrops and on stilts, is a nice place for a quiet walk. Tilting, on the far end of Fogo Island, is famous for its "vernacular" architecture, two-story houses with typically one of three floor plans. The Dwyer Fishing Premises won an award for preservation of the architectural heritage of Newfoundland and Labrador and is part of the Tilting National Historic Site (☎ *709/658–7236 or 709/658–7381* ⊕ *www.townoftilting.com*) along with the Lane House Museum, the Old Irish Cemetery, and Sandy Cove Park, open mid-June through mid-September, 10 to 8. There's overnight lodging at the four-room Foley's Place B&B in Tilting (☎ *709/658–7244 or 866/658–7244*). You can also stay in the community of Fogo at Peg's Bed and Breakfast (☎ *709/266– 2393 or 709/266–7130*). Fogo is known for its hiking trails, including Brimstone Head, one of the four corners of the earth according to the Flat Earth Society. More recently Fogo Island has begun to reinvent itself with many modern artist studios and residency arts projects (⊕ *www.shorefast.org*). To get to Fogo Island and Change Islands you must take a short ferry trip (⊕ *www.tw.gov.nl.ca/ferryservices*) from Farewell. To get to Farewell from Grand Falls–Windsor, go east on the Trans-Canada Highway to Route 340. Take Route 340 north to Route 335, which takes you through scenic coastal communities. Alternately, from Gander take Route 330 north to 331 and then to 335. Farewell is at the end of Route 335.

**ferry.** To get here, you can take a ferry from Farewell to either Change Islands or Fogo Island. ⊠ *Gander, Newfoundland and Labrador, Canada* ☎ *709/627–3492, 888/638-5454* ⊕ *www.gov.nl.ca/ferryservices* ⊠ *Grand Falls-Windsor, Newfoundland and Labrador, Canada.*

## WHERE TO STAY

*For expanded hotel reviews, visit Fodors.com.*

$ 🖥 **Hotel Gander.** You won't get lost finding this hotel right on the Trans-Canada Highway. **Pros:** vehicles with boat trailers can park easily; bright, cheerful dining room; bar has outside patio; children under 12 stay and eat for free. **Cons:** living room in suites not air-conditioned; highway traffic makes front rooms noisy. ⊠ *100 Trans-Canada Hwy., Gander, Newfoundland and Labrador, Canada* ☎ *709/256–3931, 800/563-2988* ⊕ *www.hotelgander.com* ⏎ *147 rooms, 1 jacuzzi suite, 3 regular suites, 2 extended stay* ⟡ *In-room: a/c, Wi-Fi. In-hotel: restaurant, bar, pool, gym, laundry facilities, some pets allowed.*

$ 🖥 **Sinbad's Hotel and Suites.** Sinbad's is hard to find but worth looking for if you're trying to escape highway noise. **Pros:** away from the highway; kids under 12 eat free; spacious sink area separate from bathroom. **Cons:** long corridors mean long walks dragging luggage; smoking rooms are still available. ⊠ *133 Bennett Dr., Gander, Newfoundland and Labrador, Canada* ✉ *Box 450, Gander, Newfoundland and Labrador, Canada A1V 1W8* ☎ *709/651–2678, 800/563-8330* ⊕ *www. steelehotels.com* ⏎ *100 rooms, 2 suites, 1 efficiency unit* ⟡ *In-room: a/c, Wi-Fi. In-hotel: restaurant, bar, gym, laundry facilities, business center, some pets allowed.*

4

# BOYD'S COVE

*66 km (41 mi) north of Gander.*

Between 1650 and 1720, the Beothuks' main summer camp on the northeast coast was at the site of what is now Boyd's Cove. The coastline in and near Boyd's Cove is somewhat sheltered by Twillingate Island and New World Island, linked to the shore by short causeways.

## EXPLORING

**Beothuk Interpretation Centre.** Explore the lives of the Beothuks, an extinct First Nations people who succumbed in the early 19th century to a combination of disease and battle with European settlers. A 1.5-km trail leads to the archaeological site that was inhabited from about 1650 to 1720, when pressure from settlers drove the Beothuks from this part of the coast. Walk softly to feel "The Spirit of the Beothuk," represented in a commanding bronze statue that stands almost hidden in the woods. ✉ *Rte. 340, Boyd's Cove, Newfoundland and Labrador, Canada* ☎ *709/656–3114, 800/563–6353* ⊕ *www.seethesites.ca* 🎟 *C$3* ☉ *Mid-May–Sept., daily 10–5:30.*

# TWILLINGATE

*31 km (19 mi) north of Boyd's Cove.*

The inhabitants of this scenic old fishing village make their living from the sea and have been doing so for nearly two centuries. Colorful houses, rocky waterfront cliffs, a local museum, and a nearby lighthouse add to the town's appeal. One of the best places on the island to see icebergs, Twillingate is known to the locals as Iceberg Alley. These majestic and dangerous mountains of ice are awe inspiring to see when they're grounded in early summer. With lots of lodging options, Twillingate makes a good base for exploring the many small communities in this region.

**Fish, Fun & Folk Festival.** Every year on the last full weekend in July, the town is the site of the Fish, Fun & Folk Festival, where you can enjoy fish cooked every possible way while listening to live folk music. ✉ *Twillingate, Newfoundland and Labrador, Canada* ☎ *709/884–2678* ⊕ *www.fishfunfolkfestival.com.*

## WHERE TO STAY

*For expanded hotel reviews, visit Fodors.com.*

$    🏠 **Paradise Bed & Breakfast.** Watch icebergs and whales from the patio of
B&B/INN   this modern, one-story home. **Pros:** all rooms have private bathrooms; Continental breakfast is sometimes enhanced with a hot item as well. **Cons:** no a/c; two rooms have showers, not baths; house doesn't reflect Twillingate history and heritage. ✉ *192 Main St., Twillingate, Newfoundland and Labrador, Canada* ☎ *709/884–5683, 877/882–1999* ⊕ *www.capturegaia.com/paradiseb&b.html* 🛏 *3 rooms* ⌂ *In-room: no a/c, no TV, Wi-Fi. In-hotel: parking* ⊟ *No credit cards* ☉ *Closed Oct.–mid-May* ⦿ *Breakfast.*

$    🏠 **Toulinguet Inn Bed & Breakfast.** In this 1920s-era home on the har-
B&B/INN   bor front, rooms are old-fashioned, bright, and airy. **Pros:** sunroom

and balcony overlook the harbor; all rooms have private bath/shower; away from the highway. **Cons:** smoking permitted on balcony; no air conditioning in rooms. ⊠ *56 Main St., Twillingate, Newfoundland and Labrador, Canada* ☎ *709/884–2080, 888/447–8687* ⊕ *www.bbcanada. com/9127.html* ➪ *4 rooms* ⚲ *In-room: no a/c, Wi-Fi* ⊘ *Closed Oct.– mid-May* ⑩*Breakfast.*

### SPORTS AND THE OUTDOORS

**Twillingate Adventure Tours.** Twillingate Adventure Tours conducts two-hour guided cruises (C$50) on the M.V. *Daybreak* to see icebergs, whales, and seabirds. ⊠ *Twillingate, Newfoundland and Labrador, Canada* ☎ *709/884–5999, 888/447–8687* ⊕ *www.twillingateadventuretours. com.*

**The Iceberg Shop.** The Iceberg Shop offers two-hour cruises to see whales, icebergs, and birds. Iceberg photography is the company's specialty, and there are tours that take amateur photographers out to get that perfect shot. Tours are C$44 plus tax. ⊠ *Twillingate, Newfoundland and Labrador, Canada* ☎ *709/884–2242, 800/611–2374* ⊕ *www. icebergtours.ca.*

## GRAND FALLS–WINDSOR

*95 km (59 mi) west of Gander.*

This central Newfoundland town is an amalgamation of two towns that were joined in 1991. The papermaking town of Grand Falls was the quintessential company town, founded by British newspaper barons early in the 20th century, but the mill, which shipped newsprint all over the world, closed its doors in 2009. Windsor was once an important stop on the railway, but since its demise the city has foundered.

Near Grand Falls, the turnoff to highway 360 leads to the Bay d'Espoir area along the south coast of Newfoundland. This area offers the intrepid visitor a chance to step back in time to visit roadless communities like Gaultois, McCallum, and Rencontre East that are still accessed only be passenger ferry. For ferry information see ⊕ *www. tw.gov.nl.ca/ferryservices/schedules.* The Bay d'Espoir area is also home to the island's main center of Mi'Kmaq First Nations people in the community of Conne River.

**A Logger's Life Provincial Museum.** The hard lives of those who supplied wood for the paper mill are explored in this re-created 1920s-era logging camp. ⊠ *Off Rte. 1, Exit 17, 2 km (1 mi) west of Grand Falls-Windsor, Grand Falls-Windsor, Newfoundland and Labrador, Canada* ☎ *709/486–0492* ⊕ *www.therooms.ca/museum/prov_museums.asp* ▨ *C$2.50, includes Mary March Provincial Museum* ⊘ *Mid-May–mid-Sept., daily 9:30–4:30.*

**Mary March Provincial Museum.** Mary March was the European name given to Demasduit, one of the last Beothuks. Displays trace the lives and customs of aboriginal cultures in Newfoundland and Labrador. ⊠ *24 St. Catherine's St., Grand Falls-Windsor, Newfoundland and Labrador, Canada* ☎ *709/292–4522* ⊕ *www.therooms.ca/museum/*

*prov_museums.asp* ✑ *C$2.50, includes A Logger's Life Museum*
☉ *May–Oct., daily 9–4:45.*

**WHERE TO STAY**

*For expanded hotel reviews, visit Fodors.com.*

$$ 🏨 **Mount Peyton Hotel.** Make sure you get a room on the hotel side of the highway—motel rooms are smaller, more down-at-the-heels, and cut off from the hotel and restaurants. **Pros:** VIP suite is comfortable, with lots of extras like terry bathrobes and easy chairs to lounge in, if you're upgrading; good local music on Friday night at the pub with no cover. **Cons:** front rooms very close to highway traffic. ⊠ *214 Lincoln Rd., Grand Falls-Windsor, Newfoundland and Labrador, Canada* ☎ *709/489–2251, 800/563–4894* ⊕ *www.mountpeyton.com* ⌂ *101 hotel rooms, 31 motel rooms, 16 efficiency units* ⌂ *In-room: a/c, kitchen, Wi-Fi. In-hotel: restaurant, bar, gym, parking, some pets allowed.*

# WESTERN NEWFOUNDLAND

The Great Northern Peninsula is the northernmost visible extension of the Appalachian Mountains. Its eastern side is rugged and sparsely populated. The Viking Trail—Route 430 and its side roads—snakes along its western coast through Gros Morne National Park, fjords, sand dunes, and communities that have relied on lobster fishing for generations. At the tip of the peninsula, the Vikings established the first European settlement in North America a thousand years ago, but for thousands of years before their arrival, the area was home to native peoples who hunted, fished, and gathered berries and herbs.

Corner Brook boasts a fabulous natural setting and the nearby Humber River is world renowned for its salmon fishing. To the south, the Port au Port Peninsula, west of Stephenville, shows the French influence in Newfoundland, distinct from the farming valleys of the southwest, which were settled by Scots. A ferry from Nova Scotia docks at Port aux Basques in the far southwest corner.

**GETTING HERE**

If you're coming from Nova Scotia, there's a car ferry to Port aux Basques. Otherwise, there's the airport in Deer Lake.

## DEER LAKE

*208 km (129 mi) west of Grand Falls–Windsor.*

Deer Lake was once just another small town on the Trans-Canada Highway, but the opening of Gros Morne National Park in the early 1970s and the construction of Route 430, a first-class paved highway passing right through to St. Anthony, changed all that.

**GETTING HERE**

Today, with an airport and car rentals available, Deer Lake is a good starting point for a fly–drive vacation, and is open all year. There are connections from eastern and central Canada, and from St. John's.

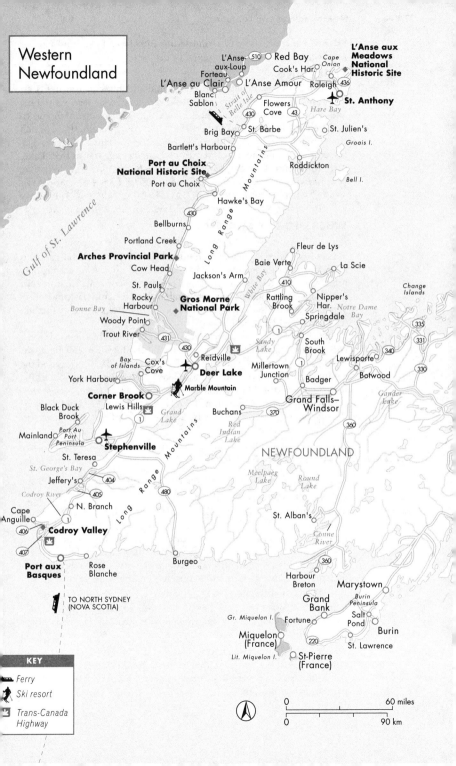

# Western Newfoundland

L'Anse aux Meadows National Historic Site

Red Bay
Cape Onion
Cook's Har.
L'Anse-aux-Loup
Forteau
L'Anse au Clair
Blanc Sablon
L'Anse Amour
Raleigh
St. Anthony
Strait of Belle Isle
Flowers Cove
Hare Bay
St. Barbe
St. Julien's
Brig Bay
Groais I.
Bartlett's Harbour
Bell I.
Roddickton

**Port au Choix National Historic Site**
Port au Choix

Hawke's Bay

Long Range Mountains

Bellburns

Fleur de Lys
Portland Creek

**Arches Provincial Park**
Baie Verte
La Scie
Cow Head
Jackson's Arm
St. Pauls
Change Islands
Rocky Harbour
White Bay
Rattling Brook
Nipper's Har.
**Gros Morne National Park**
Notre Dame Bay
Woody Point
Springdale
Trout River
Sandy Lake
South Brook
Reidville
Lewisporte
Cox's Cove
Millertown Junction
Botwood
York Harbour
**Deer Lake**
Badger
Gander Lake
**Corner Brook**
Marble Mountain
Lewis Hills
Grand Lake
Buchans
**Grand Falls–Windsor**
Black Duck Brook
Red Indian Lake
Mainland
Port Au Port Peninsula
**Stephenville**
NEWFOUNDLAND
St. Teresa
St. George's Bay
Meelpaeg Lake
Round Lake
Jeffery's
Codroy River
Cape Anguille
N. Branch
St. Alban's
**Codroy Valley**
Conne River
**Port aux Basques**
Rose Blanche
Burgeo
Harbour Breton
Marystown
TO NORTH SYDNEY (NOVA SCOTIA)
Grand Bank
Burin Peninsula
Salt Pond
Burin
Gr. Miquelon I.
Fortune
St. Lawrence
Miquelon (France)
Lit. Miquelon I.
St-Pierre (France)

Gulf of St. Lawrence

Bay of Islands

Long Range Mountains

## KEY
🚢 Ferry
⛷ Ski resort
🛣 Trans-Canada Highway

0 — 60 miles
0 — 90 km

From the airport there is a shuttle bus into Deer Lake (and Corner Brook), as well as major car rental outlets.

## EXPLORING

**Newfoundland Insectarium.** The Newfoundland Insectarium holds an intriguing collection of live and preserved insects, spiders, scorpions, and a beehive with 10,000 honeybees. The greenhouse is home to hundreds of live tropical butterflies. Check out the gift shop, which sometimes has lollipops with edible dried scorpions inside for sale. The Insectarium is one minute off the Trans-Canada Highway at Deer Lake; turn north onto Route 430. ⊠ *Rte. 430, 2 Bonne Bay Rd., Reidville, Newfoundland and Labrador, Canada* ☎ *709/635–4545, 866/635–5454* ⊕ *www.nfinsectarium.com* ▢ *C$10.50* ⊙ *July and Aug., daily 9–6; May, June, Sept., and Oct., weekdays 9–5, Sat. 10–5, Sun. noon–5.*

## WHERE TO EAT AND STAY

*For expanded hotel reviews, visit Fodors.com.*

$ AMERICAN

✕**Deer Lake Irving Big Stop.** Good home-cooked meals and burgers and fries, healthy options like salads and salmon, and clean washrooms make this chain a welcome pit stop. The adjacent convenience store sells gifts, souvenirs, some outdoor apparel, magazines, and basic motoring supplies. ⊠ *Rte. 1, Deer Lake, Newfoundland and Labrador, Canada* ☎ *709/635–2129.*

$$

▭**Deer Lake Motel.** The motel is clean and comfortable, but ask for a room in the back because the ones facing the highway can be noisy. **Pros:** easy to find, at the junction of the Trans-Canada Highway and the Viking Trail. **Cons:** restaurant more like a coffee shop; highway traffic noisy; no elevator. ⊠ *15 Trans-Canada Hwy., Deer Lake, Newfoundland and Labrador, Canada* ☎ *709/635–2108, 800/563–2144* ⊕ *www.deerlakemotel.com* ↗ *55 rooms, 2 suites* ⚁ *In-room: a/c, Wi-Fi. In-hotel: restaurant, bar, parking.*

# GROS MORNE NATIONAL PARK

*46 km (29 mi) north of Deer Lake on Rte. 430.*

## GETTING HERE AND AROUND

**Fodor's**Choice
★

Traveling north from Deer Lake, the main entry point is just before the community of Wiltondale. Continue on Highway 430 to Rocky Harbour for the park's main visitor center, as well as the scenic Western Brook Pond boat tour and Cow Head, at the northern end of the park. If you're headed to the south side of the park with its geologically spectacular Tableland, at Wiltondale turn left on Highway 431.

**Gros Morne National Park.** Because of its geological uniqueness and immense splendor, this park has been named a UNESCO World Heritage Site. Camping and hiking are popular recreations, and boat tours are available.

To see Gros Morne properly you should allow yourself at least two days, but most people, once they're here, would appreciate having a few more. Scenic **Bonne Bay**, a deep fjord, divides the park into two parts, north and south.

### Northern Gros Morne.

Head to the northern side of the park, along coastal Route 430, to visit Rocky Harbour with its range of restaurants and lodgings, plus a luxurious indoor public pool and large hot tub—the perfect place to soothe tired limbs after a strenuous day; it's open late June to early September. You'll also find the excellent **Gros Morne Visitor's Center** (*Rocky Harbour, 709/458–2417 or 709/458–2066, www.pc.gc.ca, last visit Aug. 11*), with displays and videos about the park.

The most popular attraction in the northern portion of Gros Morne is the boat tour of **Western Brook Pond.** You park at a lot on Route 430 and take a 45-minute walk to the boat dock through an interesting mix of bog and woods. Cliffs rise 2,000 feet on both sides of the gorge, and high waterfalls tumble over ancient rocks. Those in good shape can tackle the 16-km (10-mi) hike up **Gros Morne Mountain**, at 2,644 feet the second-highest peak in Newfoundland. Weather permitting, the reward for your effort is a unique arctic landscape and spectacular views. The park's **northern coast** has an unusual mix of sand beaches, rock pools, and trails through tangled dwarf forests (called tuckamore forests locally). Sunsets seen from **Lobster Head Cove Lighthouse** are spectacular. Keep an eye out for whales, and visit the lighthouse museum devoted to the history of the area. At the very north end of the park is the community of **Cow Head,** home to the Gros Morne Theatre Festival's popular summer program of theater and music. Also nearby, Shallow Bay Beach has a two-mile stretch of soft sand ready made for beach combing.

**Norris Point** is known for its Photographer's Lookout, best seen in the morning when the sun lights up the distant Tablelands.

The **Bonne Bay Marine Station** (*709/458–2874 or 709/458–2550, www.bonnebay.ca, C$6.25*), at Norris Point is a must, especially for kids. It offers a 45-minute guided aquarium tour which includes a touch tank. There is also a display area with live exhibits and a gift shop. It's open mid May to mid-October daily 9–5.

### Southern Gros Morne

Woody Point, a charming community of old houses and imported Lombardy poplars, is in the south part of the park, on Route 431. The **Discovery Centre** (*Rte. 431 on the outskirts of Woody Point, 709/458–2417, May 20–June 24, daily 9–5; June 25–Sept. 5, Mon., Tues., and Thurs.–Sat. 9–6, Wed. and Sun. 9–9; Sept. 6–Oct. 10, daily 9–5*) is the main center for interpreting the geology of the park. It also has educational programs on natural history as well as a craft shop. At the back of the center's parking lot is the fine Lookout Hills trail, a 5-km (3-mi) trek with outstanding views of Bonne Bay, Gros Morne Mountain, and the Tablelands.

On the south side of the park, rising behind Woody Point, are the **Tablelands,** a unique rock massif that was raised from the earth's mantle through tectonic upheaval. Its rocks are toxic to most plant life and have weathered to a rusty brown color. The Tablelands provide a remarkable exposure of mantle rock, rarely seen at the earth's surface; it's the main reason Gros Morne National Park has received UNESCO

World Heritage status. The small community of **Trout River** is at the western end of Route 431 on the Gulf of St. Lawrence. You pass the scenic Trout River pond on the way there. The **Green Gardens Trail**, a spectacular hike, is also nearby, but be prepared to do a bit of climbing on your return journey. The trail passes through the Tablelands barrens and descends sharply to a coastline of eroded cliffs and green meadows. ⊠ *Gros Morne National Park, Newfoundland and Labrador, Canada* ⊕ *www.pc.gc.ca* ⊠ *C$9.80.*

## WHERE TO EAT

$$
╳**Fisherman's Landing.** The wide-ranging menu here has lots of seafood

SEAFOOD
but many other options, too. Both the food and the service are good and reliable, which means that it can get busy; you can always browse the crafts shop upstairs until your table's ready. It's open 6 am to 11 pm. ⊠ *44 Main St., Rocky Harbour, Newfoundland and Labrador, Canada* ☎ *709/458–2060.*

$$$
╳**Java Jack's Restaurant and Gallery.** The pleasures of this lively, busy

CANADIAN
restaurant begin with a stroll by the meticulously kept organic garden,

Fodor's Choice
where you can see the herbs, peas, and other vegetables you'll enjoy

★
inside. Stop in to pick up a take-away bag lunch (maybe a sandwich of shredded pork with partridgeberry-honey mustard) for the boat trip to Western Brook Pond, or eat in; there are great views of the harbor. Dinner is a real treat. Wines are reasonably priced, and the menu has many seafood options—the pan-seared scallops in mild mango curry are especially good—as well as popular vegan and vegetarian dishes. The restaurant also doubles as a gallery; work by Atlantic Canadian artists (all for sale) decorates the walls. ⊠ *88 Main St. N, Box 250, Rocky Harbour, Newfoundland and Labrador, Canada* ☎ *709/458–3004* ⊙ *Closed Tues. and Oct.–mid-May.*

$$$
╳**Seaside Restaurant.** This two-story restaurant overlooking the ocean

SEAFOOD
prepares fresh seafood in traditional, innovative, Newfoundland style. A perfect meal might start with Northern scallops served on greens brightened with deep burgundy partridgeberries, followed by grilled shark. Cod tongues—a secret recipe—are popular and offered throughout the season, and the ocean catfish is also highly recommended. The boardwalk is delightful for a stroll before or after you eat, and you can watch the sunset from the upper deck. ⊠ *Main St., Trout River, Newfoundland and Labrador, Canada* ☎ *709/451–3461* ⊙ *Closed Oct. 1–May 24.*

## WHERE TO STAY

*For expanded hotel reviews, visit Fodors.com.*

$$
🛏 **A-1 Wildflowers Country Inn.** Set back from the main road on a lovely

B&B/INN
property full of trees, this grand 80-year-old clapboard house over-

★
looks the ocean. **Pros:** common room with fridge; guided back-country snowmobile tours in season. **Cons:** no a/c; some rooms have shower, not bath. ⊠ *108 Main St. N, Rocky Harbour, Newfoundland and Labrador, Canada* 🕭 *Box 291, Rocky Harbour, Newfoundland and Labrador, Canada A0K 4N0* 🖭 *709/458–3000, 888/811–7378* ⊕ *www. wildflowerscountryinn.ca* ⏎ *5 rooms, 1 cottage* ⅃ *In-room: no a/c, Wi-Fi. In-hotel: parking* ⑂ *Breakfast.*

**$** ⌂ **Blanchard House.** Built in 1904,
**B&B/INN** this spotlessly clean heritage home
has been renovated but retains
its original character, accented
by antique furniture. **Pros:** some
rooms have gorgeous bay windows; all rooms have private bath;
one hot item daily with Continental
breakfast. **Cons:** no Internet access
on-site; three rooms have shower
but no tub; small beds. ✉ *12
Blanchard La., Woody Point, Newfoundland and Labrador, Canada*
☎ *709/451–3236, 877/951–3236*
⊕ *www.crockercabins.com* 🛏 *4
rooms* ⅃ *In-room: no a/c, no TV.
In-hotel: laundry facilities, parking* ⊘ *Closed early Oct.–late May*
⦿ *Breakfast.*

> ## LEAVE THE CAR BEHIND
>
> You can drive to the pretty town
> of Woody Point, but why not leave
> the car behind and take a boat?
> Leave your wheels at Norris Point
> and take the water taxi (BonTours,
> *see below for contact info*). The
> journey takes 15 minutes, and
> you'll probably see whales and
> kayakers out on the water. In
> Woody Point, you can have lunch
> and spend the day strolling or
> stay overnight. The water taxi
> leaves Norris Point at 9 am, 12:30
> pm, and 5 pm daily and leaves
> Woody Point roughly half an hour
> later, mid-June through August
> (C$12 return).

**$$** ⌂ **Fisherman's Landing Inn.** Although
it's not on the water as the name
implies, this is a spacious, bright, and well-maintained property. **Pros:**
crafts shop off lobby; cross-country skiing and snowshoeing winter
packages. **Cons:** a bit overpriced; limited food and wine menu; 2-km
(1¼-mi) walk from most other eateries; away from the waterfront.
✉ *2129 West Link Rd., Rocky Harbour, Newfoundland and Labra-
dor, Canada* ⅅ *Box 124, Rocky Harbour, Newfoundland and Lab-
rador, Canada A0K 4N0* ☎ *709/458–2711, 866/458–2711* ⊕ *www.
fishermanslandinginn.com* 🛏 *40 rooms* ⅃ *In-room: a/c, Wi-Fi. In-hotel:
restaurant, bar, gym, laundry facilities, parking.*

**$$** ⌂ **Gros Morne Resort.** Rooms in the front of this hotel overlook the
ocean; those in the rear face the Long Range Mountains and St. **Pros:**
closest accommodation to Western Brook Pond; 18-hole golf course
that looks out on the Long Range Mountains; some rooms have views
of St. Paul's Inlet. **Cons:** no laundry facilities or service. ✉ *Rte. 430,
Box 100, St. Paul's, Newfoundland and Labrador, Canada* ☎ *709/243–
2606, 888/243–2644* ⊕ *www.grosmorneresort.com* 🛏 *12 rooms, 6
suites* ⅃ *In-room: a/c, Wi-Fi. In-hotel: restaurant, bar, parking.*

**$$** ⌂ **Ocean View Hotel.** This two-story hotel is right on the water and has
an on-site kiosk for Bon Tours, which conducts sightseeing boat trips on
Western Brook Pond and Bonne Bay. **Pros:** near craft stores and dining
options; there's a small strand of beach across the street. **Cons:** open win-
dows bring loud music from pub; pub accessible only with cover charge.
✉ *38–42 Main St., Rocky Harbour, Newfoundland and Labrador, Can-
ada* ⅅ *Box 129, Rocky Harbour, Newfoundland and Labrador, Canada
A0K 4N0* ☎ *709/458–2730, 800/563–9887* ⊕ *www.theoceanview.ca*
🛏 *47 rooms, 5 suites* ⅃ *In-room: a/c. In-hotel: restaurant, bar, parking.*

**$$** ⌂ **Sugar Hill Inn.** Host Vince McCarthy's culinary talents and educated
**B&B/INN** palate—he imports Old World wines and Italian olive oil, buys his fish
★ fresh from the fishermen, and grows his own asparagus and herbs—have

earned this inn a reputation for fine wine and food. **Pros:** cedar-lined hot tub and sauna; water comes from a spring on the property. **Cons:** exterior doesn't suggest the quality inside; surroundings could be prettier. ⊠ *115–129 Main St., Box 100, Norris Point, Newfoundland and Labrador, Canada* ☎ *709/458–2147, 888/299–2147* ⊕ *www.sugarhillinn. nf.ca* ⊅ *10 rooms, 1 cottage* ⌂ *In-room: a/c, Wi-Fi. In-hotel: restaurant, bar, laundry facilities, parking, some pets allowed* ⊘ *Closed Nov.–mid-May; from mid-Feb. will open for group bookings of 3 or more rooms* |⊙| *Breakfast.*

### NIGHTLIFE AND THE ARTS

**Gros Morne Summer Music.** Gros Morne Summer Music provides a wide range of live musical offerings from mid-July to late August. The venues include locations in Woody Point and Norris Point. The main focus is classical music but you might hear jazz or traditional music by international artists on any given evening. ⊅ *30 Elwick Rd., Corner Brook, Newfoundland and Labrador, Canada A2H 2W6* ☎ *709/639–7293* ⊕ *www.gmsm.ca.*

**Gros Morne Theatre Festival.** The Gros Morne Theatre Festival provides first-rate summer entertainment in Cow Head at the northern end of Gros Morne National Park. Most productions are dramas, though there are some comedies and musical performances based on local stories and songs. ⊠ *193 Main St., Cow Head, Newfoundland and Labrador, Canada* ⊅ *Box 655, Newfoundland and Labrador, Canada A2H 6G1* ☎ *877/243–2899* ⊕ *www.theatrenewfoundland.com.*

### SPORTS AND THE OUTDOORS

**BonTours.** BonTours runs sightseeing boat tours of Western Brook Pond in Gros Morne National Park and on Bonne Bay as well as a water taxi service between Norris Point and Woody Point. ⊠ *Gros Morne National Park, Newfoundland and Labrador, Canada* ☎ *709/458–2016, 888/458–2016* ⊕ *www.bontours.ca.*

**Gros Morne Adventures.** Gros Morne Adventures offers sea kayaking on Bonne Bay in Gros Morne National Park, as well as guided coastal and mountain hiking in the area. ⊠ *Gros Morne National Park, Newfoundland and Labrador, Canada* ☎ *709/458–2722, 800/685–4624* ⊕ *www. grosmorneadventures.com.*

## ARCHES PROVINCIAL PARK

*20 km (12 mi) north of Gros Morne National Park.*

**The Arches Provincial Park.** The Arches Provincial Park is a geological curiosity: its rock formations were made millions of years ago by wave action and undersea currents. The succession of caves through a bed of dolomite was later raised above sea level by tectonic upheaval. This is a good place to stop for a picnic, to break up your driving. ⊠ *Rte. 430, Arches Provincial Park, Newfoundland and Labrador, Canada* ☎ *709/635–4520* ⊕ *www.gov.nl.ca/parks* ⊞ *Free* ⊘ *Early June–mid Oct.*

**EN ROUTE**  **Long Range Mountains.** Continuing north on Route 430, parallel to the Gulf of St. Lawrence, you'll find yourself refreshingly close to the ocean and the wave-tossed beaches. The Long Range Mountains to your right reminded Jacques Cartier, who saw them in 1534 as he was exploring the area on behalf of France, of the long, rectangular-shaped farm buildings of his home village in France. Small villages are interspersed with rivers teeming with salmon and trout. ⊠ *Arches Provincial Park, Newfoundland and Labrador, Canada.*

### EXPLORING

**Port au Choix National Historic Site.** The remains of Maritime Archaic and Dorset people have been found in abundance along this coast, and Port au Choix National Historic Site has an interesting interpretation center about them. An archaeological dig in the area has also discovered an ancient village. Ask at the interpretation center for directions to it.

At Plum Point you have two choices: you can drive to St. Anthony via Route 430, which travels along the Strait of Belle Isle before heading inland. Alternately you can take Route 432, which joins Route 430 near the St. Anthony airport. For variety most visitors travel one way going and the other way coming back. ⊠ *Off Rte. 430, Arches Provincial Park, Newfoundland and Labrador, Canada* ☎ *709/458–2417, 709/861–3522* ⊕ *www.pc.gc.ca* ☒ *C$7.80* ☉ *June 1–mid Oct., daily 9–6.*

## L'ANSE AUX MEADOWS NATIONAL HISTORIC SITE

*210 km (130 mi) northeast of Arches Provincial Park.*

Fodor's Choice ★ **L'Anse aux Meadows National Historic Site.** Around the year 1000, Vikings from Greenland and Iceland founded the first European settlement in North America, near the northern tip of Newfoundland. They arrived in the New World 500 years before Columbus but stayed only a few years and were forgotten for centuries. It was only in 1960 that the Norwegian team of Helge and Anne Stine Ingstad discovered the remains of the Viking settlement's long sod huts. Today L'Anse aux Meadows is a UNESCO World Heritage Site. Parks Canada has a fine visitor center and has reconstructed some of the huts to give you a sense of centuries past. An interpretation program introduces you to the food, clothing, and way of life of that time. ⊠ *Rte. 436, St. Anthony, Newfoundland and Labrador, Canada* ☎ *709/623–2608* ⊕ *www.pc.gc.ca/eng/lhn-nhs/ nl/meadows/index.aspx* ☒ *C$11.70* ☉ *June–early Oct., daily 9–6.*

### EXPLORING

☾ **Norstead.** Two kilometers (1 mi) east of L'Anse aux Meadows is Norstead, a reconstruction of an 11th-century Viking port, with a chieftain's hall, church, and ax-throwing arena. Interpreters in period dress answer questions as they go about their Viking business. ⊠ *Rte. 436, St. Anthony, Newfoundland and Labrador, Canada* 709/623–2828, 877/620–2828 ⊕ *www.norstead.com* ☒ *C$10* ☉ *June–mid-Sept., daily 9–6.*

### WHERE TO EAT

$$$
SEAFOOD
Fodor's Choice ★

✕ **Norseman Restaurant.** One of the attractions of this restaurant on the harbor front is that you can pick your own lobster from a crate. The extensive wine list accompanying the menu that features fresh mussels, crab, and shrimp from the area, as well as caribou when available, is another plus. The paintings, jewelry, and carvings on display are for sale, and there's live traditional music every Tuesday and Friday in July and

August. ✉ *Turn right at end of Rte. 436, L'Anse aux Meadows, Newfoundland and Labrador, Canada* ☎ *709/623–2370, 877/623–2018* ⊕ *www.valhalla-lodge.com/restaurant* ⊘ *Closed late Sept.–mid-May.*

## WHERE TO STAY

*For expanded hotel reviews, visit Fodors.com.*

**$$$$** 🏨 **Quirpon Lighthouse Inn B&B.** This restored 1920s lighthouse is on a small (7 km by 1½ km) island off Quirpon (pronounced kar-poon), on the northern tip of Newfoundland; it's about a 3½-hour drive north of Cow Head (take Rte. 430 to Rte. 436). Getting here is half the fun. You can take Linkum Tours' regular boat service or one of the two intriguing alternatives: kayak over or be dropped at the near end of the island and walk the 5 km (3 mi) to the inn (your luggage will meet you there). Once there you can stay in the lightkeeper's house, a registered heritage structure, or next door at the 1960s house of the assistant. **Pros:** indoor whale-watching station; package includes return boat trip and all meals; visit L'Anse aux Meadows by boat. **Cons:** the only option is the full package. ✉ *Quirpon Island, St. Anthony, Newfoundland and Labrador, Canada* ☎ *709/634–2285, 877/254–6586* ⊕ *www.linkumtours.com* 🛏 *10 rooms* ⚘ *In-room: no a/c. In-hotel: restaurant* ⊘ *Closed Oct.–Apr.* ¶⊙¶ *All meals.*

**¢** 🏨 **Tickle Inn at Cape Onion.** This refurbished, century-old fisherman's

**B&B/INN** house on the beach is probably the northernmost residence on the island of Newfoundland. The setting is beautiful, and you can relax by the Franklin stove in the parlor after exploring the coast or L'Anse aux Meadows (about 45 km [28 mi] away). The atmosphere is informal, and guests often mingle. Evening meals are available at an additional cost. **Pros:** close to Burnt Cape ecological reserve; optional three-course dinner reasonably priced (C$25). **Cons:** meals served at one table with the owner hosting; small bedrooms; no rooms with private bath. ✉ *R.R. 1, Cape Onion, Newfoundland and Labrador, Canada* ☎ *709/452–4321 June–Sept., 866/814–8567, 709/739–5503 Oct.–May* ⊕ *www.tickleinn.net* 🛏 *4 rooms with shared bath* ⚘ *In-room: no a/c* ⊘ *Closed Oct.–May* ¶⊙¶ *Breakfast.*

**$** 🏨 **Valhalla Lodge Bed & Breakfast.** On a hill overlooking iceberg alley

**Fodor's Choice** 8 km (5 mi) from L'Anse aux Meadows, the Valhalla has quiet and

**★** brightly painted rooms with large windows, pine Scandinavian furniture, and handmade quilts. The rooms all have Viking names. Some fossils are part of the rock fireplace in the common room. Breakfast is a treat, especially pancakes with local berry sauce. Pulitzer Prize winner E. Annie Proulx, author of *The Shipping News*, stayed here while writing the novel. The owners of this lodge have bought and now rent out two homes in which Proulx lived; you can even take her dory for a row. The Quoyle's is a three-bedroom A-frame house with a view of the ocean, and Wavey's is a low-ceilinged Newfoundland saltbox with two bedrooms. **Pros:** view of whales and icebergs from the lodge; sauna; sitting room with fireplace and patio. **Cons:** few services and restaurants within walking distance; some bathrooms small. ✉ *Rte. 436, Gunner's Cove,, Newfoundland and Labrador, Canada* ☎ *709/623–2018, 877/623–2018, 709/754–3105 off-season* ⊕ *www.valhalla-lodge.com*

➲ *5 rooms* ♿ *In-room: no a/c, Wi-Fi. In-hotel: laundry facilities, parking, some pets allowed* ☉ *Closed Oct.–Apr.* ⦿ *Breakfast.*

**$** ⊞ **Viking Nest/Viking Village Bed & Breakfast.** Thelma Hedderson owns
B&B/INN and oversees these two B&Bs on the same property, just 1 km (½ mi) from the Viking settlement at L'Anse aux Meadows. There are four rooms at the Viking Nest, though only one has a private bathroom. The Viking Village has five rooms, which are decorated with spruce walls and Scandinavian furniture. **Pros:** proximity to L'Anse aux Meadows; en suites in the Viking Village; full hot breakfast included. **Cons:** no elevator; Nest has only one room with private bath; no a/c. ✉ *Rte. 436, L'Anse aux Meadows, Newfoundland and Labrador, Canada* ☏ *877/858–2238* ⊕ *www.vikingvillage.ca and www.bbcanada.com/ vikingnest* ➲ *9 rooms, 6 with bath* ♿ *In-room: no a/c, no TV, Wi-Fi. In-hotel: parking* ☉ *Viking Village closed Oct. 15–May 1* ⦿ *Breakfast.*

# ST. ANTHONY

*16 km (10 mi) south of L'Anse aux Meadows.*

The northern part of the Great Northern Peninsula served as the setting for *The Shipping News,* E. Annie Proulx's 1993 Pulitzer Prize–winning novel. St. Anthony is built around a natural harbor on the eastern side of the Great Northern Peninsula, near its tip. If you take a trip out to the lighthouse, you may see an iceberg or two float by, and it's a good spot for whale-watching.

## EXPLORING

**Grenfell Historic Properties.** The Grenfell Historic Properties comprise Grenfell's house and a museum and interpretation center, all focusing on his life and work. Grenfell's house is located a short distance from the museum and interpretation center. ✉ *4 Maraval Rd., St. Anthony, Newfoundland and Labrador, Canada* ☏ *709/454–4010* ⊕ *www.grenfell-properties.com* ▣ *C$10* ☉ *May–Sept., daily 9–8.*

## WHERE TO EAT AND STAY

*For expanded hotel reviews, visit Fodors.com.*

**$$** ✗ **The Light Keeper's Seafood Restaurant.** Good seafood and solid Canadian
SEAFOOD fare are served in this former lighthouse keeper's home overlooking the ocean. Halibut, shrimp, crab, and cod are usually good bets, as is the seafood chowder. Watch whales and bergs (when they oblige) as you feast on bakeapple cheesecake for dessert. ✉ *21 Fishing Point Rd., St. Anthony, Newfoundland and Labrador, Canada* ☏ *709/454–4900, 877/454–4900* ☉ *Closed Oct.–late May.*

**$** ⊞ **Hotel North.** Completely refurbished in 2011, this centrally located hotel has clean and comfortable rooms and an on-site casual restaurant that serves a variety of decent family-style food. **Pros:** most rooms have ironing boards and all have minifridges and coffeemakers. **Cons:** parking for registration is congested; no landscaping. ✉ *19 West St., St. Anthony, Newfoundland and Labrador, Canada* ☏ *709/454–3300* ⊕ *www.hotelnorth.ca/three* ➲ *44 rooms* ♿ *In-room: a/c, Wi-Fi. In-hotel: restaurant, business center, parking.*

$$ ⬚ **Tuckamore Lodge & Country Inn.** About an hour from St. **Pros:** outdoor wooden sauna; canoes available to paddle on Southwest Pond; billiard table. **Cons:** meals served at communal tables; few dining options nearby. ✉ *1 Southwest Pond Rd., Box 100, Main Brook, Newfoundland and Labrador, Canada* ☎ *709/865–6361, 888/865–6361* ⊕ *www. tuckamorelodge.com* ⇨ *9 rooms, 3 suites* ⬙ *In-room: no a/c, Wi-Fi. In-hotel: gym, parking* ⦿ *Breakfast.*

### SPORTS AND THE OUTDOORS

**Northland Discovery Boat Tours.** Northland Discovery Boat Tours leads specialized trips to see whales, icebergs, seabirds, and sea caves. ✉ *Behind the Grenfell Interpretation Centre off West St. (Box 726), St. Anthony, Newfoundland and Labrador, Canada* ☎ *709/454–3092, 877/632–3747* ⊕ *www.discovernorthland.com.*

### SHOPPING

**Grenfell Handicrafts.** Be sure to visit Grenfell Handicrafts in the Grenfell Historic Properties complex. Training villagers to become self-sufficient in a harsh environment was one of Grenfell's aims. A windproof cloth that they turned into well-made parkas came to be known as Grenfell cloth. Mittens, coats and table clothes are embroidered with motifs such as polar bears and dog teams. There is a large selection of other handicrafts and most are locally made. ✉ *4 Maraval Rd., St. Anthony, Newfoundland and Labrador, Canada* ☎ *709/454–3576* ⊕ *www. grenfell-properties.com.*

## CORNER BROOK

*50 km (31 mi) southwest of Deer Lake.*

Newfoundland's fourth-largest city, Corner Brook is the hub of the island's west coast. Hills fringe three sides of the city, which has dramatic views of the harbor and the Bay of Islands. The town is also home to a large paper mill and a branch of Memorial University. Captain James Cook, the British explorer, charted the coast in the 1760s, and a memorial to him overlooks the bay.

The town enjoys more clearly defined seasons than most of the rest of the island, and in summer it has many pretty gardens. The nearby Humber River is the best-known salmon river in the province, and there are many kilometers of well-maintained walking trails in the community.

### GETTING HERE AND AROUND

Corner Brook is a convenient hub and point of departure for exploring the west coast. It's only a three-hour drive (allowing for traffic) from the Port aux Basques ferry from Nova Scotia.

The north and south shores of the Bay of Islands have fine paved roads—Route 440 on the north shore and Route 450 on the south—and both are a scenic half-day drive from Corner Brook. Route 450 is especially lovely, and there are many well-developed hiking trails near the end of the road at Bottle Cove and Little Port.

## EXPLORING

**The Newfoundland Emporium.** Flossy, the huge and handsome Newfoundland dog, will greet you at the door of this, well, "emporium" is the best way to describe it: the store is crammed from wall to wall with Newfoundland-related stuff. The main three-level store is full of books (including ones by Newfoundlanders and about Newfoundland as well as volumes about ships and sailing), art, crafts, music, and souvenirs. They also have antique furniture, collectibles, and an art gallery. ✉ *11 Broadway, Corner Brook, Newfoundland and Labrador, Canada* ☎ *709/634–9376.*

## WHERE TO STAY

*For expanded hotel reviews, visit Fodors.com.*

**$$** 🏨 **Glynmill Inn.** This well-built, quiet, Tudor-style inn was once the staff
★ house for the visiting top brass of the paper mill. **Pros:** art gallery in hotel; pleasant setting; Deer Lake airport shuttle service (C$22). **Cons:** hard to find from the highway; small windows in many rooms. ✉ *1B Cobb La., Box 550, Corner Brook, Newfoundland and Labrador, Canada* ☎ *709/634–5181, 800/563–4400 in Canada* ⊕ *www.steelehotels. com* 🛏 *53 rooms, 25 suites* ♿ *In-room: a/c, Wi-Fi. In-hotel: restaurant, bar, gym, business center, parking, some pets allowed.*

**$** 🏨 **Mamateek Inn.** Rooms are standard, bright, and clean, but it's the panoramic view of the city and the Bay of Islands that is the selling point for this hotel. **Pros:** town and bay view from half the rooms; bright, open lobby with friendly staff; near highway. **Cons:** not much within walking distance except a mall; four TVs hang in the restaurant. ✉ *64 Maple Valley Rd., Corner Brook, Newfoundland and Labrador, Canada* 🏤 *Box 787, Corner Brook, Newfoundland and Labrador, Canada A2H 6G7* ☎ *709/639–8901, 800/563–8600* ⊕ *www.mamateekinn.ca* 🛏 *55 rooms* ♿ *In-room: a/c, Wi-Fi. In-hotel: restaurant, bar, parking, some pets allowed.*

**$$$** 🏨 **Marble Villa.** These spotless condo-style units are meant for skiers but they're perfect for a quiet off-season stay and as a base from which to make Bay of Islands and Gros Morne day trips. **Pros:** beautiful property with pond and walking trails; kitchens with dishwasher and fireplace in most units; spacious, comfortable rooms. **Cons:** cafeteria-style restaurant closed outside ski season; few eating options in area. ✉ *Exit 8 off Rte. 1, 10 km (6 mi) east of Corner Brook, Corner Brook, Newfoundland and Labrador, Canada* ☎ *709/637–7666, 800/636–2725* ⊕ *www. skimarble.com* 🛏 *29 condos* ♿ *In-room: a/c, kitchen, Wi-Fi. In-hotel: restaurant, bar, laundry facilities, business center, parking* ⏻ *No meals.*

## SPORTS AND THE OUTDOORS

**Crystal Waters Boat Tours.** Crystal Waters Boat Tours, out of Corner Brook's Bay of Islands Yacht Club, offers day and evening cruises of the Bay of Islands. ✉ *Bay of Islands Yacht Club, off Griffin Dr., Corner Brook, Newfoundland and Labrador, Canada* ☎ *866/344–9808, 709/632–1094* ⊕ *www.crystalwatersboattours.com.*

## STEPHENVILLE

*77 km (48 mi) south of Corner Brook.*

The former Harmon Air Force Base is in Stephenville, a town best known for its summer theater festival. To the west of town is the Port au Port Peninsula, which was largely settled by the French, who brought their way of life and language to this small corner of Newfoundland.

**Stephenville Theatre Festival.** The Stephenville Theatre Festival, held in July and August, presents mostly musicals, some new, some familiar. ⊠ *129 Montana Ave., Stephenville, Newfoundland and Labrador, Canada* ☎ *709/643–4982, 709/643–4553 box office* ⊕ *www.stf.nf.ca.*

**EN ROUTE**

**Codroy Valley.** As you travel down the Trans-Canada Highway toward Port aux Basques, routes 404, 405, 406, and 407 bring you into the small Scottish communities of the Codroy Valley. Some of the most productive farms in the province are nestled in the valley against the backdrop of the Long Range Mountains, from which gales strong enough to stop traffic hurtle down to the coast. They are locally known as Wreckhouse winds and have overturned tractor trailers. The Codroy Valley is great for bird-watching, and the Grand Codroy River is ideal for kayaking. Walking trails, a golf course, and mountain hikes make the area an appealing stop for nature lovers. ⊠ *Stephenville, Newfoundland and Labrador, Canada.*

## PORT AUX BASQUES

*166 km (103 mi) south of Stephenville.*

In the 1500s and early 1600s there were seven Basque ports along Newfoundland's west coast and in southern Labrador; Port aux Basques was one of them and was given its name by the town's French successors. It's now the main ferry port connecting the island to Nova Scotia. In J.T. Cheeseman Provincial Park, 15 km (9 mi) west of town on the Trans-Canada Highway, and at Grand Bay West, you may see the endangered piping plover, which nests in the sand dunes along this coast.

### WHERE TO STAY

*For expanded hotel reviews, visit Fodors.com.*

$    🏨 **St. Christopher's Hotel.** This clean, comfortable two-story hotel is minutes from the ferry and has good food at reasonable prices. **Pros:** business center; local fare such as moose stew served in the restaurant; waterfront boardwalk close by. **Cons:** limited (and overpriced) wine list; conventions/weddings/sports teams can be noisy; a/c sometimes loud. ⊠ *146 Caribou Rd., Box 2049, Port aux Basques, Newfoundland and Labrador, Canada* ☎ *709/695–7034, 800/563–4779* ⊕ *www.stchrishotel.com* ⇱ *83 rooms* △ *In-room: a/c, Internet. In-hotel: restaurant, bar, gym, laundry facilities, business center, parking, some pets allowed.*

# UNDERSTANDING NOVA SCOTIA AND ATLANTIC CANADA

---

**BOOKS AND MOVIES**

---

**FRENCH VOCABULARY**

# BOOKS AND MOVIES

## Books

**Newfoundland and Labrador** For contemporary fiction, pick up *The Shipping News,* the Pulitzer Prize–winning novel by E. Annie Proulx: it's an atmospheric and moving tale of fishing and family, set in Newfoundland (the author is American); the book is much better than the movie. Wayne Johnston is a native Newfoundlander and *The Colony of Unrequited Dreams* is a comic epic about the history of the province. His *Baltimore's Mansion* is a memoir depicting his childhood on the Avalon Peninsula. *The North Bay Narrative,* by Walter Staples (Peter E. Randall), is the true story of the evolution of a remote outpost into a bustling fishing town. *Random Passage* is historical fiction about a family of early Newfoundland settlers arriving from England; it was a best seller and the basis for a television miniseries of the same name. *The Lure of the Wild,* Dillon Wallace's account of his 1903 trek across Labrador, is a classic. Wallace's companion, Leonidas Hubbard, died on the trip, but his wife, Mina, wrote her own book: *A Woman's Way Through Unknown Labrador.*

**New Brunswick** David Adams Richards is one of New Brunswick's best-known writers. His novels *Mercy Among the Children* and *Bay of Love and Sorrows,* both set in northern New Brunswick, explore bleak themes. Richards also wrote *Lines on the Water,* a tale of the fishing community on the Miramichi River. In Beth Powning's memoir *Home: Chronicle of a North Country Life* the author and her husband relocate from Connecticut to a farm near the Bay of Fundy.

**Nova Scotia** The sweeping novel *Fall on Your Knees,* by Ann-Marie MacDonald, takes place partly on Cape Breton Island; it was an Oprah's Book Club selection. Henry Wadsworth Longfellow's long poem *Evangeline* tells the story of lovers separated when the British deported the Acadians in 1755 and has inspired a number of tourist attractions in the province.

*Island: The Complete Stories,* by Alistair MacLeod, is a collection of tales about everyday life in Nova Scotia. MacLeod's first novel, *No Great Mischief,* is the story of a Scottish family that builds a new life on Cape Breton.

**Prince Edward Island** It almost goes without saying that *Anne of Green Gables* is a must-read.

**General** Acadian culture is unique to this region, and Clive Doucet's *Notes from Exile: On Being Acadian* is a thoughtful memoir that explores what it means to be Acadian and incorporates the history of Acadie and the Acadians.

## Movies

*Rain, Drizzle, and Fog* (1998) is a documentary about Newfoundland seen through the eyes of a "townie," or resident of St. John's. *The Shipping News* (2001), set in Newfoundland, was filmed primarily in Corner Brook, New Bonaventure, and Trinity, Newfoundland. The documentary *Ghosts of the Abyss* (2003) has excellent footage of the *Titanic,* which sank off the coast of Newfoundland. Canadian director James Cameron's *Titanic* (1997) was filmed partly in Halifax.

Many lesser-known movies filmed and set in the Atlantic provinces show more of the landscape and culture. Some are *The Bay of Love and Sorrows* (2002; Miramichi, New Brunswick); *The Bay Boy* (1984; Cape Breton, Nova Scotia); *Margaret's Museum* (1995; Cape Breton, Nova Scotia); *New Waterford Girl* (1999; Cape Breton, Nova Scotia); *A Rumor of Angels* (2000; Crescent Beach, Halifax, Lunenburg, and Sambro, Nova Scotia); and *Rare Birds* (2001; Cape Spear, Petty Harbour, and St. John's, Newfoundland).

# FRENCH VOCABULARY

| | ENGLISH | FRENCH | PRONUNCIATION |
|---|---|---|---|
| **BASICS** | | | |
| | Yes/no | Oui/non | wee/nohn |
| | Please | S'il vous plaît | seel voo play |
| | Thank you | Merci | mair-**see** |
| | You're welcome | De rien | deh ree-**ehn** |
| | Excuse me, sorry | Pardon | pahr-**don** |
| | Good morning/ afternoon | Bonjour | bohn-**zhoor** |
| | Good evening | Bonsoir | bohn-**swahr** |
| | Goodbye | Au revoir | o ruh-**vwahr** |
| | Mr. (Sir) | Monsieur | muh-**syuh** |
| | Mrs. (Ma'am) | Madame | ma-**dam** |
| | Miss | Mademoiselle | mad-mwa-**zel** |
| | Pleased to meet you | Enchanté(e) | ohn-shahn-**tay** |
| | How are you? | Comment allez-vous? | kuh-mahn- tahl-ay **voo** |
| | Very well, thanks | Très bien, merci | tray bee-ehn, mair-**see** |
| | And you? | Et vous? | ay voo? |
| **NUMBERS** | | | |
| | one | un | uhn |
| | two | deux | deuh |
| | three | trois | twah |
| | four | quatre | **kaht**-ruh |
| | five | cinq | sank |
| | six | six | seess |
| | seven | sept | set |
| | eight | huit | wheat |
| | nine | neuf | nuf |
| | ten | dix | deess |
| | eleven | onze | ohnz |
| | twelve | douze | dooz |
| | thirteen | treize | trehz |

| ENGLISH | FRENCH | PRONUNCIATION |
| --- | --- | --- |
| fourteen | quatorze | kah-torz |
| fifteen | quinze | kanz |
| sixteen | seize | sez |
| seventeen | dix-sept | deez-**set** |
| eighteen | dix-huit | deez-**wheat** |
| nineteen | dix-neuf | deez-**nuf** |
| twenty | vingt | vehn |
| twenty-one | vingt-et-un | vehnt-ay-**uhn** |
| thirty | trente | trahnt |
| forty | quarante | ka-**rahnt** |
| fifty | cinquante | sang-**kahnt** |
| sixty | soixante | swa-**sahnt** |
| seventy | soixante-dix | swa-sahnt-**deess** |
| eighty | quatre-vingts | kaht-ruh-**vehn** |
| ninety | quatre-vingt-dix | kaht-ruh-vehn-**deess** |
| one hundred | cent | sahn |
| one thousand | mille | meel |

## USEFUL PHRASES

| | | |
| --- | --- | --- |
| Do you speak English? | Parlez-vous anglais? | par-lay **voo ahn**-glay |
| I don't speak . . . | Je ne parle pas . . . | zhuh nuh parl pah |
| French | français | frahn-**say** |
| I don't understand | Je ne comprends pas | zhuh nuh kohm-**prahn** pah |
| I understand | Je comprends | zhuh kohm-**prahn** |
| I don't know | Je ne sais pas | zhuh nuh say **pah** |
| What's your name? | Comment vous appelez-vous? | ko-mahn voo za-pell-ay-**voo** |
| My name is . . . | Je m'appelle . . . | zhuh ma-**pell** . . . |
| What time is it? | Quelle heure est-il? | kel air eh-**teel** |
| How? | Comment? | ko-**mahn** |
| When? | Quand? | kahn |

| ENGLISH | FRENCH | PRONUNCIATION |
|---------|--------|---------------|
| Yesterday | Hier | yair |
| Today | Aujourd'hui | o-zhoor-**dwee** |
| Tomorrow | Demain | duh-**mehn** |
| Tonight | Ce soir | suh **swahr** |
| What is it? | Qu'est-ce que c'est? | kess-kuh-**say** |
| Why? | Pourquoi? | **poor**-kwa |
| Who? | Qui? | kee |
| Where is . . . | Où est . . . | oo ay |
| the train station? | la gare? | la gar |
| the subway station? | la station de métro? | la sta-**syon** duh may-**tro** |
| the bus stop? | l'arrêt de bus? | la-**ray** duh **booss** |
| the bank? | la banque? | la bahnk |
| the . . . hotel? | l'hôtel . . .? | lo-**tel** |
| the store? | le magasin? | luh ma-ga-**zehn** |
| the . . . museum? | le musée . . .? | luh mew-**zay** |
| the elevator? | l'ascenseur? | la-sahn-**seuhr** |
| the telephone? | le téléphone? | luh tay-lay-**phone** |
| Where are the restrooms? | Où sont les toilettes? | oo sohn lay twah-**let** |
| (men/women) | (hommes/femmes) | (**oh**-mm/**fah**-mm) |
| Here/there | Ici/là | ee-**see**/la |
| Left/right | A gauche/à droite | a goash/a draht |
| Straight ahead | Tout droit | too drwah |
| Is it near/far? | C'est près/loin? | say pray/lwehn |
| I'd like . . . | Je voudrais . . . | zhuh voo-**dray** |
| a room | une chambre | ewn **shahm**-bruh |
| I'd like to buy . . . | Je voudrais acheter . . . | zhuh voo-**dray** **ahsh**-tay |
| How much is it? | C'est combien? | say comb-bee-**ehn** |
| A little/a lot | Un peu/beaucoup | uhn peuh/bo-**koo** |
| More/less | Plus/moins | plu/mwehn |
| Enough/too (much) | Assez/trop | a-**say**/tro |

| ENGLISH | FRENCH | PRONUNCIATION |
|---------|--------|---------------|
| **DINING OUT** | | |
| A bottle of . . . | une bouteille de . . . | ewn boo-**tay** duh |
| A cup of . . . | une tasse de . . . | ewn tass duh |
| A glass of . . . | un verre de . . . | uhn vair duh |
| Bill/check | l'addition | la-dee-see-**ohn** |
| Bread | du pain | dew pan |
| Breakfast | le petit-déjeuner | luh puh-**tee** day-zhuh-**nay** |
| Butter | du beurre | dew burr |
| Cocktail/aperitif | un apéritif | uhn ah-pay-ree-**teef** |
| Dinner | le dîner | luh dee-**nay** |
| Dish of the day | le plat du jour | luh plah dew **zhoor** |
| Enjoy! | Bon appétit! | bohn a-pay-**tee** |
| Fixed-price menu | le menu | luh may-**new** |
| Fork | une fourchette | ewn four-**shet** |
| I am diabetic | Je suis diabétique | zhuh swee dee-ah- bay-**teek** |
| I am vegetarian | Je suis végétarien(ne) | zhuh swee vay-zhay-ta-ree-**en** |
| I cannot eat . . . | Je ne peux pas manger de . . . | zhuh nuh **puh** pah mahn-**jay** deh |
| I'd like to order | Je voudrais commander | zhuh voo-**dray** ko-mahn-**day** |
| Is service/the tip included? | Est-ce que le service est compris? | ess kuh luh sair-**veess** ay comb-**pree** |
| It's good/bad | C'est bon/mauvais | say bohn/mo-**vay** |
| It's hot/cold | C'est chaud/froid | Say sho/frwah |
| Knife | un couteau | uhn koo-**toe** |
| Lunch | le déjeuner | luh day-zhuh-**nay** |
| Menu | la carte | la cart |
| Napkin | une serviette | ewn sair-vee-**et** |
| Pepper | du poivre | dew **pwah**-vruh |
| Plate | une assiette | ewn a-see-**et** |

| ENGLISH | FRENCH | PRONUNCIATION |
|---------|--------|---------------|
| Please give me . . . | Donnez-moi . . . | doe-nay-**mwah** |
| Salt | du sel | dew sell |
| Spoon | une cuillère | ewn kwee-air |
| Sugar | du sucre | dew **sook**-ruh |
| Wine list | la carte des vins | la cart day vehn |

# MENU GUIDE

| FRENCH | ENGLISH |
|--------|---------|

## GENERAL DINING

| | |
|--------|---------|
| Entrée | Appetizer/Starter |
| Garniture au choix | Choice of vegetable side |
| Plat du jour | Dish of the day |
| Selon arrivage | When available |
| Supplément/En sus | Extra charge |

## PETIT DÉJEUNER (BREAKFAST)

| | |
|--------|---------|
| Confiture | Jam |
| Miel | Honey |
| Oeuf à la coque | Boiled egg |
| Oeufs sur le plat | Fried eggs |
| Oeufs brouillés | Scrambled eggs |
| Tartine | Bread with butter |

## POISSONS/FRUITS DE MER (FISH/SEAFOOD)

| | |
|--------|---------|
| Anchois | Anchovies |
| Bar | Bass |
| Brandade de morue | Creamed salt cod |
| Brochet | Pike |
| Cabillaud/Morue | Fresh cod |
| Calmar | Squid |
| Coquilles St-Jacques | Scallops |
| Crevettes | Shrimp |

| FRENCH | ENGLISH |
| --- | --- |
| Daurade | Sea bream |
| Ecrevisses | Prawns/Crayfish |
| Harengs | Herring |
| Homard | Lobster |
| Huîtres | Oysters |
| Langoustine | Prawn/Lobster |
| Lotte | Monkfish |
| Moules | Mussels |
| Palourdes | Clams |
| Saumon | Salmon |
| Thon | Tuna |
| Truite | Trout |

## VIANDE (MEAT)

| | |
| --- | --- |
| Agneau | Lamb |
| Boeuf | Beef |
| Boudin | Sausage |
| Boulettes de viande | Meatballs |
| Brochettes | Kebabs |
| Cassoulet | Casserole of white beans, meat |
| Cervelle | Brains |
| Chateaubriand | Double fillet steak |
| Choucroute garnie | Sausages with sauerkraut |
| Côtelettes | Chops |
| Côte/Côte de boeuf | Rib/T-bone steak |
| Cuisses de grenouilles | Frogs' legs |
| Entrecôte | Rib or rib-eye steak |
| Épaule | Shoulder |
| Escalope | Cutlet |
| Foie | Liver |
| Gigot | Leg |

| FRENCH | ENGLISH |
|---|---|
| Porc | Pork |
| Ris de veau | Veal sweetbreads |
| Rognons | Kidneys |
| Saucisses | Sausages |
| Selle | Saddle |
| Tournedos | Tenderloin of T-bone steak |
| Veau | Veal |

## METHODS OF PREPARATION

| | |
|---|---|
| A point | Medium |
| A l'étouffée | Stewed |
| Au four | Baked |
| Ballotine | Boned, stuffed, and rolled |
| Bien cuit | Well-done |
| Bleu | Very rare |
| Frit | Fried |
| Grillé | Grilled |
| Rôti | Roast |
| Saignant | Rare |

## VOLAILLES/GIBIER (POULTRY/GAME)

| | |
|---|---|
| Blanc de volaille | Chicken breast |
| Canard/Caneton | Duck/Duckling |
| Cerf/Chevreuil | Venison (red/roe) |
| Coq au vin | Chicken stewed in red wine |
| Dinde/Dindonneau | Turkey/Young turkey |
| Faisan | Pheasant |
| Lapin/Lièvre | Rabbit/Wild hare |
| Oie | Goose |
| Pintade/Pintadeau | Guinea fowl/Young guinea fowl |
| Poulet/Poussin | Chicken/Spring chicken |

| FRENCH | ENGLISH |
| --- | --- |

## LÉGUMES (VEGETABLES)

| FRENCH | ENGLISH |
| --- | --- |
| Artichaut | Artichoke |
| Asperge | Asparagus |
| Aubergine | Eggplant |
| Carottes | Carrots |
| Champignons | Mushrooms |
| Chou-fleur | Cauliflower |
| Chou (rouge) | Cabbage (red) |
| Laitue | Lettuce |
| Oignons | Onions |
| Petits pois | Peas |
| Pomme de terre | Potato |
| Tomates | Tomatoes |

# Travel Smart
# Nova Scotia and
# Atlantic Canada

**WORD OF MOUTH**

"Just a few words to the wonderful people of Nova Scotia, New Brunswick, and PEI. We returned from our 22-day tour and want to express our gratitude to all the people there who helped us . . . make our trip unforgettable. Of all our travels in the U.S. and Canada we have never met nicer, friendlier people than in the Maritimes. Everything is so clean and nice. . . . If I were 50 years younger I would like to immigrate to your lovely country."

—tovarich

# GETTING HERE AND AROUND

## ▌ BY AIR

Flying time to Halifax is 1½ hours from Montréal, 2 hours from Boston, 2½ hours from New York, 4½ hours from Chicago (with connection), 8 hours from Los Angeles (with connection), and 6 hours from London. The flying time from Toronto to both Charlottetown and St. John's is about 3 hours; a flight from Montréal to St. John's is 2 hours. Visitors from New York can expect a 4-hour flight to St. John's, while Bostonians can expect a 3-hour trip to Newfoundland and Labrador's capital. Inside the Atlantic provinces, a jump from Halifax to Charlottetown or Moncton takes only about 30 minutes while a trip from Halifax to St. John's is about 90 minutes.

Departing passengers at all major airports must pay an airport-improvement fee (typically C$10–$20) plus a C$16 security fee before boarding, though these are usually rolled into the ticket price. All major, regional, and charter airlines that serve Atlantic Canada prohibit smoking, as do all Canadian airports.

**Airlines and Airports Airline and Airport Links.com.** Airline and Airport Links.com has links to many of the world's airlines and airports. ⊕ *www.airlineandairportlinks.com.*

**Airline-Security Issues Transportation Security Administration.** For answers to almost any question that might arise, check the Web site of the Transportation Security Administration ⊕ *www.tsa.gov* or the **Canadian Air Transport Security Authority** ⊕ *www.catsa-acsta.gc.ca.*

## AIRPORTS

The largest airport in the area is Halifax's Robert L. Stanfield International Airport (YHZ). *For information about smaller airports, see the individual chapters.*

**Airport Information Halifax Robert L. Stanfield International Airport** ☎ *902/873–4422* ⊕ *www.hiaa.ca.*

### FLIGHTS

Air Canada and its partner Jazz, which dominate the national airline industry, serve every major city in the region as well as many smaller centers. WestJet, the main competitor, serves select cities both within Atlantic Canada and elsewhere on the continent, while Porter Airlines, a comparative upstart, flies direct to Halifax from Ottawa, Montréal and St. John's with connections to other locales. As for U.S.–based carriers, American Airlines, Continental, Delta, United, and US Airways all provide service to Halifax. European budget airlines, including Condor and Icelandair, also have service to Atlantic Canada on a seasonal basis.

Among regional carriers, Air Labrador serves Newfoundland and Labrador (Provincial Airlines also connects the province to Quebec); and Twin Cities Air Service provides regularly scheduled flights between Yarmouth and Portland, Maine. Smaller outfits are worth investigating, especially when flying short distances. Contact regional travel agencies for charter companies. Private pilots should obtain information from the Canada Map Office, which has the *Canada Flight Supplement* (lists of airports with Canada Customs services) as well as aeronautical charts.

Halifax's airport is located 40 km (25 mi) northeast of downtown, and ground transportation takes 30 to 40 minutes, depending on traffic. If you're flying nonstop to the States at the end of your trip, remember that in addition to leaving time for the drive back to the airport you must also leave yourself sufficient time *in* the airport because air travelers are now required to preclear U.S. customs before departing.

**Information** **Air Canada** ☎ 888/247-2262 ⊕ *www.aircanada.ca.* **Air Labrador** ☎ 800/563-3042 ⊕ *www.airlabrador.com.* **American Airlines** ☎ 800/433-7300 ⊕ *www. aa.com.* **Canada Map Office** ☎ 800/465-6277 ⊕ *maps.NRCan.gc.ca.* **Condor Airlines** ☎ 866/960-7915 ⊕ *www.condor.com.* **Continental Airlines** ☎ 800/523-3273 for *U.S. reservations, 800/231-0856 for international reservations* ⊕ *www.continental.com.* **Delta Airlines** ☎ 800/221-1212 for *U.S. reservations, 800/241-4141 for international reservations* ⊕ *www.delta.com.* **Icelandair** ☎ 800/223-5500 ⊕ *www.icelandair. com.* **Provincial Airlines** ☎ 800/563-2800 ⊕ *www.provincialairlines.com.* **Porter Airlines** ☎ 888/619-8622 ⊕ *www.flyporter.com.* **Twin Cities Air Service** ☎ 800/564-3882 ⊕ *www.twincitiesairservice.com.* **United Airlines** ☎ 800/864-8331 for *U.S. reservations, 800/538-2929 for international reservations* ⊕ *www.united.com.* **US Airways** ☎ 800/428-4322 for *U.S. reservations, 800/622-1015 for international reservations* ⊕ *www.usairways. com.* **WestJet** ☎ 888/937-8538 ⊕ *www. westjet.com.*

## ▮ BY BOAT

Car ferries provide essential transportation on the east coast of Canada, connecting Nova Scotia with New Brunswick, PEI, and Newfoundland.

Bay Ferries Ltd. sails the *Princess of Acadia* between Saint John, New Brunswick, and Digby year-round. There is at least one round-trip per day—two in summer—and the crossing takes approximately three hours.

Weather permitting, from May through late December, Northumberland Ferries operates between Caribou, Nova Scotia, and Wood Islands, Prince Edward Island, making the 75-minute trip several times each day. Marine Atlantic operates daily year-round between North Sydney and Port aux Basques, on the west coast of Newfoundland. Thrice-weekly service between North Sydney and Argentia, on Newfoundland's east coast, is offered from mid-June through late September. Reservations are required. *For additional information about regional ferry service, see individual chapters.*

**Information** **Bay Ferries, Ltd.** ☎ 888/249-7245, ⊕ *www.nfl-bay.com.* **Marine Atlantic** ☎ 800/341-7981, ⊕ *www.marine-atlantic.ca.* **Northumberland Ferries** ☎ 877/635-7245, ⊕ *www.peiferry.com.*

## ▮ BY BUS

If you don't have a car, you'll likely have to rely on bus travel in Atlantic Canada, especially when visiting the many out-of-the-way communities that don't have airports or rail lines. Buses usually depart and arrive only once a day from any given destination. Greyhound Lines offers interprovincial service. Acadian Lines operates regional bus service throughout Nova Scotia, New Brunswick, and PEI. Buses are quite comfortable, have clean bathrooms, and make occasional rest stops.

Bus terminals in major centers and even in many minor ones are usually efficient operations with service all week and plenty of agents on hand to handle ticket sales. In some less-trafficked spots, however, the bus station is simply a counter in a local convenience store, gas station, or snack bar. If you ask, the bus driver will usually stop anywhere on the route to let you off, even if it's not a designated terminal. There are a number of small, regional bus services, but connections are not always convenient.

Tickets may be purchased in advance, but—capacity-wise—it isn't necessary to do so, and reservations per se aren't accepted. Just pick a ticket up at least 45 minutes before the scheduled departure time.

**Information** Acadian Lines ☎ 800/567–5151 ⊕ www.acadianbus.com. **Greyhound Canada** ☎ 800/661–8747 ⊕ www.greyhound.ca.

# ▌BY CAR

Your own driver's license is acceptable in Atlantic Canada for up to three months, and the national highway system is excellent. It includes the Trans-Canada Highway, the longest in the world—running about 8,000 km (5,000 mi) from Victoria, British Columbia, to St. John's, Newfoundland, with ferries bridging coastal waters at each end.

### FROM THE U.S.

Drivers must carry owner registration and proof of insurance coverage, which is compulsory in Canada. The Canadian Non-Resident Inter-Provincial Motor Vehicle Liability Insurance Card, available from any U.S. insurance company, is accepted as evidence of financial responsibility within the country. The minimum liability coverage in New Brunswick, Newfoundland and Labrador, and Prince Edward Island is C$200,000; in Nova Scotia, it's C$500,000. If you're driving a car that is not registered in your name, carry a letter from the owner that authorizes your use of the vehicle.

The U.S. Interstate Highway System leads directly into Canada along Interstate 95 from Maine to New Brunswick, and there are many smaller highway crossings between the two countries as well.

▌TIP➡ Motorists crossing into Atlantic Canada from the U.S. can check border-wait times online; they're updated hourly. Click on "Border wait times" at ⊕ www.cbsa-asfc.gc.ca.

**Insurance information Insurance Bureau of Canada** ☎ 902/429–2730, 800/565–7189 within Atlantic Canada ⊕ www.ibc.ca.

### GASOLINE

Because Canada uses metric measurements, gasoline is always sold in liters. One gallon equals about 3.8 liters. At this writing, the per-liter price of gas is C$1.31 (C$4.96 per gallon) in Nova Scotia; C$1.33 (C$5.03 per gallon) in Newfoundland and Labrador; C$1.25 (C$4.73 per gallon) in New Brunswick; and C$1.24 (C$4.69 per gallon) in PEI.

### ROADSIDE EMERGENCIES

In case of an accident or emergency call 911. If you're a member of the American Automobile Association, you're automatically covered by the Canadian Automobile Association while traveling in Canada.

**Emergency Services Canadian Automobile Association** ☎ 800/222–4357 ⊕ www.caa.ca.

▌TIP➡ Motorists should bear in mind that many roads in rural areas require attentive driving, as they are often narrow and don't always have a paved shoulder (sharply curving ones warrant special attention). That said, they're generally well surfaced and offer exquisite scenery.

### RULES OF THE ROAD

Speed limits, always given in kilometers, vary from province to province, but are usually within the 90- to 110-kph range outside cities. (As a mile equals 1.6 km, that translates into 50–68 mph.) Radar-detection devices are illegal, and speed limits are strictly enforced. Tickets start at C$75.

By law, you are required to wear a seat belt. Children must also be properly restrained regardless of where they're seated. Those under 40 pounds must be strapped into approved child-safety seats. Even children over 40 pounds who are under nine years of age and less than 145 centimeters (57 inches) in height are legally required to use child seats. This rule does not apply, however, if you're visiting from outside Atlantic Canada and driving your own vehicle, provided it complies with the child-restraint safety laws of the province or country where the car is registered.

Drinking and driving (anything over .08 blood-alcohol level) is a criminal offense. In the Atlantic Provinces, however, there are also serious penalties—including license suspension and vehicle confiscation—if you're found to have a .05 blood-alcohol level. Road-block checks are not unusual, especially on holiday weekends.

Another no-no is using a handheld cell phone while driving. All four provinces have banned the practice. Other regulations, such as those concerning headlight use and parking, differ from province to province. Some have a statutory requirement to drive with your headlights on for extended periods after dawn and before sunset. Parking rules are set by individual municipalities. In Halifax, tickets for violators are common and start at C$20.

## ■ BY CRUISE SHIP

Every season, between mid-April and late October, cruise ships sailing up from New England, and in some cases across the Atlantic from Europe, arrive in Atlantic Canadian waters. In terms of traffic, Halifax is hands down the most popular port of call, annually receiving more than 125 ships representing major lines such as Royal Caribbean, Holland America, Princess, Silversea, Carnival, Crystal, Cunard, and—new for 2012—Disney. The city's deep natural harbor is well suited to large ships, and the terminal's downtown location makes it a convenient stop for the 261,000 passengers who land here every year.

About 75 major cruise ships carrying 205,000 passengers also dock in Saint John, New Brunswick, while the ports of Charlottetown and Sydney get approximately 20 calls apiece. Cruise ships are also an emerging element of the Newfoundland and Labrador tourism sector. Right now, the province plays host to a relatively small number of major lines, and they must first dock at either Corner Brook or St. John's, the only ports with customs officers; however, there are another 30-odd outports all over the province that attract smaller, more adventure-oriented operators like Wanderbird Expedition Cruises.

**Contacts Atlantic Canada Cruise Association** ⊕ www.atlanticcanadacruise. com. **Cruise Halifax** ⊕ www.cruisehalifax. ca. **Cruise Newfoundland and Labrador** ⊕ www.cruisenewfoundland.com. **Cruise Saint John** ⊕ www.cruisesaintjohn.com. **Historic Charlottetown Seaport.com** ⊕ www.historiccharlottetownseaport.com. **Port of Sydney** ⊕ www.portofsydney.ca. **Wanderbird Expedition Cruises** ⊕ www. wanderbirdcruises.com.

## ■ BY TRAIN

VIA Rail, Canada's Amtrak counterpart, provides transcontinental rail service to Atlantic Canada, but it's limited to an overnight Montréal-to-Halifax trip, called The Ocean, which runs every day except Tuesday. The train stops in a dozen Nova Scotian and New Brunswick towns along the way, among them Truro, Amherst, Moncton, and Miramichi. There are three service classes: Economy Class, featuring an upright seat with foot- and head-rest, is the least expensive; Sleeper Class, with a berth or bedroom cabin, is the middle-of-the-road option; and Sleeper Touring (offered from mid-June to mid-October) is an upgraded version of the latter that includes cabin accommodations, meals, access to the panoramic Park Car, complimentary educational activities, and pre-boarding privileges. You can expect to pay more than double for accommodations in Sleeper Touring over seats in Economy Class.

If you're planning to travel a lot by train, look into the Canrail pass. It enables you to take seven one-way trips anywhere in Canada during a 21-day period. During the high season (June to mid-October), a standard pass is C$969, plus applicable taxes. The low-season rate (valid October 16 through May) is C$606, plus taxes. For more information and reservations, contact VIA Rail or a travel agent within the United States.

**Information VIA Rail Canada** ☎ 888/842–7245 ⊕ www.viarail.ca.

# ESSENTIALS

## ▌ACCOMMODATIONS

In Atlantic Canadian cities, you may choose between luxury hotels (whether business-class or boutique-y), moderately priced modern properties, and older ones with fewer conveniences but more charm. Options in smaller towns and in the countryside include large full-service resorts, small privately owned inns, bed-and-breakfasts, and a diminishing number of roadside motels.

Accommodations will generally cost more in summer than at other times (except those places, such as ski resorts, where winter is high season) and should be booked well in advance for peak periods. A special event or festival that coincides with your visit might fill every room for miles around. Inquire about special deals and packages when making reservations. Big-city hotels that cater to business travelers often offer weekend packages. Discounts are common when you book for a week or longer, and many urban hotels offer rooms at up to 40% off in winter.

The lodgings we list are the cream of the crop in each price category. We always list the facilities that are available, but we don't specify whether they cost extra. So when pricing accommodations, always ask what's included and what qualifies as an add-on. It's worth noting that most hotels allow children under a certain age to stay in their parents' room at no extra cost, yet some charge for them as extra adults; also ask about the cut-off age for discounts if you're traveling as a family.

Properties are assigned price categories based on the range between their least and most expensive standard double rooms at high season (excluding holidays). *Check the planner page at the front of each province chapter for the price chart.*

Most hotels and other lodgings require your credit card details before they will confirm your reservation. If you don't feel comfortable emailing this information, ask if you can fax it (some places even prefer faxes). However you book, get confirmation in writing and have a copy of it handy when you check in.

Be sure you understand the hotel's cancellation policy. Some places allow you to cancel without any kind of penalty—even if you prepaid to secure a discounted rate—if you cancel at least 24 hours in advance. Others require you to cancel a week in advance or penalize you the cost of one night. Small inns and B&Bs are most likely to require you to cancel far in advance.

### APARTMENT AND HOUSE RENTALS

Rental cottages are common in the Atlantic provinces, especially Nova Scotia and Prince Edward Island. Many of them are privately owned but only used by the family for a few weeks each summer. That leaves week after week available for rental potential, with most owners leaving the booking to an online agency or enterprising neighbor.

**Information HomeAway.** HomeAway leads the pack with more than 400 Atlantic Canadian properties. ⊕ *www.homeaway.com.* **Atlantic Canada Vacation Rentals.** Atlantic Canada Vacation Rentals scores points for its wide geographic coverage—just follow the links from "lodgings" for listings. ⊕ *www.atlanticcanada.worldweb.com.* **Canada Cottage and Cabin Rentals.** Canada Cottage and Cabin Rentals is a reliable option. Searching under "accommodations" at the individual provinces' tourism Web sites *(see individual chapters)* yields still more results. ⊕ *www.cottage-canada-usa.com.*

### BED-AND-BREAKFASTS AND INNS

Staying in smaller, more intimate spots is a wonderful way to meet people who are passionate about their communities and well versed in local events and history. Inns and B&Bs are both prevalent in

Nova Scotia, particularly in the Annapolis Valley and the South Shore, where you can stay in the magnificent homes once occupied by ship builders, politicians, and other esteemed citizens. Prince Edward Island and New Brunswick also have a number of stately lodgings.

**Information The Canadian Bed & Breakfast Guide.** The Canadian Bed & Breakfast Guide is the oldest B&B guide in Canada. ⊕ *www.canadianbandbguide.ca.* **B&B Canada.** B&B Canada helpfully divides each province into tourist regions. ⊕ *www.bbcanada.com.* **Nova Scotia Bed & Breakfast Guide** ⊕ *www.nsbedandbreakfast.com.* **Unique Country Inns.** Unique Country Inns also cover Nova Scotia. ⊕ *www.uniquecountryinns.com.* **Prince Edward Island Inns and Bed & Breakfasts.** Prince Edward Island Inns and Bed & Breakfasts has PEI info. ⊕ *www.peislandbedandbreakfast.com.* **The Inns of Distinction of Prince Edward Island.** The Inns of Distinction of Prince Edward Island is also a useful site. ⊕ *www.innsofpei.com.* **Select Inns of Atlantic Canada.** Select Inns of Atlantic Canada covers inns, B&Bs, and boutique hotels in all four provinces. ⊕ *www.selectinns.ca.*

International sites with a strong local lineup include **Bed & Breakfast.com** ⊕ *www.bedandbreakfast.com.* **BnB Finder.com.** BnB Finder.com can also be helpful. ⊕ *www.bnbfinder.com.*

## HOTELS

Although Canada doesn't have a national government-run system for rating hotels, many have joined the voluntary Canada Select program, which assigns member properties one to five stars based on strict criteria. Most hotel rooms have air-conditioning, private baths with tubs and showers, and two double beds; all those we list have air-conditioning and private bath unless otherwise noted.

**Information Canada Select** ☎ *506/458-1995 in New Brunswick, 709/722-3133 in Newfoundland and Labrador, 902/406-4747 in Nova Scotia, 902/566-3501 in PEI* ⊕ *www.canadaselect.com.*

# ▌COMMUNICATIONS

## INTERNET

It's the norm in most hotels—as well as many inns and B&Bs—to provide either a public computer or wireless capabilities to guests. In the larger centers, like Halifax, Saint John, St. John's, and Charlottetown, wireless coffee shops continue to sprout up so you can surf while you sip. Airports and ferry terminals have also jumped on the wireless bandwagon, offering travelers an option for computer time while they wait for their next flight or boat ride.

## PHONES

The good news is that you can now make a direct-dial telephone call from virtually any point on earth. The bad news? You can't always do so cheaply. Calling from a hotel is almost always the most expensive option as hotels usually add huge surcharges to all calls, particularly international ones. Calling cards usually keep costs to a minimum but only if you purchase them locally. And then there are mobile phones (⇨ *below*). As expensive as mobile-phone calls can be, they are still usually much cheaper than calling from your hotel.

Phone numbers in Atlantic Canada have seven digits. In most cases, the prefix of phone numbers denotes a certain geographical area within the province you are calling. Area codes are three numbers and are as follows: for Prince Edward Island and Nova Scotia (902), New Brunswick (506), and Newfoundland and Labrador (709). Pay phones, which cost 25¢ for each call, are still quite common in airports, hotels, and at gas stations. They can be used to make long-distance calls either by calling the operator ("0") to reverse the charges, by depositing several coins to pay for the first minute of talk, or by using credit or phone cards (some pay phones, especially in airports, are equipped to handle cards directly).

Phone cards are readily available at grocery and drug stores as well as some convenience stores and gas stations. Cellular phone stores are readily accessible all over Atlantic Canada.

### CALLING OUTSIDE CANADA

The country code for the United States is 1.

### MOBILE PHONES

If you have a multiband phone (some countries use different frequencies from what's used in the United States) and your service provider uses the world-standard GSM network (as do AT&T and Verizon), you can probably use your phone abroad. Roaming fees can be steep, however: 99¢ a minute is considered reasonable. It's almost always cheaper to send a text message than to make a call, as text messages have a very low set fee (often less than 5¢).

If you just want to make local calls, consider buying a new SIM card (note that your provider may have to unlock your phone for you to use a different SIM card) and a prepaid service plan in the destination. You'll then have a local number and can make local calls at local rates.

You can also rent a phone in Canada before you go through Cellular Abroad, Mobal, or Planet Omni. This is likely to be cheaper than relying on your own phone and paying the high roaming costs on a U.S. number because these companies let you take advantage of the low local rates, regardless of the length of your trip. However, rental prices vary drastically in price based on style and features. With a cell phone rental, you will also need to purchase a Canada SIM card.

■TIP→ If you travel internationally frequently, save one of your old mobile phones or buy a cheap one online; ask your provider to unlock it and take it with you as a travel phone, buying a new SIM card with pay-as-you-go service in each destination.

Contacts **Cellular Abroad.** Cellular Abroad rents and sells GSM phones and sells SIM cards that work in many countries. ☎ 800/287–5072 ⊕ www.cellularabroad.com. **Mobal.** Mobal rents mobiles and sells GSM phones (starting at C$29) that will operate in

170 countries. Per-call rates vary throughout the world. ☎ 888/888–9162 ⊕ www.mobal.com. **Planet Omni.** Planet Omni offers similar services, but its per-minute rates are expensive. ☎ 800/707–0031 ⊕ www.planetomni.com.

# ▌ CUSTOMS AND DUTIES

You're always allowed to bring goods of a certain value back home without having to pay any duty or import tax, but there's a limit on the amount of duty-free tobacco and liquor you can return with, and some countries have separate limits for perfumes. For exact figures, check with your customs department. The values of so-called "duty-free" goods are included in these amounts. When you shop abroad, save all your receipts, as customs inspectors may ask to see them as well as the items you purchased. If the total value of your goods is more than the duty-free limit, you'll have to pay a tax (most often a flat percentage) on the value of everything beyond that limit.

U.S. Customs and Immigration (⇨ *In the U.S.*) has preclearance services at international airports in Halifax, as well as Montréal, Toronto, Ottawa, Winnipeg, Calgary, Edmonton, Vancouver, and Victoria.

American and British visitors may bring the following items into Canada duty-free: 200 cigarettes, 50 cigars, and 200 grams (7 ounces) of tobacco; 1.14 liters (40 imperial ounces) of liquor, 1.5 liters (53 imperial ounces) of wine, or 24 355-milliliter (12-ounce) bottles or cans of beer for personal consumption. Any alcohol and tobacco products in excess of these amounts are subject to duty, provincial fees, and taxes. You can also bring in gifts valued at C$60 or less without paying duty. Neither alcohol nor tobacco products qualify as gifts, and all gifts—regardless of their value—must be declared.

Cats and dogs must have a certificate issued by a licensed veterinarian that clearly identifies the animal and certifies that it has been vaccinated against rabies during the preceding 36 months. Guide dogs are allowed into Canada without restriction. Plant material must be declared and inspected as there may be restrictions on some live plants, bulbs, and seeds. With certain restrictions or prohibitions on some fruits and vegetables, visitors may bring food with them for their own use, providing the quantity is consistent with the duration of the visit.

Canada's firearms laws are significantly stricter than those in the United States. Only sporting rifles and shotguns may be imported, provided they are to be used for sporting, hunting, or competition while in the country. All firearms must be declared to Canadian Customs at the first point of entry. Failure to declare firearms will result in their seizure, and criminal charges may be made. Regulations require visitors to have a confirmed "Non-Resident Firearms Declaration" to bring any guns into Canada; a fee of C$25 applies, and the declaration (which acts like a temporary license) is valid for 60 days. For more information contact the Canadian Firearms Centre.

**Information in Canada** **Canada Border Services Agency** ☏ *800/461–9999 within Canada, 506/636–5064 outside Canada* ⊕ *www.cbsa.gc.ca.* **Canadian Firearms Centre** ☏ *800/731–4000* ⊕ *www.cfc-cafc.gc.ca.*

**Information in the U.S.** **U.S. Customs and Border Protection** ☏ *877/227–5511* ⊕ *www.cbp.gov.*

# ▌ EATING OUT

The Atlantic Provinces are a preferred destination for seafood lovers. Excellent fish and shellfish are available in all types of dining establishments. The restaurants we list are the top picks in each price category. *This book has a price chart at the start of each province chapter.*

## MEALS AND MEALTIMES

Unless otherwise noted, the restaurants listed in this guide are open daily for lunch and dinner. Pubs generally serve food all day and into the wee hours of the night. The dinner meal at restaurants usually begins around 5 pm with seating through 9 or 10 pm.

## RESERVATIONS AND DRESS

Regardless of where you are, it's a good idea to make a reservation if you can. We only mention them specifically when reservations are essential (in short, when there's no other way you'll ever get a table) or when they are not accepted. We mention dress only when men are required to wear a jacket or a jacket and tie.

## SMOKING

Smoking in *all* indoor public places is prohibited in both New Brunswick and Newfoundland and Labrador. PEI is a little more lenient in that it allows smoking in certain designated areas (including some outdoor patios after 10 pm). Nova Scotia, on the other hand, has some of the country's toughest legislation. In addition to the public indoor ban, it has banned smoking in private cars when passengers under the age of 19 are present. It also requires stores selling tobacco products to stock them out of customers' view.

## WINES, BEER, AND SPIRITS

Locally produced wines, ranging from young table wines to excellent vintages, are offered in most licensed restaurants and are well worth trying. Provincially owned liquor stores, as well as private outlets, are operated in Atlantic Canada. Stores selling alcohol are permitted to be open on Sundays (typically from noon or 1 until 5 pm). But provinces like Prince Edward Island allow certain outlets to open on that day in peak months only. Sundays aside, most liquor stores open at 10 am and close at 9 or 10 pm. For a list of government-operated stores (including private "agents" who sell beer through convenience stores in Newfoundland and Labrador), check out the Web site for each province.

# ■ ELECTRICITY

Canada uses the same voltage as the United States, so all of your electronics should make the transition without any fuss at all. No need for adapters.

# ■ EMERGENCIES

The U.S. embassy—like all other foreign embassies—is in Ottawa, Ontario (the nation's capital). There are also seven U.S. consulates in Canada, including one in Halifax.

**Foreign Consulates** **U.S. Consulate** ✉ *Suite 904, Purdy's Wharf Tower II, 1969 Upper Water St., Halifax, Nova Scotia, Canada* ☎ *902/429–2480* ⊕ *halifax.usconsulate.gov.* **U.S. Embassy** ✉ *490 Sussex Dr., Ottawa, Canada* ☎ *613/688–5335* ⊕ *www.usembassy.gov.*

# ■ HOURS OF OPERATION

Most banks are open Monday through Friday 10 to 5 or 6. All banks are closed on national holidays. Nearly all banks have automatic teller machines (ATMs) that are accessible around the clock.

Hours at museums vary, but most open at 10 or 11 and close in the evening. Many are closed on Monday; some stay open late one day a week, and admission is sometimes waived during those extended hours. Stores, shops, and supermarkets usually are open Monday through Saturday 9 to 6, and Sunday noon to 5, although in major cities supermarkets are often open 7:30 am to 11 pm, and some food stores are open 24 hours a day. Stores often stay open Thursday and Friday evenings, most shopping malls until 9 pm. Drugstores in major cities are often open until midnight, and convenience stores tend to be open until at least that time every day.

## HOLIDAYS

Canadian national holidays are as follows: New Year's Day (January 1), Good Friday (late March or early April), Easter Monday (the Monday after Good Friday),

Victoria Day (the first Monday preceding May 25), Canada Day (July 1), Labour Day (the first Monday in September), Thanksgiving (the second Monday in October), Remembrance Day (November 11), Christmas Day (December 25), and Boxing Day (December 26).

New Brunswick, much of Nova Scotia, and parts of PEI recognize the first Monday in August as another holiday, while Newfoundlanders and Labradorians, who love any excuse to party, also celebrate St. Patrick's Day (March 17), St. George's Day (April 23), Discovery Day (the Monday nearest to June 24), and Orangemen's Day (July 12).

# ■ MONEY

## ATMS AND BANKS

Your own bank will probably charge a fee for using ATMs abroad; the foreign bank you use may also charge a fee. Nevertheless, you'll usually get a better rate of exchange at an ATM than you will at a currency-exchange office or even when changing money in a bank. And extracting funds as you need them is a safer option than carrying around a large amount of cash. The easiest way to minimize transaction fees is by making withdrawals from ATMs affiliated with your home bank. Users of Cirrus or PLUS networks can locate them at ⊕ *www.mastercard.com/ atmlocator* and ⊕ *www.visa.com/atms* respectively.

■TIP→ PIN numbers with more than four digits are not recognized at ATMs in many countries. If yours has five or more, remember to change it before you leave.

Most banks, gas stations, malls, and convenience stores have ATMs that are accessible round the clock.

## CREDIT CARDS

American visitors should note that in Canada, as in Europe, chip-and-pin cards are now widely used; however, most venues that accept credit cards are still equipped to process transactions by the traditional swipe-and-sign method as well. It's a good idea to inform your credit-card company before you leave home. Otherwise, it might put a hold on your card owing to unusual activity—not a good thing halfway through your trip. Record all your credit-card numbers—along with the phone numbers to call if your cards are lost or stolen—in a safe place, so you're prepared should something go wrong. Both MasterCard and Visa have general numbers you can call (collect if you're abroad) if your card is lost, but you're better off phoning the number of your issuing bank, as MasterCard and Visa usually just transfer you to your bank anyway.

If you plan to use your credit card for cash advances, you'll need to apply for a PIN at least two weeks before your trip. Although it's usually cheaper (and safer) to use a credit card abroad for large purchases (so you can cancel payments or be reimbursed if there's a problem), note that some credit-card companies *and* the banks that issue them add substantial percentages to all foreign transactions, whether they're in a foreign currency or not. Check on these fees before leaving home, so there won't be any surprises when you get the bill.

■TIP→ Before you charge something, ask the merchant whether or not he or she plans to do a dynamic currency conversion (DCC). In such a transaction the credit-card *processor* (shop, restaurant, or hotel, not Visa or MasterCard) converts the currency and charges you in dollars. In most cases you'll pay the merchant a 3% fee for this service in addition to any credit-card company and issuing-bank foreign-transaction surcharges.

Dynamic currency conversion programs are becoming increasingly widespread. Merchants who participate in them are supposed to ask whether you want to be charged in dollars or the local currency, but they don't always do so. And even if they do offer you a choice, they may well avoid mentioning the additional surcharges. The good news is that you *do* have a choice. You can avoid it entirely thanks to American Express; with its cards, DCC simply isn't an option.

**Reporting Lost Cards American Express** ☎ 800/297–8500 within the U.S. or Canada, 336/393–1111 collect from abroad ⊕ www.americanexpress.com. **MasterCard** ☎ 800/627–8372 within the U.S. or Canada, 636/722–7111 collect from abroad ⊕ www.mastercard.com. **Visa** ☎ 800/847–2911 within the U.S. or Canada, 410/581–3836 collect from abroad ⊕ www.visa.com.

## CURRENCY AND EXCHANGE

Throughout this book, unless otherwise stated, all prices are given in Canadian dollars.

U.S. dollars are accepted in much of Canada (especially in communities near the border). However, to get the most favorable exchange rate, change at least some of your money into Canadian funds. Major U.S. credit cards are accepted in most areas. Traveler's checks (some are available in Canadian dollars) are becoming less and less common.

The units of currency in Canada are the Canadian dollar (C$) and the cent, in almost the same denominations as U.S. currency ($5, $10, $20, 1¢, 5¢, 10¢, 25¢, etc.). The $1 and $2 bill are no longer used; they have been replaced by $1 and $2 coins (known as a "loonie," because of the loon that appears on the coin, and a "toonie," respectively).

## WORST-CASE SCENARIO

All your money and credit cards have just been stolen. In these days of real-time transactions, this isn't a predicament that should destroy your vacation. First, report the theft of the credit cards. Then get any traveler's checks you were carrying replaced. This can usually be done almost immediately, provided that you kept a record of the serial numbers separate from the checks themselves. If you bank at a large international bank like Citibank or HSBC, go to the closest branch; if you know your account number, chances are you can get a new ATM card and withdraw money right away.

**Western Union.** Western Union sends money almost anywhere. Have someone back home order a transfer online, over the phone, or at one of the company's offices, which is the cheapest option. ☎ 800/325-6000 ⊕ www.westernunion.com.

**Overseas Citizens Services.** The U.S. State Department's Overseas Citizens Services can wire money to any U.S. consulate or embassy abroad for a fee of $30. Just have someone back home wire money or send a money order or cashier's check to the state department, which will then disburse the funds as soon as the next working day after it receives them. ☎ 202/647-5225 ⊕ www.travel.state.gov/travel.

Prices throughout this guide are given for adults. Substantially reduced fees are almost always available for children, students, and senior citizens.

## ▐ PASSPORTS AND VISAS

Citizens of the United States need a passport or other WHTI-compliant document to re-enter their country when returning by air from Canada. Passport requirements apply to minors as well. As of 2009, passports, passport cards, or other WHTI-compliant documents are also required for adults crossing the border by land or sea, though children under age 16 may continue to do so using only a U.S. birth certificate. Check with U.S Customs and Border Protection (⊕ www.cbp.gov or ⊕ www.getyouhome.gov) for full details.

Anyone under 18 who is either traveling alone or with only one parent should carry a signed and dated letter from both parents or from all legal guardians authorizing the trip. It's also a good idea to include a copy of the child's birth certificate, custody documents (if applicable), and death certificates of one or both parents (if applicable). Be aware that most airlines do not allow children under age five to travel independently. Air Canada is particularly strict: children must be at least eight years of age to fly unaccompanied and can only travel on nonstop flights.

Citizens of the United States, United Kingdom, Australia, and New Zealand do not need visas to enter Canada for a period of six months or fewer. Visitors from numerous other countries are also exempt: see Citizenship and Immigration Canada's Web site (⊕ www.cic.gc.ca) for a complete list.

▐ **TIP→** Before your trip, make two copies of your passport's data page (one for someone at home and another for you to carry separately) or scan the page and email it to someone at home and/or yourself.

## ▐ TAXES

A goods and services tax (GST) of 5% applies on virtually every transaction in Canada except for the purchase of basic groceries. In PEI, a 10% provincial sales tax (PST) is also added on to most items. Newfoundland and Labrador and New Brunswick have a 13% single harmonized sales tax (HST), which combines the GST and the provincial sales tax. It is 15% in Nova Scotia.

**Information** Canada Customs and Revenue Agency ☎ 800/267–6999 ⊕ www.ccra-adrc. gc.ca.

# ▮ TIME

New Brunswick, Nova Scotia, and Prince Edward Island are on Atlantic time, which is (during daylight saving time) three hours earlier than Greenwich mean time (GMT) and one hour later than eastern daylight time (EDT). Newfoundland and Labrador are on Newfoundland time, which is –2:30 GMT and +1:30 EDT.

# ▮ TIPPING

Tips and service charges are not usually added to a bill in Canada. In general, tip 15% of the total bill (before tax). This goes for waiters and waitresses, barbers and hairdressers, and taxi drivers. Porters and doormen should get about C$2 a bag. For maid service, leave at least C$2 per person a day (C$3 in luxury hotels).

# ▮ TOURS

## SPECIAL-INTEREST TOURS

The companies listed *below* offer multi-day tours in Atlantic Canada. *Additional operators that run different-length trips with these themes are listed in each chapter either on the Planner page or with information about the specific community.*

## ACTIVE ADVENTURES

**Atlantic Canada Cycling** has excellent information to help you plan your cycle trip, posts journals of other travelers, and has its own organized adventures. **Backroads** plans biking, hiking, and cycling junkets on the East Coast and beyond. **Bike Riders Tours** offers bike trips all over the globe, including Nova Scotia's Lighthouse Route and Bay of Fundy area. **Black Spruce Tours** goes for the cold with canoeing, kayaking, snowmobiling, and cross-country-skiing tours in Newfoundland and Labrador. **Coastal Adventures** has sea kayaking options themed around icebergs and buried treasure. **Country Haven**

offers angling tours on New Brunswick's salmon-rich Miramichi River. **Eastwind Cycle** specializes in custom bike tours in New Brunswick, Nova Scotia, and PEI. **Easy Rider Tours** celebrates pedal power with bike tours in PEI and Nova Scotia. **Eureka Outdoors** in western Newfoundland offers package trips for anglers. **Freewheeling Adventures** organizes Atlantic Canadian holidays for bikers, hikers, paddlers, and yoga enthusiasts; multisport offerings for families are available too. **Fresh Air Adventure** focuses on sea-kayaking trips in New Brunswick's fabled Bay of Fundy biosphere. **Ocean Quest**, one of Canada's premier adventure expedition planners, offers cool vacations in Newfoundland and Labrador that can include wreck diving and snorkeling with whales. **Pedal & Sea** specializes in guided and self-guided bike tours in Eastern Canada.

▮TIP→ Most airlines accommodate bikes as luggage, provided they're dismantled and boxed.

**Contacts Atlantic Canada Cycling** ☎ 902/423–2453, 888/879–2453 ⊕ www. atlanticcanadacycling.com. **Backroads** ☎ 510/527–1555, 800/462–2848 ⊕ www. backroads.com. **Black Spruce Tours** ☎ 631/725–1493 ⊕ www.blacksprucetours. com. **Coastal Adventures** ☎ 902/772–2774, 877/404–2774 ⊕ www.coastaladventures. com. **Country Haven** ☎ 877/359–4665 ⊕ www.miramichifish.com. **Eastwind Cycle** ☎ 902/471–4424 ⊕ www.eastwindcycle. com. **Easy Rider Tours** ☎ 978/463–6955, 800/488–8332 ⊕ www.easyridertours.com. **Freewheeling Adventures** ☎ 902/857–3600, 800/672–0775 ⊕ www.freewheeling. ca. **Fresh Air Adventure** ☎ 506/887–2249, 800/545–0020 ⊕ www.freshairadventure. com. **Ocean Quest** ☎ 709/834–7234, 866/623–2664 ⊕ www.oceanquestcharters. com. **Pedal & Sea Adventures** ☎ 877/777–5699 ⊕ www.pedalandseaadventures.com. **Eureka Outdoors** ☎ 709/638–8098 ⊕ www. eurekaoutdoors.nf.ca.

## CULTURAL AND CULINARY TOURS

The escorted and self-guided tours that **Ambassatours Gray Line** runs throughout the region typically serve up a hefty dose of local history. **Vision Atlantic Vacations**, which specializes in Newfoundland and Labrador, offers similar fare along with more esoteric options: including a six-night "Silver Screen" tour that turns the spotlight on locally made movies like *The Shipping News*. **Maxxim Vacations** designs some of the most innovative themed packages around. For instance, it has multiday trips that focus on topics like quilting in Newfoundland, plus "Taste of the Maritimes" junkets geared specifically for foodies. Gourmets will also appreciate **Collette Vacation**'s tours, some of which include visits to wineries, lobster pounds, apple orchards, and maple sugar farms. For those who'd prefer to learn how to prepare local delicacies themselves, Nova Scotia's **Trout Point Lodge** runs a highly regarded vacation cooking school at its wilderness resort. Just so oenophiles don't feel ignored, Nova Scotian wine expeditions are also available through **TayMac Tours.**

**Contacts Ambassatours Gray Line** ☎ 902/423-6242, 800/565-7173 ⊕ www. ambassatours.com. **Collette Vacations** ☎ 800/468-5955 ⊕ www.collettevacations. ca. **Maxxim Vacations** ☎ 709/754-6666, 800/567-6666 ⊕ www.maxximvacations. com. **TayMac Tours** ☎ 902/422-4861, 800/565-8296 ⊕ www.taymactours.com. **Trout Point Lodge** ☎ 902/761-2142 ⊕ www. troutpoint.com. **Vision Atlantic Vacations** ☎ 709/686-1395, 877/847-4660 ⊕ www. visionatlanticvacations.com.

## GOLF

**Golf New Brunswick, Golf Nova Scotia,** and **Golf PEI** organize Stay and Play packages throughout their respective provinces, as well as provide details about local golf courses. **Golf Newfoundland** has compiled a course directory and offers info on "the game untamed."

**Contacts Golf New Brunswick** ☎ 877/833-4662 ⊕ www.golfnb.ca. **Golf Newfoundland** ☎ 709/424-3102 ⊕ www.golfnewfoundland.ca. **Golf Nova Scotia** ☎ 866/404-3224 ⊕ www. golfnovascotia.com. **Golf Prince Edward Island** ☎ 866/465-3734 ⊕ www.golfpei.ca.

# ▌ VISITOR INFORMATION

Provincial tourism offices *(see individual chapters for details)* are an invaluable source of information. Related Web sites are also a useful resource. Looking for specifics on museums? The **Canadian Museums Association** (⊕ *www.museums. ca*) offers a sort of cultural tour of the country. If you would rather park yourself in a national park, **Parks Canada** (⊕ *www. pc.gc.ca*) covers everything you need to know. Publications like **The Globe and Mail** (⊕ *www.theglobeandmail.com*), the country's national newspaper, help put this region into context, as do Canadian periodicals (Magazines Canada, ⊕ *www. magazinescanada.ca*, offers a link on their homepage to more than 400 of them). For current, comprehensive visitor information on Canada as a whole, visit the official **Canadian Tourism Commission** Web site (⊕ *www.canada.travel*).

# INDEX

## A

Aberdeen Cultural Centre, 146
Acadia University, 67–68
Acadia University Art Gallery, 67–68
Acadian Coast (New Brunswick), 150–162
Acadian culture, 43, 155
Acadian Festival, 161
Acadian Historical Village, 161
Acadian Museum (Moncton), 146
Acadian Museum (Summerside), 218–219
Admiral Digby Museum, 62–63
Adventure tours, 142, 214, 217, 271, 278, 307
Advocate Harbour, 82
Age of Sail Museum Heritage Centre, 82
Air Saint-Pierre, 267
Air travel, 296–297
New Brunswick, 114
Newfoundland and Labrador, 231
Nova Scotia, 22
Prince Edward Island, 184
Airports, 268, 296
Aitkens Pewter, 175–176
Alexander Graham Bell National Historic Site of Canada, 100
Alexander Keith's Nova Scotia Brewery, 32
Alma, 139
Amherst, 80–81
Amherst Shore Country Inn ×⌷, 81
Amusement parks, 65–66, 145, 157, 159
Andrew and Laura McCain Gallery, 166
Anglican Cathedral of St. John the Baptist, 240
Anna Leonowens Gallery, 32
Anna Swan, 78
Annapolis Royal, 6–67
Annapolis Royal Historic Gardens, 65
Annapolis Valley, 43–73
Anne Murray Centre, 80
Anne of Green Gables, 10, 205–206, 207, 209
Anne of Green Gables Museum at Silver Bush, 209
Antigonish, 75–76

A-1 Wildflowers Country Inn ⌷, 276
Apartment and house rentals, 300
Aquarium and Marine Centre (Shippagan), 160
Aquariums, 130, 160, 225
Archelaus Smith Museum, 57
Arches Provincial Park, 278–279
Arichat, 107–108
Art Gallery of Nova Scotia, 27–29
Art Gallery of Nova Scotia (Western Branch), 59
Atlantic Salmon Museum, 158–159
ATMs, 304–305
Avalon Peninsula (Newfoundland and Labrador), 251–258

## B

Baddeck, 99–102
Bailey House, The ⌷, 66
Balmoral Grist Mill, 79
Bank of Nova Scotia Museum, 265
Barbour's General Store, 122
Bare Bones Bistro ×, 84
Barrington Woolen Mill Museum, 57
Basilica Cathedral of St. John the Baptist, 236
Basin Head Provincial Park, 215
Basin Head Fisheries Museum, 215
Battery (St. John's), 241
Bay Vista Moteland Cottage ⌷, 206–207
Beaches, 12
New Brunswick, 127, 143, 154
Nova Scotia, 41, 54, 78, 82, 85, 91
Prince Edward Island, 202–204, 208, 209
Beaconsfield Historic House, 188
Beothuk Interpretation Centre, 270
Beaubears Island, 151
Beaverbrook Art Gallery, 10, 16
Bed and breakfasts, 300–301
Bianca ×, 244

Bicycling, 11
New Brunswick, 168
Nova Scotia, 48, 52, 56
Prince Edward Island, 184, 188, 202, 203, 217
Big and Little Tancook Islands, 46
Big Pond, 107
Bird-watching
New Brunswick, 141, 152, 153–154
Newfoundland and Labrador, 252–253
Nova Scotia, 69, 76
Bishop's Foundry, 219
Black Duck Gallery and Gifts (shop), 52
Black Loyalist Heritage Site, 57
Bluenose II schooner, 50
Boardwalk (Charlottetown), 188
Boat and ferry travel, 297
New Brunswick, 113
Newfoundland and Labrador, 231, 269
Nova Scotia, 23, 63, 98
Prince Edward Island, 185
Boat tours
New Brunswick, 165–166
Newfoundland and Labrador, 263, 278, 282, 283
Nova Scotia, 45–46, 48, 52, 58, 78, 94, 95–96, 101
Prince Edward Island, 199, 216
Boating and sailing
New Brunswick, 126
Newfoundland and Labrador, 263, 278
Nova Scotia, 45–46, 107
Prince Edward Island, 199
Bonavista, 264
Books about Nova Scotia, 13, 286
Bouctouche, 156–157
Bowring Park, 243
Boyce Farmers' Market, 170
Boyd's Cove, 270
Brackley Beach, 202–204
Bras d'oOr Lakes Interpretive Centre, 100
Bread and Roses Country Inn ⌷, 66
Bridgewater, 53
Brier Island, 63–64
Brier Island Ferry, 63
Brigus, 255

Brigus South, *253*
Brunswick Square, *127*
Burin, *265–266*
Bus travel, *297–298*
Nova Scotia, *22–23*
Prince Edward Island, *184*
Business hours, *304*

**C**

Cabot Beach Provincial Park, *209*
Cabot Links, *92*
Cabot Tower, *241*
Cabot Trail, *11, 88*
Cabot's Landing Provincial Park, *96*
Camp Gagetown Military Museum, *167*
Campobello Island, *137–138*
Canadian Museum of Immigration at Pier 21, *29*
Canoeing
New Brunswick, *175*
Nova Scotia, *40*
Cape Bear Lighthouse, *219*
Cape Bonavista Lighthouse, *264*
Cape Breton Highlands National Park, *94–95*
Cape Breton Island (Nova Scotia), *88–108*
Cape Breton Miners' Museum, *103*
Cape Chignecto, *81–83*
Cape Chignecto Provincial Park, *81–82*
Cape d'Or, *81–83*
Cape Enrage, *142*
Cape Enrage Interpretive Centre, *142*
Cape Forchu Lighthouse, *59*
Cape Sable Island, *57*
Cape St. Mary's Ecological Reserve, *258*
Cape Spear Lighthouse, *10, 241*
Cape Spear National Historic Site, *241*
Car travel, *12, 298–299*
New Brunswick, *114*
Newfoundland and Labrador, *232*
Nova Scotia, *23*
Prince Edward Island, *184–185*
Caraquet, *161–162*
Carleton Martello Tower, *122–123*
Cashel's Cove Crafts (shop), *265–266*

Casinos, *105, 192*
Castle Hill National Historic Site, *257*
Castle Moffett ⊡ , *101*
Cavendish, *204–208*
Central Coastal Drive (Prince Edward Island), *200–211*
Celtic Colours International Festival, *89*
Celtic Music Interpretive Centre, *90*
Central New Brunswick Woodmen's Museum, *159*
Change Islands, *269*
Chanterelle Country Inn & Cottages ⊡ , *98*
Charlotte County Courthouse, *130*
Charlotte Lane Café ✕ , *58*
Charlottetown (Prince Edward Island), *186–200*
Cherry Brook Zoo, *119*
Ches's ✕ , *244–245*
Chester, *46–47*
Chester Race Week, *46*
Chéticamp, *93–94*
Chez Christophe ✕ , *61–62*
Children, attractions for
New Brunswick, *119, 120, 122, 128, 130, 143, 145, 148, 154, 159, 160, 161, 162, 163–164, 166–167, 170–171*
Newfoundland and Labrador, *241–243, 253, 254, 260–261, 264, 268, 274, 279*
Nova Scotia, *29, 30–32, 33, 38, 39, 41, 46, 49–50, 54, 55–56, 59, 63, 65–66, 70, 74–75, 81, 83–84, 86, 87, 95, 97, 100, 104, 105–106*
Prince Edward Island, *188–190, 193, 203, 205, 206–207, 208, 209, 214, 215, 224*
Chives Canadian Bistro ✕ , *34–35*
Chocolate Museum, *128*
Christ Church Cathedral, *170*
Church Point, *61–62*
Churches
New Brunswick, *123, 130, 150, 152, 160–161, 170*
Newfoundland and Labrador, *236, 239, 240, 241*
Nova Scotia, *34, 61, 62, 108*
Prince Edward Island, *192–193*
Circular Road (St. John's), *240*
Clarenville, *259–260*
Climate, *8*

Coach House Museum, *150, 152*
Cobequid Interpretation Centre, *85*
Codroy Valley, *284*
Colleges and universities, *51, 61, 67–68, 75, 98*
Colonial Building (St. John's), *236*
Colony of Avalon (archaeological dig), *253*
Commissariat House, *240*
Confederation Bridge, *210*
Confederation Centre of the Arts, *188–189*
Confederation Landing Park, *191–192*
Confederation Trail, *182–183*
Connell House, *163*
Corner Brook, *282–283*
Cossit House, *103*
Court House (St. John's), *236*
Covered bridge, *165*
Cow Head, *275*
Crafts, *41*
Cranberry Cove Inn ⊡ , *106*
Creamery Square (Tatamagouche), *78*
Credit cards, *5, 305*
Cruise travel, *299*
Crystal Palace, *145*
Cuisine
New Brunswick, *115*
Nova Scotia, *23–24*
Prince Edward Island, *185*
Culinary tours, *308*
Cultural tours, *308*
Cupids, *255–256*
Cupids Legacy Centre & Museum, *256*
Currency and exchange, *305–306*
Customs and duties, *302–303*

**D**

Da Maurizio Dining Room ✕ , *35*
Dalvay-by-the-Sea, *202*
Deer Island, *136–137*
Deer Lake, *272, 274*
Deer Point, *136*
DeGarthe Memorial, *45*
Delta Beauséjour ⊡ , *148*
DesBrisay Museum, *53*
Digby, *62–63*
Digby Pines Golf Resort and Spa ⊡ , *63*
Digby Scallop Days, *62*

Dining, 5, 303. ⇨See also
   under cities and provinces
Discovery Centre, 275
Discovery Trail, 259
Dock Restaurant ✕, 262
Domaine de Grand Pré
   (winery), 68
Dorchester, 150, 152
Dory Shop Museum, 57
Downhome Shoppe and
   Gallery, 250
Drives, 12
Duckworth Street (St. John's),
   239
Dunes Café ✕, 203
Duties, 302–303

E

East Point Lighthouse, 218
Eastern Newfoundland,
   258–267
Eastern Shore (Nova Scotia),
   73–87
Eastport Peninsula, 261
Edmundston, 163–164
Electricity, 304
Elmwood Heritage Inn 🖃,
   196–197
Emergencies, 304
and car travel, 298
English Country Garden Bed &
   Breakfast 🖃, 98–99
Eptek Arts and Culture Centre,
   219

F

Faire Brayonne, 163
Fairholm National Historic Inn
   🖃, 197
Fairmont Algonquin 🖃, 132
Fairview Cemetery, 32
Farmers' Market (Annapolis
   Royal), 65
Farmers' Market (Halifax), 42
Ferry service. ⇨See Boat and
   ferry travel
Ferryland, 253–254
Ferryland Lighthouse, 253–254
Festival Acadien de Clare, 61
Festival Antigonish, 75
Festivals and seasonal events
New Brunswick, 113, 161, 163
Newfoundland and Labrador,
   231, 278, 284
Nova Scotia, 21–22, 46, 53–54,
   62, 70, 75, 76, 83, 89, 104
Prince Edward Island, 183–
   184, 220–221
Fid ✕, 35

Firefighters Museum of Nova
   Scotia, 59
Fish, Fun & Folk Festival, 270
Fisheries Museum of the
   Atlantic, 49–50
Fishers' Loft Inn 🖃, 262–263
Fishing
Newfoundland and Labrador,
   231
Nova Scotia, 55, 92
Prince Edward Island, 209–
   210, 216, 226
Five Islands, 85
Five Islands Provincial Park, 85
Fleur de Sel ✕, 50
Fogo Island, 269
Fort Anne National Historic
   Site, 65
Fort Beauséjour National
   Historic Site, 153
Fort Edward, 70
Fort Point Lighthouse Park, 54
Fortress of Louisbourg National
   Historic Site of Canada,
   105–106
Founders' Hall-Canada's
   Birthplace Pavilion, 189–190
Fredericton (New Brunswick),
   168–177
Fredericton Region Museum,
   170
French vocabulary, 287–294
Fundy Coast (New Brunswick),
   127–150
Fundy Discovery Aquarium,
   130
Fundy Geological Museum,
   83–84
Fundy National Park, 139–142
Fundy Trail Parkway, 127, 138

G

Gables, The ✕, 131
Gaelic College of Celtic Arts
   and Crafts, 98
Gagetown, 176–177
Gahan House Pub & Brewery
   ✕, 194
Gampo Abbey, 95
Gander, 267–269
Gander International Airport,
   268
Ganong Chocolatier, 128
Gardens
New Brunswick, 130, 163–164
Newfoundland and Labrador,
   242
Nova Scotia, 33, 65, 68
Prince Edward Island, 204

Gardens of Hope, 204
Georgetown, 212–214
Glynmill Inn 🖃, 283
Golf, 308
New Brunswick, 133, 141,
   149, 175
Nova Scotia, 40, 63, 92, 94,
   97, 101
Prince Edward Island, 198–
   199, 202, 207–208, 213–214,
   217, 223
Government House
   (Fredericton), 170
Government House
   (Halifax), 32
Government House (St. John's),
   239
Gower Street United Church,
   239
Grand Bank, 266
Grand Falls (New Brunswick),
   165–166
Grand Falls Museum, 165
Grand Falls-Windsor
   (Newfoundland), 271–272
Grand Manan Island, 134–136
Grand Pré National Historic
   Site, 67
Great George 🖃, 197
Greater St. John's, 241–250
Green Gables, 205
Green Gardens Trail, 276
Greenock Church, 130
Greenwich (P.E.I. National
   Park), 216–217
Grenfell Historic Properties,
   281
Gros Morne Mountain, 275
Gros Morne National Park, 10,
   274–278

H

Haliburton House Museum,
   70–71
Halifax (Nova Scotia), 25,
   27–42
Halifax Citadel National
   Historic Site, 30
Halifax Public Gardens, 33
Halifax Waterfront Boardwalk,
   10, 30
Hall's Harbour, 68
Hants County Exhibition, 70
Harbour Grace, 256–257
Harbour Station, 126
Harbourside Park, 239
Harriet Irving Botanical
   Gardens, 68
Hawke Hills, 254–255

Hawthorne Cottage, *255*
Hector Heritage Quay, *76*
Herring Cove Provincial Park, *137*
Highland Games, *75*
Highland Village Museum, *102*
Hiking and walking
*New Brunswick, 121, 175*
*Newfoundland and Labrador, 232, 248, 259, 284*
*Nova Scotia, 21, 40–41, 70, 74, 80, 85, 91, 97, 105, 107*
*Prince Edward Island, 226*
Historic Garrison District (Fredericton), *170–171*
Historic Properties (Halifax), *30–31*
Historical Association of Annapolis Royal, *64–65*
Home exchanges, *300*
Hopewell Cape, *142–143*
Hopewell Rocks, *10, 143*
Horse-drawn carriage tours, *52*
Horse racing, *192*
New Brunswick, *141*
Nova Scotia, *41, 94*
Hotel on Pownal ▦ , *197*
Hotels, *5, 162, 301.* ⇨ *See also under cities and provinces*
price categories, *24, 116, 186, 234*
House rentals, *51*
Houses and buildings, historic
*New Brunswick, 150, 152, 163*
*Newfoundland and Labrador, 239, 255, 281*
*Nova Scotia, 32, 34, 59, 103*
*Prince Edward Island, 188, 221*

**I**

Icebergs, *11, 271*
Île Miscou, *160*
India Gate ✕ , *245*
Ingonish, *97*
Inn at Bay Fortune ▦ , *215–126*
Inn at St. Peters ▦ , *217*
Inns, *300–301*
International Fox Museum and Hall of Fame, *220*
Internet, *301*
Interpretive Centre and Aquarium, *225*
Iona, *101–102*
Irish Loop, *253*
Irish Moss Interpretive Centre, *225*

**J**

Irving Eco-Centre: La Dune de Bouctouche (coastal ecosystem), *157*
Irving Nature Park, *119*

**J**

Java Jack's Restaurant and Gallery ✕ , *276*
Joggins Fossil Center, *81*
Johnson GEO Centre, *241–242*
Jöst Vineyards, *79*
Judique, *90*
Julien's Pâtisserie, Bakery & Café ✕ , *47*

**K**

Kayaking
*New Brunswick, 133, 136, 141, 175*
*Newfoundland and Labrador, 249, 254*
*Nova Scotia, 41, 45–46, 52, 63, 83, 99*
*Prince Edward Island, 203, 210, 211*
Keillor House, Coach House Museum, and St. James Church, *150, 152*
Kejimkujik National Park and Historic Site, *55–56*
Kejimkujik National Park-Seaside, *54*
Keltic Lodge Resort and Spa ▦ , *97*
King Street (Saint John), *123*
King-Edgehill School, *70*
Kings Landing Historical Settlement, *166–167*
King's Square (Saint John), *123*
Kingsbrae Arms ▦ , *132*
Kingsbrae Horticultural Gardens, *130*
Knobb Hill Gallery, *170*
Kouchibouguac National Park, *158*

**L**

La Manche, *253*
Labrador. ⇨ *See* Newfoundland and Labrador
Landmark Café ✕ , *211*
L'Anse aux Meadows National Historic Site, *279*
Lantern Hill & Hollow ▦ , *97*
Le Pays de la Sagouine (theme park), *157*
LeNoir Forge, *108*

Les Trois Pignons Cultural Center, *93*
Lester-Garland Premises Mercantile Building, *262*
Lighthouse on Cape d'Or, The ▦ , *83*
Lighthouses, *14*
*Newfoundland and Labrador, 241, 253–254, 264, 275*
*Nova Scotia, 54, 59, 74*
*Prince Edward Island, 218, 219*
Little Louis's Oyster Bar ✕ , *146*
Liverpool, *53–55*
Lobster Head Cove Lighthouse, *275*
Lodging, *5, 51, 300–301.* ⇨ *See also under cities and provinces*
Logger's Life Provincial Museum, *271*
Long Island, *63–64*
Long Range Mountains, *278–279*
Lot 30 ✕ , *194*
Louisbourg, *105–107*
Loyalist Burial Ground, *119–120*
Loyalist House, *123*
Lucy Maud Montgomery Birthplace, *205–206*
Lucy Maude Montgomery's Cavendish Home, *206*
Lunenburg, *10, 49–53*
Lutz Mountain Heritage Museum, *146*

**M**

Mabou, *90–91*
Mabou Highlands, *91*
Mactaquac Provincial Park, *167*
Maddox Cove and Petty Harbour, *243*
Magic Mountain Water Park (theme park), *145*
Magnetic Hill, *145*
Magnetic Hill Zoo, *145*
Magnolia's Grill ✕ , *50*
Mahone Bay, *48–49*
Malabeam Tourist Information Center, *165*
Malpeque, *208–210*
Marconi National Historic Site of Canada, *103*
Margaree Harbour, *92*
Margaree Salmon Museum, *92*
Maritime Museum of the Atlantic, *31–32*
Market Slip (Saint John), *120*

Marshlands Inn ☲ , 153
Mary Celeste, 82
Mary E. Black Gallery, 33
Mary March Provincial
    Museum, 271–272
Marystown, 265
Marysville, 170
Memorial University Botanical
    Garden, 242
Memramcock, 150–151
Mermaid Theatre of Nova
    Scotia, 70
Mersey River Chalets ☲ , 56
Minas Basin, 83
Ministers Island, 131
Miquelon, 266–267
Miramichi, 158–160
Mistaken Point Ecological
    Reserve, 254
Mockbeggar Plantation, 264
Moncton, 143–150
Moncton Museum, 146
Money matters, 5, 304–306
Montgomery, Lucy Maud,
    205–206, 209
Monument Lefebvre National
    Historic Site, 152
Moose, 233
Morris East ✕ , 37
Motorcycle travel, 184–185
Movies about Nova Scotia, 286
Murray Premises, 240
Museums and galleries, 13
    New Brunswick, 120, 122,
        128, 131, 141–142, 146,
        149–150, 152, 153, 158–159,
        161, 165, 166, 167, 169,
        170–171, 177
    Newfoundland and Labrador,
        239–240, 241–242, 250, 256,
        265–266, 268, 270, 271–272,
        281
    Nova Scotia, 27–29, 31–32, 33,
        46, 49–50, 53, 54, 57, 59,
        62–63, 70–71, 74, 75, 77, 78,
        79, 80, 81, 82, 83–84, 92,
        98, 100, 102, 103, 107, 108
    Prince Edward Island, 188–
        189, 200, 203, 204, 209,
        215, 218–220, 221, 222,
        224, 225
Music
    New Brunswick, 126, 148
    Newfoundland and Labrador,
        248, 278
    Nova Scotia, 62, 89
    Prince Edward Island, 198, 221
Myriad View Artisan Distillery,
    215

**N**

New Brunswick, 6, 109–177
    Acadian Coast, 150–162
    children, attractions for, 119,
        120, 122, 128, 130, 143,
        145, 148, 154, 157, 159,
        160, 161, 162, 163–164,
        166–167, 170–171
    cuisine, 115
    dining and lodging, 123–126,
        131–133, 135, 136–137,
        138–139, 140–141, 146–148,
        152, 153, 156, 157, 159–
        160, 161–162, 164, 172–174,
        177
    festivals and seasonal events,
        113, 161, 163
    Fredericton, 168–177
    Fundy Coast, 127–150
    itinerary recommendations, 117
    nightlife and the arts, 126, 148,
        174–175
    outdoor activities and sports,
        115, 126, 133, 135–136,
        137, 139, 141, 142, 149,
        152, 153–154, 162, 164, 175
    price categories, 116
    Saint John, 116, 118–127
    St. John River Valley, 162–167
    shopping, 127, 134, 143, 149–
        150, 154, 175–176, 177
    timing the visit, 116
    tours, 115, 121, 126, 133, 135–
        136, 142, 165, 169, 170
    transportation, 112, 113–114
New Brunswick Botanical
    Garden, 163–164
New Brunswick Museum, 120,
    122
New Glasgow Lobster Suppers
    ✕ , 206
New River Beach, 127
Newfoundland and Labrador,
    6, 227–284
    Avalon Peninsula, 251–258
    children, attractions for,
        241–243, 253, 254, 260–261,
        264, 268, 274, 279
    cuisine, 232
    dining and lodging, 233, 242,
        243–247, 255, 256–257, 258,
        259–260, 261, 262–263,
        264, 265, 266, 267, 269,
        270–271, 272, 274, 276–278,
        279–282, 283, 284
    Eastern Newfoundland,
        258–267
    festivals and seasonal events,
        231, 270, 278, 284

    Gander and environs, 267–272
    itinerary recommendations,
        235
    language, 247
    nightlife and the arts, 247–248,
        263, 278
    outdoor activities and sports,
        231, 232, 233, 248–249,
        252–253, 254, 263, 271,
        278, 282, 283
    packing, 233
    price categories, 234
    safety, 233
    St. John's, 234–251
    shopping, 250–251, 260, 282
    time, 234
    timing the visit, 234
    tours, 233, 238, 263, 267
    transportation, 231–232
    Western Newfoundland,
        272–284
Newfoundland Emporium,
    The, 283
Newfoundland Insectarium,
    274
Newman Wine Vaults, 240
Nightlife and the arts. ⇨ See
    under cities and provinces
Norris Point, 275
Norseman Restaurant ✕ ,
    279–280
Norstead, 279
North Atlantic Aviation
    Museum, 268
North Cape, 224–226
North Cape Coastal Drive,
    218–226
Northern Gros Morne, 275
Northern Nova Scotia, 73–87
Notre Dame de l'Assumption,
    108
Nova Scotia, 6, 17–108
    Cape Breton Island, 88–108
    children, attractions for, 29,
        30–32, 33, 38, 39, 41, 46,
        49–50, 54, 55–56, 59, 63,
        65–66, 70, 74–75, 81, 83–84,
        86, 87, 95, 97, 100, 104,
        105–106
    cuisine, 23–24
    dining and lodging, 34–39, 45,
        46–47, 48, 50–52, 55, 56,
        58, 60, 61–62, 63–64, 66,
        68–69, 71, 74–76, 77, 79, 81,
        82–83, 84–85, 86–87, 90–91,
        92, 93–94, 96, 97, 98–99,
        100–101, 103–104, 106
    Eastern Shore and Northern
        Nova Scotia, 73–87

festivals and seasonal events, 21–22, 46, 53–54, 62, 70, 75, 76, 83, 89, 104
Halifax, 25, 27–42
itinerary recommendations, 26
nightlife and the arts, 39–40, 47, 77, 85, 91, 101, 104–105, 106–107
outdoor activities and sports, 21, 24, 25, 40–41, 45–46, 48, 52, 55, 56, 58, 63, 64, 70, 73, 76, 78, 80, 83, 85, 87, 90, 91, 92, 94, 95–96, 97, 99, 101, 105, 107
price categories, 24
shopping, 41–42, 46, 47, 49, 52–53, 60–61, 67, 76, 77–78, 79, 87, 99, 105
South Shore and Annapolis Valley, 43–73
timing the visit, 24–25
tours, 24, 28, 52, 63, 64, 83, 87, 94, 95–96, 99, 102
transportation, 21, 22–23
visitor information, 24
**Nova Scotia Gem and Mineral Show,** 83
**Nova Scotia Museum of Industry,** 77
**Nova Scotia Museum of Natural History,** 33

**O**

**Oceanstone Inn and Cottages** 🖫 , 45
**Old County Court House,** 16
**Old Courthouse** (Saint John), 123
**Old Gaol** (St. Andrews by-the-Sea), 131
**Old Meeting House Museum** (Barrington), 57
**Old Sow** (whirlpool), 136
**Old Sydney Society,** 102, 103
**O'Leary,** 222–223
**Olivier Soapery,** 157
**Ottawa House-by-the-Sea Museum,** 84
**Outdoor activities and sports,** 10, 11, 307–308. ⇨ See also under cities and provinces
**Owens Art Gallery,** 153

**P**

**Packing,** 233
**Palate Restaurant & Cafe** ✕ , 173
**Panmure Head Lighthouse,** 219

**Parc de l'Aboiteau,** 154
**Parks**
New Brunswick, 119, 122, 137–138, 139–142, 145, 153, 154, 158, 159, 162, 167
Newfoundland and Labrador, 239, 243, 254–255, 260–261, 274–279
Nova Scotia, 33–34, 54, 55–56, 70, 71, 74, 81–82, 85, 86, 91, 94–95, 96, 100
Prince Edward Island, 191–192, 193, 200–202, 209, 210, 215, 216–217, 224, 226
**Parlee Beach,** 154
**Parrsboro,** 83–85
**Parrsboro Rock and Mineral Shop and Museum,** 84
**Partridge Island,** 83
**Passports and visas,** 306
**Peggy's Cove,** 43, 45–46
**PEI Potato Museum,** 222
**Perkins House Museum,** 54
**Pictou,** 76–78
**Placentia,** 257
**Plane travel.** ⇨ See Air travel
**Pleasant Bay,** 95–96
**Point de l'Eglise,** 61–62
**Point Pleasant Park,** 33–34
**Point Prim Lighthouse,** 219
**Points East Coastal Drive,** 211–218
**Pontoon boat,** 165–166
**Pope's Museum,** 161
**Port au Choix National Historic Site,** 279
**Port aux Basques,** 284
**Port Bickerton Lighthouse Beach Park,** 74
**Port-La-Joye-Fort Amherst National Historic Site,** 190–191
**Port Royal National Historic Site,** 65
**Press Gang** ✕ , 37
**Price categories**
dining, 24, 116, 186, 234
lodging, 24, 116, 186, 234
New Brunswick, 116
Newfoundland and Labrador, 234
Nova Scotia, 24
Prince Edward Island, 186
**Prince Edward Distillery,** 215
**Prince Edward Island,** 6, 179–226
Central Coastal Drive, 200–211
Charlottetown, 186–200

children, attractions for, 188–190, 193, 203, 205, 206–207, 208, 209, 214, 215, 224
cuisine, 185
dining and lodging, 185, 191, 193–198, 202, 203, 206–207, 209, 211, 212, 215–216, 217, 221, 222–223, 224, 225–226
festivals and seasonal events, 183–184, 220–221
itinerary recommendations, 187
nightlife and the arts, 198, 203, 211, 213
North Cape Coastal Drive, 218–226
outdoor activities and sports, 198–199, 202, 203, 207–208, 209–210, 211, 213–214, 216, 217, 222, 223, 224, 226
Points East Coastal Drive, 211–218
price categories, 186
shopping, 199–200, 204, 211, 223
timing the visit, 186
tours, 188, 210, 214, 222
transportation, 184–185
**Prince Edward Island National Park,** 200–202
**Prince William Street** (Saint John), 123
**Privateer Days,** 53–54
**Province House** (Nova Scotia), 34
**Provinces,** 9
**Provincial Legislature** (New Brunswick), 171
**Provincial Seamen's Museum,** 266
**Pumpkin Festival,** 70

**Q**

**Queens County Courthouse,** 177
**Queens County Museum,** 177
**Quidi Vidi,** 242

**R**

**Random Passage,** 263–264
**Rappelling,** 142
**Red Shoe** ✕ , 91
**Red Shores Racetrack and Casino,** 192
**Regent Bed & Breakfast, The** 🖫 , 81

**Restaurants** 5, 11. ⇨ *See also under cities and provinces*
dress, *303*
price categories, *24, 116, 186, 234*
reservations, *303*
smoking, *303*
wine, beer and spirits, *303*
**Reversing Rapids,** *11, 122*
**Rita's Tea Room,** *107*
**Ritchie Wharf Park,** *159*
**River Breeze Farm,** *86*
**Riverfront Park,** *145*
**Robie Tufts Nature Center,** *69*
**Rockwood Park,** *122*
**Rooms, The,** *239–240*
**Roosevelt Campobello International Park,** *137–138*
**Rosedale Manor Bed & Breakfast** 🖾 , *257*
**Ross Farm Living Museum of Agriculture,** *46*
**Ross Memorial Museum,** *131*
**Rossignol Cultural Centre,** *54*
**Ross-Thomson House & Stove Museum,** *57*
**Ryan Premises National Historic Site,** *264*

**S**
**Sackville,** *152–154*
**Sackville Waterfowl Park,** *153*
**Safety,** *306*
*Newfoundland and Labrador, 233*
**Sailing.** ⇨ *See* Boating and sailing
**St. Andrews by-the-Sea,** *128, 130–134*
**St. Ann's Bay,** *97–99*
**St. Anthony,** *281–282*
**St. Croix Island,** *128*
**St. Dunstan's Basilica,** *192*
**Saint James Church,** *150, 152*
**Saint John** (New Brunswick), *116, 118–127*
**Saint John Arts Centre,** *126*
**Saint John City Market,** *122*
**St. John River Valley** (New Brunswick), *162–167*
**St. John's** (Newfoundland), *234–251*
**St. Martins,** *138–139*
**St. Mary's Church,** *61*
**St. Paul's Anglican Church** (Charlottetown), *192*
**St. Paul's Church** (Halifax), *34*
**St. Peter's Bay,** *216–217*
**St. Peter's Cathedral,** *192–193*

**St-Pierre,** *266–267*
**St. Stephen,** *128*
**St. Thomas Anglican** (Old Garrison) **Church,** *241*
**Sainte Famille Winery,** *71*
**Ste-Cécile Church,** *160–161*
**Salmonier Nature Park,** *254–255*
**Scenic drives,** *12*
**Science East** (Fredericton), *171*
**Scuba diving,** *248–249*
**Seafood,** *14*
**Shadow Lawn Inn** 🖾 , *125–126*
**Shaw's Hotel and Cottages** 🖾 , *203*
**Shediac,** *154, 156*
**Shelburne,** *56–58*
**Shelburne County Museum,** *57*
**Shelburne Museum Complex,** *57*
**Sheraton Hotel Newfoundland** 🖾 , *247*
**Sherbrooke,** *74–75*
**Sherbrooke Village,** *74–75*
**Ship Harbour** (Newfoundland), *257–258*
**Shippagan,** *160–161*
**Shopping.** ⇨ *See also under cities and provinces*
**Shubenacadie River Runners,** *87*
**Signal Hill National Historic Site,** *242–243*
**Silent Witness Memorial,** *268*
**Sirenella Ristorante** ✕ , *195–196*
**Site of Lucy Maud Montgomery's Cavendish Home,** *206*
**Skerwink Trail,** *262*
**Skiing**
*New Brunswick, 139, 164, 175*
*Newfoundland and Labrador, 283*
**Souris,** *214–216*
**South Shore** (Nova Scotia), *43–73*
**Southern Gros Morne,** *275–276*
**Spinnaker's Landing,** *220*
**Sports and outdoor activities.** ⇨ *See under cities and provinces*
**Springhill,** *80*
**Springhill Miners Museum,** *80*
**Stephenville,** *284*
**Stephenville Theatre Festival,** *284*
**Stone Church,** *123*
**Sugar Hill Inn** 🖾 , *277–278*

**Sugar Moon Farm Maple Products and Pancake House** ✕ , *87*
**Summerside,** *218–222*
**Summerside Lobster Carnival,** *220–221*
**Summerville Beach Provincial Park,** *54*
**Suncor Energy Fluvarium,** *243*
**Sunrise Trail Museum,** *78*
**Surfing,** *41, 55, 73*
**Sutherland Steam Mill Museum,** *79*
**Swimming,** *41*
**Swissair Memorial,** *45*
**Sydney,** *102–105*
**Sydney Mines Heritage Museum and Fossil Centre,** *103*
**Symbols,** *5*

**T**
**Tablelands,** *275*
**Tantramar Marsh,** *80*
**Tatamagouche,** *78–80*
**Taxes,** *306–307*
**Telephones,** *301–302*
**Tempest World Cuisine** ✕ , *68–69*
**Terra Nova National Park,** *260–261*
**Theater**
*New Brunswick, 126*
*Newfoundland and Labrador, 248, 263, 278, 284*
*Nova Scotia, 40, 47, 70, 75, 85, 106–107*
*Prince Edward Island, 198, 203, 211, 213, 219, 222*
**Thomas Raddall Provincial Park,** *55*
**Tidal Bore** (Moncton), *145–146*
**Tim Hortons** ✕ , *16*
**Time,** *307*
**Timing the visit,** *8*
**Tipping,** *307*
**Titanic,** *31*
**Tours and packages,** *307–308*
**Train Station Inn** 🖾 , *79*
**Train travel,** *299*
*New Brunswick, 114*
*Nova Scotia, 23*
**Trinity,** *261–264*
**Trinity Church,** *123*
**Trout Paint Lodge** 🖾 , *60*
**Trout River,** *276*
**Truro,** *86–87*
**Twillingate,** *270–271*

## U

Uniacke Estate Museum Park, 71
Université Ste-Anne, 61
Upper Clements Park (amusement park), 65–66
Usige Ban Falls Provincial Park, 100

## V

Vacation rentals, 210–211
Valhalla Lodge Bed & Breakfast ☷ , 280–281
Victoria, 210–211
Victoria Park (Charlottetown), 193
Victoria Park (Truro), 86
Victoria Provincial Park, 210
Victoria Row (Charlottetown), 191
Victoria's Historic Inn and Carriage House ☷ , 69
Vikings, 279
Visas, 306
Visitor information, 308
Vocabulary, 287–294

## W

Wagmatcook Culture & Heritage Centre, 100
Walking tours
  New Brunswick, 121, 175
  Newfoundland and Labrador, 236, 238
  Nova Scotia, 28, 52, 76, 85
  Prince Edward Island, 188, 189
Water sports, 133, 199, 208
Water Street (St. John's), 240
Waterfalls, 122, 165–166
Weather, 8
Weekend crafts market (Pictou), 77
West Point, 223–224
West Point Lighthouse ☷ , 224
West Point Lighthouse Museum, 224
Western Brook Pond, 275
Western Newfoundland, 272–284
Westin Nova Scotian ☷ , 39
Whale Interpretive Centre, 95
Whale watching
  New Brunswick, 133, 135–136
  Newfoundland and Labrador, 249, 252–253, 271

Nova Scotia, 25, 52, 63, 64, 94, 95–96
White-water rafting, 87
Wild Caraway Restaurant & Café ✕ , 82
Wile Carding Mill Museum, 53
Windsor (Nova Scotia), 70–71
Windsor Hockey Heritage Centre, 71
Wineries, 11, 68, 71, 79
Witless Bay Ecological Reserve, 251–253
Wolfville, 67–70
Woods Island Lighthouse, 219
Woodstock, 166
Woody Point, 277
Wyatt House Museum, 221

## Y

Yarmouth, 58–61
Yarmouth County Museum & Archives, 59
York Street (Fredericton), 171

## Z

Zip-line tours, 126, 165
Zoos, 119, 145

# NOTES

# NOTES

# NOTES

# ABOUT OUR WRITERS

Having recently completed a trip around the world, frequent Fodor's contributor **Susan MacCallum-Whitcomb** can now say with some certainty that Atlantic Canada is her favorite place on earth. Born and bred in New Brunswick, Susan has strong family ties to Prince Edward Island, and currently resides with her husband and two children in Nova Scotia—so she pretty much has the region covered. She updated the Nova Scotia, PEI, and Travel Smart chapters along with the front matter for this edition of *Nova Scotia and Atlantic Canada.*

**Keith Nicol** has lived in and written about Newfoundland for 30 years. He has traveled by sea kayak, skis, and on foot over many parts of Western Newfoundland and has had his articles published in the *Globe and Mail, Explore, Ski Canada,* and *SkiTrax* magazine.

**Penny Phenix** moved to New Brunswick in 2009, after a long association with the province through travel writing commissions and marriage to a New Brunswicker. She has written or contributed to many guidebooks, including *Spiral Guide Canada, Key Guide Canada, Essential Canada East,* and *Explorer Canada.*